Army of the Potomac

McClellan Takes Command

VOLUME II

Also by Russel H. Beatie

Army of the Potomac
VOLUME I
Birth of Command
November 1860–September 1861

Army of the Potomac

McClellan Takes Command
September 1861–February 1862

VOLUME II

Russel H. Beatie

Da Capo Press
A Member of the Perseus Books Group

Maps by Blake Manger
Text set in 10-point Times New Roman by the Perseus Books Group.

Cataloging-in-Publication data for this book is available from the Library of Congress.

First Da Capo Press edition 2004
ISBN 0-306-81252-5

Published by Da Capo Press
A Member of the Perseus Books Group
http://www.dacapopress.com

Da Capo Press books are available at special discounts for bulk purchases in the U.S. by corporations, institutions, and other organizations. For more information, please contact the Special Markets Department at the Perseus Books Group, 11 Cambridge Center, Cambridge, MA 02142, or call (800) 255-1514 or (617) 252-5298, or e-mail special.markets@perseusbooks.com.

1 2 3 4 5 6 7 8 9—08 07 06 05 04

TO THE SAME MEN AND
THE SAME OTHERS FOR THE SAME REASONS,
especially to the two most important women in my life:

MY BELOVED NOISY FRIEND,
Julie Beatie,

and

MY BELOVED DILIGENT
AND INDEFATIGABLE SECRETARY
Esther Rosa

Contents

Contents (continued)

Contents (continued)

Contents (continued)

════════════════════════════

List of Illustrations

Illustrations appear in the Dramatis Personae

List of Maps

List of Maps (continued)

List of Maps (continued)

Army of the Potomac

McClellan Takes Command

VOLUME II

Preface

This volume covers military development, no great battles, and political domination of military affairs. None of these volumes present battle studies. They are NOT a biography or a life and times of Major General George B. McClellan. Nor are they an effort to climb on Douglass Southall Freeman's throne.

The battles are important because they reveal the discovery, development, successes, and failures of the higher-ranking officers of the Army of the Potomac. They might appear limited to McClellan, who will often occupy center stage alone and play the role of the major character. The major general has provoked such controversy over the years, and the views taken here so greatly conflict with those of many others, that the author has attempted to evaluate all the evidence—to "exhaust the field." Overinclusive? Too much of a good thing? More than the reader wants to know? Perhaps. If so, stop reading. For almost a century and a half extreme controversy has enveloped McClellan's plans, personal conduct, attitudes, strategic skills, and tactical judgment. The·debate has produced scorching heat but little illumination . . . and precious little fairness, although McClellan's supporters more often acknowledge his disabilities and failures than his detractors give him his due. If nothing else, the author has attempted to achieve fairness and balance, and the "encyclopedic" approach to the facts will hopefully allow that. The goal has not come easily, and some will certainly say it has not come at all. A debate on that score without the usual unreasonableness—and careless inaccuracies—would receive a ready welcome.

Making the task of fairness and objectivity even more difficult, the major general himself did not exude the silence that followed the Duke of Wellington's sharp snap, "Publish and be damned," or Henry Ford II's, "Don't explain; don't complain." For a man who maintained remarkable reticence on many things, McClellan—and his friends Porter, Franklin, Smith, and Biddle—left much of the written word behind to confound the search for an informed, fair conclusion; yet when his objective subordinates participating in the Second Civil War called for help on the deeply subjective facts only he would know, the cry went unanswered. In the author's opinion he did not leap to support his adherents for two reasons: First, the most honorable, he deemed the nasty back and forth beneath a gentleman; and second, more base, he could not tell the truth about his intentions and his motives without, in many cases, detracting from the credit his ardent supporters gave him when he did not deserve it. More sinned against than sinning, McClellan has been more unfairly treated by the politicians of his country, his contemporaries, and later by posterity than any other prominent American. At the same time no man so compounded the unfairness of his treatment by refusing to satisfy or by ignoring the legitimate—if some times benighted—wishes of his superior.

At the end of the beginning, when he prepared for his campaign on the Peninsula, McClellan and his superior had both undergone such rare, thorough changes in character and conduct that penetration of their thoughts and motives to the "inside" of the historical idea, as Collingwood might call it, becomes more difficult still. McClellan altered his disruptive, secretive conduct, changed his inflexibility, and modified his plans to make them serve President Lincoln's political, economic, and other needs. If the president had recognized this change, he would have thought it favorable . . . but he apparently never even saw its shadow. Lincoln, too, changed, but in a way McClellan could not have favored. Applying a new style of leadership for him, the president abandoned his practice of passive consensus building in order to exercise talents and skills he did not yet have.

Did McClellan change soon enough? Would Lincoln's foray into the world of military science produce lucky victories even though he knew nothing about the subject and had no natural talent for the work? This volume and the next will attempt to answer these questions for this part of the war.

Dramatis Personae

George B. McClellan

Called from a tiny success to assume command of his country's largest and most important army, a noteworthy position, McClellan moved higher yet. Accumulating widespread support and diverse friends, he built a great base for his growing power; and he would need them for the struggle with his strongest enemy, the general in chief Winfield Scott. McClellan worked with his political friends in the cabinet and other supporters in the government to rid himself of interference by his direct superior. Over his aged and infirm but experienced and successful superior officer, he prevailed! But did he? The stakes and the consequences, he would learn to his surprise, involved far more than military rank and assignment.

The major general's personality would also develop in an unusual way, giving overt primacy to characteristics that would ordinarily have lain well below the surface and out of sight. These features of his personality would suffer a near mortal attack from an unseen, and for McClellan an absolutely unexpected, foe. At the same time a trusted friend would mount an unplanned coup to seize his position.

Ignorant of all military doctrine and without knowledge born of experience, the president would transform his management style, a change that would have a profound effect on the major general. Surviving the assault on his life and his position, McClellan would attempt a change in character that few men would have

George B. McClellan

found possible. The changes in both the president and the major general would co-incide, but the result? A collision? A smooth partnership? Controversy? McClel-lan's plan for an offensive against the Confederates would run through all these explosive factors.

Winfield Scott

*F*ive decades of service, experience, and uninterrupted success had not prepared Scott for the vast changes in warfare that would confront him in 1861. In spite of poor health and weakened physical condition, he might have learned over time, but the American beast and the problems at hand would not allow him this educational, experimental luxury. Coordination of the two widely separated armies of Patterson and McDowell, a national strategy involving thousands of miles, communication by telegraph, and use of railroads lay beyond his understanding. With great hesitancy and reluctance along with sound personnel judgment, the president would decide that the general in chief could not continue, and in the cold rain, sharp lightning, and bleak darkness of a Wagnerian early morning, the aged general would leave the stage of his greatest challenge.

James S. Wadsworth and Philip W. Kearny

*T*wo of the few truly wealthy members of the general officer corps in the Army of the Potomac, James Samuel Wadsworth and Philip Watts Kearny came from diverse backgrounds and achieved their promotions to brigadier general in very different ways. Military lineage graced them both. To great rank in the continental army and the post-war Connecticut militia rose Wadsworth's grandfather. Kearny's older uncle Stephen Watts Kearny played a major role as a brigadier general commanding the Regular Army units that wrested California from the Mexican government during the Mexican War.

Both Wadsworth and Kearny enjoyed extraordinary intelligence; both received educations at outstanding future members of the Ivy League, Wadsworth at Harvard and Kearny at Columbia College; both inherited great wealth, Wadsworth tens of thousands of acres of farmland in western New York and Kearny more than one million dollars in cold money at the untimely death of his uncle without heirs; and both belonged to prestigious clubs in New York City, Wadsworth to the Century Association and Kearny to the Union Club.

A farmer who applied intelligent management to his sprawling lands, Wadsworth naturally involved himself in the higher levels of New York State and national politics. Dominated by a lifelong desire for the excitement of a military life, particularly the exhilaration of battle, the young Kearny rejected an offer of a large patrimony conditioned on a life in the ministry and, shortly after graduating from Columbia, entered the Regular Army as a junior company grade officer. He

Philip W. Kearny

advanced slowly but steadily until he became a captain in December 1846 and showed his extraordinary courage, if not reckless indifference to death, in a famous cavalry charge on one of the gates at Mexico City. Although Wadsworth would not have an opportunity to demonstrate these characteristics until the Union armies took the field, he shared Kearny's great courage and thoughtless indifference to death.

Their private lives reflected the vast differences in their personalities. Wadsworth found a proper wife; fathered children, including one son who would serve

James S. Wadsworth

with him in the war; and had a warm, peaceful domestic home life. Consistent with his wealth, family, station, and tempestuous personality, Kearny married a socially appropriate wife who bore him children, then fell in love with a beautiful young woman barely half his age. Unwilling to bend to custom, he sought a divorce over the ferocious opposition of his family, remarried, and began a family life that appeared to rest on social isolation.

In Paris when war seemed inevitable, Kearny returned to the United States, sought high rank from the federal government, the State of New York, and ultimately the State of New Jersey. Finally, the governor of New Jersey gave him a brigade, which became known as the "Jersey Blues." The star of a brigadier general followed.

As the smoke swirled over Fort Sumter, Wadsworth committed himself to the Union Defense Committee, a remarkably effective and highly visible civilian organization representing the great spirit of New York City by forwarding supplies and troops to the capital during its most desperate hours.

Unlike Sherman, who believed that an officer's circumstances should differentiate him from his enlisted men, Wadsworth kept humble quarters, sharing the privations and rugged outdoor existence of his farmers and his enlisted men. Although Kearny lived more like Sherman than Wadsworth, he showed the most particular care for the well-being of his men, testing their food, supplementing their diet with his own money, verifying the adequacy of their living accommodations, and supervising all aspects of their daily life.

Kearny's voluminous correspondence revealed no attitude on the issue of abolition and no involvement with the Radical Republicans, but Wadsworth would rapidly become an ardent abolitionist with close ties to the Radicals. Kearny's extraordinary ability, his long military career, and his unwillingness to accept anything less made him a strong candidate for high rank. Wadsworth, on the other hand, had been promised the two stars of a major general by New York's Governor Edwin D. Morgan when governors could commission general officers; but when the federal government changed the rules, Wadsworth willingly yielded the two stars, serving first as a volunteer aide to Scott in Washington, then as a volunteer aide to McDowell at Bull Run. In many ways these two men represented the best of the officer pools from which they were drawn, Kearny from the Regular Army officers and Wadsworth from the powerful civilians. In many other ways they represented the worst of both pools, both outspokenly criticizing their commanding general.

Irvin McDowell

*D*isgraced in the eyes of his soldiers and his countrymen by the defeat at Bull Run, McDowell still had many paths to choose. His principal alternatives offered a place in the Army of the Potomac in a subordinate position or a responsible command in another area. The rumors of cowardice and drunkenness had not convinced his original supporters, influential men like Secretary of the Treasury Salmon P. Chase, who continued their support. Choosing to remain in the theater of his failure in an attempt to erase the Bull Run blot on his escutcheon, McDowell became McClellan's primary division commander, his principal adviser, and his friend. The respect of younger officers who recognized McDowell's sublimation of his prior position and his unmitigated willingness to help McClellan he earned at once.

Irvin McDowell

During the weeks that followed McClellan's arrival, McDowell's status with the commanding general diminished as McClellan's old friends began to achieve influential positions. The final blow leading to a radical change in the relationship resulted from a series of meetings in which the political participants thrust McDowell center stage. The opportunity for full vindication and for elimination of the blot he did not resist.

John Adams Dix

$\mathcal{M}$any prominent, wealthy New York businessmen sympathized with the South during the pre-war period and hoped for a peaceful dissolution of the Union. The gunfire around Fort Sumter produced their immediate volte-face as the outbreak of hostilities unified them in support of the Union. John A. Dix, a resident of New York City and a leader of this group, represented many of the factions Lincoln believed he must unify in order to have a successful war effort. Dix's education, some at the hands of his father, some at Phillips Exeter Academy, and some at the College of Montreal, suffered interruption by the War of 1812. At the age of fourteen he obtained a commission and served as an ensign at the Battle of Lundy's Lane. Continuing in the army after the war, he rose to the rank of major but resigned in 1826 when he married.

While practicing law, he became active and successful in politics and served as adjutant general of the New York State militia. Elected to the United States Senate as a Democrat in 1845, he consistently supported the anti-slavery Free-Soilers, the Barnburner Democrats, the Wilmot Proviso, and the admission of New Mexico and California as free states during and after the Mexican War. In the 1850s Southerners of his own party blocked his appointments as secretary of state and minister to France. After a restful period in private life, a call from James Buchanan restored him to public prominence as the head of a Post Office Department disrupted by a disastrous defalcation. In response to pressure from wealthy men of the Northeast, Buchanan then appointed him secretary of the treasury in the midnight cabinet at the end of his presidency. In January of 1861, South Carolina and other states having seceded, the captain of a revenue cutter in New Orleans decided to deliver his boat to the State of Louisiana. Dix directed his local treasury official by telegraph to take possession of the cutter, saying, "If anyone attempts to haul down the flag, shoot him on the spot." Dix's service, brief, scrupulous, and successful, resulted in the delivery of a sound treasury department to his successor, Salmon P. Chase, on inauguration day.

The bustling events in New York City after the Rebels fired on Fort Sumter found Dix an active participant, his efforts and credentials being recognized by Governor Morgan's offer of a major-generalcy in the New York militia. Anxious to serve in the field, Dix forwarded his regiments to Washington as rapidly as they were ready; but his own orders to active service never seemed to arrive. He wrote to Washington twice. At this time most believed the war would be quick and easy. Dix waited impatiently in New York City for orders to the field. Soon he would find himself a major general of volunteers seeking a line command.

John A. Dix

Charles P. Stone

From his successful preparation to defend the capital at the outbreak of war, his marches up and down the Potomac between Georgetown and Harpers Ferry, and the confidence of his classmate George McClellan, Stone naturally became a division commander stationed along the Potomac, with his headquarters at Poolesville, Maryland. While in this position he had a chance for a reconnaissance across the river to Leesburg, Virginia, a swift, small unit movement, and a small battle. His strict code of proper warfare, which excluded civilians and their property from the military consequences of rebellion, came promptly to public view and to conflict with

Charles P. Stone

important political figures. To him—and to many others—the slaves of both loyal and disloyal civilians were property not involved in the war. The Radical Republicans, the zealous proponents of abolition and integration, saw the issue differently. The combination of Stone's military action, his treatment of fugitive slaves, and the Joint Committee would create an explosive environment dangerous to Stone's military career.

Edward Donald Baker

A skillful trial lawyer, an exceptional public speaker, and a successful politician, Baker represented more than one pool of candidates with claims to high rank, the foreign born, the Mexican War veteran, and the politician. He arrived in the United States from England at a young age. During his years of residence in Illinois he practiced law in partnership with Abraham Lincoln, the two

Edward D. Baker

men became best friends, and Lincoln named one of his sons after him. In the Mexican War Baker commanded a brigade in Scott's Vera Cruz–Mexico City column and acquired valuable experience for a role in the war with the South. The outbreak found him a United States senator from Oregon, a state he had saved for Lincoln in the election of 1860. The eagles of a colonel and permission to recruit an oversized regiment of volunteers for the federal government led him to assemble the "California Battalion." When standardization required that all federal volunteer regiments be assigned to the states, Baker and Isaac J. Wistar, who had done most of the recruiting, arranged for its designation as the Seventy-first Pennsylvania Infantry.

A showman, Baker would appear in the Senate in full uniform, lay his sword on his desk, and deliver an impassioned pro-Union speech. Soon, he received an offer of the star of a brigadier general, then the two stars of a major general, but acceptance of either commission, requiring confirmation by the Senate, would have compelled him to resign his seat. The single star he declined; but before he rejected the major generalcy, he found himself on the Potomac River with an opportunity to distinguish himself by capturing Leesburg on the Virginia side of the river and defeating a small force of aggressive Confederates—an independent command in battle, the dream of every self-confident man.

Andrew Atkinson Humphreys

Some men, gifted with superior intelligence, even a rare intellectual capacity, had so many talents that their elevation to high rank in the infantry traveled many paths but always with recognition of their high qualities. Andrew Atkinson Humphreys, an underachieving thirteenth in the West Point Class of 1831 and a commission in the topographical engineers, became a scientist and engineer of international reputation. Humphreys missed an active part in the Mexican War but in 1851 was assigned to study the hydrology of the ever-shifting channels at the mouth of the Mississippi River and the causes of the destructive floods in that area. Sunstroke, a tour in Europe to study other things, and various unrelated assignments delayed but did not halt Humphreys and his team. By 1861, he and his subordinate still labored to finish their written work. Without greed for personal distinction Humphreys insisted that he and Henry L. Abbott submit the *Report Upon the Physics and Hydraulics of the Mississippi River* as "our joint report." He had solved a problem that had eluded engineers of many countries for many years. So brilliant was the paper on its general subject of river hydraulics that it found translation to many foreign languages and remained the authoritative work on the subject well into the twentieth century. Memberships in the distinguished American Philosophical Society and many other illustrious scientific societies bloomed about his work.

His appearance confirmed the rigorous application of precise scientific principles that characterized his work in all fields, even as an infantry officer. Extremely neat, he constantly scrubbed himself clean and wore clean paper dickeys. Widely read and learned beyond his profession, he appeared to others to be an "extremely gentlemanly man." He would be described after his time as "a thunderbolt to all who deviated from that path which gentlemen followed."

On December 1, 1861, he was assigned to the Army of the Potomac as a staff officer with specific responsibility for the terrain features that would govern McClellan's Occoquan, Urbana, and Peninsula plans. He began the careful, if not somewhat futile, collection of detailed information about the topography, roads and railroads, rivers and streams, bridges, and man-made obstacles for the area from Alexandria to Richmond and beyond. With this knowledge he strongly preferred, as McClellan did, the Urbana route to Richmond over all others.

In due course Humphreys would find himself disgruntled at the treatment he received from McClellan, a man for whom he nevertheless developed a lifetime respect. More disruptive, he would face conflicts between his topographical engineers, the army's primary mapmakers, and Barnard's engineers, the army's only bridge-builders. Any contest—even ordinary business—with Barnard would immerse Humphreys, a scrupulously honest man, in disputes involving personal integrity.

Andrew A. Humphreys

Fitz John Porter

est Point graduate, political Democrat, and personal friend of the commander of the Army of the Potomac, Porter represented the quintessence of the Regular Army officers despised by the Radical Republicans. Not only were the Democrats from the Regular Army officer corps philosophically and politically anathema to the Radicals, they were often thought to be disloyal or traitors. In addition, Porter personified another dilemma facing the commanding general: the formation of corps. McClellan had quickly formed brigades, then divisions, but he withheld the rank of major general and the formation of corps. Although he wanted to form corps as soon as possible, he wanted his choices to command them, and assignment to corps command required the action of

Fitz John Porter

the president. McClellan had selected his brigadier generals himself, except for those left him in the ragamuffin remnants of McDowell's Army of Northeastern Virginia; but the men he wanted for corps commanders, men like Franklin, Fitz John Porter, and Andrew Porter, had little experience, no prewar seniority, no battlefield reputations, and for these reasons, little likelihood of receiving the obligatory presidential approval.

Amid these complex currents Porter quickly became the major general's most sturdy friend and supporter; and he enjoyed the support, even the public adulation, of the major general. In this unassailable position, protected by the virtual impregnability of his superior, Porter would confront, if not insult, the Radicals in their home forum, the Joint Committee on the Conduct of the War. As long as McClellan held his position, Porter stood well beyond their reach.

William Buel Franklin

*B*orn in 1823 in York, Pennsylvania, "Frank," to his friends, graduated from the Military Academy at the head of the class of 1843, entered the Topographical Engineers, and served with the Kearny expedition to South Pass, then with General Wool's command in the Mexican War. Marriage, a first lieutenancy, a captaincy, and a station for several years in Washington as supervising engineer in charge of the construction of the dome on the Capitol and the new wing on the Treasury Building followed. In the nation's capital he became an excellent example of both Scott's company grade officer rule and Colonel Browne's geographic rule of promotion. When Congress created the new regiments in May he became colonel of the Twelfth United States Infantry.

At Bull Run, one of his regiments, the Fourth Pennsylvania, claimed its discharge on the day of the battle and left his brigade. Understrength, he performed reasonably well, taking his men into the final battle line on Henry House Hill, where he found no opportunity to distinguish himself with an independent, extraordinary act. Promoted to brigadier general at the suggestion of his friend McClellan, he received command of a division one month later.

All division matters brought before him he decided impartially and on their merits. In a short time he gained the confidence and esteem of his soldiers. His continuous efforts to protect private property while the army lay in Confederate country failed to save the helpless citizens. Nevertheless, he did not take advantage of the circumstances to select a fine local house for his headquarters. After the army reestablished its position on the heights west of the Potomac River in the area of Alexandria, Virginia, he pitched his tent in an open field on the brow of a hill and remained there the entire winter. He did not communicate with the local citizens except on official matters and did not permit himself or any of his staff to occupy their houses. His tent served as his headquarters.

According to the Comte de Paris, he was "different from the others and is spiritual despite a tough appearance. He is a soldier before everything. He would gladly fight but he does not have Heintzelman's ardor. He does not care about the political aspect of the conflict and would like to have to improve his troops." Keenly susceptible to "the demands of justice and true humanity," modest and unassuming in his manners, but a rigid disciplinarian, he had a strong contempt for hypocrisy, openly rebuked it when it interfered with the discipline of his troops, and set an example for his officers by his conduct. He strongly believed that the army must fight and conquer the enemy but also protect the defenseless and the innocent. In his view the army was too much inclined to yield to unnecessary fears and "thereby bring distress upon the innocent." A considerable thinker, he realized

William B. Franklin

that moderation in enemy country would be more effective than the sword. He knew that many citizens of Virginia had been misled by their leaders and, much like his friend "Mac," was most anxious to be merciful to those who had been led astray while punishing those who had led them.

Before the end of 1861, he became a confidant of McClellan and a trusted member of his "kitchen cabinet," an association that became widely known. In the eyes of those increasingly hostile to McClellan, that fact and Franklin's treatment of Confederate civilians cast doubts on his patriotism. Some of these whisperings reached important members of government. Rumors about the loyalty of Franklin and others played on the confusion about the correct means to put down the rebellion and the proper treatment of the citizens who supported it.

Frederick West Lander

$\mathcal{A}$s a school boy he excelled at sports, showing a spirit of adventure and great personal strength. After studying civil engineering Lander chose the railroads for his career, first in the East, then on the cross-continental railroad projects of the 1850s. Powerful and tall, in fact, as tall as the president and Scott, Lander had a rugged physique that made him a visual expression of the frontiersman and mountainman he was, but he also appeared to be a contradiction: "both active and indolent, both stately and careless."

In 1853, then in his early thirties, he accepted an offer from Isaac Ingalls Stevens, a lieutenant of engineers, to be chief engineer on the survey for a northern railway route to the West Coast. That began a series of projects in which he searched for the best route between the frontier and the West Coast, many of his reports being published by Congress. But he did not simply make cross-country trips for the Department of the Interior in order to investigate railroad routes. Nor did he "go native" and remain on the frontier fighting Indians and living on buffalo jerky. He had ideas of his own.

Participation in the philosophical debates about the first railway to the Pacific swept him inevitably into the sectional controversy about the location of the route, north, central, or south. A loyal but moderate Democrat, he wrote and spoke charitably about the southern route but scorned it even while he described its virtues.

In September 1859 he attended the Pacific Railroad Convention, at which he delivered a well-received speech about the Pacific Railway project. In it he took the opportunity to compliment the contributions of James A. McDougall, the able, fiercely competitive, but too-often-intoxicated senator from California, and to espouse the central route. Just before he returned east he married an internationally renowned actress, who complemented his less well-known artistic talent as a poet.

When war erupted, the men in Washington knew his rugged, fearless skills as a railroader, frontiersman, outdoorsman, and Indian fighter would make him a talented addition to the Union effort. He wrote to General Scott to volunteer "in any capacity, at any time, and for any duty." Scott accepted.

Lincoln and Scott sent Lander to Texas, where Governor Sam Houston remained loyal to the United States. Houston's fellow citizens were a different story. Lander's assignment, which was to offer Houston military assistance, illustrated Lincoln's mistaken conclusion about the depth of loyalty to the Union in the South. The old Texan did not want assistance, and he certainly did not want the disruption of United States troops in his state. After Lander returned safely to Washington, now isolated from the northeastern states, he was sent through hostile Maryland to deliver dispatches to the military forces under Butler, Keyes, and Lefferts in Annapolis

Frederick W. Lander

on the north side of Baltimore. Of eight messengers, only Lander and one other succeeded in reaching the objective, and Lander had to escape from capture to do it.

As a colonel on McClellan's staff in western Virginia, he distinguished himself in the battle at Phillipi and earned national fame by galloping at breakneck
speed down a steep slope to perform his staff duties. He marched with McClellan
to Rich Mountain, where the major general burst on the scene with the Union's
first victory. Taking advantage of his skills as an outdoorsman, Lander led the

flanking column on an eight-hour march "through a pathless forest, over rocks and ravines in the rain."

A plan he submitted to Seward for raising a regiment of Virginia volunteers for the Union passed to Lincoln, who asked Scott to see Lander and consider his idea. The president wrote, "Col. Lander is a valuable man to us." In August, Lander received from the Adjutant General's office a commission as a brigadier general to rank from May 17, 1861; and he was assigned a brigade in Charles P. Stone's division, the Corps of Observation. The fighting at Ball's Bluff caught Lander at a meeting in the capital, but he raced to the scene in time to command a reconnaissance from Edward's Ferry the day after the battle and receive a bullet in the leg. The wound would have a curious but undetectable history.

The conference related to the east-west part of the Baltimore and Ohio Railroad, the line from Harpers Ferry to Cumberland, Maryland. From the outbreak of the war the major railroad arteries to the capital had been the lines from New York and Philadelphia in the north and the Baltimore and Ohio line from Cumberland in the west. Traffic had been interdicted since May. Given the equivalent of a division scattered over the line of track and a very long, peculiarly shaped department only thirty miles wide, Lander would have numerous encounters with McClellan's classmate Tom "Stonewall" Jackson and the famous Confederate cavalry officer Turner Ashby. The end of his campaign against them would differ from that of every other independent commander in the valley.

Chapter 1

"no excuse can be received for bringing on an action . . . without . . . instructions."

—McClellan in Instructions to General Officers

McClellan Plans His First Advance

"Here we are," said "Greasy Dick" Richardson, gesticulating toward Munson's Hill, "seventy thousand men within one hour's march of that hill, where there are not over four thousand Confederates, whose nearest supports are at Fairfax Court House. We could wipe them out in a twinkling, and yet I am ordered to make no demonstration, and if attacked, to fall back under the guns of the fortifications along Arlington Heights."[1]

Sharing the almost universal ignorance of McClellan's intentions, Richardson complained about the Union failure to snatch Munson's Hill from the Confederates. Like most of his fellow general officers and all members of the government, he knew nothing about McClellan's plans. The days had passed through September, the number of "stampedes" had declined, and the uncertainty about the safety of Maryland had faded. Now surrounded by a series of forts and protected on the west bank of the Potomac by a growing army arranged in a concave semi-circle from Alexandria to Langley, Virginia, Samuel P. Heintzelman on the left around Fort

---

1   Andrews, J. Cutler, *The North Reports the Civil War* (Pittsburgh, 1955), 151–152 (Andrews, *North Reports*), quoted from Coffin, Charles Carleton, *The Boys of '61* (Boston, 1925), 56.

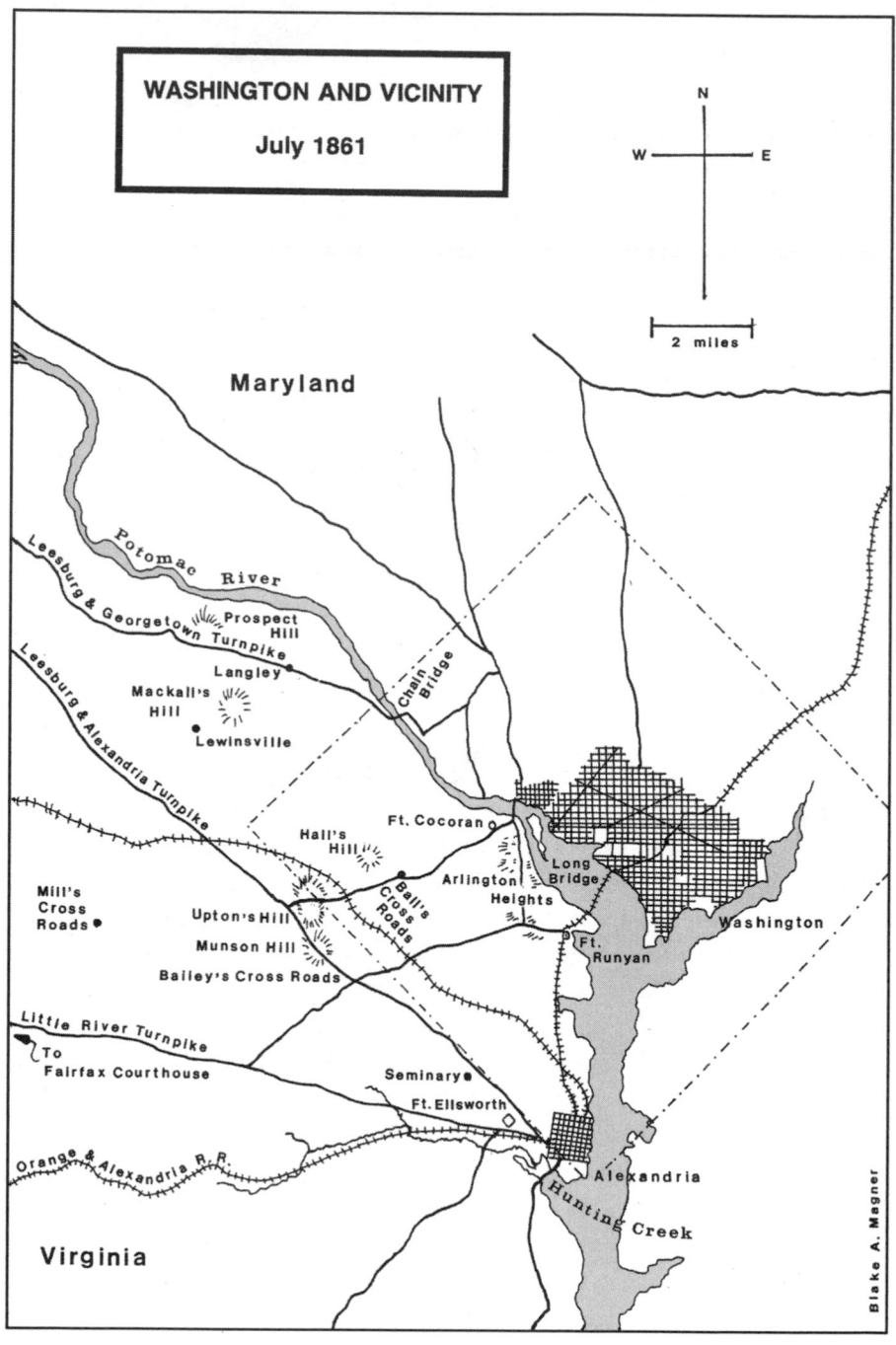

WASHINGTON AND VICINITY

July 1861

N

W — E

2 miles

Maryland

Potomac River

Leesburg & Georgetown Turnpike

Prospect Hill

Langley

Leesburg & Alexandria Turnpike

Mackall's Hill

Lewinsville

Chain Bridge

Ft. Cocoran

Hall's Hill

Mill's Cross Roads

Upton's Hill

Ball's Cross Roads

Arlington Heights

Long Bridge

Munson Hill

Bailey's Cross Roads

Ft. Runyan

Washington

Little River Turnpike

To Fairfax Courthouse

Seminary

Ft. Ellsworth

Orange & Alexandria R.R.

Alexandria

Hunting Creek

Virginia

Blake A. Magner

Lyon to William F. Smith on the right at the Chain Bridge,[2] the capital had become safe; and McClellan had begun to consider light offensive plans.

In late July, a few days after the battle at Bull Run, the Confederates had reoccupied Fairfax Court House and in early August advanced their outposts to Munson's and Upton's Hills. Together the two hills formed a north and south ridge approximately a mile in length, Munson's Hill immediately south of Upton's Hill, with Miner's Hill and Hall's Hill to the north. Formidable rifle pits with cannon in small works, all visible from the unfinished dome of the U.S. Capitol building and blocking any advance from the river, ran along the crests of Munson's and Upton's Hills, showing that the Confederates intended a long stay in a strong position. Their Stars and Bars waved contemptuously in the breeze.[3] East of the heights marked by Munson's Hill lay Ball's Cross-roads and to the south lay Bailey's Cross-Roads. With both crossroads occupied by Union pickets, the two hills lay nestled in a crook in the federal lines,[4] the configuration McClellan had inherited from General Irvin McDowell. The shallow area at Arlington Heights made the Munson's Hill-Upton's Hill area critical to the army's safety.[5]

Although the cranky old general in chief still opposed any offensive into his beloved Virginia,[6] McClellan knew that, before he could consider any larger plan, he must create a suitable buffer zone west of the Potomac by expanding his internal space. To do this he would reoccupy the Munson's Hill area and incorporate the two heights into his fortified line. Seizure of the Fairfax Court House line would follow,

2   *The War of the Rebellion: A Compilation of the Official Records of the Union and Confederate Armies prepared under the Supervision of Lieut. Col. Robert N. Scott, Third U.S. Artillery and Published pursuant to Act of Congress Approved June 16, 1880*, 145 vols. (Washington, 1880), 5, 32 (*OR*).

3   McClellan, George B., William C. Prime, ed., *McClellan's Own Story; The War for the Union: the Soldiers who Fought It, the Civilians who Directed it and his Relations to it and to them* (New York, 1886, Easton Press ed.), 73 (*M.O.S.*).

4   Philip W. Kearny MSS (Library of Congress), letter dated August 29, 1861, from Kearny to Parker; Mills, John Harrison, *Chronicles of the Twenty-first Regiment New York State Volunteers Embracing a Full History of the Regiment from the enrolling of the first Volunteer in Buffalo, April 15, 1861, to the final Mustering Out, May 18, 1862, including a Copy of Muster Out Roles of Field and Staff, and Each Company* (Buffalo, 1867), 120 (Mills, *Twenty-first New York*); Wistar, Isaac Jones, *Autobiography of Isaac Jones Wistar, 1825–1907* (Philadelphia, 1937), 359 (Wistar, *Autobiography*); Sterling, Pound (Manson, William P.), *Camp Fires of the Twenty-third: Sketches of the Camp Life, Marches, and Battles of the Twenty-third Regiment, N.Y.V., during the Term of Two Years in the Service of the United States* (New York, 1863), 25 (Sterling, *Camp Fires of the Twenty-third*).

5   *M.O.S.*, 73.

6   Comte de Paris, "McClellan Organizing the Grand Army" in Johnson, Robert Underwood, and Clarence Clough Buel, eds., *Battles and Leaders of the Civil War*, 4 vols. (New York, 1956, Youseloff reprint), 2, 112, 115 (*B&L*).

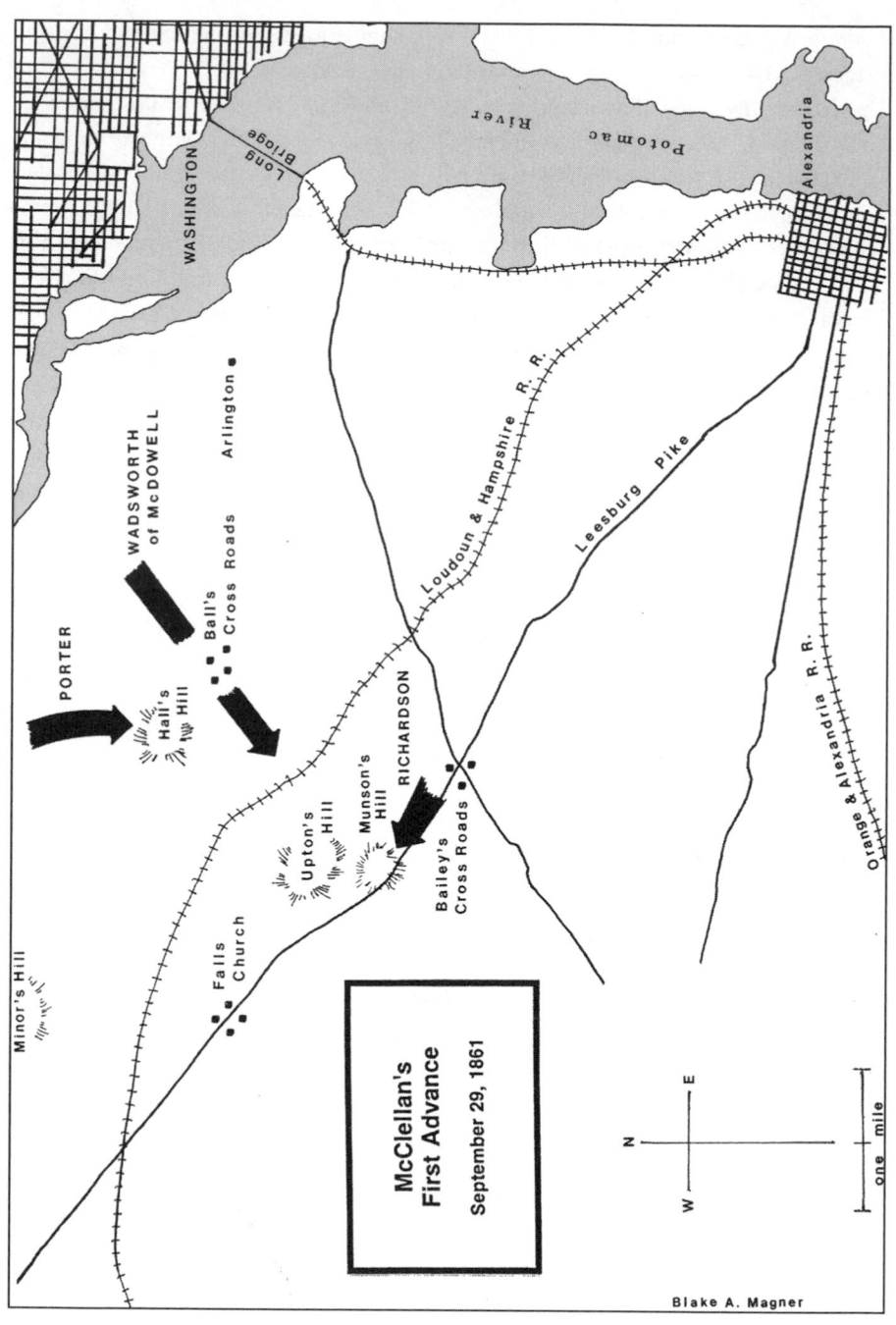

McClellan's
First Advance
September 29, 1861

N

E

W

one mile

Blake A. Magner

but his first attention he fixed on the lesser goal, the area around the two hills. An advance here would straighten his line, give his position depth to the river, and allow him to maneuver behind his front lines. By the end of September he would be ready. In three columns he would advance and capture the hills. Generals Smith, Heintzelman, and McDowell, a group that included some of his most trusted division commanders, would perform the advance.[7] The first column, Richardson's brigade of Heintzelman's division, would march north from Bailey's Cross-Roads; the second, James S. Wadsworth's brigade of McDowell's division, west from Ball's Cross-Roads, and the third, Edward D. Baker's brigade, into the open area northwest of Hall's Hill and Upton's Hill. This first aggressive act would solve many political and other problems that threatened his master plan for a strategic advance and a final Armageddon. Already conscious of security and probably concerned about interference by the general in chief, he told no one about his plans except President Lincoln and a staff officer from the War Department.[8] He would make a surprise move that would, he hoped, provoke the Rebels to attack and precipitate a "big fight."[9] But

7   Comte de Paris MS diary (large diary) (Archieve National de la Maison de France), entries dated October 11, 20, and 27, 1861; Wistar, *Autobiography*, 359, 360; Sypher, J. R., *History of the Pennsylvania Reserve Corps: a Complete Record of the Organization and of the Different Companies, Regiments and Brigades Containing Descriptions of Expeditions, Marches, Skirmishes and Battles; together with Biographical Sketches of Officers and Personal Records of Each Man during his Term of Service* (Lancaster, 1865), 108–109 (Sypher, *Pennsylvania Reserves*); Bates, Samuel P., *History of Pennsylvania Volunteers: prepared in Compliance with Acts of the Legislature*, 14 vols. (Harrisburg, 1870, Broadfoot reprint 1993) 4, 697, 788–789 (Bates, *Hist. Penn. Vols.*). Bates dates this event on September 29, but the contemporaneous diary entry of Lieutenant Charles R. Haydon, noted in Sears, Stephen W., ed., *For Country, Cause & Leader: the Civil War Journal of Charles R. Haydon* (New York, 1993) 97–99, entry dated September 28, 1861 (Sears, *For Country, Cause & Leader (Haydon Diary),* makes this virtually impossible. The confusion about the dates, September 28 or 29, probably arose from the fact that some of the incidents occurred before midnight (September 28), some after (September 29). Many writers typically used one date for an entire night.

8   George B. McClellan MSS (Library of Congress) letters dated October 25, 1869, from Schuyler Hamilton to McClellan, and October 30, 1869, from McClellan to Hamilton; Meade, George, ed., *The Life and Letters of George Gordon Meade, Major-General United States Army*, 2 vols. (New York, 1913) 1, 221, letter dated October 6, 1861, from Meade to his wife (Meade, *Life and Letters*); M.O.S., 69. The sources do not fix the date of McClellan's discussion with the president with certainty. The conversation has been placed in the chronology of identifiable dates on a logical basis. The letters do not specify Colonel Scott as Colonel Thomas A. Scott, assistant secretary of war, or Colonel Henry L. Scott, inspector general: Heitman, Francis B., *Historical Register and Dictionary of the United States Army from its Organization, September 29, 1789, to March 2, 1903*, 2 vols. (Washington, 1903) 1, 868 (Heitman, *Historical Register*).

9   Comte de Paris MS diary (large diary) (A.N. de la M. de F.) entry dated September 29, 1861; Benedict, G. G., *Vermont in the Civil War: A History of the Part Taken by the Vermont Soldiers and Sailors in the War for the Union, 1861–1865*, 2 vols. (Burlington, 1886) 1, 94 (Benedict, *Vermont in the War*).

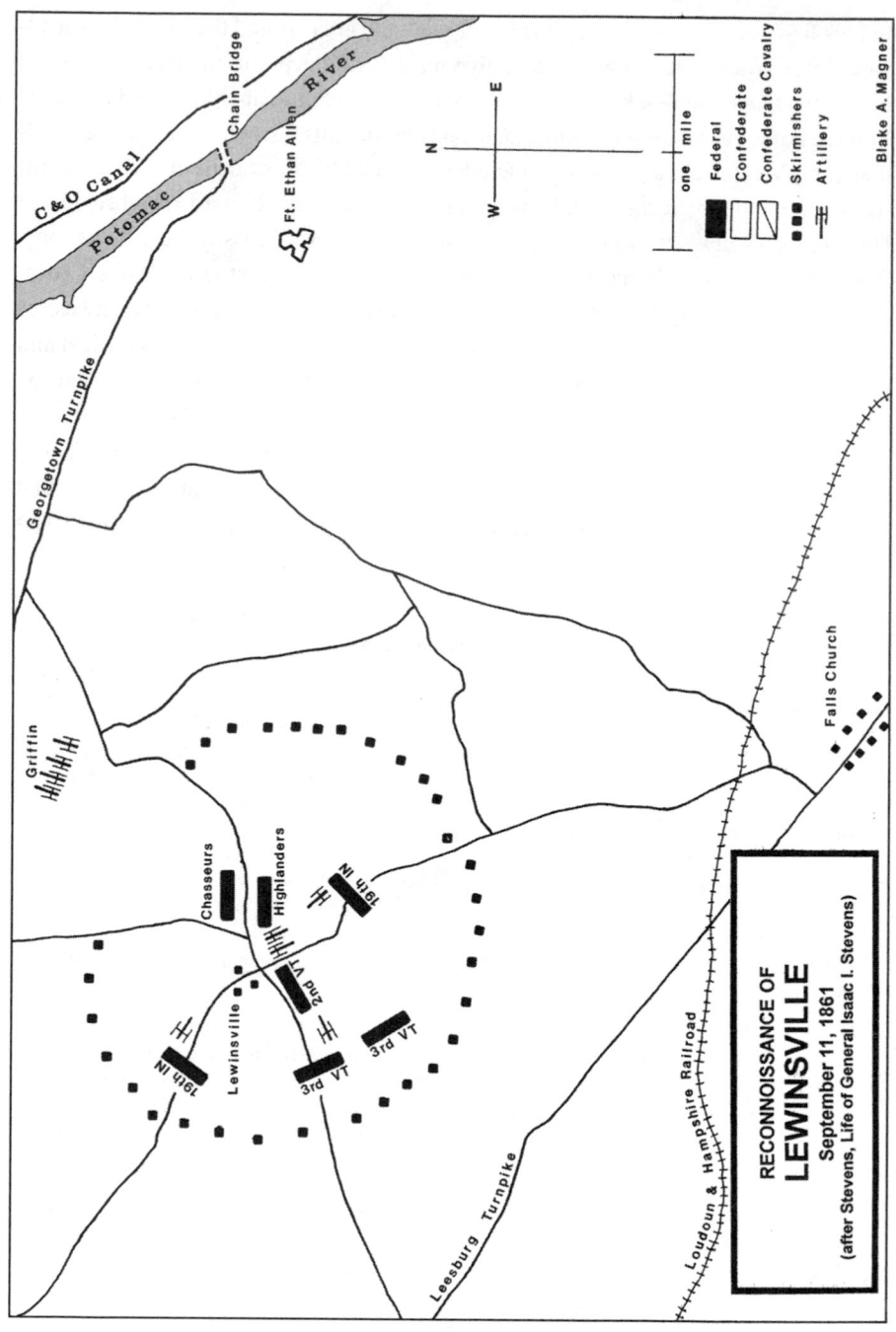

RECONNOISSANCE OF
LEWINSVILLE
September 11, 1861
(after Stevens, Life of General Isaac I. Stevens)

Blake A. Magner

first, he must reconnoiter the area to determine whether he could capture the well-fortified Rebel positions on the two heights.[10]

On August 26, the Seventy-ninth New York broke camp, headed through Washington, and camped a mile short of the Chain Bridge. Disgraced by the loss of their colors after the mutiny, the Highlanders proceeded to the music of the *Dead March* and on September 6 formed part of a large force that crossed Chain Bridge to the Virginia side of the Potomac. There, they took positions in the division under "Baldy" Smith, McClellan's right flank element in Virginia. Succeeding by seniority to command of Smith's First Brigade, Colonel Isaac Ingalls Stevens was to construct Fort Ethan Allen, a large earthwork west of the Leesburg Turnpike, and fell the woods in the vicinity.

McClellan ordered Smith to reconnoiter in force to Lewinsville, a small village six miles west of the Chain Bridge. Still concerned about unplanned meeting engagements, he told Smith to be certain not to precipitate a general engagement. Smith assigned the reconnaissance to Stevens and repeated these instructions to him.

The reconnaissance party consisted of Stevens' Highlanders, the Seventy-ninth New York; Smith's old regiment, the Third Vermont; two companies of the Second Vermont under Lieutenant Colonel George J. Stannard; four companies of the Sixty-fifth New York under Lieutenant Colonel Alexander Shaler; five companies of the Nineteenth Indiana under Colonel Solomon Meredith; four guns of Charles C. Griffin's battery; forty volunteer cavalry; and fifty Regular cavalry. All these officers would ultimately rise at least to brigade command, and Griffin would reach Appomattox at the head of the Fifth Corps.

Without mishap, the troops arrived in Vienna and formed a perimeter near the spot where the "masked battery" had embarrassed Brigadier General Robert C. Schenck in June. Lieutenant Orlando M. Poe, a young engineer officer who had graduated sixth in the West Point class of 1856, supervised the reconnaissance. Confederate artillery opened fire. Although shells landed among the infantry and inflicted some casualties, the men did not flinch or leave their positions. Griffin's four guns responded vigorously.

Hearing the firing and mindful of McClellan's instructions not to bring on a general engagement, Smith suffered "considerable anxiety" and, followed by his staff and a section of Captain Thaddeus P. Mott's Third New York Battery, galloped hotly to Stevens' position. As soon as he saw the good order of the troops, he "resumed his wonted coolness, and heartily congratulated Colonel Stevens and his

---

10   No source expressly states these inferences, but the facts all support them. Probably because the outcome of this effort embarrassed McClellan and greater events occurred afterwards, he never explained it in his report, prepared in 1863, or his postwar memoirs.

command on the well-conducted and successful reconnaissance," wrote Stevens' son after the war.

Showing even greater excitement and anxiety, McClellan and a large following of staff and escort "came tearing up the road." He, too, became calm when he learned the affair had ended, congratulated Smith, and visited the wounded. Giving further substance to Stevens' concerns about his position in McClellan's army, the major general passed about the reconnaissance force "without noticing Colonel Stevens,"[11] according to Stevens' son.

That evening McClellan had an appointment to meet Frederick L. Olmstead, the secretary, and Henry Whitney Bellows, the president, of the United States Sanitary Commission. In his absence his aides talked with the visitors. The Seventy-ninth Highlanders and two other regiments, they explained, had withstood the Confederate artillery fire superbly. The men had shown no apparent concern, although two had been killed and several wounded.

Not until late did the major general, still elated at the performance of his men, finally arrive at his headquarters. He was beginning to feel as if he had an army, he told them; had decided to report the reconnaissance to the secretary of war; and would take his guests with him if they wished. Back in Washington, sprawling on Cameron's couch and puffing on a cigar, he described the Vienna reconnaissance in a "direct, frank, and familiar" manner, Olmstead wrote to his father.[12]

A few days later the commanding general told Smith he would send the Highlanders' colors to division headquarters for restoration. Smith was to tell them they had "shown by their conduct in the reconnaissance of the 11th instant that they are worthy to carry the banner into action."[13] On September 13, he sent preliminary orders to all his division, brigade, and regimental commanders to give their personal attention to preparations for the field by eliminating all unnecessary baggage,

11   Sears, Stephen W., ed., *The Civil War Papers of George B. McClellan: Selected Correspondence, 1860–1865*, 78, Instructions to General Officers, dated August 4, 1861, by the editor (Sears, *McClellan's Correspondence*); OR, 5, 168, 171, Stevens' report; 172, Poe's report; 173, Meredith's report; 177, Stannard's report; 178, Hyde's report; Benedict, *Vermont in the Civil War*, 1, 134–135; Stevens, Hazard, *The Life of Isaac Ingalls Stevens by his Son*, 2 vols. (Boston and New York, 1911) 2, 329–331 (Stevens, *Stevens*); Heitman, *Historical Register*, 1, 795. In the segment entitled "Instructions devoted to Battles," McClellan said, "no excuse can be received for bringing on an action . . . without . . . instructions."

12   McLaughlin, Charles Capen, ed., *The Papers of Frederick Law Olmstead*, 4 vols. incompl. (Baltimore and London, 1986); Censer, Jane Turner, vol. ed., *Defending the Union: The Civil War and the U.S. Sanitary Commission, 1861–1863*, vol. 4, 196–197, letter dated September 12, 1861, from Olmstead to his father (McLaughlin, *Olmstead Letters*).

13   OR, 5, 168, letter dated September 14, 1861, from McClellan to Smith.

reducing the contents of the wagons, and assuring themselves that no wagons contained unauthorized articles.[14]

Unlike the strict discipline shown by the Confederate troops in other areas, unpredictable picket firing took place around Bailey's Cross-Roads. Confederate patrols and skirmishers had become aggressive, "closely searching our picket-lines every night," wrote a junior officer in his diary.[15] Philip W. Kearny, a brigadier general stationed in this area, thought it was diversionary activity intended to distract attention from a crossing they might make north of the Chain Bridge.[16]

In the middle of the month "Dick" Richardson arranged with his Rebel counterpart to stop the picket firing in the area around Bailey's Cross-Roads south of Munson's Hill.[17] Less than a week later Richardson's truce collapsed when the Rebels began firing all along their picket lines.[18] The Union officer in command at the crossroads, Captain James Brethschneider, a German with a thick accent, called for a flag of truce and in "high temper" crossed to complain about the unannounced change.[19]

"I know nothing about any agreement," said the Confederate officer in charge of the fort. "I came here to fire and am going to fire. Anybody is a damned fool not to fire. I want nothing more to do with you, and I will have you arrested in less than no time unless you are off."

"Very well," said Brethschneider, "you want to fire, I gives you enough of it. Good day, sir. I hope I meet you again before the war is over."

"Now, boys," he said when he returned to his lines, "you waits till they fire once, then you give them hell. Shoot at the damned rascals so fast as you can."

Heavy firing occurred before dark. At daylight next morning, September 23, 1861, brisk picket firing began again, as many as twenty rounds per man on the Union side. The road at Bailey's Cross-Roads, slightly more than two hundred yards behind the picket line, ran nearly parallel to it. The Rebel infantry fire at the picket line passed so high that many of the balls carried to the road in the rear. In

---

14   Joseph Hooker MSS (Huntington Library), Circular, dated September 13, 1861, from Headquarters, Army of the Potomac, by Seth Williams by order of General McClellan.

15   Sears, *For Country, Cause & Leader (Haydon Diary)*, 88–91, entries dated September 15, 16, 17, and 18, 1861.

16   Kearny MSS (L.C.) letter dated August 29, 1861, from Kearny to Cortlandt Parker.

17   Sears, *For Country, Cause & Leader* (*Haydon Diary*) 91, entry dated September 19, 1861.

18   As the Confederates would prove on many occasions in the future, unexplained increased activity, especially increased heavy firing, preceded and foretold their withdrawal. The Union commanders seem never to have identified this pattern and taken advantage of it.

19   Sears, *For Country, Cause & Leader* (*Haydon Diary*) 94, entry dated September 22, 1861.

the afternoon the Confederates burned two houses just beyond their lines, presumably to prevent them from being used by sharpshooters.

Richardson's pickets decided to burn the large barns and stacks of hay and grain being used by the Confederates for sharpshooting. Firing red-hot iron slugs, they finally set fire to one barn just after dark. The fire spread to the other and the stacks.[20]

On September 25, McClellan took one last look at the Confederate position, force, and temper with a mixed force of five thousand men. Once again, the trusted Baldy Smith commanded. Except for a slight artillery exchange, nothing occurred; but the Rebels had now seen two reconnaissances in force in the same area within two weeks. They needed no man of genius to conclude that the Union army had decided to attack Munson's Hill.[21] By his last reconnaissance, McClellan committed an error in judgment that Union officers would still be making in 1865: He telegraphed his "surprise" attack by obvious preparations.

Richardson, who commanded the brigade in the area around Bailey's Cross-Roads, went to his forward positions to determine how to take Munson's Hill. He concluded that Upton's Hill to the north could be taken, which would allow them to approach Munson's Hill from the flank. Headquarters sent him no response until he telegraphed that, according to his pickets, the Rebels were leaving. McClellan directed him to move forward cautiously, coordinate with McDowell on his right, and take the Hill. Richardson sent his pickets forward to the Bailey's Cross-Roads area.[22]

Having prepared carefully, perhaps too carefully, McClellan gave the orders to the appropriate senior officers for the capture of Munson's Hill and Upton's Hill. Not for the last time, two things happened: Forewarned, the Confederates acted first; and McClellan's enterprising American infantrymen and junior officers anticipated his plans.

---

20   Sears, *For Country, Cause & Leader (Haydon Diary)* 94–96, entry dated September 23, 1861.

21   *OR*, 5, 215–217, Smith's report; Benedict, *Vermont in the Civil War*, 1, 134–136.

22   *Report of the Joint Committee on the Conduct of the War* (Wilmington, 1998, Broadfoot reprint) 1, 115 (Richardson) (*C.C.W.*).

Chapter 2

"There, damn it, Colonel, there goes one of them up to the fort. There goes two more. There, by God, goes the whole of them. Colonel, all you have to do is hold these men, if you can, till it is time to let them go."

—Richardson on the spontaneous charge of his men to capture Munson's Hill

Munson's Hill (McClellan's First Advance)

Ct t 4 A.M. on September 28, already aware that the Confederates had evacuated the Munson's Hill area, McClellan sent word to his staff to join him for a trip across the river. His staff officers met him at the Georgetown Ferry. The general told them that the enemy had withdrawn and that the troops would occupy the hill. They rode past Fort Corcoran, crossed an old outpost line, then reached the ravine bottomed by Four Mile Run. Now in Rebel territory, they kept a sharp watch in all directions, paused briefly to send orders for the troops to move forward, then pressed forward until they reached a house half destroyed by the retreating enemy. From the roof of a building they confirmed that the Rebels had abandoned the fortifications on the hill. They could see a few Confederate cavalrymen leaving.[1]

From Bailey's Cross-Roads that morning, the officers and men of Richardson's Brigade could see no Confederates around the fort on Munson's Hill. The Rebels had apparently been withdrawn from their pickets during the night. The relief for

---

1 Comte de Paris MS diary (large diary) (A.N. de la M. de F.), entry dated September 29, 1861.

the Federal picket line arrived late.[2] Only six or eight cavalrymen, possibly the horsemen seen by McClellan and his staff, could be seen about the fort. A local woman passed the fort with children and furniture in a wagon. When she reached the Union line, she reported that two regiments lay concealed in the fortifications with six regiments not far beyond.

About four o'clock in the afternoon, Richardson and Orlando M. Poe, by recent appointment a colonel commanding the Second Michigan, arrived at their picket line. Richardson examined the area, then ordered a captain, a lieutenant, and twelve men from Company I to occupy a house about five hundred feet in front of a Confederate battery. They moved forward and took positions in the house or scattered along a fence. Concealed in the weeds and knowing nothing about the Confederate force or position, they lay half a mile in advance of all pickets for almost an hour and a half. Around the Confederate works they could see approximately twenty men firing occasional shots. Twenty men of the Fifth Michigan joined them, and a short time later more came through the woods to occupy a schoolhouse a little nearer the fort. On the road another party of about forty men took a position even with the Second Michigan.

Suddenly, someone called "Forward," and everyone rushed the works. Richardson and Poe could only watch with astonishment. Richardson swore ferociously. He turned and shouted.

"Is there another lieutenant here?"

"Yes, sir," said a lieutenant. "I am."

Richardson looked at the lieutenant a moment and said, "Well, by God, you look like one. You'll kill somebody yet. Where in hell is your sword, sir? Where have you been? What have you been about? Out on duty without a sword?"

The outburst paralyzed the lieutenant, who was armed only with a pistol. Colonel Poe, recently promoted from lieutenant of engineers to command of the Second Michigan, explained that the young officer had been promoted only within the last day or so and had not had an opportunity to obtain a sword.

"Ah, well," said Richardson, "can you get a sword, sir?"

Another captain handed the lieutenant his sword.

"Do you see that barricade on the road?"

"Yes," responded the new lieutenant.

"Can you lead these men there?"

"Yes."

Richardson then said sharply, "Come. Why in hell ain't you off, sir? What are you standing here for?"

2   Sears, *For Country, Cause & Leader (Haydon Diary)*, 97–98, entry dated September 28, 1861.

Pretending to be enraged but secretly "laughing in his sleeve," Richardson shouted to Poe, "There, damn it, colonel, there goes one of them up to the fort. There goes two more. There, by God, goes the whole of them. Colonel, all you have to do is hold these men, if you can, till it is time to let them go."

The old woman had lied. The works were empty. Up went the Union flag. Three cheers from the men. Other parties soon occupied the works beyond their flanks.[3] By sunset, Union pickets had "stormed and captured" Munson's Hill, the great Rebel fortress, without a shot. From the fortifications on the crest, the new occupants had a fine view of Washington and the Potomac to the east and toward the west of the high hills to the right of Manassas.[4] The men found abandoned Confederate "artillery" made of logs and cardboard, "ingeniously painted" to look like cannon.[5] The fortifications, low and worthless, would have provided scant protection for infantry.[6] An officer who viewed them the following day wrote in his diary, "The whole thing has been a grand humbug and bugaboo. Naturally it is a strong position, and our men will soon make it impregnable."[7]

In McDowell's division, Brigadier General James S. Wadsworth, who had served as a volunteer aide to McDowell during the Bull Run campaign, attempted to arrange the same kind of truce in front of his picket line[8] near Ball's Cross-Roads east of Munson's and Upton's Hills. His efforts having been futile, slight skirmishes and firing between the pickets had taken place almost constantly. While the inquisitive men of Richardson's brigade prepared for their impromptu charge

---

3   Eicher, John H., and David J. Eicher, *Civil War High Commands* (Stanford, 2003) 432 (Eicher, *Civil War High Commands*); Sears, *For Country, Cause & Leader (Haydon Diary)*, 97, entry dated September 28, 1861.

4   Comte de Paris MS Diary (A.N. de la M. de F.), entry dated September 29, 1861; Comte de Paris, "McClellan Organizing the Grand Army," in *B&L*, 2, 113.

5   Norton, Oliver Willcox, *Army Letters, 1861–1865, extracts from Private Letters to Relatives and Friends from a Soldier in the Field during the late Civil War with an Appendix containing copies of some Official Documents, Papers and Addresses of a later Date* (Chicago, 1903) 25, letter dated September 30, 1861, from Norton to "Sister L" (Norton, *Letters*); Sears, *For Country, Cause & Leader (Haydon Diary)* 97–98, entry dated September 28, 1861; Prince de Joinville, William H. Hurlbert, ed. and trans., *Army of the Potomac: its Organization, its Commander, and its Campaign* (New York 1862) 26 (de Joinville, *Army of the Potomac*).

6   James S. Wadsworth MSS (Library of Congress), six-page memorandum handwritten on lined paper in lead pencil of n.d. but apparently written shortly after McClellan set sail for the Peninsula.

7   Rusling, James F., *Men and Things I Saw in Civil War Days* (New York, 1899) 199, letter dated September 29, 1861, from Rusling to his father and friends (Rusling, *Men and Things*); Norton, *Army Letters*, 25, letter dated September 30, 1861, from Norton to his friend P. Sterling, *Camp Fires of the Twenty-third*, 25.

8   Wadsworth MSS (L.C.) six-page memorandum handwritten on lined paper in lead pencil of n.d.

onto a deserted Munson's Hill, Wadsworth recklessly reconnoitered in person with two companies of the Thirty-fifth New York. He found the same thing. The enemy had abandoned both Upton's and Munson's Hills. The only Rebel force, a small detachment of cavalry, perhaps the same one seen by McClellan and Richardson, retired when Wadsworth approached.[9]

At 5 P.M. the long roll sounded throughout Wadsworth's brigade. Anxious for a pitched battle, the men took arms and formed line, ready to go when orders for the brigade to come forward arrived. The Twenty-first New York, having the position of honor on the right, took the lead. Infantry, artillery, and cavalry crowded the road.[10] When they cleared the woods surrounding their camp and entered the open road, the Twenty-first accelerated to the "double-quick," passed Ball's Cross-Roads, passed their old picket stations, passed the new outposts, and neared the railroad where it went through a gorge with a stream.[11] As twilight verged into darkness the long columns of advancing infantry and artillery passed McClellan and his staff, and the infantrymen jokingly asked if McClellan and his party, returning to Washington, were making a Bull Run flight.[12]

Using his superb ability to generate loyalty, affection, and morale in his fighting men, McClellan made an offhand but audible comment about "the right regiment in the right place." The men of the Twenty-first New York Infantry, even though winded by their "double-quick" pace, responded with the loudest cheer they could muster.[13] This kind of praise for a unit, typical of McClellan's style of leadership throughout his time with the Army of the Potomac, he had started much earlier. After McClellan had reviewed the Sixth Wisconsin in late August, a lieutenant wrote his wife, ". . . as usual the greatest man was the plainest dressed and the most unassuming of the party, the Gen'l complimented our Reg't as being the *cleanest uniformed and guns in the best condition of any volunteer regiment in the service. . . ."*

Wadsworth and his staff joined their men on the road. Not satisfied with the "double-quick," Wadsworth took advantage of McClellan's inspirational comment

---

9   Wadsworth MSS (L.C.) six-page memorandum handwritten on lined paper in lead pencil of n.d.; Sterling, *Camp Fires of the Twenty-third*, 25.

10   Sterling, *Camp Fires of the Twenty-third*, 25; Mills, *Twenty-first New York*, 118.

11   The stream was probably Four Mile Run, which had been crossed earlier in the day by McClellan.

12   Comte de Paris MS Diary (large diary) (A.N. de la M. de F.) entry dated September 29, 1861.

13   Edwin A. Brown MSS (Civil War Institute, Carroll College), leter dated August 28, 1861, from Brown to his wife. Mills, *Twenty-first New York*, 119.

and urged the colonel to increase the pace. The colonel demurred. The long distance the regiment had already come, the "double-quick" cadence, and the condition of the men made it impossible. Wadsworth called to the regiment for two companies to go forward rapidly as skirmishers. All the men of the regiment responded with a yell and broke into a run, loading their weapons as they went. At the foot of the hill they slowed while they worked their way through Confederate obstructions, but in a short while they reached the crest.

Like the ferocious Confederate guns found by Richardson's men on Munson's Hill, the threatening cannon captured by Wadsworth and his men were discovered to be wheeled stovepipes and painted logs. Also as on Munson's Hill, the earthworks, which had foretold from a distance a desperate Rebel defense, were merely furrows of earth not high enough to protect a prone man.[14] A staff officer reported that the Confederates were falling back in every direction. The officers forbid fires though the men, soaked with perspiration and without overcoats or blankets, had reached a state of exhaustion. Several times during the night they heard firing and once a loud charge of cavalry accompanied by shouts of "Cut 'em down."[15]

That same morning, regiments on the Washington side of the river and in the Alexandria area on the left wing, as well as those in the vicinity of the two hills, formed lines, stacked arms, drew ammunition, and made ready to march. Artillery, baggage wagons, and ambulances began the tedious march from the capital to the aqueduct in order to cross to Virginia.[16] The road was continually blocked and the march delayed; some of the regiments not reaching their positions west of the river until well past dark.

When the Fiftieth New York, a volunteer engineer regiment, finally reached its new position west of Fort Corcoran—after several false halts—Colonel Charles B. Stuart, its commander, roused Captain Wesley Brainerd from his blankets and took him to the crest of a small nearby hill. More than a mile to the west, perhaps even two or three miles, a long line of fires burned.

"We are now in the enemy's country," the colonel told his company commander in a "very solemn manner," his voice trembling. "There," he said, "are the campfires of the enemy. I have selected you and your company to do picket duty

---

14   Sterling, *Camp Fires of the Twenty-third*, 25–26; Pearson, *Wadsworth*, 83.

15   Mills, *Twenty-first New York*, 118–119.

16   Roe, Alfred Seelye, *The Tenth Massachusetts Volunteer Infantry, 1861–1864, a Western Massachusetts Regiment* (Springfield, 1909) 40–41 (Roe, *Tenth Massachusetts*); Floyd, Fred C., *History of the Fortieth (Mozart) Regiment New York Volunteers which was composed of four companies from New York, four companies from Massachusetts, and two from Pennsylvania* (Boston, 1909) 83 (Floyd, *Fortieth New York*).

tonight as I know that I can trust you. Bring up your company to this spot, and I will proceed with you to the line where you are to be posted."

After Brainerd roused his sleeping company, Stuart led them half a mile to a point at which the company deployed right and left at fifty-foot intervals over a mile. Brainerd was to let no one pass without the countersign and to fire on anyone who did not have it. Stuart left.

Brainerd paced his picket line throughout the hours of darkness. Two or three times he could hear ominous heavy firing from the west, then the clatter of horses hooves on the road from the direction of the firing. Brainerd positioned a squad across the road, ordered his men to be ready with the bayonet, and prepared to receive a charge of Rebel cavalry. An oncoming body appeared in sight.

"Who goes there?" challenged Brainerd.

"Friends."

"Halt, friends. Advance one with the countersign."

One officer, a colonel, came forward. "What is this posted here, sir?" the colonel demanded.

"The outer picket line, sir."

"The *outer* picket line is it? What fool posted you here and what the devil was he thinking about with forty thousand of your own men outside of you?"[17]

Colonel Stuart was not the only man confused about his position. Intended by McClellan to be part of the advance, Baker's brigade of Smith's division was to march during daylight hours on September 28 from the two hills at the Chain Bridge until it reached a position that would protect the right flank of Wadsworth's troops on the heights. On the evening of September 27, Baldy Smith had visited Colonel Edward D. Baker's Seventy-first Pennsylvania Infantry Regiment and ordered it to march at half past nine the next night. In Baker's absence, Lieutenant-Colonel Isaac Wistar received the order. Without advance guard or flankers, Wistar was to pass Colonel Hiram Burnham at the crossroads beyond the Vanderburgh House. There, he should deploy two companies across the road as skirmishers about one hundred fifty yards ahead of the first battalion. A file of men at ten-pace intervals would cover the gap between the skirmishers and the lead battalion.[18] The rest of Smith's division would not advance until early morning on September 29, 1861.[19]

17 Malles, Ed, ed., *Bridge Building in Wartime: Colonel Wesley Brainerd's Memoir of the 50th New York Volunteer Engineers* (Knoxville, 1997) 34–35 (Malles, *Bridge Building*).

18 Sears, *McClellan's Correspondence*, 104, letter dated September 29, 1861, from McClellan to his wife. *OR*, 5, 218–219, Wistar's report.

19 Judd, David W., *The Story of the Thirty-third N.Y.S. Vols or Two Years Campaigning in Virginia and Maryland*, 53–54 (Rochester, 1864).

On the morning of September 28 the Sixty-ninth and Seventy-first Pennsylvania Infantry began their preparations to advance. At a quarter past eleven that evening, the Sixty-ninth lay peacefully tucked in its blankets. Baldy Smith reigned his horse at regimental headquarters. The colonel, Joshua T. Owen, a man of genial and generous spirit with previous experience as colonel of the Twenty-fourth Pennsylvania Infantry in the three months service, was absent.

Why was the regiment not in line and ready to march, Smith demanded.

Dennis O'Kane, the lieutenant colonel, replied that he had no orders to that effect. In fact, he had orders to cook two days' rations, strike tents, and prepare to march with the rest of Baker's brigade, at eight o'clock next morning, September 29, to Poolesville, where they would join the division under General Charles P. Stone.

Someone had distributed the orders poorly. Smith was surprised O'Kane had no orders to be in line that evening, he said. O'Kane must form the regiment, issue ammunition, march through camp, then cross the hill next to Fort Baker. O'Kane would receive further directions from the pickets he would pass. Before midnight, under dark and cloudy skies, Smith had compounded the problem by giving verbal orders that came as a complete surprise to O'Kane. But in less than forty-five minutes, the Sixty-ninth had risen, packed for the march, and headed toward the enemy on a route to be designated by "pickets along the way. . . . The officers were in entire ignorance of the purpose or direction of the movement," O'Kane wrote the next day in his report.[20]

Meanwhile, Lieutenant Colonel Wistar had begun his march with the Seventy-first about 9:30 P.M. and had a head start. By eleven he reached the Vanderburgh House. The night was dark. For the next two hours his men cleared trees that blocked the road and delayed his column. As the men passed Burnham and deployed, Smith and his staff joined the column. After a short distance it came upon the pickets of a New York regiment. Wistar was surprised. As far as he knew, he was already beyond the outpost line. A quarter of a mile later, the road turned right, where twenty pickets of the Fourth Michigan lay in position with six more about thirty yards farther. He enjoined his men to keep the strictest silence. Thick trees enclosed the road on both sides, but the moon illuminated the trees and fields enough to make distant objects visible. The skirmishers struggled in the heavy forest, especially on the left. Fifty yards past the second group of pickets, the woods on the right ended at an open field. A worm fence separated the road from the field.

---

20   *OR*, 5, 218, O'Kane's report; Benedict, *Vermont in the Civil War*, 1, 94.

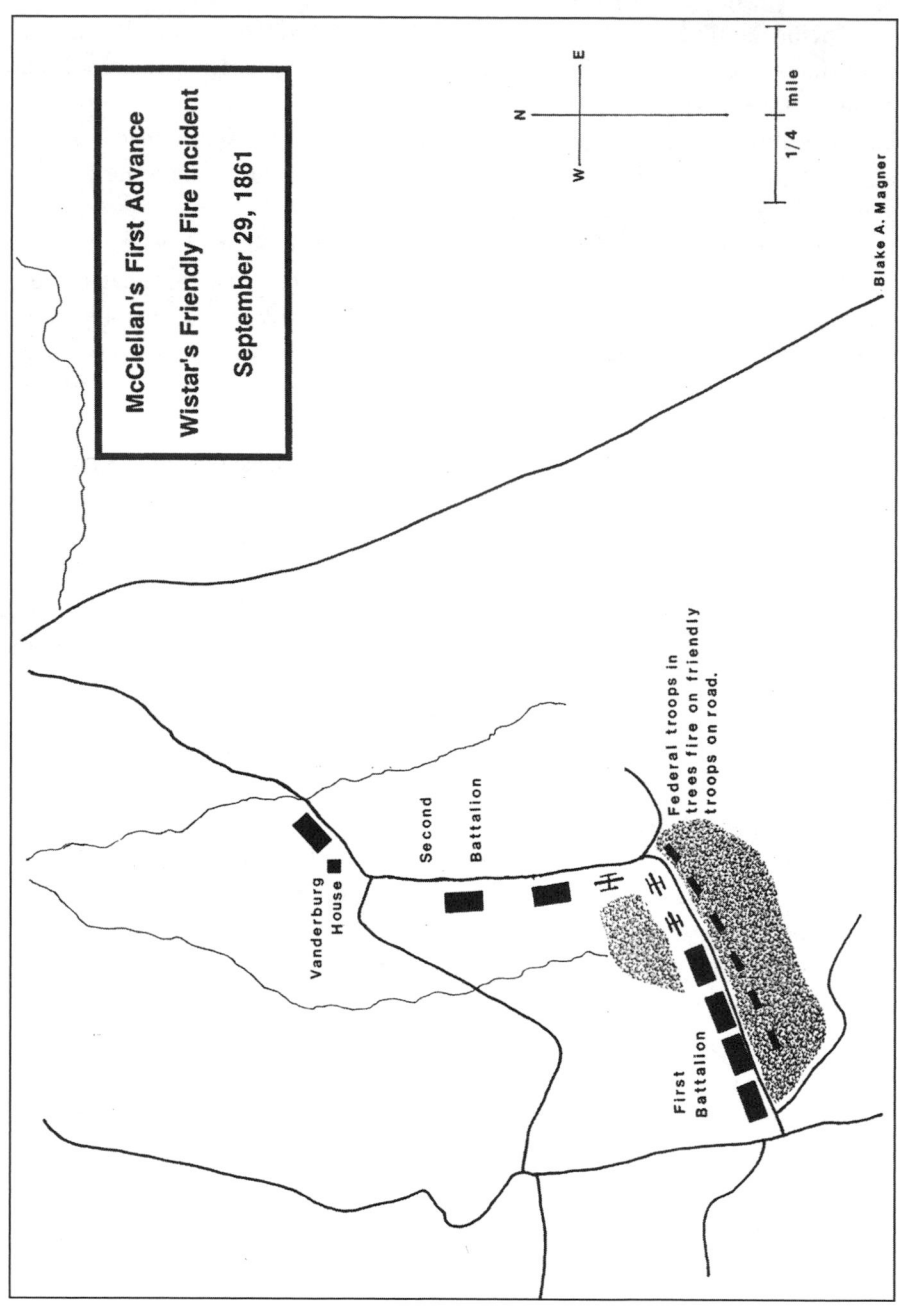

McClellan's First Advance
Wistar's Friendly Fire Incident
September 29, 1861

N

1/4 mile

Blake A. Magner

Vanderburg House

Second Battalion

First Battalion

Federal troops in trees fire on friendly troops on road.

The light of the moon now backed Wistar's column, but in the moonlight its gray uniforms made it look like Confederate infantry.[21]

Following the Seventy-first, the Sixty-ninth Pennsylvania under Lieutenant Colonel O'Kane was startled to see three horsemen ride forward along the length of the regiment.

"Take care, boys! Here they come," one of the horsemen shouted when he reached the middle of the regiment.

He fired his pistol. Simultaneously, a number of men appeared in the woods along the road. O'Kane's men opened fire from the road.

Farther forward, Wistar's Seventy-first had marched with one battalion of infantry in the lead, a four-gun battery of artillery next, and the remainder of the infantry behind the guns. Suddenly, from beyond the fence on the left, at very short range, Wistar's main column received fire, no doubt the fire heard by Captain Brainerd to the rear and Wadsworth's men to the left. Union horsemen, coming forward at a gallop from the rear, joined the melee with indiscriminate firing and shouting that added to the confusion.

Wistar knew he should have found no Confederates in this area and was convinced that friends were firing at each other. He and his company officers ordered their column to halt, face left toward the woods, and withhold fire. Only the muzzle flashes of the invisible riflemen could be seen in the dark woods. He galloped into the road between the two forces and called to both sides not to fire. A bullet struck his horse. Plunging and rearing, it became "completely unmanageable," he wrote in his postwar memoirs. Understandably, his own men returned fire for two minutes. The men in the woods retired. Wistar ordered his men to care for the wounded and straightened his line. In a few moments the mysterious infantry reestablished their position in the woods and fired another volley, this time at a range of twenty feet. Wistar's men returned the fire again.

The artillery horses pulling the guns behind the first battalion became crazed, broke loose from the caissons, and galloped to the rear through the second battalion, causing great confusion. The artillerymen wheeled their guns into position and prepared to rake the road—and the lead battalion—to their front. Hearing these sounds and realizing that a disaster was about to occur, a lieutenant of the Seventy-first organized the men near him and with "a yell of despair," he wrote in a letter, led a charge on the guns. Leaving their half-loaded pieces to be "captured," the gunners ran "in all directions." Wistar brought forward Company G, deployed it,

---

21   Acken, J. Gregory, ed., *Inside the Army of the Potomac: the Civil War Experience of Captain Francis Adams Donaldson* (Mechanicsburg, 1998) 21–22, letter dated October 15, [1862], from Donaldson to Jacob (Acken, *Inside the Army* [*Donaldson Letters*]); *OR*, 5, 218, 219, Wistar's report.

and swept the woods to the left of his column. The "enemy" troops had disappeared deep into the woods.

The firing ceased. Gradually, O'Kane and Wistar restored order, sent their dead and wounded to the rear, and assumed defensive positions. Farther to the left Keyes heard the firing, concluded that Union troops were firing at each other, and made certain that his brigade held its fire. In a short while the firing stopped.[22]

The Sixty-ninth Pennsylvania had suffered one man killed and three wounded, the "California Battalion" or Seventy-first Pennsylvania, four killed and fourteen wounded, several mortally.[23] The press had its usual field day, denouncing everyone "from the general in chief down," Wistar wrote in his memoirs.[24] Many men of the California Battalion believed Baldy Smith was to blame for the incident under the "he was in command" theory that had been applied to McDowell for Bull Run.

22 National Archives, Record Group 94, Officers' Manuscript Reports of Services (Keyes) (Off's MS Rpts); Sears, *McClellan's Correspondence*, 104, letter dated September 29, 1861, from McClellan to his wife; Wistar, *Autobiography*, 359–361; Bates, *Hist. Penn. Vols.*, 4, 679, 788–789; Banes, Charles H., *History of the Philadelphia Brigade. Sixty-ninth, Seventy-first, Seventy-second, and One Hundred Sixth Pennsylvania Volunteers* (Philadelphia, 1876) 13–14, 20–22 (Banes, *Philadelphia Brigade*); Stevens, Capt. C. A., *Berdan's Sharpshooters in the Army of the Potomac 1861–1865* (St. Paul, 1892) 8–9 (Stevens, *Berdan's Sharpshooters*); Acken, *Inside the Army* (*Donaldson Letters*) 21–26, letter dated October 15, 1861, from Donaldson to Jacob. According to Mills, *Twenty-first New York*, the "enemy" was a scouting party returning from its mission (120–121); but Benedict in *Vermont in the Civil War*, 1, 94, says it was the Fifth Pennsylvania Cavalry, which had lost its way and circled back into the advancing infantry of Smith's division. Bates in *Hist. Penn. Vols.*, 3, 568, makes no mention of the advance or the incident in the chapter for the Fifth Pennsylvania Cavalry (Sixty-first Pennsylvania Regiment of the line), nor does the "Compiled Record" for the Fifth in Part II, *OR Supp.*, 56, 774–776, but Donaldson's contemporaneous letter clearly identifies the Cameron Dragoons (the Fifth Pennsylvania Cavalry Regiment) in the marching column behind the Seventy-first Pennsylvania and states that he halted its charge when he recognized the orderly sergeant, who was about to lead the charge to "clear the road," as an old friend (26). No account identifies the "enemy" unit reliably. Samito, Christian G., ed., *Commanding Boston's Irish Ninth: the Civil War Letters of Colonel Patrick R. Guiney, Ninth Massachusetts Volunteer Infantry* (New York, 1998) 53–54, letter dated October 1, 1861, from Guiney to Jennie (Samito, *Guiney Letters*); Banes, *Philadelphia Brigade*, 20–22; or the exhaustively researched Lash, Gary G., *"Duty Well Done": The History of Edward Baker's California Regiment (71st Pennsylvania Regiment)* (Baltimore, 2001) 94–98 (Lash, *71st Pennsylvania*). Wistar believed the "enemy" troops came from Smith's division. They certainly were not Confederate troops. According to the regimental history of the Ninth Massachusetts, which participated in the advance with Porter's division but did not witness the event, the Sixty-ninth and Seventy-first Pennsylvania Regiments fired into each other, the Seventy-first having taken a position in the woods along the road, McNamara, David George, *The History of the Ninth Regiment Massachusetts Volunteer Infantry, Second Brigade, First Division, Fifth Army Corps, Army of the Potomac, June, 1861–June, 1864* (Boston, 1899) 57–58 (McNamara, *Ninth Massachusetts*); but the contemporaneous reports show the inaccuracy of this hearsay account.

23 Bates, *Hist. Penn. Vols.*, 4, 697, 789.

24 Wistar, *Autobiography*, 361.

Thought by some to have been drunk, Smith had supposedly ordered the four artillery pieces to fire into the regiment with grey uniforms in the road ahead of the guns.[25] These speculations probably found their way back to McClellan; and although they did not remove Smith from the favored list, they would have taken a place in McClellan's unforgiving mind. To McClellan, like many men in military history and many men in positions of authority, "involvement" rated as poorly as culpability. No matter that he was not to blame . . . "he was in command."

A man who ignored no lesson as far as his army and his men were concerned, McClellan probably concluded that he could not move the parts of his large army like toy soldiers with no notice, that he always needed a plan, that information should be given to more than a handful, and that well-considered orders, in writing, from him, should govern future operations of larger units over terrain he could not see and direct with a hard-riding aide on a fast horse. More small lessons would follow in the immediate future with unpleasant consequences for the commanding general, consequences inconsistent with his self-image and his personal requirement of perfection. Flickering through all this was the restless murmur for an advance against Manassas, the press showing, as always, that it had not learned from its mistakes.[26] Although moderately aggressive scouts probed almost to the Fairfax Court House line, the Confederates had flown.[27] Worse yet, rumors circulated in the capital that the Rebels had withdrawn from the area three days earlier.[28]

A few days later McClellan could not have been displeased to learn that Brigadier General Stevens had received orders to give command of his brigade to its senior colonel and report in person to General Thomas W. Sherman at Annapolis by

25   Lash, *71st Pennsylvania*, 97 and 500, n. 79. Lash blames Porter and Smith for lack of coordination and concludes that the men in the trees came from Porter's division. Whether or not Lash's case for identification of the concealed regiment is convincing, the fault really lay with McClellan for giving insufficient information and time for the participating divisions to do more than throw gear and ammunition in packs and "fall in."

26   The press representatives in Iraq busily disgraced themselves by showing that their employers did not select them for their intelligence, nor did the employers require even the most fundamental knowledge of military concepts. The military on the other hand had "gone to school" on the abysmal performance by the Department of Defense and General William Westmoreland in the Vietnam War. Major General Gene Renuart and Brigadier General Vincent Brooks showed that the spokesmen for the military had more eloquence, more intelligence, and more restraint than the fumblers of the media—and Secretary Donald Rumsfeld, still a legend on the wrestling team for his fireman's carry and his performance in the nationals when the author became a freshman two years after the future secretary's graduation, showed the graceful verbal ability to deal with accusatory questions like, "How could you allow . . . ?"

27   McClellan MSS (L.C.) letter dated September 1861, from Wadsworth to McClellan.

28   Zachariah Chandler MSS (Library of Congress) letter dated October 8, 1861, from Wade to Chandler.

daylight, October 17. As Stevens and his son Hazard rode the train from Washington to Annapolis, Stevens expressed great relief at his transfer from the Army of the Potomac and condemned McClellan's passive-defensive methods. On the issue of field fortifications, he disagreed with McClellan. Instead of obstructing the entire front with roadblocks and tracts of slashed woods to impede any Confederate attack, McClellan should have left the front clear and unobstructed for his own attacks. The obstructions, Stevens felt, held the Union troops prisoners in their works as much as they kept the Confederate troops outside. The subordinate commanders should have carefully studied and understood the ground with a view to a heavy attack on the Confederates at any weak point. Instead, McClellan restrained the natural enterprise and ardor of the troops, prohibited all hostile contact with the Confederates as if the Union troops were no match for the Rebels, and continued the cowardly aftermath of Bull Run. They should have continuously faced the Confederates through scouts, reconnaissances, and other detachments at every opportunity, Stevens continued. This would have given the troops confidence, restored their morale, developed their natural enterprise and bravery, and given officers of all ranks experience and confidence in combat situations. Stevens said he had none of the distrust of volunteers often felt by Regular Army officers, a sentiment that "undoubtedly influenced McClellan," Stevens' son wrote after the war, and caused him to suffer a fatal lack of boldness and decision. With great feeling the elder Stevens summarized his views.

"I am glad to leave McClellan's army. I am rejoiced to get out of that army. I tell you that army under McClellan is doomed to disaster."[29]

---

29   Stevens, *Stevens*, 2, 338–341. As the remainder of this volume will show, Stevens evaluated the commanding general without knowledge of his intentions and, therefore, drew many incorrect inferences and conclusions about the Washington fortifications.

Chapter 3

"I think the greatest battle ever fought on this continent will be brought to issue."

—Francis P. Blair to his daughter Elizabeth

The Rebels
Withdraw to Manassas

*A*t half past six on the morning after the friendly fire incident, McClellan and his aides saddled their horses for another trip across the Potomac to the area of Munson's and Upton's Hills. As they rode west they felt a strong sense of confidence in their advanced positions and their men. They hoped the Confederates would change their minds, attempt to re-occupy the positions they had abandoned, and provide a clean victory on the tactical defensive behind field works. But the Rebels would disappoint them.

Quietly, McDowell placed part of his division on the high ground at Munson's and Upton's Hills, leaving the bulk of his troops in their camps farther to the rear. His lines he extended north and south, at last giving McClellan enough depth between his outer defenses and the river to maneuver and reinforce in case of an attack and a breakthrough.

McDowell met McClellan on Upton's Hill. Perhaps concerned about a delayed backlash for his "failure" at Bull Run, McDowell had been thinking about the formation of corps. He could reasonably have believed they would not be created until he had been transferred to a command in the land of oblivion. He was nervous about corps, he told McClellan, and wanted to see them created.[1]

---

1   *C.C.W.*, 144 (McDowell).

Just beyond the Upton's Hill position lay the village of Falls Church. During the day after the unfortunate night march of Smith's division, Fitz John Porter learned that on several previous days Confederate Generals Beauregard and Longstreet had dined in Falls Church. They had agreed that too many lives would be lost in an assault on the Union fortifications. They would withdraw from the area and trick the Union forces into pursuing to the Rebel works being built six miles to the rear along the Fairfax Court House line, where they had one hundred seventy thousand men.[2]

McClellan planned limited new fortifications on the rear of Munson's Hill; but first, the men must clear the position of trees. The French princes on McClellan's staff found it "simply amazing how fast the Americans can cut a forest. All the trees fall in just a few minutes, one after the other," recorded one of them in his diary.[3]

According to his officers and to rumors that circulated promptly in the press, McClellan believed his plans had been disclosed to the Confederates. A few days later George Meade, who had great confidence in McClellan, wrote his wife, "I have not written you since the few lines the day we expected to have a fight. The stampede lasted for 36 hours, and I believe it is now generally known, that McClellan had planned a surprise, which if he had succeeded in, would have brought on a big fight in which our division was to have a part; but the sudden disappearance of the enemy frustrated the plan; there is no doubt they were apprized of it tho McClellan admits he did not tell even the generals who were to share in it till the very moment of action, and that he is now confirmed it is impossible to do, or attempt anything, without their knowing it."[4]

The possible culprits were few in number, McClellan having discussed his plan with no one but the president and one other man. The confused conduct of the columns, especially Baker's column, showed that McClellan had not even given the generals the plan until "the very moment of action," as Meade put it. He supposedly addressed the president about the betrayal.

"As you, President Lincoln, and Colonel Scott had been the only parties to the conference, one of the three had betrayed the confidence; and it was not yourself."

2   William B. Franklin MSS (Library of Congress) letter dated September 29, 1862, from Porter to Franklin.

3   Comte de Paris MS diary (large diary) (A.N. de la M. de F.) entry dated September 29, 1861; *C.C.W.*, 1, 144 (McDowell).

4   Meade, *Life and Letters*, 1, 221, letter dated October 6, 1861, from Meade to his wife.

At first the colonel was thought to be Thomas A. Scott, but rumors later substituted Colonel Henry L. Scott as the miscreant.[5] If the Buckner incident had not combined with the training McClellan had received from his respected West Point professor Dennis Hart Mahan to maximize McClellan's natural reserve and reticence,[6] the Munson's Hill leak closed him to all but the smallest circle of confidants.

No matter how limited the objective might have been, McClellan had been denied an opportunity to drive the Confederates by a successful advance against resistance. He had also been denied a small tactical move that might provoke an offensive Confederate response and allow him to fight on the tactical defensive. The fact that his troops had, unopposed, occupied deserted fieldworks ultimately led to derision rather than praise from those who wanted battles, fighting, killing, and the South crushed. Benjamin F. Wade, a powerful member of the Radical contingent in the Senate, wrote sharply about this to Senator Zachariah Chandler, a fellow Radical Republican.

It is very true that three days after the enemy had left their fortifications on Munson's Hill and before they had mounted any cannon upon the ramparts, General McClellan ventured out in force and we are told exultingly that our troops behaved in the most cool and gallant manner. This I believe is the only enterprise our gallant young general has ventured upon since he took command of the Army of the Potomac. He seems to have adopted the maxim of the old woman that "old boys should learn to

5   McClellan MSS (L.C.) letter dated October 25, 1869, from Schuyler Hamilton to McClellan. Although McClellan denied making the statement to the president, McClellan MSS (L.C.), draft letter dated October 30, 1869, from McClellan to Hamilton, the denial is so narrow and precise that most of the remainder of Hamilton's letter can be taken to be admitted under the Sir Thomas More rule: that which is not denied is deemed admitted. None of the events at the end of September or McClellan's intentions at that time are drawn together in any single narrative, not even *M.O.S.* or Swinton, William, *Campaigns of the Army of the Potomac: a Critical History of the Operations in Virginia, Maryland and Pennsylvania from the Commencement to the Close of the War 1861–1865* (New York, 1882, rev. ed.). But the combined references in the Comte de Paris's diary, the Hamilton letter to McClellan in his MSS, and the reference by Meade in a home letter to "the day we expected to have a fight" (September 30) make it all fit together logically.

6   Dwight Family MSS (Massachusetts Historical Society) letter dated October 11, 1861, from Wilder Dwight to his father (this letter also appears in Dwight Family, *Life and Letters Wilder Dwight, Lieut.-Col. Second Mass. Inf. Vols.* (Boston, 1868) 115 (Dwight, *Life and Letters*); William Woods Averell MSS (New York State Library), letter dated September 25, 1861, from Averell to his sister; Griess, Thomas E., unpublished MS dissertation "Dennis Hart Mahan: West Point Professor and Advocate of Military Professionalism, 1830–1871" 310; Nevins, Allan, *The Diary of George Templeton Strong*, 4 vols. (New York, 1952) vol. 3, *The Civil War, 1860–1865*, 3, 178–179, entry dated September 16, 1861 (Nevins, *Strong Diary*).

swim well before they run into the water," so the General is determined his troops shall all be veterans before he permits them to come under fire or into a skirmish. Seriously, I don't know what is to come of all of this imbecility, it is but lately that the present state of things must not be suffered to continue. We must either have peace or war. At present we have neither. It is true we have vast armies in the field maintained at prodigious and almost ruinous expense. Yet they are suffered to do nothing with the power in our hands to crush the rebellion in two months. We are in danger of having our army set into winter quarters with the capitol in a state of siege for another year.[7]

Only ninety miles apart on an imaginary straight line, Richmond and Washington held the two principal armies nose to nose;[8] but in early October the Rebels looked more and more as if they would relinquish the remainder of their positions in close proximity to the Federal capital.[9] McClellan received information that the enemy in front of him had been weakened by fifty thousand men sent to other areas. This left only forty thousand for the Potomac-Acquia Creek line, the center at Manassas, and the extreme left flank at the Blue Ridge. Once again, they intended to fight at Manassas.[10]

This information confirmed a report from McClellan's equivalent of the modern G–2 intelligence officer, E. J. Allen. The Rebel forces in Virginia, Allen believed, had been vastly overestimated because the estimates came from counting regiments and multiplying by the full strength of one thousand men each. But everyone knew no regiment in either army had its regulation number of men. In fact, according to Allen, the entire Confederate force in Virginia numbered 184 regiments of only 126,600 men, seventy thousand under Beauregard, twenty-two thousand under Johnston, and much smaller numbers scattered in western Virginia, Richmond, Norfolk, and Portsmouth. "The tactics of The Rebel General appear to be to keep their troops moving around as much as possible, probably with a view of creating the opinion that their force is much larger than it really is," Allen wrote. Because of a shortage of ammunition, the Confederate officers did not allow their men to fire their weapons, including the blank cartridges loaded in their rifles two

7   Chandler MSS (L.C.) letter dated October 8, 1861, from Wade to Chandler.

8   Comte de Paris MS diary (large diary) (A.N. de la M. de F.) entry dated October 6, 1861.

9   Caspar Crowninshield MS diary (Boston Public Library) entries dated September 19, 21, 22, and 24, 1861.

10   McClellan MSS (L.C.) letter dated October 4, 1861, from illegible to McClellan; Averell MSS (N.Y.S.L.) letter dated September 25, 1861, from Averell to his sister; Chandler MSS (L.C.) letter dated October 8, 1861, from Wade to Chandler.

to three weeks and exposed to heavy rains. Confederate deserters complained about "the indecision of the general commanding eastern Virginia."[11] This did not sound like an enemy ready to make a quick, irresistible attack.

According to an intelligence report by one of Pinkerton's operatives, the Rebels held a Council of War at Manassas on Thursday, October 3. Beauregard and the Confederate troops felt that their army on the Potomac was not large enough to cope with McClellan's forces while Johnston stated that the Confederate forces were invincible. Twenty-seven thousand men held position near Leesburg, Virginia, but they had been taken from positions near Middleburg and Falls Church and had very little ammunition. In the spy's opinion, the Confederates had no intention of crossing the Potomac River except on the upper Potomac, where they could always withdraw before being intercepted. If the Federal army could push south from Alexandria and threaten Occoquan Creek, he thought, the Confederates would retire on Manassas.[12]

Meanwhile, heavy rainfalls in watershed areas to the northwest had caused the Potomac River to rise. Before the end of September it had risen five feet, had become uncrossable, and stood as a barrier to any Confederate operation in Maryland.[13] The heavy rains continued to fall far upriver, and the river continued to rise.[14]

Before that, McClellan and many others had worried about the easily forded points between Washington and Harpers Ferry. To deal with the Confederate threat to Baltimore and the rest of Maryland, McClellan had rearranged the divisions east of the Potomac. Nathaniel Bank's division he had drawn closer to Washington; Stone's elongated division he left along the river between Tenallytown and Rocky Point; and McCall's division he kept in the vicinity of Georgetown and Tenallytown. Casey's division of recruits, scattered around Washington, would serve as an immediate reserve.[15] If the Rebels crossed, Banks, Stone, and McCall were to concentrate as fast as they could north of the capital and delay the Rebel advance long enough for the main army to come to the rescue.[16]

11   McClellan MSS (L.C.) letter dated October 4, 1861, from Allen to McClellan.

12   McClellan MSS (L.C.) dispatch dated October 6, 1861, from Buxton to Marcy.

13   McClellan MSS (L.C.) telegram dated September 27, 1861, by the curator from R. Morris Copeland, Banks' Acting Assistant Adjutant General, to Marcy.

14   McClellan MSS (L.C.) letter dated October 9, 1861, from Copeland to Marcy.

15   OR, 5, 32, 33, McClellan's report; 567–568, letter dated August 16, 1861, from McClellan to Stone; 584, letter dated September 4, 1861, from Colburn to Stone; 585, letter dated September 4, 1861, from Colburn to Banks; 587–588, letter dated September 8, 1861, from McClellan to Cameron.

16   OR, 5, 587–588, letter dated September 12, 1861, from McClellan to Cameron.

Early in October, the Rebels withdrew from the Prospect Hill area to Mackall's Hill, which was farther from the river and about two miles from Lewinsville. On Wednesday, October 9, McClellan and his staff crossed to Prospect Hill, an imposing height between the river and the Leesburg Turnpike. That evening,[17] he ordered McCall to cross the Potomac at night and occupy the Langley-Prospect Hill area. Smith, now no longer the right flank division of the Virginia forces, would no longer have responsibility for the intersection of the line and the river. He should move forward toward Mackall's Hill.

McCall crossed the Chain Bridge, turned right to the northwest, and marched out the Leesburg Turnpike to a position in the vicinity of Prospect Hill and the village of Langley. This would extend the right flank of the army, make McCall instead of Smith the extreme right of McClellan's Virginia forces, and rest his right wing on the Potomac.[18] It would also reduce the length of Stone's line along the east bank of the river and would assure that any crossing would occur farther upstream.

Mother Nature supported McClellan's decision. The rains in the mountains did not stop, and the river continued to rise. By October 10 it had risen several more feet, was still rising, and threatened to submerge the Potomac islands.[19] That day, McClellan and his staff visited Smith's and McCall's divisions in their new positions. They now held Falls Church strongly with Morrell's brigade on Maynard's Hill, the highest point in the area.[20] McClellan had occupied and fortified Upton's and Munson's Hills. His army was improving daily. McClellan felt safe from attack on his vulnerable right. Having learned that the Confederates on the Virginia side were retiring, he and his staff returned to army headquarters.

That evening President Lincoln, Secretary of State William Seward, and Lincoln's secretary John Hay visited McClellan's quarters, where they met one of the general's French aides, Captain Louis Philippe D'Orleans, the Comte de Paris.

"We just came in from a ride of all day," said the captain rapidly in his high-pitched voice.

---

17   In his account of services, NA Off's MS Rpts, McCall noted the date as "around October 1"; but the contemporaneous account by the Comte de Paris in his large MS diary (A.N. de la M. de F.) entry dated October 9, 1861, dated the order with certainty and precision.

18   NA Off's MS Rpts (McCall); Sypher, *Pennsylvania Reserves*, 123.

19   McClellan MSS (L.C.) telegrams dated October 9, 1861, from Stone to McClellan; October 10, 1861, 11:15 A.M. from Stone to McClellan; October 10, 1861, 10:20 P.M. from Stone to McClellan; and October 11, 1861, 11:10 A.M. from Stone to McClellan.

20   Comte de Paris MS diary (large diary) (A.N. de la M. de F.) entries dated October 9 and 10, 1861.

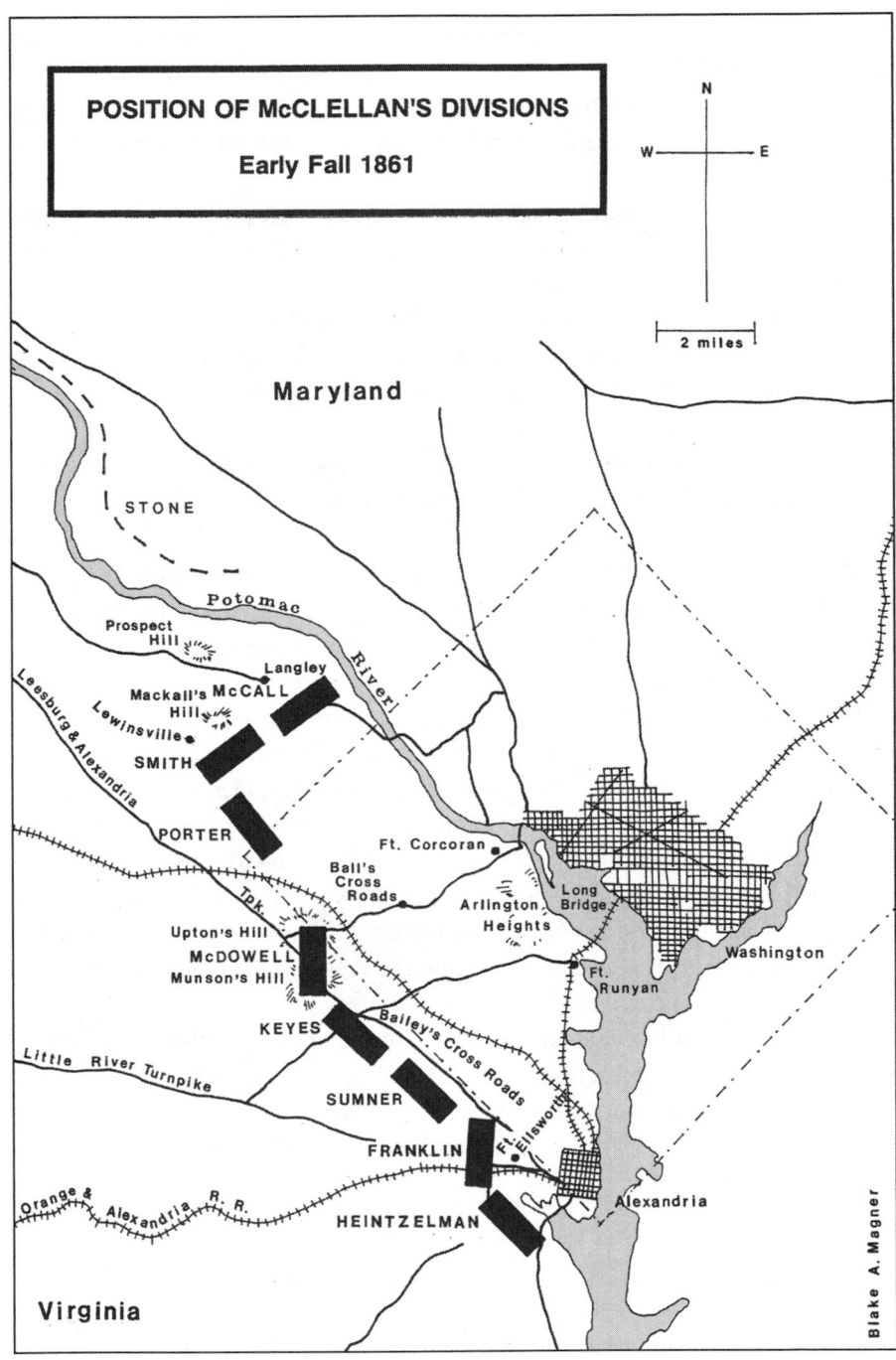

POSITION OF McCLELLAN'S DIVISIONS

Early Fall 1861

N
W   E
S

2 miles

Maryland

STONE

Potomac River

Prospect Hill

Langley

Mackall's Hill

McCALL

Lewinsville

SMITH

Leesburg & Alexandria

PORTER

Ft. Corcoran

Ball's Cross Roads

Tpk.

Upton's Hill

Arlington Heights

Long Bridge

McDOWELL

Munson's Hill

Ft. Runyan

Washington

KEYES

Bailey's Cross Roads

Little River Turnpike

SUMNER

FRANKLIN

Ft. Ellsworth

Orange & Alexandria R. R.

HEINTZELMAN

Alexandria

Virginia

Blake A. Magner

Seward introduced the president and Hay to the captain, who then went upstairs to call McClellan.

The president said quietly, "One doesn't like to make a messenger of the King of France, as that youth, the Count of Paris, would be if his family had kept the throne."

McClellan entered hurriedly and began to discuss the events of the last two days with the President. He was much pleased at the conduct of his men. They had marched without plundering or rowdyism.

As the president was leaving, the general said, "I think we shall have our arrangements made for a strong reconnaissance about Monday to feel the strength of the enemy. I intend to be careful and do as well as possible. Don't let them hurry me is all I ask."

No doubt remembering he had made a serious mistake when he sent McDowell's unready army into battle in July, the president responded, "You shall have your own way in the matter, I assure you."

Two days after McClellan sent his long strategy letter to Cameron, he and his staff rode the lines again, stopping at one headquarters after another for lunch, whiskey, and champagne. The Rebels had not been seen for some time. Information about their new positions and concentrations was important.

When he arrived at Porter's headquarters, he learned that the enemy had established new outposts all along the front. He could hear unidentifiable cannon fire, apparently from the vicinity of Smith's division. "Suddenly, there is an atmosphere of excitement all over the place," the Comte de Paris wrote in his diary. "Telegrams came in from everywhere," the troops were put on alert, and McClellan galloped in the direction of the firing. Several hundred infantry with vehicles had been seen south of Lewinsville. They could still see the bright sun reflecting from bayonets. The usual uncertainties prevailed. What troops were they, Rebel or Federal? Were the vehicles wagons or artillery?[21]

Still hoping that he could provoke the Confederates to take the tactical offensive and that he would defeat them with a tactical defense, McClellan sent the president a telegram saying that the enemy was before him in force and would probably attack in the morning. "If they attack," he added, "I shall beat them."[22] Troops and

---

21   Comte de Paris MS diary (large diary) (A.N. de la M. de F.) entries dated October 11 and 12, 1861.

22   Burlingame, Michael, and John R. Turner Ettlinger, eds., *Inside Lincoln's White House: the Complete Civil War Diary of John Hay* (Carbondale and Edwardsville, 1997) 25, entry dated October 12, 1861 (Burlingame, *Hay Diary*).

artillery in Washington he alerted to a possible engagement, and they stood to arms. As soon as William F. Barry, his chief of artillery, satisfied himself that all was ready, he sent a note to Henry Hunt.

"Please keep your horses harnessed until further orders. I go to join the General at once, but shall leave an officer *at his house* to transmit to you any order that may be received. Please send at once a reliable mounted man to be in attendance there to take out to you any message that may be received." DeRussey, Hall, Elder, and Hays, among others, had harnessed their batteries and made ready to go.[23]

Those of McClellan's staff who had not ridden with him in the morning began to arrive at Smith's headquarters. A man with a penchant for good living and decent accommodations, Smith had selected the best house in the vicinity for his headquarters, the Smoot House, just off the road from Lewinsville to the Leesburg Turnpike.[24] Present also was Smith's wife, a strong-willed, lively woman who rode "well and boldly" and who probably accounted for the meticulous appearance of his staff, all well-shaven, hair combed, and buttoned to the collar.[25]

After an evening hosted by the noticeable Mrs. Smith, Captain D'Orleans went outdoors and walked a short distance to a place near the camp. Silently, he admired the contrasts between the large fires illuminating tents, men, and horses among the trees and the tropical moonlight lighting the surrounding forest. Smoking his pipe, a poor substitute for a good cigar, he thought, the count could hear regimental musicians playing *Dixie Land* in the distance. He knew that before the war the Secessionists had tried to make *Dixie Land* a national anthem, the equivalent of a Southern *Marseillaise*. The North did not want it, and the effort failed, but the song's popularity kept it in the musical repertoire of the army. In this philosophical moment he had an Olympian view of the brothers' war in which he had taken sides. Perhaps he anticipated the thoughts he would write in his diary on this subject a few days later.

23   Misc. Civil War letters (N.Y.H.S.), letter dated October 13, 1861, from Barry to Hunt with endorsements by Hunt.

24   Comte de Paris MS diary (large diary) (A.N. de la M. de F.) entries dated October 11 and 12, 1861; Sears, *McClellan's Correspondence*, 107, letter dated October 13, 1861, from McClellan to his wife. According to the count's diary, the house belonged to Smooth; but a contemporary map of the Virginia shore area compiled by McDowell's topographical engineers, dated January 1, 1862 (author's collection), shows a house in Smith's area as Smoot and, of course, no Smooth house.

25   Comte de Paris MS diary (large diary) (A.N. de la M. de F.) entries dated October 11 and 12, 1861.

We suddenly feel the urge to see this war happen just by seeing the army organize and have its troops getting ready, feeling so close to any enemy and getting to know General McClellan and his officers. After hoping and looking for so long for an opportunity to be part of a war, (best and only school to develop a military character), I finally found it. I am sure that many people will either be resentful or sorry, whether they are friends or not, to hear that I decided to join the American army in this civil war. They will probably formulate all kinds of objections. As far as I am concerned, putting the political question aside, I do not believe that it is a bad decision to fight for the Union, which is the work of France, and to show any sympathy for a great liberal nation who will always be rich, powerful and enterprising, whatever happens. Serving under the Republican flag is an advantage rather than an inconvenience to me. I do not have any problem in wearing the uniform of a people for whom I am an equal to anyone. But had I to serve under the command of a European monarch I would. And I cannot forget my grand-father's popularity in 1815 which was mainly due to his campaigns as republican general and to his long stay in the United States.

McClellan and his men retired to their various bedrooms at the Smoot House. No doubt, none regretted more than McClellan the lack of a good cigar.[26] The day had been a busy one for the major general. Early in the morning his wife Ellen had given birth to a baby girl, and he had snatched a brief moment at Smith's headquarters to send her a short telegram expressing his thanks to God that she was safe. Now, as he tried to sleep, the fear of attack that had made him sleepless in early August had flown. He hoped for an attack from the enemy at daylight. His army was large and well trained. His fortifications were almost complete. He felt he had control. All stood in good order.[27]

While McCall crossed the Potomac and deployed, Stone, upriver in the Poolesville area, thought the Confederates were entrenching between Conrad's Ferry and Leesburg opposite Harrison's Island. Then, he learned they had strengthened their force in the Leesburg area by one or two regiments from downriver. Construction of new batteries and strengthening of old works seemed to be occurring.[28] That night, October 13, Stone reported that work had been done at Smart's

---

26   Comte de Paris MS diary (large diary) (A.N. de la M. F.) entries dated October 12 and 16, 1861.

27   McClellan MSS (L.C.) telegram dated October 12, 1861, from Mrs. Marcy to McClellan; Sears, *McClellan's Correspondence*, 107, telegram dated October 12, 1861, from McClellan to his wife and letter dated October 13, 1861, from McClellan to his wife.

28   *M.O.S.*, 181.

Mill, that the pickets near Mason's Island had been heavily reinforced, and that he anticipated an early attempt by the Confederates to capture Mason's Island or Harrison's Island, if not both.[29]

McClellan returned to Washington. On the evening of October 14, just after dinner, he and his quartermaster, General Stuart Van Vliet, met with Captain John A. Dahlgren. McClellan and Dahlgren exchanged friendly greetings. In minutes the four men, Dahlgren, McClellan, Van Vliet, and Commander Percival Drayton,[30] Dahlgren's guest for dinner, "became engaged in a quiet chat over cigars and champagne," Dahlgren wrote that night in his journal. He continued:

> Drayton did not remain long . . . The General, I soon found, has his annoyances as well as other people, for it seems that Scott insists on the direction and McClellan resist. . . . He says Scott actually had an idea of preferring charges against him for the advance of the last few days! . . . He said Scott does not wish to fight, but considers delay the policy. McClellan thinks otherwise. He says, too, that he is never consulted in the movements of the other armies. . . . One thing I noticed, that the General never became excited in speaking of these things but was always in the best temper. I only hope that there will be influence somewhere to save him from this foolish embarrassment. He is a hearty, clever gentleman, of the most moderate and proper ambition, and warm and kind in his feelings. . . .[31]

In the afternoon of October 15 the beautiful daughter of Francis P. Blair and sister of Postmaster General Montgomery Blair received an informative letter from her father. Although neither of them would have known it, the contents confirmed McClellan's worst fears about security in the government, even among strong supporters like the Blair family. Blair described the effect of McCall's division crossing to the Potomac's west bank. "About that time [Wednesday, October 16]," it said, "I think the greatest battle ever fought on this continent will be brought to issue—All our side of the River is for the most part stript of Troops & the white

---

29 McClellan MSS (L.C.) telegram dated October 13, 1861, 10:40 P.M. from Stone to McClellan.

30 The Drayton family house, Magnolia, an excellent example of aristocratic Southern architecture across the Ashley River from Charleston, South Carolina, survived Sherman's systematic destruction of the houses along the south bank of the Ashley River by trickery, author's personal visit; *D.A.B.*, 3, pt. 1, 445, 447.

31 Dahlgren, Madeleine Vinton, *Memoir of John A. Dahlgren, Rear-Admiral, United States Navy* (New York, 1891) 345, journal, entry dated October 14, 1861 (Dahlgren, *Memoirs*).

tents which yesterday covered the hills around Arlington with their snow, have during the night melted away in darkness—Several days since McClellan had driven a wedge of his force into the enemy's column opening the way out to the Leesburg Turnpike with the design evidently of cutting off the Communication between Beauregard and Johnston—" Dutifully, Elizabeth copied this part of the letter in her periodic report of events to her husband, Phillips, a naval officer serving at sea on the blockade.[32]

In the middle of the month a contraband entered the Union lines in Heintzelman's area around Alexandria with information about movements inside the Rebel lines. The Confederates had fallen back to Union Mills, south of Blackburn's Ford on Bull Run Creek. A Confederate brigade had left Sangster's Crossroads at 10 A.M. for Union Mills, where it had been positioned before the battle at Bull Run. Other troops, he reported, were also withdrawing. The Confederates expected another battle at Bull Run and had gone there to prepare. Heintzelman had already decided that this would be the course of events and believed the information given him by the contraband. All of it he telegraphed to headquarters, and at the end of the day he wrote in his diary, "All the news we get goes to convince me that the enemy is retreating."[33]

At Harpers Ferry, the far end of McClellan's line, Banks' troops had a small military action that tended to confirm the intention of the Confederates to retire. In the middle of the month, the breadbasket crops in the southwest quadrant below Harpers Ferry were ready to be harvested. On October 8, Banks created a combined arms team of infantry and artillery under Major J. P. Gould: three companies of the Third Wisconsin; a two-gun section from Battery B of the First Rhode Island Artillery; and Gould's Thirteenth Massachusetts. They were to seize the wheat collected by the Confederates around Harpers Ferry.

While Gould's troops were hard at work, General John W. Geary received "reliable information" that the Rebels were concentrating on Harpers Ferry. That evening, he, Governor William Sprague of Rhode Island, and Colonel Tompkins of the First Rhode Island Artillery went to Sandy Hook. The next day, Monday, October 14, they crossed to Virginia, where Geary supervised the collection of the wheat. Under his command he had a force of 600 men, composed of four companies of his

32   Laas, Virginia Jeans, ed., *Wartime Washington: the Civil War Letters of Elizabeth Blair Lee* (Urbana and Chicago, Illinois, 1991), letter dated October 16, 1861, from Elizabeth Blair Lee to Samuel Phillips Lee, quoting a letter from Francis P. Blair to Elizabeth (Laas, *Blair Lee Letters*).

33   Samuel P. Heintzelman MS diary (large diary) (Library of Congress) entries dated October 16 and 17, 1861.

Twenty-eighth Pennsylvania, three of the Thirteenth Massachusetts, three of the Third Wisconsin, and the gun crews for two cannon from the First Rhode Island Artillery and two from the Ninth New York Battery. Leaving one hundred Massachusetts men on the north side of the Potomac with the two Rhode Island guns, Geary placed one New York gun on the railroad opposite Harpers Ferry and the other to command the approach from Pleasant Valley, just east of Maryland Heights.

The village of Harpers Ferry rested on the river banks where the mighty Shenandoah and Potomac rivers came together.[34] The heavy rainfalls had added to their flow. The Potomac, Geary wrote home, was,

> a clear beautiful stream, its resistless tide rushing headlong over the rocky surface of the channel and roaring with "the voice of many waters." The Shenandoah is very muddy at present, and rolls its waters along with equal haste, into the same channel with the Potomac, but the waters seem to refuse to commingle and become one. The clearness and limpidity of the Potomac is discernable for miles, and the muddiness of the Shenandoah equally so in the distance, refusing to join their waters and mingle into one grand kindred stream. I cannot help thinking it resembles the condition of our country; the clear waters of the north refusing to mingle with those from the south.[35]

West of the main village lay a small knob supporting the upper village. Beyond the knob, the terrain dipped into a shallow saucer before it rose to Bolivar Heights, a ridge running two and a half miles north and south to connect the Potomac and the Shenandoah. An old, abandoned mill marked its north end on the Potomac. On the far side of the saucer the village of Bolivar rested at the eastern base of Bolivar Heights. The principal road of the area began at Harpers Ferry, crossed the saucer, bisected the village, crossed Bolivar Heights, and continued beyond to Halltown. Another road ran beside the Shenandoah on the southern edge of the promontory created by the junction of the two rivers. Rocky banks rose perhaps one hundred feet from the landward side of the road.

Union pickets extended along the crest of Bolivar Heights while work parties collected mutton, poultry, fresh pork, honey, and vegetables. Ready to return, the

---

34   Bryant, Edwin E., *History of the Third Regiment of Wisconsin Veteran Volunteer Infantry 1861–1865* (Madison, 1891) 29 (Bryant, *Third Wisconsin*).

35   Blair, William Alan, ed., *A Politician Goes to War, the Civil War Letters of John White Geary* (University Park, 1995) 13–14, letter dated September 15, 1861, from Geary to his wife (Blair, *Geary Letters*).

men in the mill had finished refining the raw grain;[36] by Tuesday night, October 15, all other work had been completed.

Geary decided he would recross the river Wednesday morning, but early that day the pickets from Bolivar Heights came scampering down the slope to the village of Bolivar. Behind them marched three Rebel columns of cavalry, infantry, and artillery. In a few minutes Geary reached Bolivar, where he rallied the retreating pickets on the main body of troops.[37] An artillery shell exploded nearby. A piece of shrapnel gashed his leg to the bone below the knee; but he considered it insufficiently serious to tell anyone or seek assistance.[38] He would remain in command. The Confederate advance guard of cavalry charged the western portion of the village while Confederate infantry took position on the heights and their artillery went into position where the Charlestown Road crossed the crest.

Giving reality to the indefensibility of Harpers Ferry, a large force of Rebel infantry and four guns appeared on Loudon Heights and opened fire on the Ferry in Geary's rear. To block the fords on the river and keep this force from crossing, Geary sent a detachment of the Thirteenth Massachusetts to his left rear, where it took position in the old rifle factory in Harpers Ferry.[39] He now had approximately 450 men. This force checked a "fierce charge" by Rebel cavalry, a second charge, then a third, all supported by artillery and infantry fire from Bolivar Heights. At 11 A.M. one piece of New York artillery arrived after running the gauntlet of fire from the Confederates on Loudon Heights.

Geary sent two companies of the Third Wisconsin under Captain Henry Bertram out the river road toward the south end of the heights. When he found no Confederates on the road, Bartram clambered up the rocky face, where he discovered to his surprise that he was on the southern flank of an enemy line moving toward the village of Bolivar. First one, then another, company of Wisconsin infantry struggled to the top, deployed, and fired a volley at the Rebels, who had by now reached the outskirts of Bolivar. The two companies advanced. The Confederates withdrew to the crest of the ridge. Bertram put part of his force into a charge, which was repulsed, but with reinforcements, he took a firm hold on the southern end of the ridge.[40]

---

36   *O.R. Atlas*, plate 29; Bryant, *Third Wisconsin*, 29–30.

37   *OR*, 5, 240, Geary's report.

38   Blair, *Geary Letters*, 19–20, letter dated October 24, 1861, from Geary to his wife.

39   *OR*, 5, 240, Geary's report.

40   Bryant, *Third Wisconsin*, 28–34.

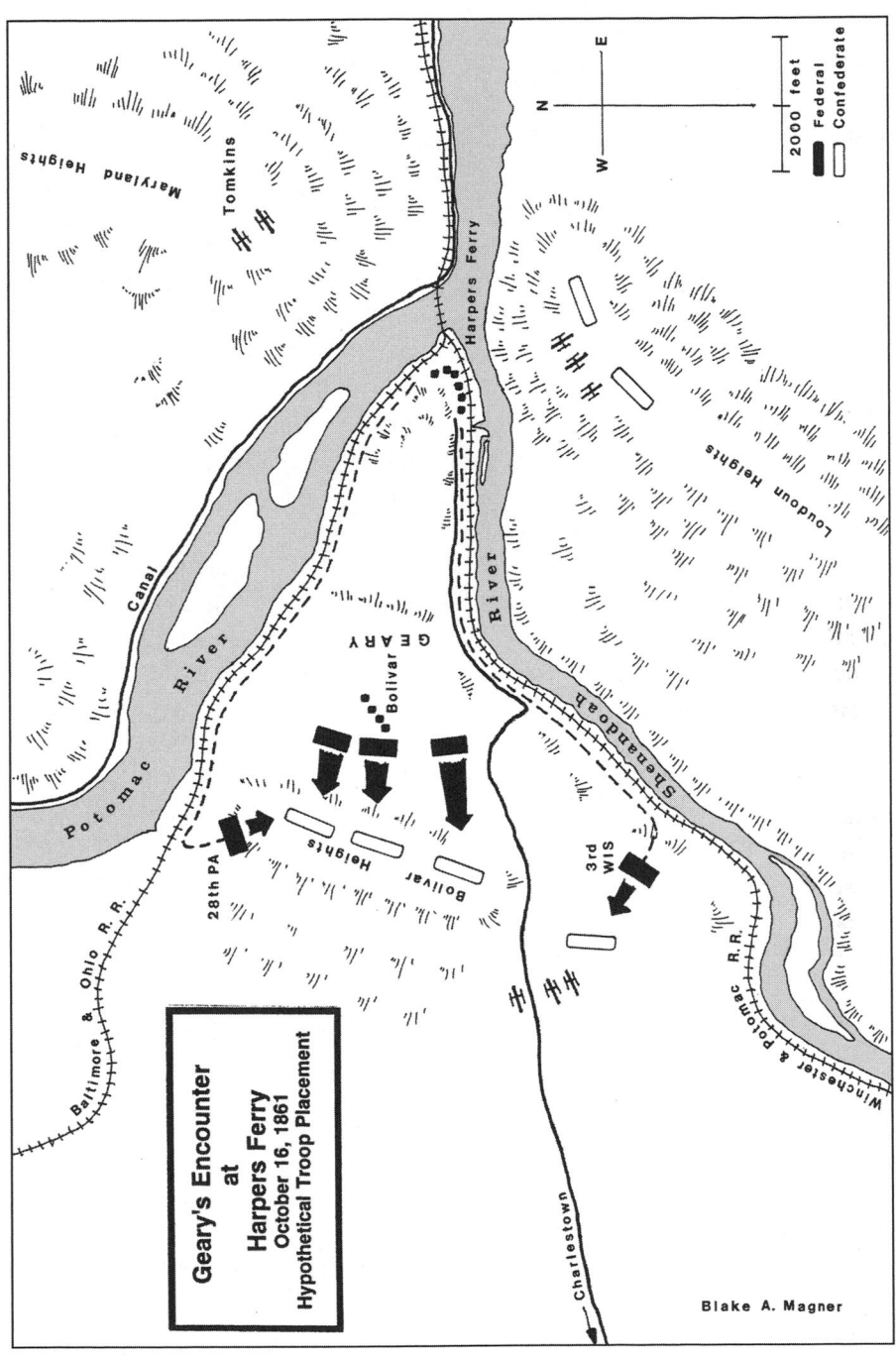

Geary's Encounter
at
Harpers Ferry
October 16, 1861
Hypothetical Troop Placement

Blake A. Magner

His right flank elements, two companies of his Twenty-eighth Pennsylvania Regiment, Geary sent to turn the Rebel left near the Potomac. The flanking force took a position on the north end of the Bolivar Heights ridge. The single piece of Union artillery opened on the Confederate guns while the fire of Captain Tompkins' two guns on Maryland Heights silenced the Confederate infantry and artillery on Loudon Heights. Seeing his right-flank force in an advantageous position on the end of the Confederate position, Geary ordered a general advance. The charge swept the crest. In their haste the Rebels broke the axle of the thirty-two pounder Columbiad. At the crest Geary halted his men and pursued the retreating Rebels with artillery fire from his New York gun and the captured thirty-two pounder. Five more companies of his own regiment came forward from Point of Rocks, two staying with Major Gould at Sandy Hook and the other three joining Geary on the field.[41]

Geary rested his dispatch book on the massive Columbiad and wrote a brief report to Banks about his success,[42] then ordered his men to rest in position. At midnight he withdrew to the Maryland side of the river.[43]

Next morning, October 17, Geary received a flag of truce from Lieutenant Colonel Turner Ashby, Stonewall Jackson's chief of cavalry. The horse of the Reverend Nathaniel G. North, Ashby's chaplain, had arrived wounded at his home the night after the battle, and his family was worried about him. Ashby asked that North, a noncombatant, be returned if he were alive. But Geary had different information about the reverend: he was hardly a noncombatant.[44] To the rear with the other prisoners he went. The Rebels withdrew past Halltown,[45] more evidence that they would not resist any forward movement along McClellan's line.

---

41   Reichardt, Theodore, *Diary of Battery A, First Regiment Rhode Island Artillery* (Providence, 1865) 24 (Reichardt, *Diary of Battery A*), entry dated October 19, 1861; *OR*, 5, 241, Geary's report.

42   Blair, *Geary Letters*, 14–15, letter dated October 15, 1861, from Geary to his wife.

43   *OR*, 5, 242, Geary's report.

44   Blair, *Geary Letters*, 19, letter dated October 24, 1861, from Geary to his wife; *OR*, 5, 241, 242, Geary's report.

45   *OR*, 5, 241, Geary's report; 245, Bertram's report.

Chapter 4

"The general [McClellan] desires that you keep a good lookout upon Leesburg, to see if this movement has the effect to drive them away. Perhaps a slight demonstration on your part would have the effect to move them."

—Colburn to Stone

Leesburg
(McClellan Advances Again)

lso confirming that the Rebels would not resist a small advance, Wadsworth reported from the Munson's Hill area on October 17 that the enemy had withdrawn from Mills Crossroads during the preceding night. He followed them with a reconnaissance of infantry and cavalry to Fairfax Court House, where he found them in force. Enemy pickets fired without effect, and he returned without loss.[1]

The same day, Baldy Smith telegraphed that a man from Richmond had just entered his lines with information that the Rebels had withdrawn to Fairfax Court House, where they intended to make their stand.[2] "We were soon sure that we did not have anyone in front of us with the Secessionists all around Manassas," wrote the Comte de Paris that night in his diary.[3]

1   Wadsworth MSS (L.C.), six-page memorandum handwritten on lined paper in lead pencil, n.d.

2   McClellan MSS (L.C.) telegram dated October 17, 1861, from Smith to McClellan.

3   Comte de Paris MS diary (large diary) (A.N. de la M. de F.) entry dated October 18, 1861.

McClellan received a report that an old black man from Fairfax Court House had seen the Rebels moving in retreat. On October 20, a Sunday, Banks reported Geary's successful encounter to McClellan[4] and enclosed a copy of Geary's hyperbolic report.[5] Geary had his tiny force of six hundred facing three thousand Rebels in four full regiments, a full battery of artillery, and Ashby's legendary cavalry, an exaggeration. In the excitement of victory Geary reported Rebel killed and wounded at one hundred fifty, also a huge exaggeration.

At Smith's headquarters, while McClellan tested experimental artillery shells under the watchful eye of numerous generals, Mrs. Smith, and a group of ladies under Mrs. Smith's wing, a reconnaissance of cavalry and artillery sought more direct intelligence about the Rebels. A short while later McClellan and his officers followed. They found Vienna abandoned and Federal pickets in possession of Annandale.

No doubt disappointed again, McClellan would not benefit from a tactical defensive in strong, prepared positions. The Confederates, he was certain, would not attack. In fact, they seemed to be withdrawing all along the line. What had caused this? Did they fear for their left? Were they too weak to hold their lines around the string of new forts? Were they trying to trick him into entering the Manassas area for another fight?

All these questions occurred to McClellan and his staff.[6] On the last one, another fight at Manassas, he would tell his most important listeners, his wife and

---

4 No evidence shows when the reports of the encounter became known to McClellan. Banks' dispatch was sent to Washington, but McClellan had been with Smith for several days. McClellan did not mention the Bolivar Heights encounter in his report or *M.O.S.*, nor does it appear in any other way in his MSS, which would be consistent with his attitude toward the Ball's Bluff disaster that followed. Nevertheless, we know that the diligent telegraph corps had wired headquarters to the divisions and that the commanding general's staff in Washington would have seen that McClellan received this information.

5 *OR*, 5, 239, Banks' report; 241, Geary's report; Blair, *Geary Letters*, 19, letter dated October 24, 1861, from Geary to his wife.

6 Comte de Paris MS diary (large diary) (A.N. de la M. de F.) entry dated October 18, 1861. An invaluable and indispensable source on McClellan, the large diary is also frustrating and difficult to use. Because the count and other staff officers often traveled with McClellan on his overnight trips to the Virginia lines, the longer entries in the large diary, which apparently did not go on these trips, were not always made daily; and the entries covering several days are not models of orderly, chronological clarity. A two- or three-day entry will often skip forward and backward several times. The count also appears to have made a simple error in his descriptions. Armies facing each other stand right flank facing left flank and vice versa. He appears to describe everyone's flanks as he would see them from his position, not as a member of each army would see his own.

his president, that he was "not such a fool as to buck against that place in the spot designated by the foe."[7] For the previous six months, the Rebels had fortified Manassas. Must they be attacked there? McDowell did not think an assault would be necessary. No doubt wanting to vindicate his earlier unsuccessful effort, McDowell believed the same movement by the right flank as he had tried at Bull Run would cut or threaten their communications with Richmond and make them evacuate.[8]

On October 15 Stone told McClellan that the Confederate movements between Leesburg and the Potomac were "apparently preparations for a resistance rather than attack"[9] and on October 18, he said that enemy pickets had withdrawn from most of their posts. Stone had sent an officer toward Leesburg the evening before. The Confederates had a small force between Leesburg and Edwards Ferry and another below Goose Creek. He would reconnoiter farther the next day if circumstances remained favorable.[10]

By the addition of McCall's Pennsylvania Reserves to the divisions already on the western side of the Potomac, McClellan had extended his right flank north along the Potomac, could reconnoiter more actively, and could collect information about the topography of the Rebel territory to the west and north. The town of Leesburg lay a bit more than thirteen miles out the Leesburg and Alexandria Turnpike.[11] An imaginary east-west line between Leesburg, Virginia, and Poolesville, Maryland, bisected Harrison's Island, a long narrow strip of land in the Potomac River near the Virginia shore. Occupying the Virginia bank as far north as Prospect Hill, McClellan could shift his Maryland forces upriver toward Harpers Ferry. This would give him better peace of mind on the continuous question about the Confederates crossing the river somewhere above the capital. The division of the reliable Charles P. Stone, its line shortened and its brigades more concentrated, would cover the area between Poolesville and Rockville.

McClellan had created Stone's division on September 12[12] and had undoubtedly kept it in this position because Stone had become familiar with the area during his march to Harpers Ferry in the Bull Run campaign and his occupation of it when

7   Burlingame, *Hay Diary*, 27, entry dated October 17, 1861; Sears, *McClellan's Correspondence*, 109, letter dated October 19, 1861, from McClellan to his wife.

8   Comte de Paris MS diary (large diary) (A.N. de la M. de F.) entry dated October 18, 1961.

9   McClellan MSS (L.C.) telegram dated October 15, 1861, from Stone to McClellan.

10   McClellan MSS (L.C.) telegram dated Octoboer 18, 1861, from Stone to McClellan.

11   Sypher, *Pennsylvanian Reserves*, 88–90, 124.

12   *M.O.S.*, 81.

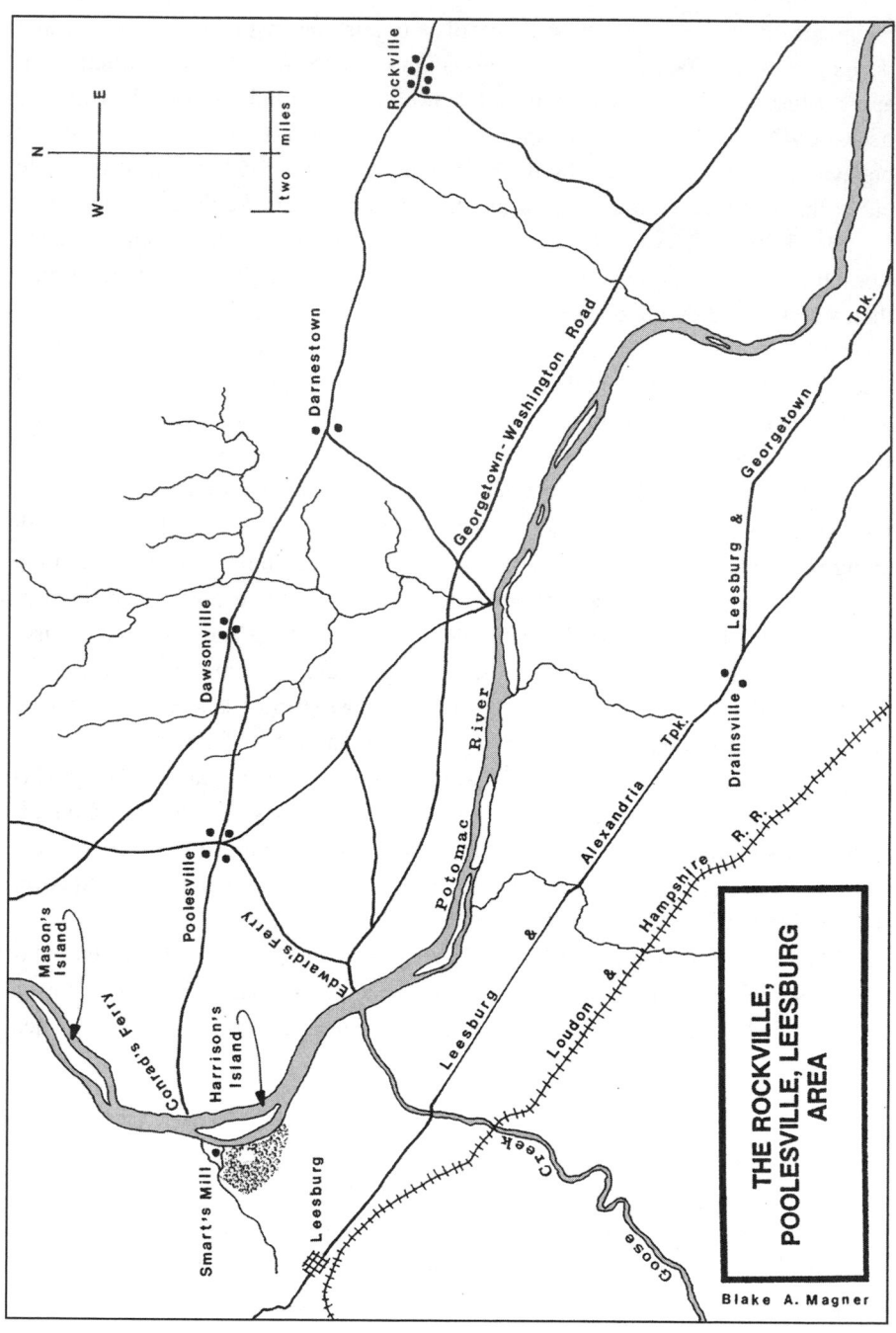

THE ROCKVILLE, POOLESVILLE, LEESBURG AREA

Blake A. Magner

McClellan first took command.[13] Originally Stone's division included infantry brigades commanded by Brigadier Generals Willis A. Gorman and Frederick W. Lander. By early October, the Philadelphia Brigade, the group of Pennsylvania regiments recruited for Colonel Edward D. Baker, had recovered from the "friendly fire" incident; marched from Munson's Hill to Poolesville on the Maryland side of the river;[14] and become the third brigade in Stone's division. Headquarters included three companies of the Third New York Cavalry under Major John Mix.[15]

On October 18, McClellan met General George A. McCall, an esteemed acquaintance from the war in Mexico,[16] in Washington and ordered him to march the next day from Langley to Dranesville along the Leesburg Turnpike. He was to reconnoiter thoroughly, map the roads, and record the topography. As he marched northwest McCall must keep a sharp watch to his left for an attack on his exposed flank.[17] Perhaps McCall could induce the Confederates to evacuate Leesburg. That would allow McClellan to extend the Virginia lines farther northwest along the Potomac.[18] McCall was to move on the nineteenth as far as Dranesville, where he would cover the work of the topographical engineers mapping that region.

13 *M.O.S.*, 79.

14 Banes, *Philadelphia Brigade*, 22–23.

15 *OR*, 5, 16, McClellan's report.

16 Myers, William Starr, ed., *The Mexican War Diary of General George B. McClellan: A Campaign Journal Written in Camp and Field, in 1846–47 and Now for the First Time Published* (Princeton, 1917) 21 ff, entries dated December 7 and 25, 1846 (Myers, *McClellan's Mexican War Diary*).

17 *M.O.S.*, 181.

18 Comte de Paris MS diary (large dairy) (A.N. de la M. de F.) entries dated October 18 and 22, 1861; Sypher, *Pennsylvania Reserves*, 124; Sears, *McClellan's Correspondence*, 109, letter dated October 19, 1861, from McClellan to his wife. Sears' volume of Selected Correspondence, by far his best contribution to the superb Civil War scholarship of our time, is careful, detailed, and reliable; and it is indispensable to the student of the period and the man. The "purifying" efforts of Mary Ellen McClellan and J. C. Prime, who edited the memoirs, did not make the work easy. "Introduction," x–xiv. But as Sears tells us on the cover and title page, the letters are "selected," though all compulsive students of the time would probably prefer that they be "complete" or "encyclopedic," especially for a man as complex and controversial as McClellan.

The only accounts of this order and conversation are in Sypher, *Pennsylvania Reserves*, 124, and *M.O.S.*, 180, the description in *M.O.S.* being shorter and less informative than the one paragraph in Sypher. They are not the same. Meticulous and careful, McClellan virtually never gave verbal orders except to his most trusted subordinates or probably when he did not want to create paper that might later embarrass him. No written order exists in *OR* or McClellan's voluminous MSS. Assuming that he never wrote an order, rather than lost or "edited" one, any account of the order to McCall must select one account over the other.

That same day Wadsworth's brigade of McDowell's division occupied Fairfax Court House, where Wadsworth found one hundred fifty abandoned tents still standing. Showing his usual reckless courage, Wadsworth had gone forward with his front elements, a fact that appeared in the written report he submitted to McDowell. By October 20 the report had reached McClellan and prompted some remarks by the commanding general.

"Being in command of the front on the day in question it was quite right when it was found the enemy had retired that the General should send a party after them. I only felt uneasy that the General had gone himself."[19]

McClellan ordered Heintzelman on the left flank to send a reconnaissance toward Occoquan Creek, some distance south of Alexandria. Heintzelman assigned the mission to Richardson. With two regiments of infantry, a company of cavalry, and half a battery of artillery, Richardson sent parties west toward the Confederate lines and south toward Accotinck Creek; but his perfunctory, unsatisfactory effort surprised Heintzelman. Nevertheless, the Rebel pickets met by the westbound column fell back; and Richardson reported the "long roll" being beaten in their camps. In his large diary, Heintzelman wrote, "The papers are full of rumors of the rebels falling back and I have no doubt there is truth in them, but not so extensive."[20]

Did McClellan intend at the outset to capture Leesburg or at least to compel its evacuation? This small question raises a most difficult historical issue about this most complex man: his credibility. Many contemporaries and historians have doubted his truthfulness, an equal number assuring us that he was a model of integrity. The resolution of this dispute would require a book, not a footnote or even an appendix. Hopefully, the narrative will sooner or later answer this large question.

In the author's opinion, McClellan was scrupulously accurate in his accounts of the facts, the events, the objectively discernible historical occurrences. When he described his intentions, he generally made the most truthful statement that would serve his purpose. But when he stated his motive for an earlier act, his credibility collapsed altogether. He usually gave a motive consistent with the result and advantageous for him, without regard for his real motives. Examples follow in the narrative.

As if to preserve his historical and personal flexibility on motive, he never gave his files to the adjutant general. In fact, after the war, when U. S. Grant, as general in chief, began to collect records from high-ranking officers whose official files were incomplete, he corresponded with McClellan and asked him to allow government representatives to review his files. McClellan refused, explaining, among other things, that he had nothing the government did not already have, McClellan MSS (L.C.) draft letter dated 1866, from McClellan to Grant; draft letter dated December 26, 1866, from McClellan to Marcy. This statement was untrue, and although McClellan did not necessarily know how false it was (we have no real way to assess this), he had many of the documents listed in *OR* as "not found." For example, in his account of Ball's Bluff, most of the dispatches he quotes verbatim in *M.O.S.* do not appear in *OR* but probably would have.

19   James S. Wadsworth MSS (University of Rochester) letter dated October 20, 1861, from Fry to Wadsworth.

20   Heintzelman MS diary (L.C.) (large diary) entries dated October 18 and 19, 1861.

His views were widely held. Two days earlier McDowell had predicted to Chase that a movement of federal troops on the Virginia side would cause the enemy to fall back on Manassas. He had drawn this conclusion, he reported, from information he considered reliable.[21]

While Heintzelman was receiving Richardson's report, McCall marched his division to Dranesville without opposition. The next day, he would cover reconnaissances in all directions.[22] When he reached a position atop Broad Hill, about eleven miles south of Leesburg, he halted to establish a base for his patrols.[23] At the same time, Smith, commanding the division to McCall's left, pushed strong parties to the surrounding heights to cover mapping parties.[24] The reconnaissances by McCall and Smith showed the area between Langley and Leesburg to be free of Rebels.

McClellan, still with Smith, sent further orders to McCall in the evening of October 19. Before retiring from Dranesville, McCall must check the roads at least two or three miles in every direction. On the Leesburg Turnpike he should send a party at least four miles to the front and another toward the Potomac River. He was to communicate fully with Smith in order to permit support if he must remain in Dranesville all day on October 20. That night, McClellan decided to remain with Smith's division.[25]

On the same day a mulatto who had deserted from the Thirteenth Mississippi crossed into Stone's lines and reported that the Confederates at Leesburg were expecting an advance and were preparing to retreat if attacked.[26] McClellan also received word from Banks' headquarters that the signal station at Sugar Loaf had seen the Confederates leave Leesburg and that a blanket of quiet covered his area.

McClellan concluded that the Confederates had taken McCall's movement to Dranesville and his reconnaissances as a threat to the flank of their Leesburg position and had abandoned the town. If he could expand his positions on the west side of the river to Leesburg, he would repeat his "capture" of Munson's Hill by seizing an unoccupied position. Just like the Munson's Hill events of the previous month, all signs told him the Confederates were withdrawing, once again to their old positions

---

21   Robert Todd Lincoln MSS (Library of Congress) telegram dated October 17, 1861, from McDowell to Chase.

22   *OR*, 5, 32, McClellan's report.

23   *OR*, 5, 290, McClellan's report.

24   *OR*, 5, 32, McClellan's report.

25   George A. McCall MSS (Pennsylvania Historical Society) letter dated October 19, 1861, from McClellan to McCall.

26   *OR*, 5, 292, Stone's report.

around Manassas and Centerville. He would take advantage of this and "drive" them from the Leesburg area. If he moved promptly, he would display an appearance of aggressive movement.

As soon as McClellan learned that the area of McCall's reconnaissance contained no Rebels, he set out with his entourage along the pike, a straight cobblestone road through hilly, wooded countryside with streams, ponds, meadows, and deep, winding ravines. Although the farm land seemed to be worn out, many pleasant cottages and small farms bordered the road. The presence of cattle and poultry showed that troops had not been in this vicinity in strength. Four to five miles north of Prospect Hill, they crossed Difficult Run on an elevated bridge, then passed some men who had straggled from Reynolds' brigade to boil coffee by the side of the road.

After riding through the village of Dranesville, where they could see the faces of the women peering at them through the windows of their houses, they finally surmounted a steep slope to reach the top of a high hill,[27] from which they could see the turnpike, the village of Dranesville, and the entire surrounding area. But they could not find McCall. The hill, an excellent defensive position, McCall could defend easily and could use to control the junction of important roads, including the Centerville road, which entered the pike just below the town. But the hill lay unoccupied. McClellan continued two miles beyond. He became impatient. Where was McCall? Finally, they arrived atop a plateau covered with junipers and surrounded by high ground, where Reynolds' brigade had lit fires and was unloading a long line of wagons. Here, at last, they found McCall.[28] Threatening McCall's route of withdrawal was a deep, muddy ravine and the strong hill position at Dranesville. McCall explained his position to McClellan and his staff officers.

"I heard the enemy is in force at Centerville," he said. "The road to Centerville runs into Dranesville, which is why I wanted to go further since I am afraid of being attacked in Dranesville."

Puzzled, McClellan wondered why McCall did not take a position at which he expected the enemy and could protect himself. Instead, McCall had marched his division three miles farther and left undefended in his rear a very defensible position at which he expected an attack. Now, the Confederates could sever his line of retreat, surround him, and pin him against the Potomac.

27   This was probably Broad Hill, where McCall had stopped, but neither the map in *O.R. Atlas*, plate viii, nor the one in the author's collection give it a name.

28   Comte de Paris MS diary (large diary) (A.N. de la M. de F.) entry dated October 20, 1861; McClellan MSS (L.C.) telegram dated October 19, 1861, from McClellan to Marcy.

When McClellan gave McCall his orders for the mapping reconnaissance, he had told him the Confederates had left the Dranesville area several days earlier; and upon arriving in the village McCall received confirmation from the inhabitants that the Rebel brigade at Leesburg had crossed Goose Creek on its way to Manassas on Tuesday. Having marched eleven and one half miles to Dranesville on Saturday, McCall spread his brigades about the area to be surveyed, two at Difficult Run a few miles short of the town and one in Dranesville. His men saw no Rebels on the Leesburg Turnpike. That evening, he sent the Dranesville brigade approximately three miles beyond the town, then brought one of the two rear brigades forward to cover the road from Centerville, his vulnerable spot.

McClellan sent Captain A. V. Colburn and the Comte de Paris to tell McCall that, if he thought the farthest position not very strong, he should withdraw the brigade to the town.

McCall thought he had strengthened his position by covering the Centerville Road. He told Colburn he considered his position very strong.

Colburn said McClellan would be better satisfied if the leading brigade returned to the village.

Taking that for what it was, a virtual order, McCall immediately returned his brigade to Dranesville. McClellan ordered reconnaissance parties sent three or four miles in every direction. The reserve brigade stationed in the town camped on the hill about a mile beyond the town on the far side of Sugarland Creek. Distant in the rear, Smith's division lay twenty-eight miles away; but the Confederates at Centerville had only fifteen miles to Leesburg. Under the orders for the reconnaissance, McCall would finish mapping on Saturday and, probably Sunday morning, return to Prospect Hill. But when he found his task unfinished at 10 A.M. Sunday, October 20, he sent a message to McClellan that he could not finish until Monday. McClellan told him to complete the task, then return. From their outer line of reconnaissance and survey the Pennsylvania Reserves lay eleven miles from Leesburg but could not reach Ball's Bluff in less than seventeen miles by any choice of roads, more than seven hours of steady marching.[29]

On McClellan's way back the miles seemed much longer. Exhausted, Judge Key could hardly stay on his horse; when they finally reached Smith's headquarters at the Smoot House, he fell asleep in one chair after another. McClellan's announcement that he would stay at Smith's headquarters rather than return to

---

29   Comte de Paris MS diary (large diary) (A.N. de la M. de F.) entries dated October 20 and 22, 1861; *C.C.W.*, 2, 267, 258, 259, 260 (McCall).

Washington delighted his men. The Comte de Paris pulled his longcoat about him and collapsed on a comfortable bed.[30]

The "capture" of Leesburg would do many things for McClellan, but most of all it would relieve him of pressure to undertake a premature offensive. All available intelligence told him the Confederates were withdrawing to Manassas or intended to withdraw on any provocation. He faced good circumstances: the roads firm, the days still long, the temperature warm, and his army by now well organized and equipped. He could take the initial steps of a campaign, and a small push would precipitate the withdrawal of any troops still in the Leesburg area. He would incur no risk because McCall would be at Dranesville in easy supporting distance on the left. Early Sunday morning, he had telegraphic orders sent to Brigadier General Charles P. Stone at Poolesville:[31]

> Camp Griffin, October 20, 1861
>
> Brigadier-General Stone, Poolesville:
>
> General McClellan desires me to inform you that General McCall occupied Dranesville yesterday and is still there. Will send out heavy reconnaissances today in all directions from that point. The general desires that you keep a good lookout upon Leesburg, to see if this movement has the effect to drive them away. Perhaps a slight demonstration on your part would have the effect to move them.
>
> A. V. COLBURN
> Assistant-Adjutant General[32]

This order reached Stone by eleven in the morning. Expecting everything in it to be accomplished that day,[33] McClellan decided that McCall's reconnaissances and Stone's "slight demonstration" would be enough work. If he had finished his reconnaissances by the end of the day, McCall could withdraw.

---

30   Comte de Paris MS diary (large diary) (A.N. de la M. de F.) entries dated October 12 and 20, 1861; McClellan MSS (L.C.) three telegrams dated October 19, 1861, from McClellan to Marcy.

31   de Peyster, John Watts, *Personal and Military History of Philip Kearny Major-General United States Volunteers* (New York, 1869) 222, letter dated December 15, 1861, from Kearny to n.a. (de Peyster, *Kearny*); *OR*, 5, 32, McClellan's report; *M.O.S.*, 180–181.

32   *OR*, 5, 290, dispatch dated October 20, 1861, from Colburn to Banks.

33   *OR*, 5, 33, McClellan's report.

Stone's troops lay some distance from the river, which was covered only by pickets.[34] The division commander ordered Colonel Charles Devens,[35] commanding the Fifteenth Massachusetts Volunteer Infantry, to move two flatboats from the canal opposite Harrison's Island into the Potomac and cross to the island with all the Fifteenth that was available. The Forty-second New York Infantry, the Tammany Regiment, under Colonel Milton Cogswell, was to proceed at once to the vicinity of Conrad's Ferry near Harrison's Island.[36] For the demonstration suggested by McClellan, Stone would put Colonel Edward D. Baker in command at Conrad's Ferry while he arranged to fake a crossing at Edwards Ferry with Gorman's brigade and two companies of the Third New York Cavalry under Major Mix.[37]

Born in England in 1811, the son of a schoolteacher, Baker came as a young boy in 1815 to Philadelphia, where he lived until 1825. After studying law, he was admitted to practice at age nineteen. In the Black Hawk War, while Lincoln received his brief military experience, Baker served as a private. Afterwards, he moved to Springfield, Illinois, where he developed and expanded a law practice, joined a group of titans at the bar and in politics, and became part of a circle including Orville Hickman Browning, Richard Yates, Stephen A. Douglas, and Lyman Trumble. As his considerable oratorical skills became sharper and sharper, so grew his political achievements. During his time in Illinois he became a close friend and law partner of Abraham Lincoln and namesake to the future president's second son. In the Mexican War, he raised a regiment of Illinois volunteers, led it to Texas, and ultimately rose to command of a brigade. In the 1850s, he was drawn to California, where his extraordinary forensic talents again made him a leader of the bar.

Devoid of all ordinary vices except his passion for cards, nevertheless "with all his rich stores of memory and transcendent talent in statement and speech, there was absolutely no trace of order or system about his character," wrote his friend Isaac Wistar after the war. "Far from keeping any pecuniary accounts, he had not even a docket of his cases, relying solely on his memory and a mass of papers carried in his hat and about his person. His office was a bare, half-furnished and desolate apartment, where nothing that was wanted could ever be found, and from whose dreary precincts he himself shrunk as from a prison cell. He cared nothing

---

34   *OR*, 5, 39, McClellan's report.

35   Also spelled Devin, Devins. The name of a Union cavalry officer (Devin) was often interchanged with "Devens."

36   Also called Swans or Sullivans Island.

37   *C.C.W.*, 2, 462 (Mix); *OR*, 5, 293, Stone's report.

for money and in spite of his great earnings, was most generally penniless. A street beggar was as likely to get from him a twenty-dollar piece as a quarter-dollar . . . "

"Ned" Baker's life followed an erratic but brilliant trail across the United States. He moved when he pleased and never settled into a way of life. When he set his mind to do something, he did it no matter what stood in the way, a perfect example of the rash, free-spirited American. And this spirit endeared him to many.

Never in his life did he gauge his audience incorrectly. With his extraordinary oratorical skills he could win a man's confidence in no time, even that of the president of the United States. The bond with Lincoln had more to it than the fact that he and Lincoln had worked together in Springfield. Baker held Oregon for the Republicans in 1860. As a result the Oregon legislature elected him to the United States Senate.

To the chief executive Baker served as close confidant and good friend. Congressmen, too, loved the Baker who in full uniform walked onto the floor of the Senate; unbuckled his sword; laid it across his desk; and denounced John C. Breckinridge, a frustrated Democratic presidential candidate of 1860, for his willingness to compromise with the Southern states.[38]

A cataclysmic event like the American Civil War could not fail to sweep Ned Baker into it. He obtained from his friend and former law partner the president an authorization, dated May 8, 1861, to raise and equip a regiment of sixteen companies of infantry.[39] His former California law partner Isaac Jones Wistar, now in Philadelphia, he telegraphed to come at once to New York.

"Well," said Wistar, "if you propose to leave your seat in the Senate to be an infantry colonel, what do you want of me?"

"Can you raise this regiment?" asked Baker.

"Not in New York. I have no acquaintances there."

"Can you raise it in Philadelphia?"

"I think I can, but I am not sure."

---

38   N.a., *He Walked With Lincoln* MS biography of Baker (Oregon Historical Society); Johnson, Allen, *Dictionary of American Biography*, 10 vols. each vol. in two parts (New York, 1927, 1964) 1, pt. 1, 517–518; Wistar, *Autobiography*, 303, 305; *New York Times*, October 23, 1861, p. 1; Baltz, John D., *Edward D. Baker, U.S. Senator from Oregon, one of America's Heroes: Colonel E. D. Baker's Defense in the Battle of Ball's Bluff, fought October 21st 1861, in Virginia and slight Biographical Sketches of Colonel Baker, Colonel Wistar, and Colonel Stone* (Philadelphia, 1888); chapter 1; Fenton, William D. "Edward Dickenson Baker," *The Quarterly of the Oregon Historical Society*, vol. IX, 1–23; T. W. Davenport, "Slavery Question in Oregon II," *The Quarterly of the Oregon Historical Society*, vol. IX, 309–373; Averell, *Recollections*, 323; Charles H. Banes, *Philadelphia Brigade*, 24–25. The quotations appear in Wistar, *Autobiography*.

39   The standard infantry regiment, ten rifle companies of one hundred men each, had been developed by McDowell and Franklin for Chase but had not then been formally proposed or adopted.

"Very well. Your private business is sure to be broken up and not worth following for a while at least. Abandon it. Go to work and raise this regiment in Philadelphia, bringing the men over here to be mustered. I cannot at this moment accept military rank without jeopardizing my seat in the Senate, but you know my relations with Lincoln; and if you will do that for me, I can assure you that within six months I shall be a major-general, and you shall have a brigadier-general's commission and a satisfactory command under me."[40]

Primarily in the Philadelphia area, Wistar raised the Seventy-first Pennsylvania Infantry, then had it mustered into the federal service at Fort Schuyler, New York. At once it became known as the California Battalion. Because he had not raised it as a New York or a Pennsylvania regiment but by direct authorization of the federal government, the military initially carried it as a Regular Army unit, Baker as colonel and Wistar, who had had military experience, as lieutenant colonel.[41]

Baker could accept the commission as colonel without compromising his seat in the Senate but could not take the stars of a brigadier or major general because they required approval of the Senate and resignation of his seat in the Senate. A brigadier general's commission he declined. A major-general's two stars? For some time he remained uncertain about accepting the higher rank, but by the middle of September he had reached his decision.[42] His thoughts on this important issue he expressed in a letter to a fellow Oregonian:

Headquarters, Baker's Brigade,
Camp Advance, Chain Bridge.

September 22, 1861

My Dear Sir:

. . . You have doubtless learned ere this of my appointment by the President, as a Brigadier-General. My duty to the state of Oregon, in my opinion, is such that I have felt compelled to decline the honor. Yesterday, I had conferred upon me an additional honor in the shape of an appointment as Major-General, but,

---

40 Wistar, *Autobiography*, 355–356.

41 Bates, *Hist. Penn. Vols.*, 4, 788.

42 Most accounts of Baker's life state that he was still considering the major-generalcy when he was killed at Ball's Bluff on October 21. In *D.A.B.*, 1, pt. 1, 518, and Heitman, *Historical Register*, 1, 183, the authors have it right.

actuated by the same motive as decided me in the former instance, I shall decline this position also.

While I am writing this, your letter of August 23 arrived. In relation to the Senatorship, be pleased to say to everyone, once for all, that I value the station conferred upon me by the state of Oregon more highly than any other in the world, that I do not intend to vacate or resign. I shall still retain command enough in the field to enable me to risk my life with honor. With that I am content . . .

E. D. BAKER[43]

Many officers, especially those who had never served before, wanted an "independent" command because it would free them of superior officers, avoid subordination to West Pointers, and give them a chance for personal glory. No doubt reacting to a request of this sort from his friend, Lincoln had sent a note to Scott saying, "Will you be pleased to cause Col. Baker to be assigned to the independent command of his own Brigade and such other troops as you or General McLellan [sic] may place with him and directing that he report to Major General McLellan [sic] directly."[44]

This request, whether or not Lincoln wrote it, contradicted every common-sense element of command. The commander of an army in the field simply could not control numerous small, independent battle units. McClellan intended to have an army exceeding one hundred thousand men in a few corps, large and self-sufficient bodies of troops. Independent brigades of four thousand men, twenty-five for an army of one hundred thousand, had no place in an army of this sort.

Too easy it would be to dismiss Baker as an ignorant, military incompetent vaulted to high rank by his friendship with the president. That would treat him unfairly and incorrectly. He had served in Mexico as a regimental commander, then

---

43   The author quotes the entire letter in *He Walked with Lincoln* MS biography (Or.H.S.)

44   McClellan MSS (L.C.) letter dated October 19, 1861, from Lincoln (?) to Scott. Although this letter is unsigned, it seems to be in the unmistakable handwriting of Lincoln; but it is not in Basler's superb and encyclopedic (with supplemental volumes) *Lincoln's Collected Works*. Giving some additional doubt to its status as a Lincoln letter is the misspelling of McClellan's name because Lincoln had spelled it correctly on many earlier occasions, e.g., Basler, Roy P., ed., *The Collected Works of Abraham Lincoln*, 9 vols. and 2 supp. vols. (New Brunswick, 1953) 4, 504 (Basler, *Lincoln's Collected Works*) 7.

as a brigade commander. There, he had learned the "drill" and the way to handle troops. At the Battle of Cerro Gordo, James Shields, his brigade commander, took a grapeshot through the lung in a charge on the fort. The brigade fell into disorder. Baker ordered his regiment forward and with it went the entire brigade in a successful assault that attracted the attention and favorable comment of Winfield Scott. At the outbreak of the Civil War, Baker had not forgotten his lessons. The historian of his Civil War brigade noted that he "personally exercised the officers in the manual of arms as well as in the school of the battalion, in both of which he displayed considerable knowledge and proficiency."[45]

With Baker temporarily absent, Devens prepared for the reconnaissance to Leesburg. He sent Lieutenant Church Howe, his quartermaster, to drag the two boats from the canal to the river.[46] Meanwhile, ten of the best shots of the Nineteenth Massachusetts crossed to Harrison's Island to reconnoiter. A scout through the tall grass, haystacks, and farm buildings revealed no Confederates. The island, about two miles long and a quarter of a mile wide, lay one thousand feet from Maryland and five hundred feet from the Virginia shore. Neither channel could be crossed without swimming or a boat. By a steep slope the Virginia shore rose one hundred fifty to two hundred feet above river level and towered over the island and the Maryland shore.[47] Opposite the island, heavy woods and thickets down to the water covered the bluff, which was cut with deep water courses, gullies, and ravines. With great difficulty an officer could ride his horse up the narrow footpath troops would use to scale the bluff. For three-quarters of a mile beyond the crest the thick woods and underbrush continued, broken occasionally by small clearings.[48]

Stone had concentrated his division in the area around Poolesville, which rested atop a hill about six miles from the river. Poolesville, the apex of an isosceles triangle

---

45   Banes, *Philadelphia Brigade*, 24; Shutes, Milton H., "Colonel E. D. Baker," 5 (California, 1938) (pamphlet reprint from the *California Historical Society Quarterly* of December 1938); Bauer, K. Jack, *The Mexican War, 1846–1848* (New York and London, 1974) 267 and n. 15, 276 (Bauer, *Mexican War*); Condon, William H., *The Life of Major general James Shields: Hero of Three Wars and Senator from Three States* (Chicago, 1900) 69–70 (Condon, *Shields*).

46   *C.C.W.*, 2, 376 (Howe).

47   John A. Roebling MSS (Rutgers University) letter dated September 1, 1862, from Roebling to n.a.

48   Quaife, Milo, ed., *From the Cannon's Mouth: the Civil War Letters of General Alpheus S. Williams* (Detroit, 1959) 218, letter dated June 20 and, by the editor, June 23, 1863, from Williams to his daughters (Quaife, *Williams' Letters*).

marked by Conrad's Ferry and Edwards Ferry on the river, spawned roads running more or less west to the two ferries.[49]

At 2 P.M., Stone's assistant adjutant general delivered orders to Colonel William R. Lee to march his regiment, the Twentieth Massachusetts Infantry, immediately for the "center pickets," the towpath between the two ferries and opposite Harrison's Island.[50] The day was autumnal and cold. The leaves were falling.

At the same time, Lieutenant French of James B. Ricketts' old battery entered the tent of Lieutenant Casper Crowninshield of the Twentieth Massachusetts in the vicinity of Poolesville. He had the usual inaccurate military information available to those below the "need-to-know" line.

"Well," he said, "I guess we shall have a little fun today, as a regiment of Rebs have been seen to go into some woods on the other side, and we have sent up for the rest of the battery, and General Stone is coming down to shell them."

"All bosh," Crowninshield wrote in his diary. He had suffered too many false alarms to believe he would have any action.

At 1 P.M., Stone mounted and rode from Poolesville to Edwards Ferry. Along the way he met Major Mix returning from an exercise ride. Perhaps the order for cavalry to be at the ferry had not reached the major. Stone asked Mix if he had received any orders.

Mix replied that he had not.

"I ordered you to be at Edwards Ferry with two companies of cavalry at two," said Stone. Pulling his watch from his pocket, he smiled. "You have only fifteen minutes to do it in. Get there as soon as you can."[51]

Continuing, the general arrived shortly at the ferry and established his command post atop the hill, from which he could see almost the entire area of both the Edwards Ferry and the Harrison's Island crossings.

About 3 P.M., Gorman arrived at Edwards Ferry with the remainder of his brigade, the Seventh Michigan, the Putnam Rangers, and a battery of Rhode Island artillery. Placing the guns on the hill, he continued the feint by deploying the Michigan regiment in sight of the enemy; pushed the balance of the Nineteenth Massachusetts toward the river where it, too, deployed in plain view; then sent his aide Major Bannister to General Stone for further orders.

---

49   Coco, Gregory A., ed., *From Ball's Bluff to Gettysburg—And Beyond: The Civil War Letters of Private Roland E. Bowen, 15th Massachusetts Infantry 1861–1864* (Pennsylvania, 1994) 19, letter dated September 13, 1861, from Bowen to his friends (Coco, *Bowen Letters*).

50   *C.C.W.*, 2, 473 (Lee).

51   *C.C.W.*, 2, 462 (Mix).

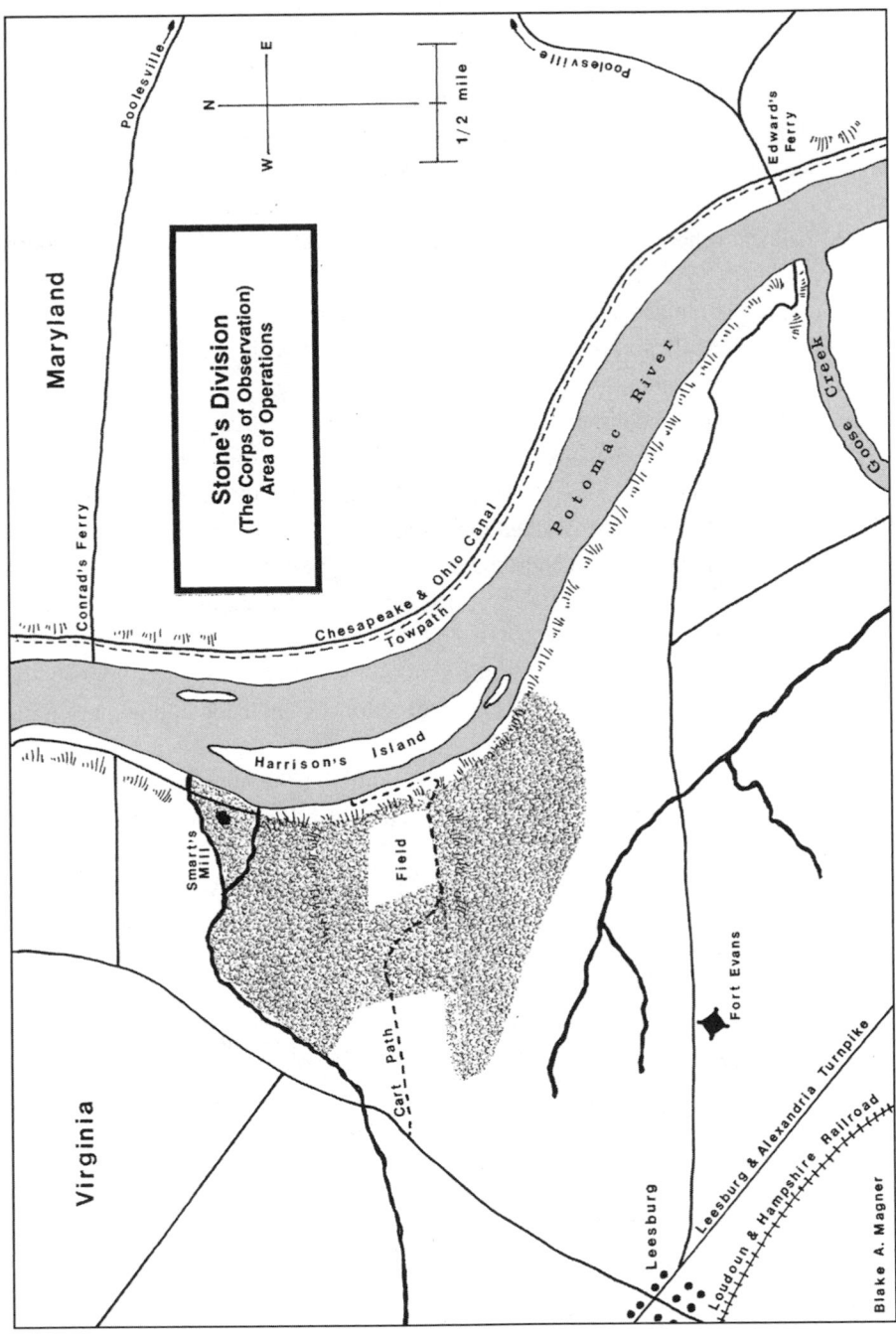

Stone's Division
(The Corps of Observation)
Area of Operations

Maryland

Virginia

Poolesville

Poolesville

Edward's Ferry

Goose Creek

Conrad's Ferry

Chesapeake & Ohio Canal

Towpath

Potomac River

Harrison's Island

Smart's Mill

Field

Cart Path

Fort Evans

Leesburg

Leesburg & Alexandria Turnpike

Loudoun & Hampshire Railroad

Blake A. Magner

N
E
W
S

1/2 mile

Gorman was to fake a crossing. Two companies of the First Minnesota readied themselves while men went into the canal to transfer three scows to the river. Over the towpath and into the Potomac they went. At 4 the artillery opened fire. The troops boarded the unwieldy craft and poled to the Virginia shore. By the end of the day he had a fleet of nine boats, composed of canal boats, flatboats, skows, and rowboats, all under the command of Quartermaster Foote of the Eighty-second New York. Overhead, shell and spherical case screamed toward the woods about the mouth of Goose Creek and other possible enemy positions.[52]

Standing on a place of vantage on the Maryland shore, Gorman peered intently through his binoculars at the terrain south of Goose Creek, then handed them to one of the officers with him.

"Take this glass, and look there, and see if you see anything. If you do, they are General McCall's men. They are within an hour's march of this place."

The two officers could see nothing but a few gray pickets scampering to avoid the artillery fire.[53] The boats reached the far side. Unlike the Virginia shore behind Harrison's Island, the Virginia shore here was low. The men scrambled ashore, deployed, and moved to the crest twenty yards inland. A few minutes passed. The artillery continued to fire. Their feint at its end, the men on the far shore could be seen reforming and clambering back into the skows.[54] The river, though falling slowly, was still swollen from the recent rains; and the swift current made poling more difficult than usual.[55]

Atop his hill, Stone watched, doubtless noticing the ease and speed of the crossing. He sent Captain Stewart to Colonel Devens at Harrison's Island to request that he reconnoiter toward Leesburg.[56] Gorman's brigade withdrew a short distance from the river under orders to be ready for a quick movement. While the troops on Harrison's Island held position to await the outcome of the reconnaissance to Leesburg, Stone reported his actions to McClellan.

---

52   *C.C.W.*, 2, 281 (Stone), 293 (Tompkins); *OR*, 5, 290, McClellan's report and Enclosure A, telegram dated October 20, 1861, from Colburn to Stone; Keillor, James A., *No More Gallant a Deed: a Civil War Memoir of the First Minnesota Volunteers* (St. Paul, 2001) 53 (Keillor, *Gallant Deed*).

53   *C.C.W.*, 2, 355 (Rea). In fact, McCall's men were more than ten miles and probably three or four hours away if they were still at Dranesville and not on their return to Langley.

54   *OR*, 5, 293, Stone's report.

55   *OR*, 5, 290–291, telegram dated October 20, 1861, from Stone to McClellan; *C.C.W.*, 2, 364 (Foote), 474 (Lee).

56   *OR*, 5, 293, Stone's report; *C.C.W.*, 2, 403 (Devens), 376 (Howe).

At 3 P.M. Crowninshield's skepticism dissipated when he saw the rest of the battery come down the road and go to the hill just to the right of Edwards Ferry, the highest ground in the vicinity and a position that commanded the low Virginia shore.

On horseback, smoking his pipe, and giving pleasant greetings with his usual cordial smile,[57] Colonel Lee assembled the remainder of his regiment hurriedly and started for the "center pickets" with 217 men, the rest being on detached duty. They passed Gorman's First Minnesota Regiment on its way to Edwards Ferry,[58] which it reached shortly after 4. By this time two companies of Devens' Fifteenth Massachusetts had taken flatboats across to Harrison's Island to reinforce the ten marksmen.

In the Harrison's Island area, Colonel Devens selected Lieutenant Philbrick, who had crossed earlier to check enemy pickets,[59] to pick twenty men and reconnoiter. He must retire if he saw Rebels. In the low light of evening, objects were unclear, especially in the shadow of the bluff towering above the river and the island. Unable to manage the path up the face of the bluff, Philbrick and his men climbed through the thick trees, brush, and boulders to the crest, then headed for Leesburg. They neither encountered nor saw any enemy. At last, some distance ahead, the men saw a row of tents, fifteen or twenty in number, atop a hill overlooking Leesburg, a camp that could belong only to Confederates. The party had completed its mission. Philbrick and his men returned to the bluff, descended, recrossed the strip of water to Harrison's Island, and reported to Devens. The colonel and the lieutenant went to the Maryland side of the island where they took a boat across to Lee's camp on the towpath.[60] Lee sent Howe to report to Stone.

Glad to have the information, the general saw a chance to strike a blow at the enemy; and his orders from McClellan gave him the latitude to do it. He could easily cross a small force, attack the undefended and unpicketed camp, and recross the river before the alarm spread.

He wrote an order and gave it to Howe for delivery. Devens was to take five companies of his regiment, surprise the camp at daybreak, rout the enemy, not pursue vigorously, and retire to the shore. If he found an excellent position defensible for a long time against significantly greater numbers, he could stay on the Virginia shore and report.

57   Crowninshield MS diary (B.P.L.), entry dated October 20, 1861.

58   *OR*, 5, 293, Stone's report.

59   *OR*, 5, 293, Stone's report; *C.C.W.*, 2, 403 (Devens).

60   *C.C.W.*, 2, 474 (Lee), 376 (Howe); the description of the bluff is in *OR*, 51, pt. 1, 48, Bramhall's report.

Colonel Lee should take four companies and two mountain howitzers to Harrison's Island, then send one of his infantry companies to the top of the bluff to cover Devens' return to the river. At the end of the order he added the kind of provision that had angered many of McDowell's men in their march to Centerville. "Great care will be used by Colonel Devens to prevent any unnecessary injury of private property; and any officer or soldier straggling from the command for curiosity or plunder will be instantly shot."[61]

Much later, Major Mix reached division headquarters atop the hill. The major got coffee, his main reason for coming, while Stone outlined his plans for the next day, October 21. A small party of infantry and cavalry from the Edwards Ferry position would make a diversionary sortie, but the major, who would command, must be careful about Devens' men. Stone told him approximately where they would be.[62]

To be prepared in case of trouble, Stone sent orders at eleven in the evening for more men to come to both crossings. Captain Candy,[63] carrying the dispatches, reached Colonel Baker, commanding the brigade at Harrison's Island, at a quarter to one in the morning. Fifteen minutes later Candy awakened Lieutenant Colonel Isaac Wistar, commander of Baker's old regiment, the Seventy-first Pennsylvania.[64] By the light of the sergeant-of-the-guard's lantern, Wistar read the order. With blankets, overcoats, and cartridge boxes his men must march at once for Conrad's Ferry and arrive at sunrise. He sent for the officer of the day and told him to carry out the order. Having gone to bed only a few minutes before and being thoroughly exhausted, Wistar went back to sleep.[65]

Because the operation was to be a surprise, the enemy must not learn about the changes in the regimental bivouacs. Knowing that all his regiments were inexperienced, Stone sent another aide to see that they left the bands behind and that the men carried unloaded weapons.[66] The general then passed the remainder of the night at his campfire atop the hill.

As dawn began to break, he could hear no firing; and he had received no message from Devens or Baker. Perhaps something had gone awry. Nevertheless, the

61   *OR*, 5, 299–300, Special Orders No. ___, dated October 20, 1861, 10:30 P.M. by Stone.

62   *C.C.W.*, 2, 462 (Mix).

63   Also called Dondee, Kendy, and Kenly.

64   This regiment, the Seventy-first Pennsylvania Infantry, had been called the California Regiment by Baker when he first publicly announced his intention to recruit it at a series of meetings in New York City in April 1861, Lash, *Seventy-first Pennsylvania*, 3.

65   *OR*, 5, 294, Stone's report; 302–303, order dated October 20, 1861, 11:00 P.M. from Stone to Baker.

66   *OR*, 5, 303, memorandum, n.d., n.a., from Stone.

Edwards Ferry feint must continue.[67] At 7 A.M., October 21, Major Mix crossed with three officers, thirty-one men of the Third New York Cavalry, and two companies of the First Minnesota Infantry.[68] The riflemen deployed to the front and right. The horsemen checked their gear, mounted, and started along the road toward Leesburg. They came upon a large, white house the Confederates had abandoned in haste, probably, during the cannonade of the previous day, Mix surmised. The road passed through thick woods and heavy underbrush. Three hundred yards from the house, the men passed a crossroads at a slow gallop. Before them, they drove some Confederate pickets toward high ground; to keep their horses fresh, they did not attempt to capture them. A black man warned them of Rebel cavalry and infantry in the vicinity. Warily, they rode a short distance farther. The glint of sun on rifle barrels revealed Rebel infantry thirty-five yards ahead. Their fire killed two horses. The horseless men mounted behind friends and rode double. An attempt to form for a charge failed, leaving no recourse but withdrawal to the ferry.[69]

Aggressive Confederate infantry and cavalry were in the vicinity. These events might have raised a question about the unwillingness of the Rebels to resist any advance, a question no one asked.

67   *OR*, 5, 294–295, Stone's formal report.

68   *OR*, 5, 335, Mix's report.

69   *OR*, 5, 335–336, Mix's report; *C.C.W.*, 2, 462 ff (Mix).

Chapter 5

"... probably seven thousand in front and around the field and to send
out two companies is to sacrifice them."
"I cannot help it," replied Baker. "I must know what is there."

—Wistar and Baker

Ball's Bluff[1]
(The Company Officer's Nightmare)

hen Major Howe of the Fifteenth Massachusetts arrived at the camp of
the Twentieth Massachusetts, he ordered all fires extinguished. Three
hundred men of the Fifteenth would cross the river to the island, now
occupied only by pickets, then cross to the Virginia shore. There, they would surprise the Confederate camp and return. Companies I and D of the Twentieth Massachusetts were to go with them, act as a reserve under Colonel Lee on the bluff, and
protect their retreat. When Major Howe told them this, the army had been so long
inactive that no one thought it could be true. Captain Casper Crowninshield went
calmly back to sleep.

---

1   Farwell, Byron, *Ball's Bluff: A Small Battle and Its Long Shadow* (McLean, 1990); Holien,
Kim Bernard, *Battle at Ball's Bluff* (Alexandria, 1985); Patch, Joseph Dorst, *The Battle of Ball's
Bluff* (Leesburg, 1958); Pierson, Charles L., *Ball's Bluff: an Episode and its Consequences to
some of us* (Salem, 1913); Baltz, John D., *Hon. Edward D. Baker, U.S. Senator from Oregon, one
of America's Heroes ... Colonel E. D. Baker's Defense in the Battle of Ball's Bluff, fought on
October 21st, 1861, in Virginia and slight Biographical Sketches of Colonel Baker and Generals
Wistar and Stone* (Lancaster, 1888). Because it involves complex war policy, political affairs,
and powerful persons, this tiny engagement has continually attracted the attention of writers and
students of the war.

At 11 P.M. the major awakened Crowninshield and the other officers and told them to rouse their men because they were to cross to the island. The men crossed the river in two flat scows. Still swollen by the rains, the river flowed rapidly, forcing the men to take the scows some distance upstream to avoid being carried below the landing place on the island. The Twentieth arrived on the island about half past midnight, went to a barnyard with five or six large haystacks, removed their knapsacks, and lay in the straw.

An hour later, the companies commanded by Frank Bartlett and Crowninshield received orders to cross to Virginia to support the Fifteenth. The men rose, marched across the island, and stopped at a house to fill their canteens. Crowninshield and Bartlett entered the house, where they found Colonel Devens and Quartermaster Howe of the Fifteenth and Colonel Lee, Major Revere, and Adjutant Pierson of the Twentieth.[2] Devens must have felt some uncertainty about his position in the regiment. If he were sensitive to the feelings of his men, he knew he had so far failed to win their confidence.[3] To Crowninshield he seemed "like a man who was on the eve of some desperate adventure, and did not seem to like to talk much. In a short time he got up and bidding us goodbye for a time, left the house."

The others stayed until half past two when Colonel Lee announced that the time had come to move. They went to the bank, found a small whaleboat that could carry sixteen men and collected two other small flat-bottom boats with a capacity of about five men each. "In these devilish tubs we were carried over," wrote Crowninshield in his diary, "and of course it took some time."

Located at the foot of the high, sharp bluff, the landing place was thickly wooded and studded with huge rocks, "wild in the extreme," Crowninshield noted. The men marched in single file along the narrow path, which wound its way to the top of the bluff, where they entered a fifteen-acre field surrounded on all sides by woods. They found the three hundred men of the Fifteenth Massachusetts in line of battle on the left of the field. The moon shed a pale, uncertain light on everything.[4]

At 3 A.M., on the Maryland shore, Lee loaded the three available skows to capacity and transferred the last of the men to the island. When all had gone, he sent word to Stone that more than eight hundred men had reached Harrison's Island,

---

2   Crowninshield MS diary (M.H.S.), entry dated October 20, 1861.

3   Coco, *Bowen Letters*, 46, letter with n.d. (early November) from Bowen to Guild.

4   Crowninshield MS diary (M.H.S.) entry dated October 20, 1861.

then crossed with the howitzers.[5] He had three-quarters of the Nineteenth and Twentieth Massachusetts and all the Fifteenth Massachusetts.

On the island he deployed part of his regiment as skirmishers and placed the other part in the ruins of an old tobacco barn, then went with Major Revere to the little house in which Devens had established his headquarters. There, he read for himself Stone's order before he went with Devens and Revere to the Virginia shore of the island, where they found two skiffs and a metal lifeboat. Cautioning stealth, Devens began to cross his men at once. To augment the inadequate transportation, he and Major Revere decided to bring one of the skows from the Maryland side. Lee returned to the farmhouse to reread General Stone's order, and Revere went to collect the boat.[6] No one seemed to realize that a crossing at Conrad's Ferry, slightly north of the island, could be made more easily and efficiently because it required one set of boats while Harrison's Island required two "fleets," one for each side. Nor had anyone thought about withdrawing from the bluff in the face of an overwhelming Confederate force. To the extent Union officers in command knew it, all intelligence forecast no force and no need for a crossing to safety, but military history abounds with examples of disaster and near disaster resulting from an uncrossable body of water in the rear of a line that failed to hold, turning a withdrawal or change of position into a rout.[7]

At 4 A.M., when the five companies of the Fifteenth Massachusetts were on the Virginia shore, Devens crossed. His troops had already ascended the bluff. For half an hour he wandered in the dark until at last he found the path to the crest. When he had assured himself that he had all in order at the top of the bluff, he descended to

---

5   Roebling MSS (R.U.) letter dated "probably" September 1, 1862, by the curator from Roebling to n.a.; but the events and times make it obviously 1861; *C.C.W.*, 1, 404 (Devens), 474–475 (Lee).

6   *C.C.W.*, 1, 404 (Devens), 474–475 (Lee).

7   For example, the Roman army under Flaminius at Lake Trasimenus, where Hannibal pinned the entire army against the lake and killed or captured all but a handful, Montagu, John Drogo, *Battles of the Greek and Roman World: A Chronological Compendium of 667 Battles from the Historians of the Ancient World*, 180 (London and Mechanicsburg, 2000); Napoleon's army at the river Berezina in western Russia during his withdrawal, Chandler, *The Campaigns of Napoleon*, 2, 832–846; and the Russian left wing at Austerlitz, unable to cross the Lake Salschan marshes and smaller bodies of water when the ferocious French breakthrough column turned to the right from the center (Marshal Devout: "Let no one escape!"), *ibid.*, 1, 431–432. Proving that, in battle as in all other aspects of life, every rule has its sound exceptions, Brigadier General Daniel Morgan chose to face the merciless Banastre Tarleton at Cowpens in the American Revolution with a river behind his left and rear. The result, a tribute to Morgan's tactical, if not his strategic, skill, was a resounding victory that destroyed 90 percent of Tarleton's army and all of Tarleton's reputation as a military leader. Ward, *War of the Revolution*, 2, 755–757, 762.

arrange the last details with Colonel Lee, who wished to command the covering force in person.

Meanwhile, Casper Crowninshield, Frank Bartlett, and approximately one hundred men of their two rifle companies, all under command of Colonel Lee, crossed the slough between Harrison's Island and the Virginia bluff. The steep bank was so slippery that ten men could not form and stand. The path, narrow at the base of the bluff, widened to cart width part way up the bluff but remained difficult to the top.

Bartlett formed his men in single file and passed up the path to the crest. There, the men walked through scrubby growth into a large, irregularly shaped field, which measured much longer than wide, the long axis being perpendicular to the river. The path from the river bank continued across the left side of the field, reentered the woods, and headed toward Leesburg. Lee found Devens anxious to start because it was already past five and growing light. His scouts had reported favorable conditions and no enemy in sight. Devens doffed his overcoat and, giving it to his adjutant, departed with Captain Philbrick in the lead for the Confederate camp.[8] The three hundred men of his Fifteenth Massachusetts marched on the cart path from the top of the bluff. As Stone had ordered, Bartlett's and Crowninshield's companies of the Twentieth Massachusetts remained behind to cover any retreat.[9] Shortly, the column entered a clearing. On the far side lay the Rebel camp.

"Are we not mistaken?" asked Devens.

The captain replied in the negative.

Devens and Philbrick walked toward the camp. The shortened distance and the brighter light dispelled all doubts. Philbrick had not seen a row of tents. He had mistaken a row of trees for tents. Perhaps Rebels were in Leesburg. A quick reconnaissance produced no reward. They could see only three or four tents and no troops about the town. They returned to the column. Sent to attack a small camp of Rebel tents, Devens had found that it did not exist. He had completed his task. Under Stone's orders, he could withdraw to the Maryland side or he could remain in Virginia and report his position to division headquarters. In either case he must retire to the river until new orders arrived. He chose to remain. Howe must go to Stone and report that he held a well-concealed position on the Virginia shore, his presence was unknown, and he could easily remain until reinforced.[10]

---

8   *C.C.W.*, 2, 405 (Devens).

9   *OR*, 5, 318, Bartlett's report; *C.C.W.*, 2, 475 (Lee); Ford, Andrew E., *The Story of the Fifteenth Regiment Massachusetts Volunteer Infantry in the Civil War 1861–1864*, 69–70 (Ford, *Fifteenth Massachusetts*); Palfrey, Francis Winthrop, *A Memoir of William Francis Bartlett* (Boston, 1878) 20–21 (Palfrey, *Bartlett*).

10   *C.C.W.*, 2, 405–406 (Devens).

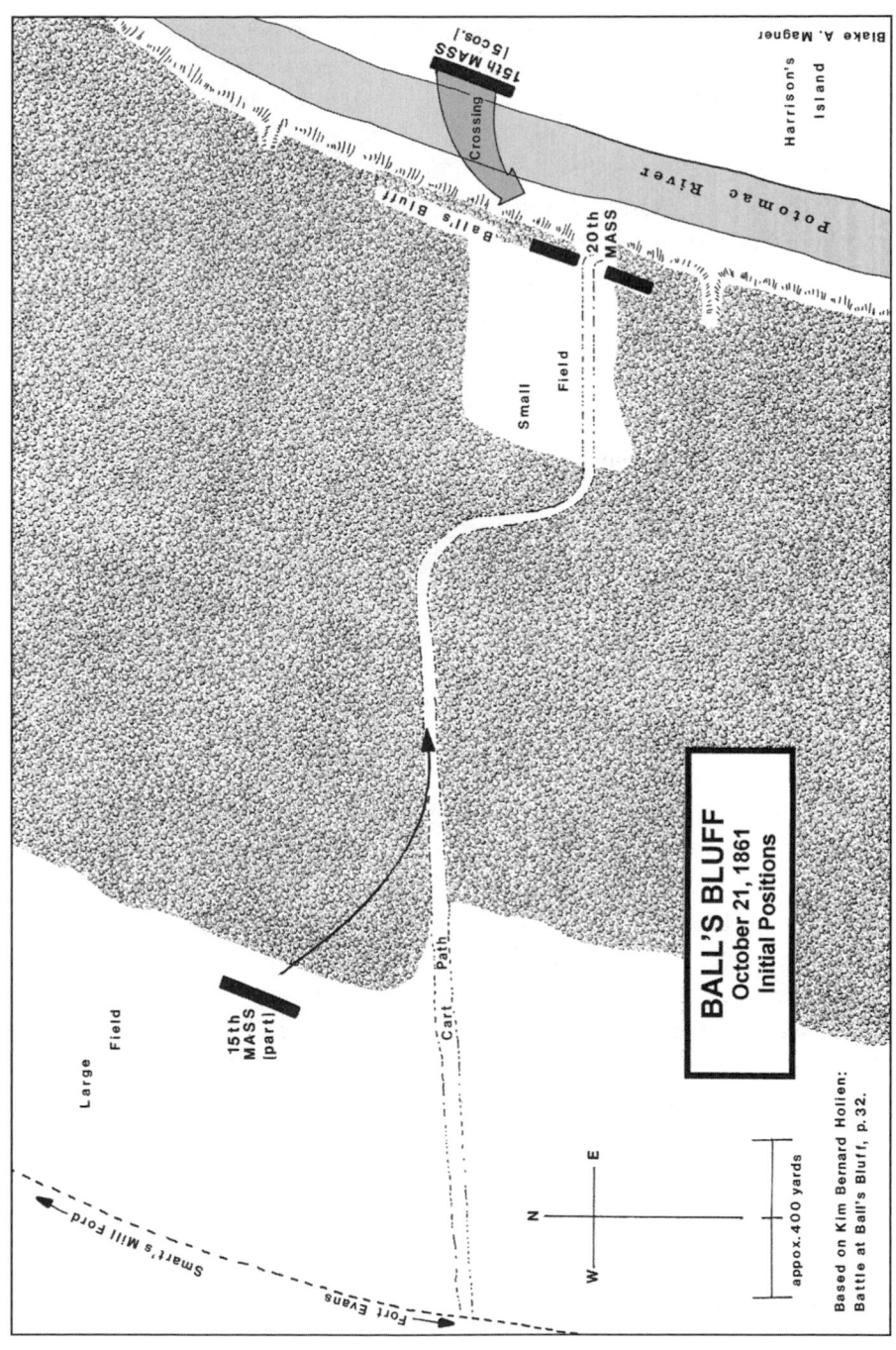

BALL'S BLUFF
October 21, 1861
Initial Positions

approx. 400 yards

Based on Kim Bernard Hollien:
Battle at Ball's Bluff, p. 32.

Finding the Fifteenth Massachusetts halted in the woods, a body of Confederate infantry apparently heading toward the diversion at Conrad's Ferry attacked, but Devens repulsed them with slight loss to his men. He sent Philbrick and Company H to attack, then another company to cut the Rebel retreat by swinging to the right and positioning itself across the road.

Philbrick's men readied themselves in the edge of a clump of trees to the right of a hill around which the Southerners must march; but when the enemy came in sight, they were not on the road. They had inclined to their left and north. Armed only with short-range smoothbores recently converted from flintlocks, the Union troops could not fire effectively unless they closed the range. They ran from the trees and across the road. The Confederates took cover in a freshly cut cornfield and opened fire. Several men in the Union line fell, but the company carried the cornfield. The Confederates went into a ditch, where they took cover again.[11] Devens sent for Captain Forehand and Company G but halted preparations to assault the ditch at a report of Rebel cavalry on the left. The three companies lay far from the main position in the field. Cavalry behind them would sever their line of retreat.

Devens decided to rejoin Colonel Lee in the field. To be safe, he awaited attack for a short while, then marched his men back along the path. In a well-ordered double column the Fifteenth reentered the field and halted on the path.

Meanwhile, to protect the position at the bluff, Colonel Lee had deployed the companies commanded by Bartlett and Crowninshield, sent out scouts, and waited for Devens to return. About 9 A.M., all officers gathered with Colonel Lee. A volley of rifle fire broke the stillness. Then another, followed by a few scattered shots. In a short while two of the scouts came from the woods on the right carrying another man. They halted and called to Lee, who shouted for them to come forward and sent men to help them. They said they had found no camp but had suddenly come upon a company of Confederates who fired a volley, then retreated. The Fifteenth's advance returned the fire, losing three killed and eleven wounded.

One hundred men of the Twentieth covered the retreat of the Fifteenth. If the Rebels were in numbers, what hope could Crowninshield and his men have of escape? No officer of the Twentieth expected to return safely to the Maryland shore. For a long time, silence reigned.[12]

---

11   The accounts confuse the geographic feature that occurs first, the ditch or the cornfield. The statement given closest to the battle and freshest in the memory is taken.

12   Crowninshield MS diary (M.H.S.), entry dated October 20, 1861; Coco, *Bowen Letters*, 46, letter with n.d. from Bowen to Davis.

When Devens reached the field, he was not pleased with his situation. Any decision lay with him,[13] as senior officer, and it was no longer black and white.[14] The enemy had discovered his troops and knew their location. He had only four hundred men on the Virginia shore, three hundred with him and one hundred with Lee. Almost any Rebel force could swallow them. Quietly thinking and obviously irritated, Devens stood in silence. Lee approached his pensive fellow regimental commander.

"If you are going to stay here, Colonel, you better form your line of battle across the road instead of leaving your battalion in column and halted in the road."

Devens did not seem to hear. He continued to think in silence. Lee persisted.[15] Scouts to the left and right had reported no enemy movements—in fact, no enemy at all.[16] With these reports and no pursuit by the Confederates, Devens decided to reoccupy his advanced position.[17]

Meanwhile, Lieutenant Howe, wearing half military and half civilian clothing, had returned Stone's orders to the Maryland embarkation point, where he found Captain Candy and ten cavalrymen about to cross. The second part of the Fifteenth Massachusetts, Lieutenant Colonel Ward's five companies, awaited its turn. The lieutenant joined the cavalry. When he reached the Virginia shore, he hurried to the crest and reported to Colonel Lee. Howe said he had just returned from General Stone, who would like to have any recent information. Lee gave a cautious reply. A good lodgement had been made for a campaign, but he needed reinforcements and supplies, plus some change or augmentation in the method of crossing the river.[18] Howe continued to Devens to report Stone's orders to maintain the position.[19] Devens ordered Howe to report to the general that they had been discovered.[20]

Once again, the lieutenant headed for Stone's command post on the hill at Edwards Ferry.[21] Having concluded that Devens wished to make a stand on the Virginia

13   Lee, although senior, acted as a subordinate until the arrival of Colonel Baker, because General Stone had placed the operation under the command of Colonel Devens.

14   *C.C.W.*, 2, 408 (Devens), 476–477 (Lee).

15   *C.C.W.*, 2, 476–477 (Lee).

16   *C.C.W.*, 2, 406 (Devens).

17   *OR*, 5, 309, Devens' report; *C.C.W.*, 2, 406 (Devens).

18   *C.C.W.*, 2, 376–377 (Howe).

19   *OR*, 5, 296, Stone's preliminary report.

20   *OR*, 5, 309, Devens' report; *C.C.W.*, 2, 407 (Devens).

21   *C.C.W.*, 2, 376 (Howe).

side of the river, Lee sent a note to Major Revere to bring the rest of the Twentieth Massachusetts across.

When Ward's half of the Fifteenth Massachusetts reached the island, it left its blankets and overcoats in the ruins of the tobacco barn next to the house, crossed to the Virginia shore, and rejoined the regiment. Now, having 650 men, Devens deployed Company C to the right toward Conrad's Ferry, Company A to the left toward Leesburg, and part of Company B to the center.[22] The main body of the regiment lay behind a fence at the edge of the clearing nearest the bluff.[23] During this deployment, Howe returned again from Stone. He had told the division commander of all occurrences, he said; and Stone had sent Colonel Ned Baker to take command of the positions around Harrison's Island.[24]

Time passed quietly. Shortly after noon Major Revere arrived with the rest of the Twentieth Massachusetts. Baker, he reported, had reached Harrison's Island. Lee started down the path, but a sudden crash of rifle fire in the direction of the Fifteenth called him back to his regiment.

Now, between the clearing and the field, Devens' front was struck by cavalry and his left by infantry, who pushed his skirmishers back toward the main body. Acting naturally but showing the skill of experienced troops behind low cover, the skirmishers lay on their bellies to fire and rolled to their backs to load. In a crouch they "ran" up fifteen feet, fell behind brush to fire, then "ran" again. As they approached the main line, the anxious, waiting infantrymen could not restrain themselves. Warfare was new to almost everyone. The men in the main unit began to open fire sporadically. One waiting member of the Fifteenth Massachusetts shouted to his comrades.

"In the name of God, will you hold on until our skirmishers get in. Don't, for Heaven's sake, kill your own men!"

The skirmishers had reached a depression behind the berm in the opening and, indefilade, were below the line of fire. Smoke from the black powder cartridges obscured everything, but the Union troops could not have seen the Confederates on the far side of the berm anyway.[25] A brisk fight continued for ten minutes until the Confederates rolled up the left flank and seized the path. The line of retreat was cut! A simple withdrawal was out of the question. The Fifteenth headed into the trees on

---

22   *OR*, 5, 309, Devens' report; *C.C.W.*, 2, 407 (Devens).

23   Ford, *Fifteenth Massachusetts*, 78.

24   *OR*, 5, 309, Devens' report; *C.C.W.*, 2, 378 (Howe), 407 (Howe).

25   Coco, *Bowen Letters*, 44–45, letter dated in November from Bowen to Guild.

the right and back to a small open space between the clearing and the field. Once again, they awaited a pursuit that did not come, then started toward the field.[26]

Earlier in the morning, while Devens lay deployed in the clearing and Lee in the field, more infantry arrived on the towpath opposite Harrison's Island. They rested on their arms and listened for infantry fire, the signal to cross. But the cornfield skirmish had occurred before their arrival, and everything continued quiet. At half past eight Colonel Baker arrived with his staff on the Maryland side of the river. He asked his old California friend Lieutenant Colonel Wistar what the orders were.

Wistar gave him unsatisfactory information.

"I reckon I had better go down to see Stone, had I not?"

"I don't know. Those are my orders," replied Wistar, adding that, because everything was quiet, he saw no reason why Baker could not go. Baker spurred his horse to a gallop toward Edwards Ferry, where he reported to division headquarters at 9 A.M.

Stone explained the situation, showed him the position, and told him the approximate positions of the troops. Together, Stone and Baker examined the map while Stone described the situation, roughly six thousand men and six guns to be reinforced by two more guns. Stone knew the Harrison's Island area well, having earlier selected defensive positions there, particularly around Smarts' Mill, because it was defensible on all sides. Giving Baker command of the division right wing, Stone told him about McCall at Dranesville. He added that he was "extremely desirous of ascertaining the exact position and force of the enemy in our front, and exploring as far as it was safe on the right toward Leesburg and on the left towards the Leesburg and Gun Spring Road." He would "continue to re-enforce the troops under General Gorman opposite Edwards Ferry," he said, "and push them carefully forward to discover the best line from there to the Leesburg and Gun Spring Road," and pointed to him the position of the breastworks and hidden battery which barred the movement of troops directly from left to right.

Baker turned to the point that interested him most.

"Then I am to have the entire command?"

"Yes."

"Please, put that in writing."

Taking a pencil and pad, Stone knelt on one knee and wrote the order. As he pulled it from the pad, the upper right corner tore away. Baker took it and prepared to leave.

---

26   *C.C.W.*, 2, 407 (Howe); Ford, *Fifteenth Massachusetts*, 78–79.

"If you use artillery there," cautioned Stone, "if you move artillery, please, see that it is well guarded. I do not like to see guns exposed to being lost. If you use guns, see that they are well supported by good infantry."[27]

As Baker left Stone on the hill behind Edwards Ferry and headed toward the Harrison's Island crossing, he turned to one of his aides.

"Did you hear that Kellen?" he asked.

"No, sir. What?"

"This order."

"No, sir. I was just behind you."

Taking a paper with the jagged upper corner, Baker read it aloud as they rode:[28]

> Headquarters Corps of
> Edwards Ferry, October 21, 1861
>
> Col. E. D. Baker, Commanding Brigade:
>
> Colonel: In case of heavy firing in front of Harrison's Island, you will advance the California regiments of your brigade or retire the regiments under Colonels Lee and Devens upon the Virginia side of the river at your discretion, assuming command on arrival.
>
> Very respectfully, colonel, your most obedient servant.
>
> CHAS. P. STONE
> Brigadier-General, Commanding[29]

Baker and his aide met Howe on his way to report that Devens had been discovered by the Confederates.

---

27 *OR*, 5, 295–296, Stone's preliminary report; 301, Stone's supplemental report; *C.C.W.*, 2, 268 ff (Stone). In his testimony before the committee, Stone described the breastwork as a fort and seemed to take the position that it barred help to Baker from the Edwards Ferry position. This was not clear to Baker and was probably not what Stone meant. His report, dated eight days after the battle and before the controversy, has been accepted here and is supported by the contemporaneous letter from Young to Lincoln, dated October 21, 1861, in Lincoln MSS, when Young had no reason to lie on this point.

28 *C.C.W.*, 2, 434 (Kellen).

29 *OR*, 5, 303, order dated October 21, 1861, from Stone at Edwards Ferry to Baker.

"I am going immediately," Baker said, "with my whole force to take command."[30]

He sent the chaplain of the California regiment ahead to order it across and shortly after 10 A.M. arrived himself. He had already decided to cross the river with his entire force and fight.[31] He floundered about the river bank, hastening everyone and looking for more boats.

During the day, Stone used the Edwards Ferry position to aid the force crossing at Harrison's Island. The entire First Minnesota crossed. While crossing his men, Colonel Tompkins of the Eighty-second New York or Second New York Militia[32] discovered in the canal a large canal boat half filled with supplies. He obtained permission to remove the cargo and use the boat in the river. Gorman placed Lieutenant Foote, the regimental quartermaster, in charge of transportation. The three skows, two skiffs, and one yawl carried a sizeable number of men. Not content, Tompkins was already placing the boat he had just emptied in the river. As the day progressed Foote seized more canal boats to a grand total of nine, the largest of which carried four hundred men. A round trip took his boatmen a little more than an hour, giving rapid and reliable transportation between the Virginia and Maryland shores. At Edwards Ferry, the Maryland shore, unlike the Ball's Bluff position, commanded the Virginia shoreline. Direct fire from artillery in position on the Maryland heights could effectively cover a force on the far shore or a withdrawal.

At a quarter to ten Stone reported the results of the Mix-Philbrick sorties. All was well. As the day progressed, Stone hoped he might have a smart little action, and minute by minute the chances looked better. Reports from upriver waxed more and more favorable. He would use his troops at Edwards Ferry to cut the line of retreat of Confederates driven toward Leesburg by Colonel Baker and capture them. This would also cause evacuation of the fort which separated the wings of his division. Success appeared imminent. He received a message from General McClellan:

---

30   *C.C.W.*, 2, 376 (Howe).

31   *C.C.W.*, 2, 307 (Wistar).

32   *Official Army Register of the Volunteer Force of the United States Army for the Years 1861, '62, '63, '64, '65* (Washington, 1865, 1987 Military Books rep.) 2, 483 and n.* (*Historical Register*).

McClellan's Headquarters
October 21, 1861.

Brig. Gen. C. P. Stone,

Edwards Ferry:

Is the force of the enemy now engaged with your troops opposite Harrison's Island large? If so, and you require more support than your division affords, call upon General Banks who has been directed to respond. What force, in your opinion, would it require you to take it today? Answer at once, as I may require you to take it today; and, if so, I will support you on the other side of the river from Dranestown.

GEORGE B. MCCLELLAN
Major-General, Commanding[33]

Stone needed no more. He had confidence in his division. He replied that he could take Leesburg against an enemy he estimated at four thousand men and four guns. McClellan was strongly considering a push by McCall to Goose Creek on the left of Stone's division. But McCall followed his orders to the letter. Although he heard the heavy firing near Harrison's Island, he formed his division and returned to his permanent camp at Prospect Hill. By not exercising his discretion and marching to the sound of the guns, he lost a critical opportunity for himself and McClellan. A report that Confederate troops were crossing Baker's front toward Edwards Ferry spurred Stone to send Gorman's entire brigade and two howitzers with their horses across to reinforce the fifteen hundred men already on the Virginia side.

Noon grew into afternoon, and reports from the right continued to be favorable. When the severe fighting began at half past two, it could be distinctly heard at division headquarters; but the flow of information ceased. At 4 P.M. Stone asked Banks to forward one brigade to Harrison's Island in case a rapid advance into Virginia territory by the troops engaged there should uncover the line of the river. To obtain direct information about events at Ball's Bluff, he sent Captain Candy.

Howe returned to the Harrison's Island area from Stone at Edwards Ferry. Gorman at Edwards Ferry and McCall at Dranesville protected the left of Baker's

---

33   *OR*, 51, pt. 1, 499, dispatch dated October 21, 1861, from McClellan to Stone. McClellan apparently confused "Dranesville" on the Virginia side with "Darnestown" on the Maryland side and used a composite of the two names, but he must have meant Dranesville, where McCall had camped his division on the mapping reconnaissance.

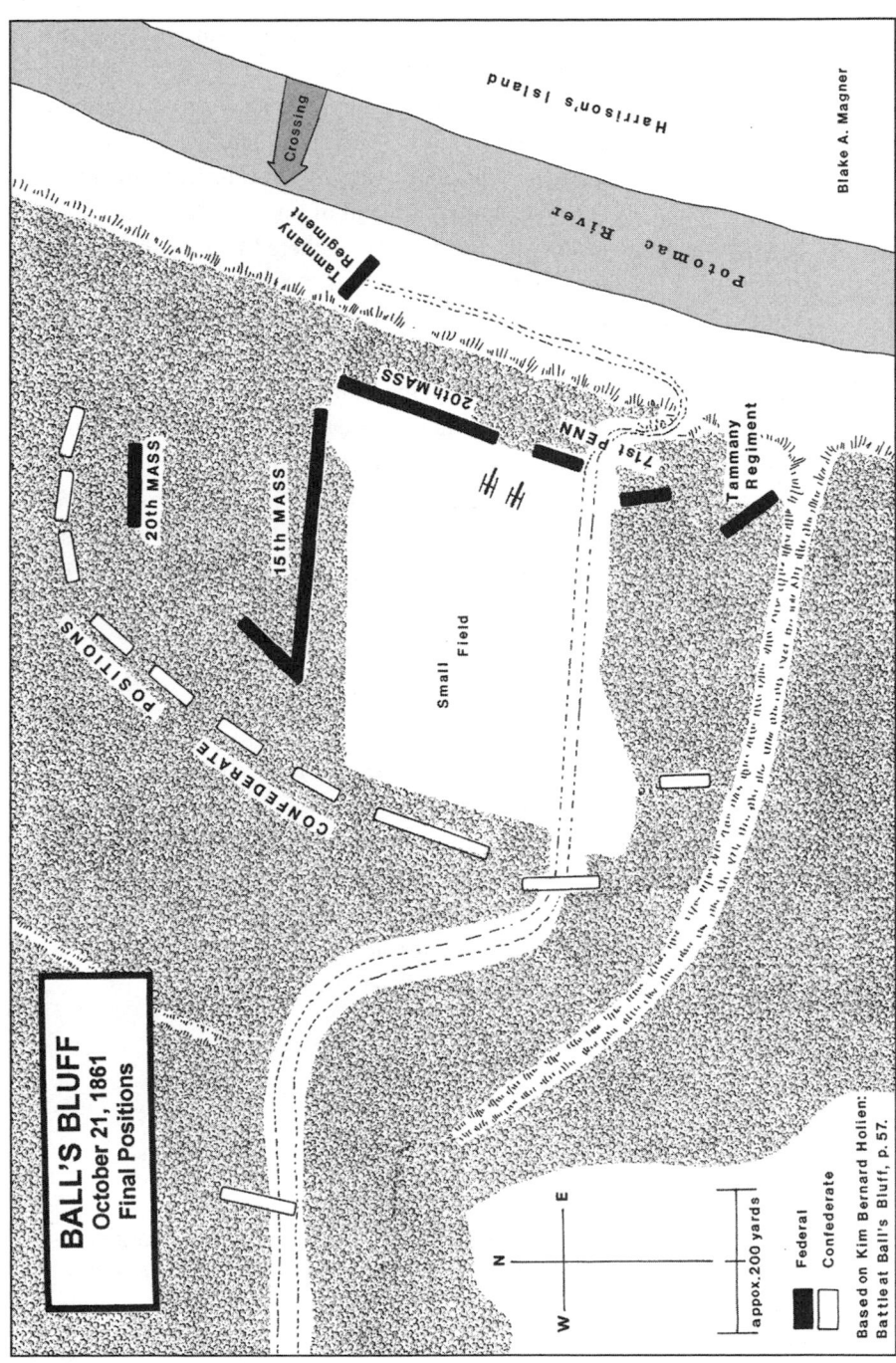

BALL'S BLUFF
October 21, 1861
Final Positions

Crossing

Harrison's Island

Blake A. Magner

Potomac River

Tammany Regiment

20th MASS

71st PENN

Tammany Regiment

20th MASS

15th MASS

Small Field

CONFEDERATE POSITIONS

Federal

Confederate

appox. 200 yards

Based on Kim Bernard Holien:
Battle at Ball's Bluff, p. 57.

position but the right lay in the air; Stone had sent an admonition to watch the right flank. Baker sent the lieutenant across to Devens and Lee. He would follow right away, he said, with the rest of his force.[34] But once again he suffered a distraction, this time a large boat he found in the canal, just the thing to increase the crossing capacity. Unlike Gorman, who had assigned these tasks to his quartermaster and retained his focus on overall command of his brigade, Baker decided that the men on the bluff could wait for him. He gathered men to drag the boat across the towpath. Lieutenant Young arrived.

"I am very glad you have come," Baker said when he saw Young. "Now, see what we can do about getting this boat out of the canal across the towpath into the river."

With 500 men, Howe set to work to drag the skow to the river. Baker stood back to watch as the men strained and sweated until success finally crowned their efforts. Young then asked if the colonel would like to go over, but Baker replied that[35] he wished to stretch a large hawser, discovered in the skow[36] just taken from the canal, across the river to steady the boat passage and make crossings more efficient. He would follow in the next boat. He took time to answer a dispatch from Edwards Ferry.

Conrad's Ferry, October 21, 1861–1:30 P.M.

General Stone

I acknowledge your order of 11.50, announcing their force at 4,000. I have lifted a large boat out of the canal into the river. I shall, as soon as I feel strong enough, advance steadily, guarding my flanks carefully. I will communicate with you often. I shall cross some guns, Rhode Island and New York, directly. As you know I have ordered down my brigade and Cogswell, who will cross as rapidly as possible. I shall feel cautiously for them. I hope that your movement below will give great advantage. Please communicate with me often.

Very respectfully,

E. D. BAKER
Commanding Brigade[37]

---

34   *C.C.W.*, 2, 376–377 (Howe); Viola, Herman J., ed., *The Memoirs of Henry Veil: A Soldier's Recollections of the Civil War and the Arizona Territory* (New York, 1993) 13 (Viola, *Veil's Memoirs*).

35   *C.C.W.*, 2, 320 (Young).

36   Although it is not stated, it seems logical, because they found no other boats, that the rope was in the skow found by Baker and hauled to the river by Young.

37   *OR*, 51, pt. 1, 502, dispatch, dated October 21, 1861, 1:30 P.M., from Baker to Stone.

When he finished this note, he left the hawser to be fixed by others and crossed to Harrison's Island, where he learned that only one company of the California Battalion had reached the Virginia shore.

"Is that all you have got across?" he asked Wistar.

"Yes, sir."

"You must hurry all you can. Get everything that can float. Cross every man you can into Virginia. I am going over now."

"Very well," replied Wistar.

Baker disappeared into one of the boats bound for the base of the bluff.[38] Around 2 P.M. he reached the crest. Where was Colonel Lee, he asked.

Revere pointed to a man with his back to them and said, "There he stands."

At the same time the figure turned toward them.

Baker rode his horse to the colonel. "I congratulate you on the prospect of a battle," he said.

Lee assumed it was Baker. "I suppose you assume command."

Baker replied affirmatively.[39]

In an orderly manner, the Fifteenth Massachusetts emerged from the trees at the far end of the field. Devens saw Baker, and turning to his major, asked, "What time is it?"

The major pulled his watch from his pocket. It was a quarter past two.

"Thank heaven he has come," Devens said with a feeling of relief. "We have been waiting eight hours and a half."

"Colonel Devens, I congratulate you on the splendid way in which your regiment has behaved this morning," said Baker heartily. "I think we better form the line here and prepare to receive them, and you shall have the right of the line."[40]

Leaving the Twentieth Massachusetts where it lay, he watched Devens place his Fifteenth Massachusetts on the right, then crossed the field in a jovial mood at the prospect of a battle.[41] As the California Regiment reached the top of the bluff, Lieutenant Colonel Wistar placed it on the left edge of the field. Baker approached him.

"Come and go around with me and look at my dispositions and plans and say what you think of them."

Amid the whine of Confederate bullets coming from the trees at the far end of the field, the two men walked through the positions of the troops, who lay prone

---

38   *C.C.W.*, 2, 308 (Wistar).

39   *C.C.W.*, 2, 478 (Lee).

40   *C.C.W.*, 2, 407–408 (Devens).

41   *OR*, 5, 301, Stone's supplemental report.

behind a rise in the ground. When Colonel Cogswell reported with the Forty-second New York, Baker received him with happiness and confidence, explained his line, and asked what Cogswell and Wistar thought of it. Cogswell replied that they held a bad position. The high ground across the ravine to the left commanded the position and should be seized right away. The most significant fighting, he asserted, would be on the left. Wistar chose not to criticize his old friend or state an opinion. He merely requested permission to adjust his skirmishers because they were useless where they were.

"I throw entire responsibility for the left wing on you. Do as you like," replied Baker.[42]

Stone had told Baker he would reinforce Gorman and push him to the left of Baker's position. The intervening breastwork and artillery Stone had described and the defensible position at Smarts Mill, Baker disregarded. He expected Gorman with reinforcements.[43] Having no reason to be much concerned about his left wing, he also ignored Cogswell's advice.

Baker returned to the center of his line, where he met Colonel Lee, who expressed no opinion about the position except that he agreed with Cogswell. The battle would be fought on the left. This was the second time someone had warned him that the main fight would occur there. This time, Baker responded. He started toward the left to make precautionary dispositions.[44]

The two howitzers had already come up the slope and reached a firing position. Bramhall had brought one rifled gun from Vaughan's Rhode Island battery to Harrison's Island. The guns and horses, too much for one skow, rode separately. The clay bank on the Virginia shore where the gun now landed had become a slippery quagmire from the passage of infantry. Only with the help of several riflemen was the gun dragged ashore, but the path up the bluff presented an impossibility. The seven horses pulled the limber, fourteen gunners carried the barrel, and infantrymen dragged the gun carriage. When all reached the crest, they restored the barrel to the carriage, hitched the reassembled gun to the limber, and drove the finished product toward the field.

As the gun entered the field, the Fifteenth Massachusetts opened a hole for it to pass. To the top of the rise in full view of the enemy it went. The Rebel infantry fire

42   *OR*, 5, 321, Cogswell's report; *C.C.W.*, 2, 308 (Wistar); Wistar, *Autobiography*, 365.

43   Lincoln MSS (L.C.) telegram dated October 21, 1861, from Francis G. Young at Poolesville to Lincoln.

44   *C.C.W.*, 2, 478 (Lee).

doubled. The two lead horses and the rider fell. Gunners fell in rapid succession as they unhitched the trail from the limber. The horses panicked and ran toward the bluff with the limber careening behind them. By the time the limber had been recovered, Lieutenant Bramhall had only two gunners left, the number-four man with the friction primers and the lanyard was nowhere to be seen, and Bramhall had not yet fired the first round.[45]

Early in the afternoon the officers of the Twentieth Massachusetts had lunch, then, under a large tree about 2 P.M., had begun to smoke and discuss the events of the morning. They were still there when the artillery started firing.

"Well, gentlemen," said Captain Driver, "I advise you all to go to your companies."

They departed at once. The two howitzers from Ricketts' old battery were already in position. Captain Crowninshield was pleased to see the cannon.

Soon after Crowninshield had taken his position, Colonel Baker rode up the hill. As Lee arrived, Baker said, "How are you, Colonel Lee? Well, I congratulate you on having a chance at them fellas."

Baker turned to Lee's men and said, "Well, boys, are you ready for them?"

He then went to Crowninshield and asked him if he liked his position and whether Crowninshield would change it in any way. Crowninshield said he was satisfied, but he, too, the third man, considered the left flank not well protected and suggested that another company be sent there. Baker sent a company of Pennsylvania troops to be deployed as skirmishers. The trees, of very recent growth and small in diameter, gave very little protection. Nor did logs or stumps of large trees offer cover.

The fighting began at a quarter to three with a shot or two on the right followed by a strong volley and rapid firing. This finally died out, then began again on Crowninshield's side, the left, where the firing, very steady and strong, wounded several of his men. The Pennsylvanians gave way. Some of Crowninshield's men, seeing them run, turned and began to run. Crowninshield managed to stop them. The fire slackened, and he led them back.[46]

Colonel Baker succeeded, during this time, in reaching Wistar on the left. With the warnings fresh in his mind, he pulled from his pocket the dispatch that warned about the enemy attacking four thousand strong from the direction of Leesburg and

45   *OR*, 51, pt. 1, 46–47, Bramhall's report; *C.C.W.*, 2, 479 (Lee); John H. Rhoades, *History of Battery B, First Regiment Rhode Island Light Artillery in the War to Preserve the Union 1861–1865*, 33–24 (Rhodes, *B, First R.I. Arty*).

46   Crowninshield MS diary (M.H.S.) entry dated October 20, 1861.

read it to his friend. Wistar replied that, with the time taken in delivery, the enemy must be right in his front and the Union troops greatly outnumbered.

"Yes, that is the bad condition of things," said Baker.

Wistar had prepared to probe the enemy, but, knowing they were in front, he decided it would accomplish no purpose. The fever of battle had excited the characteristically rash Colonel Baker.

"Colonel Wistar, I want you to send out two of your best skirmish companies to the front and feel the enemy's position, and see what is on our left[47] flank. See what is there. Make a thorough reconnaissance."

"The enemy cannot be less than five thousand[48] men and probably seven thousand in front and around the field and to send out two companies of skirmishers will be to sacrifice them."

"I cannot help it," replied Baker. "I must know what is there."

Wistar turned to Captain Markoe.[49] "Well, you hear what my orders are. Do you understand them?"

"Yes, sir."

"Don't go off in a hurry. Do you understand thoroughly what to do?"

"Yes, I do," replied the captain[50] and set his company in motion across the ravine.

Baker had no idea what he was doing. He was not skirmishing. He had ordered a tiny attack by a light force on an overwhelming force. An attack, even a light attack, to learn unknown strength in a position was a well-recognized technique, but here Baker already knew everything the destruction of the two companies could tell him. Baker, like Schenck, a political supporter of Lincoln and another of the president's military appointees, both showed themselves to be incompetent in tactical situations, even situations governed solely by common sense.

Wistar formed another company and followed Markoe in support at thirty paces. Across the fifty-yard gully they went, toward the wooded high ground com-

---

47   Baker is quoted, *C.C.W.*, 2, 308 (Wistar), as saying "right," but this could only be a misstatement or a misquote. Wistar's regiment held position on the left flank and never deployed on the right flank.

48   Neither side ever had more than approximately 1,800 men on the battlefield. In fact, the sides were unusually even in numbers. Few other encounters in the war were so evenly matched in numbers.

49   Also spelled Marco, but given in *Official Register*, 3, 884, and in Lash, *71st Pennsylvania* generally, as Markoe. He would finish his service with the regiment as its lieutenant colonel and commanding officer, Lash, *Seventy-first Pennsylvania*, 478–479.

50   *C.C.W.*, 2, 308 (Wistar).

manding the left flank of the Union line. The lead company reached the edge of the woods and moved into the trees. Still nothing happened except the incessant rattle of the sharpshooters to the right and an occasional "wham" from the six-pounder or the howitzers.

When Markoe had gone ten paces inside the trees, Confederates charged with the bayonet. His men took cover and fired. Wistar hastened his company into the trees to join them.[51] A general engagement began along the whole line,[52] with sharp firing on the right and center as well, but the main attack crushed Markoe's two companies on the left, just as Cogswell and Crowninshield had predicted. The onslaught tore apart the right of Markoe's line and scattered it. Wounded, Markoe was captured. The troops gave way and recoiled to the main body of the regiment in disorder.[53]

In the first half hour of fighting, the Confederates pressed the skirmishers on the right of the brigade line. Company I under Major Campbell went to reinforce them.[54] Lee's men would fire from behind the cover of the rise, drop back to reload, then go forward again to fire. Though both sides maintained a brisk fire on the center and right, the Confederates delivered no attacks there.

On the far left the Tammany Regiment stayed in position but, as if paralyzed by fear, did nothing. With conspicuous gallantry, Baker appeared everywhere cheering the regiment, but no effort could force action from it.[55] Finally, it broke and ran through the Twentieth Massachusetts to reassemble behind it.

Frank Bartlett walked among his men, who were lying on the ground. As he stepped over them, he talked in a joking way to take away their thoughts about the bullets, but inch by inch the Rebels drove the Twentieth Massachusetts toward the top of the bluff. The artillery fire died as the Rebels felled the cannoneers and volunteer infantry artillerymen.[56] After the remnant of Captain Markoe's men returned and resumed their places in line, the fire grew heavier and heavier. As several had predicted, the crux of the struggle developed on the left.

Wistar saw a Rebel force in column hurry across an open space to a hill sixty yards to the left, then lost sight of it. He changed the front of three or four companies

51   C.C.W., 2, 309 (Wistar); Wistar, *Autobiography*, 365.

52   OR, 5, 310, Devens' report; C.C.W., 2, 408 (Devens).

53   C.C.W., 2, 309 (Wistar); Wistar, *Autobiography*, 365.

54   C.C.W., 2, 409 (Devens).

55   OR, 5, 328, Young's report; C.C.W., 2, 309 (Wistar).

56   OR, 51, pt. 1, 48, Bramhall's report; Ford, B, *First R.I. Arty*, 34.

to the left. A gray line broke into view. The California Regiment held its fire. When the Confederates had closed the distance to a mere thirty yards, a concentrated volley broke the Rebel line and sent it back. Twenty minutes later, the Southerners tried again. They volleyed and charged. At a scant fifteen yards the first volley from Wistar's regiment smashed them to pieces. Their repeated efforts failed.[57]

Exposing himself freely and fearlessly, Baker moved over the field cheering his men by voice and example. In spite of his conspicuous, tall-crowned black hat and black feather, he seemed to lead a charmed life. Southern sharpshooters trying to shoot the officers could not touch him. Leaving Lee's regiment, he entered the trees and crossed to his old regiment, the California Battalion, on the left. It was hard-pressed. Many of the men, out of ammunition, crawled into the gully to cut cartridge boxes from the belts of dead friend and foe.[58]

The two Union howitzers had been captured by the Rebels, and the cannoneers for Vaughan's gun had fallen, some crawling under the gun and others dragging themselves with their hands.[59] Lieutenant Bramhall, the section commander, Colonel Baker, the field commander, Colonel Cogswell, commander of the Forty-second New York, the Tammany Regiment, Colonel Lee, commander of the Twentieth Massachusetts, and Adjutant Stuart served the six pounder. Eight to fifteen times they fired; but at last, the recoil drove the gun over the edge of the bluff to careen through men coming up the slope.[60]

While serving the artillery piece, Colonel Lee suffered a serious wound. His men carried him to safety behind a huge tree. The battle raging around him, he coolly lit his pipe and began to smoke.[61] Wistar had already been wounded twice, but he kept his post. His sharp eye had again detected an enemy column readying for an attack. A third bullet struck him. He staggered and dropped his sword. Coming from behind, Baker caught and supported him.

57   Wistar, *Autobiography*, 366.

58   *C.C.W.*, 2, 480 (Lee), 318 (Wistar).

59   Crowninshield MS diary (M.H.S.), entry dated October 20, 1861.

60   Roebling MSS (R.U.) letter dated "probably soon after September 1, 1862," by the curator from Roebling to n.a. During the Civil War an ordinary battery had six guns divided into three sections of two guns each. The battery was commanded by a captain, the sections by some form of lieutenant or a non-commissioned officer. In more recent years, the standard battery was six guns (105 and 155 mm.) commanded still by a captain but the standard section had one gun commanded by a sergeant.

61   *Bartlett Memoir*, 25; Roebling MSS (R.U.) letter dated "probably soon after September 1, 1862," by the curator, from Roebling to n.a.

"What, Wistar, hit again?"

"Yes, I am afraid badly this time."

Temporarily blinded by the shock, Wistar could not find his sword. Baker picked it up, put it in its scabbard, and called to a nearby infantryman.

"Here, my man. Catch hold of Colonel Wistar and get him to the boat somehow, if you have to carry him!"[62]

"There is not an instant to lose," cried Wistar, regaining his senses. "There is a heavy column deployed behind that hill, and you must see if you can stop it. You must see if you can repel that attack, for it is serious."

Baker headed toward the Twentieth Massachusetts to find support for the beleaguered California Battalion. Ordered to charge, a few men of the Fifteen Massachusetts started forward. Fifteen feet out, one of them turned, waved his hat, and called his friends forward.

"Come up! Company B, come up; and we will give them hell yet. Don't let us disgrace ourselves now."

Another shouted, "Come up, Company B! Come up!"

No charge materialized. Devens passed behind his men saying, "Fellow soldiers, if you wish to preserve your lives and the lives of your fellow men, form a line and stand still."[63]

By now it was almost 4 P.M. The military situation had finally penetrated Baker's brain. Personal bravery, which he had in abundance, would not suffice. Still indifferent to the heavy Confederate fire, he approached Bartlett.

"It's no use," he said, "It is all over with us."[64]

The Southerners had tried both line and column but had had insufficient firepower from the column and not enough power from the line. This time, firing as they charged, they appeared with their right wing in column and their left in line, an impromptu *orde mixte* formation.[65] Across the intervening space they rushed. For the first time, they gained a foothold in the Union line. The struggle became hand to hand.[66] If the flank gave way, the path to the river would be cut and the brigade trapped.

At the crucial moment two fresh Union companies joined the melee at the charge. Cheering, they burst through the Confederate line and drove the Rebels back

---

62   Wistar, *Autobiography*, 376.

63   Coco, *Bowen Letters*, 48, letter dated November 1861, from Bowen to Guild.

64   Crowninshield MS diary (M.H.S.) entry dated October 20, 1861; *Bartlett Memoir*, 24.

65   *C.C.W.*, 2, 310 (Wistar).

66   Wistar, *Autobiography*, 366.

to the hill and tried to establish an advanced Union position on it.[67] Struck by a bullet, Colonel Baker, again at the front, fell. He rose; his magical immunity failed him; and he fell again almost at once, this time struck by eight bullets.[68] Although he fell in front of Company H of his old regiment, his head resting on his hand and elbow, the smoke lay so heavily over the field that the men nearest him did not see him fall. One of his company commanders ran to the men nearest the body.

"Do you wish to leave the body of our beloved colonel in the hands of the enemy!"[69]

Baker's body became the focal point for the battle. A bayonet charge by thirty or forty men in blue managed to regain it, but disorganization made retention of the hill impossible.

Bringing the colonel's body, the men withdrew to the main line.[70] The struggle continued for another half hour while Baker's men carried his body down the bluff and took it in the skow to the island. Although the men continued to fight well and bravely as individuals, all aggressive organization seemed to have crumbled. In fact, Baker had been right. The battle was lost. Retreat remained the only course. Somehow the action had to end and the men withdraw across the river.

67   *OR*, 5, 321, Cogswell's report.

68   Crowninshield MS diary (M.H.S.) entry dated October 20, 1861; *Bartlett Memoir*, 24.

69   Acken, *Inside the Army* (*Donaldson Letters*) 34, memorandum by Donaldson and William C. Harris.

70   *Ibid.*; *C.C.W.*, 2, 310 (Wistar), 409 (Devens); *OR*, 5, 322, Cogswell's report.

Chapter 6

"By Jove! I die like a soldier. I was shot in the breast doing my duty up the hub. Afraid? No! I am proud."

—Thinking he was mortally wounded, Oliver Wendell Holmes to himself.

Another Nasty Retreat

The troops on the Virginia shore held a precarious position. With inadequate transportation behind them and attacking Confederates before, they had to recross five hundred feet of water. Over a bridge, they would have had difficulty. With one skow, a large lifeboat, and two skiffs, they would find an orderly withdrawal impossible. Their only hope lay in delaying the Rebels with a rear guard on the bluff until the main body could cross. For the covering troops at the end, every man for himself.

Assuming he was the senior officer on the field, Colonel Lee designated a rear guard to hold the bluff. Under Major Revere, two companies of the Twentieth Massachusetts, one company of the Fifteenth Massachusetts, and one platoon of the California Battalion were to take a defendable position. Lee called Devens and Cogswell to discuss the plan.[1] Devens was the first to arrive.

"I have the command," said Lee.

"Very well, Colonel, I will be happy to execute any of your orders."

"The day is utterly lost. I do not see anything that can be done but to retreat."

"Very well, I will do anything you desire in regard to it," affirmed Devens.

---

1   *C.C.W.*, 2, 480 (Lee).

Major Revere agreed with Lee. Doubtless exhausted from no sleep all night and strenuous effort all day, Devens could only say it looked bad.[2]

Captain Harvey, who had just arrived with Colonel Cogswell, interjected that he thought Cogswell was the senior officer on the field.

"Very well," Lee acquiesced. "What are your orders?"

"I think that we better try to cut our way through the enemy to our left and reach Edwards Ferry," answered the new commander.[3]

Devens said the Fifteenth Massachusetts remained in good condition. It could lead the way.

"Very well," said Cogswell, "we must make some preliminary dispositions. You bring your regiment from the right over on the left of the line, and we will push out here into the woods."[4]

Under constant fire Devens' regiment formed in column and crossed to the left flank where it took position on the right of four companies of the Tammany Regiment.[5] Working together, Cogswell and Harvey prepared for the breakout. One of them went to the front of the formation and ordered it forward.[6] The California Battalion and two companies of the Tammany Regiment started with a rush. But a coordinated effort did not occur. An officer appeared in front and waved his sword.

"Charge!"

In the confusion, Cogswell had failed to notify the other officers to be ready to attack. When Devens saw an officer on horseback order the men forward, he assumed it to be a Confederate ruse to draw the men into the open, leaped in front of his left flank, and shouted at his men who had already risen.

"For God's sake, men, stand firm where you are."

Following his lead, the major did the same on the other flank.

The full weight of the column, therefore, did not charge. The Southerners received the charge well, then drove it in confusion to the bluff. Disorganized by the retreat of these men, Devens' regiment also fell back. After several agonizing minutes, the officers reorganized the men enough to repulse a Rebel attack that looked

---

2   *C.C.W.*, 2, 409 (Devens).

3   *C.C.W.*, 2, 480–481 (Lee).

4   *C.C.W.*, 2, 409 (Devens).

5   *OR*, 5, 310–311, Stone's report; *C.C.W.*, 2, 409 (Devens); Rhodes, *B, First R. I. Arty*, 89.

6   The circumstances here are exceptionally confused. Cogswell stated in his report that he ordered the men forward, and Devens said it was a Confederate officer.

at first as if it would push the Northerners off the crest and into the river.[7] The ground smoked. Blood covered it. The noise was deafening. Men lay underfoot. Here and there a horse struggled with mortal wounds. Carts and guns lay strewn on the ground in all directions.[8] Cogswell saw these signs of defeat clearly. They could not break away to the left. They had only one choice.

"Colonel, it's no use," he said to Devens. "We must retreat here."

"Colonel, before I give the order, I will be obliged to you to repeat it in the presence of the major."

"Certainly. Retreat!" retorted Cogswell tersely.[9]

Meanwhile, Bartlett went to Colonel Lee. Gray-haired, whiskers white as snow, Lee still sat perfectly composed behind the tree. He told Bartlett they could do nothing but "surrender and save the men from being murdered." Most of them had now gone down the bank. Bartlett decided not to go that way and risk fire from the bluff. He called his company for one last rally. All those unwounded came forward with several men from another company and ten from Company H under Lieutenant Hallowell. They came face to face with a large number of Confederates. Both sides held their fire and looked at each other for twenty seconds. The Confederates fired a volley and received a Federal volley in return. The group under Bartlett then charged, only to be repulsed by overpowering numbers.

When they returned to the crest, they convinced Colonel Lee to descend and attempt to escape. Bartlett took his right arm and the adjutant his left arm to help him leave the bluff.[10]

The troops followed the darkened path while small groups covered the retreat and others scrambled down the bluff. The clock nearing six, the shadow of the bluff and the trees diminished the waning light.[11] About halfway, Devens and Cogswell, bringing up the rear, could see the skow, loaded with wounded for the return trip, through a break in the trees. They could also see more than one hundred men trying to board it. Down it went, drowning many. The only large transport was gone.

---

7   *OR*, 5, 311, Devens' report; 322, Cogswell's report; *OR*, 51, pt. 1, 48; *C.C.W.*, 1, 409 (Devens); Rhodes, *B, First R.I. Arty*, 34.

8   Bartlett, *Memoir*, 25–26.

9   *OR*, 5, 322, Cogswell's report; *C.C.W.*, 2, 410 (Devens), 481 (Lee).

10   Blight, David W., ed., *When this Cruel War Is Over: The Civil War Letters of Charles Harvey Brewster* (Amherst, 1992) 51, letter dated October 23, 1861, from Brewster to Mattie (Blight, *Brewster Letters*); Palfrey, *Bartlett*, 26–28; Townsend, Edward D., *Anecdotes of the Civil War in the United States* (New York, 1884) 72–73 (Townsend, *Anecdotes*).

11   *OR*, 5, 322, Cogswell's report; *C.C.W.*, 2, 410 (Devens), 481 (Lee).

The men had no way to cross except by swimming. Using logs, planks, or any-thing else that would float, swimmers helped non-swimmers. Some tried to swim alone. Many left the Virginia bank not to be seen again until their bodies washed ashore downstream. Chaos ruled everywhere. Men who were drowning and crying for help filled the river. "I saw many men go down with their guns in their hands, clinging convulsively to them, as if they thought they would buoy them up," Crowninshield wrote later in his diary. He went back to the top of the hill where he heard three tremendous volleys from the Confederates, but he found no Union troops except the killed and wounded. He waited a moment or two to see if the Confederates would advance, but they did not. Now, he went down the hill into a ravine that was crowded with men who had determined to surrender and who had already raised one or two white flags. They said Colonel Lee and others had gone up the river with a flag of truce. Crowninshield walked north along the river toward Harpers Ferry. After he passed beyond the position of the troops, he removed his clothing and put his watch in his mouth. Having served as a stroke oar which prac-ticed on the Charles River next to the Harvard campus, Crowninshield did not find the river unfamiliar.[12] Into it he went.

At the foot of the bluff, the sound, the wounded, and the dying crowded to-gether. Men struggling to cross filled the water, its surface like a pond in a rain storm from the firing by the Confederates on the crest. Frank Bartlett collected the remnants of his company; when he returned, Colonel Lee had gone. The major and the adjutant, he was told, had taken him across in a small boat. He saw a small boat landing on the other side and assumed Lee and the others were safe.[13] Being then the senior officer, he collected as many of the regiment as he could, made them stop to take off their clothes, and told them to take to the water. Nearly all his company could swim. Bartlett and another company officer decided they should stay with those who could not. They headed upriver with twenty men from the Twentieth Massachusetts, twenty from the Fifteenth Massachusetts, and forty from the Tam-many and California regiments. As they followed the bank north they came to a mill owned by a man named Smart, who lived in Leesburg. Here they found an old black man who told them that a boat was in the millway. They found it under water, twenty rods from the edge of the river. It could hold five persons. The men with

12   Crowninshield MS diary (M.H.S.) entry dated October 20, 1861.

13   In fact, Lee had refused to cross in a boat, instead insisting that it be used to take wounded men across. Attempting to reach the Union column at Edwards Ferry, both Lee and Cogswell were captured by Confederate cavalry. Crowninshield MS diary (M.H.S.) entry dated October 20, 1861; Townsend, *Anecdotes*, 71, n.

Bartlett declared it useless. They proposed to go into the mill to rest, then surrender in the morning, but Bartlett would not quit. He rescued the boat, had it taken from the run to the river, and prepared to transport men across. As soon as the boat lay in the river, a crowd rushed for it. Bartlett stepped in front of it, drew his pistol, and announced he would shoot the first man to move without his order. The men halted, became obedient and submissive, and waited for him to select five to cross, one man to bring the boat back. From his polyglot collection he started with men in his own company. Slowly the Twentieth Massachusetts men crossed, then the Fifteenth, and finally the men of the Tammany and California regiments.[14] Once on the other side, the men began the long walk down the tow path to the rendezvous point across from the bluff.[15]

"We shall all be destroyed here!" cried Cogswell when the skow sank. "We must do something to try to retard them."

"What shall we do?" asked Devens.

"Deploy your regiment as skirmishers over the bank."

On a small flat area part way down the bluff, part of the Fifteenth took cover among the trees. The Confederates on the bluff maintained a hot fire at the men below, but in the sunset their silhouettes showed plainly against the sky for the Massachusetts men. How long would Devens' regiment be needed? How long could it stay? How long would its ammunition last? How long before the Confederates found another way to the riverbank? The boats had a one-trip capacity of only forty men. More than one thousand had to cross. Devens went up and down his line saying the time had come to withdraw, every man for himself, and no rifles should be captured.[16] Near the spot where the men had swamped the large boat, a crowd surrounded him.

"What shall we do?" they cried.

"Brave men of the Fifteenth. You have obeyed every order I have given you today. I have done all I can for you. I can do no more."

---

14   Palfrey, *Bartlett*, 26–28; Townsend, *Anecdotes*, 72–73. The old black man who had told them about the boat had several sons who were swept along with the men crossing the river. Smart, owner of the mill, also owned the father and the sons. In Washington the sister of the black men carried over the river was a free woman who served as the nurse in the household of Scott's adjutant general, Lieutenant Colonel Edward D. Townsend. Once across, they looked for Stone as the ranking officer and for their sister in the capital.

15   Palfrey, *Bartlett*, 25–29.

16   *OR*, 5, 311, Devens' report; 322, Cogswell's report; *C.C.W.*, 2, 311 (Wistar), 410, 411, 412ff (Devens), 481 (Lee); Rhodes, *B, First R.I. Arty*, 89–90.

But in his futile efforts for the day, Devens had earned the respect and confidence of his men. In a letter home a few days later one of them wrote, "Before the sun went down he was the idol of every man."[17]

After Devens and his major had dismissed the men, they threw their swords and pistols, along with their cumbersome clothing, into the river. The colonel and Lieutenant Charles B. Eager of Company B boarded a log, and with the help of two soldiers, both of whom were good swimmers, crossed the stream. When they finally reached Harrison's Island, the current had carried them so far downstream that they landed on a tiny strip of land off the end. Exhausted, they took a short rest, then waded the twenty-five-foot gap to the main island. There they found a man face down in the clay, half in the water and half out. It was Lieutenant Derby, Company H, unconscious but not dead. Taking him along, they headed for the ruined barn to find overcoats and blankets.

As he found the men, Devens organized them for some sort of defense, until he met Colonel Edward Hinks, who had taken charge of the island during the battle.[18] Devens presented an appalling sight—no sidearms, without half his clothes, soaking wet, indescribably fatigued. He readily yielded responsibility to Hinks, saying rather disjointedly that the men were thoroughly routed and that, if the Southerners had any boats, they would cross to the island. After giving Hinks a description of the island's topography, he started for the mainland to report to General Stone.[19]

The troops on Harrison's Island were miserable. Those who had returned from Virginia were in terrible condition, no weapons, no ammunition, no supplies, some naked, most without much clothing, and useless as fighting men. They were tired and silent. Blankets hung on poles to cover the dead.[20]

In the yard about the farmhouse, which was used as a hospital, the wounded had been placed in rows as they arrived. The surgeons had worked all through the

---

17   Coco, *Bowen Letters*, 46, 49, letter with n.d. (early November) from Bowen to Guild.

18   *OR*, 5, 311, Devens's report; *C.C.W.*, 2, 411 (Devens); Rhodes, *B, First R.I. Arty*, 90 ff.

19   *C.C.W.*, 2, 412 (Devens), 436 (Hinks).

20   Roebling MSS (R.U.) letter dated September 1, 1862, from Roebling to n.a.; Morse, Charles Fessenden, *Letters Written during the Civil War* (Boston, 1898) 28, letter dated October 24, 1861 (Morse, *Letters*); NA Offs MS Rpts (Kenly); Perry, Bliss, *Life and Letters of Henry Lee Higginson* (Boston, 1921) 154 (Perry, *Higginson*); Dwight, *Life and Letters*, 120–123, letters dated October 24, 1861, and October 25, 1861, from Wilder Dwight to n.a. (his family); Hamilton, William R., "Ball's Bluff: from the diary of the late Major L. H. D. Crane, Third Wisconsin Volunteers," in *The United Service: A Monthly Review of Military and Naval Affairs*, 12–13, entry dated October 28, 1861 (vol. 12, no. 1, January 1897).

battle, continuing even when the bullets from the Southerners on the bluff began to fall about them.[21] Lieutenant Colonel Ward, Devens' second in command, had taken a ball through his lower leg. In this caricature of a hospital the medics amputated the shattered limb by the light of a two-inch candle stuck in a bottle.[22] Outside in the yard lay a delirious, fainting Isaac Wistar, thrice wounded and expecting to die. He had been struck in the jaw and had bled into his beard, giving him the appearance of a wild man. A wound in the thigh had caused so much bleeding that he had cut a hole in his boot to drain it. The third bullet had smashed his elbow.[23] Like Ricketts and Willcox at Bull Run, Wistar and other Union officers wounded at Ball's Bluff found their way without choice into a new, primitive world. In the American Civil War the number and percentage of officers wounded or killed in battle would be among the largest, if not the largest, of any American war and would be the largest by far for the higher ranking officers. More general officers were killed in the Union service than in all other American wars taken together.[24]

In his first battle, Lieutenant Oliver Wendell Holmes Jr., one of many recent Harvard graduates in the Twentieth Massachusetts, had led his company in a melee that did not allow him time for fear or personal concern. A spent bullet knocked the wind out of him. He staggered and fell. The first sergeant helped him to his feet.

"That's right, Mr. Holmes," said Colonel Lee as he passed, "Go to the rear."

According to one of Holmes' fellow Harvard graduates and company grade officers, the regiment had a number of "poor officers though, good, brave men." Holmes was one of them. The patrician's strong sense of duty, courage, and personal example drove Holmes. He did not go to the rear but returned to the front of his company where at once he was struck full in the chest. Down he went. The first sergeant opened his shirt, exposing two bullet holes, one outside the left breast and one beyond the right. A bullet was squeezed from the right hole. Holmes experienced a sickening feeling and grew faint from water someone put on his face. He could see Sergeant Merchant, covered with blood from a bullet hole in his head, lying nearby.

He was certain the left bullet had penetrated his lungs. His voracious reading had told him that, struck in the lungs, he would probably suffer great pain and die

---

21   Wistar, *Autobiography*, 303, 380.

22   Rhodes, *B, First R.I. Arty*, 93; Parker, John L., *History of the Nineteenth Massachusetts Volunteer Infantry 1861–1865*, 23 (Parker, *Nineteenth Massachusetts*).

23   Wistar, *Autobiography*, 376.

24   Brown, Russell K., *Fallen in Battle: American General Officer Combat Fatalities from 1775*, Charts A, B, C, and D. 163–205.

of hemorrhages. He spit and saw he had blood in his mouth. It must be from his lungs. He delayed taking the laudanum he carried for this kind of emergency because the pain had not begun. Half-conscious, he somehow found his way to the foot of the bluff. The skow had just departed, but a small skiff awaited its complement of passengers.

A nearby groan.

Holmes remembered that Sir Philip Sydney, wounded at Arnhem in 1586, had given his flask to an infantryman being carried past and said, "Thy necessity is yet greater than mine."

"Now, wouldn't Sir Philip Sydney have that other fellow put into the boat first?" he thought.

Confused by philosophical issues of personal survival and patrician selflessness, he could not decide the Sir Philip question before the men had put him aboard the skiff. As the boat neared Harrison's Island, he heard bullets striking the bank at the water's edge. Once ashore, he had to reach the hospital. He directed two men to make a chair of crossed hands while he put his arms over their shoulders. Then to the small house serving as a hospital. But it was filled with wounded. The floor was covered with blood and in the corner stood a pile of hands, feet, and arms "like pig's feet in a butcher shop," wrote Major Crane in his diary. Outside in the yard lay the bodies of naked men, awaiting their turn with the men digging a trench in a corner of the yard. Their clothes had been taken for the surviving swimmers. Into the barn, also serving as a general hospital, Holmes went. Men lay everywhere. A red blanket held an arm in a pool of blood. Near the entrance a patient with an unsalvageable finger and a surgeon stood while the surgeon calmly amputated the finger and the "victim" stared with a "grievous" expression.

Dr. Nathan Hayward, Holmes' regimental surgeon, examined the chest wounds.

"How does it look, Doctor? Shall I recover?" asked the patient. "Tell me the truth, for I really want to know."

"We-ell," replied the doctor evasively, "you *may* recover. General Shields did."[25] Because the bullet had obviously lodged in his lungs, causing the bleeding in his mouth, the doctor could not have had any hope for the lieutenant.

"That means the chances are against me, don't it?"

---

25   James Shields, a politician and a successful Mexican War officer, had taken a grapeshot through the lungs at Cerro Gordo, the ball exiting an inch from the spine. The wound had been "purified" by passing a silk handkerchief through it with a ramrod. *D.A.B.*, 9, pt. 1, 106–107; Howe, Mark de Wolfe, ed., *The Civil War Letters of Oliver Wendell Holmes, Jr.* (Cambridge, 1946) 25, n.3 (Howe, *Holmes Letters*); Condon, *Shields*, 69–70, 106. A lung wound was not necessarily fatal, but the bullet usually carried bits of clothing and bacteria into the wound. In a day

"Ye-es, the chances are against you," replied the medic, who had been cornered. He pulled a bit of flannel from one of the bullet holes. Nearby lay William Lowell Putnam, a fellow Harvardian and officer of the Twentieth, dying but strong enough to argue that surgery was useless and he would prefer to forego the additional pain.

Holmes had not yet come to surrender. Again he delayed taking the laudanum, then lapsed into a delirious philosophical and religious conflict in which he debated his stern father. He rejected God. He called on God for help. But he and his father had agreed, he remembered, that a deathbed recantation was "nothing but a cowardly giving way to fear." He joined "the civilized world" in the conclusion that, with his opinions, he had bought a ticket straightway to Hell.

"By Jove," he said to himself, "I die like a soldier anyhow. I was shot in the breast doing my duty up to the hub. Afraid? No. I am proud." Should he recant merely because he was dying? No. He was to take a leap in the dark. "Whatever shall happen is best . . ." he thought. "It is in accordance with a general law."

In this confused debate, he snapped at his friend "Sturge," Second Lieutenant Henry H. Sturgis, another Harvardian, "Well, Harry, I'm dying; but I'll be God damned if I know where I'm going."

"Why Homey," replied Sturgis, "You believe in Christ, don't you?" and followed it with "a brief exposition of doctrine argumentatively set forth."

If he died, Holmes said, "Sturge" should write his parents and tell them he had done his duty. An enlisted man gave him a cup of coffee. He drank; thought, "God forgive me if I am wrong"; and at last fell asleep, "perchance to dream."[26]

without antibiotics, the resulting infection was virtually always fatal. Unless the silk handkerchief had been boiled before its use, Shields survival was "a miracle." Intv. F. M. Weld., M.D., medical consultant.

26   Oliver Wendell Holmes Jr., MSS (Harvard Law School Library) letter dated October 23, 1861, from Holmes to his mother; memorandum of n.d. headed "No. 2" by Holmes; Henry Ropes MSS (B.P.L.) letter dated October, 1861, from Ropes to his family; Hamilton, William R., "Ball's Bluff: from the diary of the late Major L. H. D. Crane, Third Wisconsin Volunteers," in *The United Service: A Montly Review of Military Affairs*, 11–12, 16, entry dated October 28, 1861, vol. 12, no. 1, January, 1897. Both Holmes documents are badly paraphrased in Baker, Liva, *The Justice from Beacon Hill: The Life and Times of Oliver Wendell Holmes*, 116–119 (New York, 1991) and quoted in their entirety in Howe, *Holmes letters*, 13, 18–19, 23–33. Confused by the account in Baker and having misplaced the publication in Howe, the author called the Harvard Law School Library. Michael Austin, an extraordinarily helpful curator of manuscripts, snatched the baton, found the originals in the monstrous Holmes papers, and sent copies at once, assistance for which the author is obviously indebted and certainly grateful. Curators who go out of their way to help are infrequent. Unfortunately, many, like the retired Frauen Waffen SS of the Huntington, act as if their assignment were to make access to their collections impossible. People like Michael Austin, John Rodehamel, Tom Camden, and Peter Drummey make the finding and research grind a pleasure.

During the final stages of the defeat and far into the night, Colonel Hinks prepared the island for defense. Dominated by the bluff and surrounded by deep water, it lay in an unfortunate position. Hinks sent First Lieutenant James H. Rice of Company F to report to Stone that he was on the island with six companies of his regiment and wanted the remaining four companies from camp. But the four had already been ordered to Gorman at Edwards Ferry. Hinks should remain where he was and act under the field commander, Rice reported to him.[27] Any thought of vacating the island ended when Rice delivered the order from General Stone to hold at all costs. Organized on the island were nine companies of the Nineteenth Massachusetts, two companies of the Twentieth Massachusetts, three companies of the Tammany Regiment, and three guns[28] under an officer of the Rhode Island battery.[29]

During the night the men dug entrenchments along the Virginia side. Each time the moon appeared, sharpshooters fired from the bluff, sending the men scurrying to the nearest cover until darkness restored safety. With difficulty, Baker's hawser had been stretched across the river from the Maryland shore making crossing much easier. Command was nonexistent.

Colonel Edward D. Baker, commanding, was dead.

Lieutenant-Colonel Isaac J. Wistar, commanding the California Battalion, wounded and dying.

Colonel Milton Cogswell, commanding the Tammany Regiment, wounded and captured.

Colonel William R. Lee, commanding the Twentieth Massachusetts, wounded and captured.

Colonel Edward Hinks, commanding the Nineteenth Massachusetts, in command at Harrison's Island.[30]

Colonel Charles Devens, commanding the Fifteenth Massachusetts, was on the way to report to General Stone at Edwards Ferry.

At 5 A.M. Captain Candy returned to Stone's position at Edwards Ferry to report.

---

27   Edward F. Hinks MSS (Boston University), report by First Lieutenant James H. Rice to Hinks. Rice's report contains peculiar internal inconsistencies. He states that Hinks sent him to Stone at 10:30 P.M. and that Stone ordered him to act under Baker. By this time Baker had been dead for hours and Stone knew it. The trip must have been made much earlier in the day.

28   One six-pounder, the mate to the one lost on the bluff, and two guns of the New York battery.

29   *OR*, 5, 314–315, Hinks' report; Rhodes, *B, First R.I. Arty*, 36.

30   *OR*, 5, 312–313, Hinks' report; *C.C.W.*, 2, 422 (Merritt); Waitt, Ernest Linden, *History of the Nineteenth Regiment Massachusetts Volunteer Infantry, 1861–1865* (Salem, 1906) 24; (Wiatt, *Nineteenth Massachusetts*). Wistar would survive, rise to brigadier general, and serve to September of 1864. Heitman, *Historical Register*, 1, 1052.

"I found the body of Colonel Baker being brought off the field as I went to re- port to him," he said. "He has been killed."

"In what condition did that leave the troops?" asked Stone at once.

"They are enraged at the loss of their leader and are fighting better than before."[31]

While the fighting at Ball's Bluff was at first unintentionally, then purposefully, escalating, McClellan had returned to his headquarters on 17th Street in Washington. He received a brief report from Stone about the reconnaissance toward Leesburg from Harrison's Island and the withdrawal of the enemy's pickets to entrenchments. At 6 A.M. McCall had reported that his engineers would complete their plane table surveys and grade measurements in two hours. Thinking he had a reconnaissance in force at Dranesville under McCall and a demonstration under Stone against a retreat- ing enemy at Leesburg, McClellan responded at eight that McCall's Pennsylvania Re- serves and the engineers should finish the remaining work and return to the camp at Prospect Hill. McCall had the answer between nine and ten o'clock and began his march to his main line position between ten and eleven.[32]

A short while later McClellan learned that Stone's forces had completed two re- connaissances, one by the men at Harrison's Island and one by those at Edwards Ferry. When he learned that the cavalry at Edwards Ferry had had a sharp little fight, he responded, "I congratulate your command. Keep me constantly informed."[33]

Slowly the telegraph showed increasing engagement by increasing forces be- yond Harrison's Island and sharp fighting. Skirmishers at Edwards Ferry on the left had advanced a mile and could turn the Confederate flank across from Harri- son's Island.[34] McClellan wanted to know if the Confederate forces opposite Har- rison's Island were large and authorized Stone to call on Banks for a brigade if he needed it. More important than that, he asked Stone, "What force would it require to carry Leesburg . . . I will support you on the other side of the river from Dranestown with McCall."[35]

---

31   *C.C.W.*, 487–488 (Stone).

32   *OR*, 5, 32–33, McClellan's report; *C.C.W.*, 2, 259–260 (McCall). In his memoirs McClel- lan, probably relying on the times on the telegrams, makes slight errors in the time of McCall's movements on Monday, October 21, leaving Dranesville at half past eight and arriving at the Prospect Hill camp at eleven. According to McCall's testimony, almost contemporaneous with the events, he marched between ten and eleven o'clock, *ibid.*, 258.

33   *M.O.S.*, 182–183.

34   *OR*, 51, pt. 1, 498–499, telegrams dated October 21, 1861, 1 P.M. from Stone to McClellan and 2:20 P.M. from Stone to Marcy; *M.O.S.*, 183.

35   *OR*, 51, pt. 1, 499, telegram dated October 21, 1861, from McClellan to Stone. McClellan apparently confused Darnestown, which was on the east side of the river, with Dranesville on the west side near Leesburg. *O.R. Atlas*, plate xxxvi.

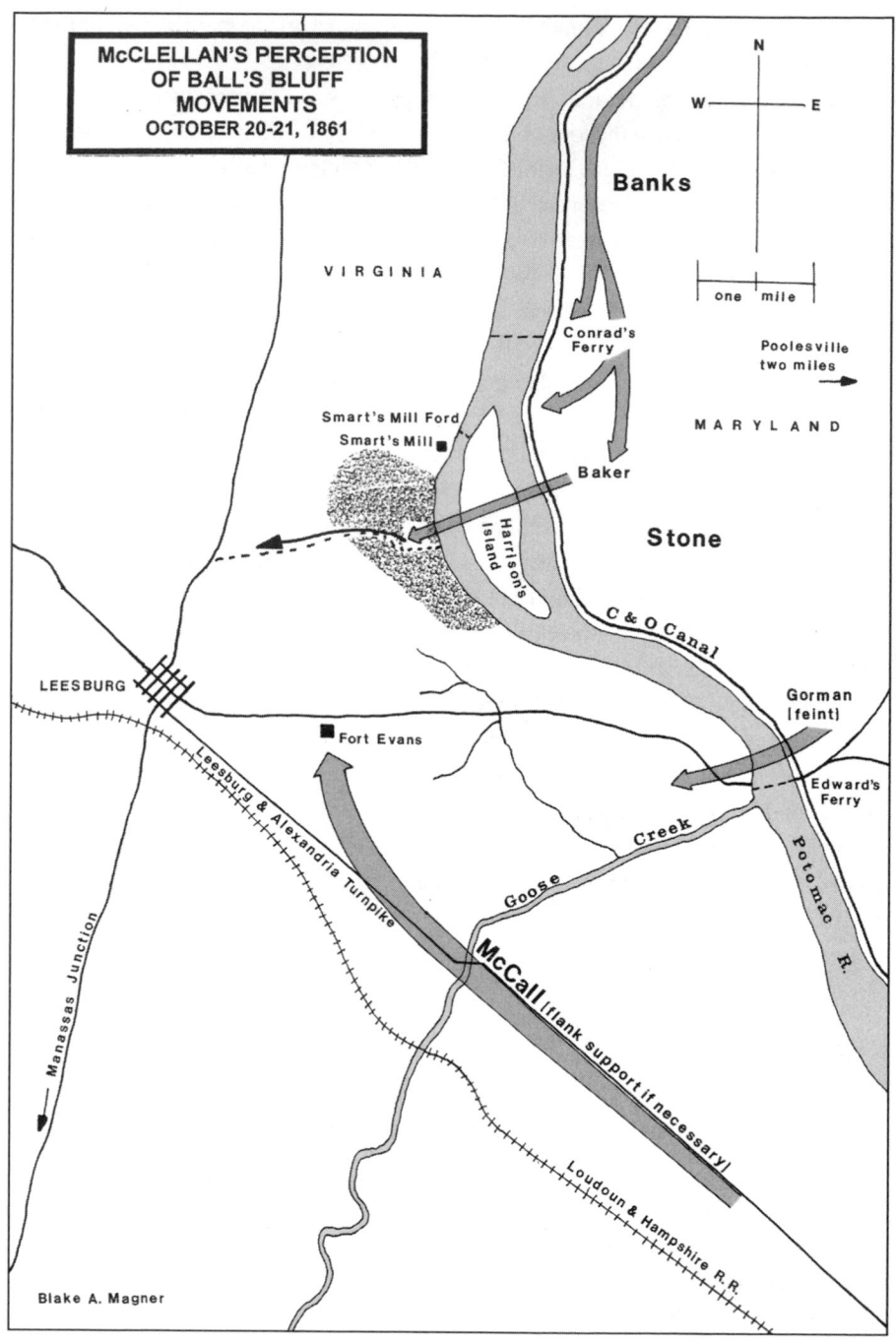

McCLELLAN'S PERCEPTION
OF BALL'S BLUFF
MOVEMENTS
OCTOBER 20-21, 1861

N
W — E

Banks

VIRGINIA

Conrad's
Ferry

one   mile

Poolesville
two miles

MARYLAND

Smart's Mill Ford
Smart's Mill

Baker

Harrison's
Island

Stone

C & O Canal

LEESBURG

Gorman
(feint)

Fort Evans

Edward's
Ferry

Leesburg & Alexandria Turnpike

Goose   Creek

Potomac R.

Manassas Junction

McCall (flank support if necessary)

Loudoun & Hampshire R.R.

Blake A. Magner

Stone was optimistic. "I believe we can occupy Leesburg with this force."

Pursuant to McClellan's authorization, Stone called for the brigade from Banks, who sent Hamilton's brigade. McClellan ordered Banks and his other two brigades to march south to Seneca Mills to be ready to support Stone if necessary. He had attempted to keep McCall at Dranesville but the order to remain had not been received until McCall arrived at his old camp at Prospect Hill.

By late afternoon and early evening, McClellan thought he had a small engagement proceeding at Harrison's Island, possibly a coordinated flank movement from Edwards Ferry, reinforcements on the way under Banks, and a clear opportunity to occupy and hold Leesburg as the Confederates departed. Cooks in units closer to Washington spent the night preparing three days' rations, and the men made ready for an advance.[36] McClellan had already been roasted for his desultory "seizure" of Munson's Hill long after the Confederates had evacuated at their leisure and increasingly criticized for not moving his army against the enemy. If Stone swept into Leesburg on the heels of the Confederates, it might look like a bona fide aggressive success against the Rebels but not require the kind of offensive movement he did not consider his army ready to undertake.[37] He had ordered Stone to call on Banks for any assistance he needed and offered to push one or two divisions from Dranesville on the inside flank of the Confederates in the vicinity of Leesburg. At last, he sent a simple direct order, "Take Leesburg."[38]

With everything well in hand and a little plaudit on its way, McClellan took the equivalent of Lincoln's carriage ride when McDowell seemed to be on the edge of victory at Bull Run. He left his headquarters, mounted his horse, and headed for Fitz John Porter's camp.

While he was gone, a somewhat incoherent message arrived over the telegraph wires in his office on 17th Street. It told of the fighting, the defeat, considerable loss, and the death of Baker.[39] Telegraph operator Thomas D. Eckert, a captain and

---

36   Blight, *Brewster Letters*, 51, letter dated October 23, 1861, from Brewster to Mattie.

37   *OR*, 51, pt. 1, 499, telegram dated October 21, 1861, from McClellan to Stone; *M.O.S.*, 184.

38   *OR*, 51, pt. 1, 500, telegram dated October 21, 1861, from McClellan to Stone.

39   Bates, David Homer, *Lincoln in the Telegraph Office: Recollections of the United States Military Telegraph Corps during the Civil War* (New York, 1907) 93–94 (Bates, *Lincoln in the Telegraph Office*). Several first-hand accounts of Lincoln's role in the events of October 21 and 22 exist, but they defy easy reconciliation. Bates, *Lincoln in the Telegraph Office*; *M.O.S.*; Burlingame, *Hay Diary*; and Coffin, Charles Carlton, *The Boys of '61 or Four Years of Fighting: Personal Observations with the Army and Navy from the First Battle of Bull Run to the Fall of Richmond* (Boston, 1896), not to mention *OR*, especially the correspondence in vol. 51, the volume for post-publication discoveries and submissions, the documents in the McClellan MSS, and the three telegrams in the Lincoln MSS.

assistant aide de camp, tried to deliver it to McClellan but found him gone. Eckert went to the stable, found "Mankiller" the only horse available, and rode nervously for Fitz John Porter's headquarters across the river. Here again, he found that McClellan had departed. He started back to the capital.[40]

McClellan had returned for dinner with Captain Dahlgren. While he and Dahlgren were conversing, the major general received a message sent by Stone fifteen minutes earlier than the telegram Eckert was lugging around the countryside. Coherently and concisely it told the entire story, including the death of Baker and Stone's intention to withdraw the Harrison's Island wing of his division from Virginia. McClellan sent definitive orders in response.

"Hold your position on the Virginia side of the Potomac at all hazards," he wrote, and he repeated it emphatically two more times.

Stone strongly recommended an advance by McCall on Goose Creek from Dranesville on the Confederate inside flank. Although McClellan had only a few hours earlier said he would move one or two divisions to that area, he reverted to the indecisive uncertainty he had shown toward the flanking column at Rich Mountain. When it was time for him to commit a major force directly under his command to the fray, he changed his intention and refused. Stone should rely on Banks for additional support.[41]

President Lincoln, too, had received word from the field about the battle. At 10:35 P.M., Stone had telegraphed directly to Lincoln, "It is impossible to give particulars of what is yet inexplicable to me. Our troops under Col. Baker were reported in good condition and position within fifteen minutes of the death of Col B."

The president had also received similar word from Francis G. Young, one of Baker's aides at Poolesville, in two more telegrams, "I have to inform you that Gen. Baker was killed this afternoon at 5:00 in an engagement with the enemy near Leesburg. Knowing your great friendship and esteem of Gen. Baker, I lose no time in apprising you of our loss."[42] The news of the death of his vigorous political sup-

---

40   Bates, *Lincoln in the Telegraph Office*, 94, does not identify the telegram he tried to deliver to McClellan; but the content described in the narrative and the implication that it was the first news of Baker's death strongly suggest that it was the 9:30 telegram quoted in *M.O.S.*, 185, but not in *OR*. If this were true, McClellan returned to his headquarters on 17th Street moments after Eckert left because the first telegram was sent and received at 9:30 P.M. while McClellan was gone. Eckert searched for him at headquarters, then left for Porter's camp, and the second telegram was sent and received thirty minutes later, at 10 P.M., after McClellan had returned.

41   Dahlgren, *Memoirs*, 347, journal, entry dated October 21, 1861; *OR*, 51, pt. 1, 500, telegrams (2) dated October 21, 1861, from McClellan to Stone.

42   Lincoln MSS (L.C.) telegram dated October 21, 1861, from Stone to Lincoln and two telegrams dated October 21, 1861, from Francis G. Young to Lincoln.

porter, his former law partner, his old friend, and the man for whom he had named one of his sons, smote him like "a whirlwind in a desert."[43] Taking his personal secretary John Hay, Lincoln paid McClellan one of his customary unscheduled visits. They spoke about Baker dying at the head of his brigade.

"There is many a good fellow that wears the shoulder straps going under the sod before this thing is over," said McClellan. "There is no loss too great to be reaped. If I should get knocked on the head, Mr. President," he added with his usual romantic hyperbole, "you will put another man immediately into my shoes."

"I want you to take care of yourself," said Lincoln.

McClellan seemed hopeful and confident. Thinking he had the enemy where he wanted them, whether or not they were in force, he began making arrangements for the following day as Lincoln and Hay left, but the truth had become painfully evident. "McClellan had no plan and not the slightest idea what he was doing," wrote Hay in his diary.[44]

After finishing his business at headquarters, McClellan went to visit the president at the White House, probably to discuss the events of the day and the course of things on the morrow. By this time, Eckert had survived his unnerving trip on Mankiller and had returned to headquarters only to find McClellan still eluding him. He walked across Lafayette Square and gained access to the president and the general, where, at long last, he delivered the message to McClellan. It certainly contained no new news. McClellan and the president had already discussed the subject. McClellan put the message away, neither discussing its contents nor showing it to Lincoln. During the night the pleasant fall weather had given way to heavy rain and high winds, just as it did forty miles upriver at the site of the battle.[45]

Meanwhile, after receiving Gorman's report about Baker's death and the good fighting of his men in spite of it, Stone sent Gorman to the right to take command, mounted his horse, and rode rapidly for the scene of the struggle. Meeting the body of Colonel Baker, he stopped to pay his respects, then rode along the towpath toward the crossing. Soon he found small clusters of men on the towpath without arms, some only partially clad and all soaking wet. According to Stone's last information,

---

43   Coffin, *Boys of '61*, 38.

44   Burlingame, *Hay Diary*, 1, 28–29, entry dated October 26, 1861.

45   Roebling MSS (R.U.) letter dated September 1, 1862, from Roebling to n.a.; Morse, *Letters*, 28, letter dated October 24, 1861; NA Offs MS Rpts (Kenly); Perry, *Higginson*, 154; Dwight, *Life and Letters*, 120–123, letters dated October 24, 1861, and October 25, 1861, from Wilder Dwight to n.a. (his family); Hamilton, William R., "Ball's Bluff: from the diary of the late Major L. H. D. Crane, Third Wisconsin Volunteers," in *The United Service: A Monthly Review of Military and Naval Affairs*, 12–13, entry dated October 28, 1861 (vol. 12, no. 1, January 1897).

Baker's men were fighting "even better than before" he was killed. These men must be cowards in flight while their comrades carried the fight.

"Men, how did you get across the river?" he demanded.

"We swam across."

Stone excoriated them for deserting their comrades, but, anxious to reach the scene, he did not delay to question them. He put spurs to his horse. More and more he passed men in the same condition. He began to fear a disaster and reined his horse to question some of them.

"We have been beaten on the other side," they told him. "We have swam the river, and those left behind are either all killed or captured. The enemy came down on us ten thousand strong."

Wild talk of fugitives? Stone rode again seeking "a cool man of whom I could learn something," he stated later. He found great confusion everywhere but soon saw the chaplain of the Fifteenth Massachusetts tending wounded.

"What happened?" Stone asked.

"According to the best information I could get from those who were fleeing across the river, the entire command is either killed or wounded."

Stone realized at once that both the right and left crossings faced danger, especially if the Rebels had ten thousand men. He could do nothing at Harrison's Island except order Hinks to secure the wounded and fugitives, hold it at all hazards until the wounded could be evacuated, and make certain not to allow a crossing to it. Gorman had only two thousand five hundred on the Virginia shore at Edwards Ferry, and Stone had no idea whether or not McCall could help. Rather than send a messenger, Stone spurred his horse again. If Gorman took position at the edge of the river and enough artillery unlimbered on the height on the Maryland side, Gorman would be safe and could begin to withdraw. With all these matters in hand, he telegraphed news of the reverse on the right to McClellan in Washington.[46]

Gorman, who had gone to bed in a nearby house because of a chill, awoke to receive orders of withdrawal. He sent an aide to the other side with the orders.

On the Virginia side Colonel Tompkins notified the men. The men carefully extinguished the campfires and began a stealthy retreat, first the howitzers, then Tompkins' Eighty-second New York Infantry or Second New York Militia, then the Thirty-fourth New York. But as the boats returned to the Virginia shore after carrying across the sharpshooters, the one regiment and one company still there noticed to their surprise that they had a full load of men. In a short while everything had returned except the two howitzers and one company of sharpshooters.

---

46   *C.C.W.*, 2, 487–488 (Stone). Slight indirect discourse converted to direct.

In the very early hours of the morning of October 22, Colonel Tompkins crossed the river to learn his orders. Were there any?

Gorman told him no.

"What shall I do?"

"Stay where you are," replied Gorman. "You need not be afraid."

"I am not afraid," said Tompkins, "but I think we will be attacked at daylight."

"No, you will not."

"Yes, we will. These men will come down and attack us."

He could see his men trapped against the river by overwhelming Rebel forces.

"No, you will not; and tomorrow you will have reinforcements from General McCall's division who are within seven miles of you."

"I don't think it," responded Tompkins, still unconvinced. "But what about those two pieces of artillery?"

Gorman replied that he could not withdraw them.

Extremely tired and anxious for his men, Tompkins protested vehemently. Like most volunteers at this time, he treated an order as if it were really the statement of an issue for debate.

"General," he started again, "those boats must be sent across the river. I must have them. I must have a little chance to get out of this thing if I am attacked."

"I can't send it across without General Stone's order," reiterated Gorman.

"Where is General Stone?"

"Up at Poolesville."

"Why, what in the devil is he doing up there?" exploded Tompkins. "Why is he not down here? I will take the boats anyway."

To relieve some of Tompkins' concerns, Gorman ordered across the Seventh Michigan. Armed only with the Belgian rifle, which would not fire reliably, the Michigan men crossed with entrenching tools instead of weapons.[47]

Meanwhile, the command structure, essentially Stone, Gorman, and, before his death, Baker, began to have a new look. Frederick Lander, in Washington attending long meetings about the Baltimore & Ohio Railroad on October 20 and 21, learned at the end of the second day that parts of his brigade had become involved in an encounter in the Edwards Ferry-Conrad's Ferry area. He mounted his horse and started toward Poolesville. For six long, miserable hours he pressed northward in the drizzling rain and darkness until at last he reached Edwards Ferry. His brigade lay divided between the two ferrys, the Twentieth Massachusetts having

---

47   *C.C.W.*, 2, 254 (Lander), 354 (Rea), 416 (Banks); *OR*, 5, 337, Abercrombie's report. The order of events involving Banks's division cannot be stated with certainty but has been arranged here on the basis of logic.

been mauled at the Conrad's Ferry crossing, and the Seventh Michigan having been sent across at Edwards Ferry without weapons.[48]

When Major General Banks reached the area, he assumed command as the senior officer on the field. Although he still lacked experience in a military crisis, the situation dictated its own solution. More than three thousand men lay on the far side of the river, one of the regiments unarmed. The Confederates might attack at any minute and with superior numbers. McClellan had given orders to hold the far shore at all hazards. The course, therefore, should have been quite evident. Reinforce at once. But Banks' troops had made a night march of some distance over roads ruined by the heavy rain. The men were exhausted.[49]

Banks, Lander, and Stone met at Edwards Ferry. Stone did not want Lander to go to Conrad's Ferry to see the Twentieth Massachusetts. He should remain in the Edwards Ferry area where he could be helpful. Uncertain in his first action, an apparent disaster, Banks asked Lander what he thought should be done.

"What are the orders from headquarters?"

"Hold the position on the other side of the river at all hazards."

"There is nothing to be done but to reinforce the men there at once."

Banks still thought he should rest his men.

"There is no time to rest. I have a regiment over there with no guns. As the position is to be held, they must be immediately supported."

"I will give the order," responded Banks.

"As I have no brigade, as my regiments are scattered everywhere, I will act as aide or reconnoitering officer, or anything you choose," Lander volunteered to Banks.

The major general mumbled a reply Lander apparently did not understand, nor did he try to understand it. Instead, he went to the river to cross. On the far side he met Gorman returning.

"Go back and press upon General Banks the propriety of withdrawing all our troops, here and now," urged Gorman.

"I have already advised carrying out the orders of the general in chief and holding the position at all hazards as I have a regiment there without arms. Having lost one regiment, the Twentieth, I believe it is about time to save another."

"The position can be enfiladed by the enemy's fire. I know the country, and it is a very risky matter."

Lander did not tarry or reply. He continued forward to the front, where he met Colonel Tompkins of the Eighty-second New York.

---

48   Ecelbarger, Gary L., *Frederick W. Lander, the Great Natural Soldier*, 134 (Baton Rouge, 2000).

49   *C.C.W.*, 2, 285 (Bannister), 399 (DeLany), 417 (Banks).

"Have you come to take command?" asked Tompkins. "If so, I am glad!"

"As you are doing well," replied Lander, "and as some of the men are marauding and I should have some of them shot if I took the command, I will not take it now. If there is fighting, however, I would take it."

Forward he continued, tinkering with the lines and positions of various units. At last, he reached the Seventh Michigan, his infantry regiment with the ineffective Belgian rifle.

"Hide your men in the ravines," he said to Colonel Ira I. Grosvenor, converting the men from nineteenth century American riflemen to sixteenth century Flemish pikemen, "and if a charge of cavalry comes down and tries to cut off the artillery, form in a hollow square behind them and use the bayonet."

"I will."[50]

At 4 P.M. the Confederates drove the Union skirmishers, and assaulted the left of the line with infantry and cavalry. A sharp action took place, but the combined fire of artillery and infantry repulsed the Rebel attack easily.[51] During the skirmish, Lander received a wound in the leg[52] and "swore like a pirate." When he went to the rear for treatment, one of his aides asked a surgeon to examine the wound. The bullet had carried Lander's bootstrap into the wound. The surgeon tugged at it, causing intense pain, a "blue streak" of profanity, and Lander's insistence that he would go to Edwards Ferry before having anything else done.[53] By this time the river had become impassable. Strong winds and heavy rain drove the boats downstream and pinned them against the shore, frustrating all attempts to cross either artillery or troops.[54]

When Lander finally reached the Maryland shore, another surgeon gave him some brandy. Having had nothing to eat for a long time, Lander became "quite tight." He was then taken to the house being used by Banks, Abercrombie, and Gorman. When he saw them, he began to curse and swear "in a most horrible manner," Crowninshield recorded in his diary.

"God damn it, there they set. Three generals on their horses, and not one of them doing a God damn thing."

---

50   *C.C.W.*, 2, 254 (Lander), part direct discourse, part indirect discourse converted to direct.

51   *C.C.W.*, 2, 254 (Lander), 354 (Rea), 416 (Banks); *OR*, 5, 337, Abercrombie's report.

52   Keillor, *Gallant Deed*, 83.

53   Hand, Colonel Daniel, "Reminiscences of an Army Surgeon," in *Broadfoot MOLLUS Minnesota*, 26, 279–280.

54   *C.C.W.*, 2, 285 (Bannister), 399 (DeLany), 417 (Banks).

He followed this with remarks to the effect that no one seemed to know what he was doing.[55]

Brigadier General Charles H. Hamilton, one of Banks' brigade commanders, and his aide Major Louis H. D. Crane,[56] having ridden ahead of Banks' column, reached Poolesville about 10 P.M. Although they could not find Stone, they found "everybody up and wakeful, but somehow . . . unaccountably silent," Crane wrote in his diary a week later. "The mounted orderlies, who are generally chatting and cracking jokes, sat on their horses dumb, and yet surely wide awake. The officers, who stood around the campfires, were silent as death, and every order given or repeated was in an undertone, as if they were afraid of waking someone."

Finally, Hamilton found an officer with orders. For a long time they spoke. Baker was dead. The crossing at Ball's Bluff had been repulsed and the regiments cut to pieces. Hamilton called Crane. He should halt the column and head for Conrad's Ferry to cover the retreat. They started at once.

As they reached the edge of Poolesville, they began to see the unmistakable signs of defeat. By now the hour hand had crawled past midnight, but although the moon had sneaked behind the clouds, they could see everything distinctly. "A double ambulance," wrote Crane in his diary, "filled with wounded, all bound and bandaged; then a single one, with it a load of mutilated men, with head or arms or legs bandaged, the clear white of the cloth stained or spotted with blood; then one with a man on the front seat with his whole body and limbs rolled like a mummy . . . then came men by twos, threes, and squads . . . some with nothing on but an overcoat, or drawers, or pantaloons—but all in silence and gloom." During Hamilton's dreary march to the river to cover the retreat, the rain, Mother Nature's tears, began to fall, a cold and pitiless rain. No sound, no talking, no singing as they usually did on the march, the only sounds being the clank of sabres, "the swash of artillery wagons through the mudholes, and the chug-chug of the horses' feet through deep mire." The rain continued "in spiteful spits for an hour or two then stops," Crane wrote.[57] The weather grew worse and worse. The crossing of Banks' other brigade halted suddenly when the Confederates attacked a small group of soldiers who had gone out without their guns to the Virginia side at Edwards Ferry

---

55   Crowninshield MS diary (M.H.S.L.) entries dated October 20, 24, 25, and 26, 1861.

56   *OR*, 5, 338, Banks' report; Crane would be killed as a lieutenant colonel slightly less than one year later at Cedar Mountain. *Official Register*, 7, 166.

57   Hamilton, William R., "Ball's Bluff: from the diary of the late Major L. H. D. Crane, Third Wisconsin Volunteers," in *The United Service: A Montly Review of Military and Naval Affairs*, 11–12, entry dated October 28, 1861 (vol. 12, no. 1, January 1897).

to gather some hay and straw. Several were killed while the remainder raced back to the lines.

As Banks' division began to arrive, Colonel George H. Gordon, commanding one of Banks' regiments, gathered some of his field officers under an apple tree. Huddled around a feeble fire, they shivered in the rain and cold. Gordon, a strict disciplinarian, interrogated an old New Englander, a private hunched over in the cold and wearing nothing but an overcoat.

"Where do you come from?"

"The river."

"What regiment?"

"Massachusetts Fifteenth."

"Did you fight?"

"Wal, I guess we did some."

"How many times did you fire?"

"Thirty or forty."

"What did you do during the day?"

"Well, at first we were skirmishing along, and I got behind a tree, and I was doing first rate. I come out once, but I see a feller sighting me, and so I got in again sudden. Then, after awhile the cavalry came down on us. I see there wa'n't much chance, and so I just dropped into a hole that was there and stayed still. Pretty soon we retreated towards the river. We got together there and formed a kind of a line, and then the fighting really began. Some fellows came out near us and says they,

"'We're Colonel Baker's men.'

"'Guess not,' says I.

"'Guess we are,' says they.

"'I know better,' says I. 'Let'er rip, boys!' and we fired on 'em. But 't'wa'n't no kind o' use. Baker got killed and we couldn't see the enemy, and they raked us like death. I finally come down the bank with the rest of 'em. I see Colonel Devens there.

"Says I, 'Colonel Devens, wot's to be done now?'

"'Boys,' says he, 'You must take care of yourselves.'

"'All right, Colonel,' says I. And the way my 'couterments come off was a caution. I swim the river. But I tell you there was a sight of 'em didn't get across.

"Do you want to go back again?" asked Gordon.

"Wal, not till I get rested."

"You're cold, ain't you?"

"I tell you, I just am."

"Don't you want some whiskey?" asked Gordon, producing a flask.

"Don't I?" responded the soggy infantryman taking the flask and pulling at it with a long, silent, intense wink to express his gratitude. He turned and seeing a shivering man approach, called to him.

"Hullo, John. I never expected to see you again. Wal, I guest we'd better go to camp."[58]

The Massachusetts regiments engaged at Ball's Bluff had many recent Harvard graduates serving as junior officers, especially the Twentieth. Major Wilder Dwight of Gordon's Second Massachusetts, also a Harvard graduate, looked for his fellow alumni. Lieutenant Harry Sturgis was in good condition. Captain Casper Crowninshield was caring for Colonel Palfrey of his regiment. In spite of his grueling adventures and his "non-reg" attire, an overcoat over his drawers, Crowninshield was calm, collected, and lucid. Holmes, he presumed, was dying of the lung shot.[59] Lowell Putnam, brought by Sturgis to the Maryland shore in spite of his wish to die on the battlefield, lay dying of the terrible wound in his groin.

With Hinks on Harrison's Island a detail from Company F of the Nineteenth under Lieutenant J. G. C. Dodge picketed the western edge of the island. Stretched along a path on the shore they could see any boat cross the water. One man took the small boat across three times to rescue fifteen men, then no one would return for the others. The wounded on the Virginia side could be heard crying for water, then pulling against the current with strong steady strokes. Little by little the strokes would become weaker until, "cold, benumbed, and almost dead," they would crawl up the bank. In worse cases the strokes became "weaker, then less steady, then mere splashes" followed by a watery sound and silence.

While making his rounds, Lieutenant Dodge heard a voice from the Virginia shore.

"Send over an officer under a flag of truce to look after your dead and wounded."

Hinks responded to Dodge's report by ordering him to take a detail across the river. Dodge's handkerchief was black. Borrowing a white one from the adjutant and wrapping himself in a ragged, dirty, gray blanket, Dodge was taken across by a volunteer from his company, his white flag held aloft on a ramrod. The wet drizzle was falling. The Virginia bank was strewn with cartridge boxes, weapons, pieces of uniform, and a few wounded calling for water. Confederates were ransacking the packs and clothing of the dead.

---

58   Dwight, *Life and Letters*, 123–124, letter dated October 25, 1861, from Dwight to n.a.

59   Dwight, *Life and Letters*, 126, letter n.d. but possibly a continuation of the letter dated October 25, 1861.

"I say, you fellow with the red blanket," Dodge called to a Rebel wrapped in a blanket with "U.S." marked on it, "where is the officer who called for a flag of truce?"

"He's on the bluff somewhars, I reckon."

"Can't you take me where I can find him?"

The Rebel agreed.

Holding his flag of truce in one hand and clutching his own blanket about him, Dodge struggled up the steep, slippery slope. The Confederate helped him. At the crest of the bluff, they found no officer.

"He was here a short while ago and went in that direction," said an enlisted man at the top.

Dodge and his escort walked here and there trying to find their elusive quarry until at last they came upon a mounted officer. Dodge asked for an officer who could receive a flag of truce. As the officer rode in search, a Rebel infantryman asked Dodge to identify a rifle he had taken from the ground.

It was an Austrian rifle, he was told.

"What's this?" he asked, showing another.

"That's an Enfield."

The Rebel patted his weapon, a Springfield. "This is the best . . . if the damned Yankees *did* make it," and he offered Dodge a plug of chewing tobacco.

A mounted officer appeared.

"Ain't you a damned Yank?" the officer asked insolently.

"I'm a Yankee."

"What do you want here?"

Dodge explained his purpose. When the officer responded with doubt, several enlisted men came to Dodge's aid.

"Oh, we know all about it. The adjutant of the Seventeenth Mississippi called out for an officer to come over under a flag of truce, and this officer came over."

"Where are your credentials?" demanded the Confederate officer.

"I have none. In our army the *word* of an officer is enough."

"How in hell do we know you're an officer?"

Dodge strode to a nearby stone, stepped onto it, drew himself to his full five feet three inches, jerked away the blanket, and pointed to his shoulder straps.

"There are my credentials!" he replied gruffly and turned his back on the Confederate.

The Rebel rode away growling, "Well, you ought to have credentials."

After being passed through several hands, Dodge finally came to Colonel Walter H. Jenifer, a Marylander with two years at West Point, service in the Regular Army, and now command of the Eighth Virginia Cavalry. Jenifer asked about his old friend General Stone. Gratuitously, Jenifer expressed astonishment that the Union forces "could have been such fools as to have made the attack as they did with everything against them." The commander on the island, he said, could send a reasonable number of men, not more than a dozen, to bury the dead. They would be placed under guard and not permitted to talk to the Confederates.

Dodge went back to the island and returned with Captain Vaughan of the Rhode Island battery and twelve men. Their orders from Hinks were to work until nightfall. Passing through a number of scares and threats, the party completed its unhappy task toward nightfall and returned to the island, where Vaughan exclaimed to one of his lieutenants, "Horrible! Horrible!"[60]

The wounded could not be left on Harrison's Island. Lieutenant Holmes, strengthened by his lifelong interest in attractive women, concluded that he had not yet had his way with enough of them and decided that he was unready to die. The hospital steward, a wall-eyed Dutchman, applied a new bandage and confirmed Holmes' determination that he would live. In fact, he had been hit once, not twice. The bullet had not entered from the front, and it had not passed through the lung. It had struck on the left side, apparently passing left to right through the flesh in front of his lungs, and made an exit hole on the right. With this joyous news, Holmes took a little whiskey, became lightheaded, and decided he could use the laudanum. Shortly, he was carried to the Maryland side of the island on a blanket and, in a coma, laid on the bank. Loaded in a boat and "swearing terrifically" when the boat nearly capsized, he made the trip across with nominal consciousness. After transfer to a canal boat, he floated south to Edwards Ferry, where he was loaded on one of the controversial two-wheeled ambulances "then in vogue as one form of torture," Holmes wrote later. Next to him lay Captain Dreher, wounded in the head, breathing heavily, and insensible. The horse balked, the ambulance was broken, and the driver incompetent. At each hill they stalled as both driver and horse fell asleep until passing infantrymen gave them a boost to start them forward again.

At the regimental hospital, Surgeon Hayward appeared again and cut away the bandage applied by the hospital steward.

"It is a beautiful face," mused Hayward.

Holmes looked over and saw Willy Putnam "calm and lovely" but now very dead. Self-reliant, dignified, modest, gentle, yet "independent in opinion and inflexible in principle," Putnam had received his commission in July one day after his twenty-first birthday. And according to his eulogy:

---

60   Wiatt, *Nineteenth Massachusetts*, 24–28; Heitman, *Historical Register*, 1, 571.

He only lived until he was a man:
The which no sooner had his prowess confirmed, In the unshrinking
  station where he fought, Than like a man he died.
Our cause of sorrow
Must not be measured by his worth, for then
It hath no end.

Probably because of his famous father, a renowned poet, author, and member of the faculty of the Harvard Medical School, Holmes received visits from Major General Banks, Colonel George H. Gordon, and Lieutenant Colonel George L. Andrews.[61]

In the capital the cabinet met Tuesday morning October 22, 1861, the battle near Leesburg a significant part of the conversation. The cabinet members knew that Baker's brigade had crossed the Potomac and been defeated with the loss of two or three hundred men. Two divisions, those of Banks and Stone, had also crossed. The Confederates would be pressed because the generals on the Union side were "heartily ashamed of inaction and inefficiency," Attorney General Edward Bates asserted in his diary. In spite of the heavy rain that had fallen for almost twenty-four hours, Bates expected hard fighting.[62] If McClellan and Stone had taken this course and committed the twenty thousand men of Banks and McCall with Stone's ten thousand, the outcome, an assured Union victory in a localized fight, would probably have averted many of the events that would befall both McClellan and Stone in the next few months. But once again, McClellan did not take this "tide in the affairs of men."

In the afternoon of October 22, Lincoln went alone to McClellan's headquarters in Washington, where two newspapermen joined him in the ante-room. Knowing both, the president greeted them cordially. But he seemed agitated, sitting down quickly and resting his head on his hand. His eyes were sunken, his countenance haggard, and his demeanor troubled. He already knew about the defeat and the death of his friend Ned Baker. The telegraph could be heard clattering in another room. An orderly emerged.

"Will you please come in here, Mr. President."

61   Holmes MSS (H.L.S.) letter dated October 23, 1861, from Holmes to his mother; and memorandum of n.d. marked "No. 2;" *D.A.B.*, 5, pt. 1, 169–176; Anon., "Lowell Putnam," 9, 10, 12–13 (Cambridge, 1863) (pamphlet).

62   Beale, Howard K., *The Diary of Edward Bates* (Washington, 1933) 198, entry dated October 22, 1861 (Beale, *Bates Diary*).

A short while later, Lincoln returned to the ante-room, his hands clasped on his chest, his head bowed, his steps faltering, and his long body bent as if under a great burden. Taking notice of no one, he left the headquarters building and trudged toward the Executive Mansion.

General Marcy came into the ante-room and confirmed the rumors the correspondents had heard.

"We have met with a sad disaster. Fifteen hundred men lost, and Colonel Baker killed."[63]

At 3 P.M., McClellan sent one last telegram,[64] then headed for Edwards Ferry to see for himself. He arrived in the evening in the rain, which had fallen all day and continued into the night. He met Stone that evening to learn the conditions. Recognizing the charged circumstances confronting him, Stone suggested that he would like a court of inquiry. McClellan had already dealt indirectly with this. He showed Stone a copy of a telegram he had sent to Lincoln. Because it vindicated Stone and placed the blame on Baker and others, Stone decided he could obtain no better vindication from a court of inquiry and dropped the request.[65]

At some point Lincoln sent McClellan a note reading, "I think Banks & Stone better not *advance at any risk*."[66] The next day, October 23, McClellan personally examined the position, ordered more artillery into position on the Maryland side at Edwards Ferry to cover the approaches to the troops on the Virginia shore, and crossed a few additional troops.[67] While meeting with Banks, he showed that he had taken stock of the situation quickly and accurately.

63   Coffin, *Boys of '61*, 37–38.

64   Probably the telegram dated October 22, 1861, from McClellan to Lincoln, which began, "From what I learn here the affair of yesterday was a more serious disaster than I thought."

65   Schoff Collection, Stone MS (William L. Clements Library, Univ. Mich.) letter dated November 5, 1866, from Stone to Lossing.

66   McClellan MSS (L.C.) letter dated October 22, 1861, from Lincoln to McClellan. This note, the original in Lincoln's unmistakable handwriting, is not in Basler, *Lincoln's Collected Works*, or the two supplemental volumes, a very reliable source. Nor is it in *M.O.S.* by text or narrative. And it is inconsistent with the ever-elusive description of intentions by McClellan in *M.O.S.*, 188. Nevertheless, it seems to be what it is even though no evidence shows that McClellan ever received it and *M.O.S.* implies strongly that he did not. Because of the problems with McClellan's explanations of his motives, *supra*, footnote 18, and *infra*, footnote 70; the fact that McClellan controlled his files; and the apparent change of mind on October 23, the author concludes it was sent by Lincoln and received by McClellan at about the time McClellan decided to withdraw.

67   *M.O.S.*, 188.

"Well, so far we seem to have applied a new maxim of war . . . always to meet the enemy with an inferior force at the point of attack."[68]

He kept his intentions and his orders to himself, but he continued his preparations to reinforce the island, the bluff, and the ferry positions. The Fiftieth New York, a regiment in the engineer brigade, had received orders to pack its gear and two days' rations and be ready to march at daybreak on October 23. "Not only our whole brigade, but the whole army who, as far as we are able to learn, are to start," wrote one of its officers in a letter home. "I hear from Colonel Stuart that this is the Forward to Richmond of McClellan and that possibly before this week is over a decisive battle will be fought. The thrill which this intelligence will send through the North is responded to by the hearts of the whole army. Such is the anxiety of the boys to push in and it is difficult to restrain them."[69]

Finally, McClellan realized that the weather, the river, and the distance between McCall and Leesburg, not to mention the Rebel fort, made any further effort on the Virginia side useless. At 6 P.M., he sent detailed instructions to Stone on the Virginia side of the river to withdraw the troops during the night. Soon after dark the movement began under Stone's personal supervision. By 4 A.M., October 24, everyone had recrossed to the Maryland shore in safety.[70]

Once he put the Poolesville area in order and reestablished his main line on the Potomac, McClellan returned to Washington, where he could assess the results. He was far less concerned about the outcome than he was about the event, even though no more serious than a minor meeting engagement; and he certainly did not want

---

68   Dwight, *Life and Letters*, 122, letter dated October 24, 1861, from Wilder Dwight to his family.

69   E. C. James MSS (Yale University) letter dated October 22, 1861, from James to his mother.

70   *M.O.S.*, 188. This is another excellent example of the dilemma McClellan poses when he discusses his motives and his intentions. The problem is especially severe in after-the-fact writings like his final report and his postwar memoirs. Everything that occurred before and during the early stages of the battle suggests that he intended to capture Leesburg, even if he had to fight for it. Everything he did immediately after the battle suggests that, unwilling to yield his foothold on the bluff, he intended to escalate his incursion into Virginia. His later accounts do not claim an intention to take Leesburg but do not deny it. They imply that Stone allowed a small reconnaissance to erupt. He puts aside his stubborn desire to continue the effort after the death of Baker by saying that, after his first personal reconnaissance, he concluded he could not defend the Virginia shore at Edwards Ferry, that he told no one, that he should not have withdrawn the troops during daylight, that everyone supposed he intended to advance on Leesburg, and that the crossings during October 23 were intended to keep the morale of the men high in case of an attack. More likely, he did not decide to withdraw until he realized later that everything, particularly the weather and the river, stood against him and when he received orders from the President not to reinforce, both probably just before he issued the withdrawal order.

any more impromptu adventures with the Rebel army, now flushed with two victories turned into routs. Instead, he would fight a set-piece battle, one large battle between the two main armies that would decide the outcome of the war in a way that would avoid minor but embarrassing mishaps beyond his personal control. Like Napoleon, he did not have a large number of subordinates he trusted to operate independently with large commands.[71] Unlike Napoleon, he did not have the exceptions to the rule—a Davout or a Lannes, men on whom he could count for judicious and victorious independent action.[72]

This was probably another reason for his reluctance to create corps and establish corps commanders. The Frederickian army had many smaller units, none of which were large enough for independent action; but Frederick's army, thoroughly and superbly drilled and disciplined, could perform the most intricate battlefield maneuvers even though the king did not have larger maneuver parts under independent commanders. Napoleon's armies, inherited from the confusion of the French Revolution, did not have this degree of precision; but their size made corps capable of independent maneuver and made battle mandatory. Even to his trusted friends and subordinates Franklin, Fitz John Porter, Andrew Porter, and Smith, McClellan was not ready to make this kind of commitment to corps. In his mind, Stone, also high on his confidence chart and a man already with some independent experience, had unfortunately validated his reluctance. McClellan's dispatches and reports expressed regret at Baker's gallant death at the head of his men. His telegrams and General Orders Number 32 expressed his thanks to and confidence in his troops for their performance in this battle, their first since he had assumed command.[73]

McClellan's investigation vindicated Stone and convicted Baker. Nor did he keep his thoughts secret. To his old friend, Franklin, commanding one of his divisions, he wrote that, even though the battle was a loss, it "was a most brilliant fight on the part of our men who displayed the utmost coolness and courage. It has given

71   Rothenberg, *Art of Warfare*, 129.

72   Chandler, *Napoleon*, 488–489, 706; "Davout" by Chandler, 94, 99–110; and "Lannes," by Donald D. Horward, 195, 200–201, 203, 212, in Chandler, David, ed., *Napoleon's Marshals* (New York, 1987). Even Napoleon, who had created a marshalate that was loyal to him for many reasons, Chandler, *Napoleon*, 2, 756, did not succeed in raising more than a few men who could operate independently, ibid., 2, 756, 939; and he would pay a high price for this deficiency at Waterloo.

73   Burlingame, *Hay Diary*, 1, 28, entry dated October 22, 1861; *OR*, 5, 626, telegram dated October 24, 1861, from Fry to McDowell enclosing a telegram from McClellan, and 291, General Orders, no. 32, dated October 25, 1861.

me the utmost confidence in them. The disaster was caused by errors committed by the immediate commander *not* General Stone."[74] James B. Fry, a captain on his staff, wrote the identical language to McDowell, whom he had served at First Bull Run, "The disaster . . . was caused by errors by the immediate commander, not General Stone."[75] Major Wilder Dwight, a civilian turned army officer, sharply and critically stated the cause of the defeat in a letter home. In his opinion, he wrote, the battle involved "the violation of every rule and maxim of military law, the exaction of the extreme penalty therefor. Such is the summing up of the massacre near Leesburg. Does it awaken you to the fact that politicians are not generals?"[76]

74   Franklin MSS (L.C.) letter dated "Washington 24th 1861." The month was obviously October, but the curator incorrectly assigned it to the month of September.

75   *OR*, 5, 626, telegram dated October 24, 1861, from Fry to McDowell enclosing a telegram from McClellan.

76   Dwight, *Life and Letters*, 120, letter dated October 24, 1861, from Dwight to his family.

Chapter 7

"I am more anxious to advance than any other person in this country—
there is no one whose interests would be so much subserved by prompt
success as myself."

—McClellan to S. L. M. Barlow

The Aftermath of Ball's Bluff

In the days immediately after the battle at Ball's Bluff, McClellan tried to determine whether his men had fought well. Although his efforts probably did not eradicate all his uncertainty about volunteers or satisfy him that his program of fortification, drilling, and reviews had made them reliable, he concluded that they had stood the test well. But he was most concerned with the work of succeeding Scott, and so was the administration.

Stone suffered a predictable effect, but it did not keep him from his responsibilities as a commanding officer. The wounded had been collected in a church and large hospital tents in Poolesville. In one of his visits he met Surgeon Daniel Hand. As he left the hospital, Stone questioned Hand about the wounded. Hand ventured into dark country.

"General, this is a most unfortunate affair."

Stone stopped his questions at once.

"How so?"

"To my eyes we have met with a heavy loss and have nothing to show for it."

Stone appeared "much depressed." He showed the uncertainty that would plague him in the next months.

"Time will tell."[1]

Some time passed before any newspapers published a comprehensive account of the fighting at Ball's Bluff.[2] On Tuesday, October 22, the New York papers carried the news of Baker's death and of "a repulse with considerable loss" on the right.[3] Though the battle had involved fewer men than the number of Union casualties at Bull Run, the people thought it an important action because it seemed to be the beginning of a large event, not the end of a small inadvertence.

The following day, Wednesday, October 23, large page-one articles in newspapers everywhere provided accounts of the battle. "The latest news tonight," said the *Herald*, "is that the whole of General Stone's column has crossed the Potomac and is in full pursuit of the enemy and that General Banks' column had reached the banks of the river and would speedily follow and support General Stone." The enemy had been driven, it said, and were saved only by Colonel Baker's death, which occurred because he disobeyed orders. There were sketches of both Baker and Stone, the two heroes.[4] To all intents and purposes a victory had been won. The newspapers devoted great line count to "accounts" and "particulars" that poured through the censor, including incidents, lists of casualties, and other items, many quite untrue. The *New York Herald* said,

> The affair near Leesburg, which came off on Monday, was undoubtedly but the prelude to an advance of General Banks' army, which in all probability will be made to-day.[5]

And on Thursday, October 24, the *Herald* reported:

> Leesburg is in the hands of the Union troops. The advance of General Stone towards that place on Monday, and General Banks across the Potomac on Tuesday, is considered by military men a decisive success, although it cost the Unionists the

---

1 Hand, Daniel, "Reminiscences of an Army Surgeon," in *Broadfoot MOLLUS Minnesota*, 26, 280.

2 Andrews, *North Reports*, 153.

3 *New York Times*, October 22, p. 1; *New York Herald*, October 22, 1861, p. 3, col. 5. The quotation is from the *Herald*.

4 *New York Herald*, October 23, 1861, p. 1, col. 2.

5 *New York Herald*, October 23, 1861, p. 4, col. 1.

loss of a gallant general and a colonel. The further development [sic] of the movement substantiated this idea, as our dispatches show that Leesburg is in the hands of the Union troops, the rebels apparently having evacuated the place and fallen back, as no further resistance was met with. General McClellan was present at General Banks' headquarters during the Union advance.[6]

Taking more space than the capture of New Orleans by Butler and Porter, a truly important victory, accounts continued to appear for a week. "Of course, everybody is on tiptoe with excitement respecting the great forward movement to take place in a few days, about which there is no concealment from Headquarters down. 'A great battle is at hand' is in everybody's mouth."[7]

The *New York Times* noted, "There are a number of prominent members of the Senate in the city,[8] and, without an exception, they represent the sentiment of the country as being impatient of further delay in the movement of the army, and the prevalence of a feeling of fear that the war is not being prosecuted with as much vigor as it should be."[9]

But a great battle was not at hand. The disappointment of the men in the army was keen. As the young officer in the Fiftieth New York wrote a few days after Ball's Bluff, "My last short note to mother was written at a time when it seemed probable that before I wrote again these two immense armies [would meet in battle] . . . a little circumstance often upsets the best matured designs. The morning upon which we were to advance came, and with it, after every preparation was made, came another order countermanding all that had gone before. It was not only a disappointment but a cruel mortification."[10]

Although McClellan had twice tried to advance, both efforts had ended unfortunately. The Munson's Hill advance had been compromised, McClellan believed, by security leaks very near the president. The Confederates had withdrawn their main forces several days before he moved, and the movement itself had produced an embarrassing "friendly fire" incident.

The Leesburg advance had been worse. McClellan mistook the distance between McCall and Stone, did not know how far McCall really was from Baker,

---

6 *New York Herald*, October 24, 1861, p. 6, col. 1; *The New York Daily Tribune*, October 23, 1861, p. 6, col. 5.

7 *The New York Times*, October 28, 1861, p. 4, col. 2.

8 New York City.

9 *The New York Times*, October 29, 1861, p. 1, col. 1.

10 James MSS (Y.U.) letter dated October 27, 1861, from James to his father.

failed to recognize that McCall's reconnaissance ended too far from Leesburg to threaten the flank of the defending Confederates, and misjudged his ability to coordinate those parts of his line not, like an army in a classic battle, visible from a height in the center. From no position could McClellan have seen Banks, Stone, and McCall at one time.

His failure at Ball's Bluff caused him to rethink many things. When he returned from his trip to Poolesville and Edwards Ferry, he said to one of his French aides, "I have learned a lot these past few days."[11] One step he reconsidered was an immediate advance. He knew one had to be made and sooner, not later. In December or January he would do it.[12] Napoleon had created a marshalate, a group of experienced corps commanders a few of whom were capable of operating independently. Lacking those men, McClellan would avoid unpredicted, unplanned, spontaneous encounter engagements. He would prepare meticulously for the great Armageddon, which would, like the battles fought by Bernard Montgomery in the next century, be a "set battle piece."[13] He had earlier shown a distaste for "meeting engagements" and "encounter" battles and a desire to prevent them when he ordered Smith and Stevens "not to bring on a general engagement" during the reconnaissance to Lewinsville. These instructions he had repeatedly given to his army for some time.[14] He would have "no more Ball's Bluffs."[15] Now confirmed in his unwillingness to allow his subordinates to precipitate an unplanned battle, he made the prohibition against "bringing on a general engagement" a byword.

On the evening of October 26, the president and his assistant visited McClellan to discuss the Ball's Bluff encounter. McClellan said he would have a report from Stone the next day. At least until then, they agreed to withhold comment.[16]

The major general had not become deaf to the public demand for a forward movement.[17] Before the first of February he would undertake his major offensive.

---

11   Comte de Paris MS diary (large diary) (A.N. de la M. de F.) entry dated December 5, 1861.

12   Shuckers, *Chase*, 445, mem entitled "Notes on the Union of the Armies of the Potomac and the Army of Virginia," written shortly after the reinstatement of McClellan on September 2, 1862.

13   Gavin, James M., *On to Berlin: Battles of an Airborne Commander 1943–1946*, 123, 139, 259 (New York, 1978).

14   Stevens, *Stevens*, 2, 446.

15   Comte de Paris MS diary (small diary) (A.N. de la M. de F.) e.g., entry dated February 28, 1862.

16   Burlingame, *Hay Diary*, 1, 29, entry dated October 27, 1861.

17   Shortly after the smoke cleared from the bluffs above Harrison's Island and McClellan spent his first long days as general in chief, he appeared to have reached a decision the Radical

A week after he assumed great, new responsibilities, he took a short break from his arduous office work to write his good friend and fellow Democrat S. L. M. Barlow. "Speaking of an advance," he wrote at 1 A.M., "let me beg of you not to be impatient (I do not know that you are)—do you & all your friends trust implicitly in me—I am more anxious to advance than any other person in this country—there is no one whose interests would be so much subserved by prompt success as myself."[18]

Meanwhile, he concluded that Stone had not committed any blunder at Ball's Bluff. In fact, the *Herald* of October 27 reported that the commanding general "does not attribute the reverse to any error of General Stone, but relieves him and his men of all responsibility for the result."[19] In fact, McClellan felt nothing but confidence in Stone's Corps of Observation, and he was very pleased with the way the men had fought under such adverse circumstances.[20]

But McClellan's exoneration of Stone did not end the controversy spawned by Ball's Bluff. Baker had earned the love of his fellow senators. As his funeral procession wound through the streets of Washington, it was a roll call for the highest levels of the federal government.[21] The scene was the same in New York as the body traveled to its final resting place in California. Baker's dashing, reckless spirit had captured the affection of the public. Because he had died at the head of his men while gallantly leading them against the enemy, Baker suffered little public blame for his abysmal tactical performance. He was a national hero. And neither his colleagues in

---

Republicans anticipated, feared, and opposed. He would allow the Army of the Potomac to go quietly into winter quarters and would not advance until spring. This meant five inactive months with no chance for the major battle that would end the war. Aside from his statements of intention to various people like Chase and Tripler, the best authority is the Comte de Paris, who says that McClellan did decide to go into winter quarters shortly after Ball's Bluff, Comte de Paris, "McClellan Organizing the Grand Army," *B&L*, 2, 114, and in his MS diary (large diary, entry dated January 6, 1862), that the December typhoid attack thwarted his plans for a December or January advance. Although McClellan's statements of intention, whether in person or in an historical account, are never reliable, the plan-frustrated-by-typhoid is supported by his conversation with Chase before the typhoid attack, his statement to Tripler, and his letter to Barlow.

18   Sears, *McClellan's Correspondence*, 127, letter dated November 8, 1861, from McClellan to Barlow; Schuckers, *Chase*, 445, mem entitled "Notes on the Union of the Armies of the Potomac and the Army of Virginia," written shortly after the reinstatement of McClellan on September 2, 1862.

19   *New York Herald*, October 27, 1861, p. 1, col. 3.

20   *OR*, 5, 291, General Orders No. 32, dated October 25, 1861, from Headquarters, Army of the Potomac.

21   *New York Herald*, October 24, 1861, p. 3, col. 3.

the Senate nor his well-wishers in the public would have him pass without an explanation for his death in a battle lost.[22]

All who had military experience and some knowledge of the event knew the
defeat had been Baker's fault. Even knowledgeable civilians believed Baker was at
fault. But the dead colonel stayed in everyone's mind, particularly the minds of his
friends in the Senate and in his brigade. The turbulent aftermath started in both
these places.

Baker's staff, like most, included friends and relatives who were partial to his
memory and wanted to preserve it in a good light. Shortly after the battle, Captain
Francis G. Young, who had already written directly to the president, wrote to Assistant Adjutant General Townsend. "At the request of the relatives and many friends
of Colonel Baker, I have the honor to submit a statement of the facts of the engagement on last Monday, the 21st instant, fought opposite Harrison's Island, on the Virginia shore." A long eulogy of Colonel Baker followed. By half-truths and twisted
facts, Young's account showed Baker to be blameless.[23]

Following a path used by McClellan in his campaign to undermine General
Scott, this document bypassed all proper military channels. But Townsend had
grown to manhood in the Old Army. He returned Young's account with an endorsement that it should be forwarded through the proper channels. When it reached
Stone, he brushed it aside with the notation, "This extraordinary production of a
fertile imagination is respectfully forwarded. I have no time to notice its misstate-
ments, but would simply call attention to the last clause in the communication,
which I am informed is true: 'There was no regularity or order in the movement of
the boats. Had there been, there would have been no disaster.'. . ."[24]

Recriminations by Baker's friends continued. Achieving no favorable verdict
in the army, they carried their campaign to the public. In matters of this sort the
ignorant press and its "penny-a-line" investigative reporters always stood ready to
participate. The day McClellan exonerated Stone for any misstep at Ball's Bluff, he
received from Stone a telegram that told much about the future when it said, "I
have just seen in the Sunday Morning *Chronicle* what purports to be a dispatch
from me to Col. Baker—it is a shameless forgery."[25] Worse was to come.

---

22   Moore, *Rebellion Record*, 3, 75.

23   *OR*, 5, 327–330, report of Captain Francis G. Young of Baker's staff, with endorsements by
Townsend and Stone.

24   *OR*, 5, 330, Stone's report.

25   McClellan MSS (L.C.) telegram dated October 24, 1861, from Stone to McClellan.

Regulations forbade giving military papers, reports, and dispatches to the press or publishing them in any other way. Nevertheless, a Washington paper printed several dispatches that it described as having been found covered with blood in Colonel Baker's hatband. Statements that finally prompted Stone to write Seth Williams, McClellan's adjutant general, followed. "The persistent attacks made upon me by the friends (so called) of the lamented late Colonel Baker, through the newspaper press, have made it my duty to call the attention of the major-general commanding to distinct violations of my orders and instructions to that officer in the affair of 21st ultimo, more pointedly than it has been my wish to do in an official report concerning one who is no more . . . ."

A more detailed account than his report followed, this time reciting the mistakes Stone thought Baker had made.[26] But Stone did not lose his austere reserve, his military bearing, his restraint, or his dignity. He did not stoop to publishing in newspapers. Satisfaction came from the vindication of his conduct by his military companions. The army believed in the main that the fault lay with Baker, and for Stone that was enough. Outsiders, particularly civilians, he ignored. Gradually, the outcry died. But not for long.

An issue dear to the Radicals and bewildering to many high-ranking officers appeared in the eddies of the battle: the status and treatment of slaves. Abolition, emancipation, and the related issue of runaway slaves reached into many corners of the government. In foreign relations the tension caused by the possibility that Britain and France might recognize the Confederacy as an independent country would be lessened if the Union abolished slavery. Abolition might cause slave uprisings, which would help the Union war effort. Many believed in abolition for its own sake. But abolition, the goal of the Radicals, was not a free card for Lincoln to play. No matter how he did it, the president feared, it would have unwanted effects. Emancipation might drive border states as political entities and slave-holding Unionists as individuals into the camp of the rebellion. Slaves who deserted their masters posed these inescapable issues. While in command at Fort Monroe, Major General Benjamin F. Butler, a shrewd lawyer if not an able general, had developed his own legal theory for the question. All slaves entering Federal lines from seceding states, being "property" of the Rebels, were to be "seized" as "contraband" of war and to become freemen.[27] But slaves could desire to be free from Unionist

26   *OR*, 5, 300, Stone's report.

27   Belz, Herman, *Emancipation and Equal Rights: Politics and Constitutionalism in the Civil War Era*, 25 (Belz, *Emancipation and Equal Rights*).\

owners just as much as they might from secessionists. What should be done with them? Should slaves leaving loyal residents of non-seceding states be reclaimable by their owners as private property?

McClellan had ordered the return of slaves who had escaped from loyal owners. This order, which came to be known as the "Maryland Slave Order," had its largest effect in Maryland and along the fringe of Virginia that bordered Maryland, because loyal owners from deeper in Virginia were few and did not come forward to declare themselves.[28] In Maryland the officer, having custody of a fugitive slave, had to determine the political leanings of the owner, Union or Secession, and act accordingly.

The observant Comte de Paris described the dilemma in his diary. "One does not know the real meaning of the word secessionist anymore. Is it the citizen of a separated state, a soldier who fights for the Confederate army or the one who works actively to dismember the Union in the loyal states? Is it any man who is a Southern sympathizer and who wishes the slave states to remain separated from the 'free soilers'? Or is it, as the extremist party pretends, anyone who shares the doctrines of the South about State Rights? Or, concerning the question of slavery, anyone who was once their ally and would like to bring them back through concessions? Sometimes one considers secession just a simple uprising and winds up fighting anyone who is a sympathizer."[29]

The abolitionists in Congress pressed for legislation covering the slaves.[30] Lincoln and the Jacobins had already tested their strength over slavery, emancipation, and abolition. The first round of the bout had been a draw.[31] Personally, Lincoln hated slavery, but he thought the black man could not survive competition with the white man and early in his presidency was a colonizationist. Later he advocated "compensated abolishment."[32] Others suffered their own confusion. William Lloyd Garrison, a longtime able and outspoken abolitionist, had to recon-

---

28   Townsend, *Anecdotes*, 72; Doster, William Emile, *Lincoln and Episodes of the Civil War* (New York, 1915) 59–60 (Doster, *Lincoln and Episodes*).

29   Comte de Paris MS diary (large diary) (A.N. de la M. de F.) entry dated December 8, 1861.

30   Nevins, Allen, *John Charles Fremont: Pathmarker of the West*, chaps. 29 and 30 (New York, 1928).

31   Williams, T. Harry, *Lincoln and the Radicals* (Madison, 1941) chap. 2 (Williams, *Lincoln and the Radicals*).

32   Nicolay, John G., and John Hay, *Abraham Lincoln: A History*, 10 vols. (New York, 1914) 4, 385–462; Donald, David Herbert, *Lincoln* (New York and London, 1995) 165–167, 633–634, n. 221 (Donald, *Lincoln*).

cile a war to free the slaves with his pacifism.[33] Benjamin Wade, Zachariah Chandler, and Charles Sumner, with the lack of confusion characteristic of religious zealots, favored outright freedom and assimilation.[34] To hold together his many diverse constituencies, Lincoln felt compelled to leave the issue unresolved in the early part of the war.[35]

Politically and militarily unstable border areas like Kentucky, eastern Tennessee, and Maryland had slaves, and many individuals in those areas were owners. At this point few of the owners intended to yield their slaves, and their willingness to support an abolitionist federal government was uncertain at best. Abolition for the sake of abolition was a moral luxury Lincoln could not afford.[36]

Through and through, abolition was a political issue. But the military could never evade it, and some did not try. Major General John Charles Fremont, in command of all forces in the West, rationalized it to be a military issue. Plagued by lack of equipment, inadequate support from the government, military failure, rampant disloyalty in his rear areas, dubious financial integrity in his military purchases, and marginal military competence, Fremont decided to stabilize his shaky position by striking a simple but direct blow at his local enemies.[37]

In the dark of early morning on August 30, he rose and went to his office. All night he had lain awake considering a proclamation. At his desk he began to write. Dawn broke. His wife, Jessie, a friend from New York, and others sought to see him.

"I want you two and no others," said Fremont to his wife and his friend.

He read the "Proclamation" to them.[38] It prescribed harsh penalties for guerilla activities, abolished civilian government, declared martial law, and decreed the

---

33 Mayer, Henry, *All on Fire: William Lloyd Garrison and the Abolition of Slavery*, 520 (New York, 1998).

34 See generally, Goodman, Paul, *Of One Blood: Abolitionism and the Origins of Racial Equality* (Berkeley, Los Angeles, London, 1998).

35 Donald, *Lincoln*, e.g., 165–166.

36 *N&H*, 4, 420–425.

37 Nevins, *Fremont*, 497–504. Going beyond primary characterization of the question as political, military, or social, *N&H* in 4, 417, 424–425, describe Fremont's motives as political in their view and charge him with political intent when he issued the proclamation. The counterarguments by Nevins, *Fremont*, 503–504, are more persuasive and are accepted by Rolle, Andrew, *Fremont, Character as Destiny* (Norman, 1991) 205 (Rolle, *Fremont*). Some current scholars call it a miliary question, e.g., Belz, *Emancipation and Equal Rights*, 25–26, 30–31.

38 John C. Fremont MS Rem. (University of California at Berkeley) n.p.; *OR*, 3, 477, letter dated September 8, 1861, from Fremont to "the President."

property of those in rebellion "to be confiscated to the public use, and their slaves, if any they have, . . . freemen."[39]

Both his wife and his friend warned him his declaration would have a hostile reception in Washington.

"General," said his friend, "Mr. Seward will never allow this. He intends to wear down the South by steady pressure, not by blows, and then make himself the arbitrator."

Fremont replied, "It is for the North to say what it will or will not allow and whether it will arbitrate or whether it will fight. The time has come for decisive action. This is a war measure, and as such I make it. I have been given full power to crush rebellion in the department, and I will bring the penalties of rebellion home to every man striving against the Union."[40]

The general issued the proclamation. Decrees of manumission for specific slaves followed.[41] Lincoln reacted with his customary apparent calm. In a short deferential note dated September 2, 1861, he called Fremont's attention to "our Southern Union friends" and said the general should "as of your own motion, modify that paragraph about the slaves."[42]

An apparently voluntary withdrawal, Fremont thought, would be a confession of error on his part. He would not risk the consequences to his unstable position by such a dramatic change. Instead, he sent his wife, Jessie, a brilliant, irascible woman fiercely loyal to her husband and born one hundred years before her time, to Washington to state his explanation personally. She was to refuse to withdraw the proclamation but state his willingness to be overridden. "I acted with full deliberation," he wrote in the note she carried, "and upon the certain conviction that it was a measure right and necessary, and I think so still."[43]

During a contentious meeting with Jessie, the president appeared to grow angrier as he spoke.

"The General ought not to have done it. He would never have done it if he had consulted Frank Blair. I sent Frank there to advise him and to keep me advised

39   *OR*, 3, 466–67, Proclamation by J. C. Fremont, dated August 30, 1861, from Headquarters, Western Department.

40   Fremont MS Rem. (Univ. Cal. Berkeley), n.p.

41   *N&H*, 4, 417.

42   Basler, *Lincoln's Collected Works*, 4, 506–507, letter dated September 2, 1861, from Lincoln to Fremont.

43   *OR*, 3, 477–478, letter dated September 8, 1861, from Fremont to "the President."

about the work, the true condition of things there, and how they were going. Frank never would have let him do it. The General should never have dragged the Negro into the war. It is a war for a great national object, and the Negro has nothing to do with it."[44]

Lincoln ordered the offending language conformed to the far less sweeping existing legislation.[45] The many who had applauded the proclamation were infuriated, freely expressing themselves for Fremont and against the administration, some even talking about making Fremont a military dictator.[46] Senator Wade, a hardened, almost violent abolitionist, wrote Fremont a letter that showed the deep division at the top level of government:

Confidential.   Jefferson October 18th. 1861.

Genl. J. C. Fremont

Dear Sir,

Amidst all your cares and perplexities, I am not about to trouble you with a long letter . . . There has no incident since this unfortunate controversy commenced, so thrilled the hearts of our people, as did that proclamation, it placed you in their estimation immeasurably in advance of all our public men, it was the right word, spoken at the right time and will be remembered, when your enemies and your rivals will be forgotten . . . What your friends fear, is that harassed, thwarted and calumniated, you may be induced to retire from the positions you have assumed and from the field of action in which you are

---

44   Herr, Pamela, and Spence, Mary Lee, eds., *The Letters of Jessie Benton Fremont* (Urbana and Chicago, 1993) 264–269. The editors quote from several versions of "Great Events," Jessie Benton Fremont's unpublished manuscript reminiscences in the Fremont MSS at Univ. Cal. Berkeley. This account differs in degree from the account in *N&H*, 4, 297–298, who were not present and who have long been recognized as excellent, even indispensable, biographers of Lincoln, but who were also biased in favor of Lincoln. Mrs. Fremont's account has been preferred even though she probably had no less bias.

45   Basler, *Lincoln's Collected Works*, 4, 517–518, letter dated September 11, 1861, from Lincoln to Fremont.

46   E.g., Lincoln MSS (L.C.) letters dated November 6, 1861, from Browning to Lincoln and November 9, 1861, from Swett to Lincoln; Chandler MSS (L.C.) letter dated September 16, 1861, from William E. Doubleday to Chandler. According to an account by Lincoln two years later, Jessie Fremont had said that, "if General Fremont should decide to try conclusions with me, he could set up for himself." Memorandum quoted in *N&H*, 4, 414–415.

engaged. Let me assure you that all your enemies have yet been able to do, has not in the least shaken the unbounded confidence which the people have ever had in you and we all hope you will persevere in the course you have thus far pursued. No greater misfortune could befall the country than that you should retire at this period. . . .

B. F. WADE.[47]

With support like this for Fremont's proclamation, the proper treatment of the escaped slave remained confused; and the confusion continued to involve the military. The Radicals, zealots if not fanatics, wanted one program; the president, compelled by personal predisposition and circumstances he could not control, another.

The military could not satisfy both and could not avoid either. Some officers willingly projected themselves into the controversy. Serving as colonel in command of the United States Chausseurs, a New York infantry regiment he had raised, was John Cochrane, a former Democratic member of the House of Representatives from New York and a man who, like Dan Sickles, had favored the South before the war but turned home when the Southerners resorted to violence.[48] In late October he traveled to New York City with Secretary of War Cameron, who received a serenade at the Astor House. The secretary addressed the audience, and Cochrane followed with a short speech in which he advocated arming the blacks, a revolutionary proposition.

By November, the two men had agreed that arming the slaves should be part of the war program. For Cameron this probably occurred as a result of calculation rather than altruism. In the middle of the month the colonel addressed his regiment with Cameron in attendance. Cochrane repeated his view about arming the slaves. Needing to replenish his political capital, which had been diminished by his incompetence and by widespread corruption in his department, Cameron followed with a speech in agreement. Cochrane's speech and its high-level support provoked a storm of controversy.[49]

Familiar with high-stakes politics and comfortable in them, Cameron included in his annual report to Congress a recommendation that an army be created of freed

47   Fremont MSS (Univ. Cal. Berkeley), letter dated October 16, 1861, from Wade to Fremont.

48   *D.A.B.*, 2, pt. 2, 252–253; Heitman, *Historical Register*, 1, 313.

49   Cochrane, John, "The War for the Union" (New York, 1879) 15–17 (Cochrane, *War for the Union*) (pamphlet); *D.A.B.*, 2, pt. 1, 438.

slaves. The draft, if not the idea, was prepared for him on this issue by Edwin M. Stanton, McClellan's Democratic friend from the prior administration. Knowing full well the controversial nature of this proposal, Cameron had copies of his report printed and released before he sent it to Congress and the president. Stanton hid in the shadows. When Lincoln discovered this intrusion on delicate federal policy, he reacted even more strongly than he had with the errant Fremont: He ordered the report recalled and the offending passage deleted.[50]

Meanwhile, headfirst into this whirlpool of deadly forces fell Charles P. Stone. In the month of November Stone published an order describing two runaway slaves and directing that they be returned to their owner if found. Lieutenant Colonel Francis Winthrop Palfrey of the Twentieth Massachusetts was one of the colonels to receive the order and pass it to his officers. On a Sunday morning in late November, Lieutenant Macy of Company I was mounting the guard when he saw the two runaways. In short work he took them into custody and reported to the commanding officer. A file of soldiers returned the two to their owner,[51] a routine occurrence in camp life except for one thing: it happened in a regiment from Massachusetts, the hotbed of abolition.[52]

A letter from one of the men in the regiment reported the entire affair with embellishments to Governor John A. Andrew.[53] Energetic, emotional, and enthusiastic, Andrew had hated slavery almost from birth. His rise to the governorship of Massachusetts marked the rise of anti-slavery political forces in the state. He led the defense of John Brown after the Harpers Ferry raid, and after Brown was hanged, he arranged a collection for the Brown family. In August 1860 the electorate of his state set him in the governor's chair by the largest majority in the history of the

---

50   Williams, *Lincoln and the Radicals*, 59; Thomas, *Stanton*, 133–134; Bradley, *Cameron*, 201–203.

51   Much confusion surrounds this incident. Accounts state variously that the two men were slaves who wished to return to their masters, or that they had not run away at all but were carried across the Potomac in the retreat from the battle, or that they were really freemen, and so on. No attempt has been made to determine their status or the incidents of their capture.

52   In general, the Massachusetts regiments opposed slavery and refused to return escaped slaves, e.g., Blight, *Brewster Letters*, 57, letter dated November 17, 1861, from Brewster to his mother. Brewster of the Tenth Massachusetts Infantry wrote, "Col. Briggs did not come here to hunt niggers and can't see that it is any part of his duty to send them back"; 61, letter dated November 24, 1861, from Brewster to his mother; 87, letter dated February 12, 1862, from Brewster to his mother.

53   *OR*, ser. 2, vol. 1, 784–785, letter dated December 12, 1861, from Cameron to Banks, enclosing letter dated December 7, 1861, from Governor Andrew to Cameron, subenclosing letter dated November 28, 1861, from n.s. to n.a.

state.[54] Stone's action could not go unheeded by a man like Andrew, especially when it involved a Massachusetts regiment.

On the seventh of December Andrew sent a letter to Cameron denouncing the use of Massachusetts troops to return fugitive slaves without any investigation. He enclosed the original letter from the soldier of the Twentieth.[55] Two days later he instructed Lieutenant Colonel Palfrey to end this "dirty and despotic work" and notify Lieutenant Macy that, had Andrew known about his part in the affair, he would not have signed the commission for Macy's recent promotion.[56]

To Stone, this was not just an unpleasant insult from a civilian. It was an intolerable intrusion on his authority as a commanding officer, and he would not ignore it. He responded with a frank, accurate, provocative, and, in the end, explosive letter. Unlike McClellan in similar situations, he loosed it into proper channels:

> Headquarters Corps of Observation,
> Poolesville, December 15, 1861

> Brig. Gen. S. Williams, Assistant Adjutant-General.

> General: I have the honor to enclose herewith the copy of a most extraordinary letter addressed by authority of a governor of a State to the lieutenant-colonel of a regiment of U.S. volunteers serving in this division, and respectfully request of the major-general commanding in the hope that he may be able to devise measures which shall in the future prevent such unwarrantable and dangerous interference with the subordinate commands of the army. The fact that most of the soldiers in the regiment referred to were enlisted into the service of the United States in the State of which the governor referred to is the respected chief magistrate does not give his excellency a right to assume control of the interior discipline of the regiment, nor does it give him authority to command the punishment of a meritorious officer for any offense, either real or imaginary.

54 *D.A.B.*, 1, pt. 1, 279–280; Hesseltine, William B., *Lincoln and the War Governors* 19–23, 110–111, 203 (New York, 1948); Browne, Albert Gallatin, *Sketch of the Official Life of John A. Andrew* (Boston, 1868) 13–14, 84 ff; Oates, Stephen B., *To Purge this Land with Blood: A Biography of John Brown*, 271, 324–328 (New York and London, 1970).

55 *OR*, ser. 2, vol. 1, 784, letter dated December 7, 1861, from Andrew to Cameron.

56 *OR*, ser. 2, vol. 1, 787–788, letter dated December 9, 1861, from Drew, assistant military secretary, to Palfrey.

Disagreeable as it may be to me to do anything distasteful to the governor of any state of the Union I do not feel that it is consistent with my sworn duty to permit any governor to give orders affecting the discipline of my regiment which the government of the nation has entrusted to my command. I am not aware that there are here Michigan, New York, Pennsylvania, Minnesota or Massachusetts troops. I do know that there are here U.S. troops collected from all those States; and they are carefully taught that their duty is to serve the United States honestly and faithfully against all those who set themselves in opposition to the Constitution and laws of the United States, whomsoever the oppressors may be.

I enclose a copy of General Orders, No. 16, of September 23, 1861, from these headquarters which will illustrate the course I have pursued here in reference to the loyal citizens of Maryland who are of course to be on a different footing from rebels in arms.

Very respectfully, general, your most obedient servant,

CHAS. P. STONE
Brigadier-General, Commanding[57]

Although Stone had honored the niceties of the system, the system did not reciprocate. His letter went to Governor Andrew, who sent all the correspondence and a tirade to Massachusetts Senator Charles Sumner.[58] This ugly exchange reached the press.[59]

Tall and well-formed even for a man younger than his fifty years, Sumner was humorless, vain, arrogant, intelligent, and self-assured. He was not a Unionist. He was not really a Radical. He was the sharpest, most extreme of the slavery haters and a confirmed proponent of immediate abolition. His skill as an orator made him an unbeatable opponent in any debate about the black man.[60] On Wednesday,

57   *OR*, ser. 2, vol. 1, 786–787, letter dated December 15, 1861, from Stone to Williams.

58   Townsend, *Anecdotes*, 74.

59   *The New York Daily Tribune*, December 13, 1861, p. 2, col. 6.

60   *D.A.B.*, 9, pt. 1, 209 ff, 213; Stryker, Lloyd Paul, *Andrew Johnson, A Study in Courage*, 40 ff; generally, Donald, David, *Charles Sumner* 2 vols. (New York, 1960 and 1970), especially vol. 2, Donald, *Charles Sumner and the Rights of Man*.

December 18, he rose on the floor of the Senate to make a vehement protest against the use of troops to return runaways. Bringing the issue to a personal level, he put one more public blot on the record of the hapless commander of the Corps of Observation.

"Brigadier-General Stone, the well known commander at Ball's Bluff," he said to his colleagues, "is now adding to his achievements there by engaging ably and actively in the work of returning fugitive slaves. He does this, sir, most successfully. He is victorious when the simple question is whether a fugitive slave shall be surrendered to a rebel."[61]

Stone took Sumner's Senate remarks personally, and for the first time he replied outside military channels. "Please accept my thanks for the speech in which you use my name," he wrote to Sumner. "There can hardly be better proof that a soldier in the field is carefully performing his duty, than the fact that while he is receiving the shot of the public enemy in the front, he is at the same time receiving the vituperation of a well known coward from a safe distance in the rear."[62]

Sumner took this letter at once to Lincoln, who had a considerable amount of personal knowledge about the battle and its progression from a reconnaissance to an escalating, voluntary engagement. He spoke his reaction to Stone's letter.

"I don't know that I should have written such a letter," he said; "but if I had wanted to, under the circumstances—under the circumstances, mind you—I would have had a right to do so."[63]

Whether or not others in important positions would see it that way remained to be seen. For now it would be just below the surface and just below boil.

61   *Congressional Globe*, 2d Session, 37th Congress, 130, December 18, 1861, col. 1 (Sumner).

62   Charles Sumner MSS (Harvard University) (a U.P.I. microfilm of Sumner's papers is in the Butler Library of Columbia University), letter dated December 23, 1861, from Stone to Sumner. My schoolmate Alfred Bakhash, who veered away to Harvard when we graduated from school, kindly found this letter for me in Sumner's massive collection in the fall of 1957.

63   Irwin, Richard B., "Ball's Bluff and the Arrest of General Stone," in *B&L*, 2, 133.

Chapter 8

"Our victory must depend on you and the men that may be placed at your disposal. Impressed with this belief and anxious to aid you with all the power of my Department, I will be glad if you will inform me how I can do so."

—Cameron to McClellan

McClellan's Friends

*M*ore than any other group of officers who served together in the war, McClellan and his friends shared the same characteristics, similar career paths, the same beliefs, the same political and philosophical leanings, the same views on the policies for the war, and similar tactical and strategic ideas. They also confronted the same demons, who pursued them because they shared McClellan's judgments and opinions, which were the focal points for their opponents. As early as November of 1861, one recorder of attitudes and rumors wrote, "If not McClellan himself, some intriguers around him already dream, nay, even attempt to form a pure military, that is, a reckless, unprincipled, unpatriotic party. These men foment the irritation between the arrogance of the thus-called Regular Army, and the pure abnegation of the volunteers."[1]

In the early part of the war McClellan and his friends personified the unresolved major policy disputes. Most often their part in the struggles represented no more than a sideshow to the larger disagreements between Lincoln and the Radical

---

1   Gurowski, Adam, *Diary*, 3 vols. (Boston, 1862, 1864, 1866) *Diary, from March 4, 1861, to November 12, 1862* (Boston, 1862) 1, 97, entry dated November, 1861 (Gurowski, *Diary*).

Republicans: how should the civilian population of the South be treated? what should be done with their property, ranging from crops to livestock to buildings to land? what should be done with their slaves? what should happen to slavery as an institution? on what terms should the war end?

These questions had as many answers as men to debate them. Each being a political question, the men of the military should have avoided them to the best of their ability, and politicians with foresight and the best interests of their country at heart should have helped them do that . . . for both altruistic and selfish reasons.[2] But the higher-ranking officers became inexorably involved in them; the higher the rank, the more the involvement. Military ability would certainly serve as a minimum test for promotion and assignment but would sometimes seem less important than the "correctness" of the officers' views on the political questions. And their answers to the questions would become entangled with the thread that had run so distinctly but with such uncertain direction through the early fabric of the war: the thread of loyalty.

Their answers to non-military, political questions made McClellan's loyal subordinates, his political friends, his advocates in the press, and his civilian "backers" important for many more reasons than they should have. Worse yet, their answers sometimes appeared to play determinative roles on questions of strategy, promotion, and assignment.

In Washington, the questions swept McClellan into the vortex of the political struggle between the Radical Republicans and the president. Because of his proximity he lived in a fishbowl surrounded by sharp-eyed onlookers of all stripes, he was readily available to all important men, and he could be at once called to account in person for every little incident. More than any other military leader

---

2   This standard, long-accepted view of relations among politics, political questions, and politicians on one side of the table and military issues, military goals, and military personnel on the other has recently been restored to the debating agenda by a number of British scholars, including Hew Strachan in *The Politics of the British Army*, who declares Gordon Craig's *The Politics of the Prussian Army* to be a ground-breaking work in civil-military relations. Craig, however, although producing an extraordinary piece of scholarship, did not believe that the principle of his study could be applied to other western societies and probably meant to say that no one had, would, or should follow the Prussian-German example. Another even more recent work, intended to blur the old, clear line and favor intrusion from the political side, does not prove its sound point, Cohen, Eliot A., *Supreme Command: Soldiers, Statesmen, and Leadership in Wartime* (New York and London, 2002). The definition of war aims must always remain in the hands of the political representatives of the body politic. The achievement of those ends by military action should remain with the military, subject to absolute overview and supervision by the civilian government. And the line between—more correctly, the gray area in which the fuzzy line should be drawn—should remain as well defined as possible and should be observed by both sides.

throughout the war, he would be a "participant" in, if not a victim of, the jerky, adversarial development of a national policy on all important questions.

The cabinet and the president had endorsed McClellan when they decided that he should command the great Union army of the Civil War. Composed of men with odd and varied political backgrounds, the cabinet exemplified the polyglot nature of the Republican Party, the Lincoln government, and the North. Several of its most important members in 1861, Secretary of Treasury Salmon P. Chase, Secretary of War Simon Cameron, and Postmaster General Montgomery Blair, supported McClellan and considered themselves his friends. But they were very different, and they treated McClellan very differently, although their conduct flowed from similar sentiments and motivations.

Salmon P. Chase, the secretary of the treasury, had been a Free-Soiler, an independent Democrat, the governor of Ohio, a United States senator, and a strong candidate for the Republican nomination for president in 1860. Chase's immediate family had distinction, one uncle the Episcopal bishop of Ohio and another the United States senator from Vermont. Three wives and six children having died after sharing his life only a short time, Chase came to Washington in 1861 a widower of almost ten years. As a lawyer he worked prominently in the confused legal activities involving fugitive slaves. As Republican governor of Ohio his reorganization of the state militia just before the war paved the way for McClellan's prompt creation of a strong military contingent from Ohio. Chase's cabinet position had been one of Lincoln's deft political efforts to draw his party together in the government. The secretary's honest philosophical differences with Lincoln strained relations between them, and his conniving with the Radical Republicans, as the war progressed, would cause ugly confrontations in the cabinet. Nevertheless, an ardent proponent, then supporter of McClellan, Chase already had great confidence in the young major general when he arrived in Washington.[3] Part of Chase's adoption of McClellan stemmed from his intense, parochial loyalty to his state and his view of McClellan as a fellow Ohioan, far more important factors in nineteenth-century thinking than the easy recognition of federal supremacy today.

The secretary of war, Scott's direct superior, was a wealthy, successful, self-made man with a string of political successes to his credit, but his financial activities had provoked sharp criticism for self-dealing. As a Democrat supported by a coalition of Whigs, Know-Nothings, and protectionists, he defeated the Democratic

<hr />

3   See generally, Schuckers, *Chase*; Niven, John, *Salmon P. Chase: A Biography* (New York and Oxford, 1995); Hart, Salmon Portland, *Salmon Portland Chase* (Boston and New York, 1890); *D.A.B.*, 2, pt. 2, 27–30.

Party candidate for senator in 1845. Two failures at reelection sent him into the Republican Party, where his financial misconduct did not impair his political strength. He, too, made a strong showing for the Republican presidential nomination in 1860. Unable to secure that, his backers traded his support for a cabinet post. Ignorant of a bargain he might not have made, Lincoln reluctantly honored the commitment. With political "necessities" too often determining his appointments and contracts, Cameron's administration as secretary of war was deplorable. Corruption in the building of the military "infrastructure" was widespread.[4]

McClellan had a comfortable working relationship with Cameron, who had precisely the motives and intentions that would earn the major general's favor. In the late fall when the New York bankers pressed Chase to secure Cameron's removal, McClellan intervened with the president on Cameron's behalf.[5] In early September, Cameron sent McClellan an unsolicited letter saying, "It is evident that we are on the eve of a great battle—one that may decide the fate of the country. Our victory must depend on you and the men that may be placed at your disposal. Impressed with this belief and anxious to aid you with all the power of my Department, I will be glad if you will inform me how I can do so."[6]

The swirl of controversy surrounding the secretary of war had little effect on McClellan's attitude toward him. As Fitz John Porter put it years after McClellan had gone, "McClellan would do nothing against Secretary Cameron to force his resignation or to cause anyone else to be selected in his place."[7] But smooth relations with the commander of the Army of the Potomac did not guarantee Cameron job security or eliminate criticism, and his conduct toward the president did not give him stability in his cabinet position. In early October, the ever-watchful Nicolay recorded the President's comments. To Lincoln, Cameron was "utterly ignorant and regardless of the course of things, and the probable result . . . selfish and

---

4   *D.A.B.*, 2, pt. 1, 437–438; generally Bradley, Erwin S., *Simon Cameron, Lincoln's Secretary of War: a Political Biography* (Philadelphia, 1966).

5   Porter MSS (L.C.) draft letter dated November 15, 1861, from Porter to Benjamin.

6   *M.O.S.*, 105, 152–153; McClellan MSS (L.C.) letter dated September 7, 1861, from Cameron to McClellan (this letter is also reproduced in *M.O.S.*, 105). This letter, known to have existed by reference to it in another letter but noted "not found" in *OR*, 5, proves again the incompleteness of the government's files, of McClellan's unwillingness to allow the government access to his files, and of McClellan's control of the available evidence for his own purposes, for example, twisted assertions about his intentions.

7   Porter MSS (L.C.) letter dated August 3, 1888, from Porter to Benjamin.

openly discourteous . . . Obnoxious to the Country. Incapable either of organizing details or conceiving or advising general plans."[8]

With a mixed Western and Eastern background, Postmaster General Montgomery Blair also had the heterogeneous political background of most Republicans. Son of Francis Preston Blair, a distinguished, influential journalist and politician, Blair graduated from the Military Academy in 1835 and served against the Seminoles. He resigned from the army and became a prominent lawyer, living in Maryland and arguing important cases before the Supreme Court. Although he became a Free-Soiler, he espoused the moderate border state view on slavery that the question should be settled peaceably. Like many, he moved briefly through the Know-Nothing Party, before he came to rest in the Republican Party. Whatever his views on slavery, he rose to public recognition when he served as counsel to Dred Scott and helped organize a defense for John Brown. Stints as a delegate to the Democratic National Convention in 1844, 1848, and 1852 did not keep him from presiding over the Republican State Convention in Maryland and being a delegate to the Republican National Convention in 1860.

Republican Party service, his family, and experience made him a cabinet officer under Lincoln, whom he supported staunchly. In the early months of the war, Blair had wisely recognized Scott's faults and their deleterious effects. He believed McClellan was a good choice for the Army of the Potomac and became friendly with some of McClellan's most trusted subordinates, including Fitz John Porter.[9]

The Radical Republican members of the House and Senate, the most intense, unyielding, and unforgiving combatants in the government, to a man possessed a masterly ignorance of military concepts. Men of rigid principles, they refused to make the typical, pragmatic compromises of work-a-day political life. They had one—and only one—answer to each critical question. Any man with a different answer was wrong, they suspected his loyalty, and they sometimes even believed him a traitor. Their unyielding unilateral views on political and military questions put them often in disagreement, it seemed, with Lincoln. The president probably shared their views on slavery from the outset. But he had other, larger questions to consider; suffered compulsion to be a statesman; and could not implement their policies

---

8   Nicolay MSS (L.C.) notes of meeting of October 2, 1861, between Lincoln and Cameron.

9   *D.A.B.*, 1, pt. 2, 339–340; generally Smith, W. E., *The Francis Preston Blair Family in Politics*, 2 vols. (New York, 1933); Fehrenbacher, Don E., *The Dred Scott Case: Its Significance in American Law and Politics*, 281–288 (New York, 1998); Gurowski, *Diary*, 1, 134, entry dated December, 1861.

on slavery until the country came to them. Like true revolutionaries, the Radicals behaved with uncompromising, unilateral zeal: anti-South, anti-Democrat, anti-slavery, they would have their program no matter what and would sweep away any who disagreed with them. Unlike the war aims pursued in most patriotic international wars, victory over the enemy army was not enough for them. Victory was one step toward a greater social end: the restructuring of Southern society by the revolutionary displacement of the Southern, landed, planter, slave-holding aristocracy and the freeing and assimilation of the slaves. This social revolution could take place only in the fires of destructive military victory and the cauldron of reconstruction. Disagreements over this goal caused constant confrontation with the president.[10] Although he probably would have chosen not to become involved, McClellan, whether he wanted to or not, participated in this politically lethal contest.

When McClellan arrived in Washington, the Radicals adopted him, showed him around the capital, and acted as if he were their discovery. Michigan Senator Zachariah Chandler, a tall, spare, but powerfully built man with a hard face crowned by a shock of unruly hair and one of the most intractable Radicals, acted as if he had a proprietary interest in the new general. He believed the appointment of McClellan as the practical successor to General Scott a wise one. McClellan's enterprise and courage in the field he took for granted.[11] Expressing confidence in the young major general and none in the cabinet, another Radical noted that he now considered the capital safe.[12]

The early friendly relationship between McClellan and the Radical Republicans arose from naivete on his part and ignorance on theirs. They had no idea who he was or what he thought. Probably, they did not care, because he was no more than a soldier. He was not to have ideas on important political questions but was to win the war by crushing the Southern armies and their Southern aristocratic lead-

10   This view of the Radicals and Lincoln, controversial and much debated, has been best stated and defended over many decades by the extraordinary student of nineteenth century America, Professor T. Harry Williams, in his *Lincoln and the Radicals* (Madison, 1941); the introduction to the 1965 reprint; xii-xiii; and in his "Lincoln and the Radicals" in McWhiney, Grady, ed., *Grant, Lee, Lincoln and the Radicals*, 92–117 (Chicago, 1964). For a brief discussion of the differing historical views, see Belz, Herman, *Emancipation and Equal Rights: Politics and Constitutionalism in the Civil War Era* (New York and London, 1978) chapters 1 and 2, especially 10–14; and "A Bibliographical Review," especially 156–158 (Belz, *Emancipation and Equal Rights*).

11   Detroit Post & Tribune, *Zachariah Chandler: an Outline Sketch of his Life and Public Services* (Detroit, 1879) 224 (Detroit Post & Tribune, *Chandler*); Williams, *Lincoln and the Radicals*, 35, 67–68.

12   Salter, William, *Life of James W. Grimes* (New York, 1876) 147 (Salter, *Grimes*).

ers, war aims shared by McClellan and others.[13] He was then to disappear from the scene and leave the politicians to their work. McClellan, of course, had no idea that he was to be their implement and never realized that his military policies might have severe political implications.

When he made his trip to the Senate to obtain legislation increasing the number of his personal aides and modernizing the engineers,[14] the legislators congratulated McClellan and treated him with great respect. Surrounded by the older generation of the Senate, he felt he had their "unbounded confidence."

"Why, how young you look," they said repeatedly, "and yet an old soldier."

While he stood in the Senate Library, from which he could look over the capital of his country, he saw a crowd gathering to watch him and realized the importance and magnitude of the task entrusted to him.[15]

These meetings cast an eerie, shadowy illumination on the future. McClellan's adoption by the Radicals brought him in contact with the most highly charged political issues of the war: slavery, abolition, and emancipation. Several times he met important Radical leaders, including Senator Charles Sumner of Massachusetts, the high priest of abolition. McClellan consistently said he was thoroughly opposed to slavery, which he considered a great evil, especially for the Southern whites. But he opposed sweeping emancipation unless it also included regulation of the relations between the races. The interests of both had to be protected.

"Were such a policy framed to my satisfaction," he said to them, "I would certainly support it."

Speaking for many of the Radicals, Sumner replied, "Such points do not concern us. All that must be left to take care of itself."

"No real statesman," responded McClellan, "would ever contemplate so sweeping and serious a measure as sudden and general emancipation without looking to the future and providing for its consequences. Four and a half millions of

13   Morgan MSS (N.Y.S.L.) letter dated May 9, 1861, from Van Vliet to Morgan; Sears, *McClellan's Correspondence*, 72, letter dated August 2, 1861, by the editor from McClellan to Lincoln.

14   *OR*, ser. 3, vol. 1, 397–398, 400, 401, General Orders No. 54, War Dept., Adjutant Genl's Office, dated August 10, 1861, publishing Public Law No. 38, sections 3 and 4, approved August 3, 1861, Public Law No. 42, approved August 5, 1861, Public Law No. 52, section 2, approved August 6, 1861, Public Law No. 53, sections 1 and 2, approved August 6, 1861.

15   Sears, *McClellan's Correspondence*, 71, letter dated July 30, 1861, from McClellan to his wife. He was even told that in Richmond, the Confederate capital, "there was only one man they feared and that was McClellan." He prayed to God for "the wisdom and courage necessary to accomplish the work." Ibid.

uneducated slaves should not be manumitted without due precautions taken both to protect them and to guard against them. Just there is the point where we differ radically and probably irreconcilably."[16]

Little more than two months later McClellan would write his friend, former business colleague, and fellow Democrat Samuel L. M. Barlow, "Help me to dodge the nigger—we want nothing to do with him. I am fighting to preserve the integrity of the Union and the power of the Gov't—on no other issue. To gain that end we cannot afford to raise the negro question—it must be incidental and subsidiary. The President is perfectly honest and is really sound on the nigger question. I will answer for it now that things go right with him."[17]

His views, never changing, became prescient. Immediately after the war he wrote to his father-in-law, "I suppose I ought to be glad to hear that the black troops look so well, for I strongly suspect that our permanent army will mainly consist of them. I confess to a prejudice in favor of my own race, & can't learn to like the odor of either billy goats or niggers, but so long as they don't conscript me into a black regiment, I must be contented."[18]

Although no one, least of all McClellan, knew it at the time, the conversation with Sumner and his private letters showed an attitude that extended well beyond military considerations. As a high-ranking military officer, where did he find the power and the discretion to "support" a policy or to keep the president "right"? Perhaps he had spent too much time thinking about the great military leaders of old: Leonidas, king of Sparta; Alexander, king of the Macedonians; Darius, king of Persia; Henry V, king of England; Frederick, king of Prussia; and Napoleon, emperor of France. These great military leaders of the past had been heads of state and had formulated the social as well as the military policies of their countries. As kings and emperors they issued military orders and political edicts.

---

16   *M.O.S.*, 33. In a real but not readily observable sense, McClellan had a more long-term and more intelligent philosophical, if not practical, view of the solution to slavery, a view the short-sighted Radicals would have supported but not one they considered in depth. McClellan thought not about abolition as the end but about assimilation and integration as complex social problems that would need solutions at the end of the war. He would not likely have embraced integration gladly, but he probably would have come to it thoughtfully in time, just as he did to frontal attacks with heavy casualties. The Radicals' ill-considered and poorly managed efforts during Reconstruction, a regrettable failure, left a festering problem for solution in the civil rights movement of the 1960s.

17   Sears, *McClellan's Correspondence*, 128, letter dated November 8, 1861, from McClellan to S. L. M. Barlow.

18   McClellan MSS (L.C.) letter dated August 20, 1865, from McClellan to Marcy.

Subject to military orders and political edicts, John Churchill, duke of Marlborough, carried his country's military flag in the War of the Spanish Succession without reverse and with victory after victory over many years. For political reasons he did not carry the flag at the end of the war, and the English "lost the peace." A general in a democratic republic not unlike the English structure, McClellan did not have the power to choose between "support" if the government's policy on slavery and emancipation suited him and "opposition" if it did not. Nor did he have the power to "answer for" that policy in the hands of the president and keep him "right" on it. These were political matters. They had the potential to destroy a military career when an errant general failed to follow the government's policy or took matters in his own hands. McClellan's duty should have been clear to him, and if it were not, he should have known enough to seek clarification. He was to do as he was directed by the president—no more and no less. His considerable powers of persuasion and his great influence on military questions he could properly ply at all times. But he had no power to make political policy, and he would undertake to influence it at his peril.

When McClellan first arrived in Washington, he established an easy working relationship with the press, which included some of his most far-flung supporters and friends in the early months. From a woman in Philadelphia he had already received severe advice about dealing with the gentlemen of the pen. "Banish all newspaper reporters from & about your camp," she wrote, "and either hang or shoot them, or threaten to do so. I constantly read the Papers, and at the commencement of the campaign, was astonished at the full reports, of the General-in-Chief's plans, being continually given . . . Doubtless there are hundreds of traitors, and spies among them; and even if there were not, it is generally conceded that penny-a-line writers, are not men of high standard of morality, that as a general thing they are a venial set, who will do anything for money, and are destitute of patriotism, morality or religion."[19]

At least in the beginning, McClellan had a different, far wiser, and far more conciliatory plan. He invited the newspaper correspondents to visit his headquarters for an interview. The newspapermen accepted this invitation as evidence of a cordial attitude. On the evening of August 1, two large omnibuses stopped in front of Willard's Hotel to collect the journalists; and when they arrived at his headquarters, they were ushered into a spacious parlor. In a short while McClellan appeared with his father-in-law and chief of staff, Colonel Randolph B. Marcy. His face was covered with

19   McClellan MSS (L.C.) letter dated July 29, 1861, from "a Philadelphia lady" to McClellan.

dust and perspiration from a long ride. He was completely unpretentious. In fact, many of the reporters failed to recognize him until the formal presentation.

McClellan gave a little talk in which he spoke flatteringly about the newspaper profession and solicited its cooperation during the trying days ahead. This was a time of great crisis, he said. Newspapermen held positions of great influence and could do much harm or good. A few correspondents had accompanied his West Virginia campaign, had conformed with his wishes, and had found no reason to complain about his dealings with them. Those at the meeting, according to McClellan, knew far better than he what should be printed and what should not. He said he was inclined to give them a wide range of responsibility and hoped they would come to an agreement among themselves to eliminate information that might help the Confederates.

After some discussion, a committee of five newspapermen agreed to convey the general's suggestions to the remainder of the press corps. As they were about to depart, one reporter suggested that the pictorial press be censured for recently publishing sketches of military fortifications. McClellan remarked breezily that he thought the pictorial press could safely be let alone, its drawings being more likely to confuse than to inform the enemy.

Within a few days lengthy accounts of this meeting appeared in many newspapers. Among those giving details of the general's personal appearance, one reporter likened him to Napoleon. This characterization caught the popular fancy, and the press afterward commonly described him as the "young Napoleon."[20] In the beginning he had the universal support of the press, which wrote laudatory coverage of his doings.[21] Wherever he went, he was "well supplied with newspaper correspondents."[22]

In his headquarters McClellan did not require strict security against the press. Telegrams and reports lay in piles on the desks, and reporters simply helped themselves. At times a document would find its way into a newspaper before it reached the addressee.[23] The reporters "wrote up" officers at all levels in a complimentary way as long as they included the reporters in the officers' counsels, gave them their inner thoughts, and kept them current on the confidential workings of the Army.[24]

---

20   Andrews, *North Reports*, 149–151.

21   Williams, Frederick D., ed., *The Wild Life of the Army: Civil War Letters of James A. Garfield* (Lansing, 1964) (Williams, *Garfield Letters*); Haupt, *Reminiscences*, 305.

22   Thomas C. H. Smith MSS (Ohio Historical Society) MS History of Second Bull Run, 53.

23   Comte de Paris MS Diary (large diary) (A.N. de la M. de F.) entry dated November 12, 1861.

24   Andrews, *North Reports*, 69.

In October, the *New York World* defended Robert Patterson and Fitz John Porter for their roles in the Valley Campaign. Porter wrote to Manton Marble, editor of the *World* and before the end of the war its owner,[25] "Be pleased to accept my grateful acknowledgment for the token of friendship presented in the prompt defense of my character which appeared in your paper, and which I accidentally saw last Monday in Washington."[26] Porter's initial contact opened a line of communication with Marble that would continue as long as Porter remained in the army; and the *World* would remain a supporter of McClellan throughout.

The meeting with the press presented another aspect of McClellan's personality. He was not given to public dispute. Long after the war had ended and the Army of the Potomac lived only in the memories of its men, he still did not enter the lists of active, public controversy. He allowed the Second Civil War, the endless debates among participants at all levels, to proceed without him. His military memoirs, undertaken much later and incomplete when he died, he did not intend for publication until after his death, if at all.[27] Although he would do nothing to halt the controversy that came to surround him, he did not do anything to stay the hands of his friends who chose to defend him. They received his tacit, if not his express, approval for their efforts on his behalf. Porter became the first and most active of this group. As time passed, he would write Marble long letters that sounded much like McClellan talking. In all probability they were.

McClellan's civilian friends were no less a source of political controversy and later divisiveness about his motives, his policies, and his goals. Samuel Latham Mitchell Barlow, the young, brilliant, successful lawyer McClellan had met during his railroad career, was a Democrat but a supporter of the Republican war effort.[28] Some would think him a Copperhead, a northern Democrat who supported the South.[29] Sporadically,[30] McClellan would write to Barlow about important policy issues and receive Barlow's advice in return. Other men of great wealth became part of his military family under the legislation allowing him an unlimited number of volunteer aides.

---

25   *D.A.B.*, 7, pt. 2, 267.

26   Manton Marble MSS (Library of Congress) letter dated October 23, 1861, from Porter to Marble.

27   *M.O.S.*, McClellan's introduction, dated November 8, 1881.

28   *D.A.B.*, 1, pt. 1, 613–614.

29   Keyes, *Fifty Years*, 441.

30   Sears, *McClellan's Correspondence*, 127–128, 154–155, 313, 360–361, 369–370, letters dated November 8, 1861; January 18, 1862; March 16, 1862; July 15, 1862; July 23, 1862, by the editor from McClellan to Barlow.

John Jacob Astor, a long-time Democrat with a great fortune and great influence in the Democratic Party, served as a colonel on his staff.[31] August Belmont, another extraordinarily wealthy Democrat with great power in the party and thought by some to be disloyal, became a McClellan supporter.[32] This did not escape observation. "McClellan under fatal influences of the rampant pro-slavery men," wrote Count Gurowski in his diary, "and of partisans of the South, as is a Barlow. All the former associations of McClellan have been of the worst kind—Breckinridgians."[33]

Edwin M. Stanton, a new acquaintance, a man of steadfast Democratic Party loyalty, was introduced to McClellan in Washington as a shrewd lawyer who could give safe advice on questions of law. They quickly became friends, Stanton working hard to ingratiate himself with McClellan and professing the warmest devotion to him.[34] A successful, wealthy lawyer, Stanton had achieved political prominence when President James Buchanan formed his twilight cabinet in December of 1860 and elevated Stanton, on the basis of his noteworthy prewar successes as a lawyer, to attorney general. When Stanton came to a new view on any issue, he embraced it, much like the ardent revolutionary Leon Trotsky, with the zealotry of a religious fanatic. Although opposed to slavery and a strong believer in the Union before the war, Stanton took a simplistic view of important questions involving slavery. For example, if a properly enacted law required the return of a fugitive slave, he believed the slave should be returned.[35]

In Buchanan's cabinet he allied himself with Jeremiah Black and Joseph Holt against the evacuation of Fort Sumter. Excitable and suspicious, fearing insurrection and assassination, he betrayed his party by passing information about confidential cabinet deliberations to high-level Republicans.[36] During all this he was a model of the insincere sycophant by flattering Buchanan continuously.[37]

---

31   *D.A.B.*, 1, pt. 1, 399; Wilson, Derek, *The Astors, 1763–1992: Landscape with Millionaires*, 97 (New York, 1993).

32   *D.A.B.*, 1, pt. 2, 170; Katz, Irving, *August Belmont: A Political Biography*, 104–114 (New York and London, 1968); Nevins, *Strong Diary*, 3, 256, 268, entries dated September 13, 1862, and October 30, 1862.

33   Gurowski, *Diary*, 1, 95, entry dated September, 1861.

34   *M.O.S.*, 151–152.

35   *D.A.B.*, 9, pt. 1, 518; generally, Deutscher, Isaac, *Biography of Leon Trotsky*, 3 vols. (New York and London, 1954–1963).

36   Thomas, Benjamin P., and Hyman, Harold M., *Stanton: The Life and Times of Lincoln's Secretary of War* (New York, 1962) 88–118 (Thomas, *Stanton*).

37   Curtis, G. T., *Life of Buchanan, Fifteenth President of the United States*, 2 vols. (New York, 1883) 2, 523.

Writing to Buchanan about the newly arrived major general, Stanton described McClellan's environment with considerable insight. "[I]f he had the ability of Caesar, Alexander, or Napoleon, what can be accomplished? Will not Scott's jealousy, Cabinet intrigues, and Republican interference thwart him at every step?"[38]

Lincoln, Stanton regarded as a buffoon and a fool. Writing about Stanton years later, McClellan said, "The most disagreeable thing about him was the extreme virulence with which he abused the president, the administration, and the Republican party. He carried this to such an extreme that I was often shocked by it. He never spoke of the President in any other way than as the 'original gorilla,' and often said that du Chaillu was a fool to wander all the way to Africa in search of what he could so easily find in Springfield, Illinois. Nothing could be more bitter than his words and manner always were when speaking of the administration and the Republican party."[39] In spite of this disagreeable characteristic McClellan began to use Stanton's apartment as a place of concealment in which he could evade the "drop-in" visits of the President and obtain sage advice and editorial assistance.[40]

Before Stanton became embroiled in the war, he had a joyous nature and a keen sense of humor. Free and eager in their enjoyment, he had a hearty and contagious laugh and enjoyed "a taste for light literature that made his conversation extremely attractive." His vivid imagination was "the larger and most potent quality of his mind."[41] His brother's suicide and the death of his wife and daughter stilled this. As disunion, then war, fell upon the country, he developed a deep pessimism. Everything, he believed, would end wrong. He foresaw failure at every turn.[42] With this morbid foreboding of disaster, would his pleasant, stimulating personality continue? Or would it take a dour and gloomy turn with an overlay of viciousness?

Although McClellan's social and business friends seemed to be Democrats by happenstance, his military friends would be Democrats by force of circumstances. Because the higher-ranking officers exemplified the "Scott Rule," brigadier and major generals would rise from the lieutenants and captains of the old Regular Army, they would probably be taken from McClellan's contemporaries at West Point, a pool numerically dominated by Democrats.

---

38   Moore, *Buchanan Works*, 11, 213–214, letter dated July 26, 1861, from Stanton to Buchanan.

39   *M.O.S.*, 152; McClellan, "The Peninsula Campaign," in *B&L*, 2, 162–163; Piatt, *Memories*, 55–56.

40   Sears, *McClellan's Correspondence*, 113, letter dated October 31, 1861, by the editor, from McClellan to his wife.

41   Piatt, *Memories*, 50–51.

42   Thomas, *Stanton*, 41; Piatt, *Memories*, 54.

Among the men selected for promotion to or appointment to colonel before he came east were William B. Franklin, Andrew Porter, Fitz John Porter, and William F. Smith, all old friends standing high in McClellan's estimation and taken early into his confidence.[43] Of these men, however, the one he inherited without choice and with whom he early developed a strong, friendly relationship was the unfortunate but intelligent and gentlemanly Irvin McDowell.

Much of the blame for Bull Run, especially in the minds of the troops, fell on McDowell. Victim of a simplistic analysis—he was in command, he must have been at fault[44]—he would do nothing to explain or justify his conduct. That was beneath him.[45] Wild, baseless charges circulated about him, drunkenness, cowardice, and disloyalty. His imperious and arrogant behavior toward his subordinates, including his enlisted men, did not help. He did not naturally capture the affection of his men, and he did not try[46] even though, like any good officer, he took good care of them. McDowell understood his duties and his division well. Daily he examined his command, passing from camp to camp to be certain that matters progressed properly and making frequent, careful inspections of his men.[47]

Emerging from his headquarters in the Arlington mansion early one cold morning, he noticed a private pacing the guard beat directly in front of the house. The private, on duty since 4 A.M., wore a pair of ill-fitting mittens knitted for him on the memory of his size as a boy.

Bareheaded, McDowell sniffed the frosty air. The private came to present arms, then shifted to right shoulder arms and proceeded to the other end of his beat. When he returned, McDowell stopped him.

"Soldier, where is your overcoat?"

Laconically the private replied, "Haven't got none."

"Well, this is a pretty cold morning to be out without an overcoat on."

43   Porter MSS (L.C.) letters dated September 26, 1893, and May 9, 1890, from Franklin to Porter; *C.C.W.*, 1, 178 (Porter) and 122 (Franklin); Kearny MSS (L.C.) letters dated February 15, 1862, and March 31, 1862, from Kearny to Cortlandt Parker; de Peyster, *Kearny*, 209.

44   Cole, *Under Five Commanders*, 20; Adams, *Story of a Trooper*, 260; Robertson, *McAllister Letters*, 133, letter dated April 13, 1862, from McAllister to his wife; Blake, *Three Years*, 33.

45   Schuckers, *Chase*, 450–451, letter dated September 4, 1862, from Chase to Bryant; Robertson, *McAllister Letters*, 133, letter dated April 13, 1862, from McAllister to his wife; Williams, *Garfield Letters*, 314, memorandum dated October 12, 1862; Gates, *Ulster Guard*, 178–179.

46   Comte de Paris, MS Diary (large diary) (A.N. de la M. de France), entry dated September 28, 1861; Gates, *Ulster Guard*, 178.

47   *OR*, 12, pt. 1, 101 (McDowell court of inquiry) (Keyes).

The private was not about to disagree. "Yes, sir."

"What regiment do you belong to?"

"To the Nineteenth Indiana." The private added that his regiment had been unable to obtain any overcoats.

McDowell responded, "I will see that your regiment is supplied with overcoats at once."

They arrived a short time later.[48]

In spite of incidents like this, some of McDowell's men even believed him sympathetic to the Confederates, if not outrightly disloyal.[49] With a better understanding of the general, Salmon P. Chase, again cleaving to a fellow Ohioan, recognized the problem and McDowell's real character. "He is too indifferent in manner, and his officers are sometimes alienated by it. He is too purely military in his intercourse with his soldiers. There is apparent hauteur: no, that is not the word—rough indifference expresses better the idea—in his way toward them, that makes it hard for them to feel any warm personal sentiments toward him . . . "[50] After Bull Run, McDowell declined command of the Army of Missouri because he viewed command in the East as unfinished business and he preferred to remain in the Army of the Potomac to redeem himself.[51]

Many of McDowell's officers still admired him and valued his judgment. "Colonel Lebedeff, from the staff of the Emperor Alexander II, and professor in the School at St. Petersburg, saw here everything, spoke with our generals," recorded one observer in his diary, "and his conclusion is that in military capacity McDowell is by far superior to McClellan," a view shared by Colonel Romanoff of the Russian corps of engineers.

McDowell's willingness to accept unfair treatment without recrimination against fellow officers who had failed him fostered a cordial and collegial spirit among the generals of the Army of the Potomac. Due in large measure to McDowell's example, they wished to help each other and suffered no jealousy toward one another. In spite of his reduced circumstances, McDowell was "not only very highly regarded in the army but also in the government, using his influence to support McClellan in the midst of the difficulties he has had to face," wrote one of the

---

48   William Roby Moore MS rem, no. 4, 92–94 (Indiana Historical Society). Moore wrote five versions of his recollections, all of which are in the collection.

49   Moore MS rem (I.H.S.) no. 1, chap. 5; T. C. H. Smith MSS, Judson MS Narrative (Ohio Historical Society); Gates, *Ulster Guard*, 178.

50   Schuckers, *Chase*, 450–451, letter dated September 4, 1862, from Chase to Bryant.

51   Comte de Paris MS diary (large diary) (A.N. de la M. de F.) entry dated November 7, 1861.

French princes in his diary. "One needs exceptional selflessness to consider his successor as a friend and not as a rival."[52]

McClellan had other reasons to be grateful to McDowell and to be favorably disposed toward him. When Governor William Dennison organized the military forces of Ohio at the outbreak, he and his advisers searched for an officer to command the Ohio contingent. McClellan was not the only person to be considered, nor was he the first. Dennison originally intended to offer the position to McDowell, to whom he was related by marriage, and wrote McDowell to tell him about his intentions. Meanwhile, prominent businessmen of Cincinnati urged the appointment of "Captain McClellan," whom Dennison had met at a railroad convention. Dennison hesitated. Pressure from Cincinnati mounted. McDowell seemed likely to be kept busy in Washington. McClellan, with high standing in the army, might have more prestige and was available. Learning that McClellan was also under consideration, McDowell showed the diffidence and self-effacement that had caused him to decline the two stars of a major general. He wrote Dennison in favor of McClellan. In relevant matters, he said, McClellan was better educated and should be appointed. After his meeting with McClellan, Dennison gave McClellan the appointment, then wrote McDowell to report his decision and his motives.

McDowell responded magnanimously. "I congratulate you on the credit which justly attaches to you for your appointment of McClellan to the chief command. Among all our graduates yet in the vigor of youth, he is of the first order. I say it in all sincerity, that though he has the place to which I aspired, the command of the troops of my native State (of which I am still a citizen), you have done better for the State, and better for the Country, than if you had adhered to your intention of appointing me."

A few hours after McDowell wrote this letter, Scott asked him about men qualified for promotion to general in the Regular Army. McDowell named McClellan and Don Carlos Buell. A short time later the May promotions took place, McClellan being promoted to major general in the Regular Army. Aware of these generous contributions to his career, McClellan was deeply grateful.[53]

Once in Washington, McClellan consulted McDowell frequently and sought from him reports on the condition of the forces on the west bank of the Potomac.[54]

52　Comte de Paris MS Diary (large diary) (A.N. de la M. de F.), entry dated October 18, 1861; Gurowski, *Diary*, 1, 94, 99, entry dated September, 1861.

53　Williams, *Garfield Letters*, 306, memorandum dated October 12, 1862; Reid, *Ohio in the War*, 1, 659. Reid quotes the letter from McDowell.

54　*C.C.W.*, 1, 131 (McDowell); *M.O.S.*, 68, 70–71.

They rode the lines together, talking about strategy, avenues for future advances, and other military issues.[55] McDowell's straightforward loyalty, his sincere efforts to make the transition to McClellan smooth, and his genuine all-round assistance did much to reduce the turmoil in McClellan's early period.[56]

Recognizing McDowell's situation, McClellan felt strong sympathy for him. He believed that, if he arranged for McDowell's transfer to another theater, McDowell would be ruined for life. To give McDowell "an opportunity to retrieve his military reputation," McClellan wrote later, he left him in command of the military forces on the Virginia side of the Potomac until he issued General Orders No 1, August 20, 1861, constituting the Army of the Potomac and assuming command of it.[57] McClellan gave McDowell eight regiments of infantry, the equivalent of a small division of two brigades. When McDowell asked if that would be a permanent or temporary arrangement, McClellan responded that it was purely temporary; and if the army were organized into corps, McDowell would have one. Nervously, McDowell awaited a major step in his climb from hell.[58]

In the wings waiting with anticipation stood an old friend, Fitz John Porter, who was serving as a major and an inspector-general in Banks' army in the Shenandoah. Balanced against his considerable talents and abilities, his position was not rewarding. On August 1, he sent McClellan a letter that, in an interesting commentary on the progress of the postal department, arrived in McClellan's hands

---

55   *C.C.W.*, 1, 131 (McDowell); Swinton, *Army of the Potomac*, 61, 69, n.

56   McClellan took from the war a lasting hatred of McDowell and blamed him for much that went wrong. The first draft of his memoirs was destroyed by a fire. When he tackled the task a second time, he intended to leave his work unpublished in the hands of his children and to avoid the appearance of "any public reply to the various criticisms and misrepresentations of which I have been the subject" (*M.O.S.*, McClellan's Preface, 27). Through all this one might expect his views on unpleasant questions to have softened. In McDowell's case, it did not happen. McDowell is one of the few men criticized and castigated in the memoirs. Much of the criticism McClellan leveled at others his family-appointed editor and friend W. C. Prime deleted after McClellan died but not the part about McDowell. The original of the second manuscript in McClellan's handwriting is in his MSS in the Library of Congress. *M.O.S.*, 70, 71, Introductory Biographical Sketch by W. C. Prime, 22–23. His animus toward McDowell had continued at a high level. He found nothing done for him by McDowell to be helpful or praiseworthy and adopted conspiracy theories about McDowell that were as preposterous as the disloyalty charges he himself suffered. The contemporary diary of the French prince, a man who had McClellan's trust during the war and who remained his friend in the years afterward, told a different, less tainted, and more reliable story. It and Reid's account, based on contemporaneous correspondence, are preferred here.

57   *OR*, 5, 575, General Orders No. 1, Headquarters of the Army of the Potomac, dated August 30, 1861, by McClellan; *M.O.S.*, 70–71.

58   *C.C.W.*, 1, 144 (McDowell).

the next day.[59] For the government not to suffer, he wrote, he consented to remain when Banks assumed command of Patterson's old army and had himself appointed acting inspector general "in order that I might accomplish what no one else here can, a reorganization of this demoralized force." Once he finished that, he would be available unless Banks' force were to enter an active campaign, "an impossibility I think—without a General. Should this campaign turn out as the last, the odium which has been thrown unjustly upon Patterson will be reflected upon me and his other advisers. Time and orders from high authority will show he was right and the country should be thankful." Porter then spoke about his juniors rising to higher positions while he plodded "in a beaten and lowly track."[60]

When Sherman received orders to the West, McClellan sent for Porter to report to Washington. At first he gave him responsibility for training new regiments of three-year volunteers, then assigned him to command Sherman's old brigade, and finally, on August 30, gave him a division of brigades commanded by George W. Morrell and John H. Martindale. A brigade under Daniel Butterfield made the division complete on September 13. For the good future of the division and its successors, the field artillery battalion went to the sharp-tongued Charles Griffin of Bull Run fame.[61]

While in position at Miner's Hill, Porter used the excellent drill condition of Butterfield's brigade to stimulate competition in his division. The program was so successful that it produced a division superior at drill. After one of the reviews McClellan issued a general order, dated November 16, 1861, in which he took the unusual course of expressing his great appreciation for the "high soldierly quality displayed by the division commanded by Brigadier General F. J. Porter during the review and evolutions on the 9th instant." The division's appearance, he said, would have done credit to veterans. The Regulars should prepare to protect their laurels if Porter's division could fight as well as it marched. "The General Commanding thanks General Porter and the officers and men of his command for their excellent military appearance on the occasion alluded to . . . let others excel it if they can."[62]

59   *M.O.S.*, 74, McClellan's report.

60   McClellan MSS (L.C.), letter dated August 1, 1861, from Porter to McClellan; *M.O.S.*, 81.

61   *M.O.S.*, 81; Powell, William H., *The Fifth Army Corps (Army of the Potomac): a Record of Operations during the Civil War in the United States of America, 1861–1865* (New York and London, 1896) 9–10 (Powell, *Fifth Corps*).

62   Fitz John Porter MSS (L.C.) General Orders No. 44, dated November 16, 1861.

Showing that Porter was one of the commanding general's favorites, this order created great jealousy in some of Porter's fellow officers. It must have had some adverse effect on McDowell because his division had been regarded by some, even some close to McClellan, as the best in the army.[63] "The reputation created during its camp on Hall's Hill was always sustained and subsequently extended to other divisions in the Fifth Army Corps of which it formed the basis," wrote Porter after the war. As further evidence of Porter's standing, McClellan assigned him additional responsibility for both Major Albert Myer and his fledgling signal corps and Professor Thaddeus Lowe's balloon corps.

Porter found the prevention of unnecessary destruction of private property and invasion of the rights of properly behaving citizens within Union lines his most difficult tasks. Other officers also confronted this problem. Porter received reports that members of Colonel Henry Wilson's Twenty-second Massachusetts Regiment of Martindale's brigade had stealthily taken outside boards and timbers from a large private dwelling within the camp area for use for floors for officers' tents. The incident had apparently been sanctioned by the colonel. Porter ordered Martindale to tell Wilson he must return the material and restore the house to proper repair. As Porter saw it, "General Martindale repeated my order in such an offensive manner as to induce the Colonel that night to abandon camp and the regiment. He never again put foot within the limits of my command."

Another of Martindale's regiments, the Thirteenth New York Volunteers, commanded by Colonel John Pickell, a graduate of the Military Academy in the Class of 1822 and an officer well advanced in age, camped at Fort Corcoran. Pickell, like Martindale, was annoyed at being commanded by a graduate of the Military Academy many years his junior. Intense abolitionists, they both curried favor with politicians in Congress by misrepresenting Porter's acts.

Colonel Pickell induced a slave to leave his master, a Union lieutenant colonel who resided in Washington, then concealed the fugitive in his house. When the lieutenant colonel appealed to Porter for the return of his servant, Pickell denied all knowledge of the servant and denied that any black man was in his house. Convinced that Pickell had the man and that Martindale had encouraged Pickell's conduct, Porter ordered the colonel to turn the man out of his house. Enticing a servant to leave a master and owner who was loyal to the Union unnecessarily aroused bad feelings and tended to destroy discipline, Porter believed. In addition, Porter said, he

---

63   Comte de Paris MS diary (large diary) (A.N. de la M. de F.) entry dated September 28, 1861.

would not knowingly permit this kind of conduct by one officer toward another. Careful not to order the fugitive returned to his master, Porter stated that, so far as the military was concerned, the black man was free to go where he chose.[64]

Self-confident and fixed in the rightness of his conduct, McClellan did not protect himself from negative appearances. From a successful relationship during his days as a railroad executive, McClellan had selected Judge Thomas Key for his staff while he was in Ohio and brought him east in July. An abolitionist, an advocate of women's rights, and a supporter of emancipation, Key, an extremely conservative Democrat, was believed by many to be pro-slavery.

A native of Kentucky, he had been "imbued from birth with the peculiar traits of the South." Impulsive but also a student of many subjects, he had natural ability which he expanded with a wide and varied store of knowledge. He became a member of the Superior Court of Cincinnati at an early age, where he "won the respect of the bar by the dignity of his bearing, his singular legal acumen, and the courage of his decisions. He procured a position on McClellan's staff, and not only won the confidence of his general, but, from an eccentricity of genius, sought to lose himself in the man. He seemed satisfied in this through the sense of power it gave, and the strong assertion of the peculiar views with which the confidential aide was penetrated," wrote Don Piatt after the war.

"A brilliant conversationalist," Key was a charming companion. "The suggestive mind given to expression in talk is apt to bore the listener with a persistency of views that either weary or offend. Key had the subtle flattery of a listening face. He practiced this on McClellan not because of McClellan's superior rank, for at the

---

64   Porter MSS (L.C.) hw narrative by Porter (n.a., n.d., n.p.) (document no. 1050). The regimental history for the Twenty-second Massachusetts gives no hint of this series of incidents, Parker, John Lord, *History of the Twenty-second Massachusetts Infantry, the Second Company Sharpshooters, and the Third Light Battery in the War of the Rebellion* (Boston, 1887) 44–49 (Parker, *Twenty-second Massachusetts*). The statement about Wilson "abandoning" his regiment was probably Porter's view but, although perceived by Porter, was probably not accurate. Wilson had recruited the regiment and served as its colonel but always with the clear understanding that he would yield command shortly and return to the Senate. Wilson had known from the time he recruited the regiment that he would remain in the Senate and perform his war service as chairman of the Committee on Military Affairs. When the regiment achieved satisfactory organization, training, and assignment, Wilson left the regiment on October 27 and resigned as colonel. Jesse A. Gove, a former captain in the Tenth United States Infantry, a native of New Hampshire, and a graduate of the Norwich Military Academy, took his place. Wilson returned to his civilian responsibilities as a member of the United States Senate and chairman of the Committee on Military Affairs, ibid., 48; *D.A.B.*, 10, pt. 2, 324; Bennett, Edwin Clark, *Musket and Sword, or, Camp, March, and the Firing Line in the Army of the Potomac* (Boston, 1900) 35 (Bennett, *Musket and Sword*). Later occurrences and Porter's general integrity suggest that the incidents took place but were not causally related to Wilson's departure.

time he was only a militia general, having been selected by the Governor of Ohio to organize the State volunteers. It was the practice of Key's life to listen much and talk little . . . Key soon possessed and controlled McClellan without the soldier's being aware of his lost identity."

Behind Key's reserved, sometimes curt, exterior stood an intelligent, thoughtful conversationalist, with broad knowledge of history and many other subjects, the kind of man who appealed strongly to McClellan. During the West Virginia campaign, McClellan asked Key to serve on his staff as a general legal adviser on questions involving civilians and the civil authorities. By his "courage, capacity, readiness, and tact," Don Piatt wrote after the war, Key earned an invitation to go to Washington with the general. Unfortunately, Key gave substance to rumors that McClellan opposed freeing the slaves and favored a negotiated peace to end the war, rather than a crushing victory. Many recognized Key as a man with influence. One of Chase's correspondents wrote, "Judge Key boasts among his friends that his influence is potential just now with Mr. Lincoln in shaping the slavery policy of the administration, and Judge Key everybody knows is as thoroughly pro-slavery as Jeff Davis or the devil could be."[65]

In the eyes of some, McClellan became a Key Democrat with a "strange mixture of abolitionism, states' rights, patriotism, and a love of the South. Key wanted the southern armies defeated and the States recognized as they were before the war. He sought to free the slaves and compensate the masters. He upheld the Government but despised Lincoln, Stanton, and Seward; in a word, he had a deep-seeded contempt for the Administration."

To Piatt, Key was McClellan's "evil genius. He shut him out from the school of generalship based on defeat, that in the end would, probably, have won him success. Looking back, it is astonishing to note the amount of important work accomplished by the man so unknown to history."[66]

McClellan held a peculiar position. A major general in his early thirties, he outranked his contemporaries and all older men except Scott, Fremont, and Halleck.

---

65   McClellan MSS (L.C.) letter dated November 14, 1864, from Burns to McClellan; Chase MSS (L.C.) letter dated December 2, 1861 from Heaton to Chase.

66   Biddle, "Reminiscences of McClellan," in vol. xi, *The United Service*, 468–469 (May, 1894); Piatt, Don, *Memories of the Men who Saved the Union* (New York, 1887) 291–295 (Piatt, *Memories*). In spite of Key's reputation for pro-slavery attitudes, Key was the draftsman and proponent of congressional legislation freeing the slaves in the District of Columbia while Lincoln was attempting to avoid the issue. Niven, *Chase Papers*, diary, 1, 317, entry dated December 12, 1861. After the South surrendered, he favored universal suffrage for the freed slaves. Ibid., 581, entry dated June 28, 1865.

One of his instructors in artillery and cavalry at West Point, Erasmus D. Keyes, was now a mere brigade commander in his army.[67] But for discussion of the most difficult questions, military, civilian, and political, he did not turn to the older, experienced men who had taught him in his youth. He looked to his trusted friends and contemporaries Porter, Smith, and Franklin on military issues and to Key on civilian and political affairs.[68]

67   Keyes, *Fifty Years*, 440.

68   Williams, *Garfield Letters*, 315, memorandum dated October 12, 1862; Piatt, *Memories*, 291–292.

Chapter 9

"Party considerations have and should have no weight. For my part I consider that the Republican Party has ceased to exist. The question now is whether a man is true to his country or not."

—Lincoln expressing his views on officer appointments

The Power to Appoint

cClellan had served notice that a huge military establishment would be necessary to defeat the South and that the main military effort, to be commanded by him, would require a large army. The superb manpower from the generous wellsprings of American manhood satisfied the extraordinary need for men.[1] But the officers? How would they be found? Who should appoint them? Who should promote them?

Of course, Lincoln would participate in the creation of all general officers because he alone had the power to make the nominations and the appointments. Cabinet officers, particularly Seward, Chase, and Cameron, had large suggestive power in the early appointments made by the president.[2] McClellan, and to a lesser extent Scott, had great powers of origination. Powerful senators, representatives, and governors spoke their wishes to Lincoln; and in the circumstances of democratic government they would be heard.

---

1   de Joinville, *Army of the Potomac*, 11.

2   Schuckers, *Chase*, 365, letter dated April 1, 1862, from Chase to n.a.; Wade MSS (L.C.) letters dated May 16, [1861], from Caleb Smith to Cameron and May 16, [1861], from John H. Young to Chase with endorsement by Chase; Lyman Trumble MSS (Library of Congress) letter

In spite of the fact that Lincoln, by law, had the power to nominate, participants in the government did not see him to be omnipotent early in the war: ". . . during the month of March, 1861," wrote Nicolay and Hay after the war, "Lincoln did not know the men who composed his cabinet. Neither, on the other hand, did they know him. He recognized them as governors, senators, and statesmen, while they yet looked upon him as a simple frontier lawyer at most, and a rival to whom chance had transferred the honor they felt to be due themselves. The recognition and establishment of intellectual rank is difficult and slow. Perhaps the first real question of the Lincoln Cabinet was, 'Who is the greatest man?' It is pretty safe to assert that no one—not even he himself—believed it was Abraham Lincoln."[3] At this time no one could say who would "run" the government, what its military policy should be, who would formulate that policy, and who would lead its military forces.

A presidential appointment, which took effect immediately, entitled the officer to assume his appointed rank at once, one star on his shoulder straps for a brigadier general, two stars for a major general, and for both the distinctive two vertical rows of buttons on their uniform jackets. In all respects, including pay and assignment, they held the elevated grade.

But all presidential appointments were subject to the "advice and consent of the Senate." If the Senate failed to confirm before the end of its next regular session, the appointment lapsed; and like Cinderella's carriage at midnight, the unapproved general would revert to his previous rank, in almost all cases that of a colonel. The Senate would apply some bizarre tests to the candidates sent them by Lincoln.

Daniel E. Sickles, a former Democratic representative from New York, recruited five regiments, became a colonel, and was appointed a brigadier general by Lincoln. Although still surrounded by a swirl of controversy, Sickles showed con-

---

dated June 7, 1861, from Allison to Trumble; Dennett, Tyler, ed., *Lincoln and the Civil War in the Diaries and Letters of John Hay*, 3 vols. (New York, 1939) 1, 59, letter dated August 1, 1862, from Nicolay to Hay (Dennett, *Hay Diaries and Letters*). Legislation passed on July 22, 1861, provided for a specific number of additional major and brigadier generals for the volunteers and that "the President shall be authorized to appoint, by and with the advice and consent of the Senate, for the command of the forces provided for in this act, a number of major-generals, not exceeding six, and a number of brigadier-generals, not exceeding eighteen, and the other officers required for the organization of these forces, except the aides-de-camp, who shall be selected by their respective generals from the officers of the Army or volunteer corps." *OR*, ser. 3, vol. 1, 381, Act passed July 22, 1861, quoted in General Orders No. 49, War Dept., Adjt General's Office, dated August 3, 1861.

3 *N&H*, 3, 443.

siderable ability as a brigade commander; but when his commission came before the Senate, his former colleagues in the federal legislature did not approve it; and he reverted to colonel in 1862.[4]

After Bull Run and the passage of the volunteer bill, the president sent letters to Cameron asking for Senate confirmation of John Pope, Jacob D. Cox, John Schenck, George McCall, and Philip Kearny as brigadier generals. Butler, Banks, and Dix he wanted confirmed as major generals.[5] But he hardly ever made original appointments. Not that he lacked the power. Although he had the most power of all, he did not use it to initiate except in unusual individual cases. And why should he? All his life he had been a lawyer and a politician. Except for the "Train Gang" and the politicians, he knew few of the men in the pools of candidates for promotion to general officer.[6] He made most of his appointments at the suggestion or insistence of others.

From the pool of politicians who wished military rank, Lincoln found a polyglot group without any identifying characteristics. Nor did he find them all "reliable" Republicans. Many Democrats of great stature wished to serve their country, enhance their political careers with battlefield exploits, or be swept along by the current of the great national event of the nineteenth century. A political career of

4   Oliver Otis Howard MSS (Bowdoin College) letter dated August 15, 1861, from Howard to his wife; Dwight Family MSS (M.H.S.) letter dated 1861 from William Dwight to family; Francis Channing Barlow MSS (Massachusetts Historical Society) letter dated July 24, 1862, from Barlow to "R"; *D.A.B.*, 8, pt. 1, 150–151; Warner, Ezra J., *Generals in Blue, Lives of the Union Commanders* (Baton Rouge, 1964) 446–447 (Warner, *Generals in Blue)*; Swanberg, W. A., *Sickles the Incredible* (New York, 1956) 132–140 (Swanberg, *Sickles)*; Pinchon, Edgcomb, *Dan Sickles, Hero of Gettysburg and Yankee King of Spain* (New York, 1945) 134–137 (Pinchon, *Sickles)*.

5   Basler, *Lincoln's Collected Works*, 4, 463, letter dated July 29, 1861, from Lincoln to Cameron.

6   Jefferson Davis had a distinct advantage over his Union counterpart in the selection and promotion of general officers because he had graduated from West Point in the Class of 1828, served in the Regular Army, commanded a regiment of volunteer infantry in the Mexican War, and become personally acquainted with the abilities of many officers who would be chosen to lead the Confederacy's brigades, divisions, corps, and armies. *D.A.B.*, 3, pt. 1, 123. Early in the war he wrote one of his correspondents, "The gentlemen named in your letter, in connection with the position of Brigadier General, I am happy to see combine these requisites, in addition to their other qualifications. Some of these gentlemen are known to me personally, and I know them to be worthy of the high praise which you bestow. Such is General Zollicoffer, for instance. Gen. Cheatham I had the honor of serving with in Mexico, and I have the highest appreciation both of his personal worth, and of his military ability. The other gentlemen are all more or less known to me by reputation." Crist, Lynda Lasswell, and Dix, Mary Seaton, co-eds., *The Papers of Jefferson Davis*, 10 vols. (incomplete) (Baton Rouge and London, 1971–) 7, 246–247, letter dated July 17, 1861, from Davis to Harris (Crist, *Davis Papers)*.

decades had introduced Lincoln to many of these men. Others he knew by reputation and standing. Their claims for rank were, at least in the early period of the war, irresistible. In his appointments from the pool of political figures Lincoln acted in a bipartisan if not an apolitical manner. Early in the war he expressed his opinion on this subject. "Party considerations have and should have no weight. For my part I consider that the Republican Party has ceased to exist. The question now is simply whether a man is true to his country or not."[7]

Lincoln's statement had a truly American ring to it. Promotion should be guided by nonpartisan merit, not by political affiliation, family prestige, or any other unearned personal characteristic. But in this war, without precedents or guiding principles, the men at the top, Lincoln on the political height and McClellan on the military height, felt compelled to heed other voices and continuously suffered bites by partisan parasites. One of Senator Wade's correspondents expressed it clearly—and bitterly. "One subject that gives the plain thinking men of our State some uneasiness is, the manner in which the President has disposed of the offices in his power to bestow, both civil and military. Many men in this State have Federal offices the gift of Mr. Lincoln who have no sympathy with his Administration whatever, and would rejoice at any misfortune that would befall it, so also with the military. Has Mr. Lincoln established the precedent that a man to get an appointment under his administration has to be a semisecessionist? . . . The true Union men everywhere are the same in sentiment. That sentiment is as broad as the Continent. *If slavery stands in the way of the restoration of the Union destroy it.* This is alone the true test of Unionism. . . ."[8]

The second group known personally to the president was the "Train Gang." Elected from Illinois, Lincoln had to travel to the capital in February of 1861 for his inauguration. The train trip, which lasted approximately twelve days, was not thought to be free of danger. Many rumors, reports, and actual threats had followed on the heels of the election. For this train ride the president-elect had a military escort, but not the usual privates and non-commissioned officers. The military members of the entourage were experienced and promising officers, Colonel Edwin Vose Summer, Colonel Ward H. Lamon, Colonel Elmer E. Ellsworth, Major David Hunter, and Captain John Pope. Each of these men had some prior connection with the president-elect, and they could not have worsened their case for promotion by

---

7   Lincoln MSS (L.C.) letter dated November 13, 1861, from John T. Doyle to Montgomery Blair (limited indirect discourse converted to direct).

8   Benjamin F. Wade MSS (Library of Congress) letter dated March 2, 1862, from Smith to Wade.

service on this long ride. If nothing else, their names on a later list of recommendations for promotion would stir a favorable memory in Lincoln's mind.[9]

In the last months of 1860 Lincoln had exchanged letters with David Hunter, and he ultimately made Hunter part of the Train Gang. On inauguration day, Hunter wrote the president that he would like to command in Washington under Scott. He felt familiar enough to suggest that he be given the brigadier-general's star made available by the dismissal of David Twiggs for treasonable conduct in Texas. He was as old as Sumner, Hunter wrote to Lincoln, and "a better soldier." Besides, Sumner was a Douglas Democrat, while he had been "persecuted on account of my love for Freedom and the Whig and Republican parties." Hunter's political supporters, including Congressman Isaac N. Arnold of Illinois, petitioned for his promotion. Arnold, too, noted that Hunter had been slighted "on account of his devotion to the Whig and Republican party." In the weeks after the inauguration, Hunter served briefly in the White House.[10] Through these activities he and Lincoln came to know each other well. In the numerous promotions occurring on May fourteenth, Hunter became colonel of the Third United States Cavalry; on May 17, brigadier general of volunteers; and on August 13, 1861, one of the few early promotions to major general.[11]

A member of the Train Gang, a West Point graduate in the class of 1842, and the inventor of the "fly" closed by buttons on men's trousers, Brigadier General John Pope came from a state with large claims for promotion of its "favorite sons." With political connections to the president through his father, a judge, Pope exemplified the Scott Rule by his early promotion from captain to brigadier general.[12] At his headquarters in St. Louis on August 23, he received a visit from Orville Hickman Browning, a newly elected Illinois senator returning from the emergency session called by Lincoln.

9   Donald, *Lincoln*, 273–279, esp. 273; generally Searcher, Victor, *Lincoln's Journey to Greatness: A Factual Account of the Twelve Day Inaugural Trip* (Philadelphia, 1960).

10   Lincoln MSS (L.C.), letter dated March 4, 1861, from Hunter to Lincoln; NA Offs' MS Rpts (Hunter); Miller, David A., Jr., *Lincoln's Abolitionist General: The Biography of David Hunter* (Columbia, 1997) 51–54, quoting the petition, among other things (Miller, *Hunter*); Warner, *Generals in Blue*, 243–244; Heitman, *Historical Register*, 1, 557; *D.A.B.*, 1, pt. 1, 368, (Arnold); ibid., 5, pt. 1, 400 (Hunter).

11   Heitman, *Historical Register*, 1, 557.

12   Cullum, George W., *Biographical Register of the Officers and Graduates of the U.S. Military Academy at West Point, N.Y. from its Establishment, March 16, 1862, to the Army Reorganization of 1866–1867*, 2 vols. (New York, 1868) 2, no. 1127 (*Cullum*); Warner, *Generals in Blue*, 376–377; *D.A.B.*,8, pt. 1, 76–77; Schutz, Wallace J., and Trenarry, Walter N., *Abandoned by Lincoln, a Military Biography of General John Pope* (Urbana, Illinois, 1990); Hassler, Warren W., Jr., *Commanders of the Army of the Potomac*, 56–57, 62–63 (Baton Rouge, Louisiana, 1962).

Pope argued that the Illinois regiments should be brigaded together and that Illinois should have a major general appointed from its candidates. Opposing the president's order sending David Hunter west to command the Illinois regiments, he slyly told Browning that, although Hunter was "a fine officer," the Illinois troops would refuse to obey him and that Governor Richard Yates of Illinois should be given the two stars. Browning was not fooled. "My own opinion," he wrote that night in his diary, "is that he is fomenting dissatisfaction with a view to getting an appointment as Major Genl himself."[13]

One area in which Lincoln apparently exercised more power and influence than others was promotion in the Regular Army. Commissions in the Regular Army and the volunteers were not the same. At the end of the war, the volunteer army would disappear, and the volunteer officers would disappear with it. The tiny Regular Army, which would have far fewer slots for general officers, would continue. Early in the war Regular Army rank was often awarded parallel to and simultaneously with volunteer rank.[14] In May, McClellan, Fremont, and Henry Halleck had been appointed major generals in the volunteer service. McDowell, Mansfield, and others had been promoted to brigadier general; and Sherman, Heintzelman, Franklin, and many others had been made colonels. On July 29, 1861, nominations of McClellan and Fremont as major generals and Mansfield, McDowell, and Rosecrans as brigadier generals in the Regular Army went to the Senate for confirmation.[15]

To the outside world the president had the supreme appointive power. He received numerous letters requesting this or that rank for an individual or supporting this or that candidacy.[16] In the early months the task of sifting the many requests was too much even for Lincoln's earnest diligence. The personnel or "human resources" department in the army was, and is today, the adjutant general's office. After a short meeting at the White House with Captain James B. Fry, the officer in charge of the

---

13   Pease, Theodore Calvin, and Randall, James G., eds., *The Diary of Orville Hickman Browning*, 2 vols. (Springfield, 1925) 1 (1850–1864), 497, entry dated August 23, 1861 (Pease, *Browning Diary*).

14   Basler, *Lincoln's Collected Works*, 4, 370, memorandum dated circa May 14, 1861, by Lincoln to n.a.

15   Lincoln MSS (L.C.), letter dated July 29, 1861, from Cameron to Lincoln.

16   Williams, *Lincoln and his Generals*, 8–9. This long-standing work by one of America's best historians continues to have the best grasp of the subject, even though a recent work has criticized and disagreed with it, Cohen, Eliot; *Supreme Command: Soldiers, Statesmen, and Leadership in Wartime*, 16 (New York, 2002). Although Williams's book has a few minor factual errors, they do not impair its great value, and many of its interesting conclusions continue today to be worthy of recognition, even if also of debate.

appointment branch of the adjutant general's office, the president turned to the vast quantity of inquiries he had not been able to consider.

"You are in charge of the Appointment Office," he said to Fry. "I have here a bushel basket full of applications for officers in the Army. I have tried to examine them all, but they have increased so rapidly that I have got behind and may have neglected some. I will send them all to your office. Overhaul them, bring only those that require further action before the Secretary of War, and file the others."

The basket of papers arrived. Fry found its contents dotted with notes, comments, and queries. On one slip of paper he found a memorandum in Lincoln's handwriting about the wife of a major of the Regular Army who had called on him. "She wants her husband made a brigadier general. She is a saucy little woman, and I think she would torment me till I have to do it.—A. L." Fry returned this note remarking that he supposed Lincoln would probably not want it placed in the official files.[17] She was not the only woman to approach the president on her husband's behalf.[18]

Most of Lincoln's few personal appointments were whimsical initiations of the process. He could be struck at the moment that someone should be given a certain rank or command. Joseph Hooker, an undistinguished twenty-ninth of fifty in the West Point class of 1837, had come to Washington from California and watched the Battle of Bull Run as a civilian. His efforts to obtain a commission failed when they reached General Scott, who had a strong animosity because of Hooker's testimony in Scott's court of inquiry at the end of the Mexican War. Briefly, Hooker despaired and decided to return to California. He called on the president to pay his respects before departure, probably with the hope that he might be able to remove the stall from his military career. General Cadwalader introduced him as "Captain Hooker."

Lincoln prepared to say the usual brief pleasantries before ending the conversation, but Hooker firmly seized the opening Cadwalader had given him.

17 Lincoln MSS (L.C.) memorandum dated August 23, 1862; Fry, James B., *Military Miscellanies*, 280–281. Williams suggests that Lincoln enjoyed being harassed by women for promotions for their men, *Lincoln and His Generals*, 9.

18 Lincoln MSS (L.C.) memorandum dated April, 1861, about Adam Slemmer; John G. Nicolay MSS (Library of Congress) letter dated May 23, 1861, from Nicolay to Therena; Andrew Atkinson Humphreys MSS (Pennsylvania Historical Society) letter dated May 1, 1862, from Humphreys to his wife. For a peculiar but accurate assessment of any president's appeal to women, even though a scoundrel, see Edward Otho Cresap Ord MSS (Stanford University) letter n.d. [but end of December], 1861, from Ord to Molly [letter no. 75].

"Mr. President, my friend makes a mistake. I am not 'Captain Hooker' but was once Lieutenant Colonel Hooker of the Regular Army. I was lately a farmer in California; but since the rebellion broke out, I have been trying to get into the service, but I find I am not wanted. I am about to return home, but before going I was anxious to pay my respects to you and to express my wishes for your personal welfare and success in quelling this rebellion."

He saw that the president was about to speak and could not restrain a prompt display of his character. "I was at Bull Run the other day, Mr. President," he said, "and it is no vanity in me to say I am a damned sight better general than you had on that field."[19]

Lincoln seized Hooker's hand and shook it. He begged the former colonel to sit, began a social conversation, and told one of his usual stories. He did not assess Hooker as a braggart but as self-confident and thought him fully competent to make good on his words. Hooker should delay his return to California, he said.

A few days later Lincoln asked McClellan for his opinion of Hooker. McClellan and Hooker were very different men. Restrained as always, McClellan objectively told the president that Hooker had earned a strong reputation in Mexico but had "fallen" after he moved to California. He scrupulously added that he had no personal knowledge about the California events and that the president should talk to officers who had served there. A few days later Lincoln, impressed with Hooker's self-assurance, appointed him a brigadier general.[20]

---

19 *Harper's Magazine*, vol. 31, 642; Warner, *Generals in Blue*, 234; Mattocks, Brigadier-General Charles P., "Major-General Joseph Hooker" in *Broadfoot MOLLUS Maine*, 18, 211–212 (Wilmington, 1993); Spaller, Roger J., ed., *Dictionary of American Military Biography*, 3 vols. (Westport, 1984) 2, 487–488 (Spaller, *D.A.M.B.*); Heitman, *Historical Register*, 540; *Cullum*, 1, no. 909; Hebert, Walter H., *Fighting Joe Hooker* (New York, 1944) 49–50 (Hebert, *Hooker*); Shanks, William F. G., *Personal Recollections of Distinguished Generals*, 182–183 (New York, 1866). Of the several different accounts of this conversation with Lincoln, including the accounts in *Harper's Magazine* and *Broadfoot MOLLUS Maine*, none by an eyewitness, the description by Shanks has more information and more collaterally corroborated information than any other and has been adopted here.

20 *M.O.S.*, 161. For reasons that are unclear the chronological facts in this period of Hooker's career are recited differently by various authors. Heitman, *Historical Register*, 1, 540, notes that he was commissioned brigadier-general on May 17, 1861; and *Cullum*, 1, no. 919, agrees. Hassler, in *Commanders of the Army of the Potomac*, 127, agrees with the date but states that Hooker visited Bull Run two months later as a "private observer," in effect, a brigadier-general without a command. McClellan's conversation with Lincoln, *M.O.S.*, 161, speaks as if Hooker had been a civilian at Bull Run and became a general afterwards. Hassler in Spaller *D.A.M.B.* says he was a civilian at Bull Run, 2, 488. Warner has him commissioned brigadier-general on August 6, 1862, to rank from May 17 (presumably 1862), *Generals in Blue*, 234. This must be a mistake in a task of monumental research or, as the text makes more likely, a typographical error. The most logical sequence is Bull Run as a civilian, McClellan conversation while a civilian, and appointment to Brigadier-General on August 6, 1861, to rank from May 17, 1861.

The appointment, promotion, and assignment of Republican Senator Edward Donald Baker was an excellent example of Lincoln's unguided, uninformed ad hoc promotions. And an excellent example Baker was, as well, of the politician who did not work his way through experience up the ladder of rank but went at once to a top rung. Baker's courageous demonstration of the deficiencies in his skill and training matched those of Schenk. Baker, however, had paid the ultimate price for his poor performance while Schenk still had other opportunities before him. The larger questions had not been answered when Lincoln appointed both Baker and Schenck. Did they have the knowledge of the Regular Army captains and lieutenants promoted under the Scott Rule? Did they know enough to exercise the discretion and judgment of a general officer acting independently in a battle situation? For others time would tell, but for both Baker and Schenck it had been told at once.

Members of the cabinet, members of Congress, and others who had direct access to Lincoln helped their causes either on the spur of the moment or by carefully devised lobbying. They, too, benefited from random, whimsical appointments. In early October, First Lieutenant William W. Averell, twenty-sixth in the West Point Class of 1851, waited in the office of Assistant Secretary of War Colonel Thomas Scott to deliver a report. A group of citizens arrived to complain about the depredations of Colonel William H. Young's Kentucky Cavalry Regiment, technically the Third Pennsylvania Cavalry Regiment, a unit well known for its unruly and undisciplined behavior.

"I wish to God I could find a Colonel who could take care of that regiment and make it behave properly!" said Scott.

The report brushed from his mind, Averell stepped forward immediately and said, "Colonel, I am your man."

"Are you in earnest, young man?" asked the assistant secretary.

"Perfectly so."

That same day Averell received an order granting him an indefinite leave of absence from the Regular Army to take command of the Third Pennsylvania Cavalry and a short time later a commission as colonel.[21]

---

21   Eckert, Edward K., and Nicolas J. Amata, eds., *Ten Years in the Saddle: The Memoir of William Woods Averell, 1851–1862* (San Rafael and London, 1958) 322 (Eckert, *Averell Memoirs*); Heitman, *Historical Register*, 1, 175; *Cullum*, 2, no. 1702; Bates, *Hist. Penn. Vols.*, 3, 360. Some confusion surrounds the dates for the incident and the commissioning. Undoubtedly working from the order quoted in the text of his memoirs, Averell dated everything October 7. *Heitman* and *Cullum*, op. cit., record the promotion to Colonel in August 1861, which would place the conversation also in August. Given the history of the organization of the regiment, described in Committee, *History of the Third Pennsylvania Cavalry, Sixtieth Regiment Pennsylvania Volunteers, in the American Civil War 1861–1865*, 16 (Philadelphia, 1905) (commission issued by Governor Curtin under date of August 23, 1861, and muster into service at that rank on October 12, p. 17), the regimental history probably has it right.

Leaving aside the spur-of-the-moment appointments like Hooker and Averell, the most common appointment by the president was a man who combined military experience, if not a West Point education, with support from powerful political sources. Isaac Ingalls Stevens, the Democratic territorial governor who had been McClellan's superior in the search for the passage through the rugged Cascade Mountains, exemplified these men. In 1861, Stevens had left the West Coast on an eastbound steamer to serve his country. From the time he arrived in the East he marshaled support from his many influential friends and family members. In August, before he faced the mutiny in the Highlanders, his kinsman E. H. Hazard had enlisted the support of both Governor Sprague and Lieutenant Governor Arnold of Rhode Island. Governor Andrew of Massachusetts expressed his desire to assist Stevens' campaign for a brigadier-generalcy.[22] On August 15, 1861, T. G. Hazard wrote "My dear Brother" to report about letters that were being written to the president and to describe other efforts by Stevens' supporters. "Gov Sprague expressed himself warmly in your favor for a Brigadiership. The recommendation was drawn up for a Major Generalship but altered at the Governor's suggestion because he knew the Government did not intend to appoint any more of that grade . . . Col. Lawton intimated that if you took command of a R.I. regiment the Gov would soon make it a brigade. I think the result of the battle in Virginia has been a decided loss of confidence in the administration, and a determination that the country shall not be ruined through the imbecility or corruption of the Government. I should think if you could take advantage of this feeling by getting a recommendation from the leading men of New England backed up by such other influences you might command, that it must have the desired effect."

Oliver Stevens obtained the support of Senator Henry Wilson of Massachusetts and his signature on a petition.[23] Additional support by Cyrus Aldrich and Morton S. Wilkinson of Minnesota, and Senator John P. Hale of New Hampshire included visits to the president.[24] A written summary of Stevens' qualifications and background went to Secretary of State William H. Seward.[25]

---

22   Stevens Family MSS (University of Washington) letter dated August 8, 1861, from E. H. Hazard to Stevens; letter dated August 9, 1861, from Lieutenant Governor Arnold to Stevens; and telegrams dated August 10, 1861, and August 15, 1861, from Governor John A. Andrew to Stevens.

23   Stevens MSS (Univ. Wash.) letter dated August 15, 1861, from Oliver Stevens to Stevens.

24   Stevens MSS (Univ. Wash.) letters dated August 28, 1861, from Cyrus Aldrich to Stevens, and September 2, 1861, from John P. Hale to Stevens.

25   Stevens MSS (Univ. Wash.) letter dated September 28, 1861, from Aiken to Stevens.

Before he crossed the Potomac River with the Highlanders, Stevens spoke to Lincoln about his rank and received an assurance that he would be promoted to brigadier general within a week. Daily, he expected the commission and an assignment to command the regiments he had trained. A short time later, three of his regiments were reassigned to a brigade created for another officer; and he was given several newer, less experienced regiments as replacements.[26] He was "deeply hurt and disappointed" by this, his son wrote years later.

In September, Lincoln wrote a short note to McClellan, "May I not now appoint Stevens a Brig. Genl? I wish to do it."[27] Always slow to forgive, McClellan had probably not forgotten that Stevens had embarrassed him by arranging for a junior officer to outperform him in the hunt for a railroad passage through the Cascades. In all probability both Stevens and McClellan found qualities they could readily dislike in each other and carried them forward from this period.

"Colonel Stevens had better remain in command of the Highlanders some time longer," McClellan wrote in response to the president's note. "They are not yet reduced to proper discipline and it would be unsafe to take away their colonel at present."[28]

Stevens' commission languished. To him, the unexplained delay and "McClellan's significant and diverted demeanor" implied an intention to deny him promotion. Angry at his treatment and the promotion of his juniors, Stevens began to consider other options. He would resign, a contemplation reported to Seward and by him to Lincoln.[29] He would relinquish command of the brigade and devote himself to making the Highlanders the best-disciplined, best-drilled regiment in the army. It would have a devotion that would make it irresistible. It would fight, he fantasized, like Cromwell's Ironsides.

A man of small height and slight build, Stevens dressed carelessly with no regard for his personal appearance. But he showed excellent talents as an organizer and administrator and worked his command well. Genial and outspoken, he had strong likes and dislikes, being a "warm friend and a bitter, unrelenting hater."[30]

---

26   Stevens, *Stevens*, 2, 332–333.

27   Original in McClellan MSS (L.C.) n.d. but dated September by the curator. It is also, of course, reprinted in Basler, *Lincoln's Collected Works*, 4, 504.

28   Stevens, *Stevens*, 2, 334.

29   Lincoln MSS (L.C.) letter dated September 25, 1861, from Aiken to Seward.

30   Leasure, Daniel, "Personal Observations and Experiences in the Pope Campaign in Virginia" in *Broadfoot MOLLUS Minnesota*, 26, 141.

Recognizing the president's great weight of care and responsibility, Stevens feared Lincoln had forgotten his assurance to him. Before embarking on a drastic course, he decided to make one last try for his star. He would send his son Hazard to see the president. Hazard was to say that, although several weeks had passed since Stevens had been assured he would soon be appointed a general officer, he had heard nothing.

Hazard rode into Washington and presented himself at the White House. Although someone took his card, he did not see the president and could not attract the attention of anyone who might help. The ante-rooms were crowded with applicants and callers. He waited. Hours passed. He noticed a black messenger entering the president's office from time to time with various cards. At last he accosted the messenger to beg for assistance in obtaining an interview. He said that he had a message of great importance. The messenger attempted to ignore him. His father, Colonel Isaac I. Stevens, he said, had sent him expressly to deliver the message to the president.

"You mean Governor Stevens?" the man asked. "Is Governor Stevens your father? I used to see him here often in Mr. Buchanan's time, and I am glad to do anything in the world I can for him. I'll take your name in the next time, and you shall see the president if I can fix it."

A short time later, the black man took Hazard to the inner office, where Lincoln received him in a kindly and fatherly way. Young Stevens was at once at ease. He delivered his father's message.

"Tell your father that I have not forgotten my promise, nor him—that I should have had his appointment before this if it had not been for General McClellan." Lincoln explained McClellan's response, then said, "But tell your father that it shall no longer be delayed."

The president took a small blank card and wrote a line on it directing the preparation of Stevens' appointment as brigadier general. He handed it to Stevens' son with instructions to take it to the War Department and deliver it to the adjutant general. Young Stevens complied, then spurred his horse into a gallop to deliver the news.

On September 28, Isaac Stevens became a brigadier general and on the following day received formal assignment to command the Third Brigade of Smith's division, which consisted of his original Highlanders regiment and the three new regiments already under his command.[31] But even in the Stevens appointment, Lin-

---

31 Stevens, *Stevens*, 2, 334. Some colloquy converted from indirect to direct discourse. The chronology is not clear and has been reconstructed in the most logical sequence.

coln did not thwart his young major-general. A short time after appointing Stevens, he transferred him to a force being collected for attacks on the Confederate coast.[32]

Others, like George Gordon Meade and Andrew Atkinson Humphreys, would also find early promotion through a similar combination of West Point education, military experience, and political influence, the influence perhaps even arranged by their wives.[33] A combination of identifiable characteristics would give any candidate a strong chance for high rank. European military experience, leadership in an American community of foreigners, political service to Lincoln and the Republicans, and personal acquaintance with the president made a commission for Carl Schurz a virtual certainty. Born in a small town on the Rhine near Köln, Schurz was headed for a professorship in history at the University of Bonn when his eloquence, natural leadership ability, and alliance with an intellectual leader of the struggle for democratic institutions led him to become a lieutenant and staff officer in the revolutionary army of 1848 during its final, unsuccessful battles against the reactionary Prussian army.

From his last post, a fortress under siege, he escaped through sewers after its surrender to the Prussians and fled his homeland for Switzerland. But the Prussians captured his intellectual mentor, sentenced him to life imprisonment, and incarcerated him in a fortified prison in Spandau. Although proscribed, Schurz reentered Germany, arranged the escape of his professor, rushed him to the coast, and caught a schooner for England.

Ultimately leaving for the United States, Schurz settled in Wisconsin, where he became a master of the English language, a lawyer, a superb public speaker in his new tongue, an abolitionist, an active member of the Republican Party, a repeated candidate for public office, and a supporter of Abraham Lincoln and Henry Wilson in the campaigns of the late 1850s. Although he and the Wisconsin delegation voted for Seward until the end of the 1860 Republican convention, Schurz campaigned vigorously and effectively for Lincoln among both native-born and foreign Americans.[34] On April 11, 1861, the day before the Confederates opened fire on Fort Sumter, Schurz wrote Lincoln that he had four regiments ready to be sent to Washington.[35] Two days later Lincoln sent Cameron an endorsement stating that the four

---

32   Stevens, *Stevens*, 2, 333–336, 341.

33   Humphreys MSS (P.H.S.) letter dated May 1, 1862, from Humphreys to "Cherie," his wife; Cleaves, Freeman, *Meade of Gettysburg* (Norman, 1960) 53–54 (Cleaves, *Meade*).

34   Schurz, Carl, *The Reminiscences of Carl Schurz*, 3 vols. (New York, 1907–1908) generally vols. 1 and 2 (Schurz, *Reminiscences*); *D.A.B.*, 8, pt. 2, 466–467.

35   Lincoln MSS (L.C.) letter dated April 11, 1861, from Schurz to Lincoln.

German regiments wished to be brigaded together with Schurz at their head. The president thought it should be done.[36] That same day he wrote to Schurz, "Get the German Brigade in shape, and, at their request, you shall be Brigadier General."[37]

Dominated by a desire to serve in the military, Schurz faced temporary frustration. Lincoln recognized his broad range of talents and decided that he could do more for his adopted country by serving as ambassador to Spain. But Schurz was already raising the First New York Cavalry Regiment, which he expected to command.[38] He wrote his wife, "I almost regret being a foreign minister. If I were only one of the multitude who could follow their impulses! Excuse me, wifey. I cannot get rid of these reflections, silly as they probably are."[39] He obtained a three-month leave of absence from his diplomatic assignment, had his unpleasant conversation about cavalry with Scott, then dutifully left for Madrid, where he spent his free time studying tactics and military campaigns.[40]

Even though his experience in 1848 had probably taught him little and he had shown no military capacity beyond raw courage, Schurz could not shake the desire for service in the field. In December he tendered his resignation as ambassador.[41] After the turn of the year he returned to the United States and met at once with the president. Following a discussion of many subjects, Schurz turned to his personal desires. He repeated his earlier statement that he wished to end his position as minister to Spain. He found it intolerable, he said, to lead a life of ease and luxury and comparative idleness while the Republic fought for its life and most of the men his age held posts of danger. Now that relations with Spain had reached a satisfactory condition and he had accomplished his business of reporting on public sentiment in Europe and lending a hand to quicken the anti-slavery current, he was anxious to enter the army.[42]

36   Basler, *Lincoln's Collected Works*, 4, 367, endorsement dated May 13, 1861, from Lincoln to Cameron.

37   Basler, *Lincoln's Collected Works*, 4, 368, letter dated May 13, 1861, from Lincoln to Schurz.

38   *D.A.B.*, 8, pt. 2, 467.

39   Schafer, Joseph, ed. and trans., *Intimate Letters of Carl Schurz, 1841–1869 Publications of the State Historical Society of Wisconsin Collections, vol. 1130* (Madison, 1929) 253, letter dated April 17, 1861, from Schurz to his wife, and, 255, letter dated April 30, 1861, from Schurz to his wife (Schafer, *Schurz Letters*).

40   *D.A.B.*, 8, pt. 2, 467.

41   Lincoln MSS (L.C.) letter dated December 23, 1861, from Schurz to Lincoln.

42   Schurz, *Reminiscences*, 1, 329. *D.A.B.* has Schurz returning to the United States in January, but Schurz dates his return precisely in his memoirs (the day after the battle between the *Monitor* and the *Virginia*, therefore March 10) and his correspondence with Lincoln in the Lincoln MSS (L.C.) tends to confirm the March date.

He thought he could be particularly helpful in the army on the issue of abolition, a concept the conservative, Democratic officers from the Regular Army would not support. To Lincoln he wrote, "We shall soon have new issues upon us. Party-machinations and the spirit of many of the leaders of the army will throw great difficulties in your way. Your endeavors of bringing about an amicable solution of *the* great question are now counteracted by many of our generals who repudiate your principles and your policy. It is for this reason that I propose to go into the army. But for this reason also I naturally desired to have a sphere of action and influence sufficiently large. This is what I gave you clearly to understand in the first conversation we had on this subject . . . In no case can you have supposed that the mere title of a general can have any charm for me. It has long since ceased to be a distinction. I am proud enough to think that an empty appellation cannot elevate me in the eyes of the people nor in my own."[43]

As the days passed, Schurz, like Stevens, became restless with the silence emanating from the White House. So did his wife. In a chance meeting with Secretary Chase she dutifully stated her husband's military desires even though she personally opposed them. She described the conversations between her husband and the president about his resignation and the position he should have in the army. Chase offered to help. In response to a letter from Lincoln, Schurz had offered his unconditional resignation as a minister and reserved to himself the right to decline appointment as a general if Lincoln could find no suitable position in the army for him. Schurz had asked the president to dispose of the matter as soon as possible. Since then, he had waited patiently for an answer that did not come. "This state of uncertainty," his wife wrote to Chase, "is most painful to both of us, especially as the recent victories of our army make it probable that the war will soon be ended." Her husband, resistant to her pressing, refused to write Lincoln again because he had nothing new to say after his last letter. "My own private wish," she continued to Chase, "is to go back to Europe. Mr. Schurz desired very strongly to enter the army and to remain here, but since things have changed so much for the better in the field as well as in politics and also since his health has become so uncertain I think he also will reconcile himself to the idea."[44]

Lincoln knew that Schurz had gone abroad reluctantly. He had already considered this and had discussed it with Seward. The secretary of state, more than satisfied with Schurz's diplomatic efforts, which had established a good position with the Spanish government, wanted him to return to Madrid.

---

43   Lincoln MSS (L.C.) letter dated April 23, 1862, from Schurz to Lincoln.

44   Chase MSS (L.C.) letter dated May 29, 1862, from Mrs. Schurz to Chase.

Lincoln asked Schurz if he would not consider the matter for a week or two or longer and also discuss it with Seward.

Schurz felt he could not refuse this request. He visited a complimentary Seward, who invited Schurz and his wife to dinner. The secretary of state strongly urged him not to give up the ambassadorship.

A short time after this meeting Schurz decided, yet again, that he must go to the field. He waited a reasonable time to avoid appearing to treat Lincoln's request lightly,[45] then, about the time his wife wrote Chase, renewed his request for a commission.[46]

Lincoln responded, "Well I hope you have not forgotten that you are giving up a large salary and a distinguished and comfortable place to take one that pays little and will bring you plenty of discomfort and danger. Have you talked the matter over with that handsome, dear wife of yours?"

"Yes," replied Schurz. "She thought it was pretty hard, but she is a good patriot."

"If she agrees, then I do," replied Lincoln. "I expected you to come to this decision, but I will send your name to the Senate with the next batch of brigadiers, and I trust we can find you a suitable command."[47]

A staff officer who met Schurz after he had taken his command saw a tall, thin man with a pale complexion, a wide forehead, a red moustache, sharp hazel eyes, glasses, and a manner that seemed effeminate. The officer considered him "a visionary, itching philanthropist and philosopher such as disturbed society everywhere with their restless conceits and babblings."[48]

---

45   Schurz, *Reminiscences*, 1, 329.

46   Lincoln MSS (L.C.) letter dated May 22, 1862, from Schurz to Lincoln.

47   Schurz, *Reminiscences*, 1, 330.

48   Eby, Cecil D., Jr., ed., *A Virginia Yankee in the Civil War—the Diary of David Hunter Strother* (Chapel Hill, 1961) 74, entry dated August 7, 1862 (Eby, *Strother's Diary*).

Chapter 10

"When you reflect that there are not more than twenty such Republican officers in the U.S. Army, it is time that those who have been true to their principles under the opposing circumstances surrounding them should be remembered."

—William E. Doubleday to Senator Chandler

The Power of McClellan and the Congress

$\mathcal{U}$nder all circumstances the Regular Army would dominate the lists of higher-ranking officers, brigadier generals and major generals. Lincoln would consistently find in its men the experience and qualities necessary for leading larger commands and conducting independent operations. A tiny manpower pool it was and one with no ability to increase its numbers. The Regular Army of 1861 had no Army War College, no Command and General Staff School, and no program for graduate degrees at great universities. Nor did it harbor many general officers.

Aside from Winfield Scott, a brevet lieutenant general, only three other general officers existed: Edwin Vose Sumner, successor to Robert E. Lee as commanding officer of the Second United States Cavalry, then commander of the Department of the West, and recent appointee to fill the gap created when the disloyal David E. Twiggs was cashiered; William Selby Harney, a successful leader in the Mexican War and commander of the Department of the West but a man whose efforts to be neutral in St. Louis had caused doubts about his loyalty; and John Ellis Wool, a highly successful veteran of the Mexican War and the commander of the Department of the East but now a septuagenarian.[1]

In most appointments to the Army of the Potomac, McClellan, as he had told Lieutenant Colonel Pisani at dinner, had the final say in one way or another.[2] In practical effect, McClellan had the most power and, given his active role, he probably contributed more to the pool of general officers who served in the Army of the Potomac throughout the War than any other man. As he described his positive efforts to the secretary of war, "In organizing the Army of the Potomac I have selected general and staff officers with distinct reference to their fitness for the important duties that may devolve upon them. Any change or disposition of such officers without consulting the Commanding General may fatally impair the efficiency of this army and the success of its operations. I therefore earnestly request that in future every general officer appointed upon my recommendation shall be assigned to this army; that I shall have full control of the officers and troops in this department, and that no orders shall be given respecting my command without my being first consulted. It is evident that I cannot otherwise be responsible for the success of our arms."[3]

A rumor, probably without any substance, showed that in the minds of the public McClellan did more to appoint officers for his army than the president. In late August George Templeton Strong recorded in his diary, "McClellan sent in his resignation last week, Lincoln having given him a list of subordinates whose appointment was a political necessity. After twenty-four hours' consideration, Lincoln concluded it would not do to let McClellan resign, and withdrew his list of appointees."[4]

At the dinner held for Prince Jerome Napoleon in early August McClellan had discussed his plans for command of the army. Lieutenant Colonel Pisani, a thoughtful observer, knew that the peacetime American military establishment had no unit larger than a regiment.

"Thus, it is impossible for us to believe," he said to McClellan, "that regiments form organized brigades with titular generals, that brigades constitute divisions,

---

1   *D.A.B.*, 4, pt. 2, 280; 9, pt. 2, 214–215; and 10, pt. 2, 513–514.

2   *M.O.S.*, 160.

3   Sears, *McClellan's Correspondence*, 97, letter dated September 8, 1861, from McClellan to Cameron; Thomas C. H. Smith MSS, MS History of Second Bull Run (Ohio Historical Society) 54–55.

4   Nevins, *Strong Diary*, 3, 179, entry dated August 26, 1861.

and divisions armies, with permanent generals of brigades, divisions, armies, and staffs. It seems to us—until proved differently—that when it is a question of any military operation—such as the occupation of a border, the attack or defense of a position, and even a battle—the general in chief, sometimes even Congress, appoints a general who assumes the temporary command of the regiments assembled for said operations. As a result, American generals pass and pass again in front of our eyes, without ever being able to follow them closely in their campaigns, as we can do with ours, whose military destiny is invariably linked to that of the troops under their titular command."[5]

McClellan well knew that units larger than regiments, created during the Mexican War, had vanished without a trace when the war ended—as had their commanding officers. He probably knew about the long-term critical transformation of the American "nation in arms" from militia to volunteer, a change that had given the war-time forces an even more temporary quality.

In all wars prior to the Mexican War the American military forces were composed of regulars, militia, and volunteers. Because the militia, the military arm of the individual states, existed in peace and war, it had some continuity through longevity. But, by law, the militia could be called into the federal service for three months and no more.

With no life except that created by military necessity and congressional response, the volunteer force had no longevity and no continuity. The government could enroll it for the length of the war whether the term were months or years. At the end of the war, its temporary reason for existence being gone, it would vanish. In the War of 1812, 520,000 men served, of whom only 34,000, approximately 7 percent, were volunteers. But in the Mexican War, reliance on the volunteer had become the rule. Of 104,000 officers and men who served in the Mexican War, 61,000, roughly 59 percent, were volunteers.[6]

Interrupting quickly, McClellan explained to Pisani that he recognized the problem, had a solution in mind, and intended to fix it. He had already given Lincoln and the Congress the first part of the repair program, a list of one hundred men for promotion to brigadier general, of whom sixty already had their commissions,

5   Joyaux, Georges J., ed. and trans., *Prince Napoleon in America: Letters from his Aide-de-Camp by Lieutenant Colonel Camille Ferri Pisani* (Bloomington, 1959) 110–112 (Pisani, *Napoleon in America*).

6   Upton, Emory, *The Military Policy of the United States* (Washington, 1904) 221 (Upton, *Military Policy*); Sellers, James G., *James K. Polk Continentalist 1843–1846*, 2 vols., 2, 438–440 (Princeton, 1966).

fifteen having been selected by McClellan for his army. Half of these men were former Regular Army officers. The brigade organization McClellan considered temporary because he intended to select division commanders from the brigade commanders who "tested" well in their brigade responsibilities. For the future, McClellan believed, a national military force could not be based on militia and volunteer organizations. Nor could it appear and disappear according to unpredictable necessity.

"With this last phase of our military constitution," he concluded, "we will have, at least for the higher organization, an army copied on the most perfect in the world, the French army."[7]

In both its positive and its negative use, McClellan's power sometimes failed altogether. He had his choice of officers for his army in most cases but not in all. An experienced cavalry officer, David S. Harney had been born in 1800, the eighth and last child of Nashville, Tennessee, parents. He entered the Regular Army as a lieutenant after the War of 1812 and progressed rapidly, serving as Scott's chief of cavalry in Mexico. Controversy with Scott, disobedience of orders, and a conviction at court martial did not confound his career. By the outbreak of the Civil War he was one of four general officers in the Regular Army, had a strong reputation for success on the battlefield, and commanded the Department of the West with headquarters in St. Louis. At this point in his career Harney was "a man of imposing physique, over six feet in height, perfectly well made and though getting along in years, as vigorous and erect as an oak . . . [To him] the prospect of an active campaign was like the sound of the trumpet to an old war horse. . . ."

McClellan wrote him, presumed he would disregard their prior disparities in rank and seniority, and tendered him a division in the Army of the Potomac. Offended by McClellan's presumptuous offer, Harney sent a sharp, insulting response: "Your telegram is just received. I consider your conduct to say the least of it exceedingly impertinent."[8]

7   Pisani, *Napoleon in America*, 111–113.

8   *D.A.B.*, 4, pt. 1, 280–281; Warner, *Generals in Blue*, 208–209; Heitman, *Historical Register*, 1, 502; McClellan MSS (L.C.) telegrams dated August 30, 1861, from McClellan to Harney (2) and Harney to McClellan; Drake, Lieutenant Colonel Samuel Adams, "The Old Army in Kansas," in *Broadfoot MOLLUS Massachusetts*, 52, 142–143. McClellan's response to Harney's refusal is printed in Sears, *McClellan's Correspondence*, 91, and the preceding exchange is in ibid., 91–92, n. 1. As the Bard said, "There is a tide in the affairs of men, which taken at flood leads on to . . ." By trying to treat both sides fairly and keep the peace in St. Louis in 1861, Harney aroused concerns about his loyalty, and his nasty rebuff to McClellan was the end of his last opportunity to take the tide at the flood.

George Cadwalader, a prominent Democrat of Philadelphia, a veteran of higher rank from the Mexican War and a participant in Patterson's ill-fated Valley Campaign, had been recommended by many for general officer rank. McClellan opposed a commission for him or, at least, his assignment to the Army of the Potomac. Cadwalader was not nominated till March 28, 1862, and not confirmed until April 25 of that year, when McClellan's power to control appointments had undergone much change.[9]

Already McClellan had advanced his best friends from the old army, Baldy Smith, Fitz John Porter, and William B. Franklin, exemplars of the Scott Rule and now brigadier generals. McClellan trusted and respected all three of them, along with Andrew Porter and one or two others. His schoolmate at West Point, good friend, and former business associate, Ambrose E. Burnside, had become a brigadier general.

In the construction of brigade and division command after Bull Run, those who had served at Bull Run were not ignored. To confirm that they would have larger commands, McClellan informally spoke with several of them while he was making his initial selections for promotion and assignment.[10]

On August 20, 1861, Winfield Scott Hancock arrived in Washington after an emotional departure from his Southern friends in the Regular Army in California and a long trip east. He had known McClellan since West Point and had served with him in Mexico. The general remembered him. He sent Colonel Randolph B. Marcy, his father-in-law and chief of staff, to Hancock with instructions for Hancock to wait at Willard's Hotel until McClellan had time to see him. Marcy was to say that McClellan intended to recommend him to Lincoln for appointment as a brigadier general.[11] At 10 P.M. McClellan summoned Hancock to his headquarters. As he had with his friend Simon Buckner, McClellan talked with Hancock till well past midnight.[12] A short time later the president nominated Hancock, and the Senate confirmed him.[13]

---

9   Basler, *Lincoln's Collected Works*, 4, 525, endorsement dated September 19, 1861, and 525, n. 1.

10   Heintzelman MS diary (large diary) (L.C.) entry dated September 5, 1861; Heintzelman MSS (L.C.) letter dated July 26, 1861, from Heintzelman to Chase (misdated by Heintzelman). *C.C.W.*, 1 (McDowell); Sherman, William Tecumseh, *Personal Recollections of General William T. Sherman*, 2 vols., 1, 191–192 (Des Moines, 1902).

11   Hancock, Almira, *Reminiscences of Winfield Scott Hancock* (New York, 1887) 78 (Hancock, *Reminiscences*).

12   Walker, Francis A., *General Hancock* (New York, 1895) 33 (Walker, *Hancock*).

13   Heitman, *Historical Register*, 496–497; *Cullum*, 2, no. 1721; Warner, *Generals in Blue*, 202–203.

McClellan had other, less-immediate ways to obtain general officers. On September 1, George D. Bayard, an 1856 graduate of West Point and a captain of cavalry, received a leave of absence to take a commission as a major in a cavalry regiment being raised in New York. When he arrived in Washington, Bayard went to McClellan's headquarters to see his friend Colonel A. V. Colburn, then an aide to the commanding general. Colburn said McClellan wanted several Regular Army officers to be colonels of regiments and would not permit Bayard to take a more junior position. McClellan insisted that Bayard not accept the major's commission, labor to put the regiment in condition, and lose the credit to his volunteer superior officer. McClellan offered Bayard a choice: serve as an aide on his staff or as colonel of a Pennsylvania cavalry regiment. Choosing the latter, Bayard was soon a colonel in command of the First Pennsylvania Cavalry, part of the Pennsylvania Reserve Division, and shortly after a brigadier general of cavalry.[14]

Another slowly developing exercise of the power to appoint McClellan—and his successors—created through the power to assign and the correlative power to shuffle units from one command to another. As the commanding general of the Army of the Potomac, McClellan could assign an officer to command a unit beyond the officer's grade; allow him to demonstrate his ability in the new, higher position by actions in the field; then present a proven candidate for promotion. Although this procedure had its critics,[15] the slowness of Congress to grant stars after the initial burst of promotions gave it de facto congressional approval. For example, instead of seeking an unassigned brigadier general to command a brigade with an opening, McClellan could allow a colonel to succeed to command on the basis of seniority.

In the late winter of 1862 a reorganization of general officers would occur and as a result command of "Greasy Dick" Richardson's brigade would become available; the brigade would still be part of Heintzelman's larger command. Serving in the brigade as a regimental commander was Hiram G. Berry, a volunteer officer with no military experience except service in the state militia, a wealthy businessman who had led the Fourth Maine to the seat of war. Berry had learned his new

---

14   Warner, *Generals in Blue*, 26; *Cullum*, 2, no. 1721; Heitman, *Historical Register*, 1, 200; Bayard, Samuel J., *The Life of George Dashiell Bayard* (New York, 1873) 186–188 (Bayard, *Bayard*).

15   See *infra*, this chapter. Of course, this procedure worked equally well at the division–senior brigade commander level, and in rare instances a division might find itself in the hands of a senior colonel, for example, Colonel Joseph Thorburn and Colonel William H. Powell at Cedar Creek in 1864. *OR*, 43, pt. 1, 128, 130.

task well and had firmly impressed the critical Heintzelman, who personally visited McClellan's headquarters to ask that Berry be given the brigade.

"No, I am reserving that brigade for an officer of the Regular Army. You already have two volunteer generals in command of your other brigades and I want a Regular officer for the third."

Heintzelman persisted.

Finally, persuaded that he should at least study the candidate, McClellan yielded. "Send General Berry to my quarters and let me look him over," he said.

Berry presented himself as instructed. Ten minutes later he reappeared in the camp of the Fourth Maine. In his pocket he carried an order assigning him to command of Richardson's old brigade.[16] In Berry's case McClellan's tacit agreement not to put a brigadier general in command of a brigade allowed Berry to move up the ladder of command without formal promotion.

At times, no brigadier general would be available for assignment to command of a brigade, and the senior colonel would not be deemed suitable for succession to command of the brigade. An alternative to natural succession, but still on the basis of seniority, virtually always passed underneath the scrutiny of the president and the Congress: swapping regiments between brigades to put a satisfactory senior colonel in the brigade needing a new commander. If a brigade commander were disabled, transferred, or promoted, the senior regimental commander would, under Article Sixty-two of the Articles of War, automatically succeed to command regardless of his qualifications. A more senior regimental commander who had better qualifications could not be transferred from his regiment in another brigade because the governor of his state controlled his regimental assignment. But the governors had no power over assignment of regiments to brigades. The more senior and more qualified colonel could be transferred with his entire regiment to the brigade needing a new commander or he and his regiment could be exchanged for a regiment from the brigade in need. As the senior colonel he would outrank the unqualified officers. If necessary, the unqualified senior officer and his regiment would participate in the swap.

The process of appointment required more than approval of candidates. Selection necessitated rejections, some of which were not necessarily easy to make. From New York, the first Alexander Hamilton had served on George Washington's

---

16 Gould, Edward K., *Major-General Hiram G. Berry: his Career as a Contractor, Bank President, Politician and Major-General of Volunteers in the Civil War together with his War Correspondence embracing the Period from Bull Run to Chancellorsville* (Rockland, 1899) 107–108 (Gould, *Berry*).

staff and, as a line officer, had lead a critical charge on the British works at York-town. Alexander Hamilton, his namesake and grandson, saw his path to high command through his fellow New Yorker Secretary of State Seward. Hamilton reported that he had recruited or contributed to the Forty-fifth New York Infantry; a battalion of experienced artillery including twenty-pounder Parrott guns and thirty-two pounder howitzers; the balance of an artillery regiment; and the Fifty-second New York Infantry, known as the Sigel Rifles and commanded by Colonel Paul Frank. Many of the officers and men had served in Europe; most of them had served under Sanford in the Bull Run period and had reenlisted because they had confidence in the officers under whom they served during the militia period. Two more regiments had been tendered to Hamilton as soon as "I shall be commissioned brigadier." Hamilton had the support of militia Major General Sanford, Adjutant General of New York Hillhouse, the collector of the Port of New York Hiram Barney, Charles P. Stone, other officers of the United States Army with whom Hamilton had served, and Thurlow Weed, an important political friend and adviser of Seward and Lincoln both. All this and military experience, support from military personnel, production of military strength, and political backing could not breathe life into his candidacy. He never became a general officer.[17]

Another candidate, one with more grand dreams, presented himself to Lincoln in November and to Cameron the next month. William G. Snethen, a citizen of Maryland, wrote McClellan to explain that he could recruit an entire division, which would include nine regiments of infantry, two of cavalry, and one of artillery, three from loyal Marylanders. If he did that, he would, in the tradition of brigadier and major generalcies for men who recruited more than one regiment, expect to be commissioned a major general and given command of his division.[18] His pursuit of a major general's commission died a quiet death by being ignored.

17   Lincoln MSS (L.C.) letter dated October 22, 1861, from Hamilton to Seward.

18   Lincoln MSS (L.C.) letter dated December 7, 1861, from Snethen to Cameron. Other strongly supported but failed candidates appear in Ethan Allen Hitchcock MSS (Library of Congress) letters dated October 16, 1861, from Grimes to Lincoln; October 21, 1861, from Harlaw to Cameron; October 24, 1861, from Rankin to Cameron; November 20, 1861, from Grimes and Harlaw to Lincoln; endorsement by Trumbull; November 23, 1861, from Grimes to Halleck; October 16, 1861, from Lowe and Wright to Cameron. In his letter to Halleck Grimes said that Halleck had twenty thousand Iowa troops in his department and that ". . . we expect you to select at least *one* of her citizens as a member of your Military family. We therefore respectfully request the appointment of General V. P. Van Antwerp for a position on your staff. His military education, and the high positions he has held in military and civil services obviate the necessity of formal or detailed commendations."

The Republicans dominated the federal government and the appointment process. Secretary of the Navy Gideon Welles, a shrewd observer with a marvelously literate pen, compared the Republican and Democratic parties in the early war period: "Party spirit and old party differences prevailed, however, amidst these accumulating dangers. Secession was considered by most persons as a political party question, not as rebellion. Democrats to a large extent sympathized with the Rebels more than with the Administration, which they opposed, not that they wished secession to be successful and the Union divided, but they hoped that President Lincoln and the Republicans would, overwhelmed by obstacles and embarrassments, prove failures. The Republicans, on the other hand, were scarcely less partisan and unreasonable. Crowds of them at this period, when the storm of civil war was about bursting on the country, thronged the anterooms of the President and Secretaries, clamoring for the removal of all Democrats, indiscriminately, from office. Patriotism was with them no test, no shield from party malevolence. They demanded the proscription and exclusion of such Democrats as opposed the Rebel movements and clung to the Union, with the same vehemence that they demanded the removal of the worst Rebel who advocated a dissolution of the Union."[19]

Whether or not they dominated the Republican Party as a whole,[20] the Radical Republicans, vociferous and bellicose about their opinion on any subject, did not pass the issues of appointment and promotion quietly; and their power gave them much say on the early appointments. They had their own unique yardstick for measuring military ability: attitude toward slavery, treatment of fugitive slaves, handling of Confederate property. To the Radicals, these characteristics foretold prowess as a battlefield commander. They would also tell much about loyalty and devotion to the cause, things the Radicals prized highly.

Abner Doubleday, twenty-fourth in the West Point Class of 1842 and an avowed abolitionist, had served with distinction and vigor as an artillery officer in Fort Sumter under Major Robert Anderson, then reappeared as an artillery officer in Patterson's Valley army.[21] The New York members of Congress placed him second on their list for promotion.[22] Assigned to the infantry, he received support from prominent family members for non-military reasons.

19   Morse, *Welles' Diary*, 1, 10.

20   Bogue, Allan G., *The Earnest Men: Republicans of the Civil War Senate* (Ithaca and London, 1981) 25–27, and generally chapter 3 (Bogue, *Earnest Men*).

21   *Cullum*, 1, no. 1134.

22   Chandler MSS (L.C.) letter dated October 8, 1861, from William E. Doubleday to Chandler.

"When you reflect that there are not more than twenty such Republican officers in the U.S. Army," wrote his kinsman to Senator Chandler, "it is time that those who have been true to their principles under the opposing circumstances surrounding them should be remembered. We ought to have officers to command our army whose heart is in the work like Captain Lyons of St. Louis and Captain Doubleday of Fort Sumter."[23]

But as one general summarized the situation in a postwar article, "one could easily count on the fingers of one hand about all the outspoken anti-slavery men among the superior officers of the army."[24] By early December, the political sentiments of Republican officers were being contrasted with those of McClellan, his friends, and his staff. The "facts" about McClellan, to the extent they were true, had been known for years but treated as if they were insignificant. Now, they assumed national importance. As Doubleday's supporter wrote in December, "It is a great misfortune that our most important military officers are strong pro-slavery men. General McClellan, Inspector General Marcy, his father-in-law, are such . . . Major Doubleday . . . can give you information relative to the sentiment of those gentlemen and also of brigadier generals Andrew Porter, Brooks, Morrell, Fitz John Porter, Newton, and fifty others whose nomination for confirmation will come before the Senate as nominations not fit to be made, while such men as Banks and Fremont are overslaughed."[25]

Many of the governors used the election process as a form of guidance, did not feel bound by it, and generally tried to appoint the best qualified men, often West Pointers, to command their regiments.[26] For command of his newly forming regiments, Governor John A. Andrew of Massachusetts abhorred the election process. On August 3, 1861, he wrote to Senators Summer and Wilson, the two senators from Massachusetts, "Can it be intended by Congress, that the volunteers in the field should fill vacancies by election? Where is to be the source of discipline,

---

23   Chandler MSS (L.C.) letter dated July 5, 1861, from William E. Doubleday to Chandler.

24   Drake, "The Old Army in Kansas," in *Broadfoot MOLLUS Massachusetts*, 52, 148; Skelton, William B., *An American Profession of Arms, The Army Officer Corps, 1784–1861* (Lawrence, 1992) 350.

25   Chandler MSS (L.C.) letter dated December 6, 1861, from William E. Doubleday to Chandler.

26   Dwight Family MSS (M.H.S.), letter dated 1861 by the curator, from William Dwight to his father.

when every candidate is seeking personal favor of the men."[27] To command his regiments, he appointed West Point graduates on active duty, resigned West Point
graduates in civilian life, Regular Army officers, and a few militia officers with outstanding military reputations. In the case of the Regular Army officers, he usually
followed the Scott Rule because he had no choice and selected company grade
Regular Army officers.

On August 4, McClellan took his first steps toward creation of higher com-
mand for his army. He began with the appointment of brigade leaders. The Bull
Run pool, West Point, and Colonel Browne's geographic rule dominated. The Scott
Rule for company grade West Point graduates was also well represented.

Among the blooded men of Bull Run, David Hunter, Samuel Peter Heintzelman, William Tecumseh Sherman, Erasmus Darwin Keyes, William Buell
Franklin, Louis Blenker, Israel Bush "Greasy Dick" Richardson, and Charles
Pomeroy Stone received brigades. Benefitting from Colonel Browne's geography
rule, Philip Watts Kearny, William Farrar Smith, and Darius Nash Couch rose from
command of new volunteer regiments that had arrived in Washington. Propelled by
the whimsy of the president, Joseph Hooker received a brigade. Some of these men
had been made brigadier generals directly by the federal government, but most had
been colonels appointed by the governors from civilian life or from company-
grade ranks in the Regular Army.

As the number of regiments and, therefore, the number of brigades grew,
McClellan turned to the larger tactical organizations he would need. From the latter
part of August; continuing through September, October, and November; and ending at the beginning of December, he created divisions. Between August 24 and
August 30, he created three divisions he gave to his favorites.

First, Irvin McDowell received a division of brigades under Keyes and Wadsworth; and in early October he was given Rufus King's brigade. William B.
Franklin kept his old brigade and was given the troublesome Philip Kearny. Also on
August 30, McClellan's old friend and confidant Fitz John Porter received two
brigades and later a third.

27   Gordon, George H., *Brook Farm to Cedar Mountains in the War of the Great Rebellion,
1861–1862* (Boston, 1883) 52 (Gordon, *Brook Farm to Cedar Mountain*); Hyndman, *History of a
Cavalry Company: A Complete Record of Company A, 4th Penn'a Cavalry as Identified with that
Regiment and with the Second Brigade, Second Division, Cavalry Corps in all the Campaigns of
the Army of the Potomac during the last Civil War* (Philadelphia, 1872) 28–29 (Hyndman, *History
of a Cavalry Company*).

In September, a busy month, Stone took command of brigades commanded by Frederick W. Lander, who had served with McClellan in Oregon, and John J. Peck, a friend and schoolmate from West Point. To this stable group was added the Philadelphia Brigade, the creation of Colonel and Senator Edward Donald Baker. From his West Virginia army McClellan had brought Don Carlos Buell, who acquired brigades under Darius N. Couch and Lawrence P. Graham, then a third brigade in the next month. The Pennsylvania Reserves, the extra division originally intended by Governor Andrew Curtin to be commanded by McClellan, arrived incomplete with George McCall in command, but gradually came to full strength as the regiments filled and arrived in Washington. Its brigade commanders were Pennsylvanians with noteworthy futures, George G. Meade, John Fulton Reynolds, and Edward Otho Cresap Ord, all three graduates of West Point. At the end of the month McClellan's friend "Baldy" Smith, a predictable and reasonable appointment, took command of brigades led by W. T. H. Brooks, a West Point graduate who succeeded Smith at the head of the Vermont Brigade, Isaac I. Stevens, and Winfield Scott Hancock, all Military Academy graduates who could not have foreseen how much Confederate lead they would collect.

Heintzelman began the month of October with a division around Alexandria composed of Richardson, Sedgwick, and Jameson, none of whom would make the consecrating march to the courthouse four years later. The always controversial Joseph Hooker had an always controversial Dan Sickles under him and passed his own brigade to Henry M. Naglee, a West Point graduate having persuasive connections with McClellan. Louis Blenker, the only original division commander in the Army of the Potomac not to graduate from West Point, commanded a division composed primarily of foreign regiments organized in brigades under Julius Stahl or Stahal, whose real Hungarian name was Serbiani, and Adolph von Steinwehr. The division would have a controversial role a year and a half later in a battle in heavy woods.

Arriving from California, the white-haired, venerable, and respected Edwin Vose Sumner, a member of the Train Gang, received brigades under Oliver O. Howard, Thomas F. Meagher, and William H. French, an odd collection of devout religion and heavy drinking. Last of all, Silas Casey had a provisional division formed by brigading his training regiments in three temporary commands in the capital. In late August when he created the first division under McDowell, McClellan created new divisions under Major General Banks off his right flank along the Potomac and in his rear at Baltimore for Major General Dix, both anti-slavery Democrats and political appointees over whose promotions he had exercised no control.

Irvin McDowell, Samuel P. Heintzelman, Fitz John Porter, William B. Franklin, Charles P. Stone, Don Carlos Buell, Joseph Hooker, William F. "Baldy"

Smith, and George McCall had all graduated from West Point. McDowell, Heintzelman, Franklin, Stone, and Porter came from the Bull Run pool. Buell had served with McClellan in West Virginia. Only Hooker, Smith, Sumner, and McCall had no combat experience in the current war.[28] Of the brigade commanders, some of whom were brigadier generals and some senior colonels, all had graduated from the Military Academy except Philip Kearny, a Regular Army officer with more experience and more personal wealth than most of his peers taken together; Stahl and Steinwehr, officers with service in European armies; and the political anomaly Edward D. Baker, who had served in the Mexican War.

By October McClellan had ideas about corps commanders, but he could not claim his candidates would be reliable in such large commands. Early, he wanted to give corps to McDowell, Franklin, and Heintzelman, but Scott would not permit it.[29] Later rumors that he intended to give a corps to Sumner waned when Sumner's severe fall from a horse made that impossible.[30] Finally, he sat down with a scrap of paper to list the corps commanders he wanted and the divisions he would assign to each. He would give the First Corps to Sumner, Second Corps to McDowell, Third Corps to the cranky Heintzelman, the Fourth to Fitz John Porter, the Fifth to Franklin, and the Sixth or Reserve Corps to Andrew Porter, all brigadier generals.

He intended to delay promotions to major general for the same reasons. In the perfectly formed army, brigadier generals commanded brigades, major generals led divisions, and lieutenant generals led corps. In McClellan's department, all division commanders except Dix and Banks, the two political appointees, were brigadier generals,[31] and many of the brigades were led by their senior regimental colonels. In December 1861, McClellan not having formed any corps or arranged any promotions to major general, one of Secretary Chase's correspondents on military appointments criticized this policy.

> With high respect for those who may differ with me, I maintain that the system of appointing Brigadiers instead of Major Generals, to the command of corps d'Armee

---

28   *OR*, 5, 15–17, McClellan's report, Organization of the Division, August 4, 1861; *M.O.S.*, 81.

29   Heintzelman MS Diary (large diary) (L.C.) entry dated February 10, 1862; Gurowski, *Diary*, 1, 108, October, 1861.

30   Heintzelman MS Diary (large diary) (L.C.) entry dated November 30, 1861.

31   Heintzelman MSS (L.C.) letter dated July 26, 1861, from Heintzelman to Stanton (this letter was obviously misdated by Heintzelman because it describes specific events in 1862); Chandler MSS (L.C.) letter dated March 8, 1862, from Gurowski to Chandler; *OR*, 5, 13, McClellan's report; *M.O.S.*, 222; *N&H*, 5, 169–170.

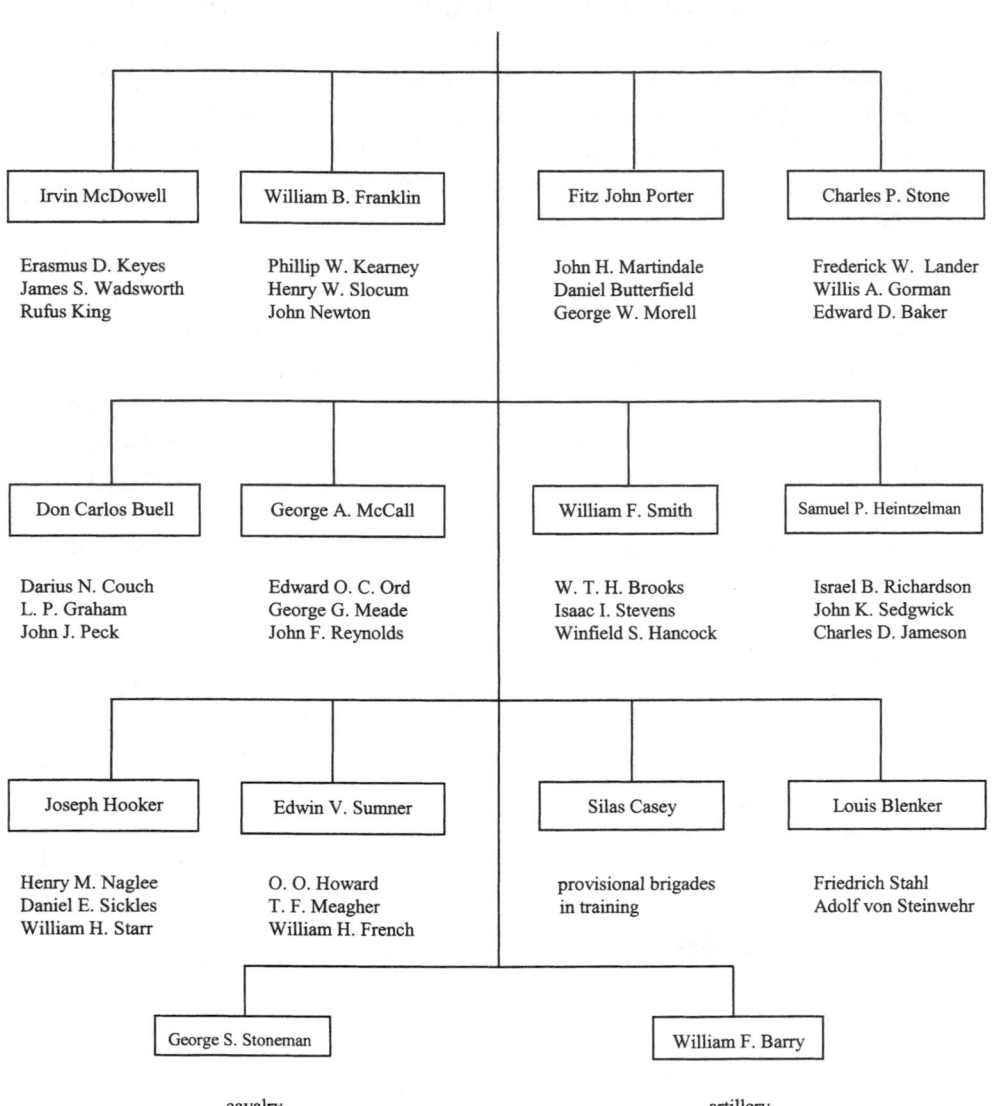

George B. McClellan

| Irvin McDowell | William B. Franklin | Fitz John Porter | Charles P. Stone |

Erasmus D. Keyes
James S. Wadsworth
Rufus King

Phillip W. Kearney
Henry W. Slocum
John Newton

John H. Martindale
Daniel Butterfield
George W. Morell

Frederick W. Lander
Willis A. Gorman
Edward D. Baker

| Don Carlos Buell | George A. McCall | William F. Smith | Samuel P. Heintzelman |

Darius N. Couch
L. P. Graham
John J. Peck

Edward O. C. Ord
George G. Meade
John F. Reynolds

W. T. H. Brooks
Isaac I. Stevens
Winfield S. Hancock

Israel B. Richardson
John K. Sedgwick
Charles D. Jameson

| Joseph Hooker | Edwin V. Sumner | Silas Casey | Louis Blenker |

Henry M. Naglee
Daniel E. Sickles
William H. Starr

O. O. Howard
T. F. Meagher
William H. French

provisional brigades
in training

Friedrich Stahl
Adolf von Steinwehr

| George S. Stoneman | | William F. Barry |

cavalry

artillery

is false in theory, and injurious in practice. If the grade of Major General should only be conferred as the reward for distinguished services, the same reason applies with equal force to regiments and companies, and the former should be commanded by Lt. Cols., and the latter by lieutenants. But without abandoning the rules laid down, its evil effects may in some measure be obviated, by only conferring the grade of Major General upon commanders of corps d'Armee, and if they prove inadequate to the trust proposed in them, they can be assigned to single divisions. The very fact that the commander of a corps d'Armee was a simple Brigadier, would indicate a want of confidence upon the part of the government, and be calculated to demoralize the troops. Besides this, the presence of a major general in any of the seceding states, would inspire greater hope and confidence among the loyal citizens, than could the presence of any Brigadier, whatever might be his ability.[32]

On McClellan's list of men preferred for corps commanders, Franklin and the two Porters came obviously from his group of favorites. He must have recognized that they were too young, too little known, and without sufficient experience, too junior in prewar rank, for an appointment of this sort. He could not have felt confident that requests for their appointment would be well received by the public, the Congress, or the president. Lacking reputations earned in the field, they could not yet be suggested for corps command. If he waited for performance, he might have his way; if he moved too soon, he would probably fail. No doubt, he did not press for them this early because he feared their candidacies would not succeed. Of all the reasons, spoken or not, for not organizing corps at this time, this was probably the strongest. He decided to wait until his choices would be acceptable,[33] created no corps, and appointed no corps commanders. Failing to gauge the outside influences accurately, he decided to delay the creation of corps and the appointment of corps leaders, which in the end allowed the issue to circle quietly to his rear, gather uncontrollable power, and overrun him.

---

32   Chase MSS (L.C.) letter dated December 17, 1861, from Morgan to Chase.

33   McClellan MSS (L.C.) mem of n.d. and n.a. in the handwriting of McClellan; Comte de Paris MS diary (large diary) (A.N. de la M. de F.) entry dated March 9, 1862; Heintzelman MS diary (large diary) (L.C.) entry dated February 10, 1862; N&H, 5, 169–170. The curator arbitrarily included the single sheet of paper in the McClellan MSS in the March 1862 volume, but it must have been created between late fall after Sumner had arrived at the Army of the Potomac (listed as a proposed corps commander) and late January when McClellan received the order to arrest Stone (listed as a division commander).

Chapter 11

"By Jesus Christ, it's a lie. Every mother's son of us will be cashiered."

—Heintzelman, on the future of the officers who served at Bull Run

The Bull Run Officer Pool

O ver its entire life the Army of the Potomac would draw more general officers from the Bull Run pool than any other. Regular, ex-Regular, militia, volunteer, politician, West Point graduate, West Point dropout, foreigner, and civilian, the Bull Run pool had them all. A West Point dropout serving as a field grade officer in Sickles' brigade probably spoke for many when he commented to his family about the performance of the Bull Run officer pool, "McDowell showed himself unequal to the command of so large an army. Americans show themselves green at war. Colonels show themselves incompetent. Line officers cowards. The men showed want of trust in their officers & that want of trust made them think they were hurt when no harm was near them."[1]

At Willard's Hotel, a five-story structure created in 1850 by consolidating several adjacent houses and recasting them as a one-hundred-room hotel, fifty officers would have jammed the bar.[2] Walt Whitman, poetically hyperbolic as always, viewed the scene there the day after the battle. "Willard's is full of shoulder-straps. I see them

---

1   Dwight Family MSS (M.H.S.) letter dated July 26, 1861, from William Dwight to his father. This analysis, perfectly logical, would have seemed superficial to more thoughtful observers like the Prince de Joinville and Frederick Law Olmstead, *infra*, Chapter 17.

2   McLaughlin, *Olmstead Letters*, 4, 127, n. 2; Eskew, Garnet Laidlaw, *Willard's of Washington: The Epic of a Capital Caravansery* 12–13 (New York, 1954).

and must have a word with them. There you are shoulder-straps!—but where are your companies? Where are your men? Incompetence! Never tell me about a chance of battle, of getting strayed, and the like. I think this is your work, this retreat, after all. Sneak, blow, put on airs there in Willard's sumptuous parlors and ball rooms or any-where—no explanation shall save you. Bull Run is your work; had you been half of one-tenth worthy of your men this never would have happened."[3]

After the battle of Bull Run, many of the officers felt concerned about the allocation of blame for the defeat. "Everybody is sick in body or in heart," Colonel Oliver O. Howard wrote his wife. "Applications for leave, resignations & discharges have been the order of the day for the last week. Grumbling, fault finding, and charges against my officers come to me from every quarter."[4]

In early August, a number of officers, unaware of McClellan's memorandum of July 29, had gathered on the first floor of the Arlington House when a lieutenant announced that he had a list of new appointments to brigadier general. Heintzelman, Keyes, Franklin, Andrew Porter, Sherman, and others from the Bull Run pool had places on the list, he said.

They were skeptical.

"By Jesus Christ," Heintzelman exclaimed, in his nasal voice, his nose almost touching his chin, "it's all a lie. Every mother's son of us will be cashiered!"[5]

By the middle of August, McDowell had received and accepted 137 resignations and had twenty-three more pending. He did not believe officers who had agreed to serve for two or three years but decided to leave after a few weeks could constitute much loss to the service if they departed or could contribute much good if they stayed. He decided to accept the pending twenty-three resignations but first wrote to Seth Williams, McClellan's adjutant general, to see if McClellan agreed.[6]

---

3   Lowenfels, Walter, ed., *Walt Whitman's Civil War*, 24–25 (New York, 1964).

4   Howard MSS (Bowdoin College) letter dated August 1, 1861, from Howard to his wife.

5   Comte de Paris MS diary (large diary) (A.N. de la M. de F.) entry dated November 7, 1861; *OR*, 5, 15–16, McClellan's report; *M.O.S.*, 79–80; Committee, *History of the Fifty-seventh Regiment Pennsylvania Veteran Volunteer Infantry, First Brigade, First Division, Third Corps, and Second Brigade, Third Division, Second Corps, Army of the Potomac* (Kearny, 1995 rep.) 26–27 (Committee, Fifty-seventh Pennsylvania); Sherman, *Memoirs*, 1, 191. In his memoirs Sherman dates the conversation as August 4. Although this date is not necessarily incorrect it cannot be confirmed. In a letter he stated that he learned about the promotions on August 3. Howe, Mark de Wolfe, *Home Letters of General Sherman* (New York, 1909) 212, letter dated August 3, 1861, from Sherman to his family (Howe, *Sherman Home Letters*). The list was published in the *New York Times* on August 7, 1861, the day after Congress adjourned the emergency session.

6   McClellan MSS (L.C.) telegram dated August 14, 1861, from McDowell to Williams.

Superficially, McDowell's approach was sound; but McClellan saw larger, longer-term issues: officers committed to the service just could not depart when the circumstances no longer suited them. McClellan's answer was simple, direct, and prompt. McDowell should accept no resignations except for physical disability, which should be determined by a medical board convened by the medical director, or mental deficiency, to be determined by a board convened for that evaluation.[7] He would not allow the Bull Run pool to suffer this kind of diminution.

In fact, the members of the Bull Run pool with West Point in their pedigree dominated the list prepared by McClellan for Lincoln when he arrived in Washington; and his choices, although they included his contemporaries and friends, covered a thirty-two-year range of classes, 1822 to 1854, not just the eight classes he would have known while a cadet. Hunter, McDowell, Heintzelman, Franklin, Sherman, Keyes, Barry, and Hunt were among those at the more senior end. Even Harvey Brown, the ante Bull-Run complainer about the geography rule, made his list. Andrew Porter, Fitz John Porter, Stone, Stoneman, and Howard added youth to the nominees.[8]

Bull Run had produced the first group of men to command divisions: Hunter, Heintzelman, Tyler, Miles, and Runyon. David Hunter, a member of the West Point pool, the Regular Army group, and the Train Gang, had been wounded early in the day while redeploying a Rhode Island regiment. In his short time on the field, he demonstrated the fault common to all officers with larger commands that day: he did not comprehend his entire command flank to flank. The serious wound in his neck required some time to heal. While he was mending, he wrote caustic letters sharply criticizing fellow officers and suggesting that McDowell had a history of cowardice.[9] A report on his own situation he wrote to his aide: "I intend to send you the first letter I have written since the battle. When we hoped to be victorious, I regretted very much that you were not with us, but when defeat came I was truly thankful that you were spared, in a measure, our great mortification. I trust that you will be able to go out with us the next time, and that you may have the pleasure of recording a glorious victory, instead of a disgraceful defeat."

7   McClellan MSS (L.C.) letter dated August 14, 1861, from Stoneman to McDowell.

8   National Archives, Record Group 94, Records of the Adjutant General's Office, Letters received, Commission Branch File (Microcopy 1064) 746-M (C.B.) 1863, memorandum dated July 29, 1861, from McClellan to Lincoln.

9   Charles Graham Halpine MSS (Huntington Library) Hunter, "Rough Notes from an Old Soldier: How the Battle of Bull Run was Lost," dated August 1, 1861, by the curator.

Although Lincoln visited him twice while he was confined with his wound, Hunter learned nothing about his own destination. The Illinois delegation had unanimously recommended to Lincoln that he be promoted to major general and assigned to command the Illinois forces. McClellan had recommended that Hunter have the star of a brigadier general, because McClellan needed brigadiers. Lincoln told Hunter that, if he accepted either, it would not interfere with the other. In the confusion Hunter did not know what they would do with him.[10]

When Hunter had healed sufficiently, Lincoln requested that he be made a major general and assigned to command a division of Illinois volunteers.[11] He then sent Hunter west to look after Fremont and to be "a sort of a father to them out there."[12]

Heintzelman had been ready on time, pressed his column at every chance, used sound tactical judgment, and kept his overall vision of the field. When the batteries on Henry House Hill fell, he rode his huge horse with great personal bravery into the teeth of the fighting to encourage his men. Yet in the final analysis, he, too, failed through lack of experience. He sent no pickets to screen his right flank and rear. There it was that the fresh Southerners attacked without warning.

Participation in the battle at Bull Run Creek did not guarantee advancement or future employment. As they should have, promotion and assignment rested on performance more than mere participation. At least two men had severely compromised their military careers in the battle. Of the four division commanders, Daniel Tyler proved that he had the least capacity for command. He repeatedly marched late and each time wrecked the schedule. He violated orders when he provoked the unfortunate encounter at Blackburn's Ford. If nothing else, that had a negative effect on the mind of the army and the men in Washington. He moved too slowly. Headed for the Stone Bridge on July 21, he needed three hours or more to march two brigades the three miles between his bivouac area and the blacksmith shop to clear the road to Sudley's Ford for the turning column. He moved so slowly that he dislocated McDowell's finely balanced timetable by more than two hours.

When the batteries under Griffin and Rickets fell, Tyler had three brigades under his command but did not even know where two of them were. Schenck, somewhere on the east bank of Bull Run, never managed to reach the battlefield.

10   Halpine MSS (H.L.) letter dated August 1, 1861, from Hunter to Halpine.

11   Basler, *Lincoln's Collected Works*, 4, 483, letter dated August 13, 1861, from Lincoln to Cameron.

12   *M.O.S.*, 137; Basler, *Lincoln's Colleted Works*, 4, 513, letter dated September 9, 1861, from Lincoln to Hunter.

Sherman, to the right and rear, had become the left flank unit of the battle line when Keyes' side slipped left to Young's Branch. Neither Sherman nor Schenck knew where Tyler was, and he gave no meaningful instructions to either. In practical effect his division had become three separate brigades and he the leader of a single brigade. He and his staff felt the isolation of their position with Keyes and recognized that they were making no contribution to the fight. They "vainly hoped from minute to minute to come again in touch with Sherman or the other divisions," wrote Henry Villard later.[13] The strongest and freshest part of the flanking column, the division with a long rest and no appreciable distance to march, Tyler's division never participated as a body in the battle.

In fact, Tyler was so detached from his other brigades that he naively confessed in his report:

> I passed [from Keyes' brigade] to the rear to find General Schenck's brigade, intending, as it was fresh, to have it cover the retreat. I did not find it in the position in which I had left it, and supposed it had moved forward and joined the retreating column. I did not see General Schenck again until near Cub Run.[14]

Tyler had proven himself unworthy of division command. He suffered a form of banishment that would become common: In spite of support from prominent men,[15] he waited in New York City without assignment. Finally, he went west. But in the Corinth, Mississippi, campaign his health broke, and he was forced to assume noncombat positions. In 1864 his wife died unexpectedly. The shock was so severe that he resigned his commission. Like Patterson, he, too, left the army under a cloud. Many blamed the defeat at Bull Run on him because of his slow march and his lack of aggressiveness at the Stone Bridge. Yet once the war ended, he, like Patterson, pursued a scrupulous business career with great success.[16]

The division commanders on the battlefield at Bull Run on July 21, 1861, had the same troublesome characteristic: they were still the small unit leaders they had been their entire careers. After the initial fighting on Mathews Hill north of the

13   Villard, Oswald Garrison, *Fighting Years: Memoirs of a Fighting Editor*, 2 vols., 1, 189 (New York, 1939).

14   *OR*, 2, 350, Tyler's report.

15   E.g., Lincoln MSS (L.C.) letter dated October 2, 1861, from Peabody to Seward.

16   Tyler, Daniel, *Damiel Tyler: a Memorial Volume, containing his Autobiography and War Record. Some Account of his later Years and with Various Reminiscences and the Tributes of Friends* (New Haven, 1883) 68 ff.

Warrenton Turnpike, they never commanded more than one brigade at a time. The attacks on Henry House Hill were made by regiment, never by brigade or division.

The most tragic figure to leave the field was Dixon Miles. McDowell did not censure him for his drunkenness, not even noting it in his report. He allowed Miles to become an "unperson" by not mentioning him in any way. As the list of officers cited for bravery and judicious action proceeded down the page in McDowell's report, it mentioned every other division and brigade commander. The hapless Miles McDowell noted only to the astute by omission.[17] Richardson, however, devoted a considerable portion of his report to an account of the drunken actions that could have led to disaster.[18] Miles requested a court of inquiry, which was granted in early August.[19]

The illness that had caused the original prescription for drinking had worsened rather than improved. When Miles, still sick, appeared before the court, Richardson attacked him bitterly. Represented by counsel, Richardson requested permission to act as prosecutor. The court overruled objections by the defense,[20] granted Richardson's request, and began the proceedings. Richardson's personal animosity was so great that the court cautioned him several times.[21] The testimony clearly showed Miles guilty of drunkenness. Although Miles tried to defend himself, Richardson had insurmountable evidence. Miles would not be vindicated by the Court of Inquiry. It would recommend a court martial he could not win.

On November 6, almost three months to the day from the time the inquiry was granted, General Orders No. 42 reported the court's verdict. The Court found:

1. That Col. I. B. Richardson was justified in applying the term drunkenness to Col. D. S. Miles' condition about 1 o'clock P.M. on the 21st July last.
2. That the evidence is clear that Colonel Miles had been ill for several days before July 21st last—was ill on that day; that the surgeon had prescribed medicines for him, and on the day of the battle had prescribed for him small quantities of brandy.

---

17   *OR*, 2, 322–323, McDowell's report.

18   *OR*, 2, 374 ff, Richardson's report.

19   National Archives, Records of the Judge Advocate General's Office (Army) RG 94 (No. II 427), Manuscript Court of Inquiry in the Case of Dixon S. Miles, letter dated July 26, 1861, from Richardson to McDowell; *OR*, 2, 439, Special Orders No. 67, dated August 10, 1861, from Headquarters, Department of Northeastern Virginia.

20   NA MS CI(Miles), letter dated August 13, 1861, from Miles to the court.

21   NA MS CI(Miles).

The court, however, considers his illness as a very slight extenuation of the guilt attached to his condition about 7 o'clock P.M. on July 21st last.[22]

The next paragraph expressed the real opinion of the three officers who composed the court. Although thoroughly in the wrong and by all rights a candidate for a court martial, Miles found his fate expressed:

> The court is of the opinion that evidence cannot now be found sufficient to convict Colonel Miles of drunkenness before a court-martial; that a proper court could only be organized in this Army with the greatest inconvenience at present, and that it will not be for the interest of the service to convene a court in this case.
>
> The court is therefore of the opinion that no further proceedings in the case are necessary.[23]

Saved! A reprieve for a condemned man! More than anything else, the vast reorganization and expansion of the army around Washington after Bull Run had probably made a general court martial impossible. Whatever the cause, Dixon Miles had kept his commission; and he was grateful. Not a drop of alcohol would he touch again, not as long as he lived. He swore it.

But the army had other ways to deal with Miles for his transgression. Since July 26, when Richardson complained to McDowell and the War Department, Miles had been "on leave of absence and awaiting orders." While his comrades in arms rose to be brigadier and major generals, he remained a forgotten colonel "on leave." Early in March of 1862, almost a year after his debacle, he received an assignment to command the brigade charged with guarding the track line of the Baltimore & Ohio Railroad. It was not a battlefield command, but it was a chance.[24]

The governors did the most to create the Bull Run pool of officers. From many diverse origins came the colonels and other regimental officers who marched with McDowell on July 16. Generally, military experience defined the sources: West Point graduates, veterans of the Mexican War, militia and volunteer officers, and veterans of foreign armies.

---

22   *OR*, 2, 438–439, General Orders No. 42, dated November 6, 1861, Headquarters, Army of the Potomac.

23   *Ibid.*, 439.

24   *OR*, 11, pt. 3, 13, Special Orders No. 83, dated March 17, 1862, from Headquarters, Army of the Potomac; *Cullum*, 1, no. 387, has a very terse sketch; Miles' posthumous court martial for his conduct at Harpers Ferry in 1862 appears in *OR*, 19, pt. 1, 248–308.

Five of McDowell's regimental commanders were United States Military Academy alumni, two of whom had been on continuous duty since their graduation and were on active duty at the fall of the Charleston Harbor defenses in April 1861. Both these men, George Sykes, the commanding officer of the Regular battalion, and Alexander McD. McCook, colonel of the First Ohio, were already battle-tested when the campaign began. The remaining three men, Isaac F. Quinby, colonel of the Thirteenth New York, Henry W. Slocum, commander of the Twenty-seventh New York, and Henry Whiting, the colonel at the head of the Second Vermont, had all resigned their commissions to enter civilian life, although Quinby and Slocum had been careful to become New York militia officers. In spite of the fact that none of these three had passed beyond the rank of first lieutenant in the Regular Army, the governors applied the "Scott Rule," apparently agreeing that their West Point education had instilled the basic characteristics necessary to command regardless of the size of the unit, a quite justifiable assumption when commissions were being awarded in the months prior to McDowell's campaign. Of the forty-three regiments[25] to march in the Army of Northeastern Virginia in July, more than 10 percent had West Point graduates in command.[26]

Mexican War veterans provided a second group of regimental commanders. The ranks held by these men during the "Rehearsal for Conflict," as the 1846 war has aptly been called, ranged from noncommissioned officer to full colonel,[27] but most important, they had acquired battle and administrative experience in command positions. Many in this group had continued in the militia after the Mexican conflict and could step into regimental command in 1861 with relatively little difficulty. Thus, the governors could anticipate that on this source they could, if not more, depend.

An excellent example of this group, Willis Arnold Gorman, commanded the First Minnesota Regiment in Franklin's brigade. Like all Mexican War veterans of any rank, Gorman was older than most. Forty-five in 1861, he had been a lawyer, a member of the Indiana house of representatives, a major in the Third Indiana Volunteers at Buena Vista, colonel of the Fourth Indiana at Puebla, a United States representative, and governor of the Minnesota Territory.[28]

---

25   This number includes the Fourth Pennsylvania, which demanded its discharge the day of the battle, but not the Regular Army battalion or the battalion of marine recruits.

26   See *Cullum*, 2, nos. 1033, 1149, 1172, 1542, 1565; for additional information on Slocum see his biography; for McCook see Reid, Whitelaw, *Ohio in the War: Her Statesman, her Generals, and Soldiers* 2 vols. (Cincinnati, 1868) 1, 807 ff (*Ohio in the War*), a hostile sketch with details.

27   J. H. Hobart Ward had been a noncommissioned officer, and Willis A. Gorman had been colonel of the Fourth Indiana, Warner, *Generals in Blue*, 178, 537.

28   Warner, *Generals in Blue*, 178.

His service at the head of the First Minnesota provoked the hostility of his men and earned the approval of his superiors. Bad food, worn uniforms, and no pay, the kind of governmental fault particularly well-recognized by thoughtful contemporaries, caused discontent among the independent-minded frontiersmen of the regiment. In letters home and to the press they accused Gorman of being unseen during the heavy fighting on Henry House Hill.[29] Meanwhile, prominent local people in Minnesota learned about Gorman's conduct at the briefing the night before the battle. Two of them wrote to Heintzelman. They had heard about the report by Colonel John B. Sanborn, Minnesota's adjutant general, to the governor of the state. According to that report, they wrote, the day before the battle, in a council of war at McDowell's headquarters, Colonel Gorman had advised that the army retire to Centerville; entrench; await a thorough reconnaissance of the enemy's works; and, if necessary, await reinforcements. His advice ignored, he made a written protest against "fighting the enemy in their strongholds the next day." The writers wished to know if this account were accurate.[30]

Waiting until his wound healed enough for him to write, Heintzelman responded on August 23. He had had a number of conversations with Gorman during the advance from Alexandria, he replied. On the day before the battle, Gorman expressed the opinion that the enemy had been largely reinforced and that the Union army should entrench and await reinforcements. "In the opinion that our force was not sufficient he was not alone. We had unmistakable evidence that at least a portion of Gen. Johnson's [sic] force had arrived in our front."

Heintzelman considered Gorman's regiment, the First Minnesota, the best in his division. By the promotion of others, but not Gorman, to brigadier general after the battle, a great injustice had been done Gorman, Heintzelman thought. "Many much less deserving has received promotion,"[31] he wrote. The accusations of cowardice lacked substance. His division commander thought well of him. His brigade commander spoke well of him in his report. Gorman's problem with his regiment resolved itself soon after the battle in an unusual way: promotion to brigadier general and assignment up the Potomac to command a brigade.[32]

29   Moe, Richard, *The Last Full Measure: The Life and Death of the First Minnesota Volunteers* (New York, 1993) 65–69 (Moe, *Last Full Measure*); Imholte, John Q., *The First Volunteers: History of the First Minnesota Volunteer Regiment 1861–1865* (Minneapolis, 1963) 57–60.

30   Heintzelman MSS (L.C.) letter dated August 15, 1861, from M. Wilkinson and Ayres Aldrich to Heintzelman.

31   Heintzelman MSS (L.C.) letter dated August 23, 1861, from Heintzelman to M. Wilkinson and Cyrus Aldrich.

32   Moe, *Last Full Measure*, 68; NA Offs MS Rpts (Gorman).

Other similar problems were not so easily solved. Concerns about the cowardice of Colonel Henry Whiting of the Second Vermont had a firm basis. In early August charges bubbled to the surface and in early November appeared in the New Hampshire legislature as a resolution calling for his resignation. He was not a Vermonter, nor was he known to anyone in the state. Although he had "many excellent qualities" and "meant to do his duty," he did not mean "to expose himself any more than was necessary." On August 12, Whiting arrested Major Charles H. Joyce and preferred charges against him for writing the Burlington *Times* a letter in which Joyce supposedly made false statements about Whiting. Major Joyce was popular. The majority of the officers and many of the men supported him. Almost all the regimental line officers signed a paper requesting Whiting's resignation. After Whiting's superiors supported him, the interest of the public bodies evaporated. But at lower levels dissatisfaction continued.[33]

Militia officers formed the largest group of regimental leaders sent to McDowell by the governors. Despite the decrepit condition of some state militias and the consequent inadequate training for the officers, the experience the men gained in these units made them valuable to the government. A peacetime, civilian officer had to train for an eventuality that might never occur, had no bond to the military, like a Regular Army officer, and knew he might never be summoned to the test. Nevertheless, the militia officers who learned the art of war during peacetime had just as much qualification for regimental command as their West Point counterparts. The experience of commanding a body of troops rendered them valuable as leaders; and because many of them had been members of their militia units over a span of years, they had acquired military capacity. In some cases the facets of military command had become second nature to them. If peacetime militia officers would not produce a large number of high-ranking commanders, they could certainly be expected to provide stable, dependable regimental and brigade commanders.[34]

The last group of experienced officers who fought under McDowell as colonels in command of regiments were foreigners who had served in European armies be-

---

33   Benedict, *Vermont in the Civil War*, 1, 88–90, 89, n. 1, Heitman, *Historical Register*, 1, 99.

34   For examples see Wilson, James G., and John Fiske, *Appleton's Cyclopedia of American Biography*, 6 vols., 6 supps. 2, 65, 261 (New York, 1887–1951); Gould, 23ff; Haynes, Martin A., *A History of the Second Regiment New Hampshire Volunteer Infantry, in the War of the Rebellion* (Lakeport, 1897) 272ff (Haynes, *Second New Hampshire*); Roe, Alfred Seelye, *The Fifth Regiment Massachusetts Volunteer Infantry in its Three Tours of Duty, 1861, 1862–1863, 1864* (Roe, *Fifth Massachusetts*); Lonn, Ella, *Foreigners in the Union Army and Navy* (Baton Rouge, 1951) 201 (Lonn, *Foreigners in the Union Army*); Bates, *Martial Deeds*; Athearn, Robert G., *Thomas Francis Meagher: An Irish Revolutionary in America* (Boulder, 1949). Officers in this category included men like Berry, Corcoran, Terry, Farnham, Marston, Lawrence, and Wood.

fore coming to the United States. Many who participated in the revolutions of 1848 had been forced to leave their homelands for America because of their political views. In America in 1861, the tendency toward ethnic enlistment produced Irish, German, Scottish, and Italian regiments; and it elevated men of these nationalities to regimental command. In most cases they had more experience than their American counterparts. [35] Though they might have been somewhat incongruous in the American military system, these men had experience in warfare, a fact not to be overlooked in granting commissions. Certainly they could be dependable in battle, and in the future they would probably produce good leaders of higher rank.[36]

Of the total number of regimental commanders who marched with McDowell from Washington, less than 20 percent and probably little more than 10 percent had no previous military experience, a small proportion considering the conditions governing creation of the Army of Northeastern Virginia. The leadership at the regimental level, while not spectacular, appeared before the battle to be dependable.

The far more numerous lower-ranking officers? What would become of those who served at Bull Run? Where would the future regiments find them? The three-year regiments created after Bull Run quite naturally drew heavily on the pool of experience created by the "three-months' campaign." Officers and enlisted men of the disbanding three-months' regiments found their way into positions of responsibility in the new regiments, and the governors had a much easier time selecting from the Bull Run pool because they had recent performance to evaluate.[37]

The Duquesne Grays, an independent rifle company organized in the Pittsburgh, Pennsylvania, area, had served during the Mexican War as Company K of the First Pennsylvania Volunteers. At the fall of Fort Sumter, it had already achieved a high state of efficiency, numbered approximately eighty men, and became Company B of the Twelfth Pennsylvania Volunteers. During the war the men of the original company

---

35   Lonn, *Foreigners in the Union Army*, 193 ff.

36   Lonn, *Foreigners in the Union Army*, sketches all foreign officers who served with the rank of colonel or above in the Union Army except for Max Einstein.

37   E.g., *OR*, ser. 3, vol. 1, 414, letter dated August 15, 1861, from Browne, military secretary to Governor Andrew, to Cameron; Albert, Allen Diehl, *History of the Forty-fifth Regiment Pennsylvania Veteran Volunteer Infantry, 1861–1865* (Williamsport, 1912) 13–17 (Albert, *Forty-fifth Pennsylvania*); Parker, John Lord, *History of the Twenty-second Massachusetts Infantry, the Second Company Sharpshooters, and the Third Light Battery, in the War of the Rebellion* (Boston, 1887) 5 (Parker, *Twenty-second Massachusetts*); Draper, William F., *Recollections of a Varied Career* (Boston, 1908) 35, 37 (Draper, *Recollections*); Waite, Otis F. R., *New Hampshire in the Rebellion containing Histories of the several New Hampshire Regiments and Biographical Notices of Many of the Prominent Actors in the Civil War of 1861–1865*, 85 (Claremont, 1870); Jordan, *Gould Journals*, 55, 65, entries dated August 19, September 30, and October 1, 1861.

produced one major general, nine colonels, four lieutenant colonels, six majors, twenty captains, and twenty-nine lieutenants, a total of sixty-nine commissioned officers.[38] The First Vermont ended its term of three-month service on August 2, 1861. It had taken to Washington 753 men, and of that number 250 later held commissions.[39]

The Twenty-second Massachusetts, Henry Wilson's three-year regiment, collected many of its officers from the Bull Run pool. Walter S. Sampson, who had served three months as captain of Company K in the Sixth Massachusetts, became a company commander. The first lieutenant of Company A, Charles O. Conant, had served two years in the Mexican War as a first lieutenant in the Second Michigan. A pensioner for wounds received in action in Mexico, he surrendered the pension in order to re-enter the service. The second lieutenant in the company was Henry Connor, who had served three months in the Eighth Massachusetts. All commissioned officers and sergeants in Company D had seen active service.

In Company B, the company commander, David K. Wardwell, had served in the war with Mexico, part of the time on the staff of General Pierce; had raised Company F, Fifth Massachusetts; and had served at Bull Run. With the field officers of his regiment disabled during the battle, he succeeded to command. At the close of the three-months' campaign, the War Department authorized him to raise an independent regiment that was ultimately assigned with his recruits to the Twenty-second. Captain Wardwell became successively lieutenant colonel of the Thirty-eighth Massachusetts, colonel of the Thirteenth Veteran Reserve Corps, and a brigadier general.

When he returned from his three months' service, Sergeant N. W. Burt of Company G, Fourth Massachusetts, recruited Company C for the Twenty-second and became its captain. He was later promoted to major in the regiment. As its first lieutenant, Company E had Nelson A. Miles, later lieutenant colonel of the Sixty-first New York, then colonel, brigadier general, and brevet major general of United States Volunteers, with command of a division of the Second Corps at the close of the war.[40] Other officers of the Twenty-second Massachusetts were William Tilton, who served periodically as a brigade commander in the Fifth Corps, and Charles Jackson Paine, who entered the regiment as captain of Company I on October 8,

---

38 Donaghy, John, *Army Experience of Capt. John Donaghy, 103rd Penn'a Vols., 1861–1864* (Deland, 1926) 13–17 (Donaghy, *Experience*); de Trobriand, Regis, George J., trans. *Four Years in the Army of the Potomac* (Boston, 1888) 64 (de Trobriand, *Four Years*).

39 Benedict, *Vermont in the Civil War*, 1, 61.

40 De Montravel, Peter R., *A Hero to his Fighting Men: Nelson A. Miles 1839–1925* (Kent and London 1998) 5–6. Reviewing his officer appointments as carefully as he always did, Andrew determined that Miles was too young to be a company commander and required him to accept a lieutenancy, something that rankled Miles the rest of his life. *Ibid.*

served with it until January 14, 1862, when he was promoted to major in another regiment, then was commissioned colonel of the Second Louisiana Infantry on October 25, 1862, and finally promoted to brevet brigadier general on July 4, 1864.[41] The history of the Twenty-second Massachusetts exemplified the pattern for the future. The governors would identify talented men from the Bull Run pool and commission them.

For good conduct at Hanover, Gaines Mill, and Turkey Bend, Morgan commissioned James C. Rice colonel of the regiment. For his good conduct at Malvern Hill and Second Bull Run, Fitz John Porter, Daniel Butterfield, and others recommended him for promotion to brigadier general.[42]

Throughout the war the Bull Run pool would be the largest single source of general officers for the Army of the Potomac. Even men who served as second lieutenants, the lowest officer's rank, first lieutenants, and captains, would rise to be major generals and brigadier generals. This group included young, unknown men like Adelbert Ames, Romeyn B. Ayres, Absalom Baird, Henry Alanson Barnum, Francis Channing Barlow, Joseph J. Bartlett, George L. Beal, John R. Brooke, George Armstrong Custer, Emory Upton, William Woods Averell, Isaac P. Rodman, John H. Hobart Ward, James C. Rice, and many others.[43] They would find themselves at lofty heights at the end of their Army of the Potomac careers.

41   Parker, *Twenty-second Massachusetts*, 3–13, 48, 582–583.

42   Morgan MSS (N.Y.S.L.) letter dated August 21, 1861, from McCurdy to Morgan; NA Offs MS Rpts (Rice); Brown, *Fallen in Battle*, 114–115; Heitman, *Historical Register*, 1, 827; Warner, *Generals in Blue*, 400–401; Norton, Oliver Willcox, *Army Letters, 1861–1865, being Extracts from private Letters to Relatives and Friends from a Soldier in the Field during the Late Civil War with an Appendix containing copies of some official Documents, Papers, and addresses of later Date* (Chicago, 1903) 165, 178 (Norton, *Army Letters*); Bacarella, Michael, *Lincoln's Foreign Legion: The 39th New York Infantry, the Garibaldi Guard* (Shippensburg, 1996) 206 (Bacarella, *Lincoln's Foreign Legion*); Jordan, *Gould Journal*, 55, entry dated August 19, 1861.

43   NA Offs MS Rpts (Rice) (Rice served as a second lieutenant in the Thirty-ninth New York, the Garibaldi Guard); NA Offs MS Rpts (Barlow); NA Offs MS Rpts (Wright), letter dated July 22, 1862 (Wright served as engineer officer to Heintzelman); Misc. Civ. War letters (H.L.) letter dated April 2, 1870, from Barlow to Farlong; NA Offs MS Rpts (Brooke); Bartlett, John Russell, *Memoirs of Rhode Island Officers who were Engaged in the Service of their Country during the Great Rebellion of the South*, 357 (Providence, 1867).

Chapter 12

"I think the Government expects that the officers of the United States Army shall be something more than mere fighting men. It expects, and has a right to expect, that they shall be thoroughly educated gentlemen. I, for one, have entertained none of the prejudice that is felt by some toward the Military Academy and those who graduate from it."

—Senator James Grimes about the qualities necessary for officers

The West Point and Regular Army Pools

*I*n the feudal era, the right, in fact the obligation, to serve as an officer or the equivalent belonged to the landed classes, the nobility.[1] But this requirement did not guarantee able military leadership or military knowledge. In the Thirty Years War, the last great European conflagration before the Age of Battles, one of the principal combatants, Albrecht Wallenstein, Duke of Friedland and Mecklenburg, found in his forces "officers . . . who corresponded in four or five languages while others could not write their names . . . Their common denominators

---

1   All land was owned by the royal ruler, king or prince, who allocated it to his nobles in exchange for performance of certain duties, one of which was to support the ruler, when necessary, with specified troops and equipment in war. The vassal owing this duty would "recruit" (supply) the men who were to compose his obligatory contingent and would generally serve the ruler at their head. If all went well, the vassal and his men would be paid by revenue from the spoils taken in war and battle, a practice that continued well into the nineteenth century. Norman, A. V. B., *The Medieval Soldier*, 103–104 (New York, 1971); generally Farwell, Byron, *Eminent Victorian Soldiers: Seekers of Glory* (New York and London, 1985).

197

were egotism, brutality, lack of friendship, and the absence of even such chivalric bonds as existed between brigands. They competed for place, emulated one another in intrigue on behalf of or against their commander in chief, and rivals in pillage."[2]

In the next two centuries the War of the Spanish Succession, the Seven Years War, and the Napoleonic Wars marked the infancy of professionalism in the European officer corps.[3] Training, study, and practice began for the first time. In America during the century after Napoleon, the development of the United States Military Academy at West Point marked the birth and growth of professionalism. The military academy became the focal point of officer development, reaching its pre-Civil War apogee in the War with Mexico.[4] Although many pools would contribute to the corps of officers that would lead the Army of the Potomac, they would have more uniformity and more focus than the military leaders of the Thirty Years War. Like Lincoln, all those who shared the power to appoint faced the formidable tasks of finding, identifying, and selecting. James Grimes, a Radical Republican Senator from Iowa, described their goals on the floor of the Senate:

> I think the Government expects that the officers of the United States Army shall be something more than mere fighting men. It expects, and has a right to expect, that they shall be thoroughly educated gentlemen. I, for one, have entertained none of the prejudice that is felt by some toward the Military Academy and those who graduate from it. That academy and the character and conduct of those who have graduated from it have sufficiently vindicated the institution from all aspersions that have been cast upon it.[5]

After mailing a series of commissions to new officers, John G. Nicolay, one of the president's secretaries, described the characteristics officers should have in a

---

2   Mann, Golo, trans Charles Kessler, *Wallenstein: His Life Narrated by Galo Mann*, 303 (New York, 1971).

3   Weigley, Russell F., *The Age of Battles: The Quest for Decisive Warfare from Breitenfeld to Waterloo*, 540–543 (Bloomington and Indianapolis, Indiana, 1991).

4   Generally, Griess, Thomas E., MS dissertation "Dennis Hart Mahan: West Point Professor and Advocate of Professionalism, 1830–1871" (UMI dissertation services, 1969).

5   Salter, William, *The Life of James W. Grimes, Governor of Iowa 1854–1858 a Senator of the United States 1859–1869*, 128 (New York, 1876). Not everyone agreed that West Point was the fount of military knowledge or leadership characteristics. Morse, John T., Jr., ed., *Diary of Gideon Welles: Secretary of the Navy Under Lincoln and Johnson*, 3 vols. (Boston and New York, 1911) 2, 85, entry dated August 17, 1862 (Morse, *Welles Diary*); Tap, Bruce, *Over Lincoln's Shoulder: The Committee on the Conduct of the War* (Lawrence, 1998) 39–41, 57–62 (Tap, *Over Lincoln's Shoulder*).

letter. "They must begin with the distinct understanding that as yet they know nothing—that they have everything to learn. That an army officer is not merely a target to be shot at by the enemy—that war is not merely a business of throat-cutting and burning and butchering. In performing the duties of an officer and in conducting the operations of war, there is ample scope and opportunity for the development and exercise of a man's highest intellectual faculties and capabilities. A good officer ought to be able to follow a trail and shoot a rifle as well as a frontiersman—make a speech as well as a politician—make surveys, maps, plans, and build roads and works as well as a railroad engineer—write as well as an author—govern as well as a statesman—and be as easy and insinuating in address as a courtier. That he should be able to endure hardships, face danger and submit uncomplainingly to severe discipline, are essential prerequisites, of course."[6]

Almost one hundred years later two worthy adversaries, Bernard Montgomery and Erwin Rommel, faced each other in another great war. Before they died, both men, revered by their troops, described the characteristics necessary for high-ranking officers. Both showed not only remarkable similarity in the factors they sought but in the characteristics that served well in the American Civil War. Bernard Montgomery, who commanded the British Eighth Army in North Africa, asked about an officer:

- where is he going?
- will he go all out?
- has he the talents and equipment, including knowledge, experience, and skill?
- will he make decisions, assume responsibility for them, and take the necessary risks?
- will he delegate and decentralize—after he creates an organization with a smooth and simple master plan that has focal points for decision?[7]

Erwin Rommel, commander of the Afrika Korps, wanted answers to the following questions:

- does he have comprehensive technical and organizational knowledge leading to independence of mind?
- will he follow mental conception by immediate action?

---

6   Nicolay MSS (L.C.) letter dated March 13, 1862, from Nicolay to Therena.

7   Montgomery, Field Marshal Bernard, *The Memoirs of Field Marshal the Viscount Montgomery of Alamein*, K. G., 75 (Cleveland, 1958).

- will he have personal and comradely contact with the men in order to capitalize on the idealism which brought them willingly to war?
- does he have the psychological strength to adjust to the non-determinative successes of the adversary? and
- will he be able to recognize the separatist tendencies of the various branches (infantry, engineers, etc.), eradicate branch ambition, and achieve unity of purpose?[8]

The men presenting either set of principles, or both melded, would produce successful high-ranking officers for any army in any war.

Describing standards of conduct lost in the dreadful, recent conduct of civilians in high places in the United States, Jefferson Davis as secretary of war wrote John G. Barnard, superintendent of the military academy, "The great purpose of the Academy is to train cadets for the high and responsible duties of officers of the army. Those to whom the honor of the country is to be entrusted should in all things be elevated to the rare standard of the gentleman, or if by their nature can not rise so high, they should be separated from the academy, and left to pursue some other occupation than that of the profession of arms."[9]

Even the press could make the correct noises on the subject, no matter what it might say in the reality of the moment. Commenting on the work of Henry Wilson's Senate Committee on Military Affairs, *The New York Herald* noted that the Senate had suggested almost one hundred fifty men for consideration as brigadier general. The committee thought it would report fifty as worthy of promotion. "In the investigation of the qualifications of each man," the *Herald* said, "the committee seem [sic] determined that no man shall receive their endorsement simply on account of political influence, family or wealth but alone on those requisite qualifications necessary to make a good officer."[10]

The relationship between the politicians and the West Point pool, an unpleasant, uneasy marriage of necessity, began long before the war. At West Point, as the politicians saw it, the cadets and, therefore, the graduates and the officers had been inculcated with secessionism. Many focused primarily on the use, or not, of a con-

---

8   Hart, B. H. Liddell, ed., *The Rommel Papers*, 516–521 (Norwalk, 1988, Easton Press ed.). One cannot read this book without seeing a much larger man than the "Desert Fox" of legend.

9   Crist, *The Papers of Jefferson Davis, 1853–1855*, 5, 136–137, letter dated November 16, 1855, from Davis to Barnard.

10   *The New York Herald*, January 20, 1862, p. 1, col. 1.

stitutional law treatise by William Rawle, a Philadelphia lawyer, who acknowl-edged the right of secession. Although some concluded that the book was used for no more than two years, 1825 to 1827, others claimed it was the standard text on constitutional law until 1861. These claims and the attitude of many toward West Point during the war show that, factual or not, many believed that the West Point curriculum treated secession as an acceptable constitutional concept. Some mem-bers of Congress made efforts during the war to terminate the annual appropria-tions for the Military Academy.[11]

With officers leaving regularly for service in the Confederacy and the leader-ship of the Rebel armies being built from alumni of the military academy, the loy-alty of the Regular Army West Point pool stood in doubt. Even though the American Civil War does not present the classic characteristics of a revolution, promotion to general officer from that pool presented many of the problems found in a revolu-tion.[12] In the French army at the outbreak of the Revolution, the nobility dominated the officer corps; the nobility was a target of the Revolution, and the Revolution treated thirty-four generals to the guillotine. Nevertheless, the pre-Revolution offi-cer corps had all the experience in high command and the expertise of war. Finally determining that it could not survive without this class of leaders, the revolutionary

11   D.A.B., 8, 400-401; Latta, James W., "Was Secession Taught at West Point" in *Broadfoot MOLLUS Pennsylvania*, 59; 239–300, esp. 239–241, 290–292 (Wilmington, 1995) generally Williams, T. Harry, "The Attack upon West Point during the Civil War" in *Mississippi Valley Historical Review*, vol. 25, March 1939, pp. 491–504.

12   See generally Brinton, Crane, *The Anatomy of a Revolution* (New York, 1965, rev. exp. ed.). The American Civil War does not satisfy Brinton's entire list of strict criteria for designation as a revolution, but it has many of them. According to one theory the French Revolution, when con-sidered as if it were the "French Revolution" only, is seen too narrowly. According to this theory, the period of 1760 to 1800, delimited by the American Revolution and the French Revolution, was a time of worldwide revolution. Palmer, Robert R. *The Age of the Democratic Revolution: A Political History of Europe and America 1760–1800* (vol. 1, *The Challenge* and vol. 2, *The Strug-gle*) (Princeton, 1959 and 1964). Although worldwide revolution is not one of Brinton's criteria, the American Civil War, when taken as part of the period from 1848 to 1870, has many of Palmer's elements. Featuring the Revolutions of 1848, especially in Germany, Italy, and France, then passing through the Unification of Italy, the wars to unify Germany, the American Civil War, the truly revolutionary Meiji Restoration in Japan in 1868, and the French Revolution of 1870, a worldwide nineteenth century Age of Revolution appears to have occurred, even if Brinton's defi-nition must be somewhat diluted. Langer, William L., *Political and Social Upheaval 1832–1852*, 319–512 (New York, 1969); Beasley, W. G., *The Meiji Restoration*, 1–2, Introduction (Stanford, 1972); Porch, Douglas, *The French Foreign Legion: A Complete History of the Legendary Fight-ing Force*, 163–169 (New York, 1991); Sperber, Jonathan, *Rhineland Radicals*, 423–430, 481–492 (Princeton, 1991).

government reluctantly struck an uneasy peace with the noble officer corps and began an unstable partnership with it.[13]

From 1917 to 1940 the Russian officer corps and the Bolsheviks suffered through the same star-crossed association. In 1918 Lenin and Trotsky decided they must have the service of officers from the czarist army and in July began to draft ex-Imperial officers, who would be controlled by political, terrorist, and collective means.[14] Although the Stalinist government executed between fifty thousand and eighty thousand officers during the Great Purge, men of noble descent nevertheless served to high rank.[15] In America, George Washington, a leader of his revolution, received his early military training from the Crown and fought for the king in his first battle.[16]

The West Point Regular Army officers and the Radical Republicans shared a very similar, unstable, and unpleasant relationship. In a democratic republic like America, executions would not occur; but scrutiny of loyalty and civilian uncertainty about devotion to the cause would compromise many careers in the early war. Like the members of the officer corps during the French and Russian Revolutions, a number of younger officers[17]—members of Scott's company-grade officer group—awaited their chance.

Whatever the relationship between the West Point pool and the members of government might have been in 1861, it had begun, in each individual case, five to

---

13   Griffith, Paddy, *The Art of War of Revolutionary France 1789–1802* (London and Mechanicsburg, 1998) 108–113, especially 109 (Griffith, *Art of War*).

14   Pipes, Richard, *Russia Under the Bolshvik Regime*, 50–53 (New York, 1993). "Collective Responsibility," a medieval Russian practice renewed in a decree prepared by Trotsky, made an officer's family (mother, father, brother, wife, and children) liable for his conduct. By November 1918, the Bolshvik regime had decreed that all officers under fifty and all generals under sixty must register for the draft. Ibid., 52.

15   John Erickson, *The Soviet High Command: A Military-Political History 1918–1941* (London, 1962) Chapter 3, 53–83, esp. 58; and Chapter 5, 113–144, esp. 114–116. Michael Tukhachevsky and B. M. Shaposhnikov, both members of the minor nobility, would rise to positions of high rank and great influence, ibid. 53, 842–843, 844–845. Shaposhnikov would survive some political missteps to die of ill health in 1945. Tukhachevsky would be executed in the Stalinist purge in 1937. Erickson stated that his execution was without trial, but Shimon Naveh in Schukman, *Stalin's Generals*, writing after the opening of the Communist records, describes Tukhachevsky's trial. This revelation stands as a negative compliment to Erickson's brilliant kremlinology in his cold war era history of the Communist high command.

16   Freeman, Douglas Southall, *George Washington: A Biography*, 7 vols. (New York, 1949–1957) generally *Young Washington* vol. 2, especially 68–81 (Freeman, *Washington*).

17   Griffith, *Art of War*, 113.

forty years earlier; and some of the office holders from the initiation remained present in 1861. Any man wishing to attend the Military Academy had to run the gauntlet of political appointment that preceded the admissions examinations. The classes graduating in the 1840s would produce the most numerous exemplars of the Scott Rule, captains and lieutenants who would become generals.

Seeking admission in the class that would graduate in 1847, Orlando Bolivar Willcox lived near the frontier in Detroit, Michigan, and chose the military over the ministry. Although orphaned at an early age when his father died of a disease contracted while hunting, Willcox and his mother seemed to have the right connections for an appointment to the United States Military Academy at West Point. William Woodbridge, the recently elected United States senator from Michigan, had given them "assurances." Jacob Howard, Michigan's only member of the House, was a "quasi-friend" of the family. During the winter of 1842–1843 Woodbridge wrote that, if young Willcox wanted an appointment, he should come to Washington at once because the Michigan delegation had severed its relations with President Tyler. Off he went, first by stagecoach, then by train, till he found himself in a room on the second floor of Willard's Hotel.

Promptly, Willcox went to see Senator Woodbridge. He should "see the President first thing," Woodbridge advised, and to do that he must "make friends" with the black man who practically held the keys to the president's reception room.

The young Willcox, only nineteen, introduced himself to the gatekeeper, described his trip from Detroit, and explained his purpose.

"God almighty," exclaimed the gatekeeper. "You come alone all the way from Michigan to see the President! Boy, you see the men sitting around the bar. They are Senators and Members, but they can wait. Some of 'em will never see him. You shall see Massa Tyler fust of all."

With trepidation Willcox entered the "Great Presence" and found a tall, slender gentleman of Virginia with blue eyes, light hair, and a prominent nose, suggesting decisiveness, if not obstinacy. Willcox explained his purpose and alluded to the problem with the Michigan delegation.

Tyler shook his hand. "My young friend, I will do the best I can for you."

Thinking his problem solved, Willcox was elated. His heart in his mouth and unable to speak, he withdrew, shook hands with his "darky stage manager," and deemed the game "as good as won." He returned to Willard's; took a letter of introduction from his trunk; and paid a social call on the general in chief of the army, General Macomb, who lived in a pretentious mansion at the corner of Seventeenth and I. He found the general not at home, Mrs. Macomb available, and his niece present. Luckily for Willcox, the niece's father was the chief clerk in the office of the Chief of Engineers. She prepared a note to her father, and promptly the next morning, Willcox presented himself and the note. The clerk was "inclined to 'aid me all he could in my quest,'" wrote Willcox many years later, "giving me the *modus operandi*, in other words, 'the ropes' for securing appointments to the Academy." So far, he now learned, he had seen no useful people. The person who controlled his destiny was Jacob Howard, his member of congress. Representatives made the nominations that secured appointments. Participation by the president would be ministerial.

"Perhaps General Totten may be able to give you some good advice how to proceed," concluded the clerk. He took Willcox into the office of the Chief of Engineers and introduced him. Totten confirmed the clerk's information, adding with a look of significance, "The sooner you see Mr. Howard the better. There may be other applicants."

Totten had shown prescience. Willcox found Howard reluctant but—in the end—willing to help.

"Oh, yes, Willcox. I'll do all I can," he said, "but I don't see why I must do it all."

He took a seat at his desk and wrote a formal letter. With youthful fervor, Willcox took the letter, thanked the congressman, and returned to the Chief of Engineers.

The general read the letter, then exclaimed, "Why, sir, this is not a nomination—but I'll fix it."

Two more times Willcox trudged through the fire with the reluctant Congressman. At last, he had the letter in proper form and could start home for Detroit.[18] The men who held the offices with which Willcox had dealt would play roles in the creation of the officer corps in 1861.

Whether by president, cabinet member, governor, or electing troops, the choice of an officer for any grade had to be made with one eye on the man and the other on his record. If he had experience or training that bore no stigma, he could be considered a valuable candidate. No one could tell how any man would perform in the test of fire. Nor could they predict that he would master the many important noncombat tasks of an officer. Local prominence suggested leadership ability. A successful career in business or at the bar implied the ability to perform the complex, frustrating, bureaucratic, administrative responsibilities of a command position.[19] Men borne upward by lofty expectations sometimes failed, but

18   Scott, Robert Garth, *Forgotten Valor: The Memoirs, Journals, & Civil War Letters of Orlando B. Willcox* (Kent and London, 1999) 42–49 (Scott, *Willcox Journals*); Robertson, James I., Jr., *Stonewall Jackson: The Man, the Soldier, the Legend*, 24–26 (New York, 1997); Waugh, John C., *The Class of '46 from West Point to Appomattox: Stonewall Jackson, George McClellan and Their Brother Officers* (New York, 1994) 3–10 (Waugh, *Class of '46*).

19   Cox, Jacob Dolson, *Military Reminiscences of the Civil War*, 2 vols. (New York, 1900) 1, 14, 17–18, 39, 168–173 (Cox, *Reminiscences*); Schurz, *Reminiscences*, 2, 330 ff.

that did not reflect adversely on the perspicacity of the chooser at the moment of choice, especially in the early days of the war. Because none of the pools presented a uniformly qualified or even an organized slate of candidates, none would be coopted wholesale for the officer corps or for higher command. Selection would be necessary; but like all other early tasks, it would be done without the guidance of experience or precedent. The sources for the hundreds of general officers who would lead the brigades, divisions, corps, armies, and independent forces in the Union Army existed naturally; but the individuals would rise from them in unpredictable, irregular, and unsystematic ways, especially early in the war.

Of course, the Regular Army, populated primarily by graduates of the Military Academy, would serve as the most obvious initial source of officers. Former Regular Army officers, men who had resigned to return to civilian life, would also form a large component of the officer corps. Already recorded on the muster rolls of Bull Run, many of them had records that could be evaluated before promotion or reappointment.

Notwithstanding the heartfelt and strident but fatuous views of the Radicals, the most reliable pool was the West Point alumni, who had a military education from, even at that time, one of the best military schools in the world. Its members had knowledge and, no matter how soon after graduation they might have resigned, valuable training. When little or no performance in the field could be evaluated, the West Point pool could be expected as a whole to provide the most predictably successful candidates. Obvious to all but the Radicals, this would form the basis for most 1861 appointments and promotions to general officer not driven by special circumstances. During this time for selection of generals, the graduates of the Military Academy caught the most stars.

No matter how the army would fight the Confederates, whether as Scott or McClellan foresaw it, the West Point pool lacked the size to supply all brigade, division, corps, and army commanders, along with the critical staff officers. Its situation was even worse than appearances because its two groups, those on active duty and those who had resigned, lost a large percentage of their constituents to the Confederacy.

Postmaster General Montgomery Blair, himself an alumnus, proposed a method for expanding the Military Academy pool. Two senior classes, a four-year class and one of the last five-year classes, were scheduled to graduate in the early summer of 1862. In the fall of 1861, Blair proposed that both classes be graduated and commissioned at once. Mahan strongly opposed this. Competent officers, he felt, developed only over a period of time. "Such men as McClellan, McDowell, Rosecrans, etc. etc.," he wrote, required extended training and discipline. Napoleon had spoken highly of the officers graduating from the officers' school in France, but after suffering a series of reverses in 1813, Napoleon finally took all students from the military schools in France, commissioned them, and put them in the army. Essentially useless, many became bitter about their lack of development because of the fundamental training they had missed.[20]

The Radicals would not have desired such a large influx of Military Academy training in their army. To them, West Point inculcated and enhanced Southern sympathies. Many of the graduates represented the Southern planter aristocracy, not the northern middle-class bourgeoisie. Equally important, if not more so, the graduates, North and South, tended to be members of the Democratic Party. Except for those few plebes appointed "at large," the members of each incoming class owed their appointment, like Willcox, to their congressional representatives. For more than three decades, the Democratic Party,[21] now the party of slavery, disloyalty, and secession, had been the dominant political party in the country; and the Democratic Congressmen had appointed sons of party members. Some candidates had, even in their young years, worked diligently for the Democratic Party. Before his appointment to the Military Academy, Hugh Judson Kilpatrick had stumped his state as an articulate young spokesman for Democratic candidates. His appointment served, at least in part, as recognition of, and expression of appreciation for, this.[22]

The country had not progressed so far from the French Revolution or from its own revolution that it remembered nothing about the old royal armies, the role of the aristocratic class, membership in the officer class as the exclusive right of the nobility, and exclusion of commoners from the corps of officers. Certainly its better read people knew that in the latter half of the eighteenth century, a growing trend of middle-class entry into the European officer ranks had been stifled in both France and Germany as the officer corps became increasingly the domain of the nobility. In France a royal edict of 1781 required future officer candidates to prove at least four generations of antecedent nobility,[23] and by the outbreak of the Revolution in

---

20   McClellan MSS (L.C.) letter dated September 3, 1861, from Dennis Hart Mahan to Chase.

21   Waugh, *Class of 1846*, 3–21.

22   Moore, James, *Kilpatrick and our Cavalry: Comprising a Sketch of the Life of General Kilpatrick with an Account of the Cavalry Raids, Engagements, and Operations under his Command from the Beginning of the Rebellion to the Surrender of Johnston*, 28 (New York, 1865); Comte de Paris, *A History of the Civil War in America*, 4 vols. (Philadelphia, 1875) 1, 17–18 (Comte de Paris, *Civil War in America*); Martin, Samuel J., *Kill-Cavalry: Sherman's Merchant of Terror: The Life of Union General Hugh Judson Kilpatrick* (Madison, 1996) 16 (Martin, *Kilpatrick*).

23   Rothenberg, Gunther E., *The Art of Warfare in the Age of Napoleon*, 29 (Norwalk, 1995, Easton Press ed.).

1789, commoners had generally been driven from the rolls of the French officer corps.[24]

In the Prussian Army this result followed direct actions by Frederick the Great, who turned to the nobility to replace the severe casualties his officers had suffered in the Seven Years War. Commoners, except a few in the engineers and artillery, he purged.[25] In the Prussian Army in 1789, eighty-five nobles and no commoners held commission as officers of the line infantry; fifteen years later the number of titled officers for the line infantry had grown to 254 while the untitled officers had remained at zero.[26] Americans must also have known that the promise of far-reaching liberal reform in Prussia had been broken after the defeat of Napoleon and that the Prussian officer corps played an important role in this march to the rear.[27]

To the Radical Republicans the West Point alumni wore the mantle of conservative elitism, like the aristocratic European officer corps before 1789 and after 1815.[28] Unlike Senator Grimes, many of them found the West Pointers anathema. As one of them wrote *The New York Tribune* in early September, "The article in your paper of the 27th on the West Point Military Academy is definitely by 'one who has seen service,' and who has reflected upon the evils which adhere to that Institution—an Institution which utterly crushes all *sabre decor*, and makes of our army a mere spiritless and mercenary mass of men. As now constituted, our army is entirely opposed to the spirit of our Government, and far more aristocratic in its tendencies than that of any other service. It might be an interesting question to determine how far the peculiar education given to our West Point graduates has tended to bring about the present unfortunate condition of affairs. My own belief is, that it has had an important influence of evil."[29] That opinion and the officers' general political affiliation with the conservative Democratic party made the Academy graduates objects of suspicion to the liberals of the period, the Radical

24   Duffy, Christopher, *The Military Experience in the Age of Reason* (New York, 1988) 36–38 (Duffy, *Military Experience*).

25   Duffy, Christopher, *A Military Life of Frederick the Great*, 330–334 (Norwalk, 1992, Easton Press ed.); Craig, *Politics of the Prussian Army*, 25–26; Duffy, *Military Experience*, 44–46.

26   Paret, Peter, *York and the Era of Prussian Reform 1807–1815* (Princeton, 1966) 263–266, Appendix 2 "Statistics on the Social Composition of the Officer Corps in the Prussian Army between 1789 and 1817," especially Tables 1 and 2, 265, 266.

27   Craig, Gordon A., *Politics of the Prussian Army, 1640–1945*, 65–81 (Oxford, 1898); Goerlitz, Walter, trans. Brian Battersaw, *The German General Staff, 1847–1945*, 52–57 (New York, 1953).

28   de Joinville, *Army of the Potomac*, 13.

29   *The New York Daily Tribune*, Sunday, September 1, 1861, p.1, col. 1, letter to the editor.

Republicans.[30] In their dealings with the volunteers, some of the West Point officers confronted problems in ways that may have justified the Radicals' doubts.

Those captains and lieutenants who benefitted from the Scott rule for promotion to general officer had enjoyed an incredible, completely unforeseeable experience. Winfield Hancock's wife expressed this sentiment to another officer, recently promoted to brigadier general.

"That's alright," he replied, "but if a cannon were fired down Pennsylvania Avenue it would strike a hundred or more newly created brigadiers."[31]

In the early stages of the war, Scott and E. D. Townsend, his adjutant general, opposed spreading the Regular Army officers through the volunteer regiments or assigning them to the new generals as staff officers. The reasons for this they never made clear, but it was indisputably their policy. Townsend had already advised McClellan to keep the tiny Regular Army an intact elite force. Probably sharing the views of Scott, his long-time superior officer, Townsend believed an expanded Regular Army would form the vital core of the military force that would give the Union victory.[32] As a consequence former Regular Army officers who had resigned their commissions to return to civilian life before the war seemed to fare better in appointments than Regular Army officers on active duty.[33] Some of the active Regulars tendered their resignations to take volunteer commissions while others sought leaves of absence from their Regular Army assignments.[34]

George Crook, a member of the West Point Class of 1852, on leave in New York City when promoted to captain in the Fourth United States Infantry in the fall of 1861, thought he would be allowed to take service in the volunteers because he was so far from California, the home of his regiment. Although older officers advised him to stay in his regiment, he went to Washington to obtain a leave of absence to enter the volunteers. He called on General Schenck, a fellow Ohioan, for

---

30   Tap, *Over Lincoln's Shoulder*, 20–21, 60, 65, 150; Weigley, Russell F., *History of the United States Army* (Bloomington, 1984) 244–246, 254–255 (Weigley, *United States Army*).

31   Hancock, *Reminiscences*, 78.

32   McClellan MSS (L.C.) letter dated October 29, 1861, from George Gibbs to McClellan; Morgan MSS (N.Y.S.L.) letter dated August 16, 1861, from Thomas to Morgan; Wilson, James H., *Life and Services of William F. Smith, Major General, United States Volunteers in the Civil War* (Wilmington, 1904) 32–33 (Wilson, *Smith*), Bayard, *Bayard*, 168.

33   Upton, *Military Policy*, 237. In fact, of the Regular officers on active duty in 1861, fifty-one percent reached the rank of colonel and twenty-five percent became general officers; but of the former Regular Army officers re-entering the service during the war, eighty percent became colonels and forty-four percent became brigadier or major-generals. *Ibid.*

34   Bayard, *Bayard*, 186.

assistance. Undoubtedly scarred by the treatment he had received for his performance at Vienna and Bull Run, Schenck was at first cool, making disparaging remarks about regulars. After a while he acquiesced and said he would go with Crook
to the president. When they started for the War Department, they met Lincoln.

Schenck explained their errand.

Lincoln advised them that, at a meeting the previous day, the cabinet had agreed
to allow one hundred officers of the Regular Army to take service in the volunteers.

Schenck asked Lincoln if he would not give an order to the adjutant general for
Crook.

Somewhat disingenuously, Lincoln refused because he never interfered with
any branches of the government, he said, "any more than he would try to mend
a watch."

Schenck and Crook continued to the adjutant general's office where they met
Adjutant General Lorenzo Thomas. Schenck explained the object of the visit and
referred to the action of the cabinet the previous day.

Thomas acknowledged the cabinet determination and stated that, if he had his
way, not a single officer of the Regular Army would be permitted to go into the volunteer service.

Schenck treated Thomas, a haughty Regular and a graduate of West Point,
more rudely than he had treated Crook, saying sharply that he thanked the Lord
Lorenzo Thomas did not have his way.

Thomas then told Crook that the governor of a state would have to apply for him.

Crook telegraphed Governor Dennison of Ohio that he could accept the
colonelcy of a regiment if Dennison had one to give.

Dennison responded that he could appoint Crook colonel of a regiment then
being organized at Columbus.

With this information, Crook obtained permission for an indefinite leave of absence and departed for Columbus, where he immediately received command of the
Thirty-sixth Ohio Infantry.[35]

Many of the active Regulars who found their way into the Bull Run army had
been called to the capital in the last days of the Buchanan administration to secure the
safety of the capital. Being handy and visible did not hurt their chances for promotion. Others, apparently "out of sight and out of mind," did not fare as well, a fortuitous, geographic basis for promotion not lost on men far away. Lieutenant Colonel

35 *D.A.M.B.*, 1, 218; *Cullum*, 2, 1573; Warner, *Generals in Blue*, 489–490; *D.A.B.*, 2, pt. 2,
563; Schmitt, Martin F., ed., *General George Crook: His Autobiography* (Norman, 1946) 84–85
(Schmitt, *Crook Autobiography*).

Harvey Brown, number six in the West Point Class of 1818,[36] had been chosen in April by Captain Montgomery C. Meigs and Lieutenant Colonel Erasmus D. Keyes to command the troops sent to Fort Pickens. A few days after the defeat at Bull Run, in a long letter to Meigs, Brown, still at Fort Pickens, vented his feelings about the promotion of officers stationed in Washington, a geographic test for promotion.

"Officers at Washington . . . have been magnificently rewarded, while none here (except those having influential friends at Washington, and *they* in my estimation very far from being the most worthy of it), have received the least promotion . . . I think of all of the Officers I have named eminently deserving promotion, and yet, being absent,—out of sight, out of mind;—not one . . . has been noticed. If Government expects good officers, they must reward *merit*, and not *residence at Washington*. I would like to know, what McDowell (except indeed the *arduous* duties of mustering recruits in service) has done or what aptitude for command he has shown, that he should be jumped from a *Major* to *General*, or Keyes or Heintzelman or Potter or F. J. Porter to be made colonels or Emory, an almost traitor, lieutenant colonel over the heads of their betters."[37]

Brown was neither alone nor a voice in the wilderness. Stationed in Detroit for duty on the Great Lakes, Captain George G. Meade gave practical expression to Brown's complaint and to the Geography Rule Brown had enunciated. Less than two weeks after Brown's letter, Meade wrote, "I went to Washington late in June, protested against being kept here . . . so much for working faithfully in the Lakes instead of hanging about Washington. If I had been in Washington for the last year, ready at the right time to maneuver & push matters I might be a col. or Brig. Genl. I do not say this as a matter of vanity—& boasting, but I mean that these things are obtained not on merit but on influence & had I have been in [sic] the ground I could have tried my hand at the latter."[38]

Nor were civilians any more pleased with the administration's appointments than Colonel Brown. As one civilian wrote to Chase, "The *Army appointments* are exciting equal interest and conversation. The whole administration is severely blamed, having suffered terribly if these appointments are continued, upon clinical grounds, or other influences, aside from *fitness*. The subject is loudly talked about every where, and denunciation unmeasured is express."[39]

---

36   *Cullum*, 1, no. 185; Heitman, *Historical Register*, 1, 251.

37   Lincoln MSS (L.C.) letter dated July 26, 1861, from Brown to Meigs.

38   Meade MSS (P.H.S.) letter dated August 5, 1861, from Meade to Dorn[?].

39   Chase MSS (U.P.I.), letter dated June 29, 1861, from Mellen to Chase.

Chapter 13

"No matter about that. His name will make up for any difference there may be, and I'll take the risk that he comes out alright. Schim-mel-fen-NIG must be appointed."

—Lincoln to Fry about commissioning a foreign officer

The Foreigner and Politician Pools

he foreign born with military experience enjoyed favor in high places during the early months of the war. Through American consuls abroad and recruiting agents sent to Europe, "Prime Minister" Seward encouraged military personnel of the Old World to seek commissions in the American military.[1] He used the far-flung operatives of the State Department to recruit German and French nobility who had military experience.

Seward also wrote, as an "old, sincere, personal friend," to Giuseppe Garibaldi to offer him a commission as a major general and sent £1,000 to pay expenses for the general and his staff to return to the United States.[2] One hopeful wrote to Lyman Trumble, a Radical Republican senator, saying, "Garibaldi I learned is to be made a general . . . I should deem it a very great favor could you procure me a position on his staff." Garibaldi would accept the offer, the letter said, if the war

---

1 *M.O.S.*, 142–143; Van Deusen, Glyndon G., *William Henry Seward*, 298, 306 (New York, 1967).

2 Lonn, *Foreigners in the Union Army*, 273–274.

were clearly and unequivocally for the abolition of slavery.[3] The American press approved this recruiting effort because of Garibaldi's long residence in the United States. They thought Garibaldi might be willing to serve the Union cause as an act of "gratitude and from interest in humanity." Rumors of Garibaldi's entry into the United States Army persisted in the European press throughout 1862.[4] He declined the offer. Others did not.

But would foreign or foreign-born officers be welcome in a mid-nineteenth century American army? The country had been colonized and developed primarily by English-speaking Protestants and in its early years of independence had a very restrictive immigration policy.[5] During the 1850s strong national sentiments hostile to foreigners and Catholics, especially in the North, coalesced in a political party that was loosely anti-foreigner, anti-Catholic, and anti-slavery.[6] If foreigners were not readily accepted in society at large, foreign officers in command of United States nationals certainly would not be.[7]

Although Europeans had a tradition of militarism and far more experience at war than Americans, most Americans believed they could do anything and believed they did not need help from Europeans.[8] Some felt the lack of need even more strongly. Expressing his opposition to foreigners in high military positions, Fitz John Porter said, "I doubt the honesty and loyalty of too many now with us."[9]

McClellan's father-in-law and chief of staff suggested to Seward that the foreign candidates apply to new generals for staff positions, but their applications had only limited success because most staff positions went to the new generals' friends and family members. In response to Secretary Seward's several communications on this subject, Marcy said, "I should regard it as highly important if the services of educated officers who speak our language could be secured with our volunteer reg-

3   Trumble MSS (L.C.) letter dated August 13, 1861, from Preston to Trumble.

4   Lonn, *Foreigners in the Union Army*, 274–275.

5   Brimelow, Peter, *Alien Nation, Common Sense about America's Immigration Disaster*, 14–16 (New York, 1995).

6   See generally Anbinder, Tyler, *Nativism and Slavery: The Northern Know Nothings and the Politics of the 1850's* (New York, 1992); Gienapp, William E., *The Origins of the Republican Party, 1852–1856* (New York, 1987).

7   Miller, Delavan S., *Drum Taps in Dixie: Memories of a Drummer Boy, 1861–1865* (Watertown, New York, 1905) 31 (Miller, *Drum Taps in Dixie*).

8   de Joinville, *Army of the Potomac*, 13.

9   Fitz John Porter MSS (Library of Congress) letter dated January 14, 1862, from Porter to Heap.

iments, and if the governors, however, of States would appoint them to the higher positions, or if they could be elected to fill vacancies, I feel confident they would contribute greatly to the efficiency of the Army."[10] The governors had their own candidates for appointment. In addition, vacancies in their regiments were filled, at least in the beginning, by elections, in which unknown foreigners were simply not realistic candidates. Tacitly recognizing them and their motivations, Emory Upton would style them "military adventurers" forty years later.

Knowing that both sides had to build their armies from the ground, Seward probably thought about the contribution of Baron von Steuben to Washington's Continental Army, knew the "foreign adventurers" would accept the first or best offer, and sought to prevent the "officers for hire" from developing the Confederate army. To preempt this potential benefit to the Confederate army he wrote a logical but impractical letter to the secretary of war, recommending that Cameron send a circular to the governors to ask that they provide places for these men.[11]

Once again underscoring the defects of the bilateral power to appoint officers with no one clearly in charge, Cameron wrote a mildly disingenuous circular to the governors of the loyal states, oddly including Virginia in the group. Leaving Seward's preemptive warehousing of foreign officers unmentioned, he wrote, "the Department deeming it of great importance that their services should be secured to volunteer forces, respectfully recommends that, when practicable, they be selected for regimental positions for which they may appear to be qualified."[12] Few regimental commanders or field-grade regimental officers emerged from this part of the foreign pool;[13] nor were the Southerners much more receptive, showing the sentiments of the defunct Know-Nothing or Native American Party to be alive and well even if a political party no longer embodied them.

Nevertheless, individual foreigners sought service, and not "entry-level" service either. Gustave Cluseret presented himself with a letter of recommendation from Garibaldi, who praised his honor and soldierly abilities in the highest terms. Cluseret sought a position with McClellan. The federal government commissioned him a colonel and assigned him to McClellan's staff. When McClellan "did not like his appearance and declined his services,"[14] the secretary of war appointed him a

---

10   Upton, *Military Policy*, 242, letter dated December 4, 1861, from Marcy to Seward.

11   Upton, *Military Policy*, 242, letter dated December 6, 1861, from Seward to Cameron.

12   Upton, *Military Policy*, 242–243, circular dated December 23, 1861, from Cameron to various governors.

13   Lonn, *Foreigners in the Union Army*, chap IX, 215–248.

14   *M.O.S.*, 143.

second time to serve as a colonel on McClellan's staff. After McClellan again declined to have him, he was sent to the Mountain Department.[15]

Having succeeded to command of a brigade, Cluseret earned the distaste of his subordinates by his low level of competence, but more by his disregard and contempt for their rights and feelings. He treated everyone with a tyrannical and despotic air. Finally, officers and men in his brigade petitioned to have him removed. "His idea of military discipline," the petition said, "appears to be simply that he is to play the tyrant over all who belong to his command. He knows nothing of the genius of our institutions or the spirit of our people and whilst he might do to command an army of European conscripts he can never command an army of American volunteers."[16]

During the fall of 1861, McClellan received a letter from a Hungarian officer recruited by Seward's agents. The officer thought it best, he said, to come to a direct understanding about the terms on which he would serve: a bonus of $100,000; an annual salary of $25,000; initial service as McClellan's chief of staff until he acquired the language, then McClellan's position as general in chief. He did not say what he intended for McClellan. When McClellan showed the letter to Lincoln, the president became angry, took it, and told McClellan not to trouble himself about it.[17]

Showing that he had the largeness of character to treat men on the basis of their individual merit rather than as a member of an undesirable class, McClellan had a much different attitude toward Louis Blenker. Before he came to the United States, Blenker had received military training in one of the many German armies and had served in Europe, first in Greece in the Bavarian Legion and later in 1849 in command of a body of revolutionary troops in Germany, where he showed great skill as a political commissar but not as a tactician or strategist. After the south German insurrection in the Rhineland failed, he migrated to the United States, where he became the traveling agent for a very popular, prosperous German weekly and a farmer in New Jersey. At the outbreak of the war, he offered his services to the federal government and very successfully organized the Eighth New York Volunteer Infantry. Immediately after Carl Schurz, another fugitive from the unsuccessful revolutions of 1848, reached New York from Washington, he called on Blenker at his hotel. Blenker received him with magnificent cordiality; offered

---

15 Warner, *Generals in Blue*, 85.

16 Robert H. Milroy MSS (Indiana Historical Society) letter dated January 3, 1863, from several officers including Colonel T. M. Harris of the Tenth Virginia (Union) to J. O. Craveris.

17 *M.O.S.*, 143.

him a glass of wine and a cigar; and when Schurz accepted, rang the bell for the waiter, saying, "Bring me a case of burgundy and a box of your best Havanas."

A few days later, Blenker invited Schurz and Schurz's wife to inspect his regiment, then camped in Terrace Garden on East Fifty-eighth Street. His fine regimental band began to play as he, in full uniform, conducted Schurz and his wife to a little platform. The regiment passed before them in parade, the officers assembled for introductions to Schurz's wife, and Blenker then dismissed them with a most imperial wave of the hand.

When his regiment, wearing light gray uniforms, presenting the finest possible appearance in equipment and bearing and marching with their regimental commander on foot at the head of it, proceeded down Broadway to the Battery to embark for Washington, as many volunteer regiments had done before it, a massive popular demonstration of New York City Germans and many other nationalities piped his men aboard. His regiment was a model regiment, and the brigade he commanded at First Bull Run, although not engaged on Henry House Hill, had stood firm.

Blenker's headquarters in the fall, the wonder and envy of the entire army, centered in a large tent designed for hospital service. After his promotion to brigadier general in August, he filled his headquarters tent with uniquely elaborate, tasteful appointments. When he took camp around Hunter's Chapel about five miles south of Long Bridge, the division found a number of houses vacant, one of which Blenker chose for his headquarters. His large headquarters and staff, composed almost entirely of foreigners, most of whom were members of the German nobility, included numerous horses and sixteen officers. His headquarters was known for its counts, barons, and other representatives of European nobility, all of whom insisted on escorts from the exhausted Fourth New York Cavalry. Officers and civilians alike came from afar to see it. Lavish in his hospitality, Blenker would provide a great and magnificent reception, serving warm champagne and a fruit punch when McClellan visited him.

His grand manner and high-flown eloquence he displayed unstintingly in conversation amused many. In singular contrast with the reserve common among American officers of his rank, Blenker's mannerisms of speech expressed an outgoing personality.

"My dear colonel," he would say.

"My good comrade."

"What a pleasure to see you here."

As John Tidball wrote in his memoirs after the war, "Blenker proved that a man could be a perfect stage general and at the same time a very efficient soldier," and his fellow officers generally respected his honorable character. "He was a brave man, an excellent organizer, and an efficient commander."

He was "not only a fine looking man but military to the back-bone," Tidball continued. "In his handsome uniform of cadet gray he looked every *inch the dashing* soldier." A fellow European but younger and born to a vastly different social stratum, the Comte de Paris, saw him as "a former mercenary German officer in every aspect of the word like those you could meet in our [country?] in the past. He is very brave, boastful, and noisy but a good man with a passion for food and beer who knows how to maintain order in his division. His soldiers, mostly German, trust him and are self-confident. They will probably fight better than the others just by self-esteem."

During the winter Chase heard that Blenker's nomination would not be confirmed by the Senate. If this were so, Chase believed, the president would nominate Schurz. The nomination of Schurz would be better for the army and the administration. Chase did not know Blenker and did not oppose him except on the issue of timing. If he were worthy, he should be confirmed without reference to Schurz; if not, he should be rejected without reference to a successor.

But Blenker had brought with him some European customs not unknown to the United States Army but certainly not accepted. He and his quartermaster bought wood from a farmer, then tried to resell it to the government at a 25 percent profit. Commissions in his brigade could be had in the usual European manner, a colonelcy for $2,000, an acting brigadier generalcy for $3,000. Other commissions: second lieutenant—$100, first lieutenant—$150, captain—$300, major—$500. Blenker sold passes for the Long Bridge to citizens for $5,000. Blenker asked the colonel of one of his regiments to make space among his officers for a count; when the colonel refused because his command needed no more officers, Blenker harassed him until he resigned his commission; and the count could take his place. As good as the division was at drill and public presentation, it was actually a band of marauders and plunderers who could not be restrained. Rather than spend the time and effort necessary to bring it into shape, Blenker "devoted more time to the sale of commissions to adventurers . . . the first two or three months pay being the consideration."

Almost 70 percent of Blenker's division in the fall of 1861 had European origins, mostly German. Created on October 12, 1861, the division had two brigades, one commanded by Colonel Julius Stahel (or Stahl), a Hungarian who had served in the Austrian army, then chosen the losing side in the Revolution of 1848; the other by Adolph Wilhelm August Friedrich Baron von Steinwehr, son of a lieutenant general in the Prussian army, educated in German military schools and colonel of the Twenty-ninth New York. The majority of the officers and men in the division had experience resulting from service in the military forces of Germany or another European country.

With this background it could early have been the best division in the Army of the Potomac. Franklin, whose division was a short distance to the south, called it the "circus"; and he and McClellan both liked to visit it to be entertained by the "pomp and circumstance" that greeted their approach. As soon as they were seen from camp, the bugler would sound "officers' call," which would summon all the brigade officers in their polyglot finery, Blenker at their head in a cloak lined with scarlet. The "most formal and polished courtesy" he would lavish on the visitors. After the initial formalities Blenker would shout, "Ordinand numero eins!" Quantities of champagne would appear, the band play, and songs resound. To McClellan, the drill and bearing of the division were excellent.

For dress parade all regimental officers presented themselves at 6 P.M. at headquarters in full dress uniform and arranged to form three sides of a square, the headquarters tent forming the fourth side. In the front rank stood the field-grade officers, the captains in the second, the first lieutenants next, and the second lieutenants as always—and today—the rear rank. With all ready and in place, "the Great Mogul"—the division commander—attended by his staff, who were followed by fifty or more bogus counts, barons, and dukes, would enter the square from a hand salute which they held until the Mogul raised his gold laced cap. The field officers approached, they saluted again, and the adjutant general delivered the orders, at which the officers dispersed to their camps. The regiments' irregular and spasmodic drills, which were without "system and proper supervision," left the division in a poor state of discipline.[18]

Officers with European military experience appeared in various subsets: immigrants living in the United States, fugitives from the Revolutions of 1848, men coming to the United States at the outbreak of the war, foreign adventurers, "soldiers of fortune," and mercenaries. Before the war foreigners had served as officers in the Regular Army; but none had risen to high rank, the most senior being a lieutenant

---

18   Tidball MS mem (USMA) 216A; Comte de Paris MS diary (large diary) (A.N. de la M. de F.) Chase MSS (UPI) entry dated November 7, 1861; 433, Shuckers, *Chase*, letter dated March 10, 1862, from Chase to Henry Wilson in the Senate; Sigel MSS (N.Y.S.H.) affidavit dated February 24, 1862, [the signature is illegible]; Schurz, *Reminiscences*, 233–234; de Trobriand, *Four Years*, 106; Sperber, *Rhineland Radicals*, 407, 423–424; *M.O.S.*, 21, 138, 141; Warner, *Generals in Blue*, 469, 530; Heitman, *Historical Register*, 1, 224. Parnell, William R., "Recollections of '61" in *The United Service: a Monthly Review of Military and Naval Affairs*, 266 (September, 1895). A thoughtful analysis of the division and a spirited defense of its "successor," the Eleventh Corps, appears in Hamlin, Augustus Choate; *The Battle of Chancellorsville: the Attack of Stonewall Jackson and his Army upon the Right Flank of the Army of the Potomac at Chancellorsville, Virginia, on Saturday Afternoon, May 2, 1863*, 26–47 (Bangor, 1896) (pam.).

colonel.[19] Many foreigners—Carl Schurz, Franz Sigel, Adolph von Steinwehr, Hubert Dilger, Regis de Trobriand, Thomas F. Meagher, and Louis Blenker, all of whom were immigrants living in the United States when the war began—would achieve prominence in the East, but only those receiving their commissions at the regimental level from the governors would succeed at higher command. Working their way to promotion on merit were Baron Phillippe Regis Dénis De Kerendern de Trobriand, Louis Blenker, Heinrich Bohlen, Alexander Schimmelpfennig, Adolph Wilhelm August Friedrich Baron von Steinwehr, Wladimir Krzyzanowski, and others relatively unknown at the beginning of the war. Hubert Dilger, to be known as "Leatherbreeches" and to earn a reputation as an artilleryman's artilleryman, would achieve widespread recognition.[20]

Of course, the foreign officers brought with them customs of the European armies that were foreign—indeed, repugnant—to Americans. Well into the nineteenth century, candidates in European armies could, even must, purchase their commissions and promotions.[21] A far cry from appointment and promotion by the governor of the regiment's parent state, this practice was even further from election by enlisted men in the case of company-grade officers or by vote of the company officers in the case of field-grade positions.

Colonel Frederick D'Utassy, commander of the Thirty-ninth New York Volunteer Infantry, the polyglot regiment of numerous nationalities known as the "Garibaldi Guard," honored the old European customs. About to become an acting brigadier general, D'Utassy claimed that Blenker had already demanded $3,000 for his brigade. He offered to sell his colonelcy for $2,000, and he regularly sold commissions in his regiment. While commanding the Thirty-ninth New York, D'Utassy sold commissions, revoked commissions wrongfully, sold government rations to his own men, declared government property lost when it was not, claimed rations

19   Lonn, *Foreigners in the Union Army*, 83; Skelton, William B., *An American Profession of Arms: The Officer Corps 1784–1861* (Lawrence, 1992) 154–163, esp. tables 9.1 (155), 9.2 (156), and 9.3 (157).

20   *M.O.S.*, 143; Lowery, Roland, *The Story of Battery I First Regiment Ohio Volunteer Light Artillery 1861–1865* n.p. (Cincinnati, 1972) (pam.); Lonn, *Foreigners in the Union Army*, chapter VIII, 175–214; Styple, William B., ed., Nathalie Chartrain, trans., *Our Noble Blood: The Civil War Letters of Regis de Trobriand Major-General U.S.V.* (Kearny, 1997) intro., vii (Styple, *De Trobriand Letters*).

21   E.g., Farwell, *Eminent Victorian Soldiers*, 22; Strachan, Hew, *The Politics of the British Army*, 20–21, 37–38 (Oxford, 1997); Reese, Peter, *The Scottish Commander: Scotland's Greatest Military Leaders from Wallace to World War II*, 170, 207, 234 (Edinburgh, 1999). In England, the purchase of commissions ended in 1871 when a deadlock between the House of Commons and the House of Lords led to a royal warrant of abolition. Strachan, 37–38.

for men who did not exist, and kept the money that resulted from these activities. His officers and men wanted him removed.[22]

Lincoln knew he must make immigrant manpower part of the war effort. If he gave some of them higher ranking commissions, he would probably bring the foreigners to serve as enlisted men under them. Early in the war he and the secretary of war discussed the appointment of brigadier generals and reviewed the many applications and recommendations. The secretary delivered a speech on the subject.

"Well, Mr. Secretary," Lincoln said, "I concur in pretty much all you say. The only point I make is, there has got to be something done that would be unquestionably in the interest of the Dutch, and to that end I want Schimmelfenig appointed."

The secretary replied, "Mr. President, perhaps this Shimmel—what's-his-name is not as highly recommended as some other German officer."

"No matter about that," said Lincoln, "his name will make up for any difference there may be, and I'll take the risk of his coming out alright." Dwelling upon each syllable of the name, he repeated it, emphasizing the last.

"*Schim-mel-fen-NIG* must be appointed."[23]

In contrast with Lincoln's unfamiliarity with the candidates for general officer from most pools, Lincoln knew most of the applicants from the political pool; and many of its members had calls on his gratitude. He would often consider them because of their contributions to his civilian political agenda. Clearly and sharply divided into Republicans and Democrats, this pool did not come to him in unitary condition.

Lincoln's appointment of Republican Senator John Schenck to be a brigadier general preceded by a short time the unfortunate but predictable embarrassment at Vienna. Other Republican politicians like James A. Garfield and Lincoln's old friend Edward Donald Baker would find their way to promotion and in some cases unwanted prominence.

---

22   Franz Sigel MSS (New York Historical Society) Affidavit dated February 24, 1862 (the signature is illegible); Carl Schurz MSS (Wisconsin State Archives) papers relating to Frederick G. D'Utassy court-martial, 1861–1863, charges and specifications; National Archives-Court Martial of Frederick G. D'Utassy-charges and specifications and findings (NA CMD'Utassy); *M.O.S.*, 142; Bacarella, *Lincoln's Foreign Legion*, 18–19, 36–37, 71, 121–122, 127–128; Burton, Richard L., *Melting Pot Soldiers: the Union's Ethnic Regiments* (Ames, 1988) 172–174 (Burton, *Melting Pot Soldiers*).

23   Fry, *Military Miscellanies*, 281; James B. Fry in Rice, Allen Thorndike, ed., *Reminiscences of Abraham Lincoln by Distinguished Men of his Time* (New York, 1888) 391–392 (Rice, *Reminiscences of Lincoln*). Schimmelfenning's entry into the military service, in spite of his military training and experience, was difficult and halting. Burton, *Melting Pot Soldiers*, 98–100.

For a unified war effort, the president needed to draw the hostile Republicans and Democrats together. Politicians certainly had no less call on his powers of military appointment than others, and the spoils system, if anything, stood much stronger in 1861 than today. Lincoln showed an openness toward Democrats by making Benjamin F. Butler, Nathaniel P. Banks, and John A. Dix major generals while Daniel E. Sickles and John Cochrane flitted about the edge of a brigadier-general's commission. But Lincoln's sound intentions about unity were not blessed at the outset with peacefulness between the constituencies and certainly not in his own party.[24]

Before the Confederates fired on Fort Sumter, many prominent, wealthy New York City businessmen sympathized with the South and hoped for a peaceful dissolution of the Union, but the outbreak of hostilities unified them in support of the Union. One of the leaders in this group was John A. Dix.[25] The War of 1812 interrupted his education in French, Spanish, Latin, mathematics, and public speaking, some at the hands of his father, some at Phillips Exeter Academy long before Butler and Porter, and some at the College of Montreal. At the age of fourteen Dix served as an ensign at the Battle of Lundy's Lane. Continuing in the army after the war, he rose to the rank of major but resigned in 1826 when he married.

While practicing law, he became active and successful in politics and served as adjutant general of the New York State militia. In 1845, he won election to the United States Senate as a Democrat. During and after the Mexican War he consistently supported the anti-slavery Free-Soilers, the Barnburner Democrats, the Wilmot Proviso, and the admission of New Mexico and California as free states. In retaliation, hostile Southerners of his own party blocked his appointments as secretary of state and minister to France. After a restful period in private life he received a call from President Buchanan to restore order to the Post Office Department, which had suffered a disastrous defalcation. In response to pressure from wealthy men of the Northeast, Buchanan appointed him secretary of treasury during the short "Twilight Cabinet," in which Dix served briefly, scrupulously, and successfully.

In January of 1861, South Carolina and other states having seceded, the captain of a revenue cutter in New Orleans decided to deliver his ship to the State of Louisiana. Dix telegraphed his local treasury official to take possession of the cutter, saying "If anyone attempts to haul down the flag, shoot him on the spot."[26]

---

24   Dwight Family MSS (M.H.S.) letter dated August 31, 1861, from Wilder Dwight to his father (reprinted in part in Dwight, *Life and Letters*).

25   Dix, Morgan, *Memoirs of John Adams Dix*, 2 vols. (New York, 1883) 2, 9 (Dix, *Memoirs*).

26   This famous incident, to which Seward referred in the conversations about the Maryland legislature, is described in detail in Dix, *Memoirs*, 1, 371 ff.

A Treasury Department restored to order and public credit in reasonably good condition he delivered to his successor Salmon P. Chase on inauguration day.[27]

The bustling events in New York City after the Rebels fired on Fort Sumter found Dix an active participant, his efforts being rewarded by an offer from Governor Edwin Morgan of a major generalcy in the New York militia. Anxious to serve in the field, Dix forwarded his regiments to Washington as rapidly as he could make them ready, but his own orders to active duty never seemed to arrive. He wrote to Washington twice. At this time most believed the war would be quick and easy.[28] Not wanting to miss it, Dix waited impatiently in New York City.

In late May, still without orders to the field, he wrote his former president, "So I am in harness for the field but the Administration take [sic] it easy, for I have not yet been accepted and there are rumors that there are too many Democratic epaulettes in the field."[29] A few days later, Dix told Edwin M. Stanton, a fellow officer in Buchanan's twilight cabinet, that he "had been so badly treated by Cameron . . . that he intended immediately to resign."[30]

Stanton replied, "Of military affairs I can form no judgment. Every day affords fresh proof of the design to give the war a party direction. The army appointments appear (with two or three exceptions only) to be bestowed on persons whose only claim is their Republicanism—broken down politicians without experience, ability or other merit. Democrats are rudely repulsed or scowled upon with jealous and ill-concealed aversion."[31]

But while Stanton wrote this letter, Dix learned that he was to become a major general in the Federal service and ordered to the front. In due course, but not as promptly as he wished, his commission as a major general of volunteers arrived, and shortly after that he received a letter from Scott asking him to come to Washington "at the first convenient moment," where he would be given "command of the Alexandria and Arlington Department, the next to the enemy, containing five brigades." He left on June 24.[32]

27   *D.A.B.*, 3, pt. 1, 325–326; generally Dix, *Memoirs*, 1, 364–383; Hammond, Bray, *Sovereignty and an Empty Purse: Banks and Politics in the Civil War*, 26–43 (Princeton, 1970).

28   In Dix, *Memoirs*, 2, 18, Morgan Dix states that his father's inability to achieve his desires was caused by younger officers who wished to keep the glory of the "six weeks war" for themselves.

29   Moore, John Bassett, ed., *The Works of James Buchanan: Comprising his Speeches, State Papers, and Private Correspondence*, 12 vols. (New York, 1960 rep.) 11, 197, letter dated May 28, 1861, from Dix to Buchanan (Moore, *Buchanan Works*).

30   Moore, *Buchanan Works*, 11, 203, letter dated June 8, 1861, from Stanton to Buchanan.

31   Dix, *Memoirs*, 2, 19, letter dated June 11, 1861, from Stanton to Dix.

32   Dix, *Memoirs*, 2, 20–21, letter dated June 19, 1861, from Scott to Dix.

After Dix arrived in Washington, he met Lincoln, who apologized for the delay, said he meant to appoint him all along, and told him he would have his orders shortly.[33] But a command in McDowell's army preparing to advance on Manassas was not to be his. Through the connivance of junior officers and the gullibility or willingness of the administration, as his son saw it, Dix received a post in the rear where he was "sequestered within the walls of Fort McHenry" in Maryland.[34]

With limited exceptions, no one could evaluate the combat performance of the political officers, but knowledge of the routine, daily aspects of military life could be seen at once, and it was poor. Banks, seeking a political solution to a problem of military discipline, had already shown how little he understood the fundamental duties of an officer. Schenck had proven his lack of ability. Gorman and Baker, Stone's two active brigade commanders at Ball's Bluff, had simultaneously shown very different characteristics in the same circumstances. Both qualified as political generals, Baker as a United States senator and political crony of the president, and Gorman as a United States representative and the governor of the Northwest Territory. Both had Mexican War experience at the level of regimental command or higher, and neither had a West Point education.

In the face of sporadically aggressive infantry and cavalry, Gorman commanded the feint at Edwards Ferry and could have had no idea about the strength of the Confederates. He assured himself that he had adequate transportation for rapid reinforcement and rapid withdrawal by ordering the regimental quartermaster of the First Minnesota to take charge of the "fleet" and enlarge it as necessary. He went at once to the high hill on the Maryland side, where he established his headquarters, had a view of his men on both sides, and placed his artillery in dominant positions.

Baker, given discretion by Stone, decided to cross the river and defend the bluff before he scouted the terrain, before he knew about his transportation, and before he knew the strength of the Rebels. When he arrived, his men had already begun a battle. Still ignorant of the terrain, relative strengths, and current circumstances, he wasted more than an hour directing the movement of a skow from the canal to the river and extending a hawser across the river to control the effect of the current while his men fought on the bluff without him.[35]

---

33   Moore, *Buchanan Works*, 11, 206, letter dated June 28, 1861, from Dix to Buchanan.

34   Dix, *Memoirs*, 2, 22–23.

35   Much of this the young Comte de Paris recognized less than a few days after the battles. Comte de Paris MS diary (large diary) (A.N. de la M. de F.) entry dated October 25, 1861.

Baker had no instinctive and no instructed sense of place. Neither did he understand his role. By instinct or thought in this tiniest of battles, Gorman knew where to place himself, what to do, and what to delegate. Aside from distances, maneuvers, and unit coordination, all of which the political generals could learn on the parade ground, much of the remainder they would derive by common sense. And this explains, among other reasons, why so many brigades and divisions had capable volunteer commanding officers when they reached the courthouse several years later. The early war phenomenon—the political general—would have superb courage, as Baker did, but no field instincts, as Gorman did but Baker, Schenck, and Banks did not, and no classroom experience, as all four did not. Being put to the test without practical or schoolroom training, the political generals early in the war received too much responsibility and rank too soon. Whether they would react like Gorman or Baker, no one could predict for these early appointments.

Chapter 14

"You have been ordered to appear before this Board for an examination of your qualifications as a cavalry officer."

—Colonel Van Alen to an officer before a review board

The Gubernatorial Pool

The next sources of general officer appointments were indirectly the governors of the states. After the early creation of generals from active and resigned Regular Army officers like McDowell and McClellan, most of them West Point graduates, the vast majority of the generals came from the regimental officers, virtually all of whom were appointed by the governors. But the governors did not believe they should be limited to the appointment of colonels. Each governor thought he should have the political power to designate men for appointment as generals in proportion to the size of his contribution to the volunteer forces.

The standard size of a brigade being four regiments, and a division, three brigades, any governor who sent four or more regiments wondered why his state did not have a brigadier general in the Federal service. If he had sent twelve or more regiments, he would wonder about a major generalcy. But governors did not limit themselves to wondering. Many lobbied for their candidates for brigadier and major general because they had supplied a certain number of regiments, not because they had a candidate of irresistible merit.[1] They were assisted by their constituents, who caucused to press slates of "favorite sons" on the president.

1   Chase MSS (L.C.) letter dated August 8, 1861, from Governor Sprague of Rhode Island to Chase; Lincoln MSS (L.C.) letter dated October 3, 1861, from William Dennison, governor of Ohio, to Montgomery Blair; Trumble MSS (L.C.) letter dated July 7, 1861, from O. M. Hotels to Trumble.

225

After the Federal government's May order deprived the states of the power to appoint general officers, the governors replaced the lost power with influence. Governor Edwin Morgan of New York, still wanting major generalcies for John A. Dix and James S. Wadsworth, traveled to Washington to meet with Lincoln. On his return he wrote to Wadsworth, "Although there has been greater delay at Washington than I could have desired, yet I have not seriously doubted that the two Major Generals, appointed by me, would be accepted by the U.S. authorities. I still think so, though I must admit, I have no assurances to that effect. This matter was, as I think, properly presented by me to the President, and to the Secretary of War, during my late visit to the seat of Government, and, while there has been a just response in respect to one, it has only served to make me the more anxious about the recognition of the other."[2]

Morgan had tried to persuade John H. Martindale to accept the colonelcy of the Tenth New York Infantry, a disorganized regiment. In unctuous if not obsequious letters Martindale stated parochial reasons for declining; most probably his reasons were his more splendid aspirations. "To accept the command of the 10th Regiment I am frank to admit would disappoint an expectation which I have cherished . . . I believe if you shall deem it expedient to recommend me for one of the brigadier generals from this state, that the appointment will be made."[3]

In early July Morgan wrote to Senator Preston King to obtain support for Martindale's request, and King began the Federal dance for a general's commission. First, he obtained support from his fellow New York Senator Ira Harris, then presented the recommendation to Lincoln. To Morgan, King reported, "Upon presenting the recommendation to the President he said he did not intend to make any more appointments till the Congress passed the proper laws, when he would be glad to consult with you personally on the subject here or to receive your advice and recommendations respecting the appointments for New York."[4]

A few days later King reported again on specific candidates. "I . . . mentioned for Brigadiers Mr. Martindale, Mr. Peck, and Mr. Kearney [sic]. He does

2   Wadsworth MSS (L.C.) letter dated June 12, 1861, from Edwin D. Morgan, governor of the State of New York, to Major-General James S. Wadsworth; Chase MSS (L.C.) letter dated May 31, 1861, from Morgan to Cameron. In this letter Morgan argued that, if the governors could not appoint general officers, as he believed the state and Federal constitutions required, he must limit camps of instruction for newly recruited troops to units no larger than a regiment. Another copy of the letter dated June 12, 1861, is in the Wadsworth MSS (Univ. of Roch.).

3   Edwin Denison Morgan MSS (New York State Library) letter dated June 20, 1861, from Martindale to Morgan.

4   Morgan MSS (N.Y.S.L.) letter dated July 6, 1861, from King to Morgan.

not seem to regard the number of volunteers from a state as a guide in appointment of Generals."[5]

Immediately after Bull Run Lincoln had his secretary John Hay send a form letter to each member of Congress asking for recommendations for general officers. Once again King reported to Governor Morgan about a conversation with the president. "I saw the President this Evening and he requested me to inform you that . . . he would be glad to have you make such recommendations as now thought proper." From New York he wanted a list of "ten or a dozen . . . from which he may appoint but says he does not know how many he shall appoint." Consistent with McClellan's policy, Lincoln and King spoke only of brigadier generals.[6]

Lincoln's statement did not change the attitude of the states or the Federal representatives of the states. In the evenings of Saturday, July 27, and Sunday, July 28, the Illinois delegation met in Lyman Trumball's quarters to "agree upon Brigadier Generals for the Volunteers" from Illinois. "It was supposed," Senator Browning noted in his diary, "we would be entitled to nine."[7] Also, at the request of the president, the New York delegation submitted a list of men for consideration as brigadier generals. Although other good candidates were known to these groups, they limited themselves to men from their own states.[8]

The process of designating regimental commanders remained a matter of gubernatorial power throughout the war, but early in the war the statutory elections often circumscribed the governors' appointive power. The governor of New York commissioned every colonel who was elected.[9] The New York State Constitution, Article Eleven, Section Two, required election of both company-grade and field-grade officers, and the governor officered the first thirty-eight regiments that way. Vacancies, also governed by state law, were another matter. The governor had the power "to appoint and commission the requisite officers to fill vacancies without election."[10] This power Governor Morgan exercised neither reluctantly nor late.

---

5   Morgan MSS (N.Y.S.L.) letter dated July 13, 1861, from King to Morgan.

6   Morgan MSS (N.Y.S.L.) letters dated July 25, 1861, and August 1, 1861, from King to Morgan. A copy of the printed form letter is also in the Morgan MSS.

7   Pease, *Browning Diary*, 1, 487–488, 490, entries dated July 27 and 28, 1861.

8   Wadsworth MSS (Univ. Roch.) letter dated August 3, 1861, from Senator Preston King to Wadsworth. The New York delegation considered nominating Erasmus D. Keyes until it learned he was a New Englander.

9   Curtis, Newton Martin, *From Bull Run to Chancellorsville: the Story of the Sixteenth New York Infantry together with personal Reminiscences* (New York, 1906) 209 (Curtis, *Bull Run to Chancellorsville*.

10   Sickles Misc. MSS (N.A.) letter dated February 21, 1863, from Evans to Sickles; Curtis, *Bull Run to Chancellorsville*, 207–208.

After the regimental elections in September, the governor made all appointments and promotions. The *New York Herald* reported the colonel of the Tenth New York Infantry, which had been recruited in April, to be Captain Morgan of Brooklyn; but W. W. McChesney prevailed in the election. The governor duly commissioned McChesney.[11] By late June, however, McChesney had failed to earn the confidence of his officers and had given other cause for not being continued in command. To the relief of his officers and men, he resigned his commission. The officers elected the regimental lieutenant colonel, Alexander Elder, colonel, and Elder assumed command. Morgan refused to confirm him and appointed John E. Bendix, who assumed command of the Tenth on September 9, Elder reverting to lieutenant colonel.[12]

After the May directive, governors no longer had the power to appoint brigadier or major generals for the federal army, but commissions for regimental officers, second lieutenants through colonels, remained in their exclusive power, except for the tiny Regular Army and the handful of regiments authorized by the Federal government. And that power continued after the government mustered the regiments into the Federal service.[13] Governor Sprague of Rhode Island wrote to McClellan's chief of artillery, Brigadier General William F. Barry, to learn the reason for sending a piece of Rhode Island artillery across the Potomac River into battle under an officer from another state. He wished to know if it were Barry's intention to allow any commanding officer in the future to detach the Rhode Island

---

11   Hall, Henry, *Cayuga in the Field: A Record of the 19th N.Y. Volunteers, and the 3rd New York Artillery, comprising an Account of their Organization, Camp Life, Marches, Battles, Losses, Toils and Triumphs in the War for the Union, with Complete Rolls of their Members* (Auburn, 1873) 79 (Hall, *Cayuga in the Field*); Cowtan, Charles W., *Services of the Tenth New York Volunteers (National Zouaves) in the War of the Rebellion* (New York, 1882) 21, 23 (Cowtan, *Tenth New York*).

12   Cowtan, *Tenth New York*, 37, 53.

13   *OR*, ser. 3, vol. 1, 381, General Orders No. 49, War Dept., Adjt. General's Office, dated August 3, 1861, quoting Act passed July 22, 1861; NA RG 393, section 3964, Division and Department and the Army of the Potomac, letters sent, vol. 1, p. 538, letter dated January 4, 1862, from Assistant Adjutant General to McCall. Section H of the statute reads in part, "The Governors of the States furnishing volunteers under this act shall commission the field, staff, and company officers requisite for said volunteers . . . " [but the president could appoint if the state authorities did not]. According to the letter, field officer appointments in the regiments lay "entirely in the hands of the Governors of the States in which the Regiments were respectively organized. Different methods prevail with different Governors—in some cases elections being ordered in the Regiments according to rules prescribed by the State Authorities and in others appointments being made by the Governor himself, with these details however the U.S. Authorities having nothing to do."

battery officers "who have been selected with great care, and who have the deepest interest in the men under their command and in their keeping the honor of the State. . . ."

Sprague asked that Lieutenant Colonel Reynolds, an artillery officer he had appointed, be detailed to supervise all Rhode Island batteries wherever they were stationed. This would allow Barry to employ Colonel Tompkins on service connected with the artillery in general. Sprague wanted these orders issued at once and his batteries assigned to brigades containing Rhode Island infantry regiments.[14]

These gubernatorial powers fed the growing group of general officers in several indirect ways. Although the Union army was controlled by the laws of the Federal government, the regimental officers, appointed by the governors, would form the most slowly developing source of general officers.

After the initial burst of elections, the governors appointed the regimental commanders, from whom, in the ordinary course of events, most brigadier generals came to their stars. For their regimental commanders appointed both before and after Bull Run, the governors drew deeply from the West Point graduates and after the battle from the experienced Bull Run pool. The Second Massachusetts was commanded by George H. Gordon, a West Point graduate in McClellan's class, 1846,[15] then by George L. Andrews, West Point, 1851, and first in his class.[16] The Seventh Massachusetts had a long, distinguished list: Colonel Thomas D. Johns, a Military Academy graduate;[17] Darius N. Couch, who graduated in McClellan's class and would rise to corps command;[18] Nelson H. Davis, West Point graduate and Regular Army officer on active duty;[19] and David A. Russell, West Point graduate and Regular Army officer on active duty, later to be a brigadier general commanding a division.[20] In the Tenth Massachusetts Regiment, Henry L. Eustis, an 1842 West Point graduate who resigned in 1849 to become a professor of engineering at Harvard,

---

14   William F. Barry MSS (Buffalo Historical Society) letter dated November 1, 1861, from Governor William Sprague to William F. Barry, chief of artillery.

15   Heitman, *Historical Register*, 1, 465; Warner, *Generals in Blue*, 177; *Cullum*, 2, no. 1314.

16   Heitman, *Historical Register*, 1, 166; Warner, *Generals in Blue*, 9; *Cullum*, 2, no. 1494.

17   Heitman, *Historical Register*, 1, 574; *Cullum*, 2, no. 1400.

18   Heitman, *Historical Register*, 1, 329; *Cullum*, 2, no. 1284; Warner, *Generals in Blue*, 95.

19   Heitman, *Historical Register*, 1, 359; *Cullum*, 2, no. 1320.

20   Heitman, *Historical Register*, 1, 852; *Cullum*, 2, no. 1268; Roe, *Seventh Massachusetts*, 22–23, 404.

began as the regimental colonel and rose to brigadier general.[21] The Thirteenth Regiment, an exception to the West Point rule for Governor Andrew's Army of the Potomac regiments, was led by Colonel Samuel H. Leonard, a highly respected militia major general with a reputation for exceptional peacetime military skills.[22] Jesse A. Gove, a captain in the Tenth United States Infantry, became colonel of the Twenty-second Massachusetts after Senator Henry Wilson, as he had promised, resigned to return to the Senate.[23] The rise of enlisted men to the commissioned ranks had more certainty in some regiments because thoughtful men like Dennis Hart Mahan knew the noncommissioned officers would supply the junior officers of the future,[24] and men like Colonel Edward E. Cross of the Fifth New Hampshire Volunteers ran twice-a-week instruction for noncommissioned officers he thought likely to make good commissioned officers.[25]

When the Seventh Maine had been recruited and was electing its officers, the company officers, summoned to the center chamber of the state capitol building in Augusta, Maine, chose field officers by ballot. The adjutant general of the state presided. One man proposed that a Regular Army officer be elected colonel because none of them knew much about military activities. From an advertisement containing the name of a captain in the Seventeenth United States Infantry, Edwin C. Mason, who was on recruiting service in Portland, they elected their colonel. Completing a term of three-months' service in the First Vermont as a sergeant, Seldon Connor looked as if he would be a man with sufficient experience to drill a company and make a good lieutenant colonel.[26]

The governors were not inexorably bound to the system of election. Governor John Andrew of Massachusetts seems not to have used it at all. Governors Morgan of New York and Curtin of Pennsylvania allowed the elections to proceed but after the initial period of recruiting ignored their results or accepted them as no more than advice. The governor of Vermont did exactly as William F. "Baldy" Smith suggested for promotions in the Vermont regiments. Many lower-ranking officers appointed by

21   Heitman, *Historical Register*, 1, 408; Warner, *Generals in Blue*, 144; *Cullum*, 2, no. 1111.

22   Davis, Charles E., Jr., *Three Years in the Army: The Story of the Thirteenth Massachusetts Volunteers from July 16, 1861, to August 1, 1864* (Boston, 1894) xiv (Davis, *Thirteenth Mass.*).

23   Bennett, *Musket and Sword*, 35; Parker, *Twenty-second Massachusetts*, 48.

24   Morgan MSS (N.Y.S.L.) letter dated August 7, 1861, from Mahan to Morgan.

25   Livermore, Thomas L., *Days and Events, 1860–1866* (Boston, 1920, rep. 1998) 39.

26   Hyde, Thomas W., *Following the Greek Cross or Memories of the Sixth Army Corps* (Boston and New York, 1894) 14–16 (Hyde, *Following the Greek Cross*).

the governors would achieve general officer rank, but would need more time than the colonels to "catch a star."[27]

The power to promote regimental officers would, rightly or wrongly, remain with the governors throughout the war. Even though they had little or no first-hand knowledge about the performance of the men they sent to the field as officers, they had their own sources of information for promotion. They would receive information about performance and advice about promotions from the brigade and division commanders, who often designated or recommended men to replace the fallen colonels, lieutenant colonels, and majors.[28] Recommending one of his particularly deserving company grade officers, Francis Channing Barlow wrote Governor Morgan of New York, "A vigorous Field Officer is needed here and if the vacancy occasioned by Col. Cone's dismissal is to be filled by promotion I am anxious to have Mr. [Nelson A.] Miles made either lieutenant-colonel or major. Officers and men know respect and obey him."[29]

Like the problem caused by assignment of a regimental officer to a staff, an officer's illness, wounding, or capture would leave a regiment with an opening that could be filled by a junior officer from the same regiment temporarily, pending his

27   *C.C.W.*, 1, 189–190 (Smith); Hyndman, William, *History of a Cavalry Company: a complete Record of Company "A," 4th Penn'a Cavalry*, 28–30 (Philadelphia, 1870); Curtis, *Bull Run to Chancellorsville*, 206–210.

28   Sigel MSS (N.Y.H.S.) letter dated June 27, 1862, from Francis Pierpont, governor of West Virginia, to Fremont; James S. Wadsworth MSS (Univ. of Roch.) letter dated March 26, 1863, from Wadsworth to Stanton; George H. Chapman MS Diary (Indiana Historical Society) entry dated November 20, 1860; Hooker MSS (H.L.) letter dated October 31, 1861, from Ritchie to Hooker; Gratz MSS Collection (Civil War Generals—Hooker) (Pennsylvania Historical Society) letter dated November 27, 1862 from Hooker to Birney; (Civil War Generals—George H. Gordon) letter dated October 20, 1862, from Governor Morgan of N.Y.; (Civil War Generals—John W. Davidson) letter dated July 17, 1862, from Davidson to General Thomas Hillhouse, Adjutant General (Civil War Generals—Barry) letter dated March 23, 1863, from William F. Barry to General George Sprague, adjutant general of New York; letter dated September 27, 1862, from William F. Barry to William Sprague, governor of Rhode Island; Misc Civ. War MSS (Huntington Library) letter dated June 26, 1862, from Francis Channing Barlow to General Hillhouse; Roebling MSS (Rutgers Univ.) letter dated Feb. 6, 1862, from W. A. Roebling to his father; James Barnes MSS (N.Y.H.S.) letter dated April 12, 1862, from William Schouler; adjutant general of Massachusetts, to Barnes; *C.C.W.*, 1, 189–190 (Smith); Stoeckel, Carl and Ellen, eds., *Correspondence of John Sedgwick, Major-General*, 2 vols. (n.p. 1903) 2, 73, 87, letters dated July 11, 1862, from Sedgwick to Seth Williams and December 5, 1862, from Sedgwick to Governor John A. Andrew (Stoeckel, *Sedgwick Correspondence*); Sears, *For Country, Cause & Leader (Haydon Diary)* 207, entry dated March 17, 1862.

29   Misc. Civ. War Letters (N.Y.H.S.) letter dated May 1, 1862, from Barlow to Edwin D. Morgan.

return. After Balls Bluff the Twentieth Massachusetts Infantry stood without a regimental colonel or lieutenant colonel, both of whom had become guests of the Confederates in Richmond. Stone wrote McClellan asking for new appointments to avoid demoralization in the regiment for lack of critical officers and leadership.[30] Headquarters replied that vacancies created by capture could not be filled. Stone must make do.[31]

Any doubt about this policy disappeared when a regimental colonel and major were captured while reconnoitering enemy lines in 1862 during the Peninsular Campaign, and the secretary of war confirmed that "the absence of an officer taken prisoner does not create a vacancy." The openings could not be filled. Once again, the lack of a central officer pool and a single appointing authority, combined with "ownership" of a slot by an unavailable incumbent, would leave a unit command structure in an incomplete, unsatisfactory, and unstable condition.[32]

Ultimately, the regimental officers, all creatures of the governors, would provide the vast majority of the brigade and division commanders and the brigadier and major generals appointed by the president and confirmed by the Senate.[33] McClellan recognized the problems caused by this bilateral system and tried to solve them in a way that predicted twentieth century practice. He sought legislation that would eliminate part of the problem caused by the two, independent sources of officers, the state and Federal governments. Under his proposal he would have the power, on his own and without permission from the governor, to transfer officers from one company to another within a regiment and to transfer officers among regiments of the same state. This would give at least the illusion of central, Federal control of officer appointments and an army-wide pool of officers. He sent Brigadier General Henry M. Naglee to Washington to suggest this radical proposition. Naglee met with the president, the secretary of war, and Governor Andrew Curtin of Pennsylvania, who happened to be present. They thought the plan was wise and said they would support it. The president and the secretary of war urged Naglee to describe the proposed legislation to members of Congress and to tell them they both supported it.

---

30   McClellan MSS (L.C.) telegram dated January 24, 1862, from Stone to Williams.

31   McClellan MSS (L.C.) endorsement without date by Colburn on telegram dated January 24, 1861, from Stone to Williams.

32   King, David H., A. Judson Gibles, and Jay H. Northup, *History of the Ninety-third Regiment New York Volunteer Infantry, 1861–1865*, 32, 35–36 (Milwaukee, 1895).

33   Developed later, exceptions to this rule would include some extraordinary senior officers.

Naglee met several of them, including Henry Wilson. All thought the proposal sound and agreed to support it. Wilson said he would propose it as soon as possible. Unfortunately, nothing happened before events directed everyone's energies to other issues.[34]

The unsystematic way in which the governors worked and the numerous appointments they had to make meant they would fail in some cases no matter how hard they tried,[35] and the early process of election would advance some unpredictably but hopelessly incompetent men. The army needed a cure for an appointment proven to be a mistake, and it had to be a Federal cure because the governors had no power to revoke a commission once the officer had been mustered into the Federal volunteer service.[36]

The day after Bull Run, Congress addressed the problem with a statute authorizing review boards for officers sent forward by the states. The regimental, brigade, and division commanders could identify an officer thought deficient, and a review board appointed by the department or army commander would then summon him for, in effect, an examination that would reconsider his commission.[37] The higher-ranking officers appreciated the value of this procedure, often called for boards, and even called for a board to be reconvened if they believed a board had not finished its work within its allotted time.

When scheduled to meet the board for their regiment, brigade, or division, some tendered their resignations before the date of their required appearance. Unit commanders were not exempt from this process. At once, many officers were driven from the army for drunkenness, inefficiency, lack of administrative knowledge, or lack of tactical skill.[38]

---

34   McClellan MSS (L.C.) letter of n.d. from Naglee to McClellan.

35   Ford, Worthington Chauncey, ed., *A Cycle of Adams Letters*, 2 vols. (Boston, 1920) 1, 206, letter dated December 21, 1861, from Charles Francis Adams, Jr., to his father and mother; 249, letter dated January 28, 1863, from Adams to his father (Ford, *Cycle of Letters*).

36   Sickles personal letters, National Archives, Record Group 393, vol. II, Polyonymous Successions of Commands, 1861–1870, No. 3, 3d Army Corps., no. 186, letters received by Daniel E. Sickles, 1861–1863, letter dated February 21, 1863, from Evans, New York Adjutant General's Office, to Sickles.

37   *OR*, ser. 3, vol. 1, 382–383, General Orders No. 49, War Dept., Adjt. General's Office, dated August 3, 1861, quoting Act passed July 22, 1861, section 10.

38   Fourth Corps MSS (New York Historical Society) Special Orders No. 102, dated April 8, 1862, and Special Orders No. 109, dated April 15, 1862, both from Headquarters of the Army of the Potomac; Hooker MSS (H.L.) letters dated November 4 and December 17, 1861, from Graham to Sickles; November 15, 1861, from William L. Small to Adjutant George Johnstone; letter

But the boards had their ironies. Designed to weed out incompetent and inefficient officers, a board might have a member who, although a candidate for scrutiny, used the board as a hiding place to avoid being hunted. The board for the examination of cavalry officers, established in Washington, met once a week. The president of the board was Colonel James H. Van Alen, a member of a prominent New York family. Other members of the board were Lieutenant Colonel Judson Kilpatrick, a West Point graduate; Captain David M. Gregg, a West Point graduate serving in the Sixth United States Cavalry; Colonel W. W. Averell, a young but experienced cavalry officer; and other competent younger officers. Van Alen had brought a cavalry regiment to Washington from New York; but when the regiment crossed to the west bank of the Potomac, the colonel took a house in Washington where he gave dinner parties for fashionable and important people. He had no military experience and knew nothing about cavalry, even theoretically; but, Averell recalled later, he was well-groomed, spoke impressively and deliberately, and presented the smooth appearance of a "typical club man."

When an officer to be examined entered the room, Van Alen would state his name and grade.

"You have been ordered to appear before this Board," he would continue, "for an examination of your qualifications as a cavalry officer. Colonel Averell, would you please conduct the examination?"

"This examination," wrote Averell in his memoirs after the war, "was of immense benefit to the cavalry service. It drove those without qualifications out of their commissions." Seven officers of Averell's regiment, including three captains, were given the alternative of resignation or examination by the cavalry board. Others followed.[39]

The Artillery Examining Board, divided into panels of three officers, received the names of three captains and five lieutenants in December. The panel reviewed the capabilities and educational attainments of each officer. One lieutenant the

dated March 1, 1862, from Lieutenant Colonel George Wells to Adjutant Joseph Dickenson; McClellan MSS (L.C.) letter dated September 5, 1861, from Seth Williams to Kearny; telegram dated November 19, 1861, from William F. Smith to Seth Williams; *C.C.W.*, 1, 227 (Keyes), 215–217 (Casey), and 203 (Rosecrans); Tyler, Mason Whiting, *Recollections of the Civil War with many Original Diary Entries and Letters Written from the Seat of War and with Annotated References* (New York and London, 1912) 16–17. In fact, the boards were indispensable because the officers, once they were mustered into the Federal service, could not be removed by the governors. Howard MSS (Bowdoin College) letters dated August 19, 1861, from Savage to Howard; August 23, 1861, from Governor Washburn to Howard; August 23, 1861, from Washburn to Cameron.

39   Averell, *Recollections*, 340.

board found lacking in every respect, another passed, and the third resigned before appearing. Captain George W. Cothran of Battery M, First New York Light Artillery, knew very little about tactics, but because he had many explanations and appeared to be a man of intellect and education, he received another chance. For Captain John W. Tamblin of Battery C, First New York Light Artillery, additional evidence was necessary because, even though he could answer all the questions, his colonel testified that he could not "impart his knowledge" to his men and lacked their respect.[40]

Thomas F. Vaughan had served at Bull Run as a lieutenant in First Battery, First Rhode Island Artillery Regiment. Governor Sprague had promoted all the officers in First Battery to higher positions in other Rhode Island artillery units. First Lieutenant Vaughan became Captain Vaughan in command of Battery A, then transferred to Battery B in the First Rhode Island Artillery Regiment.[41] He assumed command on Sunday, August 25, 1861. According to the restrained historian of Battery A, Captain Vaughan, having submitted his resignation, transferred command to one of his lieutenants on December 1, 1861, left for Washington, and was discharged.[42] Other records merely say he was "missing."[43]

Unfortunately for Vaughan, he had a rapid rise, followed by a quick reversal of fortune. After Bull Run, as the government recruited new batteries, the Rhode Island batteries became a battalion, then a regiment. First Battery, a three-month unit, was discharged; it delivered its guns to Second Battery to replace the guns lost at Bull Run. The governor received its redesignated Second Battery as Battery A, First Rhode Island Light Artillery Regiment. The new battery commanders for the new regiment came from existing units. First Lieutenant Thomas F. Vaughan became the captain in command of old Third Battery, redesignated Battery B.[44]

40   Nevins, Allan, *A Diary of Battle, the Personal Journals of Colonel Charles S. Wainwright, 1861–1865* (New York, 1982) 4–5, 7, entries dated December 25, 1861, and January 5, 1862 (Nevins, *Wainwright's Journals*); *Official Register*, 2, 388, 389, 391. Tamblin did not survive the second session, nor did the third captain, John Stocum of Battery F (spelled "Slocum" in Wainwright).

41   Aldrich, *Battery A, First Rhode Island Artillery*, 38–43. The name is spelled variously Vaughan and Vaughn. First Battery, a three-month unit, returned to Rhode Island at the end of its time. The longer-term batteries were redesignated by letters in the new regiment, Second Battery becoming Battery A, and so on.

42   Rhodes, *Battery B, First Rhode Island Artillery*, 20, 33–36.

43   *Official Register*, 1, 247.

44   Aldrich, *Battery A, First Rhode Island Artillery*, 33, 38.

After Captain Vaughan had left Battery A, Governor Sprague of Rhode Island and Colonel Tompkins, the regimental commander, visited Battery A's camp one evening to observe a parade. Captain Vaughan, too, visited his old battery that evening.

"Boys," he said, "I deserve to be kicked for ever leaving this battery because, by right, it is my battery; and I should be with you."

The men cheered loudly, then cried, "Give us our old officers, and we will show you that we can drill."

Vaughan mounted his horse, turned to his former comrades in arms, and said, "I am hanging around. It is hard for me to leave."

"We know it," the men called back. "You are a man, every inch of you."

The men followed him with nine cheers.[45] In fact, however, things were not going well for Vaughan in Battery B, his new command. He had selected the location of his camp poorly. Four or five horses died. Sixteen became unserviceable. Drinking spread. He brought his sister to camp, where she lived with him in his tent. Soon, Vaughan became one of the battery commanders pursued by the Artillery Review Board. After inspecting the battery and examining the conduct of its commander, the reviewing officers submitted a report to the Chief of Artillery.

The inspecting party found the battery in "*very unsatisfactory condition.*" The battery commander "gave few of the commands in proper form. He 'had devoted a good portion of his time for the last month, or six weeks,' the report said, 'to a woman he introduced to his brother officers as *his sister*, but it turns out to be *a prostitute* imported from Rhode Island. This fact seemed perfectly well-known by the officers *and men* of Battery A.'" Vaughan had also collected $150 from the government by submitting fictitious names as teamsters. According to the report, Lieutenant Smith of the battery stayed at a house in the village and was often seen in a state of intoxication.[46]

Brigadier General William F. Barry wrote to Vaughan enclosing a copy of Reynolds's report and advising Vaughan that he would be examined by a review board if he did not resign. He described the soft standard for cashiering an officer. The standard of scrutiny was not the lawyer's "beyond a reasonable doubt" for a criminal case; nor was it "more probable than not," the easier civil case burden. "As

---

45   Reichardt, *Diary of Battery A*, 23–24, entry dated October 15, 1861. Another briefer account of this colloquy appears in Aldrich, *A First R.I.*, 45. Although both were recorded in diaries, ibid. preface, 1, the account in Reichardt appears to be more complete and is preferred.

46   Alexander Stuart Webb MSS (Yale University) letter dated November 16, 1861, from Lieutenant Colonel William H. Reynolds to William F. Barry.

these charges are made after a careful investigation by Lt. Col. Reynolds," Barry wrote, "I do not see that you can do otherwise, than to put your commission in Gov. Sprague's hands at once. If you conclude not to resign you will be at once ordered before the Examining Board for Artillery Officers of which I am a member. The finding of this Board will not be according to technicalities but according to the convictions of members of the Board. It has full power to call all necessary witnesses. I state this to prevent your thinking that a court martial might not be able to *prove* you guilty. If you know these facts to be as charged you will do better not to join the company again except to remove your personal property."[47]

Although the boards had large discretionary powers unconfined by rigid criteria and many of their targets may have seen them as ruthless, they never reached the free-wheeling power, even to life and death, of their predecessors in the French Revolution or their successors in the Russian Revolution. Officers under investigation had to be present to confront and cross-examine their accusers and those testifying against them.[48] Like many other officers in his unenviable position, Vaughan accepted Barry's advice and resigned. His battery, under new leadership, would earn a fine record in the heavy fighting ahead.

47   Webb MSS (Y.U.) draft letter dated November 19, 1861, from William F. Barry to Captain Thomas Vaughan.

48   NA RG 393, section 3964, Division and Department and the Army of the Potomac, letters sent, vol. 1, p. 563, letter dated January 8, 1862, from Assistant Adjutant General (n.s.) to Ogle.

Chapter 15

"If in ten days McClellan is not commander in chief, the army shall have something to do with that matter."

—Quasi-public statements by several generals

The End of Scott

cClellan did not stand alone in his trouble with Scott or seeing the general in chief's powers fail. Others saw an old general who had unfortunately not received this great challenge early enough in his career to accept it. Before Bull Run, Montgomery Blair had recognized the impossibility of adopting Scott's plan for the war and his abusive treatment of junior officers. After Bull Run and Ball's Bluff some officers saw Scott as the cause of the defeat. On July 31, Lieutenant Colonel William Dwight wrote his father a letter showing that criticism of Scott was not confined to the highest quarters. "The trouble has been the want of a Genl," he said. "Scott has no more idea of the command of 300,000 men than I have. He has had no experience to aid him in such a command, he is too old to learn, . . . that battle was lost by the age & imbecility of Genl. Scott, & his utter want of capacity at any period of his life to understand so great affairs."[1]

A much older, very astute observer close to the government, Frank P. Blair, told his family General Scott was "sick—he is getting dropsical and very old."[2]

---

1   Dwight Family MSS (M.H.S.) letter dated July 31, 1861, from William Dwight to his mother.

2   Laas, *Blair Lee Letters*, 89, letter dated October 19, 1861, from Elizabeth Blair Lee to her husband.

During his trip to Washington Professor Dennis Hart Mahan had visited Scott and questioned Colonel George Washington Cullum, a member of Scott's staff, about the general-in-chief's health.

"I think I see him failing day by day," replied Cullum. "He becomes daily more drowsy."

Mahan agreed. He wondered if the president should rely heavily on a person in this condition. All this Mahan reported to McClellan.[3] The major general would have seen this information as support for his intention to unseat Scott. His differences with Scott were not just military disagreements or political impasses. At least from McClellan's viewpoint, they had sunk to outright personal hostility. By the middle of August, McClellan had described Scott as "the most dangerous antagonist I have" and insisted "either he or I must leave here."[4] In his private correspondence, his letters from the heart, he wrote, "the old General is in his dotage,"[5] and "he has become my inveterate enemy!"[6] But complaints in home letters could not produce Scott's removal as general in chief and someone's appointment in his place. Those steps must have seemed gigantic to Lincoln and the cabinet.

Scott had experience with almost every conceivable military and political question and had enjoyed a long, unbroken stream of successes. Although brilliant, charming, and impressive, McClellan was thirty-four and had under his belt one Tinkertoy campaign in western Virginia . . . in which, if a student of it were available, his subordinates, the enemy, and good fortune had saved him from critical failures.

McClellan knew he must assume the offensive, but Scott remained opposed to any advance into Virginia. Instead, he wanted the military power of the Confederacy dissipated by keeping their armies inactive, yet another position that showed his judgment severely impaired.[7] He complained to the War Department about a modest reconnaissance to Fairfax Court House even though the press, wrong again,

---

3   McClellan MSS (L.C.) letter n.d. from Dennis Hart Mahan to McClellan.

4   Sears, *McClellan's Correspondence*, 84, letter dated August 14, 1861, from McClellan to his wife.

5   Sears, *McClellan's Correspondence*, 85, letter dated August 16, 1861, from McClellan to his wife.

6   Sears, *McClellan's Correspondence*, 105–106, letter dated October 6, 1861, from McClellan to his wife.

7   Comte de Paris MS Diary (large diary) (A.N. de la M. de F.) entry dated November 2, 1861; Sears, *McClellan's Correspondence*, 95, letter dated September 7, 1861, from McClellan to his wife; Comte de Paris in *B&L*, 2, 113–114.

had begun to criticize McClellan for "want of energy." The hypercritical clerk in the State Department saw it correctly for a change. "Gen. Scott's partisans complain that McClellan is very disrespectful in his dealings with Gen. Scott. I wonder not. McClellan is probably hampered by the narrow routine notions of Scott. McClellan feels that Scott prevents energetic and prompt action . . . McClellan grows impatient, and shows it to Scott."

Always careful, always deliberate, always thoughtful, McClellan contemplated the problem for a month and a half. Finally, he decided the time had come to put an end to it. "I am firmly determined to force the issue with Genl Scott," he wrote his wife, "a very few days will determine whether his policy or mine is to prevail—he is for inaction and the defensive. He endeavors to cripple me in every way, . . . Hereafter the truth will be shown and he will be displayed in his true light."[8]

McClellan's refusal to give Scott even the most routine military information became more than Scott could bear. While McClellan watched for results from his meetings with the president and the secretary of state about Maryland, Scott directed his adjutant general to issue General Orders No. 17. Communication out of channels, it said, must cease. "It is highly important that junior officers on duty be not permitted to correspond with the general in chief or other commander on current official business, except through intermediate commanders; and the same rule applies to correspondence with the President direct, or with him through the Secretary of War unless it be by the special invitation or request of the President."[9]

On the same day Scott sent McClellan a direct order that would cure his ignorance of the military conditions in the capital area. McClellan was to give him "the position, State, and numbers of troops under him . . . by divisions, brigades, and independent regiments or detachments, which general report will be followed by reports of new troops as they arrive, with the dispositions made of them, together with all material changes which may take place in the same army."[10]

These orders had no effect. McClellan did not respond to them. Nor did he act as if he had even seen them. Three days after they were issued, he sent two important

---

8   Sears, *McClellan's Correspondence*, 167, letter dated October 13, 1861, from McClellan to his wife; Gurowski, *Diary*, 1, 103, September, 1861.

9   *OR*, 51, pt. 1, 492, General Orders No. 17, dated September 16, 1861, from Headquarters of the Army.

10   *OR*, 51, pt. 1, 492, letter dated September 16, 1861, from Townsend to McClellan. For some strange reason General Order No. 17 and the direct order seem to be haunted and, therefore, inaccurately cited; for example, *N&H*, 4, 464, cites the general order as *OR*, series 3, 1, 482.

letters directly to the secretary of war.[11] The order for reports about troops? He never sent any.[12]

On September 27, a carriage sent by Lincoln took McClellan to a meeting with the president and the cabinet in General Scott's office. McClellan's unstated program of not giving information to Scott caused an ugly discussion when the participants began to discuss the number of troops around Washington. Cameron said he did not know how many there were. McClellan said nothing. Scott said no reports had been made to him. Still, McClellan said nothing. Lincoln was disturbed by this, and he showed it. Referring to a small piece of paper, Seward stated the number of regiments that had arrived in the previous few days and the aggregate of the entire force, identifying several of the commands. He asked McClellan to verify the statement, and the general replied that it was approximately correct. Scott made no effort to conceal his displeasure.

"This is a remarkable state of things." he complained. "I am in command of the armies of the United States but have been wholly unable to get any reports, any statement of the actual forces, but here is the Secretary of State, a civilian, for whom I have great respect but who is not a military man nor conversant with military affairs, though his abilities are great, but this civilian is possessed of facts which are withheld from me. Military reports are made, not to these headquarters, but to the State Department. Am I, Mr. President, to apply to the Secretary of State for the necessary military information to discharge my duties?"

Seward replied that he obtained his information by vigilance and attention, keeping account of the daily arrival of regiments and other things.

Scott smiled grimly. At best, he was skeptical.

"And you, without report, probably ascertained where each regiment was ordered," he said sarcastically. "Your labors and industry, Mr. Secretary of State, I

---

11   *N&H*, 4, 464. This factual assertion cannot be confirmed although *N&H* probably accepted its truth from the assertion by Scott in *OR*, 51, pt. 1, 491–493, especially 492, letter dated October 4, 1861, from Scott to Cameron. No "important" letters sent by McClellan to Cameron in the week after General Orders No. 17 appear in *OR*; Sears, *McClellan's Correspondence*; the McClellan MSS; the Lincoln MSS; or the National Archives. McClellan did send a short note asking that George Cadwalader of Patterson's Shenandoah Valley Army not be confirmed as a major general of volunteers or that, at least, Cadwalader not be assigned to the Army of the Potomac. Sears, *McClellan's Correspondence*, 102, endorsement dated September 16, 1861, from McClellan to Cameron. Nevertheless, the fact remains clear. Whether or not he sent the two letters, he ignored Scott's order and left the old general in a state of ignorance.

12   *OR*, 51, pt. 1, 491–493, letter dated October 4, 1861, from Scott to Cameron.

know are very arduous; but I did not before know the whole of them. If you in that way can get accurate information, the rebels can also, though I cannot."

Attempting to arrest an incipient quarrel before it rocketed out of control, Cameron interrupted half earnestly, half ironically. Everyone knew, he said, that Seward was meddlesome and that he interfered in all the departments. He suggested that everyone go about their duties. The conversation ended, and the men rose to leave.

In the beginning, Scott and Seward had shared a reluctance to intrude on the South. Scott then had Seward's confidence and support. That had begun to wane. In this conversation Scott easily recognized his declining prestige and his loss of support. Once again, his pride was wounded.[13]

McClellan would never have raised his voice or behaved offensively—and he would, throughout the trying, confrontational year ahead, never lose his temper. Here, cool behavior came easy. He sensed he had the upper hand. He was in control, he thought. As always, he was reserved and said nothing. But why should he? He had not sought his new job in Washington and would willingly yield it at any moment—especially if he were too thwarted to be effective.

As the visitors began to leave, Scott tried to avoid the young major general; but McClellan had him cornered in his own office. Scott could not well leave merely to avoid his most contumacious but most important subordinate. McClellan walked straight toward him, looked him squarely in the eye, and extended his hand.

"Good morning, General Scott," he said.

The general in chief did the only thing he could. Irritable, hypersensitive, haughty, imperious he was. A gentleman to the core, he was as well. He took his young subordinate's hand and shook it.

"You were called here by my advice," he said. "The times require vigilance and activity. I am not active and never shall be again. When I proposed that you should come here to aid, not supersede, me, you had my friendship and confidence. You still have my confidence."

Treating all this as if it were a ritual dance, the young major general, a romantic on many scores, believed that Scott had cast his gauntlet as a challenge and that

---

13   Welles, *Diary*, 2, 241–244, entry dated February 25, 1863. The date of the meeting is unclear. Welles gives the only full account but does not date it, and its place in his diary is obviously unrelated to the date it occurred. His account of the conversation, compared to McClellan's home letters, seems to put it on September 27, 1861, Sears, *McClellan's Correspondence*, 103, letter dated September 27, 1861, from McClellan to his wife. Hassler, *McClellan*, 30, agrees.

by taking it, he had accepted an offer of personal warfare. Indifferent to the dizzy-ing heights of his new position, he was willing to risk all because he did not care about the career result of the conflict.[14] He was right. That was enough.

Scott knew he could arrest and court martial his disobedient subordinate. That would solve the problem but would show severe conflict "near the head of the army," which would encourage the Confederates and adversely affect the friends of the Union. Unable to ride or walk, paralyzed in the small of his back, he recognized the need to retire, a need that would serve both him and his government. All this he asserted in a letter of complaint to the secretary of war on October 4,[15] but he did not sit idly by the path awaiting events. Having recognized the necessity of retire-ment, he campaigned for Henry Wager Halleck to succeed him. He would feel quite easy about delivering his responsibilities to Halleck, he told people. He held McClellan in great esteem for a high command, but Halleck, ten years older than McClellan, riper in judgment, and broadly knowledgeable in the theory of the mili-tary art, would be a better choice, he thought, for general in chief.[16]

Scott was not the only knowledgeable person to prefer Halleck for this position. Even men not in the mainstream of the rumor mill were aware of the old general's imminent retirement and of Halleck as a possible replacement. The day after the fighting ended at Ball's Bluff, Dennis Hart Mahan wrote to Secretary Chase, "The rumor, that Genl Scott is on the eve of retiring from further active participation in the conduct of the war seems to be receiving stronger confirmation from his increas-ing physical infirmities. This, whenever it takes place, must leave a gap in our mili-tary matters which it will be, I fear, not a little embarrassing to fill; and, indeed, as Genl. McClellan cannot be now spared from the active duties of command, it is not easy to say how the difficulties surrounding the question are to be disposed of."

Mahan had a solution for the problem. The administration had a greater need for "an able supervisor for our general military operations than a commander. Such a man should be one of no common grasp of intellect and knowledge of the general principles of military operations . . . Now among our general officers, except Genl McClellan, I know of no one who possesses these qualifications but Genl. Hal-

---

14   Morse, *Welles Diary*, 1, 241–242, entry dated February 25, 1863; Dahlgren, *Memoir*, 348, diary, entry dated November 1, 1861; Sears, *McClellan's Correspondence*, 82, letter dated Au-gust 10, 1861, redated by editor, from McClellan to his wife; 82, letter dated August 10, 1861, from McClellan to Lincoln; *M.O.S.*, 35.

15   Stanton MSS (L.C.) letter dated October 4, 1861, from Scott to Cameron; this letter also appears in *OR*, 51, pt. 1, 491–493.

16   Townsend, *Anecdotes*, 62.

leck." As far as Mahan was concerned, Halleck had them "in a very superior degree." Although Halleck had never commanded troops in the field, he knew the general principles of military operations at a level "perhaps second to that of none of our general officers, and all of the other qualifications eminently fit him for the station in question." Although questions of rank and the issuance of orders to McClellan and Fremont might cause problems, the president could make Halleck temporary chief of the general staff. With headquarters at Washington and the aides he found necessary, he could become the head of military administration, where he would be "the medium of communication between the Administration and the army generally. Without some such functionary, I do not see how we can preserve that unity in our extensive military operations which is a prime element of success." Positions like this, he admonished, existed in all well-organized European armies.[17]

An early escape from the drudgeries of farming in western New York, where he was born in 1815, had led Halleck to live with his grandfather. Hudson Academy, Union College, Phi Beta Kappa, and appointment as a cadet at the Military Academy followed. An assistant professor of chemistry while a cadet, he graduated a distinguished third among the thirty-two men of the Class of 1839, received a commission in the engineers, and served as assistant professor of engineering from graduation until June 28, 1840. For one year after that, he was assistant to the Board of Engineers in Washington, from which the army transferred him to an engineering position on the fortifications in New York harbor. In 1843 he declined a position as professor of engineering at the Lawrence Scientific School of Harvard University, continuing in New York until 1846 except for a tour for examination of public works in Europe in 1845. During his absence in Europe, he became a first lieutenant.

Upon his return to the United States, the Committee of the Lowell Institute in Boston, Massachusetts, attracted by his published report on "coast defense," invited him to deliver a series of lectures on the science of war. These were published in 1846 under the title *Elements of Military Art and Science*. A second edition with much new material on the Mexican and Crimean Wars was published in 1861. This book, at that time the best of its kind in the English language, enjoyed great demand during the rebellion.

At the outbreak of the Mexican War, he received orders to serve as engineer for military operations on the Pacific Coast. He sailed for seven months before reaching Monterey; but during the long, tedious passage around Cape Horn, he translated Baron Jomini's multi-volume work on Napoleon.

---

17   McClellan MSS (L.C.) letter dated October 22, 1861, from Dennis Hart Mahan to Chase.

Halleck partially fortified Monterey as a port of refuge for the Pacific fleet and as a base for land operations in southern California. As secretary of state for the military governments of California, he took an active part in civil and military affairs, showing great energy, high administrative abilities, excellent judgment, and admirable adaptability to his varied and onerous duties. He accompanied several expeditions in the lower California area as military engineer and took a few mounted volunteers on a forced march of 120 miles in twenty-eight hours to surprise a Mexican garrison. In addition to his engineering duties, he served as an aide to a commodore.

After the war, he became the real head of General Bennet Riley's military government for California, initiated the movement for state organization, and pressed it forward with vigor. He served as a member of the convention to form and of the committee to draft the state constitution, of which he was the principal author. Declining a political career, he continued in the army and remained an aide on the staff of General Bennet Riley. From December 1852, he served as inspector and engineer of lighthouses and from April 1853 as a member of the board of engineers for fortifications on the Pacific coast. Promoted to captain of engineers on July 1, 1853, he resigned from the service a year later.

After leaving the army, Halleck became a practicing lawyer and a prominent partner in the firm of Halleck, Peachy & Billings, one of the first law firms formed in San Francisco. The members of the firm were "incongruous and dissimilar." Halleck was thrifty and persevering and his "distinctive characteristics were obduracy and laboriousness." Discordant nationalities promoted civil strife, a reliable source of business for the able lawyers of the San Francisco bar in the late 1850s.

While working as a lawyer, Halleck published *A Collection of Mining Laws of Spain and Mexico* in 1859, a translation of *Fundamental Principles of the Law of Mining* in 1860, and a legal treatise entitled *International Law, or Rules Regulating the Inter- course of States in Peace and War* in 1861. Because of his successful and demanding business enterprises, he declined an appointment to the highest court of California and a seat in the United States Senate but did serve as president of the Pacific Atlantic Railroad, director general of the New Almaden quicksilver mine, and major general of the California militia.

When the South fired on Fort Sumter, he headed the oldest and most prominent law firm in San Francisco, had large business interests, and owned valuable property throughout the state. Without serious regard for the preservation of his substantial assets, he immediately offered his services to the Federal government; and General Scott urged President Lincoln to give him the highest grade in the Regular Army. Halleck and McClellan, made major generals on the same day, shared similar views on some of the important questions of the day. To them, abolition was not the issue of the war, a slave insurrection would be bad for everyone, and a negotiated peace would be the most desirable outcome. The Radicals might have obstructed Halleck's promotion if they had seen a letter he wrote to Reverdy Johnson, a prominent fellow lawyer, in April. He particularly hoped, he wrote, that Maryland would not secede. "If no slave states [like Maryland] remain in the Union," he wrote, "the North will become ultra anti-slavery, and I fear in the course of the war will declare for emancipation and thus add the horrors of a servile war to that of a civil war. But if Maryland should remain in the Union, slavery will still be recognized and protected under the Constitution, and the door be kept open for a compromise or reconstruction, if either should become possible." He also thought the war would be long and bloody.

From a vantage point that provided a view unavailable to all but a few, George W. Cullum, a man of no inconsiderable intellect himself and Halleck's chief of staff during much of the war, saw Halleck's character, his skill at the military profession, and his judgment. He found Halleck to have a strong, clear intellect that gave him a comprehensive grasp of the important matters on any issue and to be industrious and self-reliant. "Indeed," Cullum continued, "determination was his most marked characteristic evinced in a calm furnace which neither entreaty nor persuasion could move from its fixed purpose. Of such a nature caution would be a prevailing quality. With these was united a modesty almost shyness; and thus perhaps he did himself injustice, as his sensitiveness to the value of sincerity caused him often to repel rather than be deemed insincere. This known temperament secured him the most valuable estimation of his instructed and ablest fellow officers. His dryness of manner was no argument of want of heart, for indeed he was a warm, true, loyal friend, and in the inner circle of his life was tender and playful, showing a keen sense of humor. His home was a scene of perfect happiness and kind hospitality. Of children he was fond; had an ardent love of nature, and indulged the expectation of closing his latter hours in a retreat in a beautiful region south of San Francisco, looking on the Pacific ocean."[18]

---

18   Wilson, James G., "General Halleck: a Memoir" in vol. 36 *Journal of the Military Service Institution of the United States*, 553; Cullum, George W., "Biographical Sketch of Major-General Henry W. Halleck of the United States Army," 3–10, 27–28 (New York, 1880) (pamphlet); *D.A.B.*, 4, pt. 2, 150–51; Ambrose, Stephen E., *Halleck: Lincoln's Chief of Staff* (Baton Rouge, 1962) 4–10 (Ambrose, *Halleck*); Keyes, Erasmus Darwin, *From West Point to California*, 78; Anders, Curt, *Henry Halleck's War: A fresh Look at Lincoln's Controversial General in Chief* (Indiana, 1999) 4–34, 27; letter dated April 30, 1861, from Halleck to Johnson (Anders, *Henry Halleck's War*).

Another observant, intelligent critic, also a member of the military and a graduate of the Military Academy, but standing on a different and more routinely available point of vantage, saw in Halleck a much less attractive person. Major General James Harrison Wilson, sixth in the Class of 1860,[19] looked at Halleck and saw a man standing five feet nine inches, weighing one hundred ninety pounds, bald in front, with a double chin, sallow eyes, flabby cheeks, a slack and twisted figure, slow deliberate movements, and sluggish speech lacking in point and magnetism.[20]

Long after the war, George D. Ruggles, another West Point graduate with long staff service, stated an equally strong view. "To my mind, he was a cold, selfish, opinionated overrated man. To me he was repellant and not magnetic . . . I knew Halleck very well, as a young officer is acquainted with his superior in military service and his senior for 15 or 20 years."[21] This unattractive image Halleck enhanced with an annoying habit of rubbing his elbows with his hands whenever he was embarrassed,[22] positioning his head with a "sideways carriage," and looking at people with "eyes wide open, staring, dull, fishy even," which gave him an "owlish" and unattractive appearance.[23]

Among the few graduates of the Military Academy who were the intellectuals of their profession and would rise to great heights in the American Civil War were Henry Jackson Hunt, whose star had already been recognized by some but had not yet risen to great heights; Andrew Atkinson Humphreys, still a virtual prisoner on shipboard on his interminable return from a far-flung post of duty in California; John G. Barnard; and George B. McClellan.[24] Halleck, too, belonged to this group.

---

19   *D.A.B.*, 10, pt. 2, 334.

20   Wilson, James Harrison, *Under the Old Flag*, 2 vols. (New York and London, 1912) 1, 99 (Wilson, *Under the Old Flag*).

21   Military Historical Society of Massachusetts MSS (John C. Ropes letters) (B.U.) letter dated April 24, 1897, from George D. Ruggles to Major W. L. Livermore.

22   Morse, *Welles Diary*, 1, 83, entry dated August 17, 1862.

23   *New York Herald*, July 21, 1862, quoted in Ambrose, *Halleck*; Wallace, Lew, *Autobiography*, 2 vols. (New York, 1900) 2, 570 (Wallace, *Autobiography*); Wilson, *Under the Old Flag*, 1, 99.

24   With considerable uncertainty the author has excluded Emory Upton, among the most recent graduates of West Point and still a junior company grade officer, from this group. A tortured but respected thinker, Upton would take his own life in a fit of despair at the thought of intellectual failure. Michie, Peter S., *Life and Letters of Emory Upton, Colonel of the Fourth Regiment of Artillery and Brevet Major General U.S. Army* (New York, 1885) 474–495 (Michie, *Life and Letters of Upton*), especially letter dated March 13, 1881, from Upton to Sara, 494, and unfinished letter of n.d. to the Adjutant-General, 495. His life and work, however thoughtful and analytical, have a quality of the mechanical, rather than the intellectual.

Unfortunately for Scott's campaign to designate Halleck as his replacement, the candidate was an abstraction on a ship somewhere between California and New York. Having set sail from California only on October 10, Colonel Brown's geography rule worked against him. No one in the government could assess Halleck's personality or character, and Scott's personnel assessments had long since become suspect, like his judgments on strategy and on the State of Virginia. Unlike McClellan, Halleck had no credits in the current war. The West Virginia campaign, no matter how small, still set McClellan apart and above.

Scott's policies, stated at the end of 1860 in his "Views" and modified in 1861 in the "Supplement," had not changed. Nor did he now give any reason to believe they had changed. His resistance to the seizure of the Potomac's Virginia shore on May 24 and subsequent resistance to McClellan's plans for offensive movements into Virginia confirmed his continued devotion to a policy of strangulation, which would, he thought, cause the Rebel military forces to wither by lack of use.[25] If his proposals did not conflict with the necessities of the Union war effort, certainly they did not serve them.

In the habit of informally visiting McClellan in his headquarters each evening, Lincoln had regular exposure to McClellan's campaign—whatever it may have been in its personal specifics—against Scott. In his possession the president had a solution to the problem of Scott's retirement. He still had the resignation Scott had given him in early August. He need only—if he could bring himself to the decision—accept it. All circumstances came together on October 18 at a cabinet meeting. Proceeding, as he almost always did, by consensus, Lincoln persuaded the cabinet to accept Scott's resignation and place him on the retired list.

---

25   The policy pursued by Scott and McClellan toward the secessionists has been recently analyzed in another of the thoughtful small books published by a university press as a policy of "conciliation." Grimsley, Mark, *The Hard Hand of War: Union Military Policy toward Southern Civilians, 1861–1865* (Cambridge, 1995) generally chap. 2, 23 ff (Grimsley, *Hard Hand*). In McClellan's case, although he foresaw a negotiated peace that would bring the Southern civilian population back to the fold without the planter aristocracy, "conciliation" is the wrong word and creates the wrong impression. McClellan meant to crush the Southern armies, no matter what was required to do it. But the devastation of the Thirty Years War with its mercenary armies and civilian horrors he meant to avoid. *OR*, 5, 611–612, General Orders no. 19, dated October 1, 1861. ("The attention of the General Commanding has recently been directed to depredations of an atrocious character that have been committed upon the persons and property of citizens in Virginia by the troops under his command . . . The General Commanding directs that in future all persons connected with this army who are detected in depredating upon the property of citizens shall be arrested and brought to trial; and he assures all concerned that crimes of such enormity will admit of no remission of the death penalty which the military law attaches to offenses of this nature.")

The implementation and publication of this decision would await the appropriate moment.[26]

Although news of the cabinet meeting did not find its way into the hands of the public at once, McClellan learned the very next day about Scott's forthcoming retirement as well as Scott's intention to promote Halleck. "The Predt & Cabinet have determined to accept his retirement," he wrote home, "but *not* in favor of Halleck."[27] Throughout the following week everyone in Washington talked about Scott's obstruction of McClellan's efforts to organize the army and his opposition to an offensive. Soldiers and civilians alike wanted a more enterprising chief.

"If in ten days McClellan is not commander in chief," a number of generals were overheard saying, "the army shall have something to do with that matter."[28]

During the last week of October, McClellan met Adam Gurowski, a scrivener in Seward's State Department. Not above a little hyperbole to achieve the desired result, McClellan described his opinions on an issue close to his heart, the formation of corps. He told Gurowski, "*how fully he is convinced* of the absolute necessity to divide the army into corps." Scott had prevented him from doing it.

"As soon as I have power," he said, "I should do it immediately."[29]

---

26   Beale, *Bates Diary*, 196, entry dated October 18, 1861. Curiously, no other account of this meeting or record of this decision seems to exist although Bates's description of it is clear. From the events that followed and their description by the participants, Lincoln and his cabinet officials seem to have been quite effective—for a change—in maintaining security on the decision.

27   Sears, *McClellan's Correspondence*, 109, letter dated October 19, 1861, from McClellan to his wife. This letter illustrates a difficulty for any student of McClellan's life. His home letters are recorded in chronological batches in *M.O.S.* but to preserve McClellan's dignity and professional reputation, they were changed and paraphrased by his posthumous editor. In fact, the originals do not seem to exist anywhere. In McClellan's manuscripts in the Library of Congress is a hand-bound collection of copies of parts of the letters he wrote to his wife entitled "Extracts from Letters to my Wife During the War of the Rebellion." The originals for the period he was on active duty are missing. The originals from 1863 and 1864, when McClellan was no longer on active service, survive. Sears states that the differences between the extracts and surviving originals were "the often personal content, such as professions of his love," Sears, *McClellan's Correspondence*, Introduction, xiii, and concludes that the earlier, active-duty deletions were similar. The extracts, however, like the letter quoted in the text, have other deletions. McClellan had, in some measure, two personalities, one public and one very private. The public personality was dignified and proper at all times. The private personality had ugly human characteristics he never revealed to the public. In *M.O.S.* the deletions from his letters, whether by McClellan or by Prime, his editor, are, in effect, an effort to eliminate the dichotomy and purify the personality. The original letter quoted in part in the text apparently had an epithet describing Scott. That has been deleted. In short, the home letters, as they have survived, are not totally reliable, but the wholesale rewriting of history by editing need not be feared because of the uncomplimentary but human personal characteristics they still disclose.

28   Comte de Paris MS Diary (large diary) (A.N. de la M. de F.) entry dated November 2, 1861.

29   Chandler MSS (L.C.) letter dated March 8, 1862, from Gurowski to Chandler.

Other events worked in McClellan's favor. Rumors circulated in government circles that the unfortunate movement on Leesburg had been ordered by Scott without McClellan's knowledge.[30]

On October 25, Postmaster General Montgomery Blair confirmed to Senators Wade and Chandler that McClellan would meet them at Blair's home that evening at 10.[31] The meeting lasted until 5 the following morning.[32] The "Jacobins," as Hay referred to them in his diary, had on their agenda immediate all-out battles, indifference to defeat in any one of them, military destruction of the Confederacy, obliteration of the Southern planter aristocracy, and emancipation of the slaves,[33] a program far removed from the negotiated peace without destructive total war desired by both McClellan and Halleck. McClellan no doubt argued that he could do nothing because of Scott's interference, and he probably did not discuss a negotiated peace. He did succeed in directing the focus to the short-term goal of removing Scott. As McClellan wrote his wife, the Radicals agreed to make, the next day, a "desperate effort . . . to have General Scott retired at once."[34]

The next evening the "Jacobin Club"—Wade, Trumbull, and Chandler—went to Lincoln. Wanting an immediate battle they began again the agitation of the early summer for an immediate advance. The president defended McClellan's deliberation. When the revolutionaries departed, Lincoln and Hay headed promptly for McClellan's headquarters. There, they found McClellan's aide and confidant, Colonel Thomas M. Key, talking about the need for an immediate battle to defeat the enemy. "He seemed to think we were ruined if we did not fight," noted Hay in his diary.

Lincoln asked what McClellan thought about it.

"The General is troubled in his mind," Key answered. "I think he is much embarrassed by the radical difference between his views and those of General Scott."

---

30   Ford, Worthington Chauncey, ed., *A Cycle of Adams Letters*, 2 vols. (New York and Boston, 1920) 1, 77, letter dated December 3, 1861, from Charles Francis Adams, Jr., to Henry Adams (Ford, *Cycle of Letters*).

31   The chronology of the three meetings that occurred here is unclear but probably not material to the departure of Scott. In a letter dated October 26, Sears, *McClellan Correspondence*, 112, McClellan told his wife that he had been at Blair's house talking "war matters" with the three Radical senators. He had, but the meeting began on October 25, Chandler MSS (L.C.) letters dated October 25, 1861, from Blair to Wade and Chandler and October 27, 1861, from Chandler to his wife.

32   Chandler MSS (L.C.) letter dated October 25, 1861, Montgomery Blair to Wade and Chandler.

33   Williams, *Lincoln and the Radicals*, 53–57.

34   Sears, *McClellan's Correspondence*, 112, letter dated October 26, 1861, from McClellan to his wife.

McClellan entered, and Key left. After discussing some preliminary military matters, Lincoln and McClellan turned to the Jacobins. McClellan said that Wade preferred an unsuccessful battle to delay and believed a defeat could be repaired by "swarming recruits." Believing the outcome of the war would turn on one great battle, McClellan said he "would rather have a few recruits before a victory than a good many after a defeat."

Lincoln expressed dismay at the popular impatience but said it should be taken into account because it was a reality. "At the same time, General, you must not fight till you are ready."

Again waxing romantic and likening himself to Harold, king of the Saxons, at Hastings, Gustavus Adolphus, king of Sweden, at Lützen, and Montcalm, commander of the French Army at Quebec, McClellan implied that, if he fought an unsuccessful battle, he would die a gallant death on the field.[35] "I have everything at stake," he said. "If I fail, I will not see you again or anybody."

Swept into McClellan's romantic ideas, the president responded, "I have a notion to go out with you and stand or fall with the battle."

The next evening Lincoln and Hay went to Seward's home, where they found Chandler and Wade. As John Hay characterized the Jacobins' views in his diary, they wanted "to get up a battle, saying that one must be fought; saying that defeat was no worse than delay, and a great deal more trash."

Henry Wilson, "a strong, healthy, hearty senator, soldier and man," wrote Hay, arrived and joined the conversation. "He was bitter on the Jacobins, saying the safety of the country demanded that the General should have his time,"[36] Hay recorded.

A "small row" followed between Scott and McClellan, one which found its way into the press and into the ranks of McClellan's soldiers, both of which, in McClellan's perception, favored him.[37] At the same time squabbles between the

---

35   Creasy, Sir Edward, *The Fifteen Decisive Battles of the World*, 107 (Norwalk, 5th Ed. 1969, Easton ed.); Weigley, Russell F., *The Age of Battles: the Quest for Decisive Warfare from Breitenfeld to Waterloo*, 33 (Indianapolis and Bloomington, Indiana, 1991); Mann, *Wallenstein*, 650–659; Parkman, Francis, *France and England in North America* (Frontenac Edition, Boston, 1902), *Montcalm and Wolfe*, 3 vols., 3, 141–143.

36   Burlingame, *Hay Diary*, 28–29, entries dated October 26 and 27, 1861. The order of events is not clear from McClellan's letter or from Hay's diary, but the content of the discussions suggests that the Radicals met first with the president, then tried to intimidate McClellan after they failed with Lincoln, who had unapproachable power. After learning about the logjam caused by Scott, the promise by Wade and Chandler, *supra* fnn. 31, 32, to discuss the succession question with Lincoln the next day and the absence of any reference to Scott in Hay's diary entry strongly suggest the order of the meetings.

37   Sears, *McClellan's Correspondence*, 112–113, letter dated October 30, 1861, by the editor, from McClellan to his wife.

staffs of McClellan and Scott became public.[38] McClellan believed the "Scott war" would end within the week and was certain about the outcome because, he wrote home, "the people will not permit me to be passed over."[39]

Events now moved at a rapid pace. McClellan met with Lincoln and probably with Cameron, the subject of his succession to general in chief no doubt a large part of the conversation. Although McClellan had stated his military views in lengthy letters dated August 2, 8, and 10 and September 8, all of which had been addressed to or forwarded to the president, Lincoln once again asked for a description of the condition of the Army of the Potomac, the measures necessary to protect the government, and a plan for the suppression of the rebellion. The president must have wanted this one last persuasion that he had the correct course: Retire General Scott, his only experienced senior officer; replace him with a younger, far less experienced officer, who already had a demanding full-time job; and reject the advice of his senior military adviser.

In all likelihood he knew, from Secretary Chase, that the president would reject the opinion of Dennis Hart Mahan, his country's most well-known and respected military theoretician. Lincoln showed McClellan the resignation letter Scott had submitted during the confrontation in early August and had refused to withdraw. His eye on the personal as well as the national goal, McClellan noted the absence of any reference to Halleck in it. The president left the meeting in an air of indecision, not about Scott, nor about McClellan's abilities, but about the monumental burdens he would place on the shoulders of his young major general. McClellan believed he had swept the field. The president would accept Scott's "offer" that evening and make McClellan general in chief at once. The major general felt "a sense of relief at the prospect of having my own way untrammeled." Although he recognized the "vast responsibility" he was about to assume, he had no special feeling about this significant event and certainly not a twinge of "gratified vanity or ambition," he wrote home.[40]

---

38   McClellan MSS (L.C.) letter dated October [1861 by the author] from illegible to "my dear George."

39   Sears, *McClellan's Correspondence*, 112–113, letter dated October 30, 1861, by the editor, from McClellan to his wife.

40   Beale, *Bates Diary*, 199, 200, entry dated November 1, 1861; Sears, *McClellan's Correspondence*, 112–119, letters dated October 30, 1861, by the editor from McClellan to his wife; October 31, 1861, by the editor from McClellan to his wife; and October 31, 1861, by the editor, from McClellan to Cameron. Nothing specifically states that McClellan was shown the August letter from Scott, but no other letter of resignation appears in *OR*, or any of the likely manuscript collections, and the August letter had no reference to Halleck, which would probably have appeared if the letter of resignation accepted on November 1 had been prepared later.

The next day, McClellan worked on the letter requested by the president. To avoid the frequent, unscheduled "drop-in" visits, he went to the quarters of his friend and confidant Edwin M. Stanton. For several hours they worked at the task,[41] Stanton drafting the beginning and rewriting the conclusion and McClellan writing the core. The additions and rewritings by Stanton had a great sense of urgency. "No time is to be lost," Stanton wrote in a new concluding paragraph, "We have lost too much already."[42]

McClellan's part was more deliberate. But he was in his element, and he was writing about things he had considered long and carefully. As always when he treated subjects he had mastered, his preferred realm of communication, his words would have come "in an even uninterrupted flow of well-constructed sentences, as fast as his rapid pen could put them on paper, with almost never a word left out or a correction required. It seemed as if writing were just enough slower than thinking to enable his thoughts to flow freely into words, and he would cover page after page without a pause except for the empty pen."[43] This kind of performance would have impressed Stanton, a glib, skillful trial lawyer with rapid means of expression.

Late in the evening McClellan quietly took aside his aide Robert D'Orleans, the Duc de Chartres, and told him to saddle their horses. He wanted the two of them to depart without being seen. Taking no escort or orderlies, they crossed the river and headed for Fitz John Porter's camp.[44] On the way McClellan told the young duke the momentous news: Scott was resigning this evening.[45] They dismounted at Porter's camp, made their way to his fire, and sat by it with Porter, where McClellan probably lit one of his evening cigars. The two men talked about many things, including, no doubt, the recent, brief past and, more likely, the uncertain and complex future.[46] With Scott no longer in the way and no other officer be-

41   Sears, *McClellan's Correspondence*, 113–114, letter dated October 31, 1861, by the editor, from McClellan to his wife.

42   Sears, *McClellan's Correspondence*, 114–119 and notes 118–119, letter dated October 31, 1861, by the editor, from McClellan to Cameron.

43   Biddle, William F., "Recollections of McClellan," in *The United Service: a Monthly Review of Military and Naval Affairs*, vol. xi, May, 1894, 461 (pam.).

44   Sears, *McClellan's Correspondence*, 114, letter dated October 31, 1861, by the editor, from McClellan to his wife.

45   Comte de Paris MS diary (large diary) (A.N. de la M. de F.), entry dated Nov. 2, 1861.

46   Sears, *McClellan's Correspondence*, 114, letter dated October 31, 1861, by the editor, from McClellan to his wife.

tween him and the president, McClellan believed he could implement almost any strategy he wanted. At last he could without impediment put his growing, improving army into a campaign on the sacred soil of Virginia. Perhaps this was the first time he and Porter discussed a radical new plan, a grandiose plan that would profit from his service in the Mexican War and his observations in the Crimea.

In all this turmoil McClellan relied, as he had continuously in recent months, on the new source of strength introduced to him by his wife. "Whatever [the result] may be I will try to do my duty to the army and to the country—with God's help and a single eye to the right and hope that I may succeed," McClellan wrote. "I appreciate all the difficulties in my path—and also I feel in my innermost soul how small is my ability in comparison with the gigantic dimensions of the task, that, even if I had the greatest intellect that was ever given to man, the result remains in the hands of God . . . I know that God can accomplish the greatest results with the weakest instruments—therein lies my hope."[47]

The next day, November 1, 1861, the cabinet met at the unusual early hour of 9 A.M. to consider General Scott's letter of resignation. Lincoln expressed doubt that he knew the correct way to proceed and uncertainty that they should have another "general in chief." The president may have considered the possibility of running the war from the White House. As always, he was far shrewder than his cabinet members. If Scott were retired but not replaced, the greatest opposition to McClellan's organization of the Army of the Potomac and an advance into Virginia would be removed. Perhaps that would be enough. Lincoln talked about the grave concern he had for the combined burden McClellan would carry as general in chief of all armies and commanding general of the Army of the Potomac. Lincoln said he remained reluctant to give the position to McClellan, if not opposed to doing it. The members of the cabinet, however, unanimously supported the young major general. A short speech by Attorney General Bates resolved the impasse.

"The general in chief or chief general is only your lieutenant," he said. "You are constitutional 'commander in chief' and may make any general you choose your second or lieutenant to command under."

This suggestion carried the day. Although no one knew it at the moment, Bates had sown the first seeds of a strange crop for the future. The cabinet passed from decision to mechanics. The president had prepared an order of retirement. Immediately after the meeting, Chase sent a note to Colonel Thomas M. Key, his old political

---

47   Sears, *McClellan's Correspondence*, 112–113, letter dated October 30, 1861, from McClellan to his wife.

confidant and source of information from within McClellan's organization, "McClellan will be commander in chief from today; Let me thank God and take courage . . . Say nothing of this act till official order is promulgated."[48]

The president and Nicolay went to visit Seward, who talked long and earnestly about the change. The secretary of state reported that he had given "a grave and fatherly lecture to McClellan which was taken in good part; advising him to enlarge the sphere of his thoughts and feel the weight of the occasion."[49] Lincoln asked that they gather at 4 P.M.

Once they reunited, the president and cabinet left the White House en masse to walk to Scott's lodgings. The aged general in chief, in full dress uniform, lay stretched on the couch in his drawing room. The visitors took seats. They exchanged preliminary compliments. Lincoln rose, took his written order from his stovepipe hat, and read it aloud.

Seward, a long-time supporter of the old general, in the main a believer in Scott's policy of inactive threatening, and an uneasy observer of McClellan's rise, summarized the crowded recent months. They had been through a great deal together. And they had survived it all.

With the assistance of Colonel Edward D. Townsend, his adjutant general, Scott rose to his feet. His voice was choked with emotion.

"President: This honor overwhelms me. It overpays all services I have attempted to render to my country. If I had any claims before, they are all obliterated by this expression of approval by the President, with the remaining support of his Cabinet. I know the president and the cabinet well. I know that the country has placed its interests in this trying crisis in safe-keeping. Their counsels are wise, their labors are as untiring as they are loyal, and their course is the right one. President, you must excuse me. I am unable to stand longer to give utterance to the feelings of gratitude which oppress me. In my retirement I shall offer up my prayers to God for this Administration and for my country. I shall pray for it with confidence in its success over all enemies, and that speedily."

Lincoln shook Scott's hand and said goodbye. Each member of the cabinet approached the reclining general, shook his hand, and exchanged words of farewell.

48   McClellan MSS (L.C.) letter dated November 1, 1861, from Chase to Key; Beale, *Bates Diary*, 199, 200, entry dated November 1, 1861; Burlingame, *Hay Diary*, 28–29, entry dated October 26, 1861; Schuckers, Chase mem. entitled "Notes on the Union of the Armies of the Potomac and the Army of Virginia," written shortly after September 2, 1862; Niven, John, *Salmon P. Chase: A Biography* (New York and Oxford, 1995) 270, and n. 52, 500 (Niven, *Chase*).

49   Burlingame, *Hay Diary*, 30, entry dated November, 1861.

They told Scott many religious associations had formed to pray daily for his health and happiness. The old general was deeply moved.

At the door Lincoln said that suitable provision would be made for Scott's personal staff, Colonels George W. Cullum, Edward H. Wright, and Henry Van Renssalaer, who were to escort the general to New York City before proceeding to other duty. He concluded that he hoped to write a letter expressing his personal appreciation for the general's services.[50]

50   Comte de Paris MS Diary (large diary) (A.N. de la M. de F.), entry dated November 2, 1861; Burlingame, *Hay Diary*, 29, entry dated October 27, 1861; *Harper's Weekly*, November 16, 1861, 722; Beale, *Bates Diary*, 199, entry dated November 1, 1861.

Chapter 16

"McClellan is invested with all the powers of Scott. McClellan has more on his shoulders than any man—a Napoleon not excepted—can stand; and with his very limited capacity, McClellan must necessarily break under it."

—Gurowski in his diary

McClellan Becomes General in Chief

On the evening of November 1 the president and his assistant visited McClellan. The general read his order about Scott's[1] resignation and his own assumption of command. The president thanked McClellan and said it greatly relieved him. In writing his general order assuming command, McClellan found the generosity to give a florid farewell to his predecessor. Not heartfelt, it was another example of form over substance, proper conduct elevated above inner feelings.

"The Army will unite with me," it said, "in the feeling of regret that the weight of many years and the effect of increasing infirmities, contracted and intensified in his country's service, should just now remove from our head the great soldier of our nation . . . While we regret his loss there is one thing we cannot regret—the bright example he has left for our emulation."[2]

---

1 Burlingame, *Hay Diary*, 30, entry dated November 1861. The edition by Dennett, 50–51, refers to "Stone's" retirement; but it must have meant Scott's.

2 Sears, *McClellan's Correspondence*, 122, General Orders No. 19, dated November 1, 1861.

McClellan had confronted an older, vastly more experienced, and well-entrenched antagonist and swept him from the field in three months. He could afford to be generous, the general order being another example of proper conduct contrary to personal feelings. The high praise he heaped on Scott probably lacking sincerity, McClellan's statements seemed almost to be gloating. He knew his order was hyperbolic. He must have intended it to be. In fact, he was writing a military obituary for a senior officer he had removed and replaced. He was not writing for or about Scott. He was writing, he wrote home, "*at* him" and "for a particular market,"[3] no doubt the market of Scott supporters who thought the country could not do without him and remained skeptical about the young Napoleon.

That evening, McClellan's aides Captains Philippe and Robert D'Orleans, the French princes, had dinner at the spacious home of Secretary of State Seward. Edward Everett, a prominent lawyer, a Democrat with the affable manners of an Englishman of the past, and an unsuccessful candidate for vice president with John Bell in 1860, also attended.

Seward held forth on his military beliefs, which, like those of Scott, favored delay and erosion. He preceded his discussion with his usual mannerism of speech, "I have a theory. . . ." While he spoke, Captain Philippe D'Orleans, the Comte de Paris, recalled the remark of Alexis de Toqueville about a man whose speeches said nothing. The captain wondered if the "retirement" of Scott would lead Seward to resign. "I am afraid his departure," wrote the prince in his diary the next evening, "would be the beginning of violent reactions bringing to power men who would be so extreme that any reconciliation would be impossible." The prince shared, if he did not simply reflect, the view of his chief that the war should end with a negotiated peace.

Sadness marked Seward's conversation that night. Emotionally, he described Scott's farewell statement, then recalled the general in chief and Buchanan in the last days of Buchanan's administration:

> I will never forget all the great trials they underwent together. I will never forget when Mr. Buchanan left us with eighteen hundred men to defend the Union's capital while the South had already brought together a great army ready to invade our territory and how he was able to organize a defense force. He will not have the opportunity to finish his work and gives his command to younger men with the mission of restoring the Union. But keep in mind, he already saved the Union once.[4]

---

3   Sears, *McClellan's Correspondence*, 122, 126; General Orders no. 19, dated November 1, 1861; letter dated November 7, 1861, from McClellan to his wife.

4   Comte de Paris MS diary (large diary) (A.N. de la M. de F.) entry dated November 2, 1861. The secretary of state also described his feelings about slavery and the black people, which were

Seward expressed something akin to nostalgia at Scott's departure. Others discussed McClellan's arrival as general in chief and did not regard it well. Experienced and observant men in the army thought Scott should not have been replaced. Philip W. Kearny, a brilliant, energetic, critical Regular Army officer of great wealth and social standing, perceived Scott as the only officer with a "habit of victory" and the temperament for handling masses. Perhaps he had in his old age become too heavily focused on detail, which he performed slowly and badly; but his numerous talents were, to Kearny, outstanding. In comparison, he thought McClellan had "undaunted, sober courage" but not "one spark of military genius."[5]

Anticipating McClellan's promotion to Scott's position, Kearny had written a friend on October 1, 1861, that orders by Scott were known to come from a man of unquestioned bravery and experience in war. "You asked me about General McClellan. I know that his mathematical talents and good sense and safe calculations and great system, are universally allowed. In the [Mexican] war he was too young in rank to be conspicuous. His has only been a 'West Point Class' reputation. I would have regarded him a good second, and a *fair promise* but as a leader superseding General Scott a most *dangerous experiment*."[6]

On November 2 at 4 A.M., McClellan, his staff, and a few cavalrymen escorted Scott to his train. In pitch darkness violent winds powerful enough to pull tent pins from the ground blew a torrential rain. The scene was Wagnerian. McClellan, the young Siegfried, said goodbye to Wotan, the aged and "defeated" former leader. Scott, ill-tempered and excessively sensitive, remained, as always, a gentleman and polite.[7] McClellan's effusive order had done much to mollify his feelings. He believed, he said, that McClellan was a superior general, if not the best that ever existed.[8] He sent kind messages to McClellan's wife Ellen and the new baby. He felt

---

even more conservative than those of McClellan. "Slavery is the most dreadful curse on a country . . . The black race can only prosper in slavery. When I was born, my father was a slave owner close to Albany. Back then, there were 50,000 Negroes and one million whites . . . A free black race cannot match the white race in intelligence. I have pity for all those poor free blacks. Whenever I need a carriage, I always pick one with a black cabman to give him a chance to earn some money."

5   de Peyster, *Kearny*, 222, letter dated December 15, 1862, from Kearny to n.a.

6   Kearny MSS (L.C.) letter dated October 1, 1861, from Kearny to Parker.

7   Comte de Paris MS Diary (large diary) (A.N. de la M. de F.) entry dated November 2, 1861; Sears, *McClellan's Correspondence*, 123–124, letter dated November 2, 1861, by the editor from McClellan to his wife; Styple, William B., ed., Nathalie Chartrain, trans., *Our Noble Blood: The Civil War Letters of Regis de Trobriand Major-General U.S.V.* (Kearny, 1997) letter dated November 2, 1861, from De Trobriand to his daughter Lina (Styple, *De Trobriand's Letters*).

8   Sears, *McClellan Correspondence*, 126, letter dated November 7, 1861, from McClellan to his wife.

very peculiar sensations, he said, leaving Washington and active life. But so he must—after serving his country honorably and successfully for fifty years. In his long military service he had never turned his back on a conflict and never failed to serve his country to a successful outcome. Now a "feeble old man scarce able to walk," wrote McClellan to Ellen, "with hardly anyone to see him off but his successor, the successor's staff, and a squadron of cavalry," he boarded the train for his trip to West Point, where he intended to live in retirement.[9]

The entire event had occurred in a manner "simple without any fuss." As the train left the station, one of McClellan's officers could be heard stating the attitude of McClellan and his staff. "He is shelved at last. *Requiescat in pace.*"[10]

The Comte de Paris was not the only officer happy to see the old general go and McClellan given complete responsibility. Wilder Dwight wrote his family, "I did not think the day would come when the country would welcome his [Scott's] loss. But I think everyone is relieved by his retirement. Now McClellan assumes an individual responsibility, and if he has courage to defy the politicians, he may yet win the laurel which is growing for the successful general of the righteous but blunder-blasted war."[11]

Less fair in tone, Count Gurowski's diary had a factually accurate characterization of the old general in chief. "He never forgot to be a Virginian, and was filled with all a Virginian's conceit. To the last hour he warded off blows aimed at Virginia. To this hour he never believed in a serious war. . . ."[12]

Always romantic in moments of peace and contemplation, McClellan understood his departing former superior's sentiments. "It may be that at some distant day," he wrote his wife, "I too shall totter away from Washin—a worn out soldier, with naught to do but make my peace with God. The sight of this morning was a lesson to me which I hope not soon to forget. I saw there the end of a long, active and ambitious life—the end of the career of the first soldier of his nation."[13] Of course, McClellan would in the passage of time repeat the departure; but that event,

9　Sears, *McClellan's Correspondence*, 123–124, letter dated November 2, 1861, by the editor from McClellan to his wife.

10　Comte de Paris MS Diary (large diary) (A.N. de la M. de F.), entry dated November 2, 1861.

11　Dwight, *Letters*, 137, letter dated November 3, 1861, from Wilder Dwight to his family.

12　Gurowski, *Diary*, 1, 116–117, November, 1861.

13　Sears, *McClellan's Correspondence*, 123, letter dated November 2, 1861, by the editor, from McClellan to his wife.

apparently an eternity in the future, lay obscured by the immediately occurring, monumental events he would control.

Was Scott's retirement a grave loss to the Union war effort? Could he be successfully replaced at the head of the Union armies by one of the captains of the old Regular Army? The answer to the first question—a grave loss?—came relatively easily and had already been stated by Postmaster General Montgomery Blair. The answer to the second question—a successful replacement?—would await the passage of time and the test of the Federal war effort in the crucible of events.

Scott's great experience, confident advice, direct manner, steady continuity, and prompt responsiveness contributed greatly to the military transition from Buchanan to Lincoln and to the early development of the Lincoln administration's army. With so much else unstable and uncertain, a person with knowledge and a firm hand did much to allow the creation and early growth of a military effort whose size had never been imagined by any American. Lincoln's great personnel skills made the president cognizant of this, and he was reluctant to do without it.

But in other ways Scott failed as general in chief. With its passivity, its practical effect of allowing the South to grow stronger by going about its business undisturbed, and its indifference to the demands of the loyal Northerners, Scott's strategy simply could not have prevailed. Immediately after the fall of Fort Sumter, Blair had likened Scott's intentions to those of a disloyal man, even though he conceded that Scott was as loyal as any man.

Even the bitterly partisan James K. Polk had shown more objective judgment than Scott. In the Mexican War, Polk had constantly tried to avoid making Scott a military hero and therefore a political threat but nevertheless had the character to give Scott command of the critical, determinative Vera Cruz-Mexico City column even though he preferred other candidates.[14] Scott could not overcome his sensitivity and reach a similar level of magnitude.

Blair had recognized the deleterious effect of Scott's treatment of the younger men who would lead the field armies. Certainly his treatment of Lieutenant Colonel Keyes, Major General McClellan, Captain David Porter, and even Brigadier General McDowell had shown a personality below the level of grand superiority necessary for dealing with rising, aggressive young leaders. Keyes, McDowell, and McClellan would become major generals, and Porter would end the war as an admiral with a reputation equaled only by David Glasgow Farragut. Talented men,

14   Sellers, Charles Grier, *James K. Polk*, 2 vols. (Princeton, 1966) 2, 439–444.

they deserved better treatment. Scott's sensitivity, unforgiving grudge-bearing, and intolerance made him unfit for a position so far-reaching.

Worst of all, the nature and scope of the war erupted beyond his experience and his ability to adjust at his age. On the blockade and the seizure of the Mississippi he had been correct. On the passive offensive he could not have been more wrong. He did not believe railroads would be important in the war.[15] Nor did he think cavalry in larger force than a company or battalion would be useful. The largest force he had led, the Mexico City column, had been less than fifteen thousand men. Napoleonic armies of more than one hundred thousand stood beyond his comprehension. If his opinion had prevailed and McClellan had created no units larger than brigades, an army of one hundred thousand men would have put its commander in the hopeless position of maneuvering more than twenty-five independent battle units, few of which could be seen at any time from any command position. The great commanders of old, Miltiades, Darius, Leonidas, Xerxes, Epaminondas, Phillip, Alexander, Hannibal, and Scipio, had been able to command larger forces in battle because they usually had at most three units to direct, a massive phalanx of infantry with separate forces of cavalry on each flank.[16] In most cases the armies fought on a large, flat, open surface, and the course of the battle followed a pre-arranged plan. Once their armies joined battle, Alexander and Hannibal became no more than exceptionally courageous infantrymen or cavalrymen fighting side-by-side with their men,[17] and the flexible adjustment to plans gone wrong was almost beyond their control.

Nor had Scott's performance in the Bull Run-Valley campaign matched the high standards of his previous work, especially his Mexico City campaign. Scott had been the oldest, most well-trained, most experienced, and most likely to succeed of the available officers on both sides. But for all that could be said about his military credentials, he, too, had embarked on a new venture, one at which he had no experience. For the first time, with minor exceptions, he was to coordinate two armies he could not see, directing them by telegraph and unable to speak face to face with their commanders. In addition, he had no identifiable elite unit for the most difficult tasks, the majority of the men in both armies being untrained, short-term troops.

---

15   *C.C.W.*, 1, 134–135 (McDowell).

16   Fraser, Antonia, *Cromwell: The Lord Protector*, 121–122 (New York, 1973); Rothenberg, Gunther E., *The Art of War in the Age of Napoleon*, 71 (London, 1977, Easton Press ed.).

17   Keegan, John, *The Mask of Command*, 61–64 (Harrisonburg, 1987); Bradford, Ernle, *Hannibal*, 37, 61 (New York, 1981).

As the coordinator of a concerted movement by two separate forces, Scott had failed, and not because of others. He did not comprehend the true nature of his old friend in the Valley until McDowell was on the march for Manassas; but before McDowell began his march, Scott should have realized that Patterson did not have the character for his assignment. He also failed to recognize Patterson's fundamental misunderstanding of his mission. In July Patterson no longer commanded the primary column; but if he had suffered defeat, held Johnston in the Valley, and made victory by McDowell possible, the trade would have been a substantial overall victory for the Union. Compounding Patterson's uncertainty, the general in chief sent unclear, contradictory orders. Alternately, Scott urged aggressiveness and caution. What caused him to order the Regulars from the Valley in the middle of June when Patterson had crossed the Potomac into Virginia? Was he showing the effects of stress? If Washington were in grave danger, why did the Regulars complete an exhausting race from Williamsport only to arrive midst the gaiety of a review and a celebration?

Scott was guilty of other specific failures as well. The general who had left his supply base at Vera Cruz and marched into the Mexican interior allowed himself to forget the campaign he had so capably handled only a decade and a half earlier. He had expected a battle on the Vienna-Fairfax Court House line on July 16 or 17, but the enemy did not resist there. He not only failed to foresee that this might happen but also did not correct the misinformation he had sent Patterson and made unjustifiable evaluations of McDowell's advance. "Old Fuss and Feathers" telegraphed Patterson that the battle would be fought on Tuesday, July 16, the day the troops began marching. To make matters worse he telegraphed at the end of that day that McDowell would probably carry Manassas Junction the next day.

Where was the enemy to be during that operation? Were they to stand aside to see if McDowell could, in one day, march his inexperienced army from its position east of Fairfax Court House all the way to Bull Run Creek, then Manassas, thirty and more miles[18] as the crow flew, let alone as the bad, unmapped roads went? If McDowell had marched with no opposition, no variables, and seasoned troops, perhaps he could have fulfilled the expectations of the general in chief, but with green troops it was highly unlikely. Scott certainly could not have expected it if he had viewed the situation realistically. Patterson had some justification for thinking on Wednesday, July 17, that the need to hold Johnston had ended. Scott's failure to

---

18   Jackson, "From Washington to Bull Run and Back Again," in *Broadfoot MOLLUS Wisconsin*, 49, 233.

make a reasonable assessment, to send accurate information, and to issue clear orders contributed significantly to the disaster. Although he did much to assure the safety of the capital and to create peace of mind for the president and cabinet, too many things compromised him, most of them of his own making. His time to retire had come.

Perhaps Lincoln, a man whose personnel and managerial skills have not been surpassed by any other president, perceived these many disabilities. Perhaps they led ultimately to the president's willingness to intervene directly in military matters well beyond his experience. And they must certainly have encouraged him to communicate outside proper channels, sanction that conduct by subordinates, and compromise Scott's position.

Although Scott made many errors in judgment, his presence, his ability to recognize the reality of the dangers of the moment, and his confidence at important times contributed greatly to the survival of the fledgling Republican government in 1861. Lincoln acknowledged this with his reluctance to retire the aged general. The fifty years of military and political contributions to his country demanded a different end, one with dignity and recognition. But the circumstances, far beyond everyone's control, dictated the bleak, dark, rain-drenched departure without the parade and the cheering throngs he deserved.

When Lincoln finished reviewing McClellan's farewell order for Scott, he added, "I should be perfectly satisfied if I thought that this vast increase of responsibility would not embarrass you."

"It is a great relief, sir!" responded McClellan. "I feel as if several tons were taken from my shoulders today. I am now in contact with you and the Secretary. I am not embarrassed by intervention."

"Well," said Lincoln, "draw on me for all the sense I have and all the information. In addition to your present command, the supreme command of the army will entail a vast labor upon you."

"I can do it all," said McClellan quietly.[19]

But could he?

The State Department gadfly Count Gurowski recognized the problem Lincoln saw. "McClellan is invested with all the powers of Scott," he wrote in his diary. "McClellan has more on his shoulders than any man—a Napoleon not excepted—can stand; and with his very limited capacity McClellan must necessarily break under it. Now McClellan will be still more idolized. He is already a kind of dictator,

19   Burlingame, *Hay Diary*, 49–50, entry dated November 1, 1861.

as Lincoln, Seward, etc., turn around him."[20] Even more than his Ball's Bluff experience, McClellan's most significant tautological event, succession to general in chief in command of all armies of the United States, proved to be much worse than he had anticipated.

When he assumed command of them, he found the condition of the forces away from the capital not unlike the military forces around the capital after Bull Run, "disorganized," "everything at sixes and sevens," "no system, no order," "perfect chaos," he wrote to Ellen. For eighteen straight hours he worked in his office at the task of introducing order.[21] The Western armies had less equipment, less organization, and less integration into a coordinated plan of campaign than his Eastern armies. All this he intended to correct. At once, he found conflict between his first love, the Army of the Potomac, and the prize he had captured, command of all the armies. Yet again, his work provoked controversy. His ever-critical engineer officer John G. Barnard thought that, in the allocation of munitions and supplies, McClellan kept the best and the most for the Army of the Potomac.[22] Others saw that his efforts to sever communication between the eastern and western Confederate armies consumed a great deal of his attention.[23]

McClellan's campaign to remove Scott—and more importantly to succeed him—had been prompted by his desire to command the Army of the Potomac without interference rather than by any ambition to reach a higher level. He did not want Scott compromising his plans, nor did he want a new complication placed over his head in Scott's place. Although he had thoughtfully sought his goal, he does not appear to have given much thought to the magnitude of the assignment he pursued. He seems to have believed that Scott's departure would solve all his problems. In reality, it changed some, increased many others, added new ones, and complicated his life in ways he did not foresee.

His new responsibilities included military forces he could not direct in person, a task new to General Scott when he undertook to direct Patterson from the capital and one the old general failed with terrible consequences. For the Army of the Potomac McClellan had collected all the best officers he could. Now he had to share his best officers with commands in other areas. Don Carlos Buell, an officer he

20   Gurowski, *Diary*, 1, 117, November, 1861.

21   Sears, *McClellan's Correspondence*, 123, letter dated November 2, 1861, from McClellan to his wife.

22   Heintzelman MSS (L.C.) letter of n.d. [1862 or 1864] from Barnard to Heintzelman.

23   Porter MSS (L.C.) letter dated September 26, 1895, from Franklin to Porter.

respected and regarded as one of his best, he sent west to assume command of the Department of Ohio.[24]

In the days that followed McClellan's assumption of overall command he found the work long, tedious, and office-bound. Devoting no time to himself, he cut his hours of sleep to the bare minimum. He took meals at his desk, and they were not luxurious, most often being a small wicker basket with sandwiches, bread and cheese, and occasionally a tart.

His responsibilities as general in chief caused a long distraction from his duties to the Army of the Potomac. Fewer daily rides. Fewer reviews. He did not see his troops and of course was not seen by them as much. Plans to sever eastern Kentucky and eastern Tennessee from Rebel armies in the East absorbed a great deal of attention and energy at headquarters. Very quickly he developed "an undue sense of responsibility resting on him as Genl in Chief and Genl commanding the Army of the Potomac."[25]

After November 2, McClellan had two major tasks: completion of the development of the Army of the Potomac, which was the main army of the Federal government, and coordination of all Union military forces, which lay scattered along a line thousands of miles long. When he took command of all United States armies, he found that Scott had maintained an office for the general in chief in New York City, then in Washington. He had kept the office for the United States Army entirely distinct from the office of general in chief. Lorenzo Thomas, the adjutant general of the United States Army, and his own adjutant E. D. Townsend maintained entirely distinct records. Townsend reported directly to him; Thomas reported to the Secretary of War. McClellan dispensed with these separate adjutant generals' offices by merging them and combining their records. In his office he kept only copies of his own letters on important subjects requiring secrecy.

The headquarters organization of the Army of the Potomac McClellan kept separate from the headquarters of the general in chief. The staff for each was distinct except for McClellan's personal aide General Marcy. Seth Williams continued to be the adjutant general of the Army of the Potomac and Lorenzo Thomas the

---

24   *M.O.S.*, 214–215; Dahlgren, *Memoir*, 348, diary, entry dated November 1, 1861.

25   Smith MS rem. (V.H.S.) first folio, n.p.; Comte de Paris MS diary (large diary) (A.N. de la M. de F.), entry dated November 7, 1861; Porter MSS (L.C.) letter dated September 26, 1861, from Franklin to Porter; Sears, *McClellan's Correspondence*, 123, 125, letters dated November 2, 1861, from McClellan to his wife; Wilson, William B., *A Leaf from the History of the Rebellion: Sketches of Events and Persons*, 15 (Philadelphia, 1888) (pam). The phrase "an undue sense of responsibility" appears in Smith MS rem.

adjutant general of the United States Army. The papers and records of the two offices remained separate. McClellan had two rooms in the War Department for his office as general in chief, to which Thomas delivered all papers and other matters requiring his attention as general in chief. Here, Thomas received his orders and from here, carried the papers back to his own office.

Colonel A. V. Colburn of McClellan's personal staff had charge of telegrams, which were copied into books or simply filed. The general kept nothing except the original rough drafts in his own handwriting or that of an aide. All written reports went to the Adjutant General's Office, then to the Secretary of War. Lorenzo Thomas' office was "simply a place for the transaction of business and not a place of record," McClellan wrote later.

The building occupied as the Headquarters of the Army of the Potomac on Pennsylvania Avenue and Jackson Square housed the telegraph office, organized under McClellan's direction. All telegraphic dispatches of any importance were sent and received in cipher and, when handed to McClellan, had been decoded. The deciphering and the encoding were done in the telegraph office. The ciphered copies, recorded in books kept in the chief telegrapher's office, never came into McClellan's possession.[26]

Except for letters drafted by McClellan in his own handwriting or dictated to Colburn, the major general kept no records in his personal office when he was general in chief. Everything remained in the Adjutant General's office or in the telegraph office. When McClellan sent a dispatch to the telegraph office, it was the only copy; and that was the last he saw of it.[27]

For McClellan, Scott's departure had an interesting aftermath. The former general in chief's candidate arrived about one week later.[28] A day or two before Halleck reached Washington McClellan's new friend Edwin Stanton warned him that Halleck, against whom Stanton had handled a large case, had indisputably committed perjury in statements under oath in court. Halleck, he said, was a scoundrel, the most bare-faced villain, and "totally destitute of principle." As McClellan recounted it later, "when Halleck arrived he came to caution me against Stanton, repeating almost precisely the same words that Stanton had employed."[29]

---

26 McClellan MSS (L.C.) draft letter dated December 26, 1866, from McClellan to Grant. This letter also appears in *M.O.S.*, 219–221.

27 McClellan MSS (L.C.) draft letter dated December 26, 1866, from McClellan to Marcy.

28 The exact date of Halleck's arrival in Washington is unclear, but it occurred before November 10. *OR*, 5, 37, McClellan's report; Ambrose, *Halleck*, 12.

29 *M.O.S.*, 137.

Chapter 17

"The confidence [of the army] in General McClellan remains unshaken.
I think the whole army only awaits his word."

—Alexander Stuart Webb to his father

Building an
Indefatigable Army

*A*t the beginning of their military careers, most of McClellan's junior officers, noncommissioned officers, and enlisted men amounted to no more than a rapidly growing number of individuals who knew few of the skills they would need in the Army of the Potomac. If this new breed received the proper training now that McClellan had more time than McDowell, would McClellan's army perform better than McDowell's army at First Bull Run? Could McClellan make the same class of volunteers fight better, harder, longer, and more effectively than they had under McDowell? And what would the proper training be? What could McClellan do after Bull Run to make the army perform better?

Many West Point alumni, familiar only with the prewar manpower of the Regular Army, had of necessity used arbitrary, despotic, and tyrannical methods of command of necessity. In 1861, the noncommissioned officers and enlisted men of the United States Army stood in poor regard, came from the lower walks of life, and were gently described by John Gibbon, a Regular Army officer, in his postwar memoirs as "not rated the highest type or the best in form."[1] Jacob D. Cox in his

---

1   Gibbon, *Recollections*, 10–15.

reminiscences described them more harshly as outcasts who had failed in life and who had succumbed to the recruiting sergeant as a desperate means of escape when every other door had closed.[2]

Thoughtful, analytical observers based their assessment of the army that fought at First Bull Run on subtle factors occurring naturally in American society. McClellan's trusted adviser without portfolio, the Prince de Joinville,[3] had a theory that explained the conduct of the men at Bull Run, the abandonment of the field, and the concluding flight. His theory rested on the relationship between the officers and men, a compact the men could abandon when, after courageous expenditure of blood and life, the compact no longer seemed to serve a purpose. Not the officers, not the commanding general, not the army, and not the government, but the men would decide when to dissolve the compact.

De Joinville saw the army and its performance dominated by an element of "consent." According to him the officer was "simply a comrade who wears a different costume. He is obeyed in every day routine, but voluntarily. In the same way the soldiers don't trouble themselves about him when circumstances become serious. From the point of view of American equality, there is no good reason to obey him. . . . The habits created by universal suffrage also play their part and are reproduced on the field of battle. By a tacit agreement the regiment marches against the enemy, advances under fire and begins to deliver its volleys; the men are brave, very brave; they are killed and wounded in great numbers, and then, when by a tacit agreement they think they have done enough for military honor, they all march off together. The colonel perhaps attempts to give a direction, an impulse, but generally his efforts are in vain. As to the officers, they never think of it. Why should they attempt it, and why should they be obeyed if the majority of the regiment has made up its mind to retreat? Obedience in such an army is like the obedience which children playing at soldiers render to him among their comrades whom they have made their captain . . . It was to remedy these vices as far as possible that General McClellan and old officers of West Point, who had become, by force of circumstances, generals of brigade or of division, devoted all their efforts."[4]

2 Cox, *Reminiscences*, 1, 166.

3 Comte de Paris MS diary (large diary) (A.N. de la M. de F.) entry dated October 22, 1861.

4 de Joinville, *Army of the Potomac*, 16–17. At least one enlisted man agreed with de Joinville so strongly that he quoted the bulk of this text almost word for word as if the concept has been his in his postwar memoirs, which were published recently in the form of a diary. Bryant, Charles E., and Nelson D. Lankford, eds., *Eye of the Storm: A Civil War Odyssey (Memoirs of Private Robert Knox Sneden)* (New York and London, 2000) 6–7 (Bryant, *Eye of the Storm (Sneden Memoirs)*).

De Joinville made his assessment from the vantage point of a monarchical European who recognized the free, democratic spirit loose in the military. The seeds of the problem, as he saw it, were the conditions that made Americans "the happiest and freest people on the earth." To create a proper army the "happiest and freest people" had to accept an autocratic system of strict discipline,[5] an acquiescence not likely to occur naturally or at once. No doubt, McClellan discussed these circumstances and the cure for them with de Joinville in the evenings when the general, exhausted from the labors of the day and the long rides to see and be seen by his men, visited the pleasant camp of his young French aides.[6]

A considerably different analysis of the mishap at Bull Run identified the same cause, the relationship between the officers and men, specifically, the inability of the officers in the turning column to hold their men to the mark even though only a small part of them had been severely handled and reduced to disorder. The United States Sanitary Commission interviewed many men of all ranks shortly after their return to the banks of the Potomac River, then produced a long pamphlet describing the results of the interviews and determining the causes of the failure.

In their report Frederick Law Olmstead and the commission gave substance to the philosophical contention that the historian's personal bias makes "objectivity" in history an impossibility. Deeply involved in the welfare of the men, the commission had scrutinized the condition of the army before the battle and identified numerous defects. After the battle the commission's further investigation validated its pre-battle analysis. The men suffered from failures in overall health, welfare, and hygiene, which caused the defeat, the commission concluded.[7] It found the government responsible—and at fault—for the deficiencies and the officers, even though many blamed them no more than whipping boys because, to the men and the public, they embodied the government.

The commission's report described "a growing want of confidence between the men and the more immediate representatives and agents of the Government— the officers—because the men were naturally disposed to hold their officers, in the

---

5   Ibid., 20.

6   Comte de Paris MS diary (large diary) (A.N. de la M. de F.) entry dated October 22, 1861; *M.O.S.*, 123, 145.

7   McLaughlin, ed., *The Papers of Frederick Law Olmstead*, "Report of the Secretary with Regard to the Origin of the recent Demoralization of the Volunteer Army at Washington and the duty of the Sanitary Commission with Reference to Certain Deficiencies in the existing Army Arrangements, as Suggested Thereby," in Turner, Jane Censor, vol. ed., *Defending the Union: The Civil War and the U.S. Sanitary Commission, 1861–1863*, 4, 169–173.

first place, responsible for the causes of their discontent. To a certain extent, but not altogether, justly so. They, however, could not distinguish between that for which the officers were justly to blame, and that which lay behind them. The consciousness of this had its effect on the officers. The company officers, especially, were acquiring habits of treating their men, some with familiarity, others with an apologetic manner, others with an insolent affectation of sternness, each according to his character, responding to the ill-will of the men in their duty to him."[8]

Like de Joinville, Olmstead had access to McClellan in the thoughtful hours of the evening after the major-general's long rides of the day.[9] McClellan must have found Olmstead, a diligent, dedicated, hard-working patrician and a contemporary, an appealing confidant. In all probability they discussed the commission's conclusions and ways to cure the problems.[10]

Both de Joinville and Olmstead described subtle causes for the nightmare at Bull Run Creek. Both found the training and care of the men, not the bravery or experience of the officers, at fault. Although the two men varied on many small points, they found command weakened in the same fundamental way. The exercise of command involved a large element of consent; when the men withdrew their consent, obedience to orders became unpredictable, if not nonexistent. At some level the element of consent exists in any command structure, but how far from its normal place could McClellan drive it? And by what means: by fortuitous circumstances? by rigorous training? by long experience?

Looking first at the best armies of the ancient world, the French theoretician and officer Colonel Ardant du Picq, who acquired fame only after his death from a random Prussian artillery shell during the siege of Metz in 1870, wrote, "The disci-

---

8   Ibid., 173. For a parallel in the Roman army of the republic, Adcock, F. E., *The Art of War under the Roman Republic* (New York, 1995 ed.) p. 38, 112 (Adcock, *Roman Art of War*).

9   McLaughlin, *Papers of Frederick Law Olmstead*, Turner, *Civil War and the Sanitary Commission*, 4, 196–197, letter dated September 12, 1861, from Olmstead to his father.

10   No direct evidence proves that conversations on this subject took place between McClellan and de Joinville or McClellan and Olmstead. Olmstead published his pamphlet in the fall of 1861 when he is known to have been meeting McClellan. The prince published his piece on the Army of the Potomac in France, and it was translated and republished in America in 1862, all within months after he left the army. This suggests that his theory had become fully developed before his departure from the United States and while serving with the Army of the Potomac, not afterwards, and could, therefore, have been discussed with McClellan during the many hours they spent together. By the reference to the fact that McClellan was working "to remedy the vices" (de Joinville, *Army of the Potomac*, 20) he clearly implies that the disability existed in the Army before McClellan's arrival. His theory was not unique (Higginson, Thomas Wentworth, "Regular and Volunteer Officers," in *Atlantic Monthly*, September 1864).

pline of the Greeks was secured by exercises and rewards; the discipline of the Romans was secured also by fear of death. They put to death with the club; they decimated their cowardly or traitorous units."[11] In the Prussian army of 1870, consent would have had a much smaller presence than it did among the American volunteers of 1861. In the modern world, the graduate of Parris Island, the Marine Corps "school," would believe, if he thought about it at all, that the consent aspect of obedience to orders stood much lower than it would for a contemporary graduate of Fort Benning, the army infantry school.

McClellan knew he could eliminate the disabilities seen by de Joinville and Olmstead; but, foreseeing the next major battle to be a single great Armageddon with final defeat of the enemy to the winner,[12] McClellan believed he could not afford to lose it. The major general could cure the root causes of the defeat at Bull Run, as both de Joinville and Olmstead defined them, by the very same program Winfield Scott had used and McClellan had watched on their way to Mexico City.

After Scott captured Vera Cruz and won the early battle at Cerro Gordo, he reached a high plateau at Puebla. Here, of necessity, he paused because his volunteers, obligated for one year, had come to the end of their enlistment and would not continue. When they departed, four thousand strong, Scott had only three thousand Regulars and the hope that eight thousand inexperienced new volunteers might arrive soon. When they did, he put them through the nineteenth century equivalent of basic individual training and basic unit training. The high plateau became, day after day, a drill ground, then a parade ground; and his army of green volunteers became, for all his needs, a skilled army of veterans ready to resume the march on Mexico City.[13] Having seen Scott create an irresistible army from nothing, McClellan knew it could be done and the way to do it: by long, thorough preparation, drill and more drill, review after review.

---

11   du Picq, Colonel Ardant, *Battle Studies: Ancient and Modern Battle* (Norwalk, 1997, Easton Press ed.) xvi, 1, 51 (du Picq, *Battle Studies*). In the original meaning of the word, an army "decimated" a unit by selecting one man in ten by lot and executing him.

12   Sears, Stephen W., *McClellan's Correspondence* 74, memorandum dated August 2, 1861, by the editor from McClellan to the president; 75, letter dated August 2, 1861, from McClellan to his wife; 115, letter dated October 31, 1861, by the editor from McClellan to Cameron; 127, letter dated November 8, 1861, from McClellan to Barlow. In the letter to Barlow he said, "I feel however that the issue of this struggle is to be decided by the next great battle . . . "

13   McCoun, Richard A., unpublished MS master's thesis, *George Brinton McClellan: From West Point to the Peninsula; the Education of a Soldier and the Conduct of War*, (1973) 71–74 (UMI dissertation services) (McCoun, *McClellan: Education of a Soldier*); Bauer, K. Jack, *The Mexican War 1846–1848*, 272 (New York and London, 1974).

First of all, he would need time; and a shrewd observer, Brigadier General William Tecumsuh Sherman, agreed he would have it. "I don't believe McClellan will be hurried," Sherman wrote home in August, "and the danger to our country is so imminent that all hands are now conscious that we must build up from the foundation."[14] The men who would exercise command over that foundation, the general officers, recognized that their future success required two things: first, the talent and devotion of their subordinate officers; and second, the proper relationship between the officers and men, specifically the ascension of "discipline" attended by the elimination of consent.

One member of the Scott Rule group who reorganized this element of command was John H. Martindale, forty-six years old, a lawyer from the Buffalo area and a graduate of the United States Military Academy, Class of 1835. Third in a class of fifty-six, Martindale had received a disappointing commission in the dragoons instead of the engineers and the next year resigned without ever serving with troops. Instead, he read law, began practice, and became a very successful attorney in the Genesee County and Rochester areas of western New York State.[15] Like most successful lawyers he developed relationships in the political arena. Prior to the battle at Bull Run Creek he corresponded with Governor Edwin D. Morgan of New York about the colonelcy of the troubled Tenth New York Infantry, an existing regiment that had been recruited in New York City.[16] Unfit, the regimental commander had to be replaced, and the governor intended to exercise his constitutional and statutory power to appoint the replacement.[17] If appointed without election by the officers, Martindale wrote to Morgan, he anticipated a failure of "consent," a "prejudice against my appointment which would render the position uncomfortable, and might impair my ability to render service. The officers might, and very likely would . . . feel chagrin, at the selection of a stranger from the western part of the State to command them, and would be disposed to inquire whether in their own ranks, or in the City of New York a suitable person with whom they are acquainted, could not have been chosen."[18] The elimination or reduction of the "consent" factor had to

---

14   Howe, *Sherman's Home Letters*, 213–214, letter n.d. to n.a., dated August by the editor.

15   *D.A.B.*, 6, pt. 2, 349; Warner, *Generals in Blue*, 312–313; *Cullum*, 1, no. 788.

16   Cowtan, *Tenth New York Volunteers*, 37, 55.

17   Curtis, Newton Martin, *From Bull Run to Chancellorsville: The Story of the Sixteenth New York Infantry together with Personal Reminiscences* (New York and London, 1986) 209 (Curtis, *Bull Run to Chancellorsville*).

18   Edwin D. Morgan MSS (New York State Library) letters dated June 20, 1861, and June 26, 1861, from Martindale to Morgan.

occur during training, but with the new and different source of manpower the training also had to be different.

Unlike the countries that had not begun the nineteenth century with democratic governments and free people, the Union did not need to revise its social or governmental structure in order to generate devoted, hard-fighting men. Naturally available in large numbers, they came forward voluntarily.[19] Cox and Gibbon agreed that the volunteers were an altogether different breed.[20] Conscious, thoughtful serving officers shared these views to a great extent. George Meade wrote his wife in early August 1861, "The material of our army—*the men*—are equal as raw material to any in the world—but to make them efficient, they must *have* discipline, organization, & that shudder to mention feeling which can only result from proper organization & confidence in officers."[21]

An officer who had served in the Mexican War as a volunteer and in the Civil War for a short time in a regular cavalry regiment before he accepted a volunteer colonelcy in 1862 regarded his new post as an experiment in which his men would test his authority. "I had been a volunteer myself in the war with Mexico," he wrote in his memoirs, "and knew something of the feeling that exists in the ranks with such troops and was aware that they must be differently handled from Regulars. They are more intelligent and sensitive, and the arbitrary and severe punishment resorted to in the Regular Service, will not do for them."[22] Cox wrote after the war, "To know how to command volunteers was explicitly recognized by our leading generals as a quality not found in many Regular officers, and worth noting when found."[23] Acknowledging this fine distinction in leadership, Major General William F. Smith later recommended a position in the Regular Army for Edward F. Hinks, who served in 1861 as colonel of the Nineteenth Massachusetts Volunteers. According to Smith, Hinks had "a rare firmness which enforced discipline without being tyrannical."[24]

19   See generally, McPherson, James, *For Cause and Comrades: Why Men Fought in the Civil War* (New York and Oxford, 1997); Cox, *Reminiscences*, 166.

20   Gibbon, *Recollections*, 14; Cox, *Reminiscences*, 1, 167.

21   Meade MSS (P.H.S.) letter dated August 5, 1861, from Meade to his wife.

22   Comtes MS memoirs (Library of Congress) 27. According to Comtes, he served as colonel of the Sixth United States Cavalry in the Peninsula campaign, then as colonel of the Second Ohio Cavalry, neither of which are consistent with *Cullum*, 2, 1203; Heitman, *Historical Register*, 1, 330; *Official Register*, 5, 3–4; or the *OR* index volume.

23   Cox, *Reminiscences*, 166.

24   Hinks MSS (B.U.) letter dated January 18, 1866, from Smith to Senator Henry Wilson.

After the Third Pennsylvania Reserves reached their position at Prospect Hill on the west bank of the Potomac, some of the men began to miss roll call, drill, and the daily training. Colonel Horatio Gates Sickel called for the delinquents to parade before his quarters. No speech! No bracing! No company punishment! No barrel and logs! Colonel Sickel marched them to the regimental parade ground and drilled them himself. The men understood, and "the kind manner in which the colonel exercised them not only effectually checked the repetition of the offense," wrote the regimental historian, "but added to their love for him whom they looked upon not only as their commander but as their considerate friend, who at first always used gentle means to induce them to act right."[25]

Patriotic, courageous, and capable of heroic action in a desperate engagement, the inexperienced American infantryman presented a new and different challenge to the West Point and Regular Army officers trained on the lesser, prewar men. When a Regular Army officer confronted his first batch of creative, imaginative, independent, and sometimes unruly volunteers, the task before him could lead to failure because of, rather than in spite of, the better material. Volunteer regiments that looked sloppy in drill could perform great feats of arms. In Cox's view, after a year of instruction and service in the field, a volunteer regiment became unquestionably superior to a Regular Army regiment.[26]

Beginning at their enlistment the men received basic individual training in the "school of the soldier": position of the soldier without arms; eyes right, left, and front; facings; the direct step in common and quick time; and the direct step in double-quick time and on the run. Then they progressed to the manual of arms: shouldered arms; load in four times and at will; firings, direct, oblique, by file, and by rank; firing and loading while kneeling and lying; and bayonet exercise. Last, they learned in groups of eight and twelve principles of alignment, direct march,

25   Woodward, E. M., *History of the Third Pennsylvania Reserve: being a complete Record of the Regiment with Incidents of the Camp, Marches, Bivouacs, Skirmishes and Battles, together with the Personal Record of every Officer and Man During their Terms of Service* (Trenton, 1883) 51 (Woodward, *Third Pennsylvania Reserves*); Marks, Rev. J. J., *The Peninsular Campaign in Virginia or Incidents and Scenes on the Battlefields and in Richmond* (Philadelphia, 1864, fourth ed.) 40–42 (Marks, *Peninsula Campaign*). The work by Marks, written by a regimental chaplain and suspect for its sanctimonious, religious attitude toward many issues, features his regiment, the Sixty-third Pennsylvania, and its commander, Colonel Alexander Hays, who, having risen to division command, would be killed in the wilderness in 1864. Eicher, *Civil War High Commands*, 290.

26   Hinks MSS (B.U.) letter dated January 18, 1866, from William F. Smith to Henry W. Halleck; Cox, *Reminiscences*, 1, 166–167.

oblique march, by-the-flank march, wheeling and changing direction, and double-quick time with arms and knapsacks.[27]

These maneuvers presented a test for the junior officers as much as for the men. An officer who gave the command of execution on the correct or the incorrect foot, with or without the correct break and inflection in the voice, soon told the men whether or not they could have confidence in him. And the men? They faced the kind of instruction that infantrymen have endured for centuries. In the Eighteenth Massachusetts Volunteer Infantry Regiment the drill leader called the commands and editorialized on the performance of his students:

"Fall into two ranks!"

"Right—dress."

"Attention!"[28]

"You, James, carry your head back and chest out!"

"Now, right—dress!"

"I say, you, Imman there, haven't you got any belly? If you have, bring it out in line."

"Front!"

In each command, the preparatory command first, a long pause, then emphasis on the command of execution.

"Company, present—arms!"

"Carry—arms!"

"Come, wake up there, David, get your gun into place before dinner time!"

"Order—arms!"

"Carry—arms!"

"Order—arms!"

The rifle butts struck the ground with a series of scattered noises.

"Why can't you bring them together and not sound like horses galloping across a forty-foot bridge!"

"Shoulder—arms!"

---

27   Casey, Brig.-Gen. Silas, *Infantry Tactics for the Instruction, Exercise, and Maneuvers of the Soldier, a Company, Line of Skirmishers, Battalion, Brigade, or Corps D'Armee*, 3 vols. (Washington, 1863) 1, 23–24, para. 86; Van Dyke, Augustus M., "Early Days; or, the School of the Soldier," in *Broadfoot MOLLUS Ohio*, 5, 19–27.

28   In the parade ground evolutions of today, still part of an infantryman's training, the words often find modification to suit their purpose and emphasis. "Attention," a soft word of command, often becomes "Attench—hut!" and the command of execution, "March," often becomes, "By the left flank—Haaarch!"

"Company, right—face!"

"Forward—march!"

"Jordan, can't you learn to step off with your left foot?"

"Halt!"

"Now, try it again."

"Company, forward—march!"

"Into four ranks—march!"

"File left—march!"

"Get round there, Martain. We ain't going to a funeral!"

"Double-quick—march!"

"Company—halt!"

"Left face!"

"Don't you know left from right, Fuller?"

"Right—Dress!"

"Front!"

"Order—arms!"

"Parade—rest!"

Hour after hour. Day after day. And extra drill for those who could not keep even with the program.[29] Although the imaginative American soldier would never lose his independence or his initiative no matter how severe the training, one enlisted man would write after the war, ". . . it was part of the drill to stamp out all the reasoning faculties a private might exercise," as if he had read and adopted de Joinville's analysis. To complain about abusive treatment by Sergeant Davis during drill, Private Thomas Mann of the Eighteenth Massachusetts Infantry visited his regimental commander.

"Colonel, Mr. Davis has . . . "

Angrily, the colonel snapped, "*Mister*? There *are* no misters in the army."

"I thought, sir . . . "

"Think? Think? What right have *you* to think. *I* do the thinking for this regiment! Go to your quarters!"[30]

Deeper and deeper did the good officers bury the need for consent.

Nor were the training and the criticism limited to enlisted men. The volunteer junior company-grade officers, as they do today, suffered their full share of abuse

29   Hennessy, John J., ed., *Fighting with the Eighteenth Massachusetts: The Civil War Memoir of Thomas H. Mann* (Baton Rouge, 2000) 13 (Hennessy, *Mann Memoir*).

30   Hennessy, *Mann Memoirs*, 37.

in the guise of training as they progressed from civilian to soldier by diverse routes of passage.

No two regiments followed the identical training path to the battlefield. The equivalents of basic unit training and advanced unit training at bayonet, skirmish, squad, company, battalion, regiment, and brigade evolutions often began in camps of instruction like Camps Curtin and Cameron in Pennsylvania and Camp Read in Massachusetts,[31] or with Brigadier General Silas Casey in Washington. The entire army "drilled like hell," wrote Corporal Thomas Mann in his postwar memoirs. Occasionally, the men tried the mock charge by regimental front, wild, out of control, men scattered over the landscape, some squads three miles beyond the line of departure, and the "wandering pieces of the machine" far from their places. At the end of the day, dress parade: best uniform, highly polished weapon, white gloves, and the colonel in epaulets and silk sash, "an inspiring sight" that produced "pride of regiment that served well, a year or two later," Mann remembered.[32]

After new regiments arrived in the capital and completed their basic and advanced unit instruction under General Casey, McClellan sent them across the Potomac to Virginia for distribution among the divisions on the west bank. The Ninety-fifth New York Infantry, known as the Ulster Guard or the Twentieth New York State Militia,[33] he ordered to Brigadier General Irvin McDowell at Arlington House; McDowell decided he would assign it to Brigadier General James S. Wadsworth's brigade on Upton's Hill. The direct distance from the Washington side by the Long Bridge or the Aqueduct Bridge required a march of only eight miles. But the route assigned to the regiment crossed the Chain Bridge, a distance of seven miles, then ran from the Chain Bridge to Upton's Hill, another seven. Without food or water, the men found the march long and fatiguing. During the last miles, visibility had become so poor that they loaded their weapons; and darkness had fallen

31   See generally, Miller, William J., *The Training of an Army: Camp Curtin and the North's Civil War* (Shippensburg, 1990); Hennesy, *Mann Memoir*, 14, n.23.

32   Miller, *Camp Curtin*, 71–74, 77; Hennesy, *Mann Memoir*, 15, 25.

33   Militia regiments that entered the three year service usually lost their militia designation and were renumbered in the volunteers. The Ulster Guard, which had been the Twentieth New York State Militia, became the Ninety-fifth New York Volunteer Infantry, *OR*, 27, pt. 1, 317; but its Colonel adhered faithfully to its militia origin when he wrote the regimental history, referring to it as the Twentieth throughout and quoting his postwar speech about the value of the militia and its elevation by the war. Gates, Theodore B., *The "Ulster Guard (20th N.Y. State Militia) and the War of the Rebellion embracing a History of the early Organization of the Regiment, its three month Service, its reorganization, and Subsequent Service"* (Albany, 1868) Appendix F, 614–615 (Gates, *Ulster Guard*).

when they finally reached their destination. Directed to a field they received orders to bivouac in it. Into the field they marched and began to pitch their tents in the darkness. Suddenly, they could see lanterns approaching from a house a few hundred feet west of the field.

"Twentieth, where are you?" a cheery voice called out.

It was Wadsworth, who cared equally for the workers on his huge family farms in western New York and the men of his military units. Anxious to assure their comfort as much as possible, he had brought with him an abundance of hot coffee prepared at his headquarters. Wadsworth ignored the chill November air, personally superintended the completion of the tasks, and, as he had with his farm hands and the bridge repair crew, remained among the troops until satisfied that he had done everything possible to make his new regiment comfortable. By thoughtful, unselfish gestures like this, he and others won the great affection of their regiments and brigades.[34]

When the Eighteenth Massachusetts reached the west bank of the Potomac and the Munson's Hill area, John H. Martindale, now a brigadier general commanding a brigade in Porter's division, greeted them with the forensic skills of a trial lawyer. Astride his "magnificent black stallion," Mann recalled, he convinced the men that each of them could overcome any five Confederates and could help end the war in six or even three months.[35]

During November and December the army kept busy with inspections, drills, and reviews.[36] Live ammunition target practice became popular, fourteen rounds per man, targets ten by fifteen inches, at ranges of one and two hundred yards.[37] All these reviews and the preparations for them suggested to the men that they had an advance in the offing. They were eager to drive the Confederates from the vicinity of Washington before winter.[38]

On November 9, a grand review of the 10,000 troops of Porter's division took place. Both Brigadier General Don Carlos Buell and Major General Henry W. Halleck, ready to depart for their commands in the West, accompanied McClellan and his staff. The division received McClellan with salutes from the batteries,

34   Gates, *Ulster Guard*, 152–154.

35   Hennesy, *Mann Memoirs*, 21-22, 36.

36   Parker, *Twenty-second Massachusetts*, 55.

37   Woodward, *Third Pennsylvania Reserves*, 59.

38   Heintzelman MS diary (large diary) (L.C.) entry dated November 13, 1861; Hard, Abner, *History of the Eighth Cavalry Regiment, Illinois Volunteers, during the Great Rebellion*, 45–46 (Aurora, 1868).

music from the bands, and cheers by the men. Rain, the infantryman's eternal enemy, wet the men thoroughly;[39] but more was at stake than "left, right, left, right" and "eyeees—riiight!"

Porter had received a set of fancy Zouave uniforms to be awarded to the best-drilled regiment in his division. A committee chosen from McClellan's staff would designate the winner from the review. McClellan said "he was highly gratified with the discipline of the troops" and that "he never saw better movements in his life." The committee unanimously selected the Eighty-third Pennsylvania for the prize.[40]

As the sun peeped over the Maryland hills the morning of November 20, McClellan's regiments began marching for Bailey's Cross-Roads, the area from which Richardson's spontaneous charge had "captured" Munson's Hill. For the grand review,[41] some units traveled fifteen miles and were on their feet thirteen hours with packs, ammunition, rations, and canteens in order to arrive at their positions in the reviewing column. They included ninety regiments of infantry, twenty batteries amounting to one hundred guns, and nine regiments of cavalry,[42] an estimated 50,000 to 60,000 men, exaggerated by some to 100,000.[43] Upon arrival, the early regiments stood ankle deep in mud for two hours waiting for the other units to take position.

The review ground, two miles long, one mile broad, and nearly level, lay in the open fields between Munson's Hill and Bailey's Cross-Roads. Cavalry, artillery, and infantry covered the fields. No fences or buildings remained, and troops had filled the ditches with earth. A large number of spectators gathered in carriages, on horseback, and on foot. Scheduled to begin at 11 A.M., the review finally began— after the usual "hurry up and wait"—late.[44]

39   Parker, *Twenty-second Massachusetts*, 55.

40   Norton, *Army Letters*, 33, letter dated November 15, 1861, from Norton to his "Friend P"; According to Judson, *Eighty-third Pennsylvania*, 25–26, Porter had been given the full kit for a regiment and awarded it to the Eighty-third "for proficiency in drill and attention to duties generally." The nature of the description and the contemporaneous dates of his letters suggest that Norton is correct.

41   Sears, *For Country, Cause & Leader* (*Haydon Diary*) 129, entry dated November 20, 1861.

42   Parker, *Twenty-second Massachusetts*, 55.

43   Bennett, *Musket and Sword*, 38; Parker, *Twenty-second Massachusetts*, 55; Curtis, *From Bull Run to Chancellorsville*, 79–82; Davis, William W. H., *History of the One Hundred Fourth Pennsylvania Regiment, August 22nd, 1861, to September 30th, 1864*, (Philadelphia, 1866) 26 (Davis, *One Hundred Fourth Pennsylvania*).

44   Heintzelman MS diary (large diary) (L.C.) entry dated November 20, 1861; Bennett, *Musket and Sword*, 38.

At noon, President and Mrs. Lincoln arrived in a barouche, a two-wheeled carriage with a retractable canopy, followed by Seward and Cameron. McClellan and his staff joined them, taking position, as the subordinate should, on Lincoln's left. Artillery fired a lengthy salute; Lincoln, Seward, and Cameron, perhaps with some trepidation, switched to horses; and preceded by the sound of a single cannon, McClellan and his staff, accompanied by Lincoln, Cameron, and Seward, followed by several regiments of cavalry and a mounted brass band, made the rounds of the entire force on horseback, beginning with the left-most division, the Pennsylvania Reserves. They rode along the front and rear of each regiment while the men stood at present arms.[45]

Looking as well as he ever had and riding his new horse, Dan Webster, McClellan passed first, followed by the president.[46] "We started off with a gallop and every reviewing general joined us along with all the aides-de-camp," wrote the Comte de Paris in his diary. "We soon found ourselves in the middle of a huge staff galloping in total disorder. General Marcy, the man of rules, was in total despair and tried his best to keep everyone at his place. In the middle of this confusion, which was increased by soldiers' screams and several frightened horses, there was the president galloping, his elbows at his side with his hat in one hand, like a blind man begging."[47] The group rode the lines for approximately four miles, McClellan sitting straight as an arrow and waving his hat to each regiment as he passed at a full gallop. The regiments presented arms and gave him cheer after cheer.

"McClellan was one of the handsomest men on horseback in the federal service," wrote a student of equestrian skill after the war. "He sat in the saddle with a grace and ease peculiarly his own. All his appointments were in the most correct taste, and his horses were full-blooded animals."[48] Soon, the general outdistanced the chief executive, who fell twenty to twenty-five yards behind. With one hand on the bridle and the other clutching the mane of the horse, Lincoln never relaxed his grip except to crowd his hat farther down over his eyes, his hair and coattails standing

45   Robertson, James I., Jr., *The Civil War Letters of General Robert McAllister*, 96, letter dated November 20, 1861, from McAllister to his wife (Robertson, *McAllister Letters*); Curtis, *From Bull Run to Chancellorsville*, 79–82; Parker, *Twenty-second Massachusetts*, 55; Davis, *One Hundred Fourth Pennsylvania*, 27; Woodward, *Third Pennsylvania Reserves*, 50.

46   Sears, *For Country, Cause & Leader* (*Haydon Diary*) 129–130, entry dated November 20, 1861.

47   Comte de Paris MS diary (large diary) (A.N. de la M. de F.) entry dated November 24(?), 1861.

48   N.a., "Generals in the Saddle: Famous Men in both Armies Who Were Good Horsemen" in *The United Service: a Monthly Review of Military and Naval Affairs*, vol. vii, 95 (January, 1892).

out horizontally and his long legs wrapped around the body of the horse. Compounding the president's difficulties, made severe enough by appearing to be all arms and legs clad in an ill-fitting black suit, each regimental band greeted him with "Hail to the Chief" while the regiment dipped its colors. Struggling with his unfamiliar position on horseback and the major general's pace, Lincoln tipped his hat each time "as on he dashed. Hardly would he get it fairly stuck on the back of his head, than another set of colors would dip," Corporal Mann recalled with clarity. Another infantrymen noted in his diary that night, "He looked as though he was determined to go through it if it killed him but would be most almighty glad when it was over."[49]

The president did not suffer alone in the review. According to the Comte de Paris, "Mr. Seward could not control his horse which was going from right to left and was a danger to his neighbors . . . he had *broken down* from the very beginning. He said it was his first time on a horse in five years and it was easy to see that he was telling the truth."[50] For more than two hours Lincoln and McClellan, escorted by their entourage, rode through the lines of infantry, cavalry, and artillery.

McClellan then took a position on horseback near a large tree, and the divisions commanded by McCall, Heintzelman, Franklin, Blenker, Porter, Smith, and McDowell passed in review in that order. Following the standard practice for reviews of switching from parade formation to battle formation, every division but one marched in a tight formation, the troops massed in close column of approximately fifty files to the front. Three batteries of artillery and a regiment of cavalry followed the infantry of each division. The divisions camped farthest away passed first in order to facilitate their return to camp. Well-dressed and well-armed, the troops marched regularly. The effect was imposing to the spectators. Thousands of cavalry, artillery, and infantry passed in review, a severe test of the endurance of the men and long afterward a subject of prideful discussion in the regiments.[51]

49   Sears, *For Country, Cause & Leader* (*Haydon Diary*) 129–130, entry dated November 20, 1861; Hennesy, *Mann Memoirs*, 56–57. Those who protested against the war in Iraq (we would all like to know what they would say to the parents of the next three thousand dead) and sneered at President George Bush's landing on a carrier (unlike the national embarrassment of watching his predecessor associate with the D-Day veterans) could take a lesson from Abraham Lincoln, who more than once reviewed his troops and who tested his rifle skills with Berdan's Sharpshooters. Stevens, Capt. C. A., *Berdan's United States Sharpshooters in the Army of the Potomac, 1861–1865*, 9–11 (St. Paul, 1892); see generally, Davis, William C., *Lincoln's Men: How President Lincoln became Father to an Army and a Nation* (New York, 1999).

50   Comte de Paris MS diary (large diary) (A.N. de la M. de F.) entry dated November 24(?), 1861.

51   Scheibert, Justus, trans. and ed. Frederick Trautman, *A Prussian Observes the American Civil War: The Military Studies of Justus Scheibert*, 57 (Columbia and London, 2001); Woodward, *Third Pennsylvania Reserves*, 49; Parker, *Twenty-second Massachusetts*, 55; Curtis, *From Bull Run to Chancellorsville*, 79–82; Davis, *One Hundred Fourth Pennsylvania*, 27.

"No problem occurred during the review, which demonstrates that the chiefs know their job and are now in full command of their troops," wrote the Comte de Paris a few days later in his large diary. ". . . When I compare them to how they were when we arrived two months ago, I have to admit that I was not expecting such fast progress . . . The advantage of such a large review is to show each division it is surrounded by others who are there to help."[52]

At the end of the review Brigadier General Samuel P. Heintzelman rode toward the reviewers to speak to Wadsworth. He found Lincoln and McClellan in conversation. Acknowledged after Bull Run as a commander who had held his troops together in the rout, Heintzelman was undoubtedly better known than he thought. The president rode forward to him, saying he could not fix Heintzelman before this, wished to shake hands with him, and would not forget him in the future.

Secretary of State William H. Seward extended his hand and identified himself. Heintzelman knew him well, he said.[53]

After the war Major General William W. Averell wrote, "The all-pervading feeling was an enthusiastic and ardent admiration for the man who had created the Army of the Potomac. In the realization of all observers, even of the most experienced officers, the army was born that day. Those who had visited its busy camps and attended the inspections and reviews of divisions had formed no adequate conception of the army as a whole . . . Everyone in and around Washington had felt the pulsations of momentous preparations and the throes of a tremendous and vigorous growth going on about them since the 1st of August, but on the day of the grand review at Bailey's Cross-Roads, the eyes of all spectators, and even of the army itself, were suddenly opened."[54]

Finally, the men reached camp, where some enjoyed a feeling of exhilaration. "I returned here to camp last night very tired from the grate [sic] review of our troops," wrote Colonel Robert McAllister to his wife. "And a grate [sic] one it was, such as this continent has never seen. It was a larger army than Genl. Scott ever commanded or reviewed—60,000 soldiers all splendidly equiped [sic], with knapsacks and blankets, haversacks and canteens—all ready, if necessary, to advance into the enemy's country."[55]

---

52   Comte de Paris MS diary (large diary) (A.N. de la M. de F.) entry dated November 24(?), 1861.

53   Heintzelman MS diary (large diary) (L.C.) entry dated November 20, 1861.

54   Eckert, Edward K., and Nicholas J. Amata, eds., *Ten Years in the Saddle: The Memoir of William Woods Averell*, 373–374 (San Raphael and London, 1978).

55   Robertson, *McAllister Letters*, 96, letter dated November 20, 1861, from McAllister to his wife.

Tired and hungry, the men found considerable new excitement when they reached their camps. A report had circulated during their absence about a large body of Rebel cavalry advancing on the pickets. The officer of the day armed every man in the camps, including the cooks and the sick; doubled the picket squads; and put three brigades on the front; but no Rebels came.

An observer with a keen eye, the Comte de Paris wrote in his diary, "I am sure the politicians do not view favorably these large troop gatherings where the General, surrounded by all his lieutenants, is acclaimed by his soldiers. I am sure that, without thinking, their instinct stimulates their mistrust. Therefore, in order to not let the General get all the day's honors, the President, Mr. Seward and the Secretary of Defense rode horses to pass in front of the troops."[56]

Reviews, parades, and retreats gave McClellan the opportunity to build the conditions that would become his greatest strengths: the professional competence of his army and its near worship for him. With his approachable demeanor, he was known informally and affectionately to his junior officers and men as "George."[57] At a smaller review of Brigadier General John King Sedgwick's brigade, which included the Fortieth New York Infantry, known as the "Mozart" Regiment, McClellan addressed Colonel Edward J. Riley, the regimental commander, in a tone audible to a wider audience. "Colonel, I congratulate you upon the looks of your regiment. Their appearance is gratifying and flattering."[58]

Later, he watched Colonel Stephen W. Stryker's Forty-fourth New York Infantry at dress parade, then said something inaudible to all but the regimental commander. When the company commanders came to the front to report, Stryker told them McClellan's comments.

---

56   Comte de Paris MS Diary (large diary) (A.N. de la M. de F.) entry dated November 24(?), 1861; Parker, *Twenty-second Massachusetts*, 55. At the critical moment every United States soldier, even though regularly a cook, mechanic, or clerk, is an infantryman with a rifle. In the fighting west of Ste Marie Eglise on June 7, 1944, General James M. ("Jumpin' Jesus Christ Jimmy") Gavin found detachments of his extraordinary Eighty-second Airborne Division in a "deteriorating" situation around the causeway at La Fiere. "I told the regimental executive of the 325th [Glider Infantry Regiment] that we were going to counter-attack with every resource we had, including himself, regimental clerks, headquarters people, and anyone we could get our hands on with a weapon." Gavin, James M., *On to Berlin: Battles of an Airborne Commander 1943–1946* (New York, 1978) 118.

57   Charles Townsend MSS (New York State Library) letter dated October 27, 1861, from Townsend to his aunt; Herdegen, *Ray Diary*, 27–28, entry dated November 27, 1861.

58   Floyd, Frederick Clark, *History of the Fortieth (Mozart) Regiment New York Volunteers, which was Composed of four Companies from New York, four Companies from Massachusetts, and two Companies from Pennsylvania*, 73 (Boston, 1909).

"Gentlemen, I have some good news for you. The commanding general says the Forty-fourth New York is the best drilled regiment in the army."[59]

And to the colonel of the Eighty-third Pennsylvania, which McClellan and his staff also observed at dress parade, the major general said, "Colonel, I congratulate you on having one of the very best regiments in the Army."[60]

One of his troops wrote his aunt, "Under our glorious young commander General McClellan we will *not* have more reverses. This is what we soldiers believe. We have the most implicit confidence in him."[61]

"The confidence [of the army] in Gen. McClellan remains unshaken," wrote Alexander Stuart Webb, thirteenth in the West Point class of 1855, assistant to the chief of artillery of the Army of the Potomac, a member of Brigadier General William F. Barry's staff, later the author of the best book on the Peninsula Campaign, and holder of the Congressional Medal of Honor. "I think the whole army only awaits his word."[62]

In all armies over time the new enlisted men would increasingly learn the rules, become rules veterans, and become sufficiently comfortable about "proper" conduct to play "rules games" with their junior officers, punctiliously "enforcing" the rules to embarrass their officers. A private of the Second United States Sharpshooters knew the officer of the day, Captain John W. Dewey, had a habit of sneaking to the guard positions to surprise the pickets. The private occupied a position on the regiment's outermost guard line near a stream. He expected the captain to walk in the water until he could surprise the private. Back and forth along the bushes at the edge of the creek the private paced his beat. After midnight he heard someone in the creek but continued to pace his beat as if he heard nothing. When the captain had reached a position well into the stream and the private knew his exact location beyond the bushes, the private stopped short and called.

"Who comes there?"

He stepped close to the stream with the point of his bayonet in the captain's face.

"A friend without the countersign," answered the officer, who then attempted to start an informal conversation. The private would have none of it and called for the corporal of the guard.

"You know me," said the captain. "I am the officer of the day, Captain Dewey." He started to leave the creek.

---

59   Nash, *Forty-fourth New York*, 55.

60   Judson, *Eighty-third Pennsylvania*, 25.

61   George B. McClellan MSS (Library of Congress) letter dated December 25, 1861, from Harrison White to "My dear Aunt."

62   Webb MSS (Y.U.) letter dated January 20, 1862, from Webb to his father.

"Halt!"

"Let me up on the bank. Then you can see who I am."

"The corporal of the guard will be along soon."

After a short while in the streambed Captain Dewey decided he had had enough of this game.

"I have the countersign," he said.

"Advance and give the countersign."

The captain complied, the guard allowed him to pass, and the captain began to walk away. After a few steps he returned and began to berate the private for not saluting. The private stood his ground.

No sign of an officer could he see, he said.

The captain threw back his cape, uncovering his sash and shoulder straps.

Still in perfect compliance with the rules, the private saluted.

"You knew me all the time," retorted Captain Dewey.

"I don't know anybody after the countersign is out," replied the private.

Acknowledging that the private had outplayed him in the "game of rules," the captain said "You are a brick," and continued on his tour of the pickets.[63]

But McClellan's officers had dissenters and some wisely waiting for conclusive proof. The thoughtful analyses of the military situation by William and Wilder Dwight, two of four serving brothers from an old Boston family, showed a sharp contrast. According to William, "The violation of the principles of war deserves to bring retribution. I hope the luck will let the rebels meet with such retribution when they deserve it, as certainly as we have met with it. There is no comprehensiveness in McClellan. There is a want of energy in the army. There are too many *can'ts*. We *can* do anything we *will* in war, it is a mere question of *Cost* in men & material."[64]

Recognizing the obstructions confronting McClellan, William's brother Wilder took a more philosophical view. "For myself I can see no other wisdom than patience & faith. I confess that now & then this seems difficult, but whether McClellan will not vindicate himself is not so clear. His difficulties have been great, his task gigantic. And if when our army moves it moves in organized obedience to a single will the wonder will not be that so much time has been spent in preparation, but that the preparation

---

63   White, Russell C., ed., *The Civil War Diary of Wyman S. White: First Sergeant of Company F. 2nd United States Sharpshooter Regiment, 1861–1865* (Baltimore, 1991) 27 (White, *White Diary*).

64   Dwight Family MSS (M.H.S.) letter dated December, 1861, from William Dwight to Wilder Dwight. Most of the letters from Wilder to his family were long ago published in Dwight, *Life and Letters of Wilder Dwight Lieut. Col. Second Mass. Inf. Vols.* (Boston, 1868). Recently, the family papers, including unpublished Wilder letters and William's letters, were donated to the Massachusetts Historical Society, like the Pennsylvania Historical Society and the Library of Congress a treasure trove, with an unusually helpful curator in Peter Drummey.

has been made. I see he has spent a day with that ridiculous Congressional Committee & hope he has given them a hint of wisdom which they need."[65] Through slightly varied approaches, McClellan engendered the same feeling in countless others. The regiments felt a warm affection for and strong confidence in their leader.[66]

Like everything else under McClellan's command, his reviews became controversial. Count Adam Gurowski, the gatherer of rumors and speculations, had an ignorant, misguided, and hostile opinion about the reviews, as he did by now for everything touching the Army of the Potomac. "Seeing these reviews," he commented to his diary, "I cannot get rid of the idea that by such shows and displays McClellan tries to frighten the rebels in Chinaman fashion."[67] In a letter marked "confidential *not to be talked about at all*," Senator Lyman Trumble said disconsolately to his wife, "I am greatly dissatisfied with General McLellan [sic]. He seems to be devoting himself to parades and military theory instead of clearing the country of Rebels. . . ."[68] A few months later Secretary of the Treasury Salmon P. Chase would try to protect McDowell from the criticism leveled at McClellan. "Permit me also to suggest the efficacy of having no more reviews," he wrote to McDowell. "The country is in no mood to hear of anything, however useful . . . , which savors of show rather than action."[69]

Watching from his position as a brigade commander, George Meade disagreed with criticism of the reviews. "An army is like a complicated machine, all its parts from the Genl. down to the private soldier must *know* & *do* their work or you will inevitably have confusion & disaster. *Soldiers* are not & cannot be made by merely putting uniforms on men & arms in their hands. You might just as well try to work a ship in a gale of wind with a lot of green lubbers."[70]

As men passed from ignorant recruit to reliable volunteer, transformations occurred at levels well above the "crunchy" or "grunt" or "mudcrusher." McClellan, a young company grade officer in the Mexican War, had drawn sharp contrasts between the Regular Army core of Scott's fighting men and the volunteers. In his diary and let-

---

65   Dwight Family MSS (M.H.S.) letter dated January 17, 1862, from Wilder Dwight to Dan.

66   Norton, *Army Letters*, 33, letter dated November 15, 1861, from Norton to his "Friend P."

67   Gurowski, *Diary*, from March 4, 1861, to November 12, 1862, 3 vols. (Boston, 1862) 1, 118–119, entry dated November, 1861 (Gurowski, *Diary*).

68   Chandler MSS (L.C.) letter dated October 12, 1861, from Trumble to his wife.

69   Chase MSS (U.P.I.) letter dated March 28, 1862, from Chase to McDowell. For a random selection of important American historical figures, U.P.I. has undertaken to locate every letter to and from the person and to put them all on a single, multi-reel microfilm. From the Civil War it has invaluably done this for Chase and Seward, the Chase reels being at the New York University Library in the Seward reels in the Columbia University Library.

70   Meade MSS (P.H.S.) letter dated August 5, 1861, from Meade to his wife.

ters he contrasted the depredations and outrages of the volunteers, whom he disdainfully described as *voluntarios*, and the firm discipline and good behavior of the regulars.[71] In a memorandum written after the Mexican War he concluded, "It is barely possible to make a decent soldier, even of Infantry in 5 years, much less of Engineers, Artillery and dragoons."[72] This background undoubtedly lay at the heart of McClellan's early doubts about his Army of the Potomac, his unwillingness to commit his men to an early general engagement, and his somewhat puzzling exhilaration when they showed sturdiness in the skirmish at Vienna and the fighting at Ball's Bluff. By embracing the reality of an army of volunteers, McClellan demonstrated the early stages of his transformation from the rigid, doctrinaire youth of the Mexican War to the slowly developing adjustable adult of the Civil War. As a consequence he would find himself engulfed by a powerful affection for his men and a sense of responsibility for their lives.[73] He described his purpose in his private, postwar memoirs.

> The frequent reviews I held at Washington were not at all for the benefit of the public, nor yet for the purpose of examining the individual condition of the men, although I did much of that even on these occasions . . . But they were to accustom the regiments to move together and see each other, to give the troops an idea of their own strength, to infuse *esprit de corps* and mutual emulation, and to acquaint myself with the capacity of the general officers. . . . What I strove for and accomplished was to bring about such a condition of discipline and instruction that the army could be handled on the march and on the field of battle, and that orders could be reasonably well carried out.[74]

Although McClellan could probably not have read the work of du Picq, a French officer and theoretician, the major general echoed the very thoughts du Picq recorded in *Battle Studies: Ancient and Modern Battle*, a study of the development of soldiers: "discipline and tactics insure unity between leader and soldier, between the men themselves . . . Esprit appears, flight is a disgrace, for one is no longer

71   Myers, *McClellan's Mexican War Diary*, 34–35, 36–37, 38–39, 43, entries dated December 27 and 30, 1846 and January 1 and 3, 1847; McClellan MSS memorandum on the Mexican War, dated January 4, 1848, quoted in Sears, *McClellan*, 25.

72   McClellan MSS (L.C.) memorandum on the Mexican War, dated January 4, 1848, quoted in Sears, *McClellan*, 25.

73   Biddle, William F., "Recollections of McClellan" in *The United Service*, 460–469, May, 1894; Herdegen, Lance J., *The Men Stood Like Iron: How the Iron Brigade Won Its Name*, 212–217 (Milwaukee, 1997).

74   *M.O.S.*, 97–98.

alone in combat. There is a legion, and he who gives way quits his commanders and his companions."[75]

None of this, McClellan knew, would occur overnight. The training of his men to serve as an army, the creation of a bond between his officers and his men, the elimination of consent in favor of obedience to orders would require time. He could use the army for light excursions in September, October, and November. A full-scale advance might be possible around Christmas, the Virginia weather permitting, but not before.

Even the youngest officers understood McClellan's program and its purpose, and they approved it because they could see its beneficial results. Alexander Stewart Webb wrote home in early October that, as a result of the training and preparation, the troops were increasing in efficiency. "They *know* their generals and they have confidence in most of them. The system of Divisions and Brigades with proper and efficient Generals is telling strongly."[76]

These basic factors remained constant in McClellan's thinking. He did not have an army of regulars. Although his troops improved through drill, training, and reviews and he tested them lightly at infrequent skirmishes like the encounter at Lewinsville, he had not progressed far enough, as he saw it, in his effort to transform a collection of undisciplined civilians into an army.[77]

A parallel from ancient history suggests that the half-hearted, often insincere, praise for McClellan's administrative and organizational ability falls far below the credit he earned. Applying a system of training and battle that depended on the natural abilities of its infantry and its centurions, the equivalents of noncommissioned officers and junior company-grade officers,[78] Roman armies of the late Republic fought well under incompetent leadership, survived battles that should have destroyed them, and won battles they probably should have lost.[79] The same quality of fighting men would give the Army of the Potomac the same performance in the future.

75   du Picq, *Battle Studies*, introduction xvi, 47.

76   Webb MSS (Y.U.) letter dated October 2, 1861, from Webb to his father; *Cullum*, 2, no. 1689; Warner, *Generals in Blue*, 544–545; *D.A.B.*, 10, pt. 1, 571–572; de Trobriand, Regis, trans. George K. Dauchy, *Four Years With the Army of the Potomac*, 122 (Boston, 1889).

77   Gurowski, *Diary*, 1, 97, 99–100, entry dated September, 1861; Sears, *McClellan's Correspondence*, 163, letter dated January 31, 1862, redated February 3, 1862, by the editor, from McClellan to Stanton.

78   Delbrück, Hans, trans. Walter J. Renfroe, Jr., *History of the Art of War*, 4 vols. (Lincoln and London, 1975 Eng. trans.) *Warfare in Antiquity*, vol. 1, 431 (Delbrück, *Art of War, Antiquity*).

79   Adcock, *The Art of War*, chap. 5, 101–102, 109, 118, 119; Delbrück, *Art of War, Antiquity*, 1, 412, 413, 430, 432.

What did McClellan make of them by drill and more drill, reviews and more reviews? What characteristics did McClellan's riflemen contribute to their army? The men McClellan trained and the battlefield force he unintentionally created for others to lead can well be compared with the armies that served in the last two centuries of the Roman Republic. Their commanders appointed by and from the Roman Senate, the Roman armies fought under inexperienced, mediocre, or worse leaders except for a few like Marius,[80] Sulla, Scipio Africanus, Caesar, and Pompey. The Roman infantrymen, by training, skill, and tenacity, often won battles the favorable outcome of which can only be attributed to their battlefield abilities, not to their leaders. Little did McClellan know that his superb training and leadership would create an implement that would survive the worst battlefield leadership in American military history. Only once would the army's great heart grow faint under these commanders—but never on the battlefield. The tests ahead would show that McClellan had the luxury of training and leading excellent manpower at the outset; that he and his officers adjusted well to this new, different manpower; and that, in the hands of others far beneath the level of leadership the Army of the Potomac deserved, his army would show the characteristics of the armies of the late Roman Republic. It would fight well above the quality of its leadership.

According to Professor Victor Davis Hanson, a classical scholar and a student of military history with a powerful imaginative streak, Western armies, the armies of Europe and America, fought better and harder, killed more effectively, inflicted more casualties, and most often prevailed in battles with armies from other parts of the globe. So too for the Army of the Potomac. But if McClellan's army had become so good by the middle of 1862, why did it not defeat the Army of Northern Virginia sooner than 1865? The other part of Professor Hanson's theory explains the time needed by McClellan's army for victory: in McClellan's case two western armies were fighting each other. Not until the Army of the Potomac had inflicted more casualties than the Army of Northern Virginia could replace did the superiority of McClellan's creation prevail over its near equal. But prevail it did, in an elongated version of Professor Hanson's theory.[81]

---

80   Marius, a commoner, had risen from infantryman to commander by natural talent and success but was unique.

81   Adcock, *Roman Art of War*, chap. 5, especially 101–102, 109, 118, 119, and 4; du Picq, *Battle Studies*, 81; Hanson, Victor Davis, *Carnage and Culture: Landmark Battles in the Rise of Western Power*, 6–24 (New York and London, 2001); Pollack, Kenneth M., *Arabs at War: Military Effectiveness, 1948–1991*, 6–24 (New York and London, 2002), *see generally* the unnumbered seventh chapter for analyses of defeat stemming from poor tactical performance in spite of superiority of numbers and equipment.

Chapter 18

"I am getting pretty familiar with my duties which thus far have been principally *paperwork*. You would be astonished to see the amount of writing & papering required of a general in the field."

—George G. Meade to his wife

The Developing Officer Corps

$\mathcal{E}$ ven after he became general in chief, McClellan's incoming personal correspondence confirmed the correctness of his policies for the Army of the Potomac. A correspondent from New York told him, "There is much impatience upon the subject of an advance movement but it is wholly undefined in the minds of those who most urge it, and the policy that you sketched to me, when once it works its way into the public mind, by the current events of the day, it will entirely satisfy those who are more clamorous for action." Knowledgeable people agreed that "great slaughter if not a second defeat" would attend "any attempt to take Manassas by force."[1]

From Philadelphia he received a strong early November letter about the timing for an advance. "Stand firm! No yielding whatever,—not a single hair's breadth. No precipitancy, not to the content of a single minute in advance of the moment when *your own* deliberate judgment (all outside influences treated as *naught*) tells you that the hour has come.—This is what you owe to your country. This is what is expected of you by her."[2]

---

1   McClellan MSS (L.C.) letter dated November 30, 1861, from Barney to McClellan.

2   McClellan MSS (L.C.) letter dated October 31, 1861, from Trist to McClellan.

On the complex problem of slavery, a knowledgeable source encouraged him to remain intractable. "I do not think, as a first, that the Radical men will be able to force a declaration of purpose as to the institution of slavery, but if any legislation occurs upon the subject of the war, it is likely to be upon the *property* of those men actually *in arms* against the government. Properly guarded an act of this sort will be unobjectionable." And McClellan would have the unqualified support of the president no matter how "violent" Congress became.[3] This view had been quite sound at the beginning of the war, when only ten to thirty percent of the men in arms believed abolition should be one of the war aims.[4] An officer of the Sixty-seventh Ohio Infantry wrote his family, "I am more strongly confirmed in my old faith that for the Constitution, the Union, and the Flag of my country I will fight to the last; I am ever ready to punish and to shoot traitors; but it was not necessary to fight for the darkies, nor are they worth fighting for."[5] Change blew in the wind by the winter of 1861–1862.

Colonel Robert McAllister wrote his wife, "There is no disguising the fact that our army is becoming more and more opposed to slavery every day. And those that will not see it will soon find themselves in the background. I never saw anything like it. Rank pro-slavery men who came here are now the other way."[6]

McClellan's attitude toward the South and its people remained unchanged. He had two conversations about the war with Peter H. Watson, a young lawyer who had

3   McClellan MSS (L.C.) letter dated November 30, 1861, from Barney to McClellan.

4   Howard, *Recollections*, 1, 191–192; Wiley, Bell I., *The Life of Billy Yank*, 40 (Indianapolis, 1952); McPherson, *For Cause & Comrades*, 117–119, 129–130.

5   Byrne, Frank L., and Jean Powers Soman, *Your True Marcus: The Civil War Letters of a Jewish Colonel* (Kent, 1995) 62, letter dated March 7, 1862, from Spiegel to his wife and children (Byrne, *Your True Marcus*).

6   Robertson, *McAllister Letters*, 122, letter dated March 10, 1862, from McAllister to his wife. Bell Wiley thought the views never changed during the war, and because the bulk of his sources and research lay in the West, he may have been correct for men from that area. But he was not correct in the East. *See*, Wiley, 41, and McPherson, *op cit. supra*. According to a more subtle, complex analysis by Professor James M. McPherson in *For Cause & Comrades*, 30 percent of the men who left a record for the early stages of the war came to believe that they could not achieve preservation or restoration of the Union, their real goal, without abolition. This subject, quantification of attitudes of enlisted men and officers toward abolition for its own sake or as a war aim, presents a large issue for any historian of this war, and many others. The letters, diaries, unpublished memoirs, and published primary material of all kinds will support every view on every issue. Almost any trend can be identified and supported, no matter how contradictory any two of them might be. For the officers, especially the higher-ranking officers, the issue appears to be more manageable because the relevant and material sources have more limits. Nevertheless, specification of a majority view on any question, even in that limited population, remains a hazardous exercise.

practiced with his new Democratic friend Edwin Stanton. In both conversations Watson expressed the opinion that the Rebels were in earnest, that a negotiated peace could not be expected, and that the Union must subjugate the Confederacy to restore the territorial integrity of the country. McClellan disagreed. The Union should avoid harshness and violence, he said. It should conduct the war in a way that would avoid offense to the civilian population as far as possible. If he thought the way Watson did, he concluded, he would feel obliged to lay down his arms.[7]

Consistent with his policies of separating the military efforts from the civilian population and not interfering with slavery, McClellan had issued a general order requiring the return of runaway slaves who could be identified by owners who were loyal to the union.[8] His officers had their own ways of construing the order, and Joseph Hooker, among others, illustrated their change of attitude over time.

Below the capital on the Maryland side of the Potomac, Hooker's division guarded the long shoreline to Port Tobacco. The residents of the county petitioned Hooker "for the delivery to the respective owners" of fugitive slaves in the camp of the Fifth Excelsior Regiment of Sickles' brigade. Hooker learned that the regiment refused to surrender the escaped slaves.

"If so," he said, "it indicates a state of demoralization in that command which it will be necessary to take in hand as soon as satisfactory evidence is given of its existence."

Whenever Hooker thought it proper, Sickles responded, he would order the delivery of the fugitive slaves to the civilians. He was certain the officers and men of the regiment would behave "like good soldiers although the duty might be repugnant to their feelings and derogatory to their just pride as soldiers."[9]

When Sickles issued the order to return all able-bodied men to their owners, an unofficial count showed that most of them had come from Virginia and that, not surprisingly, their owners had not come to claim them. Off they went to the brigade quartermaster for employment as laborers.[10]

In December 1861, Hooker sent for one of his staff officers, James F. Rusling, whom he criticized for lax enforcement of the unpopular "Maryland Slave Order."

7   Niven, John, ed., *The Salmon P. Chase Papers* 4 vols. (incomplete) (Kent and London, 1993) diary, 1, 353–354, entry dated July 27, 1862 (Niven, *Chase Papers*).

8   Porter, Fitz John, *In Memory of Gen. Charles P. Stone* (n.p., n.d.) 15 (Porter, *Stone*) (pamphlet); Rusling, *Men and Things*, 61.

9   Hooker MSS (H.L.) letter dated November 21, 1861, from Sickles to Dickenson, Hooker's adjutant.

10   Hooker MSS (H.L.) letter dated November 27, 1861, from Sickles to Dickenson.

He told Rusling he had thought of putting him under arrest for "disobedience of orders."

Rusling explained that it was only quasi disobedience because he was right and the order was wrong.

Hooker then complimented Rusling on his noncompliance and invited him to dinner and to have "a little commissary."

Over dinner and a little whiskey Hooker and Rusling became fast, long-standing friends.

A month or two later Hooker showed a clear change of position. His camps had become a place of refuge for Maryland slaves whose owners were largely disloyal; and McClellan's "Maryland Slave Order," probably the same order that had caused Porter's trouble with Martindale and Pickell, had fallen into disfavor. A party of slave owners arrived at Hooker's headquarters to claim several of their slaves in the camp of a Massachusetts regiment in his division. They pointed to McClellan's order and demanded the surrender of their property.

"Yes," said Hooker. "I have seen the order, and yonder is the Massachusetts camp. And if your slaves are there and choose to go with you and the Massachusetts boys are content, I have no objections. If they refuse and a rough occurs over there, I fear you will get into the guard house—the same as any other marauders."

"But, General Hooker, are you not going to apprehend our slaves for us?"

"Why, bless my soul, no! I am a Brigadier General U.S. Volunteers, and no nigger-catcher! I was born and bred in New England!"[11]

As winter approached with all its natural ailments, the officers had no immunity from the health problems faced by their enlisted men, and McClellan became concerned about the health of his higher-ranking officers. Baldy Smith fell ill with typhoid and was absent during November and early December.[12] Horatio G. Wright had been stricken with typhoid and, though tended by his wife, was not expected to live.[13] News of McClellan's own illness, like almost all other information, circulated throughout the army in December,[14] at first that he had a cold and that General Marcy had a fever.[15] Generals Philip Kearny and Montgomery had become so

---

11   Rusling, *Men and Things*, 61–62.

12   *C.C.W.*, 1, 186, 188 (Smith); Welsh, Jack D., M.D., *Medical Histories of Union Generals* (Kent, 1996) 313 (Welsh, *Medical Histories*).

13   Heintzelman MS diary (large diary) (L.C.) entry dated November 14, 1861.

14   E.g., Sears, *For Country, Cause & Leader (Haydon Diary)* 155, entry dated December 23, 1861; Adams, *Story of a Trooper*, 259.

15   Heintzelman MS diary (large diary) (L.C.) entry dated December 24, 1861.

ill that they returned to New Jersey to recuperate; and Kearny, not a man of robust health, was not expected to return.[16]

As Edwin V. Sumner, the most senior division commander, rode into Camp California, the camp of the Eighth Illinois Cavalry Regiment, his horse stepped in a hole, fell forward, and threw Sumner over its head, causing either a severe spinal injury or injuries to his lungs and shoulder. The "Bull Head," a name Sumner had earned in the Old Army when a bullet supposedly bounced off his skull, remounted and rode back to camp. But he was badly hurt,[17] at first not expected to live or be able to ride his horse again. Then he was thought to be only slightly injured. At last he asked to be relieved of command of his division, which was taken as evidence of a more severe injury than had been thought.

McClellan temporarily assigned Sumner's division to Heintzelman, who would then command two divisions, but that quasi-corps formation could not continue.[18] Composed of the standard three brigades of infantry regiments, the division had an odd configuration at the level of brigade leadership. Brigadier General Oliver O. Howard, an extreme example of the Scott Rule for promotion, was the senior brigade commander but had graduated from the Military Academy in 1854. "Old Nosey," Brigadier General William H. French, had graduated in 1837. Sumner asked to have John King Sedgwick, a West Point graduate, French's contemporary, and a brigade commander in Heintzelman's division, assigned to command the division.

Sumner assured Howard he did not request Sedgwick for any lack of confidence in him. He wished to avoid confrontations with French, an old army officer who would feel aggrieved if Howard were given the division. Although Howard had no special desire to command the division, he wrote home, he did not want to be "dishonored." He insisted that Sumner explain his actions in writing to army headquarters, and the division adjutant assured him it would be done. "My greatest crime," Howard wrote his wife, "has been all along my *youth*."[19]

Five days before Christmas, Captain James B. Ricketts and his wife, recently released from captivity and sent north, returned to Washington, both looking very

16   Robertson, *McAllister Letters*, 104, letter dated December 17, 1861, from McAllister to his wife; Welsh, *Medical Histories*, 188, 234.

17   August V. Kautz MS rem. (L.C.) 9; Welsh, *Medical Histories*, 329; Warner, *Generals in Blue*, 489–490.

18   Heintzelman MS diary (large diary) (L.C.) entries dated December 16, 1861, and December 20, 1861; *New York Daily Tribune*, dated December 26, 1861, p. 4, col. 6.

19   Howard MSS (L.C.) letter dated December 20, 1861, from Howard to his wife; Heitman, *Historical Register*, 1, 437, 546.

thin after their ordeal and Ricketts being still crippled by his Bull Run wounds. Mrs. Ricketts had suffered almost every indignity a woman could endure while in prison with her husband.[20] For two weeks he had lain on the floor of the small room near Bull Run Creek while his wounds verged dangerously on gangrene. At last they were taken to Richmond, Ricketts still in critical condition. He had been struck in the forehead by a piece of shell, buckshot had penetrated his shoulders and breast, and a minié ball had struck his left leg near the knee joint, shattering the bone.[21] After the couple's journey to Richmond, quite unpleasant and nearly fatal, citizens heaped insults on them at every station until they reached Richmond, where they were placed in the city poorhouse, an unfinished building with bare walls and loosely planked floors. There, surgeons decided they should amputate Ricketts' leg, but his wife refused to allow the operation.

Only once, when visited by a curious crowd that vilified the captured Yankees, did Ricketts rise from his lethargic state. A member of the group was a reverend who had come from his church in New York to damn the invaders of the South. He stopped at Ricketts' cot, where the captain lay on a stained red artillery blanket.

"This is the famous leader of Ricketts' battery wrapped fitly in the color of blood," said the reverend. "Can he be a Christian and a brother to do this thing?"

Ricketts raised his bandaged head and in a loud voice answered, "No, neither Christian nor brother to such as you."

For nearly three months of wretched prison life, made worse by the addition of prisoners taken at Ball's Bluff, Ricketts lay desperately wounded. An order sending convalescent prisoners to Charleston divided the officers who had been together since the battle. Among others, Colonel Orlando B. Willcox, whose terrible shell wound in the arm had been treated by Mrs. Ricketts, left for the south.

A short time later a messenger awakened Ricketts to inform him that he had been selected as one of the thirteen officers to be held as hostages for thirteen privateersmen then incarcerated in the "Tombs" in New York City. If the privateersmen were executed as pirates, the hostages would suffer the same fate. When the list with Ricketts' name on it was read to the assembled prisoners, a captain of the First Kentucky Volunteers said, "Is that that wounded officer, attended by such a devoted wife! Let me take his place!"

20   Heintzelman MS diary (large diary) (L.C.) entries dated December 20 and 23, 1861.

21   Struck many times by many different kinds of projectile, Ricketts left no accurate record of his wounds; and the various accounts, MS biography in Hunt MSS (L.C.) and the account in Scott, *Willcox Journal, etc.*, conflict. According to Welsh, *Medical Histories*, 279, he was "severely wounded four times . . . Details are lacking."

Mrs. Ricketts complained through a local Southern friend that her husband's wounds were too severe for him to be taken from her to the condemned cells, that it would mean certain death. The friend's influence prevailed; and Confederate commanding officer General Charles S. Winder, whose ferocity toward his former brother officers had already become well-known, exempted wounded officers from designation as hostages.

In December, a final private effort through the New York senators to exchange Ricketts, still in a deplorable condition, for a Southern officer with powerful Virginia relatives succeeded. Taken from prison to Norfolk at midnight, Ricketts and his wife went aboard the flag-of-truce boat, met in midstream the boat from Fort Monroe, sailed from there to Washington,[22] and received parole on December 17, 1861. When he reached Washington, he reported to Army headquarters. Although he had been released from his parole, his wounds still disabled him and provided orders to New York.[23]

Ricketts had graduated from the Military Academy sixteenth in the Class of 1839 and had served in the artillery throughout his career,[24] succeeding to command of "Prince John" Magruder's regular battery before Bull Run. Modest, quiet, and generous, Ricketts never spoke critically of anyone, superior or inferior in rank. In appearance, he had a fresh complexion with a "clerkly" look, pale blue eyes, a pointed chin, and light-colored whiskers that mingled with a curling mustache. On his forehead was a slight scar, somewhat like a saber cut, from one of his Bull Run wounds.[25] His wife, a woman of refinement but without beauty, was by disposition, education, and spirit a person of great strength and executive ability, thought by many to be perfectly capable of handling a corps.[26]

Ricketts became an example of two criteria for promotion that had little to do with leadership ability or tactical skill: wounds and prison. On March 21, 1862,

22   Henry Jackson Hunt MSS (Library of Congress) "Notes for a biography of General Ricketts," by Hunt.

23   NA Off's MS Rpts (Ricketts) letter dated June 30, 1873, from Ricketts.

24   Williams, *Garfield Letters*, 187, letter dated December 5, 1862, from Garfield to Harry; Warner, *Generals in Blue*, 403–404; *Cullum*, 1, no. 1001.

25   Kiefer, Joseph Warren, *Slavery and Four Years of War: a Political History of Slavery of the United States together with a Narrative of the Campaigns and Battles of the Civil War in which the Author Took Part, 1861–1865*, 2 vols. (New York and London, 1900) 2, 105–106 (Kiefer, *Slavery and Four Years*); Williams, *Garfield Letters*, 187–188, letter dated December 5, 1862, from Garfield to Harry; Bennett, *Musket and Sword*, 15.

26   Kiefer, *Slavery and Four Years*, 2, 106.

Lincoln promoted him to brigadier general.[27] Lincoln, again showing his acute ignorance of military affairs but his extraordinary personnel skills, believed promotion of a former prisoner compensated him for his suffering.[28] A wound or a period in prison, certainly a large sacrifice for any man, did not predict the man's ability as a general officer. Nevertheless, these criteria would find personification on the promotion lists well into the war, and they would produce some unfortunate results.

Although unwell for several weeks and unable to attend to his division,[29] Baldy Smith managed to take advantage of the long, mild fall that would stretch to the end of December[30] by hosting an impromptu luncheon for numerous schoolmates at the Military Academy and other fellow officers on Saturday, December 14. The capacious, double-brick Smoot House where Smith kept his headquarters served the event well. With his division flanked by those of McCall and Porter,[31] these officers would naturally make the guest list. McClellan, William B. Franklin, Winfield Scott Hancock, W. T. H. Brooks, George G. Meade, and Smith himself filled the list. After the meal, Smith invited his staff officers to join the group.

Eventually, the discussion turned to the inevitable question: the duration of the war. The consensus on this question had changed from the "walk in the sun" of earlier days to virtual unanimity that the war would last years. Franklin embellished his response by predicting the future of the ranking officers present.

"It is my opinion that the war will continue for several years," he prophesied, "and before the war is over, everyone present, with one exception, will be laid about on the shelf. That exception will be General George G. Meade. He will come out on top at the close of the war."[32]

New Year's Day, 1862, a warm and delightful day for shirtsleeves without overcoat,[33] marked the return of Philip Kearny to the army. Although not entirely well, Kearny gave a New Year's Day party to which he invited the colonels commanding

---

27   NA Offs MS Rpts (Ricketts) letter dated June 30, 1873, from Ricketts.

28   *M.O.S.*, 161.

29   *C.C.W.*, 1, 186, 188 (Smith).

30   Sears, *For Country, Cause & Leader (Haydon Diary)* 144, 145, 148, 159, 160, entries dated December 9, 11, 16, 28, and 29, 1861; Adams, F. Colburn, *The Story of a Trooper* (New York, 1865) 251 (Adams, *Story of a Trooper*); Judson, *Eighty-third Pennsylvania*, 26, col. 2.

31   *C.C.W.*, 1, 186 (Smith).

32   Scrymser, *Personal Reminiscences*, 19.

33   Potter MS Rem. (Buffalo Historical Society) the pages are unnumbered; Osborne, Seward R., ed., *The Civil War Diaries of Col. Theodore B. Gates, 20th New York State Militia* (Hightstown, 1991) 7, entry dated January 1, 1861 (Osborne, *Gates' Diary*).

his regiments, the senior captain of each regiment, the senior lieutenant of each regiment, his staff, and Generals Franklin, Heintzelman, French, and Howard.

The party, a reflection of Kearny's great wealth, took place in the home of the Right Reverend John Johns, bishop of Virginia, where Kearny kept his headquarters. The center of the table had a large frame more than three feet high entwined with evergreens stuck full of lighted candles. The heated air from the burning candles rotated a horizontal wheel in the form of a fan. Dinner consisted of many courses—oyster soup, chicken, roast turkey, venison, Irish custards, apples, and nuts. The officers then adjourned to the parlor for tea and wines served by waiters. Otis Howard and Robert McAllister, both strongly religious and firm abstainers, forsook the wines for the tea.[34]

Other officers, too, had social events during the early days of winter. Colonel William P. Maulsby, one of Banks' regimental commanders, gave a ball for officers of the division on a Friday evening. "Dickens himself could not have conjectured a better name, nor could he have caricatured a more *Dickensy* host and hostess," wrote Wilder Dwight to his family. The guests awaited the ball with anticipation throughout the preceding week. Colonel George L. Andrews and Dwight rode to it in grand costume. Numerous volunteer officers attended. Maulsby had taken a large, fine, old-fashioned house outside the town of Frederick on the road to Harpers Ferry. Built by a Tory in the Revolutionary or pre-Revolutionary period, the house supposedly had a haunted chamber where some wife had been imprisoned and starved or "worried into a restless & unquiet death. . . . I fear that much of the beauty of the capital is rebellious and traitorous. Here and there the plain but loyal maidens were varied by a beauty, but rarely," Dwight wrote home. A politician with Democratic loyalties, Colonel Maulsby was the commanding officer of the second regiment of the Potomac Home Guard. Gaunt and sharp-featured, he talked through his nose and was "overwhelmingly happy to see us." According to Dwight, Maulsby's wife "must be 30 years older than he at least. She seems a neuralgic . . . withered matron and hung at the Cols. side during the reception." When the ball opened, Colonel Maulsby and Mrs. Banks stood opposite General Banks, an excellent ball-room dancer, and Mrs. Maulsby for the first dance.[35]

Throughout the army the field officers of a regiment, colonel, lieutenant colonel, and major, hardly ever displayed uniformity in skill, aptitude, and experience.

---

34 Robertson, *McAllister's Letters*, 110–111, letter dated January 1, 1862, from McAllister to his wife.

35 Dwight Family MSS (M.H.S.) letter dated January 10, 1862, from Wilder Dwight to his mother.

Usually, one would emerge as the practical leader, and his rank varied randomly. In the Sixty-first New York, Lieutenant Colonel Francis Channing Barlow, a graduate of Harvard College, a practicing lawyer, and the best of the field-grade officers in the Sixty-first, had risen from the Bull Run Pool, starting as a private in the three-month service. Barlow's duties and responsibilities began each day with reveille at 6 A.M. when the regiment formed under arms on the color line. The rolls of the companies would be called. Barlow attended reveille each morning, he reported to his family in a letter, then washed and dressed and had breakfast. Sometimes he read tactics or wrote a letter until 9.

During this time he also tended the innumerable matters of camp regulation and answered questions. Then the regiment drilled until 11. More questions and other administrative matters preceded lunch, which lasted until 2. Drill from 2 to 4, then parade, followed by supper. During officers' school, which ran from 7 to 8:30 each night, Barlow instructed the first lieutenants. He then wrote or read until 10 or 11, when he went to bed. Because neither the colonel nor the major had the ability to make rules and regulations or to implement them throughout the regiment, Barlow did it. "I could not have desired things to go on better than they had done and I am perfectly satisfied," he wrote home.[36]

Barlow had loaded his revolver only twice and had fired it only the one time he fired all cartridges in the cylinder at a tree on his way home from picket duty. Rules forbade firing about the camp, and he never had time to go somewhere else to practice. "I do not think that a pistol would do me much good in a fight whether I were a good shot or not," he wrote.[37]

For an officer, skill with a weapon, even his performance on the battlefield, would represent a small part of his time in service. As George Meade wrote home in September, "I am getting pretty familiar with my duties which thus far have been principally *paperwork*. You would be astonished to see the amount of writing & papering required of a general in the field. A good deal of it is regular circumlocution . . . Nevertheless being upon the times one has to comply with the requirements however foolish they may seem."[38]

At the same time the younger, junior officers established their private lives, quarters, rations, and relationships. Serving in one of the abolitionist Massachusetts

36   Francis Channing Barlow MSS (Massachusetts Historical Society) letter dated December 14, 1861, from Barlow to his mother and his brother Edward.

37   F. C. Barlow MSS (M.H.S.) letter dated December 20, 1861, from Barlow to Edward.

38   Meade MSS (PHS) letter dated September 24, 1861, from Meade to his wife.

regiments, Henry Ropes, a recent Harvard graduate, reached his regiment, the Twentieth, months after it had been formed and assigned a place in the field. To his brother John, also a Harvard alumnus but victim of a childhood spinal injury that made him unable to serve,[39] Henry wrote a series of long, frank letters. To his parents, gentile Boston blue-bloods, he wrote letters on carefully selected subjects that would spare them the disturbing, harsh realities of military life and death: matters of politics to his father and housekeeping to his mother.

Of course, as any junior second lieutenant would, he expressed concern about responsibility, training, and development, not to mention his assignment. "As it is, I may be put in [Company] A, Capt. Tremlett, considered one of the very best places, Whittier 1st Lieutenant. Whittier spoke to me about it. The trouble is that Capt. Shepard likes me, for I do all the work, and he told me he had asked the Colonel for me, and the men like me too. This is of course private. As it is now, I manage the Company myself, the Captain being on the sick list. I do not know what 1st Lieutenant will be appointed here, and this is the great question with me. If there is a real good first, the Company will improve and will be well drilled, and I shall have a pleasant place. Still I should like a real soldier for a Captain, and I cannot hope but I shall be put finally in A."[40]

Then and now, one of the most important parts of an officer's life, especially in any fixed installation, was the officers' mess. Formed in each case by a number of officers who chose—or were ordered—to mess together, its members paid expenses from an account created by a periodic tithe. As one company-grade officer in the Sixty-seventh Ohio wrote home, "the Officers' Mess Room . . . is conducted on the following manner: all the Field, Line and Staff Officers [of the regiment] are united in one Mess; they appoint a committee of one Captain, and 1st Lieutenant and one 2nd Lieutenant who buy the provisions, superintend the cooking and preside at the table and render account to the Mess . . . There being 40 Officers of the Regiment, the average expenses are about from $2.50 to $2.75 per week and the boarding could not be any better. . . ."[41]

Ropes' letters to his mother and father gave partial confirmation to Surgeon Tripler's statement that the men going into the field, especially when they did not have the trappings of a permanent camp, knew little or nothing about caring for themselves. Others had done these tasks for them in civilian life, and the young

---

39   *D.A.B.*, 8, pt. 2, 152.

40   Henry Ropes MSS (B.P.L.) letter dated January 24, 1862, from Henry Ropes to his brother John.

41   Byrne, *Your True Marcus*, 24, letter dated January 9, 1862, from Spiegel to his wife.

officers had always taken them for granted. But they learned quickly to create "the general comfort of a camp," Ropes wrote. "Whittier has had a splendid log hut built, and most of the tents are floored and have fires. We mess in the tents with our Company Officers. So far I have dined at two other tents round. I am to have a stool and table made soon by the Carpenter. These, with a few tin plates and a basin etc. constitute the furniture of the tent. All log huts, stoves, and such luxuries must be left behind on a march . . . I instantly found the need of a servant, and at first thought I would have you send me one down, but I have picked up a boy here ($8 per month and board) who, I think, will do. His name is Corny, and I expect to make a good servant of him . . . You must have a boy to cook, wait, make a fire, get wood, buy things and be generally useful. Niggers are scarce here."[42]

And what better teacher for cooking than his mother, the creator of his previous "home-cooked" meals. "You know I keep house here and have my own cooking done by my boy. But will you give me a few receipts [recipes] to make some simple dishes? Tell me how to make a simple and nourishing soup. I can get rice, salt or a fresh meat, and dried vegetables, finely cut up and pressed. Tell me how you boil the rice and meat. Tell me how to make one or two simple puddings. I cannot often bake, but can always boil and fry. How is dipped toast made? How an omelet? How poached and scrambled eggs? How some simple bread puddings? . . . I forgot boiled beef. Can I make this good?"[43]

Just as Barlow, Spiegel, and Ropes, the better though not the ranking officers in their units, had more than an ordinary share of duties by default, so did Dan Butterfield and other more senior leaders. Then and now, the superior officers trained their junior officers to lead and instruct their men. Like Barlow, Dan Butterfield had begun the war as an enlisted man, first sergeant of the Clay Guards, a battalion of prominent men of the capital even though he was from New York City. By May, he was colonel of the Eighth New York, which led Sandford's column over the Long Bridge into Virginia on May 24. After service with Patterson's ill-fated column in the Valley, Butterfield's studious attention to military affairs, drill, and detail combined with his extraordinary organizational abilities to earn him a promotion to brigadier general of volunteers on September 7, 1861, and assignment to command one of the brigades in Fitz John Porter's crack division with George Morell and John Martindale, both West Point graduates.[44]

42   Henry Ropes MSS (B.P.L.) letter dated January 1, 1862, from Ropes to his brother John.

43   Henry Ropes MSS (B.P.L.) letter dated January 23, 1862, from Ropes to his mother.

44   Heitman, *Historical Register*, 1, 270–271; *D.A.B.*, 2, pt. 1, 372–373; Warner, *Generals in Blue*, 62.

At almost precisely the New Year the long mild fall weather changed to a particularly harsh winter. The balmy weather became snow, ice, rain, sleet, and the inevitable, invincible Virginia mud.[45] In this transformation of weather the business of being an army did not change. On the morning of Sunday, January 18, 1862, two companies of the Eighth Illinois Cavalry joined Howard at his headquarters at 8. Each cavalryman carried saber, carbine, and pistol. When they arrived, Howard invited Major Beveridge, Captain Medill, Captain Hooker, and Chaplain Hard into his quarters where he checked to see that the men had covered the little details.

"Have you a surgeon and an ambulance?" Howard asked. "We may have use for them."

When the column started, rain began to fall. Howard and Major Medill rode in the fog at the head of the column.

"Chaplain," Howard called, "have you no oilcloth? You had better get it out."

The chaplain dismounted, removed the oilcloth from his blanket, and donned it.

"I never saw a regiment so well mounted as yours," said Howard. "The men must take good care of their horses, or they would not look so well with their poor accommodations. Are your carbines loaded?"

"No, Sir," replied Major Beveridge. "The powder is liable to waste traveling and may become damp while it rains. They load easily."

"Yes, yes. But an attack on us will be sudden. Our response to their fire must be instantaneous or we shall be surprised and confused. A warrior must provide always against surprises. But within our lines it is not necessary. At the outpost you will all load."

The rain fell heavily as the column pressed forward. The mud was deep. First, the soldiers passed down a road, then cantered over a plain, then finally rode through woods. At Edsill's Hill two officers joined the head of the column as aides for Howard. The column now marched into a forest on a narrow path. Within half a mile they passed the outposts of the army and moved forward cautiously, never at a pace faster than a walk.

---

45   Comte de Paris MS diary (small diary) (A.N. de la M. de F.) entries dated January 16, 17, 18, 22, 28, 30, 1862; Heintzelman MS diary (small diary) (L.C.) entries dated January 2, 3, 4, 6, 7, 9, 10, 13, 14, 15, 16, 17, 19, 21, 24, 26, 30, see generally entries for February and March, 1862; William Robey Moore MSS (I.H.S.) letter dated January 23, 1862, from Moore to his sister Lizzie; F. C. Barlow MSS (M.H.S.) letter dated January 18, 1862 from Barlow to his mother; Sears, *For Country, Cause & Leader (Haydon Diary)*, 144, entry dated December 9, 1861; 159, entry dated December 28, 1861; 160, entry dated December 29, 1861; 170, entry dated January 10, 1861; 174, entry dated January 15, 1861; 175, entry dated January 18, 1861; 178, entries dated January 21 and 24, 1861; see generally entries for February and March; Judson, *Eighty-third Pennsylvania*, 26, col. 2; Adams, *Story of a Trooper*, 251.

"Major," said Howard, "send out three horsemen as far ahead as they can go within sight. Follow them with a platoon as advance guard. Behind them we will follow with a main column. But behind us let there be a rear guard of a platoon."[46]

Now, the column moved at a rapid walk, then turned from the main road.

"Send forward at full gallop two men as far as they can go and see us." Howard ordered. "Let them pause until the whole column passes, then follow on in our rear."

With this leapfrogging procedure the column continued. The countryside offered excellent opportunities for an ambush or a masked battery. The road was narrow and crooked, the forest so close that the men in the column could not see one hundred feet ahead. In the fog the heavy rain continued to fall. By twos or single-file and without talking, the column continued to move.

CRACK. A rifle on the right.

"What does that mean?" asked Howard. "Was it in our column?"

"No, Sir," replied Major Beveridge.

Silence followed.

Howard was still in command. "Send back the trusty man half a mile in the rear to the right to look out and report if any movement appears on our rear."

The column made its first halt at a stately Virginia mansion. In front was a heavy post and gate that opened to a spacious lawn with graveled roads.

"Send forward three men ahead of me. The staff and aide will go with me."

The balance of the force waited.

Howard and his group drew near the house. A well-dressed servant approached them. He was uncommunicative, cautious, and seemed to know nothing. The small group flanked the barn and drew up in front of the house. A black about twenty years old approached with a pair of steers drawing a pile of wood. Flashing his white teeth and clean gums, he smiled and seemed glad to see the column.

"My name's Noah."

"Noah?" said the chaplain.

"Yes sir, Noah. That's it." He looked as if he wished to be helpful.

They met the widow Fitzhugh, commander of all the property and a kind, communicative lady. After a pleasant discussion, she showed written "protections" signed by Scott and others. Howard and his group remounted and departed.

They met an elderly black wearing spectacles and the venerability of age. He, too, was talkative.

"I have lived here always. My wife is here, too. We never had any children but two little ones I adopted."

---

46   A platoon of infantry was half a company.

Another man appeared, this time a white man named George Seaver, a native of Hanover, Germany, and the gardener for the widow. He said that the steers pulling the wood were the only team they had. "Our whole dependence now. The carriage horses were taken from us by the Cameron Rifles."

Moving slowly and looking sharply in all directions, the column marched again. At last, it paused for dinner. Remaining mounted, each man removed his bread and meat and began to eat. Howard, the major, one of the captains, and a few others gratefully drew on the canteen of coffee carried by the chaplain.

"And now men we will strike off north towards the Fairfax Court House Road," said Howard. "Major, send out a squad to that first left-hand road. See where it leads. Look out sharp. Examine every hiding place. Forward."

Still on the road, the column now passed through open, hilly country. Near a large farmhouse it halted. The great house was empty. Howard and the chaplain went through the yard to the quarters in the back where the slaves lived. A forty-year-old black was in front of a log cabin. They asked who he was.

"My name is Alfred—Alfred Buell—dunno how old I is—was born roun here—ole marse and young massa's gone wid de army—am I for de union? Well, Gemmen, I is a fren to dem whose a fren to me—I ain't gwine to take no sides." He giggled.

Most of the men remained outside. Howard, the surgeon, a reporter, and an aide went inside. In about ten minutes Howard sent one outside.

"Chaplain, the General wishes you to come in."

The chaplain dismounted and stooped to pass through the low cabin door. Howard showed his deeply religious nature.

"Chaplain, I am warming my feet here, and have been talking to these four women about God, and about prayer. They don't pray much. Nor have any preachings or meetings of any kind. Will it be agreeable to you to unite with us who are here in prayer? It will do us all good."

The chaplain found it more agreeable than anything else he had confronted that day.

"Certainly, General Howard. Prayer is a pleasure to me anywhere. Here, most cheerfully I pray. Let us kneel."

The men in the room, including Howard, knelt with uncovered heads. As the chaplain prayed for the men, their comrades, the poor old slaves, and the country, Howard breathed an audible and earnest, "Amen."

The chaplain also prayed for freedom's triumph, for slavery's overthrow, and for peace and rest and joy for the men when they fell, whether on the field or in a quiet grave.

"And now, Lucy," said Howard to the younger black, "Do you remember that short prayer I wanted you to teach the old woman here?"

"I don't jes remember it now, Sir."

"It was this—Lord, let thy holy spirit teach me what is right and good."

"Yes, Sir, I can do that."

Howard continued. "Who do you pray to?"

"The Lord," she said.

"Who is the Lord?"

"Our Savior."

"What do you mean by that?"

"Jesus Christ."

Howard was finishing. "Well, Lucy, you must love him and pray to him and be good. Good-by old mother. Good-by Lucy."

Outside, the four men remounted. The soldier reappeared to replace the parishioner who had prayed inside the shanty. About to start, Howard reined his horse and turned.

"Oh, Alfred, here, I forgot. One question more." He leaned forward in his saddle and whispered in Alfred's ear, "Alfred, do you ever pray?"

"Sometimes, Sir."

"You ought to pray every day."

"Yes, Sir. Maybe I should."

Again, Howard spoke his own feelings. "You must not forget God, for he remembers you all the time."

Alfred had an amazed look on his face. "I guess he do."

Howard spurred his horse and dashed to the main road. The column followed. "No wonder," thought the chaplain, "that at Manassas the then Colonel Howard was as cool under a heavy fire as on dress parade, and the Third Maine was brave and true."[47]

Not so much religious harmony existed in Hooker's division, which manifested the characteristics of the division commander. Many officers had different, less politic methods of dealing with disciplinary problems than Banks. D. S. Benson, an orderly, carried a message from division headquarters for Colonel Small at the camp of the Twenty-sixth Pennsylvania Volunteers. Finding Small not at his headquarters, the orderly, an enlisted man, learned that he could find the colonel in the chaplain's tent. When Benson did not find him there, he asked a private where he could find the lieutenant colonel's tent.

The private said the lieutenant colonel was not in his tent.

---

47   Hard, *Eighth Illinois Cavalry*, 60–64.

"It does not make a damned bit of difference whether he is there or not," said Benson, "as I have been told that Col. Small is there and I want to see him."

"God damn you," the private said. "Don't insult me. I'll have you arrested."

Benson responded, "If you take that as an insult, you might and be damned."

Drunk and not in control of his horse, Benson nearly rode down one of the nearby officers, then went to the lieutenant colonel's tent, where he did not find Colonel Small. A captain repeated that the colonel was in Lieutenant Colonel van Dike's tent.

Benson knew better. He called the captain a damned liar and said, "You can kiss my ass and go to hell."

Finally, Benson found Colonel Small in the mess tent. But the private, in reality an officer, had preceded him. The officer told the colonel he wished to speak to him.

Were General Hooker's "damned messengers" allowed to insult him, he asked. Small answered, "No, by God!"

The orderly, still drunk, rude, and insolent, delivered his packet. "Arrest me, if you please," he said, "and as soon as you like."

Incensed by the orderly's conduct and provoked by his language, the colonel said he never troubled gentlemen to sit as a court martial on such a fellow but had a shorter method for disposing of them. He struck Benson soundly, then told him to leave, adding that he should leave his foul disposition behind when he visited the camp again.

Giving the drunken orderly no time to explain, Small called him a God damned son of a bitch, told him he would have him whipped through his regiment, said he did not allow any God damned general's messenger to insult his captains, and punched him twice more in the face.

"Leave here, you son of a bitch," he concluded.[48]

Other officers experienced disciplinary problems and embarrassment under more ordinary circumstances. In great numbers and in many facilities, the women invariably associated with an army gathered in Washington. On the east bank of the Potomac south of Washington, the men of Hooker's division found access to the capital easier than those linked by the heavily guarded bridges. To help the provost marshal deal with the many problems spawned by a large population of prostitutes—drunkenness, robbery, and assault—Hooker relocated many prostitutes to a

---

48   Hooker MSS (H.L.) letter dated January 24, 1862, from Small to Dickenson and memorandum dated January 22, 1862, from Benson. The text is a reconciliation or composite of the two accounts, which differ surprisingly little.

single area, which came to be known as "Hooker's Division." His name and an association with these women found expression in daily newspapers and would long outlive him.[49]

Major Alfred Napoleon Alexander Duffié, a Frenchman born in Paris, a major in the Second New York Cavalry, and a staff officer for a general, was arrested by a young junior officer of the Eleventh New York Cavalry, then serving as part of the provost marshal's forces in the capital. Aside from being in Washington without written authorization, the major suffered the misfortune of being caught without a pass on the ground floor of one of the capital's many whorehouses. Major Duffié insisted that he could solve the problem by writing a pass and signing the general's name.

The young captain asked if the general were in the city.

Duffié replied that he was.

"Have his papers been countersigned by the provost marshal of this district?"

"They do not need to be," replied Duffié. "He is a general officer and I am his adjutant general. There is the pass for the captain and myself."

The young officer took the pass, read the names, wrote them in his book, then held the pass to the open flame on the chandelier. When the paper caught fire, he dropped it on the table. It was as worthless, he said, as its smoke. He had orders to arrest all officers in the capital without authorization, up to and including the rank of brigadier general.

Stunned, Duffié and his friend looked at each other. The young officer inferred from their expression that he could find "larger game" in the vicinity.

"Gentleman, you are under arrest. Give me your parole of honor that you will report yourselves at the provost-marshal's office tomorrow morning at nine o'clock; or if you refuse, I must lock you up. Will you promise to report to the provost in the morning?"

"Yes, sir. We will report in the morning."

"All right. I won't detain you any longer."

"We are not compelled to leave this place, are we?"

"No, sir. Not unless you want to." The young officer turned to his sergeant while he kept his eye on the two miscreants. "Sergeant, I will be back as soon as I inspect the premises above stairs."

Both Duffié and the other officer flushed. Duffié tried to intercept a bad development. "We are the only gentleman in the place," he said.

---

49   Leech, *Reveille in Washington*, 262–265; Lowry, Thomas P., M.D., *The Story the Soldiers Wouldn't Tell: Sex in the Civil War*, 64 (Mechanicsburg, 1994).

If the young cavalryman had doubts about the existence of bigger prey before the obvious attempt to deflect him, they vanished. Upstairs, he found a brigadier general, who begged to be "let off" and promised to leave the city at once. After a prompt refusal, the officer went downstairs. Major Duffié had overheard the conversation.

"Lieutenant, can't you let us go?"

"No, sir. In the first place, I don't want to, and the second place I dare not. It may be that I am watched now by some secret service detective to see whether I perform my duty."

The major was furious. "Very well, sir. We may meet again under different circumstances," he threatened.

"All right, Major Duffy."

"My name is not Duffy, sir. It is spelled and pronounced D-O-U-FF-Y-A."

The lieutenant had the upper hand, would have the last word, and knew it. "All right, sir. I have got your name as you wrote it on the pass. But, major, Duffy for short is French, you know, and is good enough for me. Good night, gents."

In a rainy, cold night, surrounded by the dead and wounded of a miserable defeat, which was the nadir of the battle of maneuver in American military history, Duffié and the lieutenant would meet again. Duffié's thick accent, lack of fluency, difficulty with idioms, and poor comprehension would identify him to the young cavalryman even in the pitch darkness.[50]

---

50   NA Offs MS Rpts (Duffié), letter dated February 27, 1864; Smith, Thomas West, *The Story of a Cavalry Regiment: Scott's 900 Eleventh New York Cavalry from the St. Lawrence River to the Gulf of Mexico 1861–1865*, 39–40 (Chicago, 1897); Warner, *Generals in Blue*, 131; Heitman, 1, 386; Denison, Frederick, *Sabres and Spurs: the First Regiment Rhode Island Cavalry in the Civil War 1861–1865, its Origins, Marches, Scouts, Skirmishes, Raids, Battles, Sufferings, Victories, and Appropriate Official Papers; with the Roll of Honor and Roll of the Regiment*, 105–106 (Central Falls, 1876); Nash, Eugene Arus, *A History of the Forty-fourth Regiment New York Volunteer Infantry in Civil War, 1861–1865* (Chicago, 1911) 55 (Nash, *Forty-fourth New York*); Bryan, *Eye of the Storm (Sweden Diary)* 9, entry dated January 1, 1862. Men of the provost marshal's department—and later the military police—have bedeviled officers and enlisted men of all ranks for all time and remained immune to retaliation by officers as long as they maintained the smallest appearance of decorum. With ill-concealed delight, they performed their role as keepers of disciplinary standards and good conduct, and some, in the author's experience, made a business of pursuing officers for minor technical infractions.

Chapter 19

The Rise of McClellan's Enemies

Seeing their important goals of emancipation, abolition, and black troops supported by two such unlikely spokesmen as Fremont and Cameron, the Radical Republicans became ardent supporters of both[1] and equally ardent detractors of Stone. To them, the man who opposed emancipation was not just their political opponent, he was probably disloyal, if not a traitor. Nor were Cameron, Fremont, and Cochrane the only military personnel who believed in emancipation, abolition of slavery, an immediate advance, and all-out battles. All these Radical demands had their supporters among McClellan's general officers, with Brigadier General James S. Wadsworth, the wealthy, white-haired patrician from western New York, being one of the most outspoken.

---

1 Thomas, Benjamin P., and Harold Hyman, *Stanton: The Life and Times of Lincoln's Secretary of War* (New York, 1962) 133–135 (Thomas, *Stanton*); Trefousse, Hans L., *The Radical Republicans: Lincoln's Vanguard for Racial Justice* (New York, 1969) 210 (Trefousse, *The Radical Republicans*); Williams, *Lincoln and the Radicals*, 59–60.

A Wadsworth had lived and prospered in America since the 1600s. An earlier James Wadsworth served as a major general in the Connecticut line during the Revolutionary War and after the war as a member of the Continental Congress. In the spring of 1790, his sons William and James left Connecticut for western New York, taking with them sturdy yeomen to assist in the development of their property. With the revenues they generated they continued to buy land until a Wadsworth could ride twenty-eight miles in a single direction without leaving his property.[2] The two Wadsworth brothers created a vast, highly successful farm of crops, cattle, and sheep. When William died without children, he left everything to James and James' children.

Into this family of extraordinary landed wealth was born James Samuel Wadsworth on October 30, 1807, in the little town of Geneseo. Educated in local schools, he then attended Hamilton College for a short time. Finally, he completed his college course at Harvard, which he attended as a junior and senior in the Class of 1828. But he did not bother to obtain a degree.[3] In an indifferent attempt at the law, he attended Yale Law School a short time, read law in the office of Daniel Webster, and finished in a law office in Albany.[4]

Wadsworth focused his attention on the family's business of farming and gradually became the principal supervisor of the family estates. Although he enjoyed and indulged in the pleasures of society and elevated tastes, he used his wealth for the benefit and happiness of others. His excellent management of the farms utilized an untypical tenant system. "This system is scarcely in accordance with the spirit of our Republican institutions," wrote one of his eulogists. Liberal to his tenant farmers, he abated their rents when their crops had been destroyed or injured by insects, floods, or droughts.[5]

In 1842, a stream washed away a railway bridge a few miles east of Syracuse. A small boy and his father stood on the bank watching the workmen make repairs.

2   Pearson, Henry Greenleaf, *James S. Wadsworth of Geneseo, Brevet Major General of United States Volunteers* (New York, 1913) 3, 4–5, 10–21 (Pearson, *Wadsworth*).

3   Allen, Hon. Lewis F., *Memorial of the late Gen. James S. Wadsworth delivered before the New York State Agricultural Society at the Close of its annual Exhibit at Rochester, September 23rd, 1864* (Buffalo, 1864) (pamphlet) 10 (Allen, *Wadsworth Memorial*); Pearson, *Wadsworth*, 22–23.

4   *Proceedings of the Century Association in Honor of the Memory of Brig. Gen. James S. Wadsworth and Colonel Peter A. Porter; with Eulogies Read by William J. Hoppin and Frederick S. Cozzens December 3, 1864* (New York, 1865) 12–13 (Century Association, *Wadsworth Eulogy*) (Pamphlet); Pearson, *Wadsworth*, 22–23.

5   Allen, *Wadsworth Memorial*, 31–33 (pam.).

Walking "through mud and water directing and encouraging the laborers" was a man the boy did not recognize. He asked his father who the man was.

"My son, that is the *first gentleman* in America, James S. Wadsworth of Geneseo!"[6]

Two years later the first gentleman's father died at the age of seventy-six, "leaving his family probably the finest agricultural estate in the country."[7] James assumed management of three-fourths of the estate, the portions belonging to himself and his two sisters.

He made two trips to Europe, the second in 1854 with his wife and children. Shortly after his return he bought a house in New York City on Sixteenth Street, but his country estate in Geneseo remained his principal residence. In 1856 the young but exclusive Century Association, a private organization devoted to "philosophic inquiry and the study of literature and art" elected him to membership. In spite of Wadsworth's relation by marriage to English nobility, his fellow Century member Lathrop Motley described him as "the true, original type of American gentleman—not the pale washed-out copy of the European aristocrat."

Though his father had been a firm Whig, James became a Democrat. His father's extraordinary wealth and associations with important persons of all political parties made James a regular participant in New York's political affairs at a relatively early age. In these activities he became closely aligned with anti-slavery politicians, developing a single-minded opposition to the "peculiar institution" even though his large land holdings and great wealth made him look more like a Southern aristocrat and a conservative Democrat than a Northern businessman and a liberal Republican. Slavery he called "the one great question."[8]

In the political gyrations of these years, the Republican party developed from an amalgamation of Whigs, Free-Soilers, Know-Nothings, Temperancers, anti-slavery Democrats, and other marginal parties. One of the anti-slavery Democrats who first became members of the anti-slavery Free-Soil Party, Wadsworth found his way into the Republican Party. Early, he was designated a state elector for the party and in November of 1860 a district elector for Lincoln and his vice president, Hannabil Hamlin.

---

6   Wadsworth MSS (Univ. of Roch.) letter dated September 25, 1862, from Wilbinton to Wadsworth.

7   Pearson, *Wadsworth*, 10.

8   In his own words he was at the outbreak of the war "barely a Republican, that is, only opposed to the extension of slavery." Wadsworth MSS (Univ. of Roch.) draft letter dated September 14, 1861, from Wadsworth to David Dudley Field, Horace Greeley, S. Robinson, George Opdyke, and Thomas B. Carron.

Between fifty and sixty years of age, Wadsworth was about six feet in height and had a large, spare but well-knit frame, blue eyes, prematurely white hair and side whiskers, and a thin aquiline nose. The left side of his mouth was slightly drawn down from a paralysis suffered when, as a young man, he had ridden from Rochester to Geneseo in a furious snowstorm. Even though he had a disposition amiable, frank, firm,[9] and not quarrelsome, he was always ready to "resent insult or resist oppression." His friendships were fixed, and to assist a friend, he would risk anything. A kind, indulgent, and affectionate husband and father, he enjoyed happy domestic relations, his nature hospitable, and his manner entertaining to his guests. With his generous, liberal, humane, highly intelligent, and well educated temperament, his manner of association was direct, cordial, and genial and his style of conversation always animated, amusing, and instructive.

"If any quality of his mind was conspicuous, it was that of a vigorous common sense, coupled with a ready judgment, applied to all matters which arrested his attention," wrote one of his eulogists.[10] He had "excellent powers of mind . . . His intellectual ability developed rapidly in the later years of his life. He was an original thinker. His judgment was always clear and sound, but he disliked the details of business and the petty cares of an office. He was . . . a capital judge of character and had the art of sifting the knowledge of those who engaged in discussions with him, by putting a few pointed questions."[11]

A few days after Sumter surrendered, Wadsworth became a member of the Union Defense Committee of the City of New York. While working actively to rescue the capital in April and May of 1861, he became the centerpiece in the confrontation between Governor Morgan and the federal government over the two major generalcies and the governors' power to appoint general officers. Under the first call for troops, the number of regiments requested from New York State entitled it to two major generalcies. The first went to John A. Dix.[12] In May Governor Morgan appointed Wadsworth a "Major-General of the Volunteer force called for from this State in compliance with the requisition of the President of the United

---

9   Howard, *Autobiography*, 1, 407; Pearson, *Wadsworth*, 286, n. 1; Doster, *Lincoln and Episodes*, 49.

10   Allen, *Wadsworth Memorial*, 31–33 (pam).

11   Century Association, *Wadsworth Memorial*, 17 (pam.).

12   Pearson, *Wadsworth*, 35, 41–44, 46–47, 50, 55–60, 62; Century Association, *Wadsworth Memorial*, 14, 18, 19, 34 (pam.).

States."[13] The announcement of Wadsworth's appointment prompted the typical response to the appointment of a responsible, prominent citizen without military experience to high rank. "I offer you my very sincere congratulations on this most judicious selection of a gentleman, who whatever he may lack in military experience, possesses the great elements of success, judgment, decision and energy." Wadsworth's correspondent believed that "gentlemen of character and high position should lead in Military as well as in Civil affairs."[14]

Just when the original seventeen regiments of New York troops were about to be organized into two divisions, the first to be commanded by Dix and the second by Wadsworth, the federal general orders of May changed the system; and Secretary of War Cameron insisted that all generals receive their commissions from the federal government rather than from the states. Unless the governor yielded on this point, the secretary said, he would accept no more New York troops. Recognizing the importance of a prompt resolution of this controversy, Wadsworth magnanimously solved the problem by submitting his resignation; and the controversy ended when the federal government made Dix a major general.[15]

After a short stint as a volunteer aide on the staff of General Scott, Wadsworth served McDowell as a volunteer aide with excitable energy, reckless bravery, and considerable distinction. In his report after the battle McDowell praised Wadsworth's services and later recommended to the president that his aide be made a brigadier general of volunteers. Initially, Wadsworth refused the appointment because he had earlier been considered for a major general's commission, but his friends on McDowell's staff convinced him that he should take it and also assured him that a West Point graduate would be assigned to him as adjutant general of his brigade. A member of the Bull Run pool, he received a commission as a brigadier general on August 9 and a brigade of New York regiments with headquarters at Arlington, Virginia. The brigade was part of McDowell's division, both McDowell and Wadsworth being pleased with this assignment.[16]

13   Wadsworth MSS (L.C.) General Orders No. 40, dated May 16, 1861, State of New York, Adjutant General's Office.

14   Wadsworth MSS (Univ. of Roch.) letter dated May 17, 1861, from King to Wadsworth.

15   Wadsworth's biographer Pearson concedes that the federal government had to control the appointment of general officers and therefore reject Governor Morgan's claim on Wadsworth's behalf. *Loc. cit.*, 64.

16   Pearson, *Wadsworth*, 78, 81, 82.

From New York City's Union Defense Committee, he received an extract of the proceedings of the Executive Committee and a laudatory covering letter. They noted the Committee's "high gratification" at the "spirited conduct and gallant bearing shown by one of their number" at the recent Bull Run battle. "Having declined the Commission of Major General tendered to him by the Executive of this State, which did not confer an Active Command in the field, Mr. Wadsworth volunteered his services on the staff of the Commanding General immediately before the battle . . . The bravery and efficiency of Major Wadsworth have been warmly commended and gratefully recognized by the Government in the appointment of Brigadier General of Volunteers." In the covering letter, his correspondent said, "Permit me to add my personal congratulations on the brilliant entrance you have made into the Military Service of the Country. I sincerely hope that this brief experience may lead to still higher distinction and other equally well deserved honors."[17] To one of his fellow brigade commanders he said, "If my father was alive now and would not devote his mind, body, and estate to this cause, I could not respect him."[18]

Then—as now—some officers believed it important that their station as commanding officers be different from their enlisted men and sought their comfort when in the field. In many ways these are sound concepts of leadership, but Wadsworth did not live by them. Above any touch of affectation, he identified himself with his men, associated with his enlisted men, and wore a common, light blue army overcoat that did not set him apart. He carried a curved saber of ancient pattern, which had belonged to his ancestor Major General Wadsworth.[19] Although he appreciated the elegant things of life and the adornments of art, he did not make an idle display of luxury;[20] nor did his quarters in the field speak of high station. He generally lived like a common soldier, his furniture being limited to a few broken stools, doors taken off the hinges for tables, and boards collected from the garden as benches.[21]

As he had for his tenant farmers, he took special pains to care for his soldiers. Nothing was too trivial for his personal attention if it related to the health or comfort of his troops. Frequently, he inspected the guard house, the kitchens, the sinks, and the stables, paying particular attention to the stables because of his great inter-

---

17　Wadsworth MSS (L.C.) letter dated August 20, 1861, from Prosper Wetmond of the Union Defense Committee of the Citizens of New York to Wadsworth with enclosure.

18　Keyes, *Fifty Years*, 437.

19　Doster, *Lincoln and Episodes*, 49–50.

20　Allen, *Wadsworth Memorial*, 34–35 (pam.).

21　De Trobriand, *Four Years*, 103–104.

est in the well-being of the horses. For long hours he would stand in the snow and mud instructing his men on the building of chimneys and fireplaces. On a cold winter's morning at 4 A.M., he would rouse a regimental commander to accompany him on a tour of the camp to see if the men's huts were properly warmed and ventilated. He would enter a hut, check the stove and chimney, and sniff the air to determine whether the conditions were healthy.[22]

A sergeant and another enlisted man, after recuperating from wounds, left their hospital in Washington and went to a barber shop, where they met the general having his hair cut. After they left the barber shop, the enlisted men went to Willard's Hotel. Although officers were being served at the bar, the bartender told them that liquor could not be sold to soldiers.

In the lobby they encountered Wadsworth again. He shook his head with good humor when he saw them leave the bar.

"Well, boys, how are you enjoying yourselves? Been after something to drink, I suppose."

"Yes, General. We asked for some ale, but as we are only enlisted men and do not support shoulder straps, we have been refused though there's half a dozen officers in there already half tipsy."

"Well, well, they won't refuse me, so come along."

"A bottle of champagne and some glasses," said Wadsworth to the barkeeper. He ignored the salutes of the officers standing nearby. "Now, boys, here's to General McClellan and his army. You'll like that toast."

"Couldn't have a better one, General, if you'd tried for a week," said the enlisted man enthusiastically as he drained his glass.

"Now, sergeant, I'll bid you a good day. Good luck to you both," said Wadsworth, leaving the two enlisted men to finish the bottle.[23]

Of incorruptible integrity, he held those around him to the same high standard. A close relative held a position as commissary officer in one of the Carolina departments. He came to Washington to ask for a transfer to some other field, saying that it was impossible for an honest man to continue in the midst of such corruption.

"Then you are just the man to put a stop to it," Wadsworth responded and gave him peremptory orders to return without the transfer.[24]

22   Gates, *Ulster Guard*, 154.

23   Williams, *Bullet and Shell*, 79–82.

24   Doster, *Lincoln and Episodes*, 50.

His courage, often demonstrated by a rash indifference to the risk of death, would become legendary in the Army. The first time Keyes relieved him as general officer of the day near Munson's Hill, the Confederates held a thick wood on the far side of an open field. While showing Keyes the location of the pickets, Wadsworth began to lead him directly across the field. Keyes thought they would be foolhardy to expose themselves at short range to Confederate sharpshooters when they were both in full uniform and did not need to cross the field.[25]

With his nervous, almost hyperactive personality, Wadsworth became restless while the army lay camped in Virginia during the winter of 1861–1862. He would seek consent from headquarters to send foraging parties through enemy lines. One of his foraging expeditions was so risky that he took almost his entire brigade.[26]

But as hard as he worked, as diligently as he tried, as unstinting as he was of his personal circumstances in order to be a good officer for his men, he remained generally ignorant of military principles and struck some as an inferior commander of a larger military unit.[27] Although no one doubted his honesty or sincerity, some suspected that he adopted the military opinions of his political associates and close friends in Washington. Without regard for practical, military considerations like weather, condition of the roads, and lines of supply, he and the Radicals shared a strident desire for the army to become aggressive.[28] On Christmas, he complained to McDowell that a day or two earlier his horse had sunk to its fetlocks in mud when he rode across the parade ground after a light rain.[29] But the next day he told the Joint Committee that the roads were "remarkably good for the season. Perhaps not once in twenty years have the roads at Christmas been in as good condition as they are now. Having had this long period of dry weather, with but one rain, the roads are very good." As an apparently irrelevant afterthought, he added, "They are easily affected by rain. Even the rain of the other day had a great deal of effect upon them."[30]

25   Keyes, *Fifty Years*, 437.

26   Nevins, *Wainwright Journals*, 166, 171–172, entries dated February 8 and March 12, 1863; Gates, *Ulster Guard*, 164.

27   Nevins, *Wainwright Journals*, 171–172, entry dated March 12, 1863.

28   Gibbon, John, *Personal Recollections of the Civil War* (New York and London, 1928; Morningside edition, 1978) 15 (Gibbon, *Recollections*).

29   *C.C.W.*, 1, 133 (McDowell).

30   McClellan MSS (L.C.) letter dated January 31, 1876, from Davis to McClellan; *C.C.W.*, 1, 146 (Wadsworth).

Virginia mud left an indelible mark on the memory of every man who experienced it. Typical of the comments of many, the chaplain of the Irish Brigade wrote after the war about the area occupied by the Army of the Potomac in 1861, "Everyone who campaigned in Virginia will agree with me in the statement that the Virginia mud, after winter rains, is the worst mud he ever encountered, except, perhaps, the 'gumbo' of Dakota and parts of Texas. The soil is a reddish clay, and very porous. I have pushed down a pole with my hands, nearly ten feet in Virginia soil, and have had my powerful horse bogged in an ordinary highland corn-field . . . Our camp was laid out in streets, and the army regulations, fully carried out, conduced to make the men as comfortable as possible; but these streets, rained on continually, worked up by the tramping of the horses and the heavy wheels of the loaded army wagons, were a sight! They resembled exactly, except as to color, the mud-pits where clay is mixed for the manufacture of brick. Then, too, the roads passing back to Alexandria from the camp, and toward Washington, and even in Washington, on all the unpaved streets . . . were in a most terrible condition. One day I saw an officer attempt to cross the street in front of my tent in Camp California. When he reached the center, his boots sank so deep in the tough clay that he was obliged to call a soldier to dig him out with a spade. Even then, as he attempted to pull out one leg the other would sink, and so on, till it became impossible for him to extricate himself except by pulling his feet out of his boots and escaping in his stocking feet."[31] After a winter rain the roads would freeze and thaw, according to the local citizens, and would become so bad that no one could go to church. Wagons would cut their surface and sink; and once off the road, a wagon or a piece of artillery would sink to the axle in the mud.[32]

Nevertheless, Wadsworth believed that McClellan should begin a campaign and that he should not put the army into winter quarters. The day after Christmas he told the Joint Committee that the federal army was largely superior to the Confederates in numbers, that it had vast superiority in artillery, and that nothing had been gained by waiting the last six weeks. The troops had improved a little in drill and the officers become a little more familiar with tactics; but the general improvement was insignificant, he said. The troops themselves were in good spirits and had not abandoned the idea of an active campaign during the winter. If the army learned that it was going into winter quarters, it would become demoralized, and the volunteers

---

31   Corby, William, C. S. C., *Memoirs of Chaplain Life: Three Years with the Irish Brigade in the Army of the Potomac* (New York, 1992) 22–23 (Corby, *Memoirs*).

32   *C.C.W.*, 1, 132 (McDowell); Gibbon, *Recollections*, 15.

would be very difficult to retain. A movement, he told the committee, should be made as soon as possible.[33]

Two weeks later he wrote to Senator Charles Sumner, one of his long-time correspondents, that he considered the policy of raiding the Confederates at unguarded points to be "pusillanimous and cowardly" when the main Confederate army offered battle in sight of the Capitol, but McClellan would not accept the challenge. Wadsworth thought the army was depressed and discouraged by this. "The despondency and disgust," he wrote, "is almost universal." He thought the army had lost confidence in McClellan and the secretary of war.[34]

Wadsworth's partisan alignment with the abolitionist Radical Republicans became well-known, and if any doubt existed about his opinions on slavery, they became clearly, publicly strident for abolitionism. The *Daily Observer*, a Democratic newspaper of Utica, printed a letter from an infantryman of the One Hundred Seventeenth New York proving that the goals of the army and the politicians were not uniform. "The radicals serenaded Gen. Wadsworth the other night," the letter said, "and he made a speech in which the everlasting nigger played the principal part. It was nigger at the beginning, nigger in the middle, and nigger at the close."[35]

His attitude turned harshly against McClellan with outspoken vituperations.[36] In November, Bernard Welch of Buffalo, New York State's commissary general and a member of Governor Morgan's staff, visited Washington. Having been on very friendly terms with Wadsworth for a long time, Welch went to his camp but declined the general's offer to remain overnight. Wadsworth ordered the mess officer to prepare a supper, to which he invited the brigade staff officers and the regimental colonels.[37]

While they enjoyed the meal, the conversation turned to McClellan. Immediately, Wadsworth began to abuse the commanding general, declaring him inefficient because he did not intend to move and saying that, if the Army remained in camp all winter, a mutiny would occur before spring. The major general, he asserted, had not

---

33   *C.C.W.*, 1, 148–149 (Wadsworth).

34   Pearson, *Wadsworth*, 102, 103. This letter and others to Sumner from Wadsworth, mentioned in Pearson, *supra*, do not appear in the encyclopedic microfilm of Sumner's correspondence created by University Microfilm, Inc.

35   Jackson, Harry F., and O'Donnell, Thomas E., eds., *Back Home in Oneida: Herman Clarke and his Letters*, 44, letter from a member of the One Hundred Seventeenth New York, published in the Utica *Daily Chronicle* for October 7, 1862 (Syracuse, 1965).

36   Military Historical Society of Massachusetts MSS (John C. Ropes letters) letter dated December 19, 1893, from Franklin to Ropes.

37   James G. Bennett MSS (L.C.) addendum dated March 12, 1862, to letter dated March 12, 1862, from Calkin to Hudson.

been in any battle in West Virginia, had not planned the engagements, and had not shown the least qualification for his current position. He also insinuated that McClellan was disloyal because he refused to move even though he could, he was holding back to encourage a compromise, he wanted recognition of the South by the European powers, and he hoped for a final separation of the South. All this, Wadsworth concluded, McClellan did to preserve slavery.

Welch called him outside. That kind of talk about General McClellan before his officers, he said, was improper. He thought it would have a mutinous effect and destroy the confidence of the officers in the army commander. Seeing this had no effect, he suggested that it was in bad taste, that McClellan was his superior, and that McClellan could disgrace him at any moment. The threat of personal harm never deterred Wadsworth from any course, certainly not on matters of strong conviction. He declared Welch's points to be accurate but said he did not care who heard him.

On February 22 a member of the New York State Senate from one of the western districts visited Washington. Knowing Wadsworth well, he drove to his camp through mud and sleet that made the roads impassable for artillery and trains. He found Wadsworth growling about the peacefulness of the army. Before officers and enlisted men he denounced McClellan in bitter terms for disloyalty and incompetency. Wadsworth's complaints mirrored the points in several letters that had been published in the *Tribune*, and his language seemed identical with the most bitter of them. Either he had written the letters, the senator concluded, or the writer had received the information from him.[38]

Wadsworth did not stand alone, nor were the incidents involving him unique. Other high-ranking officers behaved in ways that were overtly hostile to McClellan.

Just as a strong clique of McClellan supporters grew in the Army of the Potomac, an active group of critics began to coalesce, and its members were not insignificant. John G. Barnard and Stuart Van Vliet, both department heads on McClellan's staff, joined line officers like Silas Casey, Joseph Hooker, and Philip Kearny.[39] Abolitionist Republican West Point graduates like David Hunter and Abner

---

38   James G. Bennett MSS (L.C.) letter dated March 12, 1862, from Calkin to Hudson. For a different interpretation of essentially the facts from the same sources, *see* Mahood, Wayne, *General Wadsworth: the Life and Times of Brevet Major General James S. Wadsworth* (Cambridge, 2003) chaps. 8 and 9 (Mahood, *Wadsworth*).

39   McClellan MSS (L.C.) letter dated November 14, 1864, from Burns to McClellan; Smith MS rem. (V.H.S.) n.p., first folio; Kearny MSS (L.C.) letters dated October 1, October 11, and December 3, 1861, from Kearny to Parker. The Smith MS rem. are in the form of a lengthy handwritten letter to his daughter on long paper. The pages are unnumbered. Long after the author completed his research in the MS rem, they were published; but citations to the MS will be used here because they appear in that form in the author's research notes.

Doubleday were few in number but sharp critics of McClellan. Others not so visible but important to the success of McClellan's efforts were hostile to him. In the War Department the officers in command of the bureaus, Commissary, Quartermaster, Engineer, Ordnance, and others, had been hostile since his arrival.[40] Quartermaster General Montgomery Meigs, having already shown great ability and initiative in the rescue of Fort Pickens, had earned the respect of the president and the secretary of state; and his opinions must have had some effect.

At the same time Radical groups played their own potentially divisive game of favorites. Delegations from the states of Pennsylvania and Maine visited Heintzelman in January to speak of his career and his future assignments. "Parties influential," Heintzelman described them in his diary, wanted to press for a separate, independent command of 50,000 men he could use to cross the Occoquan and cut Confederate communications. Some senators wanted him placed at the head of the Army of the Potomac, and one had come to his house to tell his wife that, if he would join the Radicals, he would be vaulted to the head of the Army of the Potomac in twenty-four hours. She had been in the army too long. Her husband belonged to no party and was not a Radical, she told him.[41] Cranky and outspoken but unwilling to intrigue against his commanding officer, Heintzelman himself refused their suggestions. Nevertheless, these efforts became known to McClellan, who developed "some feeling against me," Heintzelman noted later, "preventing as cordial intercourse as there might have been. I have no doubt but this colored his conduct towards me all the campaign." Although Heintzelman bore no ill feelings toward the major general, he was a caustic critic who spoke his mind at will, and with the maneuvering of others to create an independent command within McClellan's Army of the Potomac, Heintzelman must have seemed to be part of the growing hostile forces.[42] Speaking publicly and violently, Seward's clerk Count Gurowski called McClellan both a traitor and a secessionist.[43] The general's early powerful friends among the Radical Republicans had begun to turn on him.

40   Century Company MSS (New York Public Library) letter dated May 1, 1888, from Benjamin to Johnson.

41   Heintzelman MS diary (large diary) (L.C.) entry dated December 13, 1861.

42   Heintzelman MSS (L.C.) handwritten notes by Heintzelman on the pamphlet by General de Peyster "Heintzelman: the first Commander of the Third Corps;" MS diary (large diary) entries dated January 20, 1862, and May 6, 1862 [??].

43   Sparks, David S., ed., *Inside Lincoln's Army: The Diary of General Marsena R. Patrick, Provost Marshal General, Army of the Potomac* (New York and London, 1964) 59, entry dated March 22, 1862.

Much was known about McClellan in July of 1861 when Scott called him to Washington: his friendship with the southern Regular Army officers now in the rebel service, his longstanding status as a Democrat, his Democratic friendships, his opposition to unregulated abolition, and the incident with Simon Buckner. But none of these had been sufficient to prevent Lincoln and the cabinet from giving him command of the Union's largest and most important army or later putting him in command of all the armies of the United States. In the late fall and early winter these facts and others, innocent in July, became sinister evidence of disloyalty for those dissatisfied with McClellan's prosecution of the war.

His dignified reserve became a target for men willing to twist insignificant facts. Comparing him to an unsavory American adventurer in Central America, George Wilkes wrote in the *Spirit of the Times*, "what was mistaken . . . for profundity, and great reserve, was really vacuity . . . he never had a plan or could comprehend today what would be good for him tomorrow."[44]

Transformed, criticism became serious charges. Writing about McClellan's prewar activities, Wilkes said, "At an early period, we find McClellan deeply identified with filibustering schemes, and finally trace him to a prominent command in the Lone Star Association. The objects of that organization were, notoriously, the expansion and perpetuation of slavery, by the forcible conquest of Cuba and its annexation to the South."[45] Not troubled by inconsistency, the rumor mongers also made him a participant in the Quitman scheme to sever New England, the troublemaker, and replace the loss by annexing Cuba and Central America. This, too, would permit the preservation and expansion of slavery.[46]

44   Wilkes, George, *McClellan: from Ball's Bluff to Antietam* (Philadelphia, 1863) 7, article entitled "Is McClellan a Hero?" in *The Spirit of the Times* for July 9, 1862 (Wilkes, *McClellan*) (pam). Published during the war but after McClellan had been relieved from command of the Army of the Potomac, this pamphlet collects articles written by Wilkes and published in his newspaper from July 9, 1862, to March 30, 1863. Although they contain the usual protestations of sincere objectivity, they are actually a series of unsupportable, deranged charges against McClellan.

45   Wilkes, *McClellan*, 9, article entitled "McClellan inside and out" in *The Spirit of the Times* for August 4, 1862.

46   Williams, *Garfield letters*, 314, memorandum dated October 12, 1862. To consider an issue beyond the scope of this work and perhaps beyond the author, one can consider slavery and states' rights, which caused the war? Sound analytical and well-researched arguments spring forth for both historical views. But in the end the thinker cannot escape the fact that the world at this time slowly turned against slavery, just as it would against apartheid a century later, making both long-term impossibilities and disgracing the supporters as historical figures. Applying the same reasoning to the most current, similar issue, Muslims and the use of terrorism (or the supercession of infidel religious), who can take the Muslims seriously as a long-term historical

According to the *Philadelphia Daily News*, McClellan, Albert Sidney Johnston, G. W. Smith, and other officers now serving in the Confederate army had agreed to accept $10,000 each and rights in Cuba to resign from the army and join the Lone Star expedition.[47] Before this, Secretary of War Jefferson Davis had supposedly sent McClellan "stealthily" to Cuba to make "military observations." Davis also rewarded him by promoting him to a captaincy in the infantry, followed by his position as chief of the Delafield Commission, the United States group sent to report on the Crimean War.[48]

When war began, he had supposedly written Jefferson Davis to request a commission as a high-ranking officer in the Confederate Army.[49] General David Hunter's adopted daughter, married to a Confederate general and living in Georgia, supposedly reported by letter to her stepfather that she had seen evidence of McClellan's overtures to Davis.[50] Of course, this was nonsense. Although no one had any evidence to sustain the charge, it circulated as true among those who wanted to believe it.[51]

He was a Democrat, even worse, a Breckinridge Democrat.[52] This meant he had attempted in 1860 to throw the election into the House of Representatives in order to elect a candidate who would preserve slavery through compromise. Or by

---

force? Their attitudes toward other religions, dissenters' rights, and the place and rights of women have been and are being rejected worldwide, no differently than human slavery and apartheidism and segregation. Whether the correct view, as the course of events would define it, would result in regulated abolition and assimilation as McClellan foresaw it, "compensated abolishment" and perhaps colonization under Lincoln's early view, or free-fall abolition and assimilation as the Radicals pursued it awaited the historical outcome—but all headed for the end of slavery and McClellan stood firmly committed to that end. All this makes his unrecorded participation in the Lone Star scheme truly unlikely.

47   Philadelphia *Daily News*, dated July 28, 1862.

48   Wilkes, *McClellan*, 10, article entitled "McClellan inside and out" in *The Spirit of the Times* for August 4, 1862.

49   *M.O.S.*, 38.

50   Williams, *Garfield Letters*, 314–315, memorandum dated October 12, 1862.

51   This is one of the few absurd charges about McClellan's loyalty that he denied in his memoirs, *M.O.S.*, 38; and the incredible nook-and-cranny research devoted to the American Civil War, especially in the last few decades, has produced nothing to prove that he wrote to Davis at all, let alone to request a commission in the Confederate army. For inconclusive negative evidence, see generally Crist and Dix, *Papers of Jefferson Davis*, 7, which shows nothing from McClellan in spite of extraordinary research.

52   After he graduated from West Point, he and his schoolmate William W. Burns, Class of 1847, spent one of McClellan's long evenings with Breckinridge, McClellan MSS (L.C.) letter dated October, 1885, from Burns to McClellan; Warner, *Generals in Blue*, 56.

splitting the Democratic Party between Douglas and Breckinridge he would assure the election of Lincoln, thus giving the Southern states their excuse for secession and independence.[53]

His best friends in the Army of the Potomac in the fall of 1861, Baldy Smith, Fitz John Porter, and William B. Franklin, Democrats, graduates of West Point, and men of suspect loyalty,[54] attracted the hostile attention of the Radical Republicans as well. Rising in importance were others who would serve in the Army of the Potomac throughout the war and remain loyal to McClellan after it became dangerous to their careers,[55] superior men like John Gibbon and Andrew Atkinson Humphreys, both of whom would end the war as skillful and successful corps commanders; Henry Jackson Hunt, the finest artilleryman on both sides; and James C. Duane of the Corps of Engineers.[56]

Outside the army his friends and associates included too many Democrats and men thought to be copperheads, men like Clement Vallandigham, Samuel L. M. Barlow, August Belmont, and John Jacob Astor. Men of great wealth, Barlow, Belmont, and Astor had become his confidential advisers, served on his staff, or fomented presidential aspirations in his mind.[57]

The Buckner incident had proven two things: McClellan believed he could do anything with a pure heart and suffer no adverse consequences, and he was truly naive. If McClellan's account and the supporting letters of Douglas and Key were to be believed—they should have been and they apparently were—he had acted in a

53   Wilkes, *McClellan*, 10, article entitled "McClellan inside and out" in *The Spirit of the Times* for August 4, 1862. McClellan considered himself a Douglas Democrat, the wing of the Democratic Party loyal to the Union and generally located in the North. *M.O.S.*, 34–36. Breckinridge had favored compromise with the South on slavery and independence; and it was known that McClellan, as a young officer, had met Breckinridge and been friends with him. McClellan MSS (L.C.) letter dated October (n.d.), 1885, from Burns to McClellan.

54   Fitz John Porter MSS (L.C.) letters dated May 9, 1890, and September 26, 1893, from Franklin to Porter; White, Leonard D., *The Jacksonians: A Study in Administrative History, 1829–1861*, 208–212 (White, *Jacksonians*).

55   McClellan MSS (L.C.) letter dated January 12, 1865, from Gibbon to McClellan. Gibbon, by that time a major-general in command of a corps, wrote, "I suppose one may correspond with you now without subjecting himself to the charge of being a traitor."

56   Chandler MSS (L.C.) letter dated July 5, 1861, from Doubleday to Chandler; Niven, *Chase Correspondence*, 3, 211–214 letter dated June 17, 1862, from Keyes to Chase; Skelton, *American Profession of Arms*, 350–351; Hoffman, Edward M., *The Old Army: A Portrait of the American Army in Peacetime, 1784–1898* (New York and Oxford, 1986) 92–96 (Coffman, *Old Army*).

57   Keyes, *Fifty Years*, 441; Smith MS rem. (V.H.S.) n.p., first folio. Smith described Barlow, probably unfairly, as "an avowed sympathizer with the South."

most loyal and devoted way without political guile. Now, however, the Buckner incident proved that he could not rise above conduct that appeared wrong even if he
did have a pure heart. To his enemies it proved that he had remained neutral toward
Kentucky while its governor Beriah Magoffin tried to achieve secession. The day
Buckner's letter became public a Philadelphian urged Chase to take prompt action
against the Magoffin-McClellan "compact." He wanted McClellan "removed at
once. I urged Blair before the meeting of the Cabinet to take action . . . Can that
Maj. Gen. not be cashiered if that be true?"[58]

If not from general knowledge, certainly from the Buckner incident Lincoln
and the government knew that McClellan had not limited his friendships in the military to Northerners or to men of unimpeachable Union loyalty. A European officer
who briefly visited both armies a few days after Bull Run and who met Beauregard,
Johnston, McDowell, and McClellan described the alumni of West Point and the
comradeship existing among them. "The whole affair seems to be in the hands of
friends . . . On both sides, they know each other intimately, and I must add that we
found in both camps—almost everywhere, indeed—sentiments of mutual esteem
for former friends, now implacable enemies."[59]

The attitude of the Southerners toward McClellan, particularly of the higher-
ranking Confederate officers who had known him before the war, worked against
him. Proud of the respect his adversaries gave him, McClellan held that pride, uninterrupted, long after the war.[60] Others saw Confederate respect in a different
light. "We can not understand," wrote Wilkes in the *Spirit of the Times*, "the secret
of that wondrous approbation with which the high appointment of the young captain was received by Southern generals and Dixie journals. The veil was lifted, too,
from what had puzzled us the most, and that was, the miraculous unanimity with
which every man of secession principles and doubtful loyalty among us, agreed
upon his transcendent talents as a chieftain . . . Throughout the South the same sentiment was visible, and we would continually hear the Confederate Journals saying,
that the Yankees had but one great general, and the Abolitionists were trying to
crush him."[61]

58   Chase MSS (U.P.I.) letter dated June 24, 1861, from Stone to Chase.

59   Pisani, *Napoleon in America*, 109.

60   Sears, *McClellan's Correspondence*, 71, letter dated July 30, 1861, from McClellan to his
wife; *M.O.S.*, 35–36.

61   Wilkes, *McClellan*, 10, article entitled "McClellan inside and out" in *The Spirit of the
Times* for August 4, 1862.

In fact, many of McClellan's prominent admirers in 1861 were Northerners with Southern principles.[62] This would not have concerned Scott. It probably never concerned Lincoln. Seeing McClellan in the afterglow of the North's first significant military victory, the cabinet and the members of Congress suffered no distress when they brought him East. They accepted these associations as an immaterial characteristic of their best military hope.

But some came to believe he did not wish to crush the South in battle. To be sure, he wanted to win battles, they thought; but in the end he sought to prevail by "strategy," wanted to terminate the war by a negotiated peace that would preserve slavery, and even wanted to confirm the South's independence. The Radicals wanted a war that would not end until one combatant lay dead on the ground, the other standing over him, bloody but victorious.[63]

In many cases the "charges," drawn from indisputable facts like the Buckner incident, could not be disproven because the objective facts stood clear and the inferences remained a matter of free choice. In others, like the alleged correspondence with Jefferson Davis about a commission in the Confederate service, McClellan's supporters could hardly disprove the charges by obtaining evidence from Davis and his staff in 1861 and 1862.

Meanwhile, McClellan's early romance with the press came to an end. By November, the unanimous support had evaporated, and some of the newspapers had begun to criticize him for his failure to advance, the lack of battles, his policy on slavery, and "factual" discoveries casting doubt on his loyalty. They depicted him as part of the West Point aristocracy that displaced more able men like John Fremont and Franz Sigel.[64]

Gradually, the representatives of the press became pro-McClellan or anti-McClellan. His loyal supporters, in the army and out, tried to maintain favorable

---

62   Keyes, *Fifty Years*, 441.

63   Porter MSS (L.C.) letter dated January 21, 1892, from Franklin to Porter; draft letter dated July 10, 1892, from Porter to Scott of the *Atlantic Monthly*; Wilkes, *McClellan*, 10–11, article entitled "McClellan inside and out" in *Spirit of the Times*, for August 4, 1862; James G. Bennett MSS (L.C.) letter dated March 12, 1862, from Calkin to Hudson; Fahrney, Ralph Ray, *Horace Greeley and the Tribune in the Civil War* (Cedar Rapids, Iowa, 1936) 97 (Fahrney *Greeley*).

64   Fahrney, *Greeley*, 96–97. A member of the Republican Party with a strong distaste for the southern aristocracy and a resulting hostility to slavery as a pillar supporting the southern, planter upper class, Sigel benefitted on repeated occasions from Radical support rising from his political and social opinions rather than his battlefield successes in Europe or America, another example of the military incompetence of the Radicals. Generally, Engle, Stephen D., *Yankee Dutchman: The Life of Franz Sigel*, 41–42 (Fayetteville, 1993).

press relations for him; and some papers would support him to the end. Others like George Wilkes' *Spirit of the Times* and Horace Greeley's influential *Tribune,* would drift slowly from support to opposition, then to criticism, and finally to hostility.[65] Emerging from the embarrassed silence that followed his "Forward to Richmond" cry, the Bull Run defeat, and his subsequent suggestion to Lincoln that the Union capitulate, Greeley began to return to the manger of dogs baying at the moon for an advance.[66] By the middle of October the *Tribune* had begun to express a decline of confidence in McClellan.[67]

As fall grew into December and the days grew colder, the anti-McClellan forces became more openly critical. They also began to work together, taking strength from each other.[68] Unfortunately, the press wrote about McClellan while it had surrendered to "intemperate personal controversy" and "partisan distortion of the news."[69]

When he had his first meeting with the press in August, McClellan discounted the maps and diagrams of the pictorial press. They created no threat to security, he had said. But events after that changed his attitude. He believed leaks had compromised his plan to capture Munson's and Upton's Hills. His intelligence officer Allan Pinkerton complained that press coverage disclosing his identity, among other things, made the performance of his function increasingly difficult.[70]

On December 4, the *New York Times* published a rough map of the federal works on the Virginia side of the Potomac and gave the location of the divisions there.[71] McClellan's tolerance had come to an end. Enclosing a copy of the offending issue of the *Times* with a letter, he asked Cameron for the equivalent of the

---

65   Wilkes, *McClellan*, 3, publisher's preface; 7, article entitled "Is McClellan a hero" in *The Spirit of the Times,* for July 9, 1862.

66   Andrews, *North Reports*, 149–155; Williams, *Lincoln and the Radicals*, 31; Horner, Harland Hoyt, *Lincoln and Greeley*, 231–235 (Urbana, Illinois, 1953); Fahrney, *Greeley*, 83–84; Ingersoll, L. D., *Life of Horace Greeley*, 394–395 (Chicago, 1873).

67   Fahrney, *Greeley*, 91.

68   Smith MS rem. (V.H.S.) n.p., first folio. Noting that McClellan's enemies were heterogeneous, Smith commented that they, "taken together and working for a common purpose, were formidable."

69   *D.A.B.*, 8, pt. 1, 407–408; Maverick, Augustus, *Henry J. Raymond and the N.Y. Press* (Hartford, 1870) 170ff (Maverick, *Raymond*).

70   McClellan MSS (L.C.) letters dated October 10, 11, 12, and 13, 1862, from Pinkerton ("E. J. Allen") to McClellan.

71   *New York Times*, December 4, 1861, p. 1.

death penalty for a newspaper. "This is clearly giving aid comfort and information to the enemy, and is evidently a case of treasonable action, as clear as any that can be found . . . I have therefore to represent that the interest of our arms requires the suppression of this treasonable sheet, and urgently recommend that the necessary steps to suppress the paper may be taken at once."

Cameron thought McClellan's complaints "just," but he was unwilling to precipitate a struggle with the press so early in the war with the Confederacy. He was also skeptical about the charges of treason and intentional aid to the enemy. Suppression of a major daily newspaper he would not do; but he wrote an informal note to Henry J. Raymond, the editor and co-founder of the *Times*, in which he noted the importance of avoiding conduct of this sort in the future.[72] If the press had not been divided about McClellan before this, it certainly split now. He had called for the suppression of a major daily newspaper in one of the most important cities in the country. An unforgivable act.

The incident passed, but the participants did not forget it, nor did it pass without effect. Raymond wrote to Wadsworth a short time later, "I have very carefully abstained from criticizing Army matters partly because the public mind is morbidly averse to such criticism—or has been until very lately—and partly because McClellan for some reason or other has conceived a special spite against the *Times* and has been watching a chance to do us essential damage."[73]

Other sources than the press contributed the hostile written word. During the next twenty-four months a number of critical pamphlets, followed by small hostile books, appeared, and the authors covered a broader range than the penny-a-line newspaper reporters. Charles Ellet, an engineer with an international reputation and a writer of widely read scientific works, was a skillful controversialist with a venomous pen. Fifty-one years old, tall and slender, cursed with uncertain health after the age of thirty, intimately familiar with the geography of Virginia, and self-taught on military strategy, Ellet had lived since 1857 in the District of Columbia, where his considerable engineering achievements[74] made access to presidents and other important officials relatively easy. He believed he knew exactly how to save the Union.

---

72   Raymond MSS (N.Y.P.L.) letter dated December 11, 1861, from Cameron to "the proprietor of the *New York Times*"; Raymond responded with a defense of his conduct and an explanation of his sources, all, he claimed, legitimate and public. Ibid., letter dated December 13, 1861, from Raymond to Cameron; *D.A.B.*, 8, pt. 1, 408–409.

73   Wadsworth MSS (L.C.) letter dated February 9, 1862, from Raymond to Wadsworth.

74   *D.A.B.*, 3, pt. 2, 87–88.

Meetings with Lincoln, members of the cabinet, General Scott, "gentlemen of his staff," and important citizens[75] he could have at will. McClellan? A much different and more difficult matter. Ellet obtained a letter of introduction from Secretary Chase to Colonel Thomas M. Key, who scheduled a meeting later in the day. For an unstated reason Key failed to keep the appointment.

"On further reflection," Ellet wrote to Chase, "I think it would not be prudent to spread my views at this time, beyond yourself and the President. The full and certain success of my plan requires *absolute secrecy*. General McClellan, whose cooperation is necessary, is alone to be informed and consulted about it."[76] He extracted a letter of introduction to McClellan from Lincoln and called on the major general. But this was the time, August and September, that McClellan declined to meet anyone other than the president and a small list of important government officials.[77] Ellet did no better than meet with one of McClellan's aides to whom he described his program—a program, he thought, for a virtually foolproof, almost bloodless defeat of the Confederate armies in Virginia.

After endless preliminary presentations Ellet finally qualified for a few unsatisfactory, inconclusive moments with the commanding general. Although Ellet's idea bore a faint resemblance to McDowell's earlier suggestion to Chase, a later recommendation by McClellan, and practical usage by Grant, it had overall the kind of absurdity one would expect from a self-taught, civilian strategist. In the short time he spent with Ellet, McClellan must have made his attitude unmistakably clear. Brushed aside, Ellet reacted with hostility and sarcasm. The tenor of the pamphlet that followed hard on the heels of the meeting with McClellan showed that Ellet had felt slighted and had left the meeting in an angry mood.[78] He raised his pen, but he could not make short shrift of McClellan because he could not resist returning to him repeatedly for additional slurs. ". . . [T]he General at [the Army's] head, though respectable as a man, is not a *superior man*, and therefore unequal to his great task."[79]

75   Ellet, Charles, Jr., *The Army of the Potomac and its Mismanagement* (Washington, 1861) (Pamphlet) (Ellet, *Army*) letter dated October 9, 1861, from Ellet to the president of the United States. Ellet's complaints were written as a letter to the president in early October of 1861, delayed in publication by the editor of *The New York Times*, and published in early December 1861, with an introduction dated December 4, 1861. Ellet, *Army*, introduction, 3, 5.

76   Chase MSS (U.P.I.) letter dated September 17, 1861, from Ellet to Chase.

77   Lincoln MSS (L.C.) letter dated September 20, 1861, from Ellet to Lincoln; Ellet, *Army*, 6–7 (pam.).

78   Ellet, *Army*, 6, 7 (pam.).

79   *Ibid.*, 4.

"When vast masses of troops are thrown into confusion by imbecile attempts to carry out imperfectly digested arrangements, such as we have already seen and shudder to look on, the greater the numbers in the field the greater is the danger . . ."[80]

"I propose to demonstrate that *he is not equal to the command of the two hundred thousand patriotic volunteers said to be contained in the present Army of the Potomac . . .*"[81]

"You [President Lincoln] have, in fact, more men now assembled in the one army than your General has the capacity and experience to put in active motion."[82]

In Ellet's view McClellan had carelessly allowed the Rebels to blockade the Potomac with artillery near Acquia Creek, had planned the battle at Ball's Bluff for three months but botched its execution, had allowed the Rebel army to do pirouettes and cartwheels at will in sight of the Union fortifications, had left the forts unoccupied when he advanced his army toward the Rebel army, had failed to repair the Long Bridge, and had failed to follow Ellet's suggestion that he build an alternate bridge nearby.

Ellet's plan for bringing the Confederacy to its knees in Virginia rested on two beliefs: that the Rebel military forces could not live without the supplies brought to them by the principal railroads and that he could cripple them. He would need no large force. A small force of Union troops would land on the west bank of the Potomac early in the morning, march rapidly to the Orange and Alexandria Railroad by several country roads, destroy the telegraph wires, seize the first train, destroy the nearest bridges to prevent pursuit from Manassas Junction, move rapidly south toward Gordonsville, send trains forward to meet any other trains that might approach, and seize them in order to mount all his troops on trains. He would then be able to travel south faster than any pursuing force could follow. At Gordonsville he would destroy the railway station and stores, then turn toward Charlottesville and Staunton to demolish the two high bridges. "I proceed on the supposition that the forces of the rebels are concentrated *here* in front of Washington, or distributed mainly around the borders and roads of Virginia, to make front against the several divisions of the National Army; and that, consequently, interior points in the shade will be but feebly garrisoned . . . Secrecy—*perfect secrecy—is very essential to a safe and successful issue and with secrecy the work at each point will be done before the rebels are aware that it is in progress.*"

80   *Ibid.*, 5.

81   *Ibid.*, 6.

82   *Ibid.*, 13.

The small force breaking the railroads north of Richmond would operate in undefended terrain; and as it neared Richmond, would not suffer attack by Confederates from the Manassas-Centerville area because it would have severed the railroads they would need. A slightly larger force could interdict the numerous railroads that fanned west and south below Richmond. In either event he would defeat the Rebels in Virginia without bloodshed.

"The remedy, in my opinion, is to let General McClellan *stay here* and garrison and defend the thirty-two fortifications around Washington—which, with daily reviews and parades, will abundantly occupy his time and give the fullest scope to his capacity—whatever that may be . . . "[83]

At the end of December the pamphlet appeared on every congressman's desk. It found circulation in the army. In his diary, Heintzelman noted, "I am sorry to say there is much truth in it, in my estimation. Gen. McClellan may be a great General but so far I have not seen it exhibited in his acts."[84]

Yet another of the major general's friends, Salmon P. Chase, the secretary of the treasury and one of McClellan's earliest and most vigorous proponents, became torn. Chase's duties at the treasury required him to pay for the war, and his ability to do that rested on McClellan. First, he had to buy the necessary equipment, a vast capital outlay. Then, to pay the staggering daily cost, a vast cash outflow. By December, he feared he could not raise the funds necessary to pay the expenses of McClellan's army or negotiate his way delicately among the methods of payment, gold specie, bank check, treasury note, and other currency.[85] Having played a major role in mili-

---

83   *Ibid.*, 6–11; Chase MSS (U.P.I.) letter dated September 17, 1861, from Ellet to Chase. Ellet was not a gadfly and a fool. He was a brilliant engineer who could not always distinguish fantasy from practicality. In the Crimean War he had persuaded the Russians to build a fleet of steam powered rams, then sold a program of countermeasures to the English and French. In America he tried unsuccessfully to persuade the Navy Department to build rams but without success until the wand of reality sanctified his idea when the *Virginia*, impervious to close range broadsides, rammed and sank Union ships in Hampton Roads in 1862. Lincoln commissioned him to build a fleet of river rams in the West. After his new fleet of rams won a battle that resulted in the sinking of four Confederate ships and the capitulation of Memphis, he was wounded by a pistol ball in the knee; his wound apparently became infected; and he died, the only Union casualty, as his boat docked at Cairo on June 21, 1862. *D.A.B.*, 3, pt. 2, 88; Ellet, Brigadier General Alfred E., "[Charles] Ellet and his Steam Rams" in *B&L*, 1, 457–459.

84   Heintzelman MS diary (L.C.) (large diary) entry dated December 28, 1861.

85   Hammond, Bray, *Sovereignty and an Empty Purse: Banks and Politics in the Civil War*, 79–86, 94–95 (Princeton, 1970); Gordon, John Steele, *The Great Game: the Emergence of Wall Street as a World Power*, 1653–2000, 91–93 (New York, 1999). The availability of enough gold specie to pay government obligations always gave Chase serious concern. The average daily drafts on the Treasury in early October amounted to one and three-quarter million dollars, a prodigious amount at the time. *Hammond*, 125.

tary affairs, been heavily involved in the promotions of the two most important officers in the Army of the Potomac, and displaced Seward as the primary cabinet voice on the military, Chase wielded influence at the highest level of government. Lincoln would not ignore his needs. At the insistence of the president, McClellan called on Chase in the fall to explain his plans. As the commanding general described them, he would use secrecy, speed, and the navy to interpose the Army of the Potomac between the Confederate army and Richmond, thus capturing the tactical defensive.

McClellan asked how early Chase needed an advance in order to maintain financial stability. Under the existing arrangements, the secretary said, he could manage financial affairs until about the middle of February. McClellan assured Chase he would finish the entire movement before the first of February. He had already begun, he said, to accumulate the necessary shipping at Annapolis.

This concept satisfied the secretary. Without complete secrecy and great energy the plan had no chance, but with them it seemed certain to succeed. When Chase met with the vitally important New York City bankers a few days later, he expressed complete confidence in McClellan and assured them that the army would not go into winter quarters.[86]

Although the Union war effort had suffered from Ball's Bluff and the seizure of Mason and Slidell in the *Trent* incident[87] and McClellan's failure to advance had eroded his universal support, Chase had no choice but to continue his support for the major general. But if the difficulty of financing the war continued to grow, McClellan could not expect the secretary's backing to last. And in Chase's mind, a replacement would be available at once, another fellow Ohioan in whom he still had great confidence, Irvin McDowell.[88]

Of all the many enemies McClellan managed to collect, the slowest to develop and the one who did him the most harm was his president. The major general and the president could not have been more different. Socially, they stood poles apart. McClellan, smooth, polished, and reserved, came from a prominent Philadelphia family. Lincoln, affable, informal, and approachable, had risen from humble Midwestern beginnings. McClellan found Lincoln's "stories" low class. Driven by moral

---

86   Schuckers, *Chase*, 445, mem entitled "Notes on the Union of the Armies of the Potomac and the Army of Virginia," written shortly after the reinstatement of McClellan on September 2, 1862; Niven, *Chase*, 268–273; *M.O.S.*, 157–158, 203. McClellan's account, contained in his posthumously published, postwar memoirs, differs in minor details from Chase's memorandum, e.g., McClellan says Chase came to see him. Chase's earlier, almost contemporaneous, account has been accepted.

87   Niven, *Chase*, 269–273; Hammond, *War and the Empty Purse*, 123.

88   Chase MSS (U.P.I.) letter dated March 8, 1862, from Chase to McDowell.

and military imperatives he could not or would not modify, McClellan proceeded with rigid purpose guided only by right or wrong, correct or incorrect. The president followed the old saw "politics is the art of the possible," which meant nothing was fixed. Compromise, acceptance of a lesser result until the desired result became possible, and adjustment of the goal to the realistic abilities of the participants? Indispensable to the president, they formed no part of McClellan's personality. The major general considered Lincoln to be his social, intellectual, and of course military inferior. He had already begun to evade the president and had much earlier referred to him in his letters home as an "idiot."[89]

Nevertheless, he still observed the rules of form and appearance. On November 9, Lincoln had an appointment to see McClellan, who was visiting Porter's camp. The general returned to headquarters feeling unwell and canceled the appointment. That evening his father-in-law and de facto chief of staff, General Marcy, wrote Lincoln to apologize for the major general's failure to keep the appointment and to explain that the general had gone to bed early with a fever.[90]

McClellan would talk to Chase about confidential military matters because the secretary was his supporter and had a specific need to know, but he did not think Lincoln qualified for a similar open relationship on either score. Scarred by the Munson's Hill incident, McClellan did not believe the president could keep anything secret[91] and refused to entrust him with his plans for an offensive.

On the evening of November 13, McClellan and many other high-ranking officers attended the wedding of Colonel Frank Wheaton of Rhode Island at the headquarters of Don Carlos Buell. A large and distinguished crowd, including Secretary of War Cameron, Brigadier General Heintzelman with his wife and daughter, and Surgeon Tripler and his wife, blessed the event with their presence.[92]

Late in the evening Lincoln, Seward, and Hay went to McClellan's house for a "drop-in" visit. The servant at the door said McClellan was at a wedding and would return soon. The visitors waited. About an hour later, McClellan arrived. Hay recorded the incident in his diary. "Without paying any particular attention to the

---

89   Sears, *McClellan's Correspondence*, 85, letter dated August 14, 1861, by the editor from McClellan to his wife.

90   Lincoln MSS (L.C.) letter dated November 9, 1861, from Marcy to Lincoln. Marcy's letter complied with all the rules of "form over substance." Operating with American informality and egalitarianism, McClellan felt no compulsion to meet with Lincoln when he was inconvenienced by a fever; nor did Lincoln believe that was necessary.

91   *Infra*, ch. 24, "The Coup Fails."

92   Heintzelman MS diary (large diary) (L.C.) entry dated November 13, 1861.

porter who told him the President was waiting to see him, [McClellan] went upstairs passing the door to the room where the President and Secretary of State were seated." Undoubtedly tired, the general had perhaps drunk a bit too much at the festivities. He knew that Lincoln would not be offended if he made himself unavailable. He must have remembered that he had, only a few days earlier, excused himself with an appropriate letter of apology. Most of all he did not care if his convenience were an inconvenience for the president. Downstairs, Lincoln, Seward, and Hay waited about half an hour, then sent a servant to remind McClellan they awaited him. The servant returned to say the general had gone to bed.

On the way home Hay commented adversely about the incident. But Lincoln had paid no attention to it. It was better at this time not to make points of etiquette and personal dignity, he said. Stunned by the general's behavior, Hay, who was not privy to the course of conduct between the president and the general in chief, wrote, "I merely record this unparalleled insolence of epaulets without comment. It is the first indication I have yet seen of the threatened supremacy of the military authorities."[93]

The incident did not lessen Lincoln's reliance on McClellan as general in chief, nor did it result in a diminution of the commanding general's military responsibilities.

---

93   Heintzelman MS diary (large diary) (L.C.) entry dated November 13, 1861; Burlingame, *Hay Diary*, 32, entry dated November 13, 1861. When Dennett edited the Hay diaries, he followed the annoying nineteenth century custom of deleting names and substituting initials in the place of the last name, e.g., 52–53. In most instances the names can be determined from the content of the entry. Here, they are confirmed by Heintzelman's diary and by Burlingame. This incident escapes no one who writes about McClellan, and it has been interpreted in many ways. James G. Randall in his multivolume biography of Lincoln suggests that McClellan was somewhat the worse for wear after the festivities and not, therefore, guilty of an intentional snub. Randall, James G., *Lincoln the President*, 4 vols. (New York, 1956) 2, 68, 72 (Randall, *Lincoln*). In his more recent biography of McClellan, Stephen Sears allows no incident that shows McClellan in a bad light to pass unnoticed, and he uses this incident to further his ends. Sears, Stephen, *George B. McClellan: The Young Napoleon* (New York, 1988) 133 and n. 10, 425–426. The explanation in the long footnote in Burlingame, *Hay Diary*, 288–289, ns. 122 and 123, depicts Lincoln's patience and McClellan's rudeness. But is that true or fair? McClellan's standard practice was to see no one without a special purpose and an appointment. He had, from the beginning, declined dinners with, invitations from, and visits by important career-makers—and breakers. He had treated the president this way on several occasions in the past, and he had been exceptionally polite only a few days earlier. Nothing required him to act differently on this occasion, and if Randall were correct, the general had a positive reason not to struggle downstairs, even if he were only slightly disabled. The president had no appointment. By now, McClellan did not like the "drop-in" visits. The demands of his new position, atop those of the old one, were almost more than one man could satisfy. He was generally exhausted and even more tired, no doubt, from the festivities. He had declined to meet the president on several occasions in the past. Why should this time require different conduct?

On November 12, David Dixon Porter returned to Washington for the first time since he had boarded the train to New York with Lieutenant Colonel Keyes in April.[94] Imaginative and creative, Porter had a new plan and through circuitous channels managed to explain it to Secretary Welles and President Lincoln.[95]

In the evening of November 15, Gideon Welles, Assistant Secretary of the Navy Gustavus V. Fox, and Porter arrived at the headquarters of the Army of the Potomac and home of General McClellan at the corner of H and Fourteenth Streets. Simultaneously, Lincoln arrived in his carriage.[96]

As soon as the servant announced the President, McClellan came downstairs. At once he recognized Porter, an old friend and acquaintance[97] and a kinsman to Fitz John Porter.[98]

"Why, do you two fellows know each other? So much the better!"

In a moment McClellan gave a lucid, brief explanation of Porter's plan for the capture of New Orleans.[99] They discussed the proposal, eliminated any resistance, and reached a general agreement. The president and the secretary would leave the naval and military details to Porter and McClellan.[100]

"You must find the troops and a general of good administrative abilities to hold the City of New Orleans after the navy shall have captured it," concluded Lincoln to McClellan. "Now, time flies; and I want this matter settled. I will leave you two gentlemen to arrange the plans, and will come over here at eight o'clock this evening to see what conclusion you have arrived at."

He then left McClellan and Porter to discuss the project and devise a plan.[101] Mansfield Lovell, a West Point graduate, held the Confederate command in New Orleans, the largest, wealthiest, and most important city in the Confederacy. Two huge forts, one rated by McClellan as the most powerful in the country, guarded the

---

94   Hearn, *Porter*, 68.

95   Porter, *Incidents*, 63–65; David D. Porter MS "Private Journal of Occurrences" (L.C.), 1, 169; Hearn, *Porter*, 66–68.

96   *N&H*, 5, 254; Hearn, *Porter*, 72–73.

97   Porter, *Incidents*, 65.

98   *D.A.B.*, 8, pt. 1, 88, and 8, pt. 1, 90.

99   Porter, *Incidents*, 65.

100   David Porter MS Journal, 1, 169; Hearn, *Porter*, 72–73.

101   Porter, *Incidents*, 65. Porter has the matter resolved in one day in his memoirs but over a much longer period (more likely in this case) in his MS Journal.

Mississippi River below the city.[102] Knowing the river well, Porter explained to McClellan the significance of places on it, the places ships could go, and the places an army could be useful. They devised a plan for the capture of the city by a naval force and an army. They would take the army by water, capture the forts, send part of the troops north to Vicksburg to capture it, too, and join the Mississippi squadron and the western army. "The President and Mr. Seward were present at several of these interviews, although McClellan and myself, generally discussed the thing in its different bearings, while alone," Porter recorded in his journal. "We consulted all the maps and plans and obtained the opinion of Genl. Barnard that, with a force of steamships as specified and the plan of attack I proposed, the place could be taken."

"I remember one evening I was smoking with him upstairs," wrote Porter, "discussing the New Orleans expedition until it was quite threadbare" when the president sent up his name.

"Let him wait," said Little Mac, "I am busy."

"Oh," said Porter, "Don't send such a message to the President. He is very much interested in this matter, and it is not respectful to keep him waiting. Remember that he is our commander-in-chief."

"Well," said McClellan, "Let the commander-in-chief wait. He has no business to know what is going on."

Unaware of McClellan's history with the president, Porter was somewhat horrified at McClellan's conduct and wondered if McClellan "would come to grief before long," he wrote in his large journal. "However he went downstairs as I requested and did his best to entertain the President. McClellan really meant nothing by his talk, he was only letting off a little gas!"[103]

Drop-in visits by the president and McClellan's increasing evasion showed many undesirable and provocative characteristics in both men. Lincoln was guilty of violating the old saw, "A watched pot does not boil," and Lincoln pursued a disruptive course that showed he had forgotten the massive burdens he had reluctantly allowed McClellan to assume. Lincoln should have known that McClellan routinely worked long hours, carried important conferences into the wee hours of the morning, and would be disrupted by frequent unscheduled visits. While Lincoln had an absolute right to know everything about his military effort, he failed to recognize the

---

102   David Porter MS Journal (L.C.), 169–170; Hearn, *Porter*, 73; *OR*, 6, 655–658, 677–678.

103   David Porter MS Journal (L.C.), 174.

disruptive effect of his informal conduct. Although the war effort was the most important aspect of his presidency at this time, he should have left his principal soldier to perform his heavy duties without unannounced, unscheduled visits for conversations without agendas. Then, before, and since, no president has ever done this to his primary military commander. It was not a good leadership technique, nor was it one that would enhance the performance of its victim.

McClellan, however, had created this problem by putting his headquarters in the capital and could have curtailed it by moving them across the river to his army. Taking the conditions as they existed, the major general did not respond to the annoying visits as he should have. Having already taken advantage of Lincoln's ignorance of military etiquette to subvert Scott, McClellan should have known that Lincoln simply knew no better; and because this practice—irritating to be sure— caused no immediate harm, he should have risen above it. Of course, this amounted to a large demand on a man so young dealing with his head of state. But McClellan's conduct, if it were intentional and meant to snub the chief executive, could be no more than childish and immature. He had already received sound advice on this issue and would receive more.

More important than these insignificant characteristics of both men, McClellan's distrust of the administration's ability to preserve security grew to giant proportions. It led to his refusal to tell his president anything about the use of the country's most important army. In fact, these differences and their consequences would have much more severe effects on the critical working relationship between president and general in chief. Familiar and inoffensive to the president, McClellan's avoidance of the frequent, informal contacts with his chief executive unfortunately operated to the general's detriment. Lincoln did not lose the desire to support his young military leader, but the lessening of their association would make McClellan's problems harder and harder to manage as the hostility of his enemies gathered force and their contact with the president increased.

The chief executive did not intend harm and it need never have occurred. Ironically, "Lincoln the enemy" never existed except as a creation of the general's mind. As one of McClellan's supporters wrote long after the war and some years after McClellan had died, "the General's single mistake, that was the source of all his misfortunes, was his distrust of Lincoln. Had he understood and treated Lincoln as his friend, as I know Lincoln was, he could have mastered all his combined enemies."[104]

---

104   McClellan MSS (L.C.) letter dated January 13, 1892, from A. K. McClure to Mrs. McClellan; McClure confirmed this opinion at some length in his book *Lincoln and Men of War Time*, 213 ff.

When McClellan arrived in Washington in July, he had the adulation and support of almost everyone connected with the war. This enhanced two personal characteristics that would have much to do with his future: a belief that he was right, if not infallible, in all his judgments on all major questions; and a somewhat cavalier attitude toward orders that conflicted with his judgment. For the good of his country, he believed, he should follow his own determination no matter what his orders might be. This mindset did not, however, rest on a foundation of stone. Heralded as a savior, he had to do something to be a savior.

In early December the Senate and the House convened for their regular sessions. McClellan's exclusion of the president from his councils was gentle compared to his treatment of the members of Congress. In human circumstances, the man who knows and the man who does not stand differently, the one who lacks knowledge often developing hostility to the person responsible for the lack. The man with the lack attacks to acquire knowledge even though he cannot use it. Still remembering Bull Run, still stinging from Ball's Bluff, and doubting the loyalty of those who did not wish to crush the South, the House and Senate haphazardly decided to form a joint committee to cure their lack of knowledge. They would investigate the causes of both losses. Senator Grimes of Iowa suggested that the committee's charge be broadened to "the conduct of the present war," and that became the committee's mandate. Supported initially by both conservative Democrats and liberal Republicans of both houses, the Joint Committee on the Conduct of the War came uncertainly into being, but most certainly under the domination of the Radicals.[105] When Congress formed the Joint Committee, no House and only three Senate votes opposed. The idea was not new, but the power it wielded certainly was. According to its definition, it should spur the war effort and investigate

---

105   Senate, *Executive Journal*, 26, 27; *Cong Globe*, 37th Cong., 2nd sess., 6, 16, 29, 30, 32, 40, 110; Williams, *Lincoln and the Radicals*, 62–64; Trefousse, *The Radical Republicans*, 182–183; Tap, *Over Lincoln's Shoulder*, 21–24. Belz describes this in the larger frame of reference as a struggle by the legislature to balance the executive and legislative branches of the government, Lincoln in the early months having essentially established a democratic despositism by his executive acts. Belz, *Emancipation and Equal Rights*, 4–17, 24–25, especially 15–16, 24–25. Whether this conflict involved political supremacy, military policy, or constitutional theory, McClellan and his plans for achieving victory certainly became embroiled in it. The twentieth century historiography of the Committee is concisely discussed in Tap, *Over Lincoln's Shoulder*, in the Introduction, 3–5. The men of the Committee and the officers they hounded all made important contributions to the Union's ultimate victory in one of the most important wars of the nineteenth century. But when all is said and done, the men in blue uniforms did one thing the Radical committee members never did: they regularly and routinely put at risk their most irreplaceable assets—their lives.

irregularities involving slaves.[106] A product of the Radical Republicans, it recruited its members almost entirely from their ranks. At the top of its agenda stood Generals Stone and McClellan, West Point graduates, classmates, and Democrats.

Treating the Comte de Paris as a foreign visitor of distinction, Senator Charles Sumner introduced him "on the floor" of the Senate while the committee was being created. Speaking frankly to Sumner, the young captain expressed serious concern about a civilian committee supervising military affairs. He thought the history of France's wars during its Revolution proved that this would lead to unfortunate results. Only generals no longer in command should be investigated. "If you trust your generals, rely on them," he commented wisely in his diary. "Otherwise remove them from command. But if you argue about their actions while leaving them in command, you not only weaken their authority but you also take their initiative and responsibility away from them." Of course, he had little effect on Sumner; and he knew it.[107]

Congress created the committee as much for legislative supervision of Lincoln's management of the war as it did to scrutinize the general in chief and the Army of the Potomac.[108] McClellan probably knew nothing about these legislative activities and cared even less. Very quickly, however, he would find the Joint Committee an enemy of considerable proportion.

The chairman was barrel-chested Benjamin Franklin Wade, a violent, foul-tempered senator from Ohio. In the early days of 1861, Wade had kept a sawed-off shotgun in his desk on the floor of the Senate and had tried to provoke Southern members to a fight. A slight stoop, white hair falling straight back from his forehead, dark skin, and a protruding jaw gave him a ferocious appearance to accompany his ferocious disposition.[109]

Zachariah Chandler, a Radical Senator from Michigan, a creator of the Republican Party, and Wade's closest friend and right-hand man, would combine with Wade to steer the committee. By the time the committee was created, Chandler had grown to hate McClellan and to admire Banks and Fremont. "Little Mac" repre-

---

106   Comte de Paris MS Diary (large diary) (A.N. de la M. de F.) entry dated December 8, 1861; *OR*, 5, 346.

107   Julian, George W., *Political Recollections 1840 to 1872* (Chicago, 1884) 201–202 (Julian, *Political Recollections*); Blaine, James G., *Twenty Years of Congress* (Norwich, 1884, 1886) 1, 379 ff (Blaine, *Twenty Years*).

108   Belz, *Emancipation and Equal Rights*, 11–12.

109   Williams, *Lincoln and the Radicals*, 65 ff; Pratt, Fletcher, *Stanton: Lincoln's Secretary of War*, 154 (Pratt, *Stanton*); *D.A.B.*, 10, pt. 1, 303–305.

sented the small, closed circle of detestable West Pointers. McClellan's desire to avoid an investigation of Ball's Bluff seemed to Chandler to be one Regular Army officer covering for another. As far as Stone was concerned, Chandler already had opinions about him. A letter from a man born and raised in Stone's home town had told him that "it seems impossible to avoid the suspicion that his sympathies are actually on the side of our enemies."[110] With representatives and senators from Massachusetts, Michigan, New York, Indiana, Tennessee, and Pennsylvania, the committee's geographic diversity belied its unity of thought.

Among the critics and enemies rising around McClellan in his army, his chief engineer recorded an interesting insight in one of the small, nasty books he would write during the war. "Had Gen. McClellan been a Napoleon, with the prestige of a hundred victories—or even a Scott—old in the regard of the people—old in experience of war even upon a comparatively limited scale, but rejuvenated in years—had he been either of these—he might with propriety, if he thought the case demanded it, have drawn heavily upon the indulgence so freely extended. Being neither, it was important that he should make the lightest possible draft; that, at the very earliest moment, he should *do* something to confirm, continue, and justify the nation's confidence. Of all Gen. McClellan's faults and incapacities, nothing . . . furnishes a clearer proof of the lack of those qualities which make a great general or a great statesman, than his failure to do this."[111]

To silence most of his critics on military affairs, McClellan needed only the constant skirmishes and encounters whose lack had been decried by Isaac I. Stevens as he left the Army of the Potomac. By them, the army would have acquired battle seasoning, the encounter at Ball's Bluff would have been no more than one of many small events, and the willingness of his men to fight would not have been a question in his mind as it had been on September 12 and October 21. But he had determined that he should fight only when he had made his army perfect and that he would fight one enormous Napoleonic battle to end the war. This policy did not permit small-encounter engagements.

The draft McClellan made on the early, virtually universal, confidence and support had already in November and December become too great in many minds,

110   Chandler MSS (L.C.) letter dated January 9, 1861, from Newton to Chandler; Pratt, *Stanton*, 154; *Biographical Dictionary of the American Congress 1774–1927*, 801; Williams, *Lincoln and the Radicals*, 67–78; Julian, *Political Recollections*, 201; Harris, *Public Life of Zachariah Chandler 1851–1875*, 57 ff, 62.

111   Barnard, John G., *The Peninsular Campaign and its Antecedents as Developed by the Report of Maj. Gen. Geo. B. McClellan and other published Documents* (New York, 1864) 7–8 (Barnard, *Peninsular Campaign*).

and it caused him to lose the support of some of his earliest friends. Hardly more than a week after he became general in chief, the ultimate rumor began to circulate: He would be replaced as commander of the Army of the Potomac. "Cump" Sherman would come from Kentucky to take his place. This report "shelves him," Heintzelman wrote in his diary.[112]

Curiously, McClellan's most intractable and implacable foes developed from his early friends. They simply could not continue their uncompensated support as long as he demanded; and when they turned against him, they did it with a vengeance. In time, these men would willingly believe anything about him and draw the most absurd inferences from the most innocent facts. Like all things in life, absurd thoughts were not limited to his enemies. Confronted with the hostility of the major-general's foes, those who supported him began to believe in the "Great Conspiracy": the Radicals would do anything to prevent McClellan from winning the war quickly because they feared that a quick victory would leave the Southern planter aristocracy and slavery intact and would vault McClellan into the presidency to the eternal detriment of the Radical Republicans and their agenda. According to the Great Conspiracy theory, the Radicals believed the war must last longer and be won later by someone other than McClellan, but not until they had established the Radical platform, including abolition.

The important event in history is recorded in the accounts of numerous participants. The Great Conspiracy provided proof to those who believed in it by a series of incidents, each one usually reported by a single witness whose account found no confirmation in accounts by other participants. Lacking the usual historical confirmation, the conspiracy theory had no substance; but it became a strong belief of McClellan and his supporters.[113]

To implement their program, the members of the Great Conspiracy had to risk military defeat, perhaps even permanent destruction of the Union. A man like Stanton, an excitable coward, lacked the nerve, the courage, and the restraint demanded by such a dangerous game. Nevertheless, the theory had life and substance in the minds of McClellan, his strongest supporters, and his closest advisers; and in the heat of the moment the alleged conspirators made occasional intemperate statements that tended to confirm the conspiracy.

112   Heintzelman MS diary (large diary) (L.C.) entry dated November 8, 1861.

113   Porter MSS (L.C.) draft letter dated August 3, 1888, from Porter to Benjamin; *M.O.S.*, 149–155; Sparks, *Patrick Diary*, 44–46, 48, and 48–49, entries dated February 27, 1862; March 3, 1862; and March 7, 1862.

Perhaps the earliest event in the conspiracy was a meeting in the Washington offices of McClellan's ardent foe the *New York Daily Tribune* one evening in the winter of 1861. *Tribune* correspondents and twelve to fifteen members of Congress had gathered to discuss of the war. Benjamin Wade, Henry Wilson, Elihu Washburn, Thomas Corcoran, and others agreed that good statesmanship would not allow the immediate suppression of the rebellion. Under the true policy of the country and of the Republican Party, the war should last till the people of the North were "educated, or exasperated, to the point of demanding emancipation as one of the necessary results" of the war and until Southern power and influence had been so shattered that the Republican Party would retain control of the government for many years. Therefore, they should spare no effort to rid themselves of McClellan, whose only idea was to end the war quickly. Worse yet, if he became a successful general, he would rise as the natural choice of the people for president, like George Washington, Andrew Jackson, William Henry Harrison, and Zachary Taylor; but he would not support the Republican Party's policies. McClellan, they agreed, was too popular with the citizens and the army to oppose openly. They had to assail him in other ways.[114]

114   McClellan MSS (L.C.) letter dated June 16, 1886, from A. R. Waud to E. C. Prime; Porter MSS (L.C.) letter dated June 13, 1881, from Burns to Webb; letter dated January 21, 1892, from Franklin to Porter; Military Historical Society of Massachusetts MSS (John C. Ropes letters) (Mugar Library, Boston University) letters dated August 8, 1881, and November 30, 1893, and March 25, 1894, from Porter to Ropes; McClellan, "The Peninsula Campaign," in *B&L*, 2, 163–165; *M.O.S.*, 150, McClure, *Lincoln and Men of War Times*, 213–217. Porter and McClellan would carry their belief in the Great Conspiracy to their graves, but Franklin would write to Ropes that the claims of conspiracy were "absurd." Ropes letters, letter dated December 7, 1893, from Franklin to Ropes. For an interesting and illuminating contrast of "inferences" from and "characterizations" of facts, see the letters describing Franklin's meetings with Stanton and McDowell, at which Porter was not present. Ropes letters, letter dated December 19, 1893, from Franklin to Ropes, and letter dated November 30, 1893, from Porter to Ropes.

Chapter 20

"I think if they come out of their rat holes about Bull Run and give us a fair chance half way . . . the question may be settled in one grand battle."

—George G. Meade to his wife

Dranesville

Watershed events in the career of Major General George B. McClellan and the developing officer corps of the Army of the Potomac had occurred before the end of 1861. One was obvious, one notorious but more important and insidious than anyone could tell, and the last secret enough to work out of sight.

The first and obvious event: McClellan's promotion to general in chief. For its immediate effects, it solidified and validated many existing conditions. Scott, who had unfortunately outlived his usefulness and his capacities, slipped aside in the torrent of events. His departure and McClellan's elevation created a proper, direct channel of communication between McClellan and the president and cleared the path toward McClellan's goals. He could create corps and, of course, suggest corps commanders. He could develop a strategic offensive plan and a military goal without the confounding sensitivity for Virginia, all of which he anticipated with satisfaction.

The prospective effects of McClellan's appointment as general in chief? Another matter altogether. Given the president's sensitivity about eastern Tennessee and the Shenandoah Valley, among other places, McClellan would not find geographic concentration possible. He could, however, develop concentration in time by moving all his armies at once. In command of the armies nationwide, McClellan had inherited an administrative maelstrom he never foresaw. To his surprise he found the Western military forces ill-equipped, poorly commanded, missionless, and motionless. The moving parts of his twenty-thousand-man army at Rich Mountain had produced at the least decisional uncertainty. Now, he confronted an exponential enlargement of those conditions.

If he found one army in his strategic plan unready, could the others continue? Or should he abort the plan as he had aborted his frontal attack at Rich Mountain and delay them all? His deeply set need for perfection would face new circumstances in which the chance for miscarriage of a part of the plan would be great. In battle, the ultimate burden of military responsibility, he had shown himself a problem-finder, not a problem-solver. But the great military commander must solve the problem—whatever it might be—on short notice . . . and often without time for deliberate, careful thought. He had to recognize that an alert, active enemy would always attempt to disrupt him and that he must react and overcome. He had disposed of Scott in order to remove interference, not to increase his empire or achieve self-aggrandizement. But he had not foreseen the severe confusion and the grave increase in burden he would find in the new office.

Second, the notorious, insidious event: the encounter on the bluff overlooking Harrison's Island on October 21. Its insidious effects developed over months, contributed to a consequential change for McClellan, and lead circuitously to a personal disaster for his favorite subordinate and best friend. Ball's Bluff brought together his worst enemies in Congress, gave them a focus for their complaints, and created a group more powerful than the sum of its individual members. Operating under rules of secrecy open to "interpretation," the Joint Committee on the Conduct of the War began with a limited agenda, expanded it, then redefined it to achieve political goals. Given the military knowledge and judgment of the members of the committee and the focus of their efforts, one must look hard—and in vain—to find anything constructive achieved by the committee beyond the marvelous, extensive record it left for the historian.[1] Nevertheless, nothing did more to give McClellan's enemies method and power than the creation of the committee. It would unsettle the officer corps. Before it, the constant complaints about disloyalty would become charges of treason.

Third, the secret factor, the new plan McClellan began to consider early in November, a secret plan that would take the army by water to a landing in short striking distance of Richmond. He would avoid the huge casualties of an overland campaign, he would shorten the time to the decisive battle, but he would shackle

---

1   The two best students of the Joint Committee agree, see generally, Williams, *Lincoln and the Radicals*, and Tapp, *Over Lincoln's Shoulder*.

Treasury Secretary Chase with an immense financial burden. This plan would produce divided opinions among his staff officers and revive President Lincoln's old monster, a Washington not covered by the major army.

Each of these factors would rise and fall in importance, but all would remain continuously important after the first of November. And rightly or wrongly, all three would involve the officer corps of the Army of the Potomac.

Meanwhile, the day-to-day life of the army and its officers continued, and the unstable geographic areas would remain unchanged, including the Leesburg breadbasket, where a rich bounty of crops continued to supply both sides with each resenting its use by the other. The right-flank division of the army on the west bank of the Potomac, the Pennsylvania Reserves under George A. McCall, remained nearest to this area. The reconnaissance and mapping excursion in October had made McCall familiar with it and left him an awkward relationship with the commanding general. From his advantageous Dranesville position, ten thousand men near the Confederate flank at Ball's Bluff, McCall could have converted the October battle into a nice little victory. The major general's attitude toward McCall after the battle showed one of his characteristics. Men who failed to produce a beneficial result when they could have "let him down" and went immediately to the blacklist. These failures of initiative would produce all-round criticism, even hostility. Like the incident with Lieutenant Tower and General Pillow during the Mexican War, McClellan's reaction could apply to an officer who did not seize the initiative, even though contrary to orders, when an opportunity for advantage presented itself. Certainly McCall had a chance to violate his orders in October, and in retrospect, his division could have turned the tide against the Confederates on the bluff opposite Harrison's Island, saved Baker's life, saved Stone's career, and prevented the vicious criticism McClellan suffered.

Born in Philadelphia, Pennsylvania, around the turn of the century and graduating from the Military Academy an undistinguished twenty-sixth in the forty-man Class of 1822, McCall had almost reached the age of sixty when the war began. His commission in the infantry led to the usual assignments, including service in the Seminole War in Florida and in the Mexican War. In the latter he won brevets to major and lieutenant colonel for gallantry and served as chief of staff to Patterson. In 1853, after more than twenty years of continuous service, he resigned his commission because of "broken health" and retired to Belair, his country estate in Pennsylvania.[2]

---

2   NA Offs MS Rpts (McCall) letter dated February 25, 1864; *Cullum* 1, no. 311; Warner, *Generals in Blue*, 289.

When the Civil War began almost a decade later, McCall tendered his services to Andrew Curtin, governor of Pennsylvania. On April 16 Robert Patterson asked Governor Curtin to call for twenty-five thousand men. He did, and a huge response followed. Lincoln's decision to take only a total of seventy-five thousand three-month men from all states and allocate limited numbers to each state caught many Pennsylvanians on the way to camps and assembly points where the army could not take them.

A man with foresight, Curtin obtained legislative authorization for funds, officers, and the Reserve Corps of Pennsylvania Volunteers, a full division of infantry, cavalry, and artillery beyond the amount Lincoln allocated to the state.[3] After unsuccessfully offering command of the division to McClellan, Curtin finally tendered command and a commission as major general in the Pennsylvania militia to McCall,[4] who accepted, received confirmation, and took his place at once. Two days later McCall received a commission as a brigadier general of volunteers from Lincoln.[5] More than enough men to create the division had come forward. McCall ordered the surgeon to give the most strict health examinations to all candidates and took men from those parts of the state that, abounding with game, taught skill with the rifle. The colonels of its regiments ranged from West Point graduates through militia officers and Mexican War veterans to lawyers, newspaper editors, and other responsible citizens.

Just before July 16, the day McDowell began his march, Curtin tendered the reserves to the federal government, but it refused them. On July 18, Curtin tried again and again suffered a rebuff. As McDowell retreated from the Rebel positions along Bull Run Creek, both Union armies, his and Patterson's, faced dissolution by expiration of the three-month terms of service. Now, circumstances had changed and Curtin's prescience had become clear. Several times on July 21, Winfield Scott and Thomas A. Scott telegraphed for the reserves, finally saying peremptorily, "Tomorrow won't do for your regiments. We must have them tonight. Send them tonight. It is of the utmost importance."[6] Taking six regiments of infantry, McCall headed for Washington.[7]

3　Sypher, *Pennsylvania Reserves*, 58–60.

4　McCall MSS (P.H.S.) letters dated May 15, 1861, from Curtin to McCall; and July 23, 1861, from Curtin to Lincoln.

5　Warner, *Generals in Blue*, 289.

6　Sypher, *Pennsylvania Reserves*, 56–95, telegrams dated July 21, 1861, from Winfield Scott to Curtin, and from Thomas A. Scott to Curtin.

7　McCall MS (P.H.S.), letter dated July 23, 1861; NA Off's MS Rpts (McCall) letter dated August 25, 1864; Warner, *Generals in Blue*, 289.

With dyed hair and beard, McCall was tall, handsome, and older than most of his fellow general officers in the Army of the Potomac. "His strange outfits, large hats, flasks slung across the shoulder, and guns hanging from every side" differentiated him from them as well. His principal staff officer, Captain H. J. Biddle, a sharp contrast from the military-looking division commander, was short and fat. The few white hairs on his small head he covered with a large felt hat. Non-reg opera glasses buttoned underneath his tunic made him look even fatter than he was. He, too, carried a large whiskey flask on his back. But despite his odd appearance, everyone thought him a good officer.

On September 16 McClellan designated McCall's Pennsylvania Reserve regiments as a division but without two brigade commanders. Not until November did the last of these three brigade commanders report for duty. McCall organized his infantry regiments into three brigades, one regiment of cavalry, and four batteries of artillery.[8] The First Brigade received Bayard's cavalry regiment and, after some jurisdictional squabbling between McClellan and John E. Wool at Fort Monroe, John Fulton Reynolds, West Point Class of 1841, as the brigade commander.[9] To lead the second brigade McClellan selected George G. Meade, Class of 1835.[10] The Third Brigade, temporarily without a leader, had to wait until November for the arrival of General Edward Otho Cresap Ord, Class of 1839, a temporary prisoner on shipboard from California with Major General Henry W. Halleck, Colonel Henry M. Naglee, and an unorganized collection of civilians and army wives. When Ord took command of his brigade, he probably thanked the greater power that he would no longer hear the evening ballads, "My Old Kentucky Home," "Carry Me Back to Old Virginnie," and "Maggie by My Side," performed by the impromptu singing group on deck.[11]

8   Sypher, *Pennsylvania Reserves*, 118–119; Comte de Paris MS diary (large diary) (A.N. de la M. de F.) entry dated October 20, 1861. The Comte de Paris records Biddle as a colonel but entries in *O.R.*, 5, 476, McCall's Report, dated December 22, 1861, and 500, Ord's report, dated December 21, 1861, refer to him as a captain and the *O.R.* Index to vol. 5 lists him as J.H., 1115.

9   *M.O.S.*, 81; *OR*, 5, 17, McClellan's report; Sypher, *Pennsylvania Reserves*, 118–119; *ibid.*, 118; *OR*, 5, 17; Nichols, Edward F., *Toward Gettysburg: a Biography of General John F. Reynolds*, 75–77 (New York, 1958); *OR*, 4, 581, letter dated September 9, 1861, from Wood to Scott, and 612, letter dated September 14, 1861, from Wool to Thomas; Heitman, *Historical Register*, 1, 825.

10   Cleaves, Freeman, *Meade of Gettysburg*, 55 (Norman, 1960); Sypher, *Pennsylvania Reserves*, 118; Heitman, *Historical Register*, 1, 700.

11   Ord MSS (Stanford Univ.) letter dated October 19, 1861, from Ord to "My Dearest Molly Darling"; Heitman, *Historical Register*, 1, 759; Sypher, *Pennsylvania Reserves*, 119.

After the battle above Harrison's Island McClellan sent McCall a letter severely criticizing "the state of discipline in his division." Meade thought the "report of the officers who inspected us unfair and illiberal. Whilst I am aware our discipline is much below what it ought to be, yet I deny the assertion that we are worse than the rest of the army. McCall was very much mortified . . . "[12] For all its travails with McClellan, the division's senior officers would finish their war careers with many accolades, high positions, and successes; and they would not wait long for their first opportunity.

On November 26, Colonel Bayard received orders to take part of his regiment, the First Pennsylvania Cavalry, under the Pennsylvania designation system the Fifteenth Pennsylvania Reserves or the Forty-fourth Regiment of the Line, to reconnoiter the area between Difficult Creek and Dranesville along the Leesburg Pike and descend on Dranesville.[13] At 9 P.M. his column began a long, tedious night ride. At 5 in the morning, two troops took position on the pike north of the town. The other eight, under Bayard, went to the east between the town and the Potomac River, capturing two pickets and six citizens of the "bitterest secessionist stamp." On the return march the head of the column passed a thick pine wood from which it received fire that wounded an assistant surgeon and a private,[14] inflicted two slight wounds on Bayard, and killed his horse.[15] Bayard ordered the woods surrounded and sent men who had carbines into them, where they captured four more Rebels and killed two.[16]

A few days later McCall took brigades under Meade and Reynolds toward Dranesville, Reynolds in the lead. There, they collected fifty wagons of forage but saw no enemy in force. The next day, McCall and Meade left the division campground and rode into the capital on personal business. Meade met a number of friends, who told him about a military rendezvous at Ship Island in the Gulf of Mexico. He speculated rightly that an expedition would soon move against New Orleans.

Next morning, December 5, Meade drew his pay, returned to camp after breakfast, and found orders from McCall for another march toward Dranesville.[17] Following the standard practice of rotation for the march and duty in general, Meade would

---

12   Meade, *Meade Letters*, 1, 226, letter dated November 7, 1862, from Meade to his wife.

13   Bates, *Hist. Penn. Regts.*, 2, 1014.

14   *OR*, 5, 448, McCall's report and Bayard's report.

15   Bayard, *Bayard*, 191, letter dated November 29, 1861, from Bayard to "Mother."

16   *OR*, 5, 448, Bayard's report.

17   Meade, *Meade Letters*, 1, 233, letter dated December 5, 1961, from Meade to his wife.

take his turn in the lead with Easton's battery and a battalion of cavalry. Ord's brigade would follow close behind him with a train of wagons to collect forage. Meade was to march to the area of Gunnell's farm, which lay two miles from Dranesville, arrest secessionists in the area, capture two men sniping across the Potomac River,[18] and collect Gunnell's crops before he could deliver them to the Rebels.

On December 6, he marched his brigade ten miles, arriving about noon, captured the secessionists, and in two hours loaded the wagons with everything that might be useful to the Confederates. Believing the secessionists should be punished, Meade's men concluded that "the more injury they inflicted the more successful was the expedition." Gunnell was absent, but his wife, the house servants, and the farm workers helplessly suffered the indignities while the Federal troops stripped the farm. Two days later, when Meade wrote his wife, he still had the scene emblazoned on his mind. "I never had a more disagreeable duty in my life to perform . . . It made me sad to do such injury, and I really was ashamed of our cause, which thus required war to be made on individuals."[19]

Shortly after his peaceful foraging expedition, Meade learned that a Rebel brigade of infantry and a battery of artillery in the Dranesville area had concluded that his expedition was an attack and fled, abandoning the guns. Meade's disappointment at not taking the guns he expressed to his wife in terms that mirrored McClellan's desire for one grand Armageddon. "We were in ignorance of their presence, or of their stampede, or we might have had a glorious and bloodless capture . . . I think, if they come out of their rat holes about Bull Run and give use a fair chance halfway, that McClellan will eagerly seize it, and the question may be settled in one grand battle . . . The sooner this thing is settled the better, and it can only be settled by one side or the other gaining a most decisive and complete victory."[20]

McCall sent a brief, one-paragraph report of Meade's foray to army headquarters.[21] Wounded by McClellan's criticism, he felt compelled to add a postscript that addressed his gnawing concern about the harsh letter from McClellan. "It is with pleasure," he wrote, "that I refer to the very exemplary conduct of all the troops on this occasion, and can commend from personal observation the good discipline maintained. There was no straggling or lagging behind during the march out or returning."[22]

---

18   *OR*, 5, 456, McCall's report.

19   Meade, *Meade Letters*, 1, 234, letter dated December 8, 1862, from Meade to his wife.

20   Meade, *Meade Letters*, 1, 235–236, letter dated December 11, 1861, from Meade to his wife.

21   *OR*, 5, 455–456, McCall's report.

22   *OR*, 5, 456, McCall's report.

On the evening of December 19, McCall learned that Confederate pickets had advanced to a position about four or five miles from the Union lines and had carried off two Union supporters. The Rebel reserve supposedly lay in the neighborhood of Dranesville. Reynolds and Meade had already led forays to Dranesville. McCall ordered Brigadier General Ord to move his brigade, augmented by Kane's regiment, Easton's battery, and two squadrons of cavalry, "in the direction of Dranesville" at 6 A.M. the following day to surround and capture the Confederate party and at the same time collect more forage from secessionist farms.[23] The column was to march to Dickey's and Gunnell's farms between Dranesville and the river in order to strike the Confederate rear. At Gunnell's the troops should gather corn and hay, then return without staying overnight.[24] Reynolds' brigade, now second in the rotation, would march to Difficult Creek on the highway and be ready to support Ord if a strong force appeared.

That same night Colonel Thomas L. Kane, commanding the First Reserves, lay severely ill and hospitalized in Washington. He demanded that his staff take him to camp as soon as he learned about McCall's orders. Stealthily, they carried him, wrapped in blankets, to an ambulance, and the following day at 5 A.M. he appeared on horseback at the head of his regiment.[25]

Thoughtful, sharply critical, seventeenth in the West Point Class of 1839, Ord would help the men of his brigade learn the ways of outdoor life—how to pitch and ditch a tent, how to build a trench fireplace, a chimney, and a bunk for a tent. An orderly selected for him from the Ninth reserves reported for duty and received the usual mistaken-identity treatment when he asked "an elderly man" wearing a soldier's uniform and overcoat for the general's tent. When the orderly finally found the correct tent, a well-dressed officer led him to the "old gentleman."

"Here, General, is the man Colonel Jackson has sent you for an orderly."

The new orderly thought he should sink into the ground, but the general told him to take an unoccupied place in one of a group of tents, then gave him instructions about the proper way to fix it and told him to make himself comfortable. The orderly asked about his duties. "I will tell you when I want you," replied Ord with the clear implication that "no more would be necessary for now."[26]

---

23   *OR*, 5, 474, McCall's report; 480, Ord's report.

24   *OR*, 5, 481, orders dated December 19, 1861, from McCall to Ord.

25   *OR*, 5, 474, Ord's report; 484, McCalmont's report.

26   *Cullum*, 1, no. 1002; Warner, *Generals in Blue*, 349–350; Heitman, *Historical Register*, 759; Viola, *Veil Memoirs*, 12–13.

At 6 A.M. on December 20, Ord marched his brigade on the familiar Leesburg Turnpike toward Dranesville.[27] Expecting to find Rebel cavalry pickets at Dranesville, Ord assigned three companies of the Tenth Pennsylvania Reserves and twenty cavalrymen to the foraging party headed for Gunnell's. With the remainder of his force he continued to Dranesville, "satisfied that, though I might be exceeding the letter of my instructions, should I find the enemy and pick up a few you would not object," he stated in his report to McCall. He pressed forward with the head of the column, a small advance guard of artillery, cavalry, and infantry, through Dranesville and a short distance beyond the town. Confederate cavalry pickets fled as the Union troops entered the town.

His column now strung along the Leesburg Turnpike from slightly northwest of Dranesville to some distance southeast of it,[28] Ord learned from a guide that a full brigade of Confederate infantry without artillery lay at Herndon's Station, 500 infantry and cavalry at Hunter's Mill, and 200 infantry between Dranesville and the Potomac River. Ord had sent the First Reserves, under Colonel Thomas L. Kane, north of Dranesville to the woods surrounding the Reppin house. As the senior officer, Kane commanded his regiment and the nearby Sixth Reserves, which would together hold the right flank of the brigade as it faced south. While he returned to Dranesville in response to a message from Ord, he crossed a small height north of the Leesburg Pike. McCall had made his headquarters in the brick house on the hill at the time of Ball's Bluff. Now, Kane occupied it. A local citizen had already warned him about Confederates in the area. He saw men in motion south of the village where he knew no Northern troops should be. Soon, he saw the Stars and Bars.[29]

Southeast of the town Ord and Colonel John S. McCalmont of the Tenth Reserves detected the same large force to the left. McCalmont halted his regiment and the two regiments behind him on the pike.[30] At the rear of the brigade a scouting party also reported the force to Colonel John H. Taggart. Approximately four Confederate regiments lay in a field about a mile to the left of the line. Taggart halted his regiment, the Twelfth Reserves, and formed a line of battle facing the Confederates, but found they had no disposition to engage. The regiment waited some time, then resumed its march toward Dranesville. As Taggart neared the village, Confederates in a dense pine thicket to the left drove the flanking parties into the column;

---

27 *OR*, 5, 477, Ord's report.

28 *OR*, 5, 478, Ord's report; Woodward, *Third Pennsylvania Reserves*, 53–54.

29 *OR*, 5, 481, 482, Kane's report.

30 *OR*, 5, 478, Ord's report; 483–84, McCalmont's report.

and scouts reported that troops concealed in the woods had fired on them. A large force of Confederates showed itself and pursued the scouts toward the left of the regiment. Taggart halted and formed line with his right resting on the hill just before Dranesville and his left opposite a brick house west of the pike. He sent the regimental adjutant through the town to the right wing of the brigade to tell Ord that the brigade rear had come under attack.

Confederate artillery opened fire, but the shells exploded harmlessly behind the line. About fifteen minutes later the Rebel guns reduced the range, and the shells began to burst overhead. Still they produced no injury.[31] The Rebel guns lay in the road to Centerville. As the brigade faced southwest from its position along the pike, its rear, now the brigade left in line of battle, received fire from the thick wood. Ord took direct command. The brigadier general was an old artillery officer. "Carefully observing their fire," he stated in his report, he easily and quickly identified the best gun position from which to fire on the Rebel battery, then ordered Easton to it. Easton went to a gallop. One of his guns capsized. Ord left Easton to right the overturned piece. In the excitement the other guns raced past the position Ord had designated. A quick correction of position and into battery with the remaining three guns in an enfilading position near a fork in the pike.[32] Acting the part of the modern forward observer, fire direction center, and section chief, Ord "gave the gunners the distance and elevation [and] observed the result." After two rounds, the Confederate fire slackened, then continued ineffectively.

"Keep at that!" he told his gunners.[33]

He sat his horse next to the battery. Now and then he exclaimed excitedly.

"Give it to 'em, boys! That's a good shot!"

"That made one of their old caissons fly!"

"There! That knocked a gun!"

"Hurrah, boys!"[34]

Then he ordered Colonel Conrad F. Jackson to march his regiment into the woods, form line of battle, and attack. With difficulty Jackson restrained his men from taking the double-quick.[35] Others, including the First Pennsylvania Reserves

---

31   *OR*, 5, 487, Taggart's report.

32   *OR*, 5, 478, Ord's report; 483–484, McCalmont's report; 487, Taggert's report; 488–489, Easton's report.

33   *OR*, 5, 479, Ord's report.

34   Hill, Archibald F., *Our Boys: the Personal Experiences of a Soldier in the Army of the Potomac* (Philadelphia, 1864) 173 (Hill, *Our Boys*).

35   *OR*, 5, 476, McCall's report.

under Lieutenant Colonel Kane, joined the pursuit. As soon as he could see that his men were to confront the Rebels south of the pike, he rose in his stirrups and shouted to them.

"Forward, Bucktails! There's fun ahead!"

In pursuit in the woods, Kane took a bullet through the upper jaw. A halt. But just for a moment—just long enough to tie a makeshift bandage around the wound. Back to the head of the regiment.[36] Again he advanced, this time until he saw and heard troops ahead of him. He halted and formed his right.

Every officer would have known about the ugly "friendly fire" incident in late September and would have worried about firing into his own men. Someone reported that the troops opposite were the Bucktails. Unable to identify them definitely, Colonel Jackson restrained his men from firing.

Someone yelled, "Don't fire on us."

One of the men shouted, "Are you the Bucktails?"

"Yes, we are the Bucktails," the answer came back. "Don't fire."

But a volley and a report from a captain who had a clear view proved them to be Confederates. Jackson ordered his men to fire. Most of them promptly obeyed, but some still doubted the identity of the targets, causing considerable confusion in the ranks.[37]

Prior to the encounter, Reynolds, who was some distance to the rear on the pike, veered off the left of the road before he reached Difficult Creek and took a position on a high hill a quarter of a mile short of the bridge prior to the encounter. The troops stacked arms and broke ranks. After resting for several hours, they heard the heavy booming of Easton's guns from the direction of Dranesville.

"Fall in! Fall in! Take—arms!" cried Reynolds.

In a moment the troops formed line with their weapons.

"Right—face! Forward! . . . Double-quick—march!" he shouted in his shrill, high voice and took position at the head of the brigade.

Intending to move overland and strike the flank and rear of the Confederates, he led his men across the country southwest of the pike, the very flanking movement

---

36   Thomson, O. R. Howard, and Rauch, William H., *History of the "Bucktails" Kane Rifle Regiment of the Pennsylvania Reserve Corps (13th Pennsylvania Reserves, 42nd of the Line)* (Philadelphia, 1906) 73–74, 75, 77 (Thomson, *Bucktails*). The regimental history denominates Kane's regiment as the Thirteenth Reserves, Forty-second of the line; *OR*, 5, 481, lists it as the First Pennsylvania Reserve Rifles. Bates, *Hist. Penn. Regts.*, 2, 907, agrees with the regimental history.

37   *OR*, 5, 482–483, Jackson's report.

McCall had failed to make in October. Almost two years later, Reynolds would do this again to the west of a small town in Pennsylvania. In a few minutes an officer from McCall's staff rode after him.

"Stop, general!" he shouted. "Not this way—the pike, the pike!"

Reynolds knew what he was doing. McCall did not.

"Euchered!" exclaimed the brigade commander, no doubt in disappointment or irritation.

By obeying the order from McCall, Reynolds abandoned his effort to strike the flank or rear of the Confederates. He ordered his men to file to the right toward the pike and cross the creek anywhere. His battery crossed the bridge at a gallop.[38]

About one in the afternoon George Meade, in the rear of the division, heard the same heavy firing from the direction of Dranesville. According to his orders, he should prepare himself to march forward the moment he received word. Unlike McCall in October, however, he decided to do the right thing even if not completely consistent with his orders: He would march to the sound of the guns.[39]

After receiving a short field dispatch sent by Ord to report his engagement, McCall and his staff mounted and with a cavalry escort rode forward to overtake Ord's brigade. He stopped for a few moments with Reynolds at Difficult Creek and reminded him to be ready to come forward to support Ord if necessary. About two miles from Dranesville he heard artillery fire, apparently by the Confederates, and he could hear Easton's battery answering. He rode rapidly until he reached Ord's brigade deployed along the Leesburg Pike. Easton's guns were firing at will at the Confederate battery about five hundred yards down the road to Centerville. McCall watched the artillery duel from a distance, then sent an aide forward to find Ord. He could see Rebel infantry and cavalry emerge from cover to the left of the road. He warned Colonel McCalmont's regiment about this, but its intervention was unnecessary because a few shots by Easton checked the Rebels and drove them back to cover.[40]

Having heard nothing from Ord, McCall turned in the direction of the brisk firing. Captain Scheetz of his staff arrived to report that he had found Ord in front of the center where the Kane Rifles and part of the Sixth Reserves were engaged with the Confederates.[41]

---

38   Hill, *Our Boys*, 471–473.

39   Meade, *Meade Letters*, 1, 237, letter dated December 21, 1861, from Meade to his wife.

40   *OR*, 5, 474, Ord's report; 484, McCalmont's report.

41   *OR*, 5, 475, Ord's report.

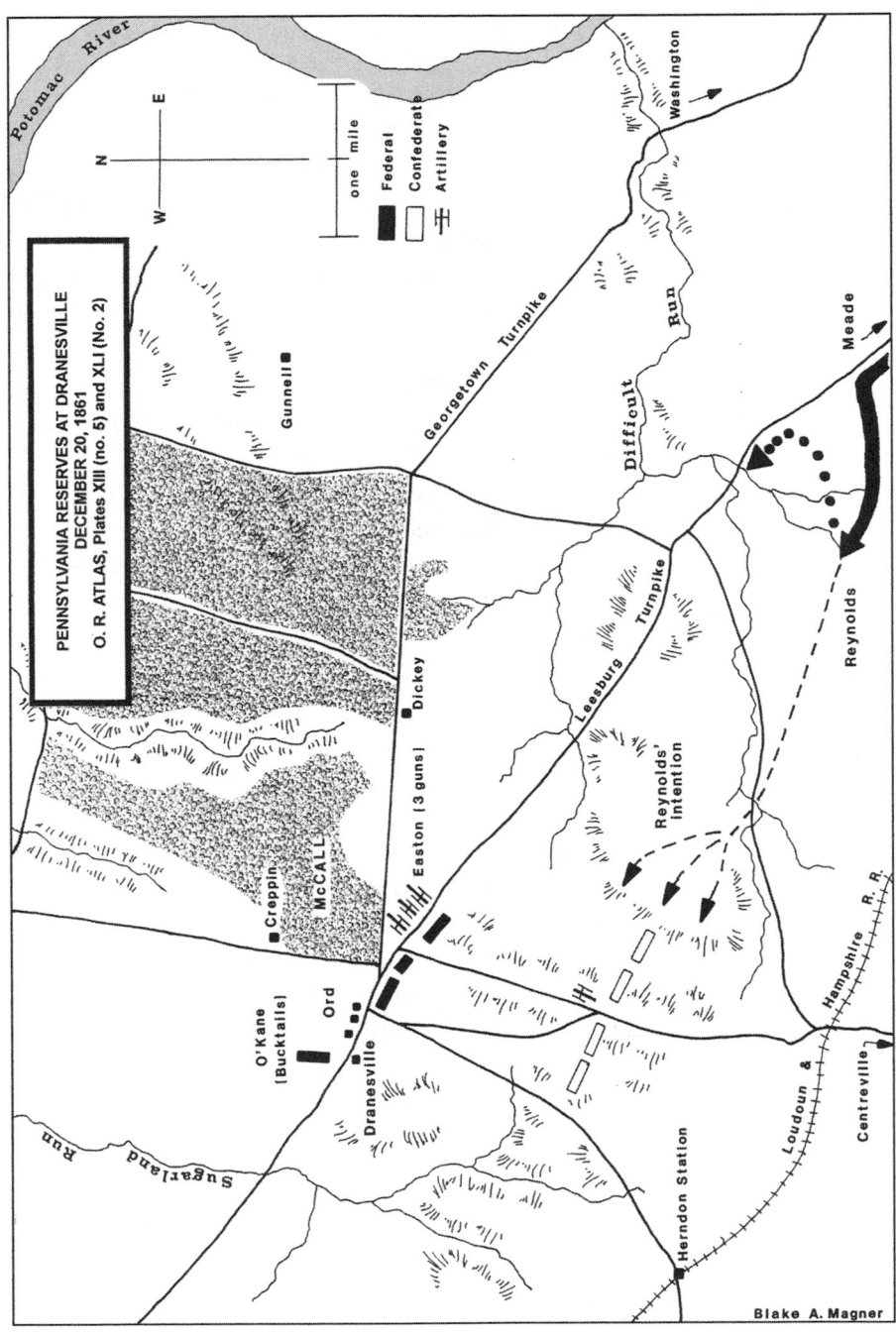

PENNSYLVANIA RESERVES AT DRANESVILLE
DECEMBER 20, 1861
O. R. ATLAS, Plates XIII (no. 5) and XLI (No. 2)

Federal   Confederate   Artillery

one mile

N E W

Potomac River

Washington

Georgetown Turnpike

Difficult Run

Meade

Gunnell

Reynolds

Dickey

Leesburg Turnpike

Reynolds'
Intention

McCALL

Easton (3 guns)

Creppin

Hampshire R. R.

O'Kane
(Bucktails)

Ord

Dranesville

Herndon Station

Loudoun & Centreville

Sugarland Run

Blake A. Magner

Meanwhile, Ord had told Colonel Taggart to dismount and lead his regiment on foot from the right wing in order to capture the Confederate battery. The troops went into the woods but found no Confederates, then advanced with a battalion front to the left, where they heard musketry. Before they emerged from the wood the firing ceased. They halted and awaited orders. Ord sent them into yet another wood to take the Confederate battery thought to be a short distance ahead. The wood revealed nothing but Confederate dead and wounded. Pursuit for a considerable distance met no Confederates but revealed "a precipitate flight, arms, ammunition, clothing, and provisions being strewed [sic] in every direction,"[42] Taggert noted in his report.

A rifle ball whistled past Ord's ear and tore one of the buttons from his cap. He remarked coolly, "A miss is as good as a mile! But I shore do hope they have no better marksman than that fellow."[43]

Ord and McCall simultaneously reached the former position of the Confederate battery where they met for the first time on the field.[44] They found the road strewn with disabled men and horses. One caisson had exploded, and another had been damaged. The Confederates had left behind artillery equipment, small arms, and a quantity of heavy clothing and blankets. Ord requested permission to pursue, and McCall granted it. Forward half a mile. But the Confederates outdistanced him. McCall then recalled him and prepared to return to his camp. He ordered the harness removed from the dead Confederate horses in the road while he collected the good caissons and the limber. As Reynolds and Meade approached the field together, "We knew Ord would be the first to win a fight," Reynolds said.[45]

By the time Meade had reached a position within a few hundred yards of the village, the firing had ceased. The brigade had arrived just in time to see the Confederates disappear down the Centerville Road with the Bucktails, the Sixth Regiment, and the Ninth in pursuit[46]—too late to take part.

McCall evaluated his situation. Ord had depleted his ammunition supply. During the night the Confederates could interpose between his Dranesville position and the Army of the Potomac. He decided to return to his main camp. In the approaching darkness the column began the march back. McCall brought with him

42   *OR*, 5, 487, Taggert's report.

43   Hill, *Our Boys*, 173.

44   *OR*, 5, 475, McCall's report; 479, Ord's report.

45   Ord MSS (Stanford Univ.) letter dated December 24, 1861, from Ord to his wife.

46   Hill, *Our Boys*, 472.

his killed and wounded and as many of the Confederate wounded as possible,[47] but left twenty-one of the most severely wounded Rebels in nearby houses.[48]

The encounter—hardly a battle—served McCall well. He had not found a place on the major-general's July list of candidates for promotion,[49] he had a strained relationship with McClellan probably because he had not saved the major general from himself at Ball's Bluff, and he had been victimized by "tittle-tattle" about the condition of his division. Not above self-aggrandizement at the expense of his subordinates, he took as much credit for the result as he could.[50] He received a congratulatory letter from Secretary of War Cameron.[51] McCall was "much pleased," Meade wrote his wife, and thought he would be "reinstated in favor."[52]

Ord's adversary had been none other than the glory-seeking J. E. B. Stuart, who had a fair ability at exaggeration himself. But McCall's zeal to reestablish himself, at least in part at the expense of his brigade commanders, did not pass without private recrimination. In his "after action report" to his wife, Ord took sharp note of this. "The papers will have told you of *my* fight at Dranesville on the 20th," he wrote a few days later. "By the time McCall (without troops) rode up the fight was over & they were in full run for Centreville . . . General McCall, who rode up while I was urging my men in pursuit, claims to have been *in* the fight before their flight & his toadies have filled the papers with accounts of McCall's battle at Dranesville but I have pretty strong friends among the officers & they know. . . ."[53] One of Ord's regimental commanders sent "me, not McCall, the *New York Times* marked as you see in the slip. I am quite tickled at the compliments. . . ."[54]

In General Orders No. 63 from Headquarters of the Army of the Potomac, McClellan expressed his thanks to Ord and the troops of his brigade for their part in the battle.[55] Writing home several days after the encounter, Ord showed a vainglorious

---

47   *OR*, 5, 475, McCall's report.

48   Ord MSS (Stanford Univ.) letter dated December 24, 1861, from "Ord to his wife."

49   NA Records of the Adjutant General's Office, Letters Received, Commission Branch file (Microcopy M 1064) (C.B.) 1863, memorandum dated July 29, 1861, from McClellan to Lincoln.

50   Meade, *Meade Letters*, 1, 240, letter dated December 27, 1862, from Meade to his wife.

51   *OR*, 5, 476–77, letter dated December 28, 1861, from Cameron to McCall, 477, General Orders No. 63, dated December 28, 1861, from Headquarters, Army of the Potomac.

52   Meade, *Meade Letters*, 1, 238, letter dated December 22, 1861, from Meade to his wife.

53   Ord MSS (Stanford Univ.) letter dated December 24, 1861, from Ord to his wife.

54   Ord MSS (Stanford Univ.) letter dated December 24, 1861, from Ord to his wife.

55   *OR*, 5, 477, General Orders No. 63, dated December 28, 1861, from Headquarters, Army of the Potomac.

streak of his own without breaching any duty to his fellow officers. Honoring the holiday season, he wrote on Christmas Eve, "Molly, darling, home-home-home! Especially Christmas times honors success are nothing to it. Twas duty brot me here, Molly mine, and not honors. I don't care for all of it as much as for one day's pleasant, cheerful, happy smiles from my wife."[56]

This encounter must have buttressed the conclusion McClellan had formed after Ball's Bluff. His training had achieved its purpose. His men had become soldiers. They would stand to the mark. He could rely on them in battle. But in the eyes of others, Dranesville offered more subtle and, for one of them, less final lessons. On its face the encounter might have confirmed the optimistic view McClellan had expressed about his developing infantry after the skirmish at Vienna and the engagement at Ball's Bluff. But only half so in the eyes of George Meade. To his wife he wrote that the infantry left much to be desired. "Had the artillery of the enemy been served as well as ours was, and committed the same devastation, he [Ord] could not have kept his command together five minutes. In other word, it is success in the beginning of an action which keeps volunteers together, and disaster or being checked is sure to throw them into confusion or cause them to run."

The artillery was a different story. The Rebel artillery had been "miserably served," according to Captain Hezekiah Easton,[57] and "unmanned by our third fire," most of their shots falling behind the guns in the road.[58] [59] When the Rebels finally found the range, their fire was harmless.[60] Commissioned in the artillery at graduation from West Point and serving in it during the Mexican War,[61] Ord came to Dranesville an experienced and skillful artilleryman. He posted and directed Easton's guns himself, causing numerous casualties and much devastation among the Confederates.[62]

---

56   Ord MSS (Stanford Univ.) letter dated December 24, 1861, from Ord to his wife.

57   Meade, *Meade Letters*, 1, 237, 238, letter dated December 21, 1861, from Meade to his wife.

58   *OR*, 5, 489, McConnell's report; 487, Taggart's report.

59   *OR*, 5, 489, Easton's report.

60   *OR*, 5, 487, Taggart's report.

61   *D.A.B.*, 7, pt. 2, 48.

62   Meade, *Meade Letters*, 1, 238, letter dated December 21, 1861, from Meade to his wife; *OR*, 5, 488, Taggart's report.

Stuart would, no doubt, have risen to the occasion if he had read the other part of Ord's family report.[63] "My artillery slaughtered them—while they were cooped up & jammed in a road which I raked. It was the old story—they had an ignoramus for a general, a fool for an artillery capt'n, took it for granted we would run, made no reconnaissance, posted their artillery just where I would have placed it to smash it soonest. . . ."[64]

This minor engagement presented a contrast between the Union and Confederate artillery that bore watching. The solid core of Regular batteries, scattered among the divisions, would quickly lead the Federal volunteer artillery and its middle-class, bourgeois officers to superiority over the Rebel artillery. Less than a year later its highly effective fire down a long grassy slope would make infantry combat virtually unnecessary. In the desperate fighting ahead the Federal gunners would deserve great plaudits. Less than two years later they would hold positions below a long ridge in Pennsylvania, would fire double cannister without sponging, thus risking a "cook-off" while still at the muzzle, and use rammer staffs to defend their guns in hand-to-hand fighting against veteran infantry.

63   *OR*, 5, 490–494, Stuart's report.

64   Ord MSS (Stanford Univ.) letter dated December 24, 1861, from Ord to his wife.

Chapter 21

"It might be one of the most brilliant events of the war. The expedition could not fail."

—Heintzelman commenting in his diary on his version of the Peninsula Campaign

McClellan's Plans

*I*f McClellan's largest difficulty with his developing enemies was the need for an immediate major offensive movement, he would solve that problem soon. He had a new plan, and he intended to execute it before the end of January. Furthermore, it was a plan with precedent behind it, with historical approval by the federal government, with recognition of the unwillingness of his countrymen to endure the casualties of repeated frontal assaults, and with reliance on the Union's clear naval superiority. Last, its historic antecedents, the Crimean War campaign and the Vera Cruz-Mexico City column in the Mexican War, he knew well from personal observation and participation.

At the beginning of the Mexican War, Zachary Taylor won a series of battles along the Rio Grande River, but President James K. Polk and his cabinet saw them as indecisive and feared the American people would refuse to endure prolonged fighting of this kind—even if it produced an uninterrupted succession of tactical victories.[1]

---

1   Bauer, *Mexican War*, 232–235; Eisenhower, John S. D., *So Far From God: The U.S. War with Mexico 1846–1848* (New York, 1989) 253–257; Elliott, *Scott*, 433–435; Eisenhower, John S. D., *Agent of Destiny: The Life and Times of General Winfield Scott* (New York, 1997) 229–230 (Eisenhower, *Agent of Destiny*). In his memoirs Thomas Hart Benton described the government's goal as a "small war, just large enough to require a treaty of peace and not large enough to make military reputations dangerous for the presidency," Benton, Thomas Hart, *Thirty Years View: or, a History of the Working of the American Government for Thirty Years, from 1820 to 1850*, 2 vols. (New York, 1908) 2, 680.

Polk decided he should assign Taylor the tactical defensive along the Rio Grande and launch a decisive offensive against the enemy's heart, the capital at Mexico City. The navy would land an army near Vera Cruz on the Mexican coast. The army would besiege and capture the port and make it the base for a march inland against Mexico City.[2] With great reluctance Polk gave command of the expedition to Scott.[3] McClellan served in it as a young engineer officer, and that service must have played some role in the formulation of the plan he ultimately pressed on the administration.

After he assumed command in the East, McClellan gave immediate thought to assuming the offensive. The junction of two streams, Cedar Run from the west and Bull Run from the north, formed the Occoquan River at Wolf Run Shoals. South of Wolf Run Shoals lay Maple Valley, uneven, heavily wooded, without a good road system, and unsuited to movements by a large military force. In August and September McClellan developed his Occoquan–Cedar Run plan for a movement southwest from Alexandria, a modified version of the plan used by McDowell in July. He would cross the Occoquan south of Alexandria, continue south through Maple Valley, and swing in separated columns toward Brentsville on Cedar Run. While he and McDowell were riding one day, he explained his plan, and at various times in September he described it to Andrew Porter, William B. Franklin, and Fitz John Porter.[4] McDowell probably reported it to Chase or Lincoln or both.

The president would have had a long time to digest this plan, consider its political implications, and accept it. Throughout the war sound proposals, even radical ideas, would find him receptive if he had time for peaceful and protracted thought. New ideas presented on short notice he was unlikely to accept. With the Occoquan plan in his mind for a long time, he had come to embrace it, and it had taken a firm place in his mind, almost as if it were his own. This, too, was a characteristic of the president. An idea, once firmly in his mind, could not easily be displaced.

---

2   Bauer, *Mexican War*, 232; Elliott, *Scott*, 433–434; In his memoirs Scott claimed vaguely that he originated the plan for the Vera Cruz-Mexico City column, Scott, Winfield, *Memoirs of Lieut.- General Scott, LL.D. Written by Himself*, 2 vols. (New York, 1864) 2, 403–404; and Eisenhower accepted his statement in *So Far From God*, 253–254, but Polk and his cabinet originated the plan long before Scott began writing his memoranda on execution. Johnson, Timothy D., *Winfield Scott: The Quest for Glory* (Lawrence, 1998) 156–158 (Johnson, *Scott*); Eisenhower, *Agent of Destiny*, 229; Elliott, *Scott*, 433; Bauer, *Mexican War*, 232; Sellers, *Polk-Continentalist*, 2, 429–430. A mistake about the role of the administration and the general in chief in the creation of the plan probably caused an important miscalculation by McClellan in the development of his own plans.

3   Elliott, *Scott*, 435–440; Johnson, *Scott*, 150–160.

4   Stanton MSS (L.C.) memorandum of n.d. of conference of general officers on stationary of Headquarters, Army of the Potomac; Heintzelman MSS (L.C.) (large diary) entry dated March 8, 1862 (description of events on March 9, 1862).

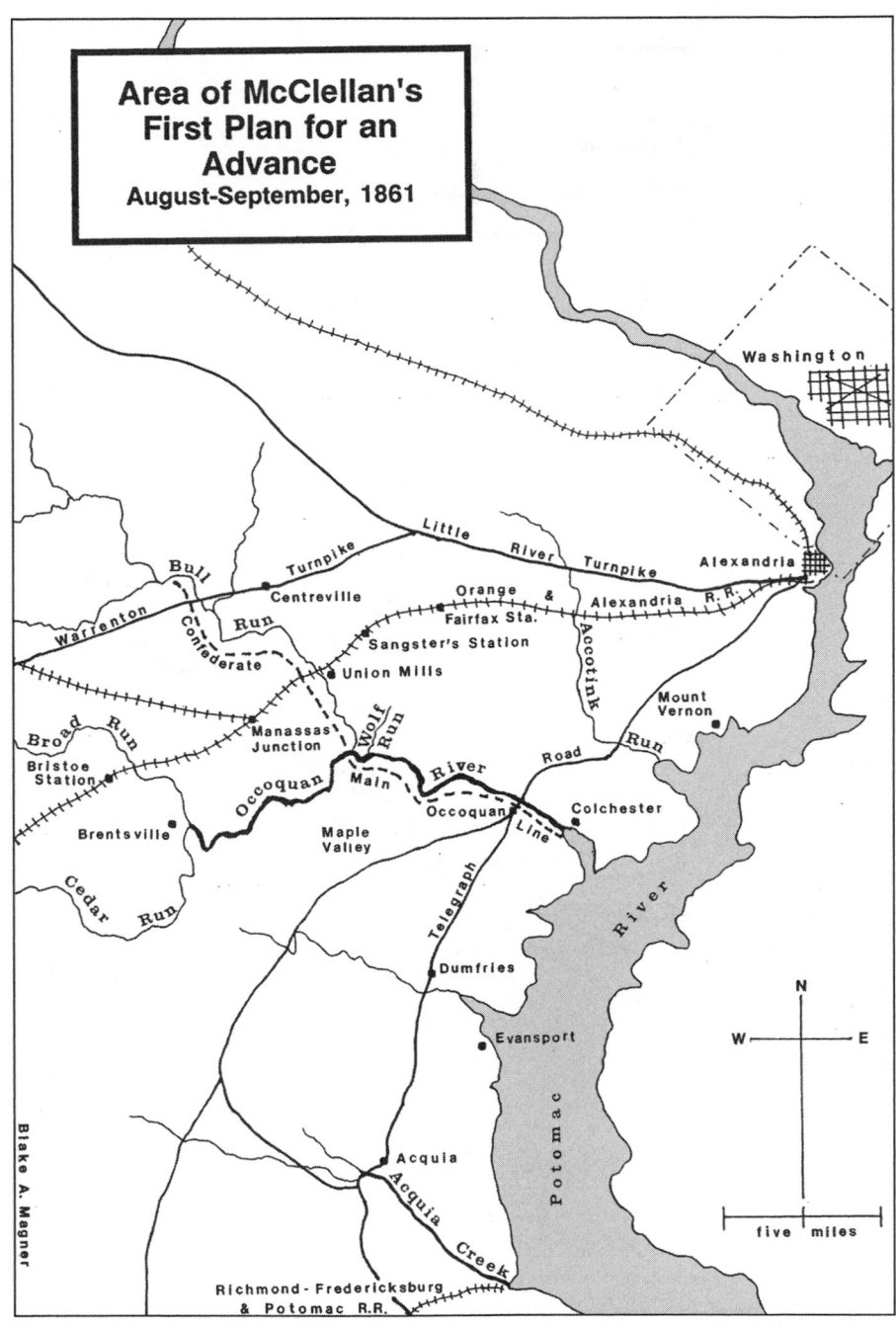

Area of McClellan's First Plan for an Advance
August-September, 1861

Washington

Little   River   Turnpike   Alexandria

Bull   Turnpike
Warrenton   Centreville   Orange   &
Confederate   Run   Fairfax Sta.   Alexandria   R. R.

Sangster's Station

Union Mills   Accotink

Broad   Run   Wolf   Mount
Vernon

Bristoe   Manassas   Run   Road   Run
Station   Junction

Occoquan   Main   River
Brentsville   Occoquan   Colchester
Maple   Line
Valley

Cedar   Telegraph   River

Run

Dumfries

Evansport   Potomac

N
W   E

Acquia

Acquia   Potomac

Creek

Richmond - Fredericksburg   five   miles
& Potomac R.R.

Blake A. Magner

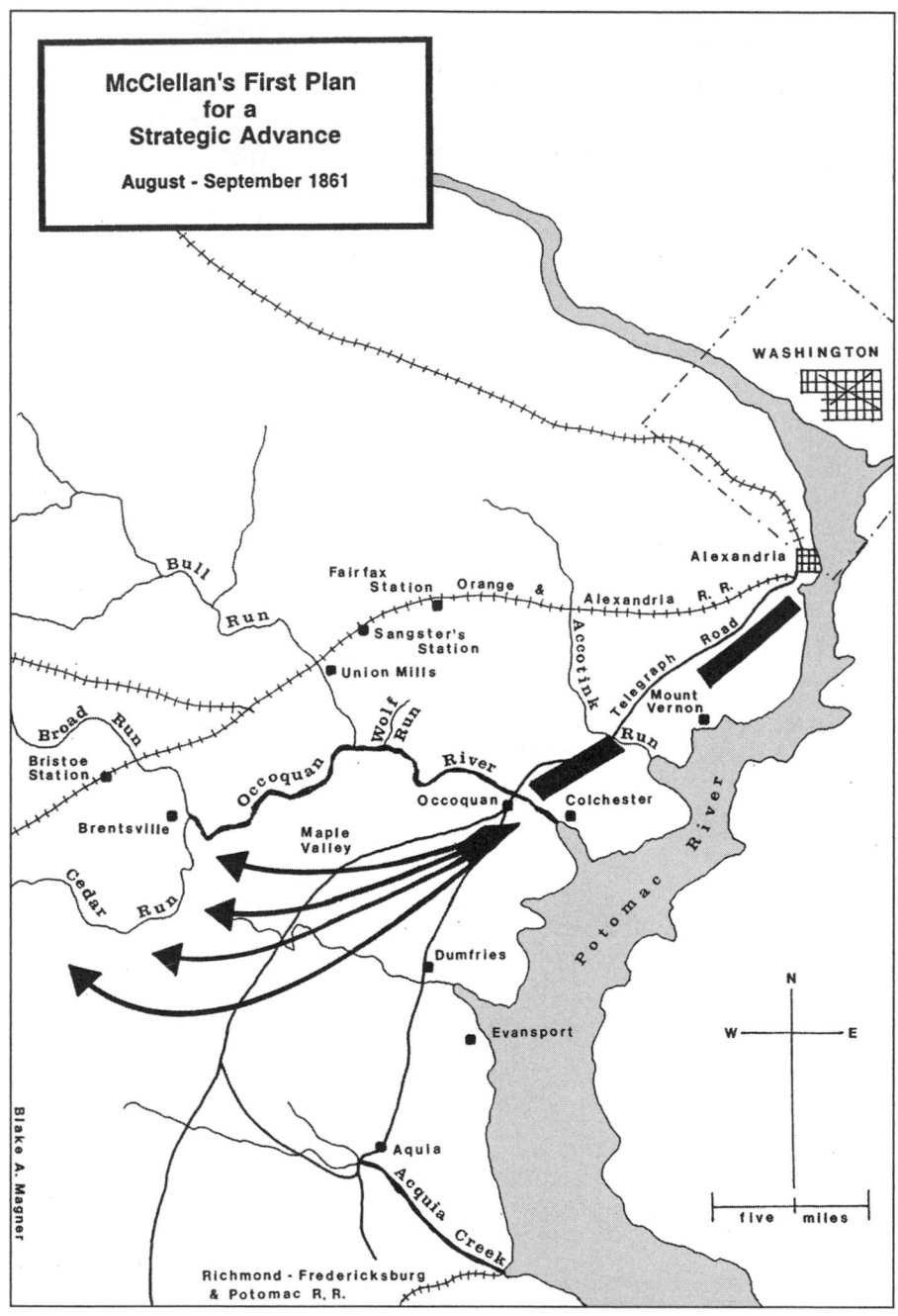

McClellan's First Plan
for a
Strategic Advance

August - September 1861

WASHINGTON

Alexandria

Fairfax
Station   Orange   &   Alexandria   R. R.

Sangster's
Station

Union Mills

Mount
Vernon

Bull   Run

Wolf   Run

Accotink   Run

Telegraph   Road

Broad   Run

Bristoe
Station

Brentsville

Occoquan   River

Maple
Valley

Occoquan

Colchester

Potomac   River

Cedar   Run

Dumfries

Evansport

N

W —— E

Aquia

Acquia   Creek

Richmond - Fredericksburg
& Potomac R. R.

five   miles

Blake A. Magner

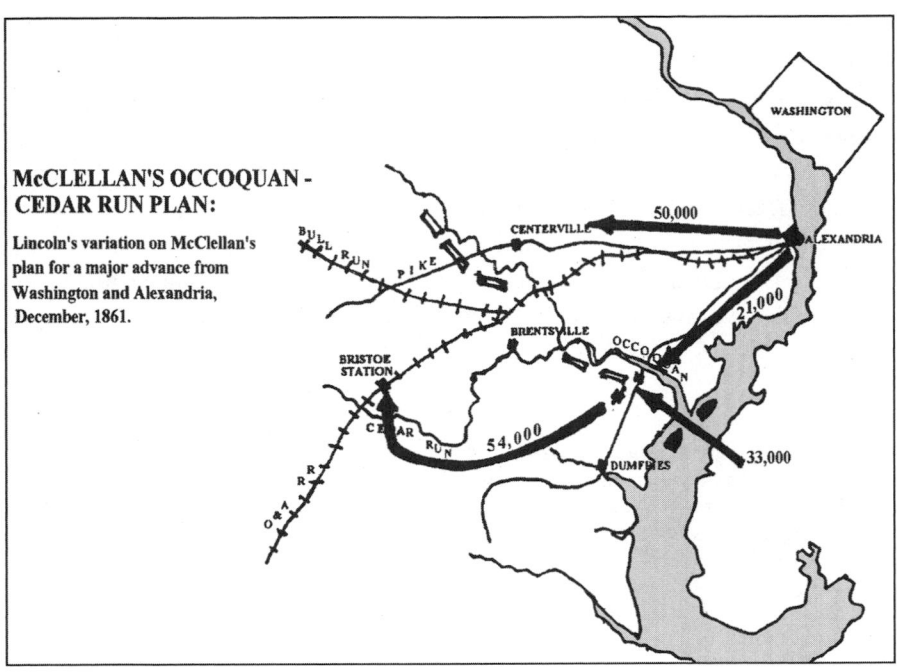

**McCLELLAN'S OCCOQUAN -
CEDAR RUN PLAN:**

Lincoln's variation on McClellan's
plan for a major advance from
Washington and Alexandria,
December, 1861.

Knowing McClellan's plan, Lincoln probably was not concerned about the general's penchant for secrecy. He would also have learned much later from Chase that McClellan changed his offensive concept to a movement against Richmond by water.[5] Bull Run, the disaster, had been fought too soon. Early February would be soon enough for this advance. But the president's ever-curious mind pushed him onward. By early December, harassed by the Radicals, he wanted more specific information and had taken the liberty of developing ideas of his own. Combining aspects of both

---

5   No direct evidence shows that Chase described the plan to Lincoln, but with all the concern about an advance Chase would not have kept it from the president. Three facts support the inference that Chase disclosed it to Lincoln shortly after McClellan described it to him: (1) Chase described the plan in early January to McDowell and Franklin, *C.C.W.*, 1, 270 (McDowell); (2) at the meeting after McClellan's recovery from his illness, the president was peaceful about McClellan's flat refusal to describe his plan; and (3)McClellan claimed in his memoirs that, when he refused to reveal his plans, he added that Lincoln "and the Secretary of the Treasury knew in general terms what my designs were." *M.O.S.*, 158; McDowell's memorandum quoted in Swinton, *Army of the Potomac*, 84–85 (a handwritten version of this invaluable document, marked as if by an assistant adjutant general, "a true copy," is in the Chicago Historical Society but has been "misfiled" and at this writing cannot be found).

McClellan's plans but not taking the army so far from the capital, he sent a "fill-in-the-blanks" series of questions to the major general around December 1.[6]

McClellan answered them in pencil, wrote a short paragraph at the end, and returned the note to Lincoln on December 10.[7] If the bridge trains were ready, McClellan wrote, he might be able to move as soon as December 15, but more probably December 25. After providing a proper garrison for the capital, he would have a movable force of slightly more than one hundred thousand men, seventy-one thousand from his army in Virginia and thirty-three thousand from Maryland and the capital. Lincoln's variation added an advance in the nature of a pinning move-

6   This is the first of a series of notes, memoranda, and letters relating to McClellan's plans for an advance. The original of this note from Lincoln is in the Lincoln MSS (L.C.) and is reprinted in *N&H*, 5, 148–149, and Basler, *Lincoln's Collected Works*, 4, 34–35. Its precise date is uncertain as is the date it was returned by McClellan with his notations in the blanks. An undated memorandum of questions from Lincoln, which is combined by Basler with Lincoln's letter to McClellan, dated February 3, 1862, is printed in *Lincoln's Collected Works*, 4, 118–125. The original is in the Stanton MSS (L.C.). Ives' very long letter to Bennett, dated January 15, 1862, recording his interviews with McClellan in January is in the James G. Bennett MSS (L.C.). Lincoln's note containing five questions, dated February 3, 1862, is in the Stanton MSS and is reprinted in *OR*, 5, 713. McClellan's letter to Stanton, dated February 3, 1862, is the last of the group. The dates of delivery of the documents to and from Lincoln are analyzed at length in Basler, *Lincoln's Collected Works*, 4, 119–125, and Sears, *McClellan's Correspondence*, 170–171, n. 1. No first-hand evidence exists. The author's views on these matters will be plain from the text. Matters on which the author disagrees with Basler and Sears—they are few and insignificant—will be treated in later footnotes except the undated "Suppose the enemy . . ." memorandum of three questions. It was probably prepared shortly after the December exchange, not in February.

7   Basler states that the final pencil entry of fifty thousand for the Centerville column is not in McClellan's handwriting. Basler, *Lincoln's Collected Works*, 4, 35, n. 5. The text is reproduced verbatim with editorial comment in *N&H*, 5, 148–149. In one of their worst examples of McClellan bashing, N&H depict a thoughtful president patiently communicating with his cavalier young subordinate, who was so indifferent that he contumaciously held the note ten days, then carelessly used a pencil to fill the blanks, an affront of some undefined sort to the chief executive. In their view Lincoln's idea had been "so scantily considered and so curtly dismissed" that the response was an insult. Of course, to them, the ten days meant nothing and could never have been used for thought. The original of the note, the circumstances, and the very lengthy letter at the end of January refute this criticism. In addition, they find the president's plan, rejected at this time, to have been later proven "eminently wise and sagacious"; but no one, not even their hero Ulysses S. Grant, adopted a small part of the president's plan. Without saying it, they may have been offended by the fact that McClellan found the time to write a long letter to the secretary of war at the end of January describing and analyzing both the Occoquan plan and the Urbana plan in considerable detail. They would have known about this letter because it found its way to Lincoln and to his MSS in the Library of Congress, letter dated January 31, 1862, from McClellan to Stanton. A letter of this sort McClellan should have addressed to his superior, the secretary of war, and with Scott on the shelf McClellan no longer had any reason to ignore protocol. But he could have been certain that it would go to the president, and he undoubtedly assumed it would, even if he did not actually arrange it.

ment on Centerville. In the blank McClellan suggested fifty thousand for it. As Lincoln saw it, the unused portion of the Virginia force, twenty-one thousand men, would again march down the Telegraph Road and cross the Occoquan River at the town of Occoquan. There, the thirty-three thousand from Maryland would join them after crossing the Potomac just below the mouth of the Occoquan. Where the Telegraph Road from Alexandria crossed the Occoquan River, the Rebels, they knew, had emplacements for artillery and entrenchments for infantry extending along its south bank toward the Potomac.[8] The combined force of fifty-four thousand men would move to positions southwest of Brentsville, cross Cedar Run, and swing north toward Bristoe Station.

The president thought his strategy would work with relative ease for two reasons: the Centerville column, a feint, would hold the largest Rebel force in the Centerville fortifications, from which it could not reinforce the Occoquan line; and the two columns converging just below the Occoquan would take the Confederates in front and flank no matter how the Rebels deployed to resist. He even considered the need for retreat. If necessary, the Centerville force could fall back fighting into the Torres Vedras works about the capital; and the Occoquan force could retire to the cover of the unassailable fleet on the Potomac.

McClellan's answers on the note did not keep Lincoln from further thinking. Prompted at least in part by Radical harassment, he had written a note seeking information about an offensive. Only Union movements had been considered. After he received McClellan's pencil responses, he wrote a second note,[9] which showed more subtlety. He considered reactions by the enemy. Once the movement began, the Rebels might attack the flank of the column on the march to the Occoquan. The president decided to forego the Centerville pinning attack and perhaps even the water crossing, combine all three forces, and march them together. Originally, the army was to follow the Telegraph Road, which crossed the river at the village of Occoquan. To reduce the danger and effectiveness of any Rebel attack, Lincoln moved the crossing from Occoquan to the village of Colchester, two miles farther downstream. Naively, he believed a march of an extra two miles would weaken any

8   *O.R. Atlas*, plate viii, prepared for Irvin McDowell, January 1, 1862.

9   The date of this note is unknown, and no other document prepared by Lincoln or McClellan suggests a date, *OR*, 5, 713, and n. By placement and notes Basler in *Lincoln's Collected Works*, 5, 119–120; n. 2, 125, suggests that it was sent to McClellan with, or around the time of, the clearly dated note of February 3. Sears agrees, Sears, *McClellan's Correspondence*, n. 1, 171, letter dated February 3, 1862, from McClellan to Stanton. The texts of the various notes suggest that the undated note related to the fill-in-the-blanks note or, as Sears suggests, to an earlier conference, ibid., n. 1, 170–171, and was, in effect, an addendum to that exchange.

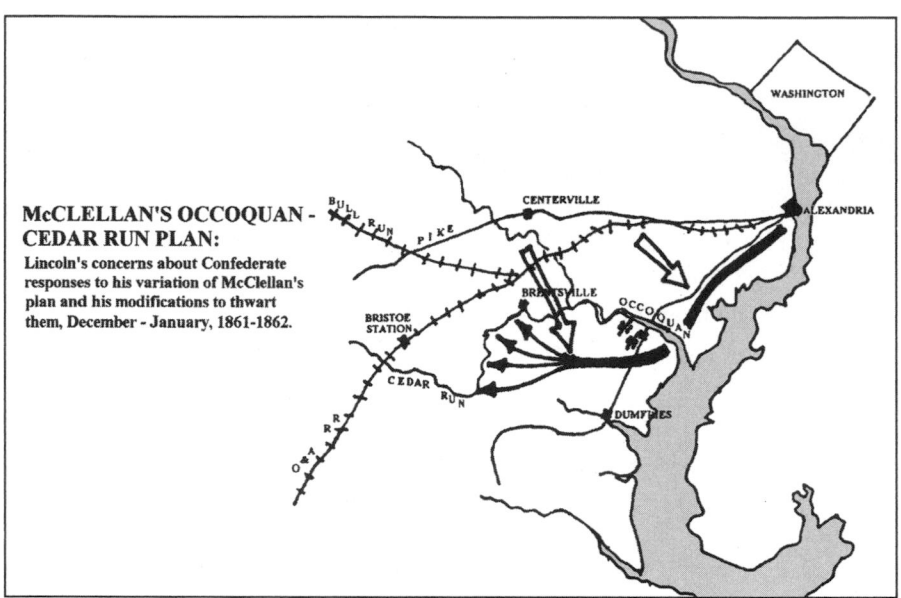

**McCLELLAN'S OCCOQUAN -
CEDAR RUN PLAN:**
Lincoln's concerns about Confederate
responses to his variation of McClellan's
plan and his modifications to thwart
them, December - January, 1861-1862.

Rebel response. Last, he was concerned that, if the Union forces reached Maple Valley beyond the Occoquan and began to break into five or six columns for the march to Cedar Run, the Rebels might use the roads from Manassas to attack them.

McClellan had already considered these rudimentary questions, thought about many other disabilities in the plan, and begun to suffer a growing disenchantment with it. He knew he could march from Alexandria to the Accotink without danger, but during the remainder of the march to the Occoquan he would expose his right flank to attack from Fairfax Station, Sangster's Station, and Union Mills along the line of the Orange & Alexandria Railroad. To protect against this, he must post a flank screen and leave it in position as long as the army drew supplies by road from Washington or until he won a battle.

Confederate infantry guarded the fords of Occoquan Creek below the mouth of Bull Run Creek at Wolf Run Shoals and had batteries concealed in woods on the heights behind them. By entrenching the heights from the vicinity of Sangster's Station on the Orange and Alexandria Railroad toward Evansport on the Potomac, the Rebels demonstrated that they expected the Occoquan movement. Any pinning column moving toward Centerville would be too far away to give support.

As he marched south from the Occoquan, passed through Maple Valley, and approached Cedar Run, the terrain and the poor road system would divide his army into five or six columns. At least one column would seize Dumfries in order to force the Confederates to abandon the batteries on the Potomac and to cover his left flank against an attack from Acquia Creek. He would need to prevent the Confederates from crossing the Occoquan below Wolf Run Shoals, where Bull Run and Cedar Run came together, and falling on the army's right flank. Once again, he would deplete his army by posting a blocking force on the Occoquan, this time from Wolf Run Shoals to Brentsville.

The weather and the roads, which would undoubtedly combine to delay his movement, prevented the selection of any definite time for an advance. McClellan believed that in mid-winter the roads would be useless. His concerns had justification. A short while later, he wrote, "The roads have gone from bad to worse. Nothing like their present condition has ever been known here before—they are impassable at present. We are entirely at the mercy of the weather."[10]

Flank exposure, detachments, bad weather, poor roads? The decline of McClellan's reliance on the Occoquan plan showed that he still adhered to the fundamental rules of Napoleonic warfare taught him by Dennis Hart Mahan: concentration, central position, and interior lines.[11] "This . . . brings out in bold relief the great advantage possessed by the enemy in the strong central position he occupies," McClellan wrote later, "with roads diverging in every direction and a strong line of defense, enabling him to remain on the defensive with a small force on one flank, while he concentrated everything on the other for a decisive action."

Even if the movement were successful, would great results follow? He thought not, and he had influential support for this opinion. On Friday, November 1, while he prepared to assume command of all armies, he and Francis P. Blair Jr., the brother of Postmaster General Montgomery Blair, discussed the disadvantages of an overland advance from the Potomac, particularly the results he could expect from any success on the Occoquan-Cedar Run line. Even if McClellan maneuvered successfully, fought a major battle, and won an overwhelming victory, Blair felt, the Confederates would have many naturally strong lines of defense in their rear areas.

McClellan told Blair his ideas had value. Over the next day or two Blair gave more thought to the discussion and on November 4 sent McClellan a memorandum

---

10   Sears, *McClellan's Correspondence*, 169, letter dated January 31, 1862, redated February 3 by the editor, from McClellan to Stanton; Bryant, *Brewster Letters*, 77, letter dated January 15, 1862, from Brewster to his mother, 85, February 19, 1862, from Brewster to his mother.

11   Unpublished MS Masters Thesis (U.M.I.) McCoun, Richard A., "General George Brinton McClellan: from West Point to the Peninsula; the Education of a Soldier and the Conduct of War" (1973) 51–52 (McCoun, *McClellan*).

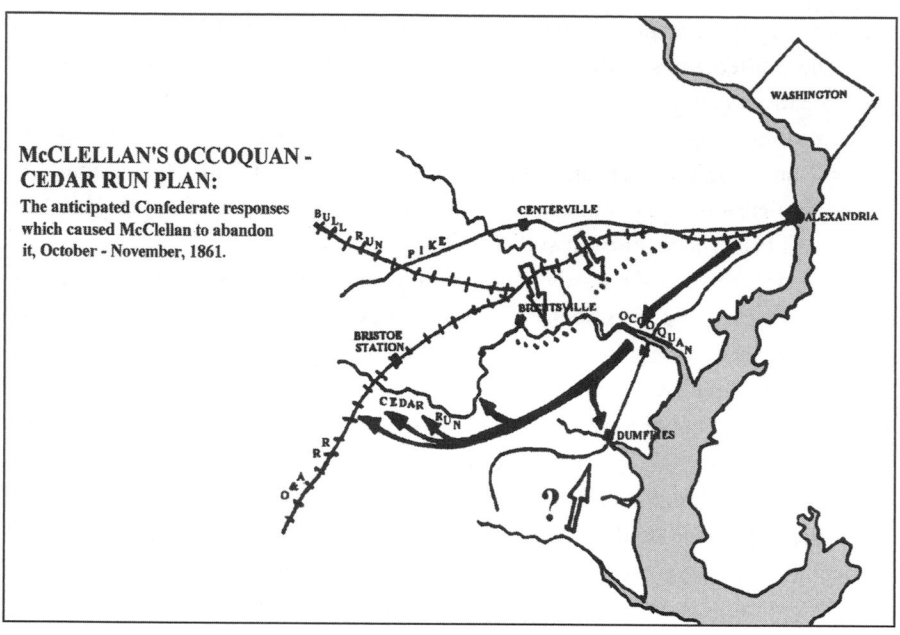

elaborating on their conversation. If McClellan attacked the heavily entrenched position at Manassas, the Confederates would most probably decline to fight and would retreat to their next position, the Occoquan River, a larger, more formidable barrier than Bull Run, Blair thought. If hard pressed there, they would fall back to the line of Acquia Creek. Falling back again, they would deploy behind the Rappahannock and would continue this until they reached Richmond. Each step would take McClellan farther from his base of operations, reduce his front line forces by detachments to guard the rear, delay his movements, and increase the burden on his transportation and commissariat.[12]

By the end of November, McClellan had abandoned his original ideas. Ever thoughtful, he had assessed the status of his army and concluded that it lacked the experience to undertake an overland campaign through Centerville and Manassas against a determined enemy. "[A]n . . . army reliable in defense," he wrote in a long February letter, "may not necessarily be reliable in offensive maneuvers until further training has been completed. Many weeks, I may say many months ago, this

---

12   Lincoln MSS (L.C.) memorandum dated November 4, 1861, from F. P. Blair, Jr., to McClellan.

Army of the Potomac was fully in condition to repel any attack. But there is a vast difference between that and the efficiency required to enable troops to attack successfully an army elated by victory, and entrenched in a position long since selected studied and fortified."

If he fought a great battle and won, the Confederates would withdraw; he would possess the battlefield; and his army would enjoy the heightened morale of a victory. But the victory would not be decisive because it would not destroy the enemy. As the Confederates retreated, they would absorb fresh units from their rear areas; they would destroy the bridges over the many rivers; and "We would probably find ourselves," McClellan wrote, "forced at last to change the whole theater of war, or to seek a shorter land route to Richmond with a smaller available force and at an expenditure of much more time, than were we to adopt the short line at once."[13] He had already hinted at "the short line" when he endorsed Lincoln's "fill-in-the-blanks" note: "I have now my mind actively turned towards another plan of campaign that I do not think at all anticipated by the enemy, nor by many of our own people."[14]

McClellan's plan for his army rapidly produced another torrent of controversy, and his increasing secrecy after the problem at Munson's Hill made it highly important to many important men. He told no one about his plans except those who had a strong "need to know" and his inner circle of trusted friends, Franklin, Andrew Porter, and Fitz John Porter. To the interested men about him, particularly the civilians with a hand in the war, he imparted nothing. If McClellan would say nothing, others would be pleased to submit their "strategic" plans to persons in authority. In fact, the persons in authority would solicit them.[15]

---

13 Lincoln MSS (L.C.) letter dated January 31, 1862, from McClellan to Stanton; Heintzelman MS Diary (L.C.) (large diary) entry dated March 8, 1862; *C.C.W.*, 1, 424 (McClellan); Swinton, *Army of the Potomac*, 69, n. McClellan's Occoquan-Cedar Run plan was a more advanced and sophisticated form of McDowell's original plan in July. Both would sideslip from their left and threaten to sever the communications of the Rebel army at Centerville-Manassas. Probably because the plan would vindicate his original idea, McDowell favored it over all others, especially over the water route, *C.C.W.*, 1, 259–260 (McDowell). This difference, especially as it was expressed in the January meetings, was probably the beginning of the severe decline in relations between McDowell and McClellan.

14 Lincoln MSS (L.C.) note dated December 1, 1861, by the curator, and reprinted in *N&H*, 5, 149.

15 The Detroit Post and Tribune, *Zachariah Chandler: An Outline Sketch of his Life and Public Services* (Detroit, 1890) 213–214, letter dated November 15, 1861, from Chandler to n.a. (Detroit Post and Tribune, *Chandler*); Stanton MSS (L.C.) letter dated January 30, 1862, from James Shields to Stanton; Swinton, *Army of the Potomac*, 80, McDowell Memorandum dated January 10, 1862.

In his final contest with Scott, McClellan had circumvented proper military channels of communication and violated the rules of military courtesy by addressing correspondence directly to important civilians like Lincoln, Chase, and Cameron rather than to Scott, his direct superior. If McClellan thought about it at all, he appears to have believed this unhealthy practice would end at Scott's departure, that no one would have the temerity to do it to him, and that it would never harm him. But it did not, they did, and it did. Almost every one of his division commanders had the ear of someone in the government. Because the men in the government heard nothing from McClellan and, therefore, had nothing to consider or discuss, they created their own material; and they would willingly receive "plans" from others. This extended the life of the back-staircase channel of communication McClellan had used so well himself, and it had the same deleterious effect on him that it had had on Scott. It undermined his relationship with Lincoln.

Always fearful that the Rebels would learn his plans, McClellan had better security than he thought. The garrulous rumor collector Count Adam Gurowski discussed an advance with McDowell in November. By this time McClellan had grown away from McDowell and had withheld his new plan to change his base by water to Urbana. Gurowski mentioned Occoquan and Brentsville. Knowing that the two towns were pivotal in the only plan McClellan had described to him, McDowell honored the major-general's desire for secrecy by responding evasively that "perhaps something similar will be under consideration."[16]

Even the Comte de Paris, probably McClellan's favorite young staff officer, did not know the new plan. At the end of November after the grand review at Bailey's Cross-Roads, the count wrote in his diary, "Now that the army's organization is well advanced, we all hope we will embark on a campaign within two weeks. There is no doubt the campaign's plan will be as we always thought it would be: to go through between Manassas and the Potomac passing Occoquan and Acquia Creek, taking Fredericks Burg and advancing from there on to Richmond."[17]

McClellan should have risked the leaks and explained his plans to the most involved government officials and his highest-ranking officers in order to pre-empt the field and make his ideas the focal point for discussion. Even if he decided that this would risk too much, he certainly should have begun the slow process of persuading the president. Without McClellan's competition for his attention, Lincoln developed his own strategic plans.

---

16   Gurowski, *Diary*, 1, 126, entry dated November 1861.

17   Comte de Paris MS diary (large diary) (A.N. de la M. de F.) entry dated November 24(?), 1861.

The vacuum created by McClellan's silence drew ideas from extraordinary persons. Disregarding the indisputable dominance of the Eastern theater, both North and South, Zachariah Chandler would have an Eastern general act strictly on the defensive with the Eastern troops, and "select one hundred thousand men of your city regiments which look well on parade, and keep them for reviews," he said. "Send the balance to the gulf states. We want none of them out West." Northwestern troops on the Potomac should be sent west where the active military forces would concentrate for an early December march. "Give the order 'forward,'" he wrote, "and *then cut the wires*. This army would march from New Orleans by way of Memphis and Richmond to Washington," which it would reach by the first of May.[18]

McClellan's subordinates, many of them older and more experienced than he, had ideas of their own for an advance. In May, McDowell had given Secretary Chase alternative overall plans for the war. Moving the main Eastern army by water to the Virginia peninsula between the York and James rivers, followed by a short march on Richmond, was one of them. In August or September, McDowell suggested this short, peninsular route to McClellan, who responded blandly that he thought it was a sound idea. Probably more for vindication than anything else, McDowell remained firmly wedded to his original march from the Potomac to Bull Run, then a slip left to interpose his army between the Rebel army at Manassas and its life-support system in Richmond.[19]

Others contributed. Heintzelman had a good idea, he thought. Thirty thousand men should sail to Fort Monroe, where they would pretend to prepare to go down the coast. He would circulate rumors to that effect. Suddenly, they would sail up the York and James rivers, bypass the Yorktown fortifications, cut off and capture the force under Magruder, and attack Richmond or Norfolk. This would force the Confederate army at Centerville and Manassas to retire. So pleased was Heintzelman with this plan that he wrote in his diary, "It might be one of the most brilliant events of the war. The expedition could not fail." He would suggest it to the general in chief.[20]

18   Detroit Post and Tribune, *Chandler*, 213–214, letter dated November 15, 1861, from Chandler to Cameron.

19   Stanton MSS (L.C.) undated memorandum on the stationery of Headquarters, Army of the Potomac (probably the minutes of the March 8 meeting of officers); *C.C.W.*, 1, 141, 259–260 (McDowell). Yet another plan was suggested by James Shields, *OR*, 5, 700–702, letter dated January 10, 1862, from Shields to McClellan.

20   Heintzelman MS Diary (L.C.) (large diary) entry dated November 25, 1861; *C.C.W.*, 3, 120 (Heintzelman).

During November he visited army headquarters to explain his idea but suffered the frustrations of others. Repeatedly, the major general could not see him.[21] When McDowell commanded the army, Heintzelman remembered, they had had long, open conversations about plans. Even the most eminent generals in history, he thought, wanted to know the opinions of their division commanders about maneuvers for such a large army. But not McClellan. Heintzelman did not know anything about McClellan's plans, he complained. He did not even know within fifty thousand the number of troops around Washington.

In early December, he went again to headquarters. Once again, McClellan was unavailable. He went to Marcy, found him unavailable, then returned to McClellan's office, where he sent in his card. Finally, a meeting. But it was interrupted when McClellan developed a chill. In despair Heintzelman explained his plan to Marcy, who said he thought it would be "a good move."[22]

Of course, Philip W. Kearny, separated by his independent personality, his social position, and his rebellious nature, and widely separated by his enormous wealth, could not be assimilated by the Army of the Potomac and could not await a plan devised by someone else. He had his own plan. A pinning force should advance on Manassas while the main force, composed of all other troops, even those from Baltimore, drove south up the Shenandoah Valley. This would force the valley Rebels either into Manassas or farther up the valley. The Federal army in the valley could then swing left, come behind Manassas, force the Confederates to leave their fortifications, and fight them in the open.

Kearny's other plan began with the same pinning movement but combined a march by forty thousand men from the left across Occoquan Creek to Acquia, which would dispose of the thirty thousand Rebels in the Acquia-Dumphries area. A second, short march would occupy Fredericksburg, Virginia, on the Rappahannock River, leaving the main force free to cooperate with columns on the York or James rivers for an attack on Richmond.[23]

Plans from other people involved a limited assault on Norfolk, Virginia; but this would not produce the decisive finality McClellan wanted. McClellan treated it as if it were an idea of no consequence, little better perhaps than the Manassas idea.

---

21 Heintzelman MS diary (L.C.) (large diary) generally, entries for the month of November.

22 Heintzelman MS Diary (L.C.) (large diary) entry dated December 6, 1861. By this time McClellan's similar Urbana plan was well developed, had supplanted the Occoquan-Cedar Run concept, and was undoubtedly known to Marcy, who could not have failed to note the similarities of the two.

23 DePeyster, *Kearney*, 211, 213.

Norfolk lay so far from the active area of his plans that it needed no consideration. And it was contrary to his defined purpose for the army; he did not wish to detach thirty thousand men for any purpose.

McClellan's friends in the navy tried to help with their ideas. David Dixon Porter, with whom McClellan had already spent much time discussing the attack on New Orleans, had been assigned command of the mortar fleet for the attack. On the way it could help McClellan capture Richmond. "When the mortar fleet was ready," Porter wrote in his journal, "I was to let the General know. He was then to embark thirty thousand men, in steamers, and I was to sail with the fleet, for Hampton Roads. Arriving there I was to open a bombardment on the point opposite the Ripraps, and he was to land the thirty thousand men as if for an attack on Norfolk. It was well known of what importance the latter place was to the rebels, until they could remove all the eighteen hundred heavy guns at the navy yard, and fit the 'Merrimack' for service, since upon that vessel they depended for annihilating our navy and laying Washington city under contribution. One hundred thousand men would embark at Annapolis, as soon as operations commenced with the mortar fleet, and move by telegraphic signals, as soon as they were needed. If the rebels did send their 60,000 men to save Norfolk there would be our 30,000 to amuse them until the 100,000 could be embarked and hurried up the James River."[24]

Curiously, the ideas of McClellan's officers had one thing in common: none proposed an attack on Centerville and Manassas, and the majority moved the army by water to the Peninsula between the York and James rivers. But the proponents of these plans, unlike McDowell, had no old failure to overcome. Continuous discussions of all these plans occurred among McClellan's generals, but because he did not communicate with them, they had nothing from him to consider. Limited communication had lasted through the period of reviews in fall, but after that, no one could see him.[25]

At the lowest levels rumors circulated throughout the army about the future. Whether they rested on leaks with substance or hypothesizing with logic, they covered the same gamut. One had the army going south. A more precise one had it moving to Fort Monroe for an advance on Richmond. One with accuracy that was probably accidental said the army would cross the Potomac with thirty to fifty thousand men to the mouth of the Occoquan, advance the forces on the river in front of Washington, and send Banks downriver, all putting two hundred thousand troops in

24   David Porter MS Journal (L.C.), 201–203.

25   Heintzelman MS diary (large diary) (L.C.) entry dated November, 1861.

three armies into a major conflict with an equal number of Confederates. Still others, less creative, thought the army would take the old but well-fortified route through Manassas. Some thought the army would stay just where it was.[26]

McClellan had long ago discarded the Manassas route. He had no desire to be tarred with a second failure of the "McDowell plan," and he knew he would find the Centerville position naturally strong, well fortified, armed with cannon, and well manned. The village lay on the back slope of a long north-south ridge with a gradual slope east, the kind of position that would expose the advancing attacker to infantry and artillery fire over a long approach. This movement would have appalled Dennis Hart Mahan. One of Pinkerton's spies, claiming to have had dinner with Jefferson Davis, Judah P. Benjamin, the Confederate secretary of state, and William M. Browne, Confederate assistant secretary of state, had learned that the Confederates had eighty thousand men under Johnston, Beauregard, and Smith at Centerville and 175 to 200 guns in strong fortifications. They expected the next major battle to be fought there.[27] Two months later, Pinkerton drew on conversations with seventeen contrabands, fugitives, and others to confirm this. Johnston had a total of one hundred sixty thousand men in Virginia, with fifty thousand at Centerville.[28] From their fieldworks the Confederates could use artillery and infantry fire to great advantage.[29]

In all McClellan's thinking he wanted the principal Rebel army to remain in the Centerville field works until he moved somewhere else with his main army.[30] If he succeeded capturing the strategic offensive, he could seize the best position, prepare impregnable field fortifications, force the Confederates to attack him, and maximize his chance of victory by fighting on the tactical defensive.[31]

26　Robertson, *McAllister Letters*, 95, letter dated November 17, 1861, from McAllister to his daughter Sarah; Blight, David W., ed., *When this Cruel War Is Over: The Civil War Letters of Charles Harvey Brewster* (Amherst, 1992) 49, letter dated October 15, 1861, from Brewster to "Pary" (Blight, *Brewster Letters*).

27　McClellan MSS (L.C.) letter dated October 28, 1861, from Allen to McClellan; Lecomte, Ferdinand, *Campagnes de Virginia et de Maryland en 1862: Documents Officiels Soumis au Congres Traduits de L'Anglais avec Introduction et Annotations* (Paris, 1863) fn. 15 (Lecomte, *Campagnes de Virginie*). In fact, the Rebels at Manassas believed this and reported it to Richmond. Crist and Dix, *Papers of Jefferson Davis*, 7, 320–321, letter dated September 3, 1861, from J. E. Johnston to Davis.

28　McClellan MSS (L.C.) letter dated January 7, 1862, from Allen to McClellan.

29　McClellan MSS (L.C.) letters dated October 28, 1861, January 6, 1862, and January 27, 1862, from Allen to McClellan.

30　Manton Marble MSS (L.C.) letter dated March 17, 1862, from Porter to Marble; *M.O.S.*, 203; Lecomte, *Campagnes de Virginie*, 28, n.

31　Sears, *McClellan's Correspondence*, 167–168, letter dated January 31, 1862, re-dated February 3, 1862, by the editor, from McClellan to Stanton.

When McClellan became general in chief in early November, the vistas before him became unlimited, and his vision changed. Now he could coordinate armies all over the United States without concerns about departmental boundaries. Relieved of the departmental system, he could take his army anywhere he chose, and he could use any means available. The extraordinary feat of his old chief in Mexico and of the English in the Crimean War would guide his new thinking. In the West, Fremont, a Radical favorite,[32] had failed and lost his command. McClellan sent Don Carlos Buell, his friend and trusted subordinate, to command the Department of Ohio. In the same general orders Henry W. Halleck, Scott's unsuccessful candidate for general in chief, received the Department of the Missouri.[33] Using the Cumberland River as a dividing line, McClellan put the eastern part of Kentucky in Buell's hands and gave the western part to Halleck.[34] As he had when he sent his first strategic suggestions to Scott, McClellan saw the force under his direct command as the determinative army. But with larger concepts available, he developed a strategic plan that would include the armies under Buell and Halleck and would effect concentration.

McClellan expected the Western forces to be in good condition with proper organization, arms, and equipment.[35] But Buell found the army in Kentucky "in the most deplorable state," and in his instructions to Halleck, McClellan acknowledged that he had been sadly mistaken about that army as well. Halleck was headed for "chaos . . . , a system of reckless expenditures and fraud perhaps unheard of before in the history of the world, [and] many general and staff officers holding illegal commissions and appointments not recognized or approved by the President or Secretary of War."[36]

At the end of November McClellan still thought he could begin a major campaign soon. He wrote Buell, "I doubt whether all the movements can be arranged

---

32   Williams, *Lincoln and the Radicals*, 20, 84, 105; Trefousse, *The Radical Republicans*, 191–192, 241–242; Tap, *Over Lincoln's Shoulder*, 83–86, generally chap. 3, esp. 81–87; Flower, Frank A., *Edwin McMasters Stanton*, 123, letter dated January 7, 1862, from Stanton to Barlow (Akron, 1905); Nevins, *Fremont*, 543–549; Blue, *Fremont*, 201–217.

33   *OR*, 4, 349 and 3, 567, General Orders No. 97, dated November 9, 1861, from the Headquarters of the Army, Adjutant General's Office; *M.O.S.*, 201–202.

34   The new departments, formed from older divisions commanded primarily by Fremont, were defined in General Orders No. 97, Headquarters of the Army, Washington, dated November 9, 1861, but printed in two volumes of *OR*, according to relevance. *OR*, 3, 567, and *OR*, 4, 349.

35   Sears, *McClellan's Correspondence*, 163–164, letter dated January 31, 1862, redated February 3 by the editor, from McClellan to Stanton.

36   *OR*, 3, 568, letter dated November 11, 1861, from McClellan to Halleck.

so that the grand blows shall be struck in less than a month or six weeks from the present time. . . . Unless circumstances render it necessary, do not strike until I too am ready. Should I be delayed, I will not ask you to wait for me."[37] Buell responded several times that he had deficient facilities and equipment, especially his transportation. Their need for augmentation delayed him.[38]

Assuming that his able subordinates could cure these deficiencies, McClellan included their armies in his expanded plans for an advance. Every hour, he thought, saw an improvement for the Northern forces and a proportionate decrease in the strength of the South. McClellan believed, as Scott had before him, that Union sentiment in North Carolina, Tennessee, North Georgia, and several counties in South Carolina was rapidly increasing, together with great dissatisfaction with the Confederate government.[39] The period of service of eighty thousand Rebel troops would expire in the near future, and, McClellan thought, "it may be assumed safely that not over ten thousand of them will reenlist . . . Much suffering, possible disaster, and great carnage would be saved if the federal armies could continue to increase in efficacy, preparation, and discipline until about April; and the war might be ended at a blow." But political considerations, financial necessity, sagging national confidence, and precarious foreign relations forced him to conclude that an immediate victory had become indispensable. The president, Seward, and the cabinet believed together that they could restore the country to a safe and healthy condition only by prompt success on the battlefield.

Movements on the Mississippi River and other movements would produce no decisive results. McClellan intended them to confuse the enemy but only as feints. Buell's army in Kentucky would begin the real effort while a coastal expedition by General Ambrose Burnside would capture Roanoke Island and drive inland to Knoxville. These movements would hold Confederate forces in eastern Kentucky and Tennessee, would distract attention from the main effort, and would prevent Confederate concentration in force against McClellan's Army of the Potomac in Virginia.[40]

---

37   *OR*, 7, 458, letter dated November 29, 1861, from McClellan to Buell.

38   *OR*, 7, 504, letter dated December 18, 1861, from Buell to McClellan; 520, letter dated December 21, 1861 from McClellan to Buell; 530, letter dated January 7, 1862, from Buell to the president.

39   Over time, numerous military planners have depended on dissident citizens of the enemy to rise and assist them; and in virtually all cases they have been wrong, an excellent example being Kennedy's ill-fated attack on Cuba. Widen, Peter, *Bay of Pigs: The Untold Story*, 309 (New York, 1979).

40   James G. Bennett MSS (L.C.) letter dated January 15, 1862, from Ives to Bennett.

Although he probably still believed he could begin the culminating movement of the Army of the Potomac by late January or early February, he must have realized that he now controlled a machine with many working parts and that the co-operating movements of the distant parts depended on his ability to direct the skills and vigor of distant subordinates, the task Scott had failed with Patterson. The difficulties presented by eastern Kentucky and eastern Tennessee absorbed his energies[41] while his own army, with the exception of a few divisions, was not ready for a major offensive movement.[42] These factors made an immediate advance by the Army of the Potomac impossible. But could he wait? A junior officer recognized McClellan's difficulty when he wrote in his diary at the end of November, "I have some little fear that we will go into winter quarters here, but I hardly believe Gen. McClellan dare risk his reputation in such a move."[43]

Frustrated by the inability of Buell and Halleck to achieve readiness, by his inability to use the new possibilities available to him, and by the problems presented by his original plan, McClellan lost interest and began to develop a new one. Doubtless, his experience as a young lieutenant in Scott's Vera Cruz-Mexico City campaign, his tour as a more senior officer in the Crimean Peninsula, and the possibility of coordinating the Western armies contributed to this change. If he followed Scott's example, he could take advantage of the Union's absolute naval supremacy, make a major water movement, move directly against the Confederate capital, force the Confederate army to attack him, fight on the tactical defensive, reduce his casualties to those of a defensive contest, and win the great battle that would end the war in negotiations for peace.[44] He must have known from his first consideration of this plan that, if nothing else, the accumulation of sufficient shipping alone would delay his movement past December if not until spring.

41   Porter MSS (L.C.) letter dated September 26, 1885, from Franklin to Porter; *OR*, 5, 41, McClellan's report.

42   Webb MSS (Y.U.) letters dated April 23, 1881, and June, 1881, from Humphreys to Webb.

43   Sears, *For Country, Cause & Leader (Haydon Diary)*, 128–129, entry dated November 25, 1861.

44   Lincoln MSS (L.C.) letter dated January 31, 1862, from McClellan to Stanton; *C.C.W.*, 1, 425 (McClellan). Disagreements and debates about frontal assaults had existed before the Mexican War, McCoun MS Masters Thesis, "McClellan: Education of a Soldier," 39–47, and had occurred during the Mexican War in the final battles at Molino del Rey and Chapultepec outside Mexico City. In most cases, the Napoleon-Jomini claim for the immediate value of the costly frontal assault prevailed. Bauer, *Mexican War*, 308–318; especially, 311–312, Eisenhower, *Agent of Destiny*, 189–196. Mahan opposed them whenever an alternative was available, Hagerman, Edward, *The American Civil War and the Origins of Modern Warfare: Ideas, Organization, and Field Command* (Indianapolis and Bloomington, 1988) 9–10, 23–24 (Hagerman, *American Civil War*).

However much McClellan derived from the ideas McDowell and Heintzelman had discussed with him, he improved on them.[45] While he considered alternatives to the Occoquan plan during the early days of November, he received information from his intelligence service that tended to confirm the viability of the route from Old Point Comfort and Fort Monroe up the peninsula formed by the James and York rivers. The Confederates had only two fortified strongholds on the route, York-town, where the British had surrendered in 1781, and Gloucester Point, directly across the river on the left bank. Less than a mile apart, they had fortifications, heavy caliber guns of position, and supplemental outworks.

The Confederate encampment at Gloucester Point had two regiments of infantry, one in board shanties inside the entrenchments for winter quarters and the other in canvas tents about half a mile outside the entrenchments. It also had two companies of cavalry and one field battery of mixed guns. A heavy earthwork on the beach had twelve mounted guns ranging from thirty-two to sixty-four pounders. The entrenchments enclosed an area of about fifteen acres bounded by a breast-work of split pine logs "set up endways inside with an earth bank outside about twelve feet at the base." Earth shoveled against the outside of the log barricade had increased the height of the breastworks by creating a ditch five or six feet deep. At the end of the breastworks a sixty-four pounder traversed their outside face and en-joyed a clear field of fire across seven hundred cleared acres bounded by timber on the north and the York River on the south. On the point, the Confederates had be-gun construction of a heavy earthwork on an elevation fifty yards from the water, thirty to thirty-five feet above water level, and about two hundred yards below the batteries. The main fortifications, now partly finished, stood eight to ten feet wide at the top and five to six feet deep with a perpendicular face. This battery was in-tended to hold four thirty-two pounders and two sixty-four pounders.

At Yorktown, John B. "Prince John" MacGruder, now a general in the Confed-erate service, maintained his headquarters in the town. The landings lay in front of a hill that rose about twenty-five feet above the beach. Atop the hill in front of the town stood an earthwork mounting thirty-two to sixty-four pounder guns. The Yorktown battery lay about three quarters of a mile from and nearly opposite the Gloucester battery but a short distance downriver.

The distance across the peninsula between Yorktown and Grove Wharf on the James River required a ride of approximately ten miles. A few miles below Grove

45   As diverse and extensive as they are, the sources provide no clue about the origin of the wa-ter movement to the Chesapeake Bay. McDowell was the first to suggest it in a surviving writing, but McClellan may or may not have conceived the idea independently. Certainly, his life had enough suggestive events to support a claim of origination by him.

Wharf a point of land in the James River had a very heavy battery and an equally heavy battery on the opposite shore.[46] Between Yorktown and Fort Monroe on the east or north side of the peninsula and between Warwick Court House on the west or south side and Newport News, small creeks and inlets emptied into both the James and York rivers cutting the peninsula. Covering the roads south of Yorktown, breastworks holding guns ranging from eighteen to sixty-four pounders stood on the high ground between the headwaters of the various creeks.

Before the war no man had contemplated a need for military maps to fight his brother. Few accurate and no current maps existed. The technology to convert aerial photographs to topographical maps with contour lines did not exist. With much effort that he concealed to avoid disclosing the new plan under consideration, Major Andrew Atkinson Humphreys managed to find an 1815 map of the Peninsula.[47]

Like all coast defenses, the Rebel heavy guns on the York River covered the water. From his intelligence officer, McClellan knew that the few land emplacements could not stop a substantial land force on either side of the peninsula. Union forces could land in an area controlled by the Fort Monroe garrison and its guns. The Confederates, known to be only fifteen thousand to twenty thousand strong,[48] lacked the strength to drive a well-supported landing force into the water.[49]

McClellan could land on Old Point Comfort by Fort Monroe, then march up the peninsula, bypassing Yorktown. This would give him a secure base of operations, a safe line of supply on the James River, and landing facilities vastly superior to any others available. If Yorktown remained occupied by an active Confederate force, he could take a blocking position to the north and besiege it with a small force. By landing a strong force in the rear of Gloucester, he could move freely up the left or north bank of the York River. Of the various alternatives he deemed this one the most safe and most secure, characteristics that would have appealed to him.[50]

---

46   McClellan MSS (L.C.) letter dated November 15, 1862, from Allen to McClellan.

47   Webb MSS (Y.U.) handwritten half-page memorandum of n.d. (approximately 1881) by Humphreys.

48   McClellan MSS (L.C.) letter dated November 15, 1861, from Allen to McClellan.

49   Butler, J. R. M., ed. *History of the Second World War (United Kingdom Series)*, Kirby, Major-General S. Woodburn, *The War Against Japan: The Loss of Singapore*, 1, 403–404 (London, 1957).

50   Military Historical Society of Massachusetts MSS (John C. Ropes letters) (Mugar Library, Boston University) letters dated November 26, 1893, November 30, 1893, and March 18, 1894, from Porter to Ropes and November 16, 1893, from Webb to Ropes; Porter MSS (L.C.) letter dated November 29, 1893, from Franklin to Porter. Participants agree to disagree about this preference, e.g., Ropes letters, letters dated December 7, 1893, from Franklin to Ropes and November 21, 1893, from Porter to Ropes. And the participants even appeared to disagree with

After more thought McClellan probably changed his mind in early December and decided against the peninsula because that route presented disabilities he could avoid. The Confederates held nearby Norfolk with a substantial, dangerous naval force. They were known to be constructing an ironclad vessel on the hull of the ineptly destroyed *Merrimac*, a former United States frigate.

If McClellan could turn the forts at Yorktown and Gloucester, known to be heavily armed and well constructed, he need not assume the risk of a siege or a bypassed enemy force in his rear. To use a better, faster, and safer movement by water,[51] he would leave the "Torres Vedras" fortifications around Washington, march secretly to Annapolis, take ship with fifty thousand men, sail down Chesapeake Bay, turn into the Rappahannock River, land unopposed at Urbana on the south bank of the river, send the ships back at once for another fifty thousand men, and with a rapidly assembled army of one hundred thousand, march unopposed to a position a few miles north of Richmond. Agents would destroy the railroad bridges between Richmond and Manassas. The Confederates, still massed along the Centerville Ridge-Bull Run Creek line, he would take by surprise in their rear.

This would avoid the batteries on the Potomac River, evade the Norfolk naval forces, trap Magruder in the Peninsula, force evacuation of the fortresses at Yorktown and Gloucester Point without siege, and interpose the Army of the Potomac between the Confederate capital and the Rebel army withdrawing from the Bull Run line. Of course, he would position himself on ground of his choosing—ground suitable for the tactical defensive—and end the war with a great battle.[52]

themselves, e.g., Ropes letters, letter dated November 26, 1893, from Porter to Ropes ("Although not so expeditious or so brilliant as were the anticipated results via Urbana, McClellan always had a preference of movement upon Richmond via the Peninsula") and letter dated December 9, 1893, from Porter to Ropes ("he [McClellan] thought well of the route via Fortress Monroe but preferred via Urbana *as most rapid and more brilliant in probable results . . .*" [Porter's emphasis]). Because Porter was the closest to McClellan and was scrupulous about the facts even though "imaginative" about the inferences he drew from them, the only explanation that accounts for these different views is that McClellan originally preferred the Fort Monroe-Peninsula route, then changed his mind in favor of the Urbana route. This also explains the ease with which he switched back to the Peninsula route in March. Smith's contrary view does not necessarily conflict with Porter's. The early choice of the Peninsula by McClellan for his flanking movement by water is supported by Franklin's description of it in the conversations with Lincoln during McClellan's illness, *infra.*

51   Military Historical Society of Massachusetts MSS (John C. Ropes letters) (B.U.) letter dated December 7, 1893, from Franklin to Ropes.

52   Heintzelman MS diary (L.C.) (large diary) entry dated March 8, 1862; *C.C.W.*, 3, 422–425 (McClellan), 388 (Barnard), 178 (Porter, F-J); Barnard, *Peninsular Campaign*, 51, Appendix. McClellan had seen the value of defensive field works during the siege of Sebastopol in the Crimean War. In the face of developments in firepower (range, accuracy, and rapidity), he and his mentor Dennis Hart Mahan preferred the tactical defensive.

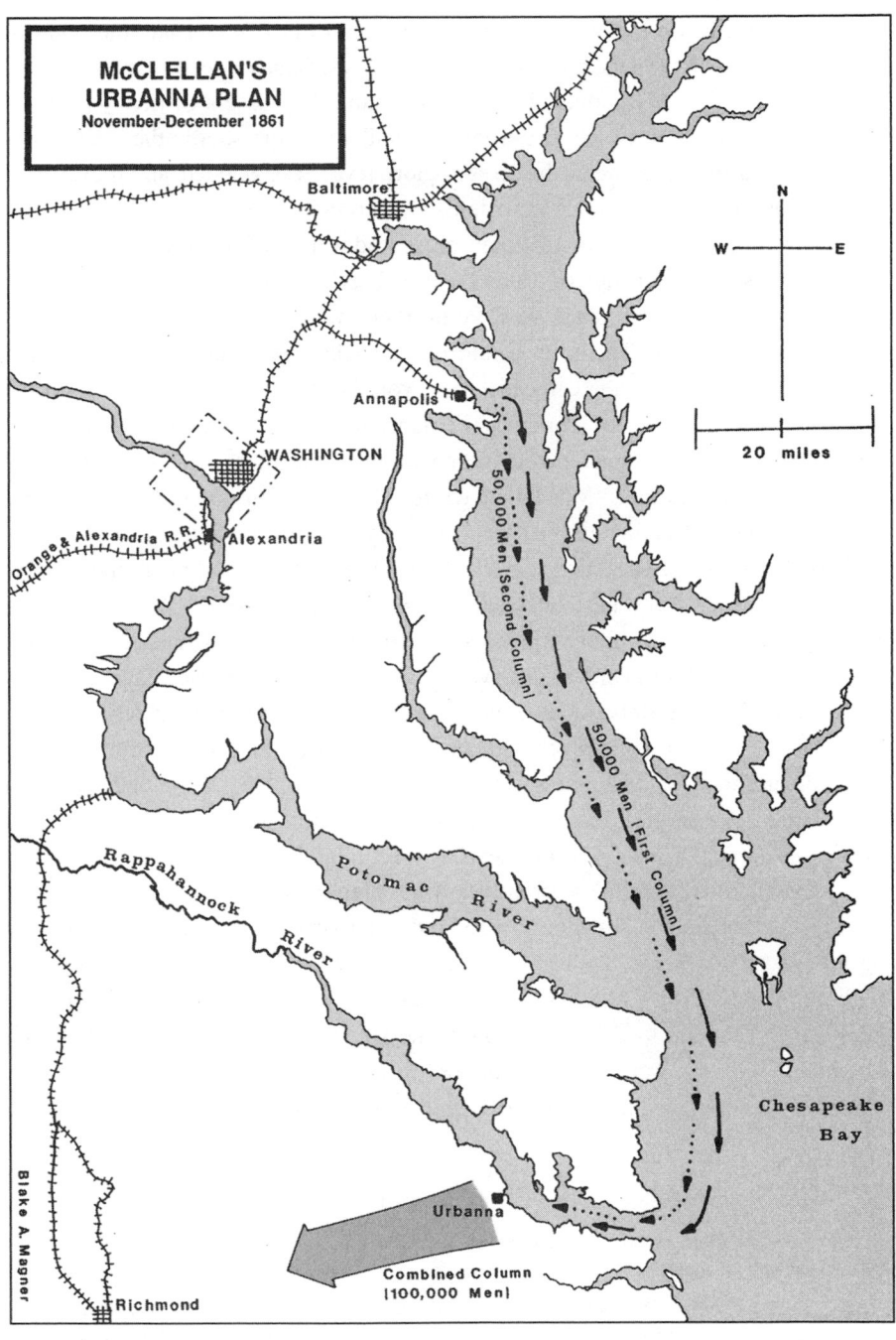

McCLELLAN'S
URBANNA PLAN
November-December 1861

N
W — E

20 miles

Baltimore

Annapolis

WASHINGTON

Orange & Alexandria R.R.   Alexandria

50,000 Men (Second Column)

50,000 Men (First Column)

Rappahannock
River

Potomac   River

Chesapeake
Bay

Blake A. Magner

Urbanna

Combined Column
(100,000 Men)

Richmond

"Should it be determined to operate from the lower Chesapeake, the point of landing which promises the most brilliant results is Urbana on the lower Rappahannock," he thought. "This point is easily reachable by vessels of heavy draft."[53] Spring came two or three weeks earlier. The soil was more sandy; the roads passable in all seasons of the year; the ground more level, less wooded, and more clear; and the country more favorable for offensive operations.

By McClellan's analysis, this plan presented a host of other advantages. The Confederates did not occupy or watch the area between Urbana and Richmond. By one long march he could reach West Point, the key to the region. Then, two short marches to Richmond. The army would reach Richmond before the Rebels could strongly reinforce it. Strategically, his army would connect Burnside's coastal force on the left with the Western armies on the right, and his advancing line would compel the Confederates to abandon the entrenchments at Manassas for a race to Richmond. "He must do this," McClellan wrote, "for should he permit us to occupy Richmond, his destruction can be averted only by entirely defeating us in a battle in which he must be the assailant . . . Should we fail in that, we could with the cooperation of the Navy, cross the James and throw ourselves in rear of Richmond thus forcing the enemy to come out and attack us, for his positions would be untenable, with us on the southern bank of the river."[54] If the Urbana movement were successful, he would cut the Rebel lines of communications; control Chesapeake Bay, the James River, and the York River; impose federal power in Virginia; and force the Confederates to abandon Tennessee and North Carolina. "Should we be beaten in a battle, we have a perfectly secure retreat down the Peninsula on Fort Monroe, with our flanks perfectly secured by the fleet."

McClellan had familiar alternatives if his plan were not satisfactory. "Should circumstances render it not advisable to land at Urbana, we can use Mob-Jack Bay or—the worst coming to the worst we can take Fort Monroe as a base, and operate with complete security, although with less celerity & brilliancy of results, on the Peninsula." The total force to be put on the new line would be somewhere between one hundred ten thousand and one hundred forty thousand men. "I hope to use the latter number by bringing fresh troops into Washington, and still leaving it quite

53   Sears, *McClellan's Correspondence,* 168, letter dated February 3, 1862, by the editor from McClellan to Stanton.

54   The correctness of McClellan's analysis would await its proof until 1864 when another general having a different relationship with Washington would implement this plan after a much different preparatory campaign.

safe. I fully realize that in all projects offered time is probably the most valuable consideration. It is my decided opinion that in that point of view the [Urbana] plan should be adopted." As this campaign progressed, McClellan thought, he would finally corner the Confederate army in Louisiana. He would lead the army that would destroy the last remnants of rebellion in their refuge in New Orleans.[55]

<hr>

55   James G. Bennett MSS (Library of Congress) letter dated January 15, 1862, from Ives to Bennett; Sears, *McClellan's Correspondence*, 168, letter dated January 31, 1862, redated February 3, 1862, by the editor, from McClellan to Stanton.

Chapter 22

"General McClellan is so unwell that he will be unable to perform his engagement with you today."

—McClellan's aide to the Joint Committee

The Plans Fall Ill

$\mathcal{J}$he plan for a water movement? McClellan at his best! Although perhaps unrealistic in his opinion about the time needed for delivery of the second fifty thousand men, McClellan did not hypothesize a plan of unrealistic numbers. When he first arrived in Washington, he suggested an army of two hundred seventy-five thousand men as the main battle force, a number without practical reality. Now he planned for a realistic mobile force of one hundred forty thousand. He assumed that completion of his version of the Torres Vedras lines around the capital would allay concerns about its safety.

In the middle of December, he turned to one of the most important aspects of his plan, transportation, and asked his quartermaster Stuart Van Vliet how much time he would need to collect the necessary vessels. Van Vliet finished his calculations just after the new year and sent McClellan a letter on January 3. Having already prepared Burnside for the coast and Butler for the mouth of the Mississippi, the government had stripped the harbors clean of shipping. Van Vliet believed he could collect enough to move a division in fifteen days, and he might be able to move forty thousand men in one month. And if the ships taking Burnside and Butler became available, he could shorten the time.[1]

---

1   McClellan MSS (L.C.) letter dated January 3, 1862, from Van Vliet to McClellan.

Unfortunately, Van Vliet underestimated the strength of a division by three regiments and two batteries, the two artillery units alone requiring six sailing vessels and three tugs for towing. As a result he underestimated the shipping needed to move forty thousand men at one time by at least 20 percent.[2] This news must have been distressing because McClellan had believed the shipping could be easily and routinely collected.[3]

Meanwhile, McClellan's preference for the Urbana route received at least private reinforcement from a well-regarded source. An 1831 graduate from the Military Academy, where he stood thirteenth in his class, Major Andrew Atkinson Humphreys had become a scientist and an engineer of international note. In 1851 he received an assignment to study the hydrology of the ever shifting channels at the mouth of the Mississippi River and the causes of the destructive floods in that area. Sunstroke, a tour in Europe to study other things, and various unrelated assignments delayed but did not halt Humphreys and his team. By 1861, he and his subordinate Henry L. Abbott, hard at work, finished the written report.

Without greed for personal distinction Humphreys insisted that he and Abbott submit it as "our joint report." Their final product, *Report Upon the Physics and Hydraulics of the Mississippi River*, produced a solution that had eluded engineers of many countries for many years. Brilliant on its general subject of river hydraulics, it found translation into many foreign languages and remained the authoritative work on the subject for decades into the twentieth century. To his memberships in the distinguished American Philosophical Society and the American Academy of Arts and Sciences, he added the Imperial Royal Geological State Institute of Vienna, the Geographical Society of Paris, the Italian Geological Society, the Society of Austrian Engineer Architects, and the Lombardian Institute of Science and Letters.[4]

Humphreys' appearance confirmed the rigorous application of precise scientific principles that characterized his work. Extremely neat, he constantly scrubbed himself, wore clean paper dickeys, a narrow cravat of brilliant red, and shoes and gaiters rather than boots. Widely read and learned beyond his profession, he appeared to others to be an "extremely gentlemanly man" and would be described after his time had come as, "a thunderbolt to all who deviated from that path which gentlemen followed." A eulogist wrote, "Humphreys was a gentleman without effort, one whose

---

2   McClellan MSS (L.C.) letter dated January 3, 1862, from Van Vliet to McClellan.

3   *OR*, 5, 46, McClellan's report.

4   *D.A.B.*, 5, pt. 1, 371; *Cullum*, 1, no. 642; Humphreys, H.H., *Andrew Atkinson Humphreys*, 56–61 (Philadelphia, 1924) (Humphreys, *Humphreys*).

natural qualities would neutralize any caste of bigotry, such as so often seriously in-
jures the graduates of an exclusive institution, which covets all the influence and advantages in *its* line. . . ." Noting the combination of the gentleman and the
thunderbolt, the eulogist continued, "The only thing which puts him out of humor is
an order not carried out, or a dangerous blunder committed in action. Then arises a
tempest, the more violent because ordinarily kept under command. To give it vent,
the General has recourse to flaming soliloquies, in the course of which all the known
and unknown energies of our language hurtle forth and burst like bombs . . ." followed by "his habitual calm."[5]

On December 1, 1861, Humphreys was assigned to the Army of the Potomac
as a staff officer[6] with specific responsibility for the terrain features that would govern McClellan's Occoquan, Urbana, and Peninsula plans.[7] Carefully collecting detailed information about the roads and railroads, rivers and streams, bridges,
topography, and man-made obstacles, he began preparation of reports on all these
subjects for the area from Alexandria to Richmond and beyond.[8] With this knowledge he confirmed McClellan's judgment: The Urbana route had no fortified or
defended positions like Yorktown and Gloucester. It was, therefore, probably unsus-
pected by the Rebels. It was the shortest route to Richmond, and it had no naturally
strong lines that could be easily defended or easily fortified. Humphreys did not,
apparently, consider the Dragon Swamp, which the army would cross on the way
to West Point, an insurmountable or even a severe hurdle. He preferred this route to
all others.[9]

---

5   Agassiz, George R., ed., *Meade's Headquarters 1863–1865, Letters of Colonel Theodore Lyman from the Wilderness to Appottomax* (Boston, 1922) 6–7, letter dated September 5, 1863, from
Lyman to his wife Elizabeth (Agassiz, *Lyman's Letters*). Although Lyman corresponded with several members of his family, the editor did not identify the recipient of each letter. The Lyman family papers reside in the Massachusetts Historical Society in Boston, which, through the kindness
of Peter Drummey, the curator, were made available to a busy lawyer in a way that allowed comparison of the book and the originals; Humphreys, *Humphreys*, dedication page; dePeyster, Bvt.
Maj. gen. John Watts, "Andrew Atkinson Humphreys, Brevet Major-General U.S.A., Brigadier-
General and Chief of Engineers U.S.A., Major-General U.S.V., etc.," in *The United Service: A
Monthly Review of Military and Naval Affairs*, vol. 1, no.3 (March, 1884) 265, 266.

6   *Cullum*, 1, no. 642.

7   Webb MSS (Y.U.) letter dated April 23, 1881, from Humphreys to Webb.

8   Copies of the numerous reports are in the Humphreys MSS in the Pennsylvania Historical
Society.

9   Webb MSS (Y.U.) letters dated June, 1881, from Humphreys to Webb and April 23, 1881,
from Humphreys to Webb, and handwritten half page memorandum of n.d.; Webb, Alexander S.,
The Peninsula (New York, 1881) 22 (Webb, *Peninsula*).

Dragon Swamp an impediment or not, McClellan knew this plan would cure one of his nagging problems: the blockaded navigation of the Potomac River. In June, a flotilla of Union ships from the Potomac fleet, some armed with monstrous fifteen-inch guns, attacked a Confederate shore battery at Acquia Creek. The heaviest guns having short range, their ships took them as close to shore as the depth of the water would permit. At point-blank range they suffered minor damage but not enough to drive them from their firing positions. The Rebel troops sprinted along the beach to safety. The Confederate gunners, too, abandoned their posts. Skeletal gun crews would sneak into their fortifications, load the weapons, unleash counter-battery fire, and flee to safety.[10]

After their victory at Bull Run, the Confederates came haltingly forward to the banks of the Potomac south of the Occoquan and ultimately built fortifications where the navigation channel came particularly close to the Virginia shore. As shipping passed north and south, Confederate guns sometimes did not fire at all; and when they did, their accuracy and effect were small.[11] Hooker wrote to headquarters, "It is not in their power to present any formidable barrier to the most uninterrupted passage of vessels up and down the Potomac. I am aware that a different opinion prevails among those whose experience should entitle their opinion to

10   Acquia Creek MSS (Library of Congress) report dated May 31, 1861, by Captain J. H. Ward; report dated June 1, 1861, by Captain J. H. Ward; report dated June 1, 1861, by M. M. McCluskey; and report dated June 2, 1861, by Commander S. C. Rowan. The fifteen-inch Dahlgren, both the Passaic and the Tecumsch classes, had a range of 2,100 yards. The Dahlgrens, eleven-inch, ten-inch, and nine-inch, had ranges greater than three thousand yards, and some of the smaller Parrotts, Columbiads, and Brooke rifles had ranges from three thousand to more than six thousand yards. Ripley, Warren, *Artillery and Ammunition of the Civil War*, Appendix C, "Tables of Statistics," 368, 369, 370, 371 (New York, 1970).

11   Roebling MSS (R.U.) letter dated February 16, 1862, from Roebling to his father; Rush, Lieutenant Commander Richard N., ed., *Official Records of the Union and Confederate Navies in the War of the Rebellion* (Washington, 1894, Broadfoot rep.) 4, 692, report dated September 26, 1861, from Haggerty to Montgomery; 718, report dated October 15, 1861, from Craven to Welles; 722–723, report dated October 16, 1861, from Wyman to Craven; 747, telegram dated November 6, 1861, from Dahlgren to Navy Department; 750, report dated November 11, 1861, from Macaw to Harrell; 752–753, report dated November 11, 1861, from Williamson to Dahlgren; 761, telegram dated December 2, 1861, from Craven to Welles; 762–770, abstracts from logs of U.S.S.E.B. *Hale*, U.S.S. *Pawnee*, U.S.S. *Pocohantas*, U.S.S. *Satellite*, and U.S.S. *Union* for various periods between April and December (*N.O.R.*); *OR*, 5, 652–753, letter dated November 15, 1861, from Hooker to Williams; 663, report dated November 22, 1861, from Hooker to Williams (*N.O.R.*); New York *Herald*, January 20, 1862, 1, col. 1, article entitled "The Situation." On November 15, Hooker reported to Army headquarters, ". . . It is not in their power to preserve any formidable barrier to the most uninterrupted passage of vessels up and down the Potomac." After Hooker took command on the lower Potomac, the Confederates managed only two hits, one in a sail. *OR*, 5, 653, letter dated November 15, 1861, from Hooker to Williams.

more consideration than my own, and for that reason it is with some reluctance that I advance it; nevertheless, it is my conviction."[12] Hooker, perhaps to the level of annoyance, pestered McClellan about attacking the Confederate positions and raising the blockade.[13]

In September, Barnard made a water reconnaissance of the growing Confederate batteries on the river with Lieutenant R. H. Wyman, commander of the Potomac flotilla. Going all the way to Mathias Point, where the Potomac entered the Chesapeake Bay, Barnard concluded that raids to destroy individual batteries would be useless. "As long as the enemy is master of the other shore he can build and maintain as many batteries as he chooses," he said. As a temporary solution McClellan could build counter-battery positions on the Maryland shore to "cause him to abandon his effort," but Barnard recommended against this. He did not believe the Rebels would put their guns in the best places, Mathias Point and the bluff north of Pope's Creek. For "counter-batteries for the portion of the river between High Point and Evansport, I would wait until the disposition and ability of the enemy seriously to molest is more fully developed. . . ."[14] Toward the end of October, civilian vessels still sailed up the Potomac, but only "at their own risk."[15] A short time later the navy deemed the river "closed."

Like so many things during McClellan's military career, the "closing of navigation," probably the first curse laid upon him by his chief engineer and the navy, became an issue that would weigh heavily against him even though it had no substance. As the perceptive naval officer John A. Dahlgren wrote in his journal entry for November 1, "The trade by the river is closed, not so much by the batteries as by our own vessels which will not allow craft to take the risk."[16] McClellan saw the solution clearly, as he did for most military problems: the Rebel river emplacements had no impact on the Union war effort because they did not detrimentally affect the navigation of the river. In daytime, ships suffered no danger because the ineffective Rebel artillery could not hit them. If their aim improved, all craft could travel at night or deliver their cargoes to the capital by the back door at Annapolis.

12   *OR*, 5, 653, letter dated November 15, 1861, from Hooker to Williams.

13   Heintzelman MS diary (L.C.) (large diary) entry dated May 6, 1862.

14   *OR*, 5, 606–608, report dated September 28, 1861, from Barnard to McClellan.

15   *N.O.R.*, 4, 740, letter dated November 1, 1861, from Welles to Adams; 742, order dated October 31, 1861, from Welles to Craven.

16   *N.O.R.*, 4, 747, order dated November 8, 1861, from Dahlgren to Reale; Dahlgren, *Autobiography*, 348, journal entry dated October 24, 1861; November 1, 1861; Gurowski, *Diary*, 1, 102, entry dated September, 1861. In fact, Gurowski deemed it closed much earlier. At the end of September he wrote in his diary, "The Potomac closed by the Rebels! Mischief and shame!" Ibid.

Among the many reasons McClellan paid little attention to this issue was the simple—and immediate—cure he intended to apply to it. His movement to Urbana would put a huge army on the flank and rear of the skimpy Rebel forces along the river. As soon as they saw his plan develop, they would run for their lives—and "open" the river.

But once again, the general in chief failed to give weight to the opinions of his fellow countrymen or, more importantly, to the attitudes of important leaders in Congress. Nor did he consider the pressure this question would inflict on the president, and he simply did not perceive Lincoln's need for relief as something important to his country or his own position. The Radical Republicans saw the navigation of the Potomac differently. To them it was a severe embarrassment or worse. And it demanded an immediate solution.[17]

Wisely, McClellan did not try to implement his Urbana plan without testing it on others. In November, he met with Fitz John Porter, Andrew Porter, and Franklin.[18] In a general way he presented his idea, but he was probably no more specific than to say that he proposed to move the army by water from Annapolis down the Chesapeake Bay to a point that would place him a short distance from Richmond.[19] Because it would require massive naval support, he discussed it with John A. Dahlgren, commander of the Washington Navy Yard.[20] This was also the

---

17   *C.C.W.*, 1, 82–85 (Journal); *OR*, 5, 41, 47; Hassler, *McClellan*, 30–31, 63–64; Trefousse, *Radical Republicans*, 189.

18   No one identifies the participants in this meeting, although some of them can be known by testimony before the Joint Committee. McClellan would have included William F. "Baldy" Smith in the group, Porter MSS (L.C.) letter dated May 9, 1895, from Franklin to Porter; but Smith had typhoid, was incapacitated throughout November, *C.C.W.*, 1, 186 (Smith); Welsh, *Medical Histories*, 313, and probably could not have attended. During the conferences in early March, Stanton asked Fitz John Porter when he first learned McClellan's plans for an advance. Porter knew about the Occoquan plan in September and the Urbana plan in November. Franklin and Andrew Porter also knew about it. Heintzelman MS diary (large diary) (L.C.) entry dated March 8, 1862.

19   *C.C.W.*, 1, 178 (Porter, F. J.).

20   The entry in Dahlgren's journal, Dahlgren, *Memoirs*, 350, journal, entry dated November 30, 1861, is frustratingly brief and unspecific. He wrote only that, after Lincoln left, "we discussed the various expeditions south, and the new idea of general campaign was talked over." This does not conclusively establish that McClellan disclosed the change of base by water, but two facts seem to make that clear. First, by November 30, the date of the entry in Dahlgren's journal, McClellan had abandoned his Occoquan-Brentsville plan. Second, according to an entry on October 21, *ibid.*, 347, "the General told me plainly his plan of campaign." This conversation occurred while the Occoquan-Brentsville plan was still in place and before any record shows the emergence of the Urbana plan. In addition, McClellan never had more than two well-developed plans for an advance, and the November reference to a "new" plan after another had been noted suggests strongly that the second reference was to the change of base plan.

month he explained the plan in detail to Chase in preparation for the secretary's conference with the New York bankers.[21]

Both McClellan and Halleck had been encouraging an older comrade in arms from Scott's Mexico City column, Scott's Inspector General Ethan Allen Hitchcock, to reenter the army and accept a commission of high rank.[22] McClellan wrote to him to explain the change of base to the lower Chesapeake. Hitchcock responded, "To execute successfully the operations you propose with a moderate army (say 20 or 30 thousand men) to be afterwards reinforced, depends upon auxiliary aids which *may* fail. If the railroad bridges are not destroyed—or but imperfectly—the enemy may overwhelm our expeditionary army—while to execute the difficult operation of transferring at once a *large* army—say 100,000 men to that line, I look upon as almost impracticable, if not otherwise imprudent. . . ." Hitchcock recommended a different operation, an army of thirty thousand men landing between the Elizabeth and Nansemond rivers to capture Norfolk. This would trap the Confederate Army in Norfolk. The "Nansemond and Dismal Swamp would, I should judge by the map, give us a defensive line against the enemies re-inforcements (breaking the rail-road as far as possible) and the capture of Norfolk would be, if not brilliant and decisive as what you propose, yet a great blow—particularly if, at the same time, we captured its Army."[23]

In early December McClellan addressed an essential new ingredient in his plan, the participation, in fact, the vital support, of the navy. He described his plan, even mentioning Urbana, to Rear Admiral Louis M. Goldsborough, commander of the naval forces at Fort Monroe on Old Point Comfort and of the North Atlantic Blockading Squadron. McClellan would march to West Point on the York River, where he would begin his operations. An expedition under General Ambrose Burnside would sail up the York River, heading for West Point as well.[24] Although many questions remained unasked and unanswered, McClellan probably left this meeting with a sense of confidence that he would have the naval support he needed.

21   Chase MSS (U.P.I.) memorandum entitled "Notes on the Union of the Army of the Potomac and the Army of Virginia" written shortly after the reinstatement of McClellan on September 2, 1862.

22   Ethan Allen Hitchcock MSS (Library of Congress) letters dated February 10, 1862, and February 10, 1862, at 8:30 P.M. from Halleck to Hitchcock; Croffut MSS, tr. Hitchcock MS Diary, entries dated May 6, 1861 and February 2, 1862.

23   Hitchcock MSS (L.C.) draft letter dated December 6, 1861, from Hitchcock to "Gen'l." This letter, not found in final in the McClellan MSS, Hitchcock probably sent to McClellan. It discusses the Urbana plan as if it had been explained to Hitchcock in some detail, and by its wording it appears to have been addressed to the proponent of the plan.

24   *C.C.W.*, 1, 631 (Goldsborough).

At the end of November, McClellan found himself working at headquarters. Also at work was his chief engineer, Brigadier General John G. Barnard. No one else was present. Barnard's incipient hostility had not reached a point that made professional communication difficult. Given Barnard's skill and experience, and McClellan's apparent respect for his intellect, Barnard might make a valuable contribution to the new plan. Casually, McClellan described it to him.[25] Barnard did not respond.

Barnard pondered the general in chief's idea over the next several days but did not try to catch the busy McClellan to discuss it. He knew better than that. He would follow Professor Mahan's advice. He wrote a memorandum that he finished and delivered on December 5. Only a short time earlier Barnard had reported to Congress that approximately twenty-two thousand men would suffice to hold the capital. Barnard and Barry had then reported to McClellan not once but twice their manpower calculations for defenses like the Torres Vedras lines: they said that 33,795 men could defend Washington against any Confederate force.[26] In one of their reports they had written "The more probable supposition is that the army moves from here in force, fully occupying the bulk of the enemy's forces by its own movement, leaving the capital so strengthened by its defensive lines as to prevent danger of sudden seizure by a strategical movement of the enemy, and enable it to be held a reasonable time in case of serious reverses to our own arms in the field."[27]

In the December 5 memorandum, Barnard did a full volte-face. Like the plan to clear the Rebel batteries from the Potomac, he did not like McClellan's new plan for a strategic offensive. He thought it had severe risks and did not think it would succeed. Even though he had earlier written, "The more probable supposition is that the army moves from here in force," he now said McClellan would leave the capital unsafe if he moved the main army from Washington. The great mass of Confederates would remain in front of Washington. The departure would expose the federal capital to attack if the Confederates in the Manassas-Centerville area were willing to trade the defense of Richmond for a desperate lunge at Washington. A large army must be left in Washington, he thought, until the Confederates withdrew far enough to make a surprise approach impracticable.

25   Barnard, *Peninsular Campaign*, 51, Appendix; *C.C.W.*, 1, 387, 388 (Barnard).

26   *OR*, 5, 622, orders dated October 18, 1861, from Williams to Barnard; 624, report dated October 22, 1861, from Barry and Barnard to Williams; 626–627, report dated October 24, 1861, from Barry and Barnard to Williams.

27   *OR*, 5, 626–627, report dated October 24, 1861, from Barry and Barnard to Williams.

The task of moving so many men troubled him. The difficulty of transportation, the inexperience of the troops, and the confusion at their landing required that the first wave be comparatively small, twenty thousand, or at most thirty thousand, men, not the one hundred thousand contemplated by McClellan. And it should move in three columns from three places, not a single force from one place in two deliveries. This would conceal the objective because the three forces would threaten the Potomac, the Rappahannock, Norfolk, and the southern coast.[28]

McClellan had probably forgotten his contest with Barnard for the hand of Ellen, the unflattering comparison by the Army's chief engineer, and Barnard's complaints about McClellan's interference with the growing engineer forces of the Army of the Potomac. Nor had Barnard's nasty pen, a mean-spirited, self-appointed implement, performed against McClellan. But this memorandum showed Barnard's intellectual dishonesty and hinted at his hostility toward McClellan. In it he disregarded the reproduction of the great Torres Vedras works, which he knew would make the Army of the Potomac independent of the capital's defenses and allow it to campaign away from Washington. With the "great mass of the enemy in front of Washington," Barnard said, "it would not be safe to leave it guarded by less than 100,000 men. . . ."[29]

This was the time McClellan became hostile toward some of his earlier friends in the press. On December 4, a map showing the locations of McClellan's divisions and of many forts appeared on the front page of the *New York Times*. McClellan's demand for suppression followed. But the offending newspaper unintentionally supported his idea by speaking of "the impregnable lines on the Virginia side," "these masterly defenses," and "an impassable barrier . . . It is enough to say," according to the article, "that officers of European armies, skilled in the latest results of military engineering, pronounce the works in front of Washington as absolutely impregnable against any assailing force, if held by no more than fifty thousand men."[30]

---

28   *OR*, 5, 671–673, memorandum dated December 5, 1861, by the author from Barnard to McClellan. According to *OR*, it was delivered on December 1 but the editors note the date with uncertainty because Barnard did not himself date the document. In the Appendix to his piece on the Peninsular Campaign, published long before *OR*, Barnard reprints three memoranda he wrote in response to McClellan's discussion and dates the delivery of this one, probably from personal files or personal recollection, as December 5. With Barnard having better access to the facts and no reason to lie on this point, his date is accepted over that of *OR*'s editors. The other two dispatches were not included in *OR*.

29   *OR*, 5, 672, memorandum for McClellan from Barnard.

30   *New York Times*, December 4, 1861, 1, cols. 1, 2, 3.

First, Barnard had said twenty-two thousand or thirty-three thousand men could defend; now he claimed the capital needed an army of one hundred thousand. First, he said, the main army could leave the capital while the Rebels sat just outside; now it must remain until the Rebels withdrew. Barnard had tripled or quadrupled the number for defense and insisted that the army remain near the capital until the Confederates departed, exactly what McClellan did not want.[31] This plainly dishonest response the chief engineer compounded by suggesting that the Army of the Potomac send approximately thirty thousand men against Norfolk,[32] a move that would satisfy no one and solve no strategic or political problem. McClellan intended a Napoleonic effort by his entire army, the only kind of "advance" that would quiet his critics and certainly the only kind that would bring the war to an end.

But forces at work behind the scenes did not care about plans, battles, slavery, abolition, or war. The weather had been unusually fair for this time of year.[33] The clamor for an advance was loud and growing louder.[34] Christmas was less than a week away. On December 19, McClellan met once again with his friend William B. Franklin to discuss his plans.[35] Then he took one of his customary rides, this time in unusually foul weather.[36]

The next day, Friday, December 20, the Joint Committee on the Conduct of the War held its organizational meeting, electing Benjamin Wade chairman.[37] On Saturday, it sent McClellan the following letter:

Washington, D.C., December 21, 1816

Sir: You are aware that a joint committee has been appointed by the Senate and House of Representatives to inquire into 'the conduct of the war.' Our

---

31   *OR*, 5, 672, memorandum from Barnard to McClellan.

32   *OR*, 5, 673; memorandum for McClellan from Barnard. *C.C.W.*, 1, 386–388 (Barnard); Barnard, *Peninsular Campaign*, 54, Appendix, memorandum dated December 6, 1861, from Barnard to McClellan.

33   *C.C.W.*, 1, 423 (McClellan).

34   Michie, General Peter S., *General McClellan*, chapter 7 (Michie, *McClellan*); Sears, *McClellan*, chapter 6; Hassler, Warren W., Jr., *General George B. McClellan, Shield of the Union*, 36 (Baton Rouge, 1957).

35   *C.C.W.*, 1, 122 (Franklin).

36   *C.C.W.*, 1, 423–424 (McClellan).

37   *C.C.W.*, 1, 67 (Journal, entry dated December 20, 1861).

committee, at a meeting held this morning, unanimously expressed a desire, before proceeding in their official duties, to have an interview with you at our room, at the Capitol, at such time as may suit your convenience, in view of your pressing engagements.

Our place of meeting is the room of the Committee on Territories of the Senate.

I remain, very respectfully yours,
B. F. WADE, CHAIRMAN.
Major General George B. McClellan,
General Commanding Army of the United States.[38]

While the letter was being prepared and sent, McClellan and Cameron reviewed Porter's division of fifteen thousand men at Ball's Crossroads. Small in comparison with the Bailey's Cross-Roads spectacle, it had a splendor of its own that only Fitz John Porter could produce. The Twenty-second Massachusetts and Eighty-third Pennsylvania appeared in their new uniforms with a new stand of colors. After the review the division drilled and performed a mock battle.[39] That evening McClellan and his wife, Ellen, hosted the president and Senator Orville Hickman Browning of Illinois for half an hour of pleasant discussion in which Ellen performed well the role of nineteenth-century wife to a man of importance.[40]

On Sunday McClellan responded to the Joint Committee's note saying that he would, as the committee wished, attend on the next day, December 23.[41] But something more severe replaced the chill that had caused him to excuse himself from his meeting with Heintzelman earlier in the month. The next morning, McClellan did not appear at headquarters for his regular staff meeting.[42] His body dehydrated, he

---

38   *C.C.W.*, 1, 68–69 (Journal).

39   Parker, *Twenty-second Massachusetts*, 61–62.

40   Pease, *Browning Diary*, 1, 517, entry dated December 21, 1861.

41   *C.C.W.*, 1, 69 (Journal, entry dated December 23, 1861).

42   Comte de Paris MS diary (large diary) (A.N. de la M. de F.) entry dated December 23, 1861; Comte de Paris MSS (A.N. de la M. de F.) galley proof of *B&L* article. Typhoid has a very brief incubation period, twenty-four hours or less. Medical Consultant Francis M. Weld, M.D. The exact day McClellan fell ill is not clear, even from the Comte de Paris' diary. The Count's *B&L* article says "approximately December 21" and his diary entry for January 6, 1862, also mentions December 21, *loc. cit.*

lay in his bed in his house, ill with a potentially fatal case of typhoid.[43] His aide Colonel Thomas Key notified the committee, "General McClellan is so unwell that he will be unable to perform his engagement with you today. I do not think he will leave his house at all."[44]

Tuesday, the day before Christmas, the committee took its first testimony. The field lay open for McClellan's enemies.

---

43   Comte de Paris MS diary (large diary) (A.N. de la M. de F.) entry dated January 6, 1862; Comte de Paris in *B&L*, 2, 120. In 1861 typhoid was a generic diagnosis for the large family of diarrheal diseases, including bacterial and viral diseases now known by specific etiologic names. Typhoid fever is a specific illness caused by the bacterium *salmonella typhosa*. The diarrheal illnesses rampant in military encampments included other non-typhoid subspecies of *salmonella*, e.g., *salmonella typhimurium*, *et al.*, and many Shigella species (the classic scourge of prison camps), as well as enteropathogenic *Escherschia coli*. Medical consultant F. M. Weld, M.D.

44   *C.C.W.*, 1, 70 (Journal).

Chapter 23

"There is no doubt but officers of the U.S. Regular Army are now in the pay of the Confederate government."

—*Hiram G. Berry to his wife*

The Elusive
Concept of Loyalty

*I*ncreasing doubts about the loyalty of his fellow generals plagued McClellan. In January, Samuel Heintzelman met Senator Henry Wilson on the street in the capital. They walked together; and, as always, the conversation turned to military subjects. Wilson said that the loyalty of some of the brigadier generals would be investigated, including that of Philip St. George Cooke, a Virginian who had been born in Leesburg and had already had a loyalty scrape while on his prewar frontier post.[1] But concern about loyalty did not stop at politicians like Wilson, Wade, and Chandler. Members of the officer corps believed that disloyalty existed in their ranks.[2] Colonel Hiram G. Berry, soon to become a volunteer brigadier general, believed the worst. "There is no doubt but officers of the U.S. Regular Army are now in the pay of the Confederate government," he wrote his wife. "They are among us, and we know them not. We can do nothing that Jeff Davis does not know, even more than

---

1   Heintzelman MS diary (large diary) (L.C.) entry dated January 13, 1862; Warner, *Generals in Blue*, 89.

2   Howard, *Autobiography*, 1, 192.

405

our most prominent generals. We are betrayed daily."[3] Well aware of McClellan's penchant for secrecy and his restrictions on access to the high command, Kearny wrote, "There is so much indiscretion, even treachery, that McClellan has made a rule to see few officers."[4]

This widespread belief in disloyalty did not bode well for Brigadier General Charles P. Stone. After the battle at Ball's Bluff and the unfortunate death of Senator Baker, the embarrassment of the defeat combined with existing suspicions and circulating rumors put Stone in a dangerous position. Rumors about Stone, even his personal appearance, worked against him. "As the tug passed by my post [on the Potomac] (about 12 o'clock in the day)," wrote Henry Ropes in a letter home, "it stopped a few moments for the ice, and the gentleman came out of the little cabin and stood a few moments looking round, and then went back to the cabin. He wore an Officer's overcoat, without the cape, had on a knit worsted cap, and was smoking a cigar. One of my men recognized him and told me it was Genl. Stone. I approached and saluted, thinking he wanted to ask some question. He bowed but said nothing and soon returned to the cabin. He is [a] good looking man, with full black (or nearly black) beard. He looks like a cool, steady man . . . and I am sorry to add, not like a man in earnest about a great thing. He looked to me like what I imagined some good French Officer to be, who was brave, but not foreseeing, able, but not ever trusting, he does not look like a traitor at all, but like a man who had no very particular sense of duty in anything beyond his mere military station and duties."[5]

In the middle of November, McClellan's intelligence officer reported that "Shanks" Evans, the Confederate commanding officer at the Harrison's Island crossing, had disobeyed orders in order to defeat Baker. A West Point graduate and the Rebel officer in command at Ball's Bluff, Evans had been directed to withdraw in order to lure the Union right wing across the river where Johnston could annihilate it while it had no effective support from the rest of the Federal army. Supposedly, the Confederates even gave thought to court-martialing Evans. Stone and Evans had been at West Point together, Stone as a member of the faculty and Evans as a student in the Class of 1848. They had become good friends.[6] Could Stone have intentionally played into Evans' hands? Absurd speculation? Of course. But it was a speculation with a future.

---

3   Gould, *Berry*, 92, letter dated January 9, 1862, from Berry to n.a.

4   dePeyster, *Kearny*, 226, letter dated February 19, 1862, from Kearny.

5   Henry Ropes MSS (B.P.L.) letter dated January 14, 1826 from Ropes to his brother John.

6   McClellan MSS (L.C.) letter dated November 15, 1861, from Allen to McClellan; *Cullum*, 2, nos. 1237 and 1404.

Controversy about Stone found its way into the press. The general granted the friends of a deceased captain a flag of truce to recover his body. When this became known, scores of letters and telegrams from widows, brothers, and friends of the Ball's Bluff dead requested the same favor. The demand was so great that Stone decided to refuse all further requests "for obvious reasons."[7]

According to the *Tribune*, the wife of Michael Gerety, a captain in the Tammany Regiment, received a letter stating that her husband had been killed at Ball's Bluff. Then she learned that he was only wounded and a prisoner. She sent a friend, with letters of introduction, to see Stone about a flag of truce to cross the river and confirm that the captain was alive. Stone refused the request. But Mrs. Gerety would not quit. Armed with "influential letters," she went to Poolesville where she stayed at the house of Dr. Poole. When she presented her request in person, Stone refused again but, the *Tribune* said, in a haughty tone and manner.

"Madam, your husband is dead! Captain Gerety was buried by the Rebels."

"Buried by the Rebels? How can that be? When Captain Vaughan was sent to bury our dead, why should the *rebels* bury him?"

"The account they give is that Captain Vaughan left him on the field, and they buried him. He was lying about two yards from Captain Alden."

"It is strange they should so soon bury him."

"They did it for *my* sake," said Stone.

"It is not likely, General," she argued, "that Captain Vaughan would bury one officer and leave another unburied not two yards from him. This is not to be believed. If the Rebel is the only source from which you have gained the account of my husband's death, I do not credit it, for they are not to be believed or relied upon at all."

"Madam," said Stone sternly, "you surprise me. What better source could you wish? The Rebels are *gentlemen* and are to be believed and relied upon. I wish you to know that many of them are my *intimate friends* and I believe everything they say respecting your husband. You are very much mistaken in your ideas, Madam!"

"I am sorry we differ so much in opinion respecting them, General. If they are what you represent them to be, there was no occasion to go to war with them. I do not believe my husband is dead; and if he is, you will not refuse me a flag of truce to see the spot where he is buried and to obtain his body."

"I cannot grant it, Madam."

"*Cannot* grant it, General?" she demanded.

"No, Madam, it cannot be done."

---

7 *New York Times*, December 28, 1861, 3, col. 3, article entitled "Justice to General Stone."

She asked if she were not entitled to the same favor as the wife of a Confederate officer who was allowed to pass back and forth for a much lesser reason. Stone turned pale and lost his stern manner but not his resolve. The widow, very excited, ended her assault with an insulting remark.

"Had my husband died on the field of battle and in so doing had he benefitted his country, I could be resigned, but he was not led *to battle* but *to slaughter*."

"Madam, do you intend that remark for me?" responded Stone.

"The blame rests upon *someone*; and whoever the cap fits may put it on."

"When we get to Virginia, I will make every investigation you desire," said Stone, trying to mollify her.

"When we get to *Virginia*? That does not look likely to happen soon. *You*, General, may be in Virginia before we can be," she said, implying desertion or treachery by Stone in the near future.[8]

The *Tribune*, a servant of the Radicals, reported that "in an ungentlemanly-like and haughty manner the general abruptly refused" to allow her a flag of truce for her mission. According to the *Times*' very different account, the widow went to Poolesville, where she and a doctor visited the general and asked permission to obtain her husband's body. Stone told her about the numerous applications and gave his invariable reply. He described the circumstances of her husband's death and said he had died as any soldier would wish: fighting gallantly at the head of his men and winning the admiration of friend and foe. Stone was particularly courteous and kind, the *Times* reported. They parted with no annoyance on her side or incivility on his.[9]

The *Times*, a friend to McClellan, published an article on December 27 entitled "Justice to Gen. Stone" saying, "This assertion is coupled with gratuitous insults to Gen. Stone, intimating very broadly that he is in sympathy with the rebels, and enjoys their intimacy."

Other events, born of the complicated circumstances of civil war, gave Stone a suspicious appearance. In the area covered by his Corps of Observation and Banks' division, civilians on both sides of the Potomac depended on longstanding cross-river trade for the goods and supplies necessary to life. Banks and Stone had diffi-

---

8   Wade MSS (L.C.) letter dated December 28, 1861, from Greeley to Wade; *New York Daily Tribune*, December 26, 1861, 5, cols. 4–5, letter dated December 20, 1861, from "A Soldier's Mother." The name given in the newspaper articles and letters is "Garrett;" but according to the appropriate entry in *Official Register*, 2, 483, no Garrett served in the Tamanny or Forty-second New York Infantry Regiment, but "Captain Michael Gerety [was] killed in action at Ball's Bluff, Va., October 21, 1861."

9   *New York Times*, December 27, 1862, 3, col. 3, article entitled "Justice to Gen. Stone."

culty distinguishing between civilian and military activity. Banks wrote Stone he would "cheerfully render every aid in my power to the People on the line of the canal to carry on their business or to supply themselves with all the necessaries of life. The difficulty we find is that the People living on the line do not apply for such privileges. It is invariably demanded by men who propose to trade for them, and who are, so far as they are known to us, of doubtful loyalty." If a farmer wanted a dozen sacks of salt, no harm would be done by allowing the transaction. But if a speculator claimed to be supplying many farmers and wanted to ship three hundred to five hundred bags, was the recipient civilian or military? Banks had to be certain. The best solution, he thought, was to allow people to trade for themselves and supply their own wants, but to exclude the speculators—to the extent they could be identified. "I will cheerfully accord to any arrangement that may be necessary to save loyal men from suffering—which shall also protect the Government."[10] Resolving the same kind of uncertain question, Stone concluded that the owner of Smart's mill, just north of Ball's Bluff, was loyal and did not order the mill destroyed.[11]

Against this background, the Senate showed that it had not forgotten its departed member and might still search for evidence establishing accountability. On Wednesday, December 11, Senator James Nesmith of Oregon announced the death of his colleague Edward D. Baker and submitted two resolutions that were adopted by unanimous consent. From a sincere desire to show every mark of respect due to Baker's memory, the members of the Senate went into mourning by wearing crepe on the left arm for thirty days; and, as an additional mark of respect, it would adjourn.[12]

As the Joint Committee of both House and Senate warmed to its task and prepared for its initial sessions, well-wishers suggested witnesses who might be helpful.[13] One visible and vocal candidate was the outspoken malcontent Samuel P. Heintzelman. A Radical Republican wrote to Zachariah Chandler, "Do you know General Heintzelman who commands south of Alexandria? I wish you could talk with him. I believe he is an officer of the right stamp and has the right ideas about conducting the campaign. I think it lucky when you find an army officer who is in the right direction, to talk with him, encourage him, and strengthen his back. Those

10   Misc. Civ. War Ltrs. (N.Y.H.S.) letter dated January 8, 1862, from Banks to Stone.

11   McClellan MSS (L.C.) letter dated February 12, 1862, from Lander to McClellan.

12   Senate, *Executive Journal*, 38, Wednesday, December 11, 1861.

13   Wade MSS (L.C.) letter dated December 28, 1861, from Greeley to Wade; letter dated December 30, 1861, from Buckingham, governor of Connecticut, to Wade; letter dated December 29, 1861, from Greeley to Wade; letter dated January 2, 1862, from Goddard to Washburn and referred to the Joint Committee by endorsement; Chandler MSS (L.C.) letter dated December 8, 1861, from William Doubleday to Chandler.

Regular officers are so accustomed to bow down to slavery they don't know any better and however honest they are they have lived so long in an atmosphere corrupt and dark as Egypt they are ignorant on these questions as we are on the dialect of the Hottentots."[14]

Chandler took the advice and arranged to meet Heintzelman on December 16 at Willard's Hotel. They left Willard's, probably for Chandler's office, where the senator closed and locked the door. For two hours he and Heintzelman discussed the Army of the Potomac and the general in chief. Early in the discussion Chandler raised a question he and the committee considered important: Had McClellan ever called a council of war? Heintzelman believed not. At all events, the general in chief had never consulted Heintzelman on any military subject. Taking advantage of his first opportunity to air his list of complaints, which long predated McClellan's arrival, Heintzelman said he had proposed several courses of action since the war commenced but none had been accepted. Finally, he had left them with General Marcy, the chief of staff. Undoubtedly, he described his strategic idea for a change of base to the Virginia peninsula. Like all others just outside the highest command, he believed that, if his advice had been taken, the Potomac would not have been blockaded, and the army would not have sustained a defeat at Manassas. Heintzelman believed that the attack at Manassas was an advantage because it "gave rise to this fine Army." He then explained his views about "carrying on this war" and the mistakes he thought had been made. "He don't want me to speak of our interview," he wrote that night in his diary.

The day before Christmas, while McClellan lay desperately ill, the Joint Committee heard its first testimony. For a congressional investigation the committee had established unusual goals: It wished to "convict" some members of the military, exonerate others, and influence military affairs. The ordinary trial in American jurisprudence—then, before, and now—is adversarial: Each side is represented by counsel, the dispute is defined by "charges" and "defenses" that are stated to the other side, each side may produce its own evidence, and each side may attack the evidence submitted by the opponent. With these bilateral protections both sides know the thrust of the case; both can prepare; they avoid the unfair methods of the Inquisition and the Star Chamber; and unlike Kafka's hero, the accused does, in fact, know he is the accused. These rules, the bedrock of the judicial systems of the English-speaking peoples for hundreds of years, assure at least a minimum of fairness to the defendant. Not bound by these rules and certainly uninterested in adopting them, the Joint Committee ignored or violated all of them and many more. Its effect on the

---

14   Chandler MSS (L.C.) letter dated December 8, 1861, from William Doubleday to Chandler.

military could not be predicted with any certainty in 1861, although the Comte de Paris had drawn on his knowledge of French history to suggest that no good would come from it. Stone, therefore, now headed for an experience that would rival the best of Franz Kafka.

A Swiss officer who served on McClellan's staff returned to Europe, translated the committee's first report, and evaluated its performance in lengthy footnotes. "The great accounts collected show that the committee did not fear the task, but it does not necessarily prove that this task was done conscientiously, that is marked by impartiality and justice. The choice of certain accounts and the turn of the questions posed indicates, to the contrary, that the committee believed it was less charged with clarifying for Congress the real conduct of the war than with constructing an inquisition against General McClellan and his friends. To this special task the committee devoted itself, we believe, with an inexhaustible zeal and a skill worthy of the greatest investigations. But that is still not impartial and wanting to claim the seal for this passionate work is a rhetorical ruse that all readers would recognize from the first pages."[15] Once again the collector of rumors and other "public information" commented in an enlightening way on the "confidential" work of the Joint Committee, "The Investigating Committee has made the most thorough disclosures of the thorough incapacity of McClellan."[16]

For Stone and McClellan the investigation began inauspiciously. Unable to see the committee at the outset, McClellan lost any chance to blunt its efforts or direct its focus.[17] Heintzelman appeared as one of the two witnesses on the first day of testimony, restating much he had said to Chandler on December 16.[18] The committee questioned him and many others about McClellan's failure to convene councils of war,[19] their knowledge of McClellan's plans,[20] the uselessness of expensive cavalry,[21] the ratio of troops for attacks on entrenchments,[22] the number of required

15 Lecomte, *Campagnes en Virginie*, 1–2, fn.

16 Gurowski, *Diary*, 1, 147–148, entry dated January, 1862.

17 Tap, *Over Lincoln's Shoulder*, 103–105.

18 *C.C.W.*, 1, 113 (Richardson) and 117, 121 (Heintzelman).

19 *C.C.W.*, 1, 113 (Richardson), 117 (Heintzelman), 122 (Franklin), 131 (McDowell), 146 (Wadsworth).

20 *C.C.W.*, 1, 178 (Porter, F. J.), 131 (McDowell), 117–118 (Heintzelman).

21 *C.C.W.*, 1, 113–115 (Richardson), 119 (Heintzelman), 124 (Franklin), and 139–140 (McDowell).

22 *C.C.W.*, 1, 115 (Richardson) and 118 (Heintzelman).

staff officers,[23] the Rebel batteries on the Potomac,[24] the necessary size of the army on the west bank of the Potomac,[25] and the effect of road conditions on an advance.[26]

As the questioning progressed, the members of the committee showed that they knew nothing about military affairs, had no idea what Congress could do to help the army, and had a political agenda dominated by preexisting hostilities and absurd preconceptions.[27] In addition, the committee showed a strong strain of congressional deceit. Occasionally, a witness would appear reluctant to cooperate. To push him the last inch, the members spoke about their rules of operation. They were strictly enjoined to secrecy. Their oath prohibited them from revealing any information they received from a witness. They would keep everything in confidence.[28] Many of the witnesses gave the members evidence they probably did not want, but the committee could not be confused by the facts. Testimony that pointed to an unsatisfactory conclusion it simply ignored.

For example, by dispatch and messenger Patterson had warned Scott that, on July 18, three days before the battle, Johnston had begun to leave the Valley. When members of the committee pilloried Patterson on the floor of Congress, Frank Blair, even though not Patterson's great supporter, announced that Patterson had alerted Scott.

"I say that General Patterson never telegraphed any such thing to General Scott," countered committee member John Covode of Pennsylvania falsely.

Even though Patterson's dispatch had been given to the committee,[29] Representative Daniel W. Gooch, another member, agreed with Covode and demanded Blair's authority for his assertion.

"I know the fact," responded Blair, adding that both Scott and Lincoln were aware of the information and that, although Lincoln wanted to halt McDowell's advance, Scott "disregarded the wish and advice of the president on the subject."

Possessing the "confidential" information collected by his Star Chamber, Covode again demanded that Blair disclose his source.

23   *C.C.W.*, 1, 114 (Richardson).

24   *C.C.W.*, 1, 115 (Richardson) and 118 (Heintzelman).

25   *C.C.W.*, 1, 116 (Richardson) and 118 (Heintzelman).

26   *C.C.W.*, 1, 118 (Heintzelman) and 146 (Wadsworth).

27   Tap, *Over Lincoln's Shoulder*, 45–47, 49–50, 253–259.

28   *C.C.W.*, 1, e.g., 122 (Franklin).

29   Tap, *Over Lincoln's Shoulder*, 48–49.

"The gentleman had better call me before his secret committee," retorted Blair snidely.[30]

The committee's charter directed it to investigate the conduct of the war, especially at Bull Run and Ball's Bluff, but its secret agenda covered broader, more complex subjects: the proper selection of generals, the loyalty of West Point Regular officers, Fremont and slavery and abolition, McClellan and the Army of the Potomac. In a welter of confusion simplified only later by the editor of the committee's transcripts, the committee investigated many subjects, assigned and unassigned. On the Army of the Potomac, after taking testimony from Richardson and Heintzelman, it switched to a man who could answer the difficult questions about McClellan's plans, his friend and subordinate William B. Franklin. After insignificant preliminaries, Senator Wade turned to the foolish subject that, he thought, strongly indicted the major general, his unwillingness to wage war by committee.

"How often has General McClellan held councils of war with the generals of his army?" he asked Franklin.

"He has never held a council of war, to my knowledge."

"How often has he consulted the principal officers of his army upon the subject of the prosecution of the war?" persisted Wade.

"I can only answer in regard to myself. He has consulted me quite often; I cannot tell the precise number of times. We must have had a dozen conversations, perhaps more."

"Conversations?"

"Yes, sir; they were private, confidential communications."

"But no council," repeated Wade, "with other officers at the same time?"

"No, sir; never any formal council."

"Do you know anything in regard to the plans of the general in chief with relation to the operations of this army?" Wade had touched the sensitive subject but had not yet asked the most sensitive question.

"I do know something in regard to it."

"Are you willing to disclose what you know to the committee? We are all sworn to secrecy. We want to know what the plans of the commanding general are."

"Before doing so," responded Franklin politely and deferentially, "I would prefer, if the committee will permit me, to see General McClellan on the subject, because

---

30 *Cong. Globe*, 37th Cong., 2nd Sess., 838–842, quoted in Tap, *Over Lincoln's Shoulder*, 51–52 and 53. In a spirit of charity in spite of his criticism of the Committee, Tap discusses Patterson's dispatch as if it were misplaced or forgotten rather than ignored or suppressed by the Committee, *op. cit.*, 53.

I do not think he has made known his plans to anybody, unless he has done so to one or two of his general officers. And he gave us these plans with the understanding that we were to keep them to ourselves. If the committee will permit me, I would much prefer to see him before saying anything to anybody about it."

"How long since you have had such conversations with General McClellan?"

"The last particular conversation I had with him was a week ago today."

"I will waive that matter for the present then," acquiesced Wade.[31] Others could solve his problem.

After Franklin, the persons most likely to know McClellan's private thoughts and his plans were his friends and subordinates Irvin McDowell, Fitz John Porter, and William F. Smith.

On the same day, McDowell testified. If the committee thought he would color his responses because he was jealous of a younger officer who had taken his place, it suffered a disappointment. Everyone testified that the general in chief had called no councils of war, and the West Point Regulars spoke of councils in disfavor.[32] McDowell went further and in the course of his responses defended the major general.

"Are you in possession of any plans of movement now?" asked Wade.

"No, sir," replied McDowell.

"Have you held any communication with the general in chief upon the subject?"

"We have had many conversations—more formerly than latterly—but they have been somewhat of a general nature. I have had my own general views upon the subject, which I have expressed to him."

"Has he called any council of war of his generals commanding divisions?"

"I am not aware that he has. I think I should have been aware of it if he had done so, because he has always expressed himself so kindly towards me personally that I am satisfied he would have called upon me if he had had such a council."

"So that you are not in possession of any general plan of operations?"

"I cannot say that I am. I will state that some time ago I expressed to the general in chief what I had thought would probably be the best course to take. It was a mere general statement, a desultory thing, while we were riding on horseback; and I thought that in a general way he coincided with those views. That was some time ago, and no doubt things are very much changed since then."

---

31   *C.C.W.*, 1, 122 (Franklin).

32   *C.C.W.*, 1, 178 (Porter); 131 (McDowell); 113 (Richardson); 215 (Blenker); 130 (Franklin); 145–146 (Wadsworth); 168 (McCall); and 117–118, 122 (Heintzelman).

"Do you think that a general council of war of generals of division would be useful?" The members of the Joint Committee received little help from McDowell on this issue.

"People differ very much about councils of war. I myself never have inclined towards them; and from all that I have read, and from my general opinion of councils of war, I do not think well of them. But this is a mere matter of opinion. I think it would be proper for the general in chief to call upon any particular officer or officers in command or upon the staff whom he might suppose had knowledge that would be useful. I have no doubt that he would do so, too. Councils of war, where all the officers get together, and the question is discussed backwards and forwards, and voted upon, from all that I have ever learned, have always proved to be of little account, even if they have not been injurious."

"I suppose the general in chief could overrule them all." Trying to create something useful where the answers would not allow it, Wade continued. "Still they might make important suggestions to him?"

But McDowell, a man of hardened integrity, would not be led or coerced. "They might give him information. But men are all alike. If they were to express an opinion and he were to go against it, it would embarrass him; and if he went for it, it would not help him."[33]

Two days after Franklin and McDowell testified, Fitz John Porter answered questions from Chairman Wade and Senator Andrew Johnson of Tennessee.

"Now, we are endeavoring to ascertain of military gentlemen what disposition they think should be made now in relation to the army. Should it retire into winter quarters, or should it attempt an enterprise to dislodge the enemy?"

"That is a question I cannot answer."

"I merely ask your military opinion."

Franklin had responded deferentially and politely. He had declined to answer these questions in a precatory manner. Porter as much as told the committee to mind its own business.

"I decline to give a military opinion on that point. I am in possession of information in regard to intended movements—rather a portion of General McClellan's plans, a small portion only—and I decline giving any information whatever in relation to future movements, or what they ought to be. I do not think it is my business to do so, and we are forbidden by our regulations to discuss or express opinions on these matters. I have refused and have failed to express any opinion upon them in my division. I am there ready, and the division is ready, to move at a moment's

33   *C.C.W.*, 1, 131–132 (McDowell).

notice. And when those in charge are prepared, we will move. I say the army is not ready to move, is not prepared to move."

"That, perhaps, answers the question I want."

"We have not what is requisite to move; we are not prepared to move."

"We want to know the reasons why, that we may aid you if possible," commented Wade disingenuously.

"You ask a question that I also decline to answer. I know these things will be ready and are getting ready."

In spite of Porter's intractable manner, the questions continued. "Is there anything that Congress could do to facilitate you?"

"Not that I am aware of. I believe that General McClellan is carrying out his plans as rapidly as he possibly can. What those plans are it is not for me to say— that is, I think it better for you to get them from him."

"I have not asked you at all for his plans even if you know them," responded Wade, who did not take well to refusals. "I have only asked you, as a military gentleman of high experience and science, what your own opinions were with regard to the movements of the army."

"I will tell you one thing. I do not think I ought to answer such a question for this reason: I am not cognizant of what is passing throughout the army, and no man can judge what this army ought to do unless he knows all its operations throughout its various ramifications here, and knows them so as to be able to put them in connection, one with another. There is a great deal I only get from newspapers, which tell an immense number of falsehoods."

"To be sure, you can only give an opinion upon the information you have in regard to the condition of the whole army. I had supposed that a man in high military command would be very well informed as to the condition of the whole army. I did not suppose he would know all about it, but still a great deal about it. But, as you say you do not, we will not press that matter."

Porter simply could not leave well enough alone and leaped upon a course that would have made a trial lawyer crawl under the counsel table. Although Wade had pretended to believe that Porter did not know enough to answer the questions, Porter felt compelled to tell him that some higher law required congressional ignorance. "I do know a great deal, I suppose; but we know very little but what we see in passing through the different divisions, and we cannot form an estimate of the condition of a division by merely riding through."

"Can you approximate to anything like the strength of the enemy in what is called their army of the Potomac?"

Porter answered with the obvious. "I only know from spies—mere reports, that are varied."

"It is uncertain, then?"

"I do not think it is uncertain, but I think these statements are very varying."

"And, consequently, unreliable, in your estimation?"

"In some respects. At least, I form my own opinion on these various reports," Porter responded.

Senator Odell took the "prosecutor's" seat to ask meaningless questions. "Where are you stationed?"

"At Hall's Hill and Minor's Hill, on the right of Upton's Hill."

Andrew Johnson, a War Democrat from Tennessee, but as Radical as the best Republican, returned to Wade's line of questions.

"From the information you have received from these various and varying channels, have you formed any opinion of your own, based upon that information, as to the strength of the enemy now immediately in front of us?"

"Yes, sir; I have."

"Would you consider that it would be out of place to give your opinion as to their strength?"

"I should suppose that their strength, extending from Leesburg down to beyond the Occoquan, was about one hundred sixty thousand men—something near that. I think immediately in front of us, at Centerville and Manassas, there are from eighty thousand to ninety thousand men. They may run down. This information continually varies. We may get information to-day, and may not get any more for two weeks; and in that time they may receive forty thousand men. I do not think their strength consists in mere numbers, but in their fortifications. Their numbers are nothing."[34]

Porter's evasive answers and outright refusals showed the arrogance of a man protected by unchallengeable power. The committee members kept at the questions long and stubbornly. They must already have thought that Porter, McClellan's closest friend, could be their best source of information. Finally, at the very end, Wade tried again to squeeze the plans from a witness who had conceded he knew them.

"Has there been any consultation among officers here," he asked, "any council of war of the principal high officers of this army, taking their opinion in regard to the condition of the army and as to what should be done?"

Porter referred to the November meeting. "I was present once when a plan was proposed."

This was news to Wade. "Present together with officers of your own rank, I suppose?"

---

34   *C.C.W.*, 1, 171–173 (Porter).

"Yes, sir."

"To consult?"

"Yes, sir."

"Were all the commanders of divisions present?" asked Andrew Johnson, once again putting his finger on an issue that would loom larger and larger.

"No, sir."

"What number were present?"

"Three or four of us were present. The propositions were presented to us as a mere matter of discussion, sufficient for one to form an idea of what General McClellan's plans were, or some of them."

"I thought you said a while ago that a portion of his plans were in your possession, but not all?"

"I have just said 'some of his plans.'"[35]

Franklin had been polite and deferential. He had respectfully requested permission not to answer without express permission from McClellan. The committee had been willing to honor his request. Porter had flatly refused. Although he had known much information early after McClellan first arrived, McDowell no longer had open and full communication with the major general.[36] He did not know the answers to many of the questions. That left "Baldy" Smith, but he had been ill for the past five weeks and most of that time not with his division. He knew no more than McDowell.[37]

Although the members of the committee were after McClellan, they found plenty of time and energy to pursue Charles P. Stone for his role in the death of Senator Baker, his status as a Democrat, his anti-abolitionism, and his treatment of fugitive slaves. The first Ball's Bluff witness was Frederick W. Lander, a brigadier general of volunteers. Lander had begun his rise as a personal acquaintance and a staff officer of McClellan at Rich Mountain in West Virginia. Outspoken and confidant in his military skills,[38] Lander criticized practically every participant in the battle. In his account, although he never saw the battlefield, had not reached Edwards Ferry until the morning after the battle, and had commanded no troops in the action, he had been a Ball's Bluff hero thwarted by men who would not listen. He managed to condemn both Stone and McClellan.[39]

---

35   *C.C.W.*, 1, 178 (Porter).

36   *C.C.W.*, 1, 131 (McDowell).

37   *C.C.W.*, 1, 186 (Smith).

38   *M.O.S.*, 190–191.

39   *C.C.W.*, 2, 253 ff (Lander).

The following day General George A. McCall, commander of the Pennsylvania Reserve Division, took the stand, the target of the seven congressmen: "Little Mac." With all their skill they managed to create damaging evidence against an unrepresented and uncharged defendant.

The testimony of the division commanders stationed near Ball's Bluff unintentionally suggested inaction, loss of an excellent opportunity to advance, inability to reach a decision, and all those things which could—and later would—contribute to the termination of McClellan's military career.[40] At the beginning of the investigation Stone had lain invisible in the shadow of a larger target. McClellen, not knowing the committee pursued him, maintained his obsession with secrecy.

On December 28, 1861, Stone telegraphed McClellan, "I am ordered to appear before a Joint Committee of the Senate and House of Representatives on the Conduct of the War. Shall I obey the order?"[41] Knowing he was a target, he sent another telegram the same day, this time to Seth Williams. He did not think "the responsibility of fixing the time of my leaving my command ought to rest with me should anything unforeseen occur during my absence. The abuse which has already been heaped on me teaches me what the result would be to my reputation."[42]

Scheduled to appear on January 5, Stone arranged a half-hour appointment with McClellan[43] for the day before his testimony. At army headquarters he learned McClellan lay ill with typhoid and could not tend to his affairs. Seth Williams told Stone that McClellan wanted all officers to "refrain from stating anything which would make known any of your plans or anything concerning positions and movements afterwards directed by you," Stone wrote later to McClellan.[44]

Rumors circulated in willing circles inside the army that Stone was a traitor. When signal lights, like those seen by Crowninshield in September, appeared in a house on the Confederate side, Stone would go into the river, they believed, and meet men from the Virginia side.[45]

On January 5, the first Sunday of the New Year, Stone took the witness chair. His interrogation began with general questions and specific innuendoes. Amazingly,

40   *C.C.W.*, 2, 257 ff (Smith and McCall).

41   McClellan MSS (L.C.) telegram dated December 28, 1861, from Stone to McClellan.

42   McClellan MSS (L.C.) telegram dated December 28, 1861, from Stone to Williams.

43   McClellan MSS (L.C.) telegram dated January 3, 1862, from Stone to Williams.

44   McClellan MSS (L.C.) letter dated January 13, 1863, from Stone to McClellan; *C.C.W.*, 2, 489 (Stone).

45   Adams, *Nineteenth Massachusetts*, 17.

the seven men did not start with Ball's Bluff. Wade fired a salvo of hostile questions aimed at the general in chief.

Could a move be made in the winter season?

Why was one not made?

Where should it be tried?

What would Stone recommend?[46]

Stone could never have seriously considered these questions except as a personal matter, but they gave him an opportunity to turn the investigation away from himself by criticizing his superior. His personal character, his integrity, his military bearing, his sense of discipline, his respect for McClellan, and his instructions from his commanding officer all demanded evasive answers to these questions or no answers at all. If he saw an opportunity to curry favor with the committee, he declined to take it. For the moment he had shielded McClellan from the committee's wrath and left himself the only significant target in the open. The seven men continually returned to damaging questions about McClellan, but Stone, if he could not evade, simply refused to answer. He and Porter must have left the Radicals particularly frustrated—and furious—by their blunt, almost caustic, refusals to recognize the magisterial power of such important men.

Two days later Roscoe Conkling, a representative from New York, took the floor of the House.[47] Strongly dissatisfied by McClellan's response to the House inquiry early in December, he asked, "Was anything being done to identify the culprit—if one existed—for Ball's Bluff?" A withering indictment based on one of the Radicals' favorite points of complaint followed.

"The House is, no doubt, aware that the Battle of Ball's Bluff, like many other things, has been made the subject of an issue between the Regular Army and the volunteers. Brigadier-General Stone . . . is an officer of the Regular Army, and Colonel Baker . . . was a volunteer . . . the cause has been espoused as if its appropriate office was to fasten some stigma on the volunteer service, and to determine certain questions of precedence and merit between West Point and the volunteers for the Union." In his cry for investigation, he announced the following "facts":

- the officers planned the advance for many days;
- they built boats for the crossing in advance, but not enough;
- they did not use a large supply of lumber available at Smart's Mill;

---

46   *C.C.W.*, 2, 265 ff (Stone).

47   *D.A.B.*, 2, pt. 2, 346.

- Stone intended to cross seven thousand five hundred men, but sent only one thousand eight hundred;
- Stone ordered Baker to cross;
- the Rebels watched the crossing and attacked when just the right insufficient number had reached the top of the bluff;
- readily available with eleven thousand men, McCall never had an order to support Baker;
- another division, under Banks, was to support Baker but found itself on the wrong side of the river.[48]

Conkling never accused Stone of negligence, incompetence, or treachery, but that was not necessary. His speech, laden with factual inaccuracies, made its point clear. Certainly it was clear to Stone. When he read it the next day, he wrote to one of McClellan's staff officers, "I have seen Mr. Conkling's speech in the House yesterday and think that I ought to ask for a Court of Inquiry—what is your advice?"[49]

At the next opportunity, McClellan showed Stone the dispatch to Lincoln absolving him of all blame, and in December the army had increased his responsibilities by adding the Chesapeake and Ohio Canal to his command, hardly the treatment of a man to be held culpable for a military disaster.[50] Stone decided that McClellan's letter vindicated him as much as any court of inquiry could.[51]

After the death of Baker, McClellan assigned Brigadier General William W. Burns, a West Point schoolmate who had stood next to him in formation in the Corps of Cadets, to command the dead senator's Philadelphia Brigade. The men did not receive him well. "Our new General Burns is not liked as well as Colonel Baker," wrote a member of the brigade. "He is not near so sociable and kindly dispositioned." And he granted no furloughs.[52]

An incident occurring in the Philadelphia Brigade raised again the awkward problem posed by the multi-headed monster making officer appointments. Francis G. Young, already making trouble about Baker and Ball's Bluff, had been charged

---

48   *Cong. Globe*, 37th Cong., 2nd Sess., 189, January 6, 1862, cols. 1, 2, and 3 (Conkling).

49   McClellan MSS (L.C.) letter dated January 7, 1862, from Stone to Hardie.

50   *OR*, 5, 686, Special Orders No. 322, dated December 6, 1861, Headquarters, Army of the Potomac.

51   Schoff Collection (Stone MS) (Univ. Mich.) letter dated November 5, 1866, from Stone to Lossing.

52   Vanderslice, *Beidelman Letters*, 51, letter dated December 4, 1861, from Beidelman to his father; *Pennsylvania at Gettysburg*, 4 vols. (1893–1938) 1, 383, speech by Burns.

with absence without leave, ordered to report for trial ten days earlier, and become a fugitive under charges. Now Lincoln had appointed him a captain and quartermaster. "Is it possible that such a blow to the discipline of Burns' Brigade has been struck with a knowledge of all the facts?" Stone wrote to army headquarters.[53]

Stone's other brigadier general, Willis A. Gorman, presented a different problem. The slave issue raised its head once again. What effect might it have on two competent officers? The First Minnesota Regiment, Gorman's original regiment, had ready access to alcohol because the regimental commander allowed the sutler to sell it, at exorbitant prices. Several men managed to find a cheaper source outside the regiment, three nearby slaves. Unfortunately for all of them, Gorman learned about an excursion to the slaves and sent a detachment to arrest them all. Sparing the oldest of the three blacks, he had the other two tied to posts in the regimental camp, ordered the would-be purchasers to administer twenty-one lashes, and stood nearby while his men began the whipping.

Finding their efforts desultory and unsatisfactory he began to curse the men for not whipping hard enough.

An onlooker berated him.

"Insubordination, sir! Insubordination!" shouted Gorman. "Another word from you and Goddamn my soul to hell if I don't have you whipped, too."[54]

This incident found its way into the *New York Daily Tribune*, which described it in an article reporting that Gorman had impressed a fugitive slave into his personal service, become dissatisfied with him, and had him whipped too.[55] Rumors of this spread throughout the brigade, except that Gorman supposedly acted on the orders of General Stone, his division commander.[56]

With his more than run-of-the-mill political background, Gorman felt comfortable enough to respond at the highest levels of the Senate. He wrote to the chairman of the Committee on Military Affairs Henry Wilson. "I see in the *New York Tribune* what I suppose to be an attack on me for surrendering fugitive slaves and other allusions of a kindred nature . . . The occurrence of flogging negroes for sell-

---

53   McClellan MSS (L.C.) letter dated January 9, 1862, from Stone to Hardie.

54   *New York Daily Tribune*, December 28, 1861, 6, col. 5, letter dated December 16, 1861, from "A Little More Grape" to the *Tribune*; Wright, *Memoirs*, 87.

55   *New York Daily Tribune*, December 13, 1861, 6, col. 1, editorial.

56   Greeley MSS (N.Y.P.L.) letter dated December 23, 1861, from Dodge to Greeley; *New York Daily Tribune*, December 13, 1861, 6, col. 1, editorial; December 28, 1861, letter dated December 16, 1861, from "A Little Grape;" and December 28, 1861, 6, col. 6, editorial.

ing whiskey to soldiers took place more than *three months* since under direct order from my superior officer."[57]

One of Senator Lyman Trumble's correspondents commented that an attack on Stone or McClellan or both would serve the cause of abolition. "Col. Gorman has written a letter to our Senator Wilkinson *acknowledging the truth of the charges against him* but says that he *whipped the negroes by order of his superior.* Now, we are well satisfied there is no truth in this statement but as Stone wants his (Gorman's) help to get himself (Stone) out of the blame for the noble Baker's death at Ball's Bluff, he may even go so far as to father the act . . . Of course, if Gorman did it by command of his Superior then Stone is the responsible man."

The correspondent continued, "It is very important that we succeed in defeating G's confirmation as it is *the first case of the kind* & will become a *precedent*. It will have a *tremendous influence upon all the officers* & the *army*. And do more than any other one thing can, to compel them to abandon their 'nigger-driving' practices and positions. What they all want is *promotion & the honors*. Once let them understand that such practices will defeat those aspirations, and there is the end, at once, of the practices. Hence you see how important this case is. *The prospect is that he will be defeated.* The officers are evidently much frightened about it. We have got them now where 'the hair is short' emphatically! Don't let up on them an inch.—Push this case through & it is the end of their game. I warrant you, you'll never hear of another similar case in the army, if he is defeated now. Let us do this, & we will 'shape the policy of the army, whatever the administration may do, or fail to do.'"[58]

More men testified before the committee—the total would eventually reach thirty-nine—but as the chance of reaching McClellan waned, the committee members concentrated on Stone. They did not want for testimony favorable to Baker and adverse to Stone. In virtually all accounts of any historical event, no matter how false the intended statement, some grain of truth forms the foundation. Captain Francis G. Young, Baker's brigade quartermaster and aide, defied this rule. Wistar, commanding the Seventy-first Pennsylvania, and Young arrived at Conrad's Ferry at sunrise of Monday, October 21, Young testified. Wistar ordered Young to go to Stone, report the arrival of the regiment, and obtain orders.

Young spurred his horse, galloped down the towpath, and found Stone at his hilltop command post staring intently at the skirmishers deploying near Goose

57   Henry Wilson MSS (Library of Congress) letter dated December 22, 1861, from Gorman to Wilson.

58   Greeley MSS (N.Y.P.L.) letter dated December 23, 1861, from Dodge to Greeley.

Creek on the Virginia side. Stone recognized him, Young thought, but said nothing. Young delivered the message, then began to feed his horse. Finally Stone approached him, saying, "Your order is, sir, that the California battalion will stand fast until you shall hear firing, and then immediately cross."

Young remembered that, when he had reached Conrad's Ferry, he sparred with the "Massachusetts boys" about the two flatboats, their fleet for crossing. He explained to the committee that he thought Stone would have further orders about better means for crossing. "General, have you any further orders?" he asked. Imperiously and curtly, as Stone always spoke, Young testified, he snapped, "You have your orders, sir!"

Intimidated, Young mounted his horse and returned to Wistar. He delivered the orders. Wistar wanted them repeated. Young gave them again, literally. "Are you sure you are right?" queried Wistar. "There is no mistake."

Young then continued up the towpath to give the report to Baker. He met the colonel coming south.

"That can't be," Baker responded when he heard he should cross as soon as he heard firing.

With a new message from Baker for the remainder of the brigade, Young prepared to head for camp.

Baker called him back. "Young, are you sure you understood Stone?"

"Colonel, I understood that the matter was very important, and I paid great attention to it. I don't often make mistakes; and I made no mistake in this, I think."

Young's testimony, which continued at great length, described written orders that never existed and conversations inconsistent at best with accounts by numerous other participants. According to Young, reinforcements would come from Gorman on the left, Stone had told them the Rebels numbered five thousand, the men lay under cover without firing, and Adjutant General Townsend withheld the account Young wrote at the request of Baker's brother and son.[59]

The credible testimony made the proper conclusions obvious: When Baker finally reached the Conrad's Ferry area, he did not go directly to the battlefield to assess conditions, he did not reconnoiter, nor did he evaluate the terrain. When he reached the open field across the river, he made no effort to examine the position of his troops. He left them generally as they lay except that he took some from the cover of trees and placed them in the open. As he saw it, the trees marking the far side of the clearing were protection for his men, not cover for the enemy. His

59   *C.C.W.*, 2, 318, 319–320, 321–323 (Young).

mind's eye could see no more than his physical eye. Topography out of sight had no relevance. His topographical short-sightedness precluded recognition of the excellent defensive position at Smarts' Mill, even though Stone had described it to him. Like others with no more than untutored, intuitive military ability, he kept his men in front of the enemy; and without a flicker of concern he exposed himself to enemy fire.

In the afterlight of Munson's Hill, McClellan had decided he would not be made the fool a second time. He concluded on the spur of the moment that he would take advantage of the Confederate withdrawal being forecast by his intelligence. For the first and only time in his military career, McClellan had turned opportunist and would accept a meeting engagement. He would follow the retreating Confederates with vigor, strike a blow at them, and advance in an area he had long considered one of his most vulnerable. If Baker, McCall, and McClellan had done anything right, McClellan's snap decision would have produced commendable results. But Baker had done virtually everything wrong; McCall had not marched to the sound of the guns; and in the major general's one impromptu adventure he had done nothing to provide against Baker's failure. He had not told Stone that McCall's true assignment was mapping rather than support, that McCall had been ordered away on Sunday, and that he had returned to his position on the right flank of the army in Virginia the morning the fighting began. Stone had been led to believe that McCall was close enough to help on the left flank if necessary.

After Baker became fully engaged, McClellan massed two full divisions and prepared to cross them. Only the foul weather and the river prevented it. McClellan's conduct at Edwards Ferry suggests dichotomous thought processes. Once the battle had been lost, he seemed to lose control altogether; but like McDowell at Centerville in July, he wished the foothold held.

He had a chance to refuse defeat in this encounter by putting McCall into the battle on the left, crossing Stone's remaining regiments under Gorman and Lander at Edwards Ferry, and crossing Banks' division of three brigades onto Stone's right,[60] a force of approximately thirty thousand men. The wind and rain delayed

---

60   McCall was across the Potomac with his entire division. Stone could have crossed Gorman and Lander more rapidly and more effectively than Baker could his smaller brigade-size force and with artillery cover from high ground. With a full division of three brigades, about ten thousand men plus artillery, Banks could have crossed north of Smart's Mill. This would have pitted approximately twenty-five thousand men against approximately five thousand Confederates under Nathan G. "Shanks" Evans, who had orders to retreat, McClellan MSS (L.C.) letter dated November 15, 1861, from Allen to McClellan. Presumably, Banks' water transportation would have been no more questionable than Baker's; but the union numbers would have been self-sustaining, if not overwhelming.

him long enough for his normal, deliberate personality to reassert itself. Evacuation followed.

The Radicals refused to recognize the obvious truth. Instead, Baker's death and the fugitive slave issue made Stone a vulnerable target. Although the evidence showed conclusively that Stone had given Baker discretion about crossing, the seven men concluded that Stone had heedlessly ordered Baker across the river with woefully inadequate transportation.

Could the engineers have built a bridge?

Was that not a main part of their job?

How much time would have been required to accumulate the materials?

How much to construct one?

These questions ignored the true situation. "What military reasons," asked Wade of a mere captain, "could a man have for sending troops across there with only such means of transportation as you had? Was it not culpable neglect?"[61]

At one point the Committee encouraged a colonel so much that he began his answer, "If I was in command . . . ",[62] and his answer targeted Stone, not Baker. The committee steered itself in a pre-determined direction, conducting neither an "investigation" nor an adversarial proceeding but an old-fashioned lynching. The questions did not seek information. They stated conclusions. Several of Baker's friends perjured themselves. Those men who wished to speak in Stone's favor the committee quickly diverted to another subject. A "search for the truth," the platitudinous byword of the American judicial system, did not occur.

Much testimony was not even devoted to Ball's Bluff but to attacks on Stone's character and integrity: He aided the enemy, a Confederate colonel across the river had been his classmate at West Point, he had sent communications to the Confederates about Union movements, he was too friendly with Southerners in general, he was too lenient on secessionist citizens, Southern soldiers thought highly of him. Evidence to support these charges and others, though outweighed in quality and quantity by favorable reports, was obtained en masse from the testimony of officers from one regiment.

Wade used George T. Brown, sergeant at arms of the Senate, to gather evidence against Stone, and Brown discovered a herd of willing assistants when he came upon Colonel G. W. Tompkins and his Second New York State Militia or Ninety-second Infantry Regiment. Colonel Tompkins helped Brown by identifying

---

61   *C.C.W.*, 2, 423 (Merritt).

62   *C.C.W.*, 2, 455 (Dana).

men in his regiment who would testify against Stone.[63] The task was not difficult. His regiment had one characteristic the committee wanted: widespread dislike of Stone. The general had worked them hard, and they resented it. Colonel Tompkins led his men in ill will toward Stone.[64] The regiment had crossed at Edwards Ferry and taken no part in the fighting. In spite of its insignificant role, its officers provided almost 20 percent of all those witnesses called. They were questioned about Stone's "traitorous" activities. Although none had seen any disloyal act with their own eyes, they had all "heard" of many which, they vowed, were true.

The testimony about Ball's Bluff continued into late January. Consistent with the power of congressional investigation, the committee never allowed Stone to confront his accusers. In fact, it never accused him of anything. Nor did it allow him to know any of the "evidence" against him or give him a chance to speak in his own defense. For an ordinary congressional investigation, none of this would have been unusual or improper, but the Joint Committee defined for itself a different task. The committee had made itself into a prosecutor, judge, and jury, but neither Congress nor the committee had created any defense counsel.

The seven men concluded that Stone had ordered Baker to cross the river. They "proved" that the forces at Edwards Ferry and Ball's Bluff were intended to unite and that they never united because of the division commander's negligence—or worse. By the end of January the committee had, to its satisfaction, confirmed its predispositions about Stone. He had knowingly sent Baker and his men to their deaths. He was a traitor.

---

63   McClellan MSS (L.C.) letter dated January 5, 1862, from Brown to Lander; Lincoln MSS (L.C.) letter dated March 17, 1862, from Brown to Wade.

64   *C.C.W.*, 2, 358 ff (Berry) and 289 ff (George W. B. Tompkins).

Chapter 24

"General, what shall I do? The people are impatient. Chase has no money, and he tells me he can raise no more. The general of the army has typhoid fever. The bottom is out of the tub. What shall we do?"

—*Lincoln to Meigs*

McDowell's Reluctant Coup

*A*t prodigious expense the government maintained huge armies east and west—huge idle armies. Both McClellan and his father-in-law lay incapacitated with potentially fatal cases of typhoid, Marcy's case being worse than McClellan's.[1] Unfortunately, McClellan had no second-in-command who could assume responsibility for the Army of the Potomac, no senior division commander he had designated as an alternate leader, and no corps commander with a clear claim to primacy. Nor had McClellan, as far as Lincoln knew, taken any of his officers into his confidence about his plans. With McClellan and Marcy ill, the Army of the Potomac lay leaderless along the Potomac River and the war in the East had come to a standstill. Difficult enough it had been to provoke an offensive when McClellan was well. Now it had become impossible.

On Friday, December 28, the *Tribune* reported that two New York doctors, one of them Marcy's brother, had been specially summoned to treat the two men and had returned to New York City. "They report that both are getting on well," noted

---

1 S. L. M. Barlow MSS (H.L.) letter January 3, 1862, from Arthur McClellan to Barlow; Sparks, *Patrick Diary*, 26, entry dated January 4, 1861; and 30, entry dated January 11, 1862.

the *Tribune*, "and that General McClellan will be back in his saddle by Saturday or Monday next."[2] Fantasy!

Cautioned against placing too much reliance on McClellan and giving him too much power, Cameron frankly spoke the simple truth.

"What shall we do? Neither the president nor I know anything about military affairs."[3]

On the last day of the year, a beautiful day, the cabinet met, according to Attorney General Edward Bates, for a "bald disjointed chat" about McClellan's illness and his plans.[4] When the cabinet and the president had considered McClellan's appointment to replace Scott as general in chief, Bates had stated that Lincoln the president should act as the constitutional "commander in chief." This had not been a transitory idea for Bates, and as time passed, he belabored Lincoln with his view of the president as the military leader of his country, urging him to create "a military organization about his own person" with two, three, or four aides "to write and carry his orders, to collect information, to keep . . . papers and records and to do his bidding generally . . . I insisted that, being 'Commander in chief' by law, he *must* command—especially in such a war as this," Bates added to his diary. "The Nation requires it, and History will hold him responsible."

Bates saw no reason to have a general in chief. Perfectly appropriate it had been to humor Scott with the title in a time of peace when he headed a tiny army and faced no active enemy. Taking the disadvantageous side of the Scott Rule, he knew that none of the ranking generals in Lincoln's armies had commanded ten thousand men under fire and that none had "any personal knowledge of the complicated movements of a great army."

As he urged his unknown but farsighted structure on Lincoln, Bates could not have predicted how accurately, how precisely, he sketched the next century. "If I were President," he wrote, "I *would* command *in chief*—not in *detail*, certainly— and I would know what army I had and what the high generals (my Lieutenants) were doing with that army."[5]

---

2   *The New York Daily Tribune*, December 28, 1861, 5, col. 1.

3   Gurowski, *Diary*, 1, 117, entry dated November, 1861.

4   Beale, *Bates Diary*, 219, 220, entry dated December 31, 1861. The published diary contains two entries dated December 31; and the entry before the first December 31 entry is December 28; they appear to record the thoughts and events of two days, probably December 30 and 31. In the notes the two will be differentiated by the page citations and "no. 1" or "no. 2."

5   Beale, *Bates' Diary*, 218–219, entry dated December 31, 1861, no. 1.

On all these subjects Bates lectured the president during many cabinet meetings. How much these lectures contributed to Lincoln's experiments as a civilian leader of his country at war, how much cause and effect Bates could claim for future events, how much of Lincoln the commander in chief in 1862 he created, no one can ever know. Lincoln stood forever silent on the subject. But almost everything Bates proposed in his diary in the last day or two of 1861 would occur in the next few months as Lincoln and McClellan both metamorphosed.

The cabinet confronted the fact that "all military operations were to stop, just because Genl McClellan is sick," Bates wrote. Some favored a council of war of generals who should know "something about the army and be able to command" it if that became necessary. Fixing his attention on McClellan's secrecy about his plans, the ignorance of the president, and the requirements of the constitution, Bates disagreed about a council. As commander in chief Lincoln did not have a *privilege*, he had a *duty*, to command, a duty "to *know* the true condition of things." The secretary of war should serve as Lincoln's adjutant general and, as he had urged many times before, at least two "active . . . skillful officers should serve as his aides . . ." All these things he pressed on Lincoln repeatedly in the cabinet meetings.

After the meeting on December 31, Bates returned to the comforting solitude of his personal record. The last few hours of the first year of the war waned as Bates, whose position as attorney general did not make him a natural adviser on military affairs, sat disconsolately before his open diary. Perhaps he had shown acute foresight, even suggested rudimentary forerunners of the joint chiefs of staff, secretaries of war like Henry L. Stimson, Robert F. McNamara, and Donald H. Rumsfeld, strong presidential leaders like Franklin D. Roosevelt, John F. Kennedy, and George W. Bush in times of dominant military concerns. If he thought he had suggested these things, he felt an air of futility. In despair that his ideas would never feel the breath of life, he addressed his diary for the last time in the year, "I fear that I spoke in vain. The Prest. is an excellent man, and in the main wise, but he lacks *will* and *purpose*, and, I greatly fear he . . . has not *the power to command*."[6]

New Year's Day, the next day, the man whom Bates admired but who left him in despair met a second time with his partners, the officers of the United States Army. As he had at his inauguration, he received them, and many others, at the White House. First, the cabinet and their family members. Then, the diplomatic corps. The justices of the supreme court. Next, the officers of the army and navy.[7] The grueling,

6   Beale, *Bates Diary*, 230, entry dated December 31, 1861, no. 2.

7   Miers, *Lincoln Day by Day*, 87 (1862).

mortal stress foretold at his inauguration reception in March had not diminished, and Lincoln's relationship with his officer corps had, if anything, become strained.

Outside, Marsena R. Patrick, a graduate of the Military Academy with active service, now an upstate farmer, an aspirant for a commission in the great volunteer army, and a brigadier general in the New York State militia, watched from a position of exclusion[8] as Washington society exchanged the visits of the day. Men in dress and women in elegant finery filled the streets.

Erasmus D. Keyes, who had recently assumed command of William S. Rosecrans' division, gathered his three brigade commanders, Darius N. Couch, John J. Peck, and Lawrence P. Graham, for the walk to the White House. Lacking Keyes' sense of familiarity and informality, the three brigade commanders, two from West Point, all three Regular Army, wore full-dress uniforms. In shoulder straps rather than epaulets, boots, trousers tucked into the tops of them, a cover on his forage cap, and an ordinary day uniform, Keyes led with the air of a man entering familiar, friendly territory. From his adventures in the preservation of Fort Pickens he knew the president well. When he returned to headquarters, he commented humorously on the splendid, formal attire of his officers and jokingly told his staff he would return them to their regiments if they repeated anything he said.[9]

Meanwhile, Bates' president and Keyes' commander in chief did not fail to make his best effort at presidential war leadership as he defined it. An earnest diligent man motivated to do his best, Lincoln tried to see McClellan at his house time after time. Each time the household staff turned him away because of the general's illness;[10] and although Lincoln soon learned that McClellan was not dangerously ill, he still believed on New Year's Day that McClellan could "not yet be disturbed with business."[11] Next day, he was at last able to visit the general in person and was

---

8   Sparks, *Patrick's Diary*, 26, entry dated January 1, 1862.

9   Rhodes, Robert Hunt, *All for the Union: The Civil War Diary and Letters of Elisha Hunt Rhodes* (New York, 1985) 48, entry dated November 10, 1862, and 51, entry dated January 1, 1862 (Rhodes, *Rhodes' Letters and Diary*); Warner, *Generals in Blue*, 95, 180, 364; *OR*, 11, pt. 1, 282. When Keyes arrived to take command of Rosecrans's division on November 10, 1861, the division staff snapped to attention as he entered the headquarters building in Washington. Accustomed to Rosecrans's martinette bearing, the men relaxed when Keyes explained the new regime.

"Sit down, boys; and attend to your work. I don't want you to stand up for me. When I come in, you say, 'Good morning, General'; and I will say 'Good morning, boys'; and that is all that I require." Rhodes, *op. cit. supra*, 48, entry dated November 10, 1862.

10   *M.O.S.*, 155.

11   Basler, *Lincoln's Collected Works*, 4, 86–87, telegrams dated January 1, 1862, from Lincoln to Buell, and January 1, 1867, redated 1862 by the editor from Lincoln to Halleck; and letter dated January 1, 1862, from Lincoln to Halleck.

so encouraged that he reported to Chase, "I have just been with General McClellan; and he is very much better."[12]

The president had relied on Scott. He was gone. Now, he relied on McClellan; but he was incapacitated. He turned to the Library of Congress—it would always respond—for standard texts on strategy and military affairs, including Halleck's *Elements of Military Art and Science*.[13] In his isolation he began to delude himself into thinking he could take the field as a military commander.[14] After all, the best constitutional thinkers saw the president in that role; and four of his fifteen predecessors—Washington, Jackson, Harrison, and Taylor—had been successful battlefield commanders. Rumors began to circulate within the army that the president was considering the possibility of leading the army himself. Officers who discussed this proposition expressed unmistakable disapproval. The issue reached the enlisted men, who joined their officers in disapproval.[15]

While Lincoln grappled with the problems caused by McClellan's illness, the Joint Committee took steps of its own. On New Year's Eve five members of the Committee visited the president for an hour and a half. During the session Wade stormed at the president. "You are," he said, "murdering your country by inches in consequence of the inactivity of the military and want of direct policy in regards to slavery."[16]

The senators' general statements directed at Lincoln had not made their intentions and their hostility toward McClellan clear. Next day, Lincoln wrote to the general in chief, perhaps somewhat disingenuously, "You may be entirely relieved on this point . . . I found them in a perfectly good mood. As their investigation brings them acquainted with facts, they are rapidly coming to think of the whole case as all sensible men would."[17]

12   Basler, *Lincoln's Collected Works*, 4, 88, letter dated January 2, 1862, from Lincoln to Chase.

13   *N&H*, 5, 155–156; Library of Congress Archives, Borrowers Ledger, 1861–1863, cited in Miers, *Lincoln Day by Day*, January 8, 1862.

14   Donald, *Lincoln*, 329; Pease, *Browning Diary*, 1, 523, entry dated January 12, 1862. According to Browning the president also had ideas about ways to defeat the Rebels. The ideas were childish and by the end of the war would be proven so: He would threaten all Rebel "positions at the same time with superior force, and if they weakened one to strengthen another, seize and hold the one weakened . . . ," or he would "shell them out of their entrenchments" with guns able to fire a large shell more than two miles, a range beyond Confederate counterbattery fire. *Ibid.*

15   Adams, *Story of a Trooper*, 259–260.

16   *C.C.W.*, 1, 72 (Journal), entry dated January 4, 1862; Trefousse, Hans L., *Benjamin Wade*, 159 (New York, 1963).

17   Basler, *Lincoln's Collected Works*, 5, 88, letter dated January 1, 1862, from Lincoln to McClellan.

But on Saturday, January 4, the committee appointed a subcommittee of Gooch, Chandler, and Odell to arrange meetings with Lincoln and Cameron.[18] The next day Zachariah Chandler visited Chase at his home to demand that the baton be taken from McClellan, that McDowell be put at the head of the Army of the Potomac, and that McDowell be given charge of military affairs generally.[19] More likely than not, Chandler also told Chase the committee wished to meet with the president; and Chase reported that to Cameron. When the subcommittee called on Cameron that same day to arrange a meeting with Lincoln, the secretary of war had preceded them. Having previously learned that the committee wanted a conference with the president and the cabinet, he had already gone to Lincoln, who had fixed the next day at half past seven in the evening for a meeting of the full cabinet and the full committee.[20] The next evening Wade, Chandler, Johnson, Odell, and Covode no longer disguised their opinions about McClellan and the war effort. They strongly urged promotion of McDowell to major general and his assignment to command the Army of the Potomac. They wanted vigorous prosecution of the war.

Chase had not yet lost faith in his protégé. McClellan was the best man for the position, he said. He believed that, if McClellan had not become sick, he would, by this time, have satisfied everyone in the country. The general, he said, had worked himself too severely. No physical or mental vigor could withstand the strains he imposed on himself, often riding nearly all day and transacting business in his rooms nearly all night. With a slight echo of the general's critics, he noted that the general should confer freely with his ablest and most experienced generals to have the benefit of their counsel. He also felt that McClellan should give his generals a full description of his plans. If he had done that, his illness or incapacity would not have interrupted the movements of the army. He added the opinion the president had expressed when he made McClellan general in chief: no person could perform the specific duties as commanding general of the Army of the Potomac and the overall duties of general in chief. By trying to do both, McClellan had undertaken a task he could not perform. Chase concluded the very long discussion with an announcement that he would call on the young commander to learn his views about the division of his responsibilities.[21]

---

18   *C.C.W.*, 1, 72 (Journal), entry dated January 4, 1862.

19   Niven, *Chase Papers*, diary, 1, 321, entry dated January 5, 1862.

20   *C.C.W.*, 1, 73 (Journal) entry dated January 6, 1862.

21   Niven, *Chase Papers*, diary, 1, 321–322, entry dated January 6, 1862. The exact words in the diary are "division of the commands." Given the context, which was a discussion of the great burdens McClellan bore, the words, none too clear, probably refer to separation of commanding general of the Army of the Potomac and general in chief of all armies.

Although no longer in danger of dying, McClellan lay far from good health, and he continued unable to resume work from his sickbed until January 6, more than two weeks from the day he was stricken.[22] The president still had, however, his pet project for the Unionists in Kentucky and eastern Tennessee, and it had been part of McClellan's grand offensive plan.[23] Lincoln decided he might be able to satisfy the clamor for an attack on the Rebels if he could organize one by the western forces under Henry Halleck and Don Carlos Buell. He wrote to them, saying they should communicate with each other, develop a plan, and cooperate.[24] The correspondence was brief, unproductive, and unsatisfactory. It ended in frustration. Buell said he needed assistance from Halleck; Halleck responded that he knew nothing about Buell's plans and that he lacked the resources to cooperate with Buell. On Friday, January 10, Lincoln sent Cameron a copy of Halleck's letter[25] with the endorsement, "It is exceedingly discouraging. As everywhere else, nothing can be done."[26]

That day, the cabinet convened, as it usually did, in the morning. McClellan was still ill and his plans still a secret. Arriving hastily from a frustrating adjournment in the Supreme Court, Attorney General Bates stated that he believed the general in chief had no plans at all. He made a flurry of recommendations about restructuring various command relationships, then resumed his insistence that Lincoln select his own military advisers and that he exercise the powers imposed on him by the constitution.

22   *OR*, 7, 531. Although neither is encyclopedic or complete, neither *OR* nor *McClellan's Correspondence* resume until this date or later.

23   *OR*, 5, 38, letter dated November 7, 1861, from McClellan to Halleck; 39, letters dated November 7 and 11, 1861, from McClellan to Buell; 7, 468, letter dated December 3, 1861, from McClellan to Buell.

24   Basler, *Lincoln's Collected Works*, 7, 71, letter dated January 1, 1862, from Lincoln to Halleck; *OR*, 7, 524, letters dated December 31, 1861, from Lincoln to Halleck and Buell; 526, letters dated January 1, 1861, from Buell to Lincoln, from Lincoln to Buell; and from Halleck to Lincoln. In fact, Lincoln had described some of his ideas for eastern Tennessee, Kentucky, and part of North Carolina in his annual message to Congress earlier in the month. Basler, *Lincoln's Collected Works*, 37, Annual Message dated December 3, 1861.

25   *OR*, 7, 532–533, letter dated January 6, 1862, from Halleck to Lincoln.

26   Basler, *Lincoln's Collected Works*, 7, 95, and 95, n. 1, endorsement dated January 10, 1862, on letter dated January 6, 1862, from Halleck to Lincoln; the endorsement also appears in *OR*, 7, 533. From this point forward in the narrative some events are given precise dates by the participants and some are given general dates. The relationship between the meetings about the Army of the Potomac and the replacement of Cameron by Stanton are discussed in no primary source. The chronology has been reconstructed in the most logical way the sources will permit.

Lincoln and Secretary of War Cameron objected, not because the proposals were wrong but because they thought "the Generals would get angry, quarrel, etc.!"

"Of course the Generals—especially the Chief—would object," responded Bates, who delivered a tirade that recognized the Scott Rule for promotion. "They wish to give, but not receive, orders," Bates continued. "If I were president and I found them restive under the command of a *superior*, they should soon have no *inferiors* to command. All of them have been lately made of comparatively raw material, taken from the lower grades[27] of the army officers or from civil life. The very best of them—McClellan, McDowell, Halleck, etc., until very lately, never commanded more than a battalion. They have no experience in the handling of large bodies of men and are no more to be trusted in that respect than other men of good sense, lately their equals in rank and position. If, therefore, they presume to quarrel with the orders of *their superior*, their constitutional commander, for that very reason they ought to be dismissed, and I would do it in full confidence that I could fill their places with quite as good men, chosen, as *they* were chosen, from the lower grades of officers, from the ranks of the army, or from civil life."[28]

But Bates gave the military servants of the government the benefit of the doubt. They would, he said, "object and grumble" about his proposal, then yield a "moral and peaceful triumph once it had been taken. Those who resisted too long would give proof positive of unfitness to command and . . . ought to be instantly removed."

Like a lawyer delivering an appellate argument for a case he had tried and won in the court below, he repeated the arguments he had made in numerous earlier cabinet meetings. A staff of skillful military advisers for the president? Absolutely essential. A general in chief? "I see not the slightest use for it." The Army of the Potomac? "Quite enough for any one man to command in detail, and more than almost any one can do with assurance of good success."[29]

Knowing that McClellan was now conducting regular business from his sickbed,[30] Lincoln made another attempt to see him. Still ill and suffering long periods without sleep, the major general was asleep when Lincoln called. As al-

---

27   The diary says, "gratis."

28   In his diary Bates presents this speech and more with the introductory phrase, "I answer," as if he were recording direct discourse; and it has been treated in that manner here although one must doubt that he addressed his president in so strident a way.

29   Beale, *Bates Diary*, 223–226, entry dated January 10, 1862.

30   McClellan MSS (L.C.) letters dated January 7, 1862, (by the curator) from McClellan to Banks; January 7, 1861, 1:00 P.M., from McClellan to Banks; telegram dated January 7, 1861, from McClellan to Banks; telegram dated January 7, 1861, from McClellan to Banks; Sparks,

ways when the president found McClellan indisposed or asleep, his staff said the general could not see him.[31] Lincoln had a powerful bent for the realistic and the pragmatic.[32] He decided he should turn to one of the men who had served him best at the outbreak and who was available, Montgomery C. Meigs.

After Meigs and Keyes had overcome the many complexities of reinforcing Fort Pickens, the government had promoted Meigs to brigadier general and made him quartermaster general of all Lincoln's armies. The president had then assigned Meigs and Montgomery Blair the delicate task of reviewing the financial operations of John Charles Fremont's quartermaster department, which committed massive frauds in the acquisition of war materiel. The train carrying Meigs and Blair west passed Jessie Benton Fremont's train bound for her unpleasant meeting with Lincoln about her husband's emancipation proclamation. Fremont imprisoned Blair for criticizing him, Meigs confirmed the irregularities, and Fremont's military forces suffered some minor reverses. By the end of the month of October Blair had been released; Fremont had been relieved of his command; and Meigs had returned to Washington, where he acted on the periphery of Chase's early program of emancipation, education, employment, and integration of blacks in the Atlantic coast Sea Islands. With McClellan ill, perhaps Meigs could help the president again.[33]

Lincoln went from McClellan's house to Meigs' office. The balmy weather of the unusually long fall had ended, changing in the early days of January to snow, freezing temperatures, and rain. A first lieutenant in the Second Michigan Infantry wrote in his diary, "The ground is plastered with mud knee deep. We can have no drills or parades and can hardly stir out of our tents. There is no knowing whether we shall get out of this." Although the thermometer on January 10 did not register

---

Patrick's Diary, 26, 30, entries dated January 2, 1862 and January 14, 1862; Niven, *Chase Papers*, diary, 1, 321–322, entries dated January 5, 1862, and January 6, 1862; *OR*, 7, 527, dispatch dated January 3, 1862, from McClellan to Halleck; and 531, dispatch dated January 6, 1862, from McClellan to Buell.

31   *M.O.S.*, 155; McDowell memorandum reprinted in Swinton, *Army of the Potomac*, 79–80, entry dated January 10, 1862; *N&H*,5, 156. McDowell's memorandum is also reprinted in Raymond, Henry J., *The Life and Public Services of Abraham Lincoln*, 772–774 (New York, 1865); and a handwritten copy marked in the traditional adjutant's style as "a true copy" with a date is in the Chicago Historical Society but was misfiled after the author first saw it and not later available for re-examination.

32   Donald, *Lincoln*, 15.

33   Niven, *Chase Papers*, diary, 1, 324, entry dated December 11, 1861; Blue, Frederick J., *Salmon P. Chase: A Life in Politics*, 180–185 (Kent and London, 1987); Weigley, Russell F., *Quartermaster General of the Union Army: A Biography of Montgomery C. Meigs*, 191–195 (New York, 1959).

bitterly cold, a heavy fog hung everywhere[34] as the president trudged to Meigs' office. He took a chair in front of the fire burning in Meigs' fireplace.

"General," he said, "what shall I do? The people are impatient. Chase has no money, and he tells me he can raise no more. The general of the army has typhoid fever. The bottom is out of the tub. What shall we do?"

"If General McClellan has typhoid fever, that is an affair of six weeks at least," replied Meigs. "He will not be able sooner to command. In the meantime if the enemy in our front is as strong as he believes, they may attack on any day, and I think you should see some of those upon whom in such case or in case any forward movement becomes necessary, the control must fall. Send for them to meet with you soon and consult with them. Perhaps you may select the responsible commander for such an event."[35]

At the cabinet meeting on December 31, some members had suggested consultation with high-ranking officers who might be able to take command of the Army of the Potomac.[36] Probably relying on personnel suggestions from Chase, the president decided to seek advice from Irvin McDowell and William B. Franklin. He had Assistant Secretary of War Thomas A. Scott send McDowell a note and Franklin a telegram stating that, if they could safely leave their posts, he wished to see them that evening at the White House at 8. The note reached McDowell at Arlington while he was at dinner. A short time later he received a "private and confidential" letter from Meigs, who alerted him to the fact that Lincoln wished to see him.[37] Both McDowell and Franklin sent Scott telegrams stating that they would present themselves at the designated hour.[38]

---

34   Heintzelman MS Diary (small diary) (L.C.) entries dated January 2, January 3, January 4, January 6, January 9, and January 10, 1862; Pease, *Browning Diary*, 1, 523, entry dated January 10, 1862; Sears, *For Country, Cause, and Leader (Haydon Diary)*, 170, entry dated January 10, 1862; Wittenberg, Eric J., ed., *"We Have It Damn Hard Out Here": The Civil War Letters of Sergeant Thomas W. Smith 6th Pennsylvania Cavalry*, 8, letters dated January 7, 1862, from Smith to his sister, and January 15, 1862, from Smith to Joe (Kent and London, 1999); Thomas, Mary Warner and Richard A. Sauers, *The Civil War Letters of First Lieutenant James B. Thomas, Adjutant, 107th Pennsylvania Volunteers*, 26, letter dated January 4, 1862, from Thomas to his sister (Baltimore, 1995).

35   Meigs in *A.H.R.*, 292. Meigs MS Diary, entry dated January 10, 1862, and supplemental entry dated May 22, 1888, *ibid.*, 302.

36   Beale, *Bates Diary*, 220, entry dated December 31, 1861, no. 2.

37   William B. Franklin MSS (L.C.) telegram dated January 10, 1862, from Scott to Franklin; McDowell memorandum in Swinton *Army of the Potomac*, 79, entry dated January 10, 1862.

38   Lincoln MSS (L.C.) telegrams dated January 10, 1862, from Franklin to Scott and from McDowell to Scott.

Promptly at 8 McDowell appeared at the White House. Lincoln was alone. They went to a small room in the northeast corner of the building where Franklin, Seward, Chase, and Thomas Scott soon joined them.[39] Cameron did not attend and presumably had not received an invitation. Lincoln began the discussion by describing his conversation with Meigs: The treasury lacked funds, the public credit stood low, foreign relations were delicate, military affairs in the west seemed paralyzed, Buell and Halleck refused to cooperate, and Congress abused him for military inaction. He complained about the rise in the price of gold, the unreasonableness of Congress, the virulence of the press, and worst of all, the illness of General McClellan. In a plain, blunt way he spoke of all that depressed him. Franklin found the president in anguish and his anguish touching.

"I am in great distress," Lincoln continued. "I have been to General McClellan's house, and the general did not ask to see me. As I must talk to someone, I have sent for you to obtain your opinion as to the possibility of soon commencing active operations with the Army of the Potomac. If something is not soon done, the bottom will be out of the whole affair. And if General McClellan does not want to use the army, I would like to *borrow* it, provided I can see how it can be made to do something."[40]

As the cabinet officer in charge of disloyal persons and as a temporary replacement for the secretary of war, Seward had the latest intelligence.[41] Early in the winter an Englishman had presented himself at the War Department to suggest that he enter the Confederate lines as a spy, go to Richmond, and obtain information about

---

39   Donald in *Lincoln*, 330, says that the assistant secretary of war who attended the meeting was Peter H. Watson, not Scott. Of the accounts, two by McDowell and one each by McClellan, Meigs, and Chase, only McDowell lists the persons in attendance and he states that the War Department official was an "Assistant Secretary of War" but does not name him. The invitations to attend were sent to both McDowell and Franklin by Assistant Secretary of War Thomas A. Scott, Franklin MSS (L.C.) telegram dated January 10, 1862, from Scott to Franklin, and both sent telegrams to Scott stating that they would present themselves at the President's house at 8:00 P.M., Lincoln MSS (L.C.) telegrams dated January 10, 1862, from McDowell and Franklin to Scott. Hence, the Scott must have been the assistant secretary of war mentioned in McDowell's memorandum.

40   Franklin, William B., "The First Great Crime of the War," in A. K. McClure, ed., *The Annals of the War written by Leading Participants North and South*, 76 (McClure, *Annals*); McDowell memorandum in Swinton, *Army of the Potomac*, 80, entry dated January 10, 1862. According to McDowell, Lincoln also mentioned difficulties with the "Jacobins of Congress"; but when Swinton showed a copy of McDowell's memorandum to Lincoln in the summer of 1864, Lincoln stated that he did not recall any reference to the Radical Republicans. Swinton, *Army of the Potomac*, 80, fn.

41   Van Deusen, *Seward*, 288–289.

the Confederate army. He claimed that he had been a captain in the English army and asked to work as part of the secret service. The War Office sent him to Major General Wool at Fort Monroe. "With his usual caution," Wool first thought the Englishman might be sympathetic to the Confederates, but after careful consideration, he decided to allow him to cross into enemy lines.

In January the Englishman returned to Fort Monroe under a flag of truce and reported to Wool about the extent and condition of the defenses of Norfolk, Petersburg, and Richmond. He said that the force at Manassas numbered in its entire strength about thirty-eight thousand men. The Confederates "all along our front" could mass on short notice slightly more than one hundred thousand men "well shod, clothed, and fed." He said he had dined with Generals Beauregard and Johnston four days earlier and that Jackson was to march with about seventeen thousand troops into the Shenandoah Valley to attack Lander near Harpers Ferry and destroy the Baltimore and Ohio Railroad.

The following day Wool sent the Englishman to Washington under surveillance and prepared an official dispatch of the information. Seward described to the group meeting with Lincoln the content of the report from the spy. Franklin concluded that Johnston could mass seventy-five thousand men at Centerville.[42] When Seward had finished, the president had a question.

"What can soon be done with the Army?"

"The question as to the *when* must be preceded by the one as to the *how* and the *where*," responded McDowell, who had probably already been primed for the meeting by Meigs. McDowell must have seen this meeting and McClellan's illness as a legitimate opportunity to escape the dungeon in which he had suffered since Bull Run, sit once again in the highest military councils of his country, and obtain vindication for his original plan. With McClellan felled by typhoid, it might even present a chance for restoration to command of the main army.

He would not allow the opportunity to escape unused.

"I would organize the army into four corps," he continued, "placing the five divisions on the Washington side on the right bank; place three of these corps to the front—the right at Vienna, the left beyond Fairfax Station, the center beyond Fairfax Courthouse—and connect the latter place with the Orange and Alexandria Railroad, now partially thrown up." He had not forgotten the supply difficulties that

42   Webb MSS (Y.U.) letter dated May 10, 1882, from LeGrand B. Cannon to Webb; Franklin, "The First Great Crime of the War" in *Annals of the War*, 76–77; Cannon, LeGrand B., *Personal Reminiscences of the Rebellion, 1861–1866* (New York, 1895) 139–140 (Cannon, *Personal Reminiscences*).

plagued his army at Centerville because he could not use the railroad, nor had he forgotten Scott's cavalier dismissal of railroads as an important element in modern war. "This would enable us to supply these corps without the use of horses, except to distribute what was brought up by rail and to act upon the enemy without reference to the bad state of country roads. The railroads all lead to the enemy's position. By acting upon them in force, besieging his strongholds if necessary, or getting between them if possible, or making the attempt to do so; and pressing his left, I think we could in the first place cause him to bring up all his forces and mass them on the flank most pressed, the left. And possibly—I think probably—we could again get them out of their works and bring on a general engagement on favorable terms to us, at all events keeping him fully occupied and harried.[43] The fourth corps, in connection with a force of heavy guns afloat, would operate on his right flank beyond the Occoquan, get behind the batteries on the Potomac; take Acquia, which, being supported by the third corps over the Occoquan, it could safely attempt; and then move on the railroad from Manassas to the Rappahannock, having a large cavalry force to destroy the bridges." In grandiose substance with slight modification from experience and political expediency, he wished to repeat his Bull Run campaign, and deep in his soul, but probably not recognized even by him, he wanted vindication.

Like McClellan, McDowell, too, believed he should have an army of Napoleonic size, but unlike McClellan, he did not have a strong distaste for the casualties of frontal assaults on fortified Rebel positions like Centerville. "I think by the use of one hundred and thirty thousand men thus employed, and the great facilities which the railroad gives us, and the compact position we should occupy, we must succeed by repeated blows in crushing out the force in our front, even if it were equal in force and strength. The road by the Fairfax Courthouse to Centerville would give us the means to bring up siege mortars and siege materials; and even if we could not accomplish the object immediately, by making the campaign one of positions instead of one of maneuvers, to do so eventually and without risk. This saving of wagon transportation could be effected at once by connecting the Baltimore and Ohio Railroad with the Alexandria roads and by running a track over Long Bridge. When all this could be commenced, I could better tell when I knew something more definite as to the general condition of the army."

---

43 In McDowell's memorandum, at 81, Swinton used the word "harrowed;" but this must have been a slip of the pen on his part or a typographical error. Because the "true copy" in the Chicago Historical Society is "missing, presumed misfiled," it cannot be used to verify or correct.

McDowell had obviously given great thought to the use of the Army of the Potomac, including ideas made possible by its much larger size than the army he had led to Centerville. But he was still dominated by his original thinking and the demons he had created in July. He wanted to repeat the right flank maneuver, once again causing the Confederates to mass on their left—just as they had on Henry House Hill. This time he would have a surprise for them. In his original plan he was to fight the Confederates on the Fairfax line, turn their left flank at Vienna, drive them out the Warrenton Turnpike toward Centerville and the Stone Bridge, then slip to his left when he reached the Centerville area. But he now knew the terrain south of Centerville precluded this. McClellan's Occoquan plan had been a more splendid and more thoughtful version of McDowell's original plan. A slip to the left at the outset would bypass the rugged terrain south of Centerville. McClellan's keener eye and his understanding of Union naval supremacy had led him to plan the shift to the left earlier, longer, and faster, along the Potomac, not at Centerville or at Occoquan. Although McClellan had concluded that the Telegraph Road-Occoquan-Maple Valley route would be indecisive, he believed it vastly superior to McDowell's July route. Now, McDowell would take advantage of the huge nine- and eleven-inch guns carried by the navy, land a corps below the mouth of the Occoquan, clear the Rebel guns along the Potomac, combine this force with the corps beyond Fairfax Station, and move to the Rappahannock. McDowell's current plan, by correcting the deficiencies of his July advance, would vindicate his judgments about an attack on Centerville and the significance of the railroads.

Lincoln heard this with a receptive ear. He probably paid no attention to McDowell's unstated plea for personal vindication or to the stubbornness of his thinking. He needed to solve a problem created by refusals to cooperate in the West and severe illness in the East. He had two military advisers in the room and had heard from one. He turned to Franklin for his opinion about "doing something" with the Army of the Potomac.

Two and a half weeks earlier Franklin had been grilled by Chairman Wade of the Committee on the Conduct of the War. In that experience, a test of his loyalty to McClellan, he had declined to discuss McClellan's plans before he cleared the subject with the general.[44] Even with the president, Franklin maintained his first loyalty to McClellan.[45] He claimed to be ignorant of too many things to have any opinion. He knew only about his own division, which he considered ready for the field.

44   *C.C.W.*, 1, 122 (Franklin).

45   *M.O.S.*, 157.

Lincoln had not been a trial lawyer for so many years without developing an acute ability to elicit the information he wanted from a reluctant witness. He changed his approach. He did not need plans with a McClellan label.

"As to a plan of operations," he continued, "have you ever thought what you would do with this army if you had it."

"I have." Although he was describing his own plan, Franklin was, as always, completely loyal to McClellan. Without attributing his idea to the major general, he described McClellan's plan for the army as he understood it. "It is my judgment that it should be taken, what could be spared from the duty of protecting the capital, to York River *to operate on Richmond.*"

That raised an important question: the availability of the means to transport a large army by water. Assistant Secretary Scott said the available shipping had been severely strained to provide transportation for the twelve thousand men of the coast expedition that had included Isaac Stevens. Collecting sufficient shipping within a reasonable time would tax its capacities to the limit.

Both Franklin and McDowell had denied sufficient knowledge to discuss the role of the service bureaus in any movement. Lincoln said he wished them to gather again the next night at eight o'clock. In the meantime he wanted McDowell and Franklin to meet in order to obtain any further information they might need from the chiefs of the staff departments of the Army of the Potomac. Immediate orders were given to build a railway line across the Long Bridge.[46]

The next day, Saturday, January 11, 1862, Franklin and McDowell met at the Treasury Building, where they discussed the operations which, in their judgment, would be best under the circumstances. They deferred consideration of timing for the moment. Season, present position of the forces, and present condition of the countryside directed their thinking.

Intent on the adoption of his plan, McDowell tried to undermine the York River-Virginia Peninsula idea suggested by Franklin. Unwilling to stoop to his own defense for Bull Run, no wielder of the after-the-fact pen, convinced about the correctness of his own thinking, not privy to McClellan's new thinking, and perhaps even thinking that he proposed no more than a modified version of McClellan's plan as he had heard it earlier in the fall, McDowell probably exercised his most powerful

---

46   McDowell memorandum in Swinton, *Army of the Potomac*, 81–82, entry dated January 10, 1862; Franklin, "The First Great Crime of the War" in *Annals of the War*, 77. In the various accounts of the meetings on January 10, 11, 12, and 13, much of the discourse is given in the form of direct discourse. The indirect discourse seems to be very close to the words used by the speakers and has, without a footnote in each case or any apparent damage to the substance, been converted to direct discourse.

motivating force, his personal desire for vindication. He argued against the York River route. There, at West Point, the army would find fortifications that would require a naval force with large guns and large works. Nor was Richmond to be had for the asking. The Rebels had fortified it. The Federal army could not walk into it after a victory in the field. It would need a siege train. Even if the Federal army could do all this, it would require time, which would allow the Confederates to mass their forces. The difficulties the Union forces would confront would not differ from those they now faced before Alexandria, Munson's Hill, and Prospect Hill, but they would impose costs in time and money with a less certain base of operations, fewer handy facilities, a smaller operating force, and a larger foe. They would fight a war of position, McDowell said, until they succeeded in penetrating the enemy's line.

If they could overcome the Rebels at Centerville or cut their communications with the interior, the moral and physical result would prostrate their army, thus permitting easy future operations that had a certainty of success. In order of time and importance, the Federal forces must overcome the army in their front, the army that beleaguered the capital, that blockaded the Potomac, that cursed them day by day with the reproach of impotence, and that made them small in the eyes of foreign observers and the people of both North and South.[47] His arguments failed to understand the real purpose of McClellan's plan and failed to grasp its point. But given his choice, he would, like McClellan, impose a singleness of purpose on the Union war effort. All resources would be concentrated in the Army of the Potomac. Only those things that would help the execution of his plan would go to another army.

Though he alone knew it, Franklin carried McClellan's flag on this question, and he did not surrender. "In view of what we are charged to do," he said to McDowell, "might not Governor Chase tell us where General Burnside's expedition has gone?"

They had not in the Treasury Building. McDowell had a close relationship with his fellow Ohioan Secretary Chase. He left for Chase's office to ask if the secretary would tell them the destination.

"Under the circumstances," replied the secretary, "I think I ought to. It is destined for Newbern, North Carolina, by way of Hatteras Inlet and Pamlico Sound to operate on Raleigh and Beaufort or either of them. General McClellan has, by direction of the President, acquainted me with his plans, which are to go with a large force of this Army of the Potomac to Urbana or Tappahannock on the Rappahannock and then with his bridge trains move directly to Richmond."

---

47   McDowell memorandum in Swinton, *Army of the Potomac*, 82–83, entry dated January 11, 1862. Indirect discourse converted to direct.

McDowell took this information back to Franklin. They agreed they should consider both the York River and the Urbana routes in their inquiries.

A gentleman, a man without guile, Franklin had neither the personality nor the experience for this kind of back-staircase political activity while McDowell seemed to have them in an abundance. Franklin also lacked the "feminine obstinence" that enabled McClellan to resist contradictory forces regardless of their source. Unfortunately for Franklin and his chief, his superior intelligence, first in the West Point Class of 1843, could not overcome these lacks.[48]

"In deference to General McClellan, should we not inform him of the duty we are ordered to perform," wondered Franklin aloud.

Because McClellan was unavailable, command of the Army of the Potomac might be reassignable. Perhaps as little as telling him about the discussions might bring him from his sickbed and end McDowell's chance for restoration and vindication.

"The order I received was marked 'private and confidential,'" McDowell said; "and as they came from the president, our commander in chief, I conceive, as a common superior to both of us, it is for the president to say this, not us. I will consult the Secretary of the Treasury, who is at hand, and can tell us what is the rule in the cabinet in such matters."

Once again, McDowell trooped the corridors to Chase's office. The secretary believed the matter "lay entirely with the president." McDowell should direct no inquiry to the major general.

Before they could determine if "something could be done" with the Army of the Potomac, Franklin and McDowell needed the kind of information they could obtain only from staff bureau heads. They went to see Colonel Charles P. Kingsbury, chief of ordnance of the Army of the Potomac; Brigadier General Stewart Van Vliet, the army's chief quartermaster; and Major Alexander Shiras, its commissary of subsistence.[49] McClellan had always conversed freely with his heads of departments, each of whom knew the exact condition of the army and had authority to give any proper person any necessary information.[50] They supplied the information McDowell and Franklin needed. At some point in this process, McDowell carried

---

48   Heitman, *Historical Register*, 1, 434; *Cullum*, 2, no. 1167; Adams, *Story of a Trooper*, 203–05; *D.A.B.*, 3, pt. 2, 601–602.

49   McDowell memorandum in Swinton, *Army of the Potomac*, 82–83, entry dated January 11, 1862. Indirect discourse converted to direct.

50   *M.O.S.*, 156.

the day with Franklin. The time necessary to move the army to a new base of operations and probably the urgency expressed by Lincoln induced Franklin to surrender the York River and Urbana ideas to McDowell's land campaign west from the Potomac.[51]

Meanwhile, Chase had other visitors, one of them his political and judicial friend from prewar days,[52] McClellan's aide Colonel Thomas M. Key. About to meet with McClellan, Key wanted to know what he should recommend. Chase replied that McClellan should relieve himself of the charge of nepotism and favoritism in the selection of his staff; should "not allow the President to wait on him," but should send one of his aides regularly to discuss affairs with the president; and should take counsel with his most experienced and able generals. Chase felt McClellan should also promptly insist on the appointment of McDowell as a major general.[53]

---

51 McDowell memorandum in Swinton, *Army of the Potomac*, 83, entry dated January 11, 1862.

52 Niven, *Chase*, 153.

53 Niven, *Chase Papers*, diary, 324, entry dated January 11, 1862.

Chapter 25

The Coup Fails

*E*arlier, rumors had circulated that Sherman would replace McClellan. They expanded to a more realistic proposition when new rumors joined the information mill that the president had sent privately for McDowell and Franklin to consult with them in order to determine whether McClellan had a plan, whether it was good, and whether the government could rely on its execution. Another rumor followed that McClellan had been relieved and McDowell appointed to take his place. Widespread dissatisfaction flowed from these rumors, particularly the one about McDowell. "Officers of all ranks," wrote one officer a short time later, "openly declared him a failure, arraigned his management of the first battle of Bull Run, and threatened to throw up their commissions than to serve under him." As hard as he had tried, McDowell had failed to regain the confidence and respect of the army. Franklin would have been acceptable to both officers and men because they considered him McDowell's mental superior and he already had a reputation as a good soldier and a patriot.[1]

Born in 1823 in York, Pennsylvania, William B. Franklin, "Frank" as he was known to friends like McClellan, graduated from the U.S. Military Academy at the head of the Class of 1843, a classmate of U.S. Grant. His commission in the topographical engineers took him to a survey of the Great Lakes, the Kearny expedition

---

1   Kearny MSS (L.C.) letter dated February 15, 1862, from Kearny to Parker; Adams, *Story of a Trooper*, 260.

to South Pass, and General Wool's command in the Mexican War. In 1852 he married, and the next year received promotion to first lieutenant. Becoming a captain in 1857, he was stationed for several years in Washington as supervising engineer in charge of the construction of the dome on the Capitol and the new wing on the Treasury Building. When Congress created the new Regular Army regiments in 1861, it promoted him to colonel of the Twelfth United States Infantry, a perfect example of both the Scott company-grade officer rule and the Browne geography rule.

At Bull Run, the regiment that claimed its discharge on the day of the battle, the Fourth Pennsylvania, had come from his brigade. With his understrength brigade, he performed reasonably well, taking his men into the final battle line on Henry House Hill, where he created no opportunity to distinguish himself with an independent, extraordinary act. After the battle he was assigned to Brigadier General Theodore Runyon at Alexandria, and when Runyon was restored to civilian oblivion in New Jersey, Franklin replaced him on July 31. Promoted to brigadier general at the insistence of his friend McClellan, he received command of a division one month later. His three brigades were posted in the vicinity of the Theological Seminary on the finger ridge that ran west from Alexandria. All matters brought before him he decided impartially and on their merits. In a short time he gained the confidence and esteem of his soldiers.

He made continuous efforts to protect private property while the army lay in Confederate country, but even his most stringent measures failed to save the helpless citizen. The men had plundered Fairfax Seminary of its valuable library, its works of art, its scientific and musical instruments, its furniture, and every other thing of value. Unlike Baldy Smith or Phil Kearny and in some ways more like McDowell, Franklin did not take advantage of the circumstances to select a fine local house for his headquarters. After the army reestablished its position west of the Potomac River and occupied the area around Alexandria, he pitched his headquarters tent in an open field on the brow of a hill and remained there during the entire winter. He did not communicate with the local citizens except on official matters and did not permit any of his staff to occupy their houses.

According to the Comte de Paris, Franklin was "different from the others and is spiritual despite a tough appearance. He is a soldier before everything. He would gladly fight but he does not have Heintzelman's ardor. He does not care about the political aspect of the conflict." Some thought he was superior in ability and military skill to all his commanders except McClellan. Keenly susceptible to "the demands of justice and true humanity," modest and unassuming in his manners, but a rigid disciplinarian, he had a strong contempt for hypocrisy, openly rebuked it when it interfered with the discipline of his troops, and set an example for his officers by his conduct. He strongly believed that the duty of the army was to fight and conquer the enemy but also to protect the defenseless and the innocent. In his view the army yielded too much to unnecessary fears, "thereby bringing distress upon the innocent." Also a considerable thinker, he realized that moderation in the enemy's country would be more effective than heavy use of the sword, and believing that many citizens of Virginia had been misled by their leaders, he was anxious to be merciful to those who had been led astray, while punishing those who had led them.

As a consequence of his attitude toward Southern civilians, some people whispered doubts about his patriotism, and some of these whisperings reached important members of government. Rumors about Franklin and others played into the confusion about the correct means to put down the rebellion and the proper treatment of the citizens swept into it.

Because he had worked to create uniformity for new regiments, had worked with the Union Defense Committee in New York City, and had guarded the Treasury Building before Bull Run, he was known to and respected by Secretary of the Treasury Chase. A brief schoolmate of McClellan at West Point, Franklin and the major general were good friends and comrades in arms with mutual respect. He and McClellan had spoken on many occasions about McClellan's early plans, but about the major change of base to Urbana he knew only that McClellan planned a movement by ship to an unidentified place that would give the army a short march to the Rebel capital. A Democrat, he had the same attitude toward the slaves as McClellan. As he wrote Baldy Smith later, "I shall not have any niggers to command, that is one comfort." Loyal to his friends, particularly to McClellan, he was an uncomplicated, ingenuous, straightforward, completely honest officer of engineers leading a division of infantry.[2]

2   Comte de Paris MS diary (large diary) (A.N. de la M. de F.) entry dated November 7, 1861; Smith MSS (V.H.S.) letter dated August 3, 1863, from Franklin to Smith; NA Off's MS Rpts (Franklin); Eby, Cecil D., *A Virginia Yankee in the Civil War: The Diaries of David Hunter Strother* (Chapel Hill, 1961) 120, entry dated October 1, 1862 (Eby, *Strother's Diary*); Franklin MSS (L.C.) letter dated March 10, 1865, from McClellan to "My dear Frank"; McClellan MSS (L.C.) letter dated September 24, 1867, from Franklin to McClellan; draft MS memoirs, 43; Smith MSS (V.H.S.) letter dated August 3, 1863, from Franklin to Smith; *Ropes-Gray Letters*, 137, letter dated June 27, 1863, from Ropes to Gray; Curtis, *Bull Run to Chancellorsville*, 291–292; Adams, *Story of a Trooper*, 201–205, 260; Curtis, *Bull Run to Chancellorsville*, 291; *Cullum*, 2, no. 1167; Snell, Mark A., *From First to Last, the Life of Major General William B. Franklin* (New York, 2002) generally 1–67 (Snell, *Franklin*); Heitman, *Historical Register*, 1, 434; Warner, *Generals in Blue*, 159–160; *D.A.B.*, 3, pt. 2, 601–602; Powell, *Officers of the Army and Navy*, 146; Beach, William H., *The First New York (Lincoln) Cavalry from April 19, 1861, to July 7, 1865*, 64 (New York, 1902).

As a subordinate junior in age, rank, and West Point class, he had served under Heintzelman at Bull Run and around Alexandria, then been promoted to brigadier general with the same date of rank as Heintzelman and made a division commander. Now he had become Heintzelman's equal in everything but age and seniority.[3] Critical of everyone who might compete with him, Heintzelman thought his former subordinate not fit to be anything but a topographical engineer and too lazy even for that.[4] Others with the same complaints, age, rank, seniority, experience, dissatisfaction, and jealousy, had similar comments. Philip W. Kearny had expected political influence to give him command of all New Jersey troops and the two stars of a major general. When the federal government asserted the exclusive power to commission general officers, the governor of New Jersey could no longer deliver the commission. In addition, the promotion of another New Jersey officer, William R. Montgomery, West Point Class of 1825,[5] had compromised the plan because he outranked Kearny and would precede him on the promotion and assignment lists. To keep Montgomery from being given a division of two New Jersey brigades, Kearny thought, McClellan and Cameron adopted a policy of mixing the regiments in each division, leaving Kearny to labor as a brigade commander in Franklin's division.

Kearny firmly believed he was wiser, smarter, and better than any of his contemporaries.[6] Most importantly, in his mind he had unusual skills as a leader of men. When assigned to Franklin's division, he found Franklin to be one of the many respectable but deficient officers around him. "It was a great misfortune," he wrote, "that I was ever interfered with by being placed in Division with Franklin, who ranked me—although I have a high opinion of his abilities. Still he *never* commanded a soldier & fails in small details, which trifles in themselves, are ruinous if misdirected. I fear too a great spirit of jealousy of my brigade, & the superior comforts I have derived for them by the possession of the Seminary & that plateau."[7] Kearny saw jealous enemies everywhere, enemies who perverted the truth about his outstanding brigade of New Jersey regiments and gave credit for it to the wrong

---

3   Heitman, *Historical Register*, 1, 434, 521. In fact, as brigadier generals of volunteers and Regular Army colonels they were both promoted to rank from the same days, May 14 and May 17. Their seniority would be determined by their place on the list or by date of commission for an earlier, lower rank.

4   Heintzelman MSS (large diary) (L.C.) entry dated April 8, 1863.

5   Warner, *Generals in Blue*, 329–330.

6   *D.A.B.*, 5, pt. 2, 271–272; Warner, *Generals in Blue*, 258–259; Welsh, *Medical Histories*, 188; generally dePeyster, *Kearny*, 40–200.

7   Kearny MSS (L.C.) letter dated December 3, 1861, from Kearny to Parker.

man. "It is true that it is mortifying to find the excellencies peculiar to my own Brigade attributed to Franklin. Franklin, a superior officer in some respects, from never having served in the line, has done much to injure my efficiency. . . . His ignorance of practical detail, his want of energy, his want of habit of command, has resulted in there being so many unwatched, independent, unregulated quotas—ceasing to improve."[8]

While the rumors and complaints about command circulated, other events, apparently unrelated, took place. The secretary of war, strangely absent from the meetings prompted by McClellan's illness, had ever since the scrape with the president over his report known that his days in the cabinet would not last long and that he must leave the government. But other events and the president's uncertainty about a replacement delayed the process. Lincoln preferred Montgomery Blair, the postmaster general. Chase and Seward both wanted Stanton, who had managed to conceal his role in Cameron's objectionable report. In an unfortunate twist of fate for McClellan, Lincoln accepted a man he did not prefer and yielded his candidate Blair.[9] In January, the ambassadorship to Russia, a post in which Cameron had previously expressed interest, became available. During the meetings about the army, Lincoln sent letters to Cameron proposing that he have the post in Russia.[10]

An important contributor to the case for Stanton's elevation,[11] Chase must have told him about the meetings taking place in the White House. Stanton went to McClellan to warn him about hostile developments in the White House meetings about the army. "They're counting on your death and are already dividing among themselves your military goods and chattels," he said.

8   Kearny MSS (L.C.) letter dated December 24, 1861, from Kearny to Parker.

9   Meneely, A. Howard, ed., "Three Manuscripts of Gideon Welles," in *American Historical Review*, 31, 491 (1926); Thomas, Benjamin P., and Hyman, Harold M., *Stanton: The Life and Times of Lincoln's Secretary of War* (New York, 1962) 134–137 (Thomas, *Stanton*); Bradley, Erwin Stanley, *Simon Cameron: Lincoln's Secretary of War: A Political Biography*, 201–210 (Philadelphia, 1966).

10   Lincoln MSS (L.C.) copy of a note dated January 11, 1862, from Lincoln to Cameron, and letter dated January 11, 1862, from Lincoln to Cameron.

11   The replacement of Cameron with Stanton as secretary of war, rightly regarded by most historians of the period as an important step by Lincoln, has been described in detail by many, e.g., *N&H*, 5, 123–144; Thomas, *Stanton*, 129–142; Stanley, *Cameron*, 201–210, Meneeley in *American Historical Review*, 31, 491 ff. With his skeptical New Englander's eye, Welles analyzed the replacement in an unusual way. He saw the conniver Chase actively promoting Stanton and taking the "credit" for his elevation, but he believed the real force behind the removal of Cameron and his replacement by Stanton was the wily New Yorker William H. Seward, who was content to let Chase strut but who achieved his own end. Meneeley in *American Historical Review*, 31, 490–492.

No doubt, Stanton had learned about the meetings at the White House in confidence, but while McDowell and Franklin collected information from the staff bureau heads on January 11, Stanton warned McClellan about the meetings and specifically told him the participants would reassemble the next day.

After all he had done to help McDowell recover from his defeat at Bull Run? McClellan's anger at McDowell's participation reached uncharacteristically high levels. Stricken with his illness only three weeks earlier, McClellan still had, by Meigs' prognostication, three more weeks before he could return to his duties. Nevertheless, the general in chief decided to intervene. Like Lazarus, he would rise and go to the White House the next day. Perhaps he would catch the culprit McDowell at work.[12]

A short while before the White House meeting scheduled for the evening, Chase took a few moments to scribble, in his wretched, vertical scrawl, a short note to his beautiful daughter Kate. He did not tarry long enough to date the letter. "My dearest Katie," he began, ". . . I have only a moment to write as I must go to the President's to be in a consultation on military matters. Everybody prowls dreadfully—worse I think than ever. And the President is trying to put life and motion into the inert army. The truth is McClellan's sickness has cost the country more than can be estimated & the loss is aggravated by the fact that he has had no men 'of his counsel' thoroughly conversant with his plans, able to comprehend & able in event of disease or disaster to him to execute them. Here has been his first error."[13]

---

12   *M.O.S.*, 156. W. C. Prime, the editor of McClellan's postwar, posthumously published memoirs, speculated about Stanton's motives for giving this information to McClellan with an equivocal assertion that Stanton did it to prevent or abort a powerful alliance of Chase and McDowell in his primary domain, *M.O.S.*, 159, n. Prime was as much susceptible to the Great Conspiracy theory as the Radicals were to the McClellan-and-West Point-Traitor theory, both equally absurd in retrospect. Applying the ordinary trial lawyer's rules for evaluating testimony (every story has an original basis in fact, no story is an entirely fictional invention, a story that is adverse or embarrassing to the teller has more truth in it, people generally try to tell the truth except for hyperbole, a very few people should not be believed on any controversial point) the normal expectations of life are the most reliable. Here, Stanton was not yet secretary of war, he had not yet formed an alliance with the Radicals, he needed all the help he could develop to become secretary of war, he was a coward filled with doubt, McClellan could help him return to the government at a high level, and a man's self-interest is the best litmus test of his motives and his credibility. Stanton sought to curry favor with McClellan and earn his gratitude, in effect, to put him in debt, by telling McClellan about the meetings of the cabal and giving him a chance to strike for himself. Prime's speculation about Chase and McDowell is too unrealistic and predates Chase's first real loss of faith in McClellan, which was just around the corner.

13   Chase MSS (U.P.I.) letter of n.d. from Chase to his daughter Kate. Even though it is without date the letter can be placed in the chronology by its text. It appears to have been written after the meetings began but before the Sunday, January 12, meeting, which is described in another letter to Kate.

Ignorant of McClellan's intention to participate the next day, the group—Lincoln, Seward, Chase, Scott, Meigs, McDowell, and Franklin–reassembled that night in the White House. A short while later Montgomery Blair joined them. McDowell had come fully prepared. Between the investigation with the bureau heads and the evening meeting, he had created a full presentation in written form. Holding it before him, he read it to the group: Still pursuing personal vindication, he proposed an advance to Manassas, then to the Rappahannock.

Blair's younger brother Frank had already written a lengthy piece showing the disadvantages of this route. Montgomery Blair, too, opposed it. He thought the army should go to the York River or to Fortress Monroe and attack Richmond or capture Suffolk in order to cut off Norfolk. That was, in his opinion, the decisive stroke.

"The plan of going to the front from this position is Bull Run all over again," he said, recognizing McDowell's attempt to vindicate the earlier advance and erase the stigma of the battle. "It is strategically defective as was the effort last July. As then, we will have the operations upon exterior lines. It involves too much risk. There is not so much difficulty as has been supposed in removing the army down the Chesapeake. Only from the Lower Chesapeake can anything decisive result against the army at Manassas. To drive them from their present position by operating from our present base will only force them to another behind the one they now occupy, and we will have all our work to do over again."

"If we only had a victory over them," the nonpartisan Seward commented, "it would answer whether obtained at Manassas or further south."

Keeper of the purse strings, Chase gave the financial response. All else equal, the moral power of a victory over the enemy in his present position would be as great, he thought, as anywhere else. The danger of the change of base lay in the probability that the Union army would lose time and spend millions while it found as many difficulties to overcome below as it now had above. Desperate for something to show the bankers who were financing the war, he would take a tactical victory anywhere on any terms, no matter that it had no beneficial strategic consequences.[14]

Lincoln said very little but he seemed to be impressed with the statement by Blair, the only cabinet member with a West Point education and any claim to military experience. He wished to hear about transportation by water. Franklin and McDowell should see Meigs in the morning, and the group should meet again at three in the afternoon.[15]

14   McDowell memorandum in Swinton, *Army of the Potomac*, 83, entry dated January 11, 1862.

15   Franklin in *Annals of the War*, 78.

During his illness McClellan had retained his clarity of mind and had tried to keep at his paperwork. Although weak, thinner, careworn, and still somewhat ill,[16] he took advantage of his strong constitution, rose early Sunday morning, dressed, and took a carriage to the White House. When he arrived, he found Lincoln and Seward already at work. Having sent them no notice of his intention, he now took his turn for a "drop-in" visit; and when he entered, he noticed that his appearance had "the effect of a shell in a powder magazine." The beneficiaries of his surprise looked, he thought, as if they had been caught doing something they considered shameful.

Unaware of Chandler's visit with Chase, the meeting of the Joint Committee with the cabinet, and the demands for his removal, McClellan had been misled by Lincoln's New Year's Day note. He believed that no opposition group had formed against him and that he faced no serious opposition as general in command of the Army of the Potomac or as general in chief of all Union armies. He had heard "slight murmurs" of impatience at delay, but as far as he was concerned, sensible, well-informed men knew he could not begin a campaign in this season of snow, rain, mud, freezing temperatures, and impassable roads. He approached this confrontation as if McDowell were his enemy. About the reason for his visit he said nothing, and he received no explanation about the White House meetings. In a "general and casual way" he explained his military intentions. At the end of the discussion Lincoln suggested a conference at the White House the next day, invited McClellan to attend, but told him nothing about the meeting scheduled that afternoon.[17]

Meanwhile, Franklin and McDowell met at Meigs' house to perform their transportation assignment. Once again, McDowell proselytized, this time making Meigs his target on the need to support his campaign for vindication: the Army of the Potomac should concentrate its efforts on the immediate enemy at Centerville. Meigs agreed, but he had also done his homework: he could assemble water transportation for thirty thousand men in four to six weeks. They adjourned to the afternoon meeting at the White House. After a few of them had gathered, Seward arrived in an excited state and threw aside his hat.

"I have seen General McClellan and *he is a well man*. I think that the meeting would better adjourn."

---

16   Nevins, *Strong Diary*, 3, 203, entry dated January 29, 1862; Eby, *Strother's Diary*, 4, entry dated February 29, 1862; *M.O.S.*, 155.

17   *M.O.S.*, 155–156.

Lincoln and Seward described the brief, earlier visit by McClellan, reporting that he was looking quite well and could now resume active charge of the army. The daily meetings were no longer necessary, nor were the services of the group. The meeting the next day would be a formality at which Lincoln would confirm that McClellan held the baton.[18]

Editorializing once again, Mother Nature's aide, the weather, produced cold, unpleasant conditions the next day.[19] In the morning Stanton met Malcolm Ives, a reporter for the *New York Herald*. Stanton already knew Ives from the time at the end of Buchanan's administration when Stanton used his cabinet position to obtain important information he could leak to the Republicans. Ives confirmed that Stanton would be nominated that day for secretary of war. Ives had come to Stanton, he said, for the express purpose of being relieved of the obligation of secrecy. He wanted to give the information to his editor, James Gordon Bennett. They discussed developing cabinet matters.

"Tell Mr. Bennett everything, orally, in New York," Stanton then said, "but do not write it." Then he added, "If I do receive the appointment, I will show that I am no middle measures man but will throw overboard the rest of the presses and cling to the *Herald* alone." He promised Ives he would arrange an interview with McClellan.[20]

That afternoon, McClellan apparently went to the meeting at the White House in a foul humor. In an uncharacteristic way he brimmed with hostility for McDowell, who, he believed, had betrayed him and wanted to replace him as commander of the army. Franklin, who had done nothing more than follow orders and who had loyally tried to involve McClellan in the secret program, he would never suspect of doing anything wrong.[21]

Chase and McDowell arrived together. Looking pale and weak, McClellan joined them a short time later. The entire group, Lincoln, Seward, Blair, Meigs,

---

18   McDowell memorandum in Swinton, *Army of the Potomac*, 84, entry dated January 12, 1862; Niven, *Chase Diary*, 326, entry dated January 12, 1862; Franklin, "The First Great Crime of the War" in *Annals of the War*, 78.

19   Heintzelman MS diary (small diary) (L.C.) entry dated January 13, 1862.

20   James G. Bennett MSS (L.C.) letter dated January 15, 1861 (undoubtedly misdated in year; because of the content it should be dated 1862), from Malcolm Ives to Bennett. Indirect discourse converted to direct. According to Thomas, *Stanton*, 137, Lincoln appointed Stanton on January 14; but *N&H* say, 5, 129, that his nomination was sent to the Senate on January 13, a date far more consistent with the chronology of events in other narratives.

21   *M.O.S.*, 155–156.

Franklin, McClellan, and Scott, attended.[22] McClellan took a seat between Blair and Meigs and began to converse with them about unrelated subjects. Lincoln described the purpose of the meeting. Chase and Blair both gave short talks. But all looked to McClellan for something definitive. This was an excellent opportunity for him to explain his plans and create powerful support for them, but, intent on disposing of McDowell, he failed to recognize it. The major general sat silently with his head down. The participants whispered among themselves, especially Chase and Lincoln. The silence became awkward.[23] Lincoln pointed to a map, asked McDowell to explain the plan he had described earlier, and briefly outlined the circumstances under which he had come to solicit help from McDowell and Franklin.

Knowing that he should be as brief as possible, McDowell described the activities he and Franklin had undertaken, the plans they had considered, and the time necessary to launch each: three weeks from the present base and four to six weeks if the base of operations were moved to Fort Monroe or Urbana. Concluding with an apologetic explanation of the awkward position in which he found himself, he disclaimed any purpose hostile to McClellan. He had acted only because of the general's critical illness.

McClellan cut the explanation short, saying that the restoration of his health changed the case and that the examination must now cease. As far as McDowell's statement of his plan was concerned, McClellan said, "You are entitled to have any opinion you please."

When he gave his opinion in favor of the Peninsula, Franklin said, he knew that his judgment coincided with General McClellan's view. McDowell claimed complete ignorance about the major general's plans, and Franklin dissented about the time for operations from the present base. He did not think the roads would be in order in three weeks.

22   McDowell memorandum in Swinton, *Army of the Potomac*, 84, entry dated January 13, 1862; Franklin in *Annals of the War*, 78–79; *M.O.S.*, 157. According to McDowell, McClellan was rude and curt when he spoke about contrary opinions and directed his remarks to McDowell. McClellan's account in *M.O.S.* does not convey any sense of gentle treatment, but Franklin's account suggests that McClellan referred to everyone's opinion, not pointedly to McDowell's. Although Franklin was a devoted McClellan partisan all his life, he never overworked the facts like Porter, whose inferences and characterizations require great care before they can be used. He would have had easy access to McDowell's memorandum because it was published in full in Swinton's history of the Army of the Potomac (date of publication 1866). *M.O.S.* was not published until 1886. McDowell's words have been accepted except when they differ from Franklin, the least biased of the participants who left an account.

23   Meigs in *A.H.R.*, 26, 292.

"*Commence* operations," McDowell restated, "in all of three weeks."

Franklin agreed that was possible.[24] This made the difference in time between commencement of McClellan's Urbana Plan and McDowell's Centerville Plan negligible at best.

The major general quietly resumed his conversation with Blair and Meigs and awaited further developments.

The whispering began again, especially between Lincoln and Chase.[25] Meigs moved his chair close to McClellan and urged him to speak.

"The President evidently expects you to speak. Can you not promise some movement towards Manassas? You are strong."

He replied, "I cannot move on them with as great a force as they have."

"Why, you have near two hundred thousand men. How many have they?"

"Not less than one hundred seventy-five thousand according to my advices."

"Do you think so?" Meigs responded. "The President expects something from you."

"If I tell him my plans, they will be in the *New York Herald* tomorrow morning. He can't keep a secret. He will tell them to Tadd."

"That is a pity, but he is the President,—the commander in chief. He has a right to know. It is not respectful to sit mute when he so clearly requires you to speak. He is superior to all."[26]

In a very excited tone and manner, Chase said he understood the purpose of the meeting to be for McClellan to explain his military plans in detail, then and there, which would allow the group to approve or disapprove. His manner seemed to McClellan unnecessarily violent. In spite of the fact that he had already been openly rude to McDowell, McClellan was surprised by Chase's demeanor, but as he had in the confrontation with Scott, he determined to keep perfectly cool. He merely remarked that the purpose stated by Chase was entirely new to him and withdrew to a technically sound but politically foolish position when so much rested on the mutual goodwill of the men in the room. He did not recognize the secretary of the treasury as his official superior, he said, and denied Chase's right to question him about military affairs. The president and the secretary of war, and they alone, had the right to interrogate him. McClellan then resumed his conversation with Blair and Meigs and

24   McDowell memorandum in Swinton, *Army of the Potomac*, 84, entry dated January 13, 1862.

25   *M.O.S.*, 157.

26   Meigs in *A.H.R.*, 26, 292–293.

took no further notice of Chase. So far, no-one had addressed the purpose of the meeting as McClellan understood it—the disposition of the military goods and chattels of a sick man.

Weeks before this meeting McClellan had explained to Chase his proposed movement to Urbana, and the plan had pleased Chase greatly. The secretary had seemed very grateful for the confidence McClellan reposed in him and to appreciate McClellan's thoughtful attempt to relieve his anxieties. Now, he seemed much different. McClellan could account for the secretary's unprovoked irritation only by concluding that Chase intended an intrigue in which McDowell would carry this new plan into effect. McClellan thought his unexpected recovery had frustrated Chase's intentions. Nevertheless, the general believed he had "disposed of the Secretary of the Treasury," he wrote years later in his memoirs.

Chase resumed his whispering with Lincoln. A few minutes passed. Finally, Lincoln said, "Well, General McClellan, I think you had better tell us what your plans are."

"If you have confidence in me," replied McClellan, taking a completely improper position, "it is not right or necessary to entrust my designs to the judgment of others, but if your confidence is so slight as to require my opinions be fortified by those of other persons, it would be wiser to replace me by someone fully possessing your confidence. No general commanding an army would willingly submit his plans to the judgment of such an assembly, in which some are incompetent to form a valuable opinion and others incapable of keeping a secret so that anything made known to them would soon spread over Washington and become known to the enemy." He then asserted that the president and the secretary knew his designs in general terms and concluded by refusing to disclose any further information unless Lincoln gave him an order in writing and assumed responsibility for the results.[27]

During this colloquy, Blair, Franklin, and McDowell had gathered in the window recess. When McClellan declined to disclose his plans, Blair turned to Franklin, saying, "Well, if that is Mac's decision, he is a ruined man."[28]

The participants urged the major general to relent. At last he described the stagnation in Kentucky and East Tennessee, not the Army of the Potomac. Although this problem had driven Lincoln to convene the group in the first place, the response could not have been satisfactory to anyone except the president.

27   *M.O.S.*, 157–158. Indirect discourse converted to direct discourse.

28   Franklin, "The First Great Crime of the War" in *Annals of the War*, 79.

"The movement in Kentucky," McClellan said, "is to precede any one from this place; and that movement might now be *forced*. I have directed General Buell, if he can not hire wagons for his transportation, he must take them."

The general paused—then stated his earlier concern, a concern of long standing.

"I must say I am very unwilling to develop my plans, always believing that in military matters the fewer persons who know them the better. I will tell them if *ordered* to do so."[29]

A long silence followed.

Finally, Lincoln broke it by asking if the major general had matured a plan for the movement of the Army of the Potomac.

McClellan said he had.

Another long silence.

"Then, General," said the president, "I shall not order you to give it."[30]

A little more whispering between Lincoln and Chase. Seward rose, buttoned his coat against weather that presaged twenty degrees and snow that night, and laughed.

"Well, Mr. President, I think the meeting had better break up. I don't see that we are likely to make much out of General McClellan."[31]

"Well, on this assurance of the general that he will press the advance in Kentucky, I will be satisfied and will adjourn this council."[32]

Chase continued his whispering with the president. When that ceased, McClellan walked to Lincoln, begged that he not yield to improper influences but trust him. If Lincoln would leave military affairs to him, he said, he would be responsible for bringing matters to a successful issue and free the president from all his troubles.[33]

29   *M.O.S.*, 158; McDowell memorandum in Swinton, *Army of the Potomac*, 85, entry dated January 13, 1862.

30   Franklin, "The First Great Crime of the War" in *Annals of the War*, 79. In his account, which could be a different recollection of the colloquy described by Meigs and McDowell but seems not to be, Franklin wrote that Chase made the statement about McClellan; but in a footnote added later he stated that he could not recall whether it was Blair or Chase. The circumstances, including the fact that McClellan had described the Urbana plan to Chase, suggest that it was Blair.

31   Heintzelman MS diary (small diary) (L.C.) entry dated January 14, 1862; *M.O.S.*, 158.

32   Meigs in *A.H.R.*, 26, 292.

33   *M.O.S.*, 158–159.

Chapter 26

"Gen'l Lander is too suggestive & critical."

—*McClellan to Banks*

Lander Protects the Baltimore and Ohio

$\mathcal{I}$n the first year of the war, Frederick West Lander was not quite forty years old. As a school boy he excelled at sports, showing a spirit of adventure and great personal strength. In build, he was tall and powerful, in fact, as tall as the president. After studying civil engineering he chose the railroads for his career, first in the East, then gradually moving to the ultimate challenge of the cross-continental railroad projects of the 1850s. His rugged physique made him a visual expression of the frontiersman and mountainman he was. Yet he presented an uncertain, confusing physiognomy, appearing "both active and indolent, both stately and careless."[1]

In 1853, then in his early thirties, he accepted an offer from Isaac Ingalls Stevens, a lieutenant of engineers, to be chief engineer on a survey for a northern railway route to the West Coast. That began a series of projects in which he searched for the best route between the frontier and the West Coast, many of his

---

1 Casper Crowninshield MS Diary (Boston Public Library) entry dated September 16, 1861; *D.A.B.*, 5, pt. 2, 569–570; Lander, Edward, "A Sketch of General Frederick W. Lander," *Historical Collections of the Essex Institute*, 40, 313–315 (October 1904, no. 4); Glad, Paul W., "Frederick West Lander and the Pacific Railroad Movement," *Nebraska History*, 35, 176–178.

reports being published by Congress.[2] But he did not simply "go native" and make cross-country trips for the Department of the Interior in order to investigate railroad routes. Nor did he remain on the frontier fighting Indians and living on buffalo jerky. He had ideas of his own.

He believed the railroad should, in the beginning, be temporary and inexpensive, first a wagon road, then wooden rails on roughly finished roadbeds. In public addresses he advocated a trackline adapted to the needs at the time of construction, the central route being a light, rough line and the northern the shortest because it would run from the navigable eastern rivers to Puget Sound. The northern route would struggle through the rugged Cascades, with their challenges of infinite tunneling, diversion along the Columbia River, winter snow and ice, and competition from a Canadian railroad.[3]

Participation in the philosophical debates about the nature of a first railway to the Pacific swept Lander inevitably into the sectional controversy about the location of the route, north, central, or south. A loyal and moderate Democrat, he wrote and spoke charitably about the southern route, but by the end of the decade, his sharp, sarcastic wit would dispose of the southern route even while he described its virtues. "If across the undulating country of Texas," he wrote, "this road is difficult of construction,—if labor is high, if contractors cannot fulfill their engagements, if fuel is scarce, if timber cannot readily be furnished to the road, if there is no local traffic to sustain it when built, so much the more reason for direct and efficient aid to it by the Government of the United States. If it needs twice the amount to sustain it that the central route does, let it have it."[4]

He thought an inexpensive, evolutionary beginning would suffice, military needs would justify federal aid, and money could be generated by limited sales of land along the right of way. Immediate railway communication with the Pacific

2   Lander, F. W., *Synopsis of a Report of the Reconnaissance of a Railroad from Puget Sound via South Pass to the Mississippi River* (Washington, D.C., 1856) (reprinted as House Ex. Docs., no. 129, 33 Cong., 1 Sess. and Senate Ex. Docs., 33 Cong. 2 sess., XIII, pt. 2); Lander, F. W. *Remarks on the Construction of a First Class Double Track Railway to the Pacific* (Washington, D.C., 1854); Lander, F. W., *Practicability of Railroads through South Pass* (House Ex. Doc. no. 70, 35 Cong., 1 Sess. IX, 18); Lander, F. W., "A Bill to Provide for the Construction of a Railroad from the Missouri River to the Pacific Ocean" (Washington, D.C., 1860).

3   Glad, "*Lander*," in *Nebraska History*, 35, 177–181, 185.

4   Letter dated 1860, from Lander to Rep. R. E. Fenton, reprinted in the *New York Times Supplement*, March 28, 1860, second page (the pages are unnumbered in the *Supplement*), cols. 3 and 4. In fact, he strongly opposed the southern route and had announced his intention to tell Secretary of War Davis it should not be adopted. Ambrose, Stephen E., *Nothing Like It in the World: The Men who Built the Transcontinental Railroad 1863–1869*, 34–35 (New York, 2000).

stood first. Improvement could follow over time. Inconsistent with the prevailing national spirit, without appeal to the government, but prophetic on economics, Lander's plans would have avoided several national financial disasters and would have treated the frontier landowners in a way consistent with their anti-government attitude and their opposition to the patronage given by government to capital.

In September 1859 Lander attended the Pacific Railroad Convention, at which he delivered a well-received speech about the Pacific Railway project. In it he took the opportunity to compliment the contributions of James A. McDougall, the able, fiercely competitive, but too-often-drunk senator from California, and to espouse the central route.[5] Just before he returned East he married an internationally renowned actress, who complemented his less well-known artistic talent as a poet whose works sounded messages of loyal nationalism.

When war erupted, the men in Washington knew his rugged, fearless skills as a railroader, frontiersman, outdoorsman, and Indian fighter would make him a talented addition to the Union effort.[6] Having dealt with government at the highest levels, corresponded with Secretary of War Jefferson Davis, and served on explorations with Isaac I. Ingalls, George B. McClellan, Cuvier Grover, and other rising army officers, he wrote to General Scott to volunteer "in any capacity, at any time, and for any duty." Scott accepted.[7]

Lincoln and Scott sent Lander to Texas, where Governor Sam Houston remained loyal to the United States. But Houston's fellow citizens were a different story. Lander's assignment, which was to offer Houston military assistance, illustrated Lincoln's mistaken conclusion about the depth of loyalty to the Union in the South. Arriving at the end of March, Lander went to Houston only to learn that the old Texan did not want assistance and certainly did not want a concentration of United States troops in his state.[8] After Lander returned safely to Washington, which seemed to be separated from the northeastern states, he was sent through hostile Maryland to deliver dispatches to the military forces under Butler, Keyes, and Lefferts in Annapolis

---

5   Glad, "Lander," in *Nebraska History*, 189–919; Lander, "Lander," in *Historical Collections of the Essex Institute*, 40, 314–316; Branch, E. Douglas, "Frederick West Lander, Road Builder," *Mississippi Valley Historical Review*, 16 (September 1929).

6   Lander, "Lander," in *Historical Collections of Essex Institute*, 40, 316; *D.A.B.*, 5, pt. 2, 569–570.

7   Stevens, 1, 306–307; Lander, "Lander," in *Historical Collections of Essex Institute*, 40, 316; Crist, *Davis Papers*, 5, 363–364.

8   *OR*, 1, 550, 551, 551–552; *D.A.B.*, 5, pt. 2, 569; Nevins, Allan, *The War for the Union*, 4 vols. (New York, 1959), *The Improvised War, 1861–1862*, 1, 29.

on the north side of Baltimore. Of the eight messengers, only Lander and one other succeeded in reaching the objective, and Lander had to escape from capture to do it.[9]

As a colonel on McClellan's staff in western Virginia, he distinguished himself in the battle at Phillipi,[10] then marched with McClellan to Rich Mountain, where the major general burst on the wartime scene with the Union's first victory. Taking advantage of his skills as an outdoorsman, Lander led the flanking column on an eight-hour march "through a pathless forest, over rocks and ravines in the rain."[11]

Having served well on the mission to Texas, succeeded in the mission to Annapolis, served with distinction and gallantry under McClellan, been mentioned with high favor in dispatches and reports, and come East to Washington with McClellan, Lander was emboldened to submit to Seward a plan for raising a regiment of Virginia volunteers for the Union. On May 2, Seward reported it to Lincoln, who asked Scott to see Lander and consider his idea. The president wrote, "Col. Lander is a valuable man to us." In August, Lander received from the adjutant general's office a commission as a brigadier general to rank from May 17, 1861,[12] and a brigade in Charles P. Stone's division, the Corps of Observation.[13] The fighting at Ball's Bluff caught Lander at a meeting in the capital, but he raced to the scene in time to command a reconnaissance to Edwards Ferry on October 22 and receive a wound in the leg.[14] One of his aides asked a surgeon to examine the wound. The doctor found that a piece of Lander's bootstrap had been carried into his leg by the bullet. He pulled it out. Lander unleashed his titanic profanity and swore "a blue streak," remembered the surgeon after the war, then demanded that the ferry take him to the Maryland side before anything else be done to the wound. Uneasy with such a "restless and intractable patient," the surgeon declared himself after the war "glad to get him off my hands."[15]

---

9   Swinton, William, *History of the Seventh Regiment*, 2 vols. (New York, ?) 1, 489–490.

10   *OR*, 2, 66, letter dated June 10, 1861, from McClellan to Scott.

11   *OR*, 2, 215, 218, Rosecrans' report.

12   Frederick W. Lander MSS (L.C.) letter dated August 13, 1861, from the Adjutant General to Lander; *Heitman*, 1, 613; Basler, *Lincoln's Collected Works*, 4, 355, endorsement of n.d., on letter dated May 2, 1861, from Seward to Lincoln; *OR*, 2, 66, McClellan's report; 67, Morris' report; 207, McClellan's report; 215, Rosecrans' report; 218, Rosecrans' report; and 288, McClellan's report.

13   *M.O.S.*, 81.

14   Lander, "Lander," in *Historical Collections of Essex Institute*, 40, 317.

15   Hand, Colonel Daniel, "Reminiscences of an Army Surgeon" in *Broadfoot MOLLUS Minnesota*, 26, 279–280.

The conference in which he had been participating had considered the opening of the Baltimore and Ohio Railroad between Harpers Ferry and Cumberland. From the outbreak of the war two major railroad arteries had served the capital: lines from New York and Philadelphia in the north and the Baltimore and Ohio line to Cumberland in the west. By early 1862, the line of track from Baltimore to Harpers Ferry had become generally safe except for guerrilla activity. At Harpers Ferry it crossed the Potomac into Virginia, where it forked, one branch running the short route southwest to Winchester and the other first looping away from the Potomac River, then into rugged terrain where it hugged the southern shore until it passed Cumberland and recrossed to the north side. In May and early June Thomas J. Jackson's Confederate troops had held Harpers Ferry and had thoroughly crippled the railroad by taking rails, cars, and locomotives south, destroying bridges, and terrifying employees. At 4 A.M. on June 4, gunpowder explosions followed by fires destroyed the main bridge over the Potomac. This and the demolitions to the west made the line useless.[16]

Responding to the increasing public pressure for some kind of offensive move in the East and the need for coal, oil, and grain from the West,[17] Secretary Chase sent J. H. Sullivan to investigate the possibility of an offensive move at the bottom of the Shenandoah Valley. Chase gave Sullivan a kind and complimentary note of introduction. Banks and Sullivan had a long conversation in which Banks described the "plans of his contemplated occupation of Harpers Ferry & Martinsburg, as far as was consistent with the reserve due to his position and responsibilities." Sullivan thought a movement forward on those two places entirely practicable. If Banks moved with force, he could easily carry both points and could supply and quarter his troops on an open road, which would be more comfortable and inexpensive for their maintenance than using the nearby town of Frederick, Maryland. Kelley concurred. Sullivan believed this was true in spite of a recent show of force by a large body of Confederates at Martinsburg. From information he had obtained, Sullivan believed Confederate forces numerically superior but not effective, most of them being conscripts pressed into service by military squads seizing citizens of surrounding counties by threats and violence. As far as Kelley was concerned, the more militia Jackson had, the worse his situation.[18]

---

16   Hungerford, Edward, *The Story of the Baltimore & Ohio Railroad 1827–1927*, 2 vols. (New York and London, 1928) 2, 7–8 (Hungerford, *B&O*); Hearn, Chester G., *Six Years of Hell: Harpers Ferry During the Civil War* (Baton Rouge, 1996) 70–71, 74–75 (Hearn, *Six Years of Hell*); Jones, Ray, *Harpers Ferry*, 146 (Gretna, 1992).

17   Summers, Festus P., *The Baltimore and Ohio in the Civil War* (Gettysburg, 1993) 51–104 (Summers, *B&O*); Hungerford, *B&O*, 3–19; *O.R. Atlas*, plate cxxxvi.

18   Chase MSS (L.C.) letter dated December 18, 1861, from Sullivan to Chase.

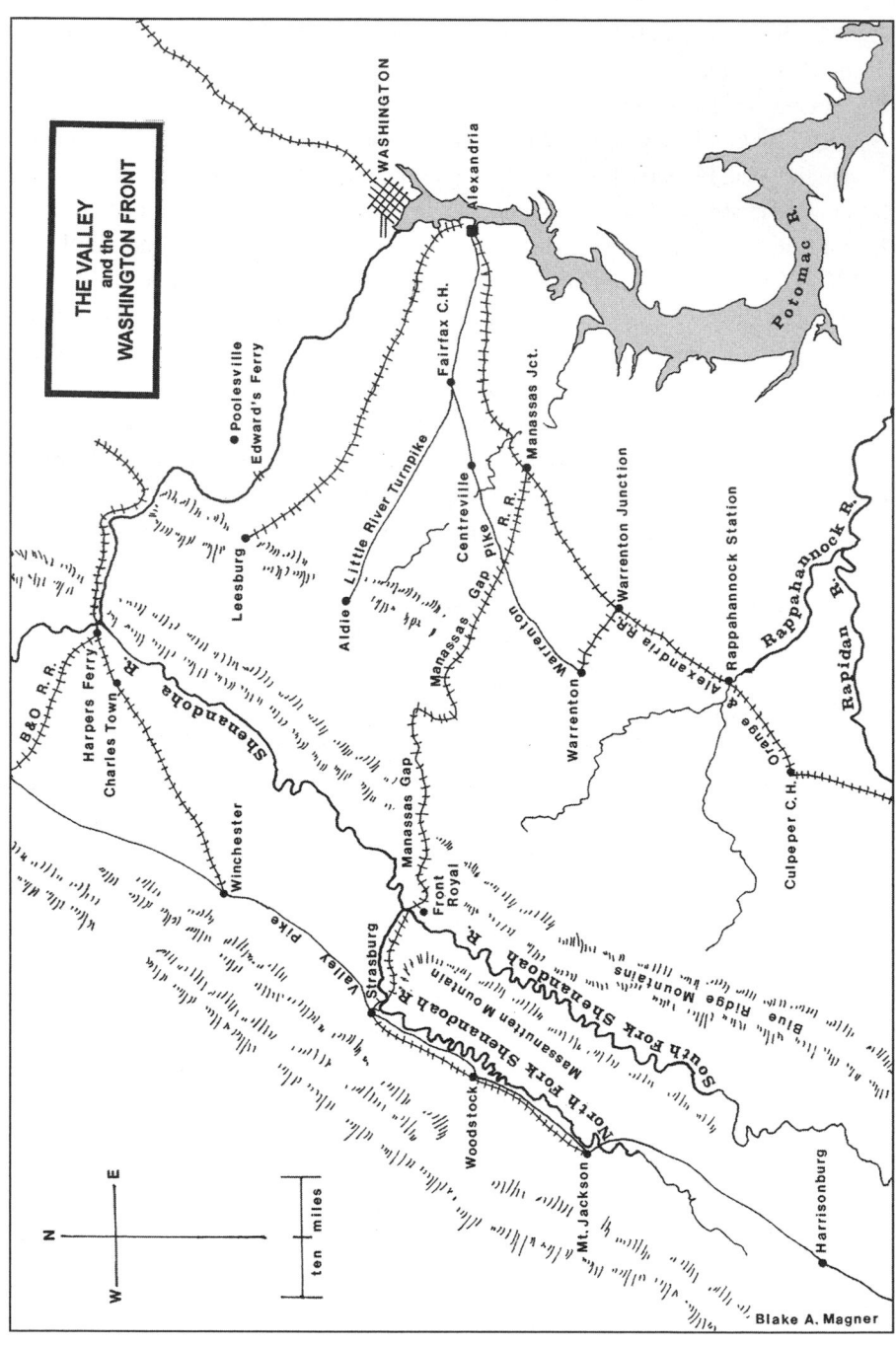

THE VALLEY
and the
WASHINGTON FRONT

Blake A. Magner

ten miles

Cameron decided that the Baltimore and Ohio west from Harpers Ferry to Cumberland could not remain closed. McClellan should open it. But the major general opposed this because he believed a movement against the left wing of the Confederate line in Virginia, the Shenandoah Valley position, would threaten the rear of the Confederate position at Manassas and Centerville and induce them to evacuate. If they withdrew to the next natural position, the line of the Rappahannock and Rapidan rivers, Fredericksburg, and Gordonsville, they would shorten their march to Richmond and frustrate the new plan under consideration. Although he knew a new Rebel line at the Rappahannock would compel abandonment of the Potomac River batteries, "open" the river in an easy, bloodless way, and satisfy a strong desire of the administration, McClellan did not believe this either necessary or desirable. Unable to hit anything on the Potomac, the inept Confederate batteries had not "closed" the river. Water access to the capital existed through Annapolis, and he would put the river batteries to flight whether he used his original plan for an advance or the new idea in formation.[19] Nevertheless, if something must be done for the railroad line, he had a natural idea for the disorganized, mixed force of Ohio, Virginia, and Pennsylvania regiments that lay scattered in the vicinity of Romney.[20]

Meanwhile, Cameron asked Lander for his views on a way to reopen the Baltimore and Ohio. Lander prepared a general memorandum and sent it to the secretary. The Confederates under Jackson had advanced, it said, down the Valley into the bulge in the line of the Potomac River at the town of Hancock. Muddy valleys, rugged mountains, and rutted roads separated Jackson's Confederate army from his support areas at Winchester and Strasberg. Rosecrans' column, useless at Grafton, should reinforce Kelley in the Cumberland-Romney area. Banks could cross the Potomac by boats, occupy Loudoun Heights, hold the Leesburg and Winchester Turnpike, and receive reinforcements from Baltimore and Annapolis. Cavalry from Banks could sever railroad connections with Manassas by burning the Manassas Railway bridge near Strasberg, "even at the sacrifice of a regiment." McCall should advance toward Leesburg with a strong column to help Banks if Jackson's march north from Winchester proved to be an attempt to turn the army's right flank. The advancing Union forces should take Winchester, then turn north toward Jackson's rear near Hancock on the Potomac River. Every country road across the Blue Ridge

---

19   McClellan MSS (L.C.) part of an account of the Army of the Potomac probably from a draft of the final report or *M.O.S.* in McClellan's handwriting, dated December 1861 by the curator but obviously written later than that. *OR*, 5, 47–48, 50–51, 54, McClellan's report; *M.O.S.*, 197, 203.

20   McClellan MSS (L.C.) part of an account of the Army of the Potomac probably from a draft of the final report or *M.O.S.* in McClellan's handwriting, dated December 1861 by the curator but obviously written later than that.

had to be covered by a reconnaissance party to watch Jackson. If the Confederates marched westward toward Romney, New Creek, and Cumberland, Kelley's Union forces should fight them in the mountain passes.

"To recapitulate," he wrote, "Jackson's force is estimated at 15,000. I deny it, but if he has them, all the better. They are either fed from the Shenandoah Valley or trains, & camp equipment will fall into our hands. . . . Can we not risk something to relieve the Union men of [the] Shenandoah Valley, engage the enemy's attention by endangering his rear & above all open for public use the Balt & Ohio RR . . . The most dangerous and assailable part of this movement is at Harpers Ferry." With great perspicacity he asked the critical question for the near future: "Will Loudoun Heights fortified & a pontoon bridge across the Potomac secure this or will it not?"[21]

It was an aggressive plan in the spirit of the man who devised it. Lander would not maneuver with Jackson. He would drive him. He thought twenty thousand men could do it. And if he did not have twenty thousand men he would "beg, borrow, or steal" them. The time for allowing Jackson to run up and down the Valley at will should end. This memorandum foretold a problem Lander would create for himself again and again. He always wanted more men than he had, and he would "beg, borrow, or steal" them from anyone within reach, most often from adjacent commands.

The federal government decided it should do something to reopen the westbound track.[22] In October, the government created the Department of Harpers Ferry and Cumberland, which covered the line of track and a strip of land thirty miles wide on the south side of the Potomac. Commander of the department was a natural choice, Brigadier General Frederick West Lander,[23] who was about to com-

---

21   Lander MSS (L.C.) undated memorandum with n.a. dated by the staff of the Library in December 1861 with a question mark but probably correct.

22   An undated, handwritten document in McClellan's papers states that Secretary of War Cameron determined to undertake the Baltimore and Ohio project in December. McClellan MSS (L.C.) handwritten page in McClellan's handwriting, n.d., n.a., dated in December by the curator apparently by content and probably part of the manuscript for McClellan's final report or his memoirs but separate from them. McClellan states imprecisely that in December the decision had been made but does not give a specific date. Other events strongly imply that it was earlier, e.g., the meeting on October 21, the Lander submission on October 25, and others by Babcock. *OR*, 5, 630–631, letter dated October 28, 1861, from Lander to Scott; 677–678, letter dated December 7, 1861, from Banks to Marcy, and from Babcock to Marcy; and 692–693, letter dated December 26, 1861, from Babcock to Marcy.

23   Welcher, Frank J., *The Union Army, 1861–1865: Organization and Operations*, 2 vols. (Bloomington and Indianapolis, 1989) 1, *The Eastern Theater*, 16 (Welcher, *Union Army*); Lander, "Lander" in *Historical Collections of Essex Institute*, 40, 317. The National Archives has no record collection for this department, thus making the McClellan MSS even more indispensable than usual.

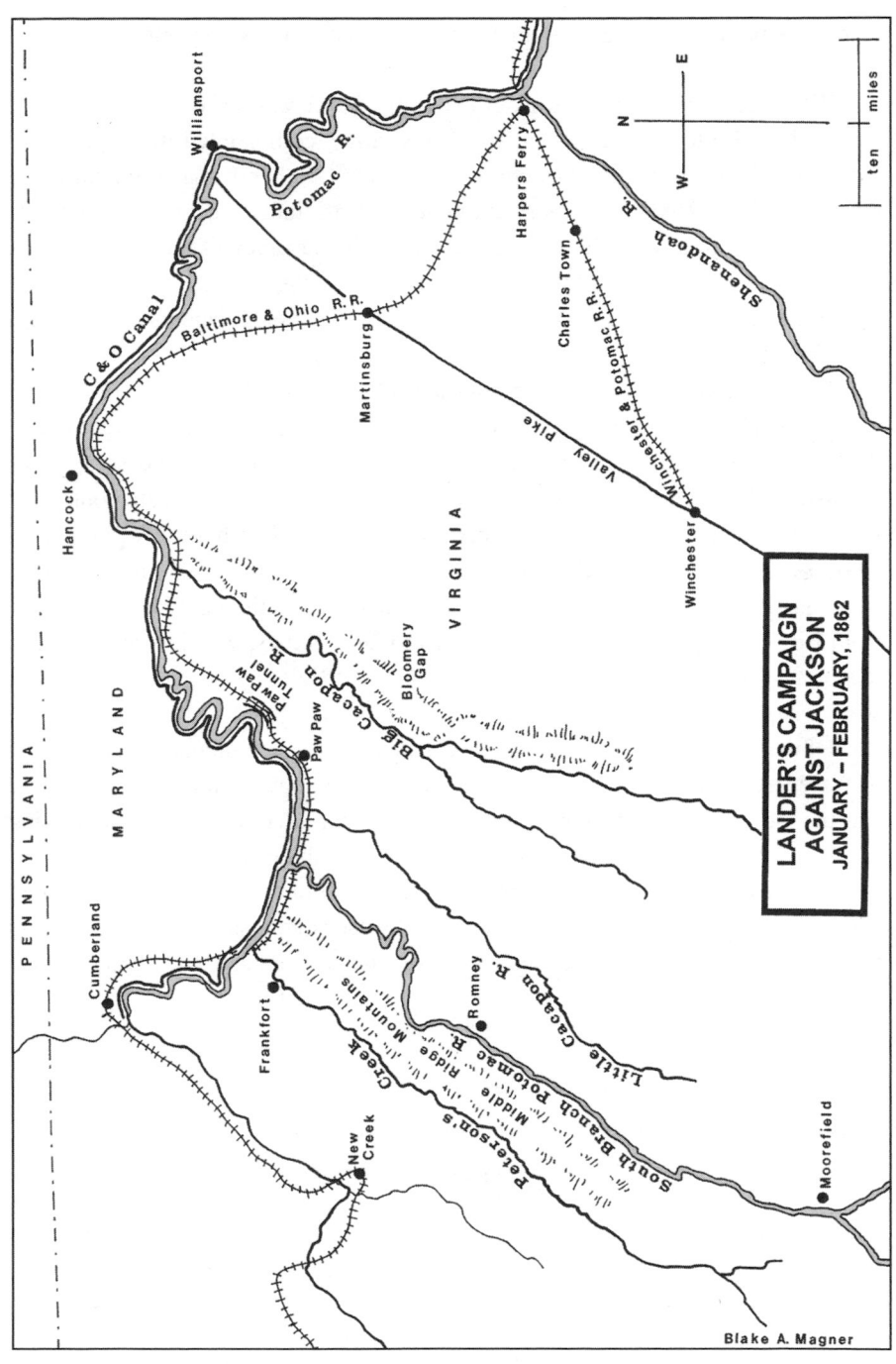

LANDER'S CAMPAIGN
AGAINST JACKSON
JANUARY – FEBRUARY, 1862

Blake A. Magner

bine his experience as a railroad man with his rambunctious, hyperactive, instinctive military capacities.

While Lander recuperated from his Ball's Bluff wound, Brigadier General Benjamin F. Kelley, an officer in Rosecrans' army, commanded the department temporarily.[24] In a brilliant little action at the end of October, Kelley used untrained infantry and the Ringgold Cavalry, an understrength, independent troop of Pennsylvania horse, to capture the village of Romney in the valley of the South Branch of the Potomac. After he had put the Confederates to flight,[25] Kelley established a "United States outpost" in the town under Colonel Samuel H. Dunning of the Fifth Ohio Infantry.[26]

Lander wrote to Scott that Kelley should be supported at once. His success, he said, was "a blow in the very face of the rebels." Brave and in the right place, Kelley needed experience and a little caution, "which he does not possess," Lander wrote. He asked for Henry W. Benham, who had caused truly ugly controversies with personal animosities at every assignment he had held. McClellan, on whose staff Benham served in western Virginia, had left him behind when he came east. Lander also requested two regiments, the Tenth and Thirteenth Ohio, from Rosecrans' column. As if he intended to keep Kelley, who also belonged to Rosecrans, he added gratuitously that Benham and Kelley were on excellent personal terms.[27]

Of the valleys formed by the three principal north-south mountain ranges west of Winchester, the wide, long valley bottomed by the South Branch of the Potomac was the most important. One hundred miles long and filled with excellent growing fields, it held the town of Romney, the county seat, which boasted a population of only five hundred. Romney had three substantial buildings, a courthouse, a bank, and a church. The courthouse had been used by Jackson to store rotting meat, and the streets "oozed" with raw sewage. One of Jackson's men had described the town as a "hog pen."[28]

---

24 *OR*, 5, 625, dispatch dated October 22, 1861, from Scott to Kelley.

25 Elwood, Sgt. John W., *Elwood's Stories of the Old Ringgold Cavalry 1847–1865* (Cool Center, 1914) 61–66 (Elwood, *Ringgold Cavalry*).

26 Farrar, Samuel Clarke, *The Twenty-second Pennsylvania Cavalry and the Ringgold Battalion 1861–1865* (Pittsburgh, 1911) 29 (Farrar, *Twenty-second Pennsylvania Cavalry*).

27 Lander MSS (L.C.) letter of n.d. from Lander to Scott, dated by the staff at the end of October and probably correctly.

28 Robertson, James I., Jr., *Stonewall Jackson: The Man, the Soldier, the Legend* (New York, 1997) 301, 315 (Robertson, *Jackson*).

After losing Romney, Jackson regrouped and began a series of raids on the railroad, the canal, and the important facilities of both. The raids, temporarily successful, severed the east-west traffic. At the end of December, Jackson marched north in two columns toward the town of Bath. South across the Potomac went the Thirty-ninth Illinois, part of the Eighty-fourth Pennsylvania, and two guns under Lieutenant Muhlenburg to delay Jackson's approach to the town of Hancock, which lay north of Bath and just across the river.[29]

McClellan believed that he could not make the railroad safe and that repair was a waste of time unless he could fight and win a major battle or occupy and hold both Winchester and Strasberg.[30] Either would require a force sufficiently large and a leader sufficiently skillful to neutralize his classmate Tom Jackson and the Confederate Army of the Valley.[31] Like the Rebel batteries along the Potomac, the Baltimore and Ohio Railroad McClellan did not regard as a severe or long-term problem. In early August, when he first described to Lincoln a strategic plan for the war, McClellan wrote that the Baltimore and Ohio line should be reopened and that his developing army would protect Harpers Ferry and the track line because, "as soon as our force in this vicinity [Washington] becomes organized, strong and efficient," it would stand on the flank and the line of retreat of any Confederate army in the Valley and north of Washington.[32]

In spite of his youth, McClellan almost always showed sound, superior judgment on military matters; but here he failed. He had not reckoned on a blitzkrieg on foot in the Valley, had overestimated the deterrent or reactive power of his force around Washington, and did not take into account a valley held by a mobile, imaginative adversary. The protection to be provided the railroad by any army around Washington, even if it assumed an advanced position along the Rappahannock River, remained to be seen. Not much time would pass before Lincoln would try this technique and learn whether it worked.

Although Lander's appointment occurred in October, he did not undertake his mission at once because he had lost a great deal of strength as a result of the leg

29   Marvin, Edwin E., *The Fifth Regiment Connecticut Volunteers: a History compiled from Diaries and Official Reports* (Hartford, 1889) 47–49 (Marvin, *Fifth Connecticut*); Summers, *B&O*, 106–109.

30   McClellan MSS (L.C.) four page handwritten memorandum with n.d. and n.a.; *OR*, 5, 48, McClellan's report; *M.O.S.*, 192.

31   Waugh, *Class of '46*, 46.

32   Sears, *McClellan's Correspondence*, 72–73, Memorandum for the Consideration of His Excellency the President submitted at his request, dated August 2, 1861 by the editor.

wound received at Edwards Ferry.[33] Two months later the effects of the wound had not disappeared. On December 22 his doctor told him the wound had healed but the leg was still weak. The physician urged him to avoid exertion for a week or ten days.[34] In fact, something insidious in the healing wound was probably at work undetected. The doctor was wiser than he knew—but not wise enough. Lander knew the importance of the railroad and would not allow a simple wound in the calf of his leg to keep him from an opportunity for independent command. He ignored the doctor's letter and reported for duty with two thoughts in mind: command the area west of Harpers Ferry and reopen the Baltimore and Ohio railroad.[35] McClellan ordered Lander, as the recently appointed department commander for the Baltimore and Ohio line, to take position with his command on the Potomac River between Harpers Ferry and Romney.[36]

In early January Lander, the scattered parts of his division, and reinforcements headed for Hancock, a small town on the north bank of the Potomac west of Harpers Ferry at the top of the "bulge" and at the head of Jackson's line of advance. Although the orders clearly described the geography of Lander's command, none stated the units to serve in his department. Applying an imaginative, fuzzy definition of his command, he would grasp at troop units as large as brigades and divisions if within marching distance.

Over the last eight miles to Hancock, hills and ridges with precipitous slopes wedged the wagon road against the north bank of the Potomac River. The heights scattered on the south side of the river commanded the tiny town and the entire eight miles of road; Hancock lay "but a stone's throw" from the high hills, and the road ran well within range of infantry fire. Lander faced a vulnerable supply line along the road[37] and a precarious position in the town.

Driven north while superbly delaying Jackson's ten thousand men, the Eighty-fourth Pennsylvania, Thirty-ninth Illinois, and Lieutenant Muhlenburg's guns crossed the Potomac River by fording the icy, armpit deep water or taking the rickety ferry. In Hancock the One Hundred Tenth Pennsylvania joined them, and on the evening of January 4 Lander arrived to assume command. Altogether, he had about

33   Lander MSS (L.C.) letter dated December 22, 1861, from John F. May, M.D., to Lander.

34   Lander MSS (L.C.) letter dated December 22, 1861, from May to Lander; Lander, "Lander," in *Historical Collections of Essex Institute*, 40, 317.

35   Lander, "Lander," in *Historical Collections of the Essex Institute*, 40, 317.

36   McClellan MSS (L.C.) part of an account of the Army of the Potomac probably from a draft of the final report or *M.O.S.* in McClellan's handwriting, dated December 1861 by the curator but obviously written later than that.

37   Quaife, *Williams' Letters*, 54–55, letter dated February 3, 1862, from Williams to "Lew."

four thousand men. From positions on the heights fringing the south bank of the river, Rebel artillery fired steadily until midnight.

Next morning at 10 A.M., Turner Ashby, the commander of Jackson's cavalry, approached the Potomac under a flag of truce. Lieutenant Colonel O. L. Mann of the Thirty-ninth Illinois, provost marshal for the day, crossed the river with a small detachment to meet him. Ashby wished to deliver a message from General Jackson to the commanding officer. Mann brought him across. On the way Ashby questioned the men in the detachment.

"What regiment do you belong to?"

"The Thirty-ninth Illinois."

The previous day part of the Thirty-ninth had skillfully ambushed and bloodied Ashby's cavalry as they led Jackson's columns toward the river.

"My God," replied Ashby, "where in hell is not the Thirty-ninth! They seem to be ubiquitous."

Once on the north bank, they met Colonel William G. Murray of the Eighty-fourth. Murray had Ashby blindfolded and took him to the headquarters of Company B. When they removed the blindfold, Ashby spoke: "Who did you say was in command here?"

"I do not think I said *who* is in command," replied Murray.

Seeing that he would learn nothing, Ashby delivered Jackson's message: If the town did not surrender in two hours, Jackson would bombard it.

Murray put Ashby in the custody of a sergeant, then went to the telegraph office to give Lander the message.

Jackson could cross the river by the means the delaying column had used, the slow, ancient ferry, or wading the deep, icy water. Concerned about a Confederate assault on inexperienced troops, Lander asked Murray how long his men could stand the fire. Murray thought about the recent successful ambushes and the steady conduct during withdrawals.

His men had already behaved very well under fire, he said.

That was enough for Lander. He would stand and fight.

A man with a colorful vocabulary, Lander emphatically refused the demand to surrender, saying that, if Jackson wanted the town, he could "come and take it."

Murray then brought Ashby to Lander in the telegraph office. Concerned that Ashby might understand telegraphic signals, Lander moved the group to another room where he read the message.[38] Jackson demanded the surrender of the Union

---

38   The text of Jackson's demand and Lander's response are quoted in full in Ecelberger, *Lander*, 170–171, 172, and the originals are in the Lander MSS (L.C.).

forces in the town, it said. He intended to cross the river. If he were opposed, he would fire on the town. But he would allow two hours for the citizens to depart. Lander delivered an "emphatic, forcible and characteristic reply."

"Colonel Ashby, give my compliments to General Jackson and tell him to bombard and be damned. If he opens his batteries on this town, he will injure more of his friends than he will of the enemy, for this is a damned secesh place, anyhow."

Mann thought the interview had come to an end. He began to replace the blindfold. But Lander reconsidered his tirade.

"Hold on!" he said. "Take a seat, Colonel Ashby. General Jackson has addressed me in a polite and soldierly manner, and it demands a like reply. I take back all that I have said and will write what I have to communicate."

Lander began to write. He placed the finished product in Ashby's hand.

"General Jackson and yourself, Colonel Ashby, are gentlemen and brave men without a question; but you have started out in a God damned bad cause!"

Lander shook hands with Ashby, Murray took him to the river, and the citizens began evacuation to places beyond artillery range. Making no specific preparations, Lander's men waited patiently. Two hours later, the Thirty-ninth Illinois put its garrison flag on the liberty pole in the town.

Silence.

At last the sound of two guns.

But harmless.

A captain collected a six-pounder round shot from the ground for a souvenir. Rebel artillery fire continued intermittently all day with desultory response from Lander's artillery.

Lander telegraphed for reinforcements and heavier parrott guns. "Delay will kill us," he wrote. "186 campfires in view." If he could have five regiments by forced march, he would cross the river and defeat the Confederates; but in his present condition, he probably could not hold his position, he said.[39]

By the end of the next day most of the artillery fire came from Union guns, a modest verification of the superiority demonstrated by the Union artillery at

39   McClellan MSS (L.C.) telegram dated January 5, 1862, 11:20 A.M. or P.M. [illegible] to Banks from Lander at Hancock; Merchant, Captain Thomas E., *Eighty-fourth Regiment Pennsylvania Volunteers* (Philadelphia, 1889) 21–25 (Merchant, *Eighty-fourth Pennsylvania*); Lander, "Lander," in *Historical Collections of Essex Institute*, 40, 317; Clark, Charles M., M.D., *The History of the Thirty-eighth Illinois Volunteer Veteran Infantry (Yates Phalanx) in the War of the Rebellion (1861–1865)* (Chicago, 1889) 42–48 (Clark, *Thirty-ninth Illinois*). The narrative is a composite of the accounts in Merchant, Lander, and Clark, which are different but inconsistent only in very small details, the inconsistencies being resolved according to the apparent quality of the sources available to the author of each account.

Dranesville. Jackson's artillery "lost a good many men . . . from our Parrott guns, which were admirably served, every shot landing plump into his batteries, upsetting his guns, killing his horses, and throwing his men into confusion," Lander wrote to army headquarters. "On their side, the firing was miserable. They literally did no damage to the town, though some shots passed through roofs of houses and some shells exploded in the streets. Not a man was wounded. Most of their shot fell short or passed high over the town into the hills beyond."[40] By January 7, Lander could report that the Confederates were withdrawing, and the danger had passed. "Had not Banks better cross & get in rear of such a prize [Jackson's Army]," he telegraphed from Hancock. ". . . If not, may I not be reinforced heavily & ordered to cross."[41]

McClellan, Banks, and Lander all knew that Jackson did not mean to retreat. He intended to withdraw, turn west, cross the mountains, recapture Romney,[42] burn Martinsburg, Hancock, and Romney, and take winter quarters at Winchester. Lander wanted orders to cross the river that night with three thousand men and fall on Jackson's rear. Williams' brigade of Banks' division, on the way forward, should rest four hours, Lander wrote, then cross to reinforce him. Banks should be heavily reinforced from Baltimore and marched through Martinsburg to the Rebel rear. The current distribution of the troops, Lander felt, prevented him from doing anything.[43]

If Jackson reached Romney before Kelley could establish a defensible position, he would seize the Romney supply depot and capture Kelley's force.[44] Lander knew that Kelley had insufficient strength to engage a large force and that reinforcements could not reach him in time. Kelley should come east to Bloomery Gap in one of the mountain ranges, block the Confederate route west, hold the pass as long as possible, and fall back fighting.[45] A rapid pursuit from Hancock might bring Jackson to bay by forcing him to deploy and fight, thus creating time to reinforce Kelley.[46] Once Alph Williams' brigade arrived, Lander would have five thousand effective men, two batteries of artillery, and approximately two thousand

---

40   Quaife, *Williams Letters*, 58, letter dated February 3, 1862, from Williams to "Lew."

41   McClellan MSS (L.C.) telegram dated January 7, 1861 [1862?], from Lander to Marcy.

42   McClellan MSS (L.C.) telegram dated January 7, 1862, from Seth Williams to the commanding officer in Romney.

43   McClellan MSS (L.C.) telegram dated January 7, 1862, from Lander to Banks.

44   McClellan MSS (L.C.) telegram dated January 7, 1862, from Lander to Banks.

45   McClellan MSS (L.C.) telegram dated January 7, 1862, from Banks to Williams enclosing a telegram from Lander to Banks; telegram dated January 7, 1862, from Lander to Banks.

46   McClellan MSS (L.C.) telegram dated January 7, 1862, from Lander to Banks.

green recruits armed with "that curse to the army, the Belgian rifle," he wrote. He pressed Banks to ask McClellan for permission to cross and engage the rear of the enemy by a forced march.[47]

Lander irritated McClellan, Banks, and Williams by insisting that he have additional troops from Banks' division in the area of Harpers Ferry and from Kelley at Cumberland, Romney, and New Creek. He simply treated their flank units as if they belonged to him. In addition, he gave his tactical and strategic ideas to Banks and McClellan, both of whom were major generals. Even though not dominated by extraordinary vanity, as Winfield Scott was, McClellan did not appreciate unsolicited advice from anyone outside his personal "kitchen staff" of respected friends. Banks did not have enough experience, seniority, or longevity to be more than miffed. But in spite of its peculiar shape, the Department of Harpers Ferry and Cumberland qualified as a military department, and Lander was its commander. Lander's positions as a colleague on the Pacific Railroad route project, a much lauded former aide to the general, and a department commander authorized a sense of familiarity few others could exercise. These characteristics, unrecognized by Williams, Banks, and McClellan, explained, if they did not justify, his actions. In these circumstances his behavior was rational and, in the main, proper. He sought support from the departments on either side of him. But the men with whom he dealt did not see him in this light.[48] Provoked by Lander's advice, plans, and suggestions, McClellan wrote to Banks, "It would be folly to cross the river at Hancock under present circumstances, except with a small corps of observation . . . "[49] At this time McClellan, still quite ill

47   McClellan MSS (L.C.) telegram dated January 7, 1862, from Banks to Williams enclosing a telegram from Lander to Banks; telegram dated January 7, 1862, from Lander to Banks.

48   McClellan MSS (L.C.) omitted segment from McClellan's draft of his final report. The report has a peculiar omission which could have been by oversight or intent. Prepared by McClellan and his staff after McClellan had been relieved by Burnside, the report covered his entire time in Washington. Although it was published in its entirety by private publishers and the Government Printing Office in early 1864 and can still be found today in that form, the editors of *OR* chose to break it into segments more or less defined by campaigns and more or less corresponding to subheadings by McClellan himself. The first major segment, *OR*, 5, 5–66, chaps. I and II, ends with the first few paragraphs of "Military Incidents of the first Military Period." The omitted Lander segment appears to have come from this part. While describing the events of February, this part of the final report says, "About the 20th of February, 1862, additional measures were taken to secure the reopening of the Baltimore and Ohio Railroad. The preliminary operations of General Lander for this object are elsewhere described in the final version." McClellan apparently drafted the description, changed his mind about its location, but forgot to put it in the final version. *OR*, 5, 48. The "elsewhere" apparently did not survive the editing process because the preliminary operations are not described.

49   McClellan MSS (L.C.) telegram dated January 7, 1862, from McClellan to Banks.

with typhoid, would never have given discretion to a volunteer brigadier general commanding a division so far away. He would not risk another Ball's Bluff, another river crossing with an active Confederate force in front. Instead, he issued the usual cautious instructions. Kelley, the commanding officer in Romney, was in danger of being attacked by Jackson from the east. He should keep his pickets well out in that direction and look to his rear. The heavy baggage and perhaps the entire force should move to a point closer to the railroad.[50] Banks should not risk crossing the river unless he saw the certainty of a great success and the certainty of re-crossing at his leisure. With Jackson withdrawing up the Valley and turning west toward Romney, Cumberland, and the South Branch of the Potomac, McClellan did not want Lander to pursue and risk a battle with Jackson. Lander should go to Romney and if Romney were seriously threatened, fall back toward the railroad and the river. "Lander is too young a general," the general in chief wrote to Banks, "to appreciate the difficulty of a river behind an army."[51]

Galled by the refusal to allow him to pursue, the outspoken Lander complained openly about his orders. Although he addressed his telegram to Banks, he spoke as if Banks were a third party and phrased many of his statements as if he were making them directly to the general in chief or his chief of staff. "General Banks should have been moved on Martinsburg," he wrote. "He would then have been ready to help me on the rear of the enemy . . . How can I get to Romney in time to serve any real purpose. This ought to be read to General McClellan by the officer receiving it for I cannot believe if he has received my dispatches but what the mistake of Jackson's moving his artillery and baggage into this Peninsula would have been taken advantage of."[52]

Annoyed well beyond his usually large capacity to absorb, McClellan did not dictate the answer to this dispatch to a member of his staff, who would have begun, "The commanding general wishes." Instead, he took the time to write in his own hand a telegram to Banks expressing his annoyance at Lander's presumptuous conduct. "Say to General Lander," he wrote, "that I might comment very sourly on the tone of his dispatches but abstain. Give him positive orders to repair at once to

---

50 McClellan MSS (L.C.) telegram dated January 7, 1861 [1862?], from McClellan to the commanding officer at Romney.

51 McClellan MSS (L.C.) telegrams dated January 7, 1861, from McClellan to Banks and January 7, 1861, 11:00 P.M. from McClellan to Banks.

52 Chase MSS (L.C.) letter from Barstow to Mrs. Lander; McClellan MSS (L.C.) telegram dated January 7, 1862, from Lander to Banks. The mass of telegrams in the McClellan MSS defy chronological organization, but some approximation at order can be achieved on the basis of content. That has been done here.

Romney and carry out the instructions I have sent already to fall back on the Railway . . . Genl Lander is too suggestive & critical."[53]

In his commentary to army headquarters, Banks said, "I have not thought it my duty to encourage General Lander's views in regard to our crossing the river. Had the event indicated in my instructions occurred, to wit, the passage of the Potomac by the enemy, the call would have been more imperative and reasonable; but we have thought from the first that he had no such purpose."[54]

On January 8, after a grueling all-night march in zero temperature, sleet, and snow, Williams, his brigade, and other miscellaneous units reached Hancock,[55] where Williams assumed control of the town and the troops. A steady, stolid man, Williams found everything chaotic, confused, and "non-reg." He put his brigade, five regiments of infantry, six pieces of artillery, and two companies of cavalry, in barns on the edge of the village.[56]

In his earlier letters to McClellan, Lander had written about the excellent condition of his troops. "My command is in [an] advanced state of discipline," he had said, along with other declarations that he deemed his little army battle-ready.[57] Williams, however, wrote home, "I found here five regiments of the newest and most mobish species . . . Food, furniture, forage, fuel, and all had been used and destroyed without thought or decency. Three of the regiments were new[58] . . . They knew nothing of garrison, or other military duty, and were literally a mob—firing their guns right and left and generally playing the devil."[59]

53   McClellan MSS (L.C.) note or telegram from McClellan to Banks, dated approximately January 7, 1862, by the curator but possibly written that day or later. Nothing clearly shows that this telegram was sent or received. It is not in *OR*, the Banks MSS, or the Lander MSS; but an incident during the fighting at First Winchester strongly suggests that it was sent, *infra*, vol. III, chapter on First Winchester.

54   *OR*, 5, 694, letter dated January 7, 1862, from Banks to Marcy.

55   Quaife, *Williams Letters*, 53–54, letter dated February 3, 1862, from Williams to "Lew"; Marvin, *Fifth Connecticut*, 54; Camper, Chas., and J. W. Kirkley, *Historical Record of the First Regiment Maryland Infantry, with an Appendix containing a Register of the Officers and Enlisted Men, Biographies of deceased Officers, etc., War of the Rebellion, 1861–1865* (Washington, 1861) 25 (Camper, *First Maryland*).

56   Quaife, *Williams Letters*, 54–55, letter dated January 31, 1862, from Williams to "My dear Daughter."

57   McClellan MSS (L.C.) telegrams dated January 5, 1861 [1862] from Lander to Marcy and January 7, 1862, from Lander to Banks.

58   Probably the Thirty-ninth Illinois, Eighty-fourth Pennsylvania, and One Hundred Tenth Pennsylvania.

59   Quaife, *Williams Letters*, 54, 52, letter dated February 3, 1862, from Williams to "Lew"; letter dated January 31, 1862, from Williams to "My dear Daughter."

Without any real explanation Lander had also said, "I ask you for one efficient regiment the Nineteenth Massachusetts—as an example & for Provost service on this account." Could Colonel Grover, with whom he had served under Isaac Stevens, join him as the provost marshal of his command, he asked McClellan. This would aid in "promoting its efficiency."[60] The duty of the provost was, among other things, to keep order and assure proper separation of the military and the civilian spheres. In whatever "advanced state of discipline" Lander's troops might have been, he lacked an effective provost force until, steady and well-disciplined, the men under "Old Pap" Williams arrived to serve, de facto, as a provost guard for the hapless town and citizens of Hancock.

On January 9, Lander headed west over the mountains for Romney in a two-horse wagon with his adjutant, Simon F. Barstow, another graduate of Harvard University, the "little West Point" in Cambridge, Massachusetts. Near Cumberland they crossed the Potomac and headed south into the valley of the South Branch of the Potomac.[61] On January 10, they reached Romney, where Lander assumed command. As McClellan had ordered, and this order, too, galled Lander, he would withdraw from Romney. The men spent the entire day striking tents, loading commissary stores in wagons, and packing. In the afternoon a cavalry scout reported a heavy column of Confederate infantry, artillery, and cavalry approaching through Bloomery Gap on the road from Winchester. Having been stationed in Romney since October, the members of the Ringgold Cavalry had made many friends among the townspeople. The horsemen paid their respects, said their goodbyes, and took position to mask the withdrawal to the mouth of Patterson's Creek.[62]

All night Lander's Romney units marched north up the valley of the South Branch, then turned west toward Patterson Creek. Rain had fallen continuously for several days, swelling Patterson's Creek to a torrent. When Lander reached the ford, the water had climbed over the banks. Lander was drunk.

"The next time I undertake to move an army and God Almighty sends such a rain," he raged, "I will go around and cross hell on the ice."

He ordered Lieutenant H. A. Myers across the boiling stream. The lieutenant put his horse into the water and started toward the other side. The current, raging no less than the general, separated Myers and his horse. Both headed north toward

---

60   McClellan MSS (L.C.) telegrams dated January 5, 1861 [1862?], from Lander to Marcy and January 7, 1862, from Lander to Banks.

61   Hunt, *Brevet Generals in Blue*, 35; Clark, *Thirty-ninth Illinois*, 55.

62   Chase MSS (L.C.) letter dated January 24, 1862, from Barstow to Mrs. Lander; Elwood, *Ringgold Cavalry*, 85–86.

the Potomac. Myers luckily grabbed the limb of a tree growing on the bank and came ashore. The horse caught the bank some distance downstream.[63]

Finding a naturally strong position on the south bank of the Potomac River beyond the mouth of Patterson's Creek, Lander camped and reported the safety of his command. He believed he could hold this position against twenty thousand men.[64]

Like all men with strong, external personalities, Lander provoked controversy. His orderly, a religious man, still bore the shock of the blasphemous tirade years later. "While he was perhaps a brave man and no doubt could handle troops," he wrote, "he was one of the wickedest men I ever met . . . The Bible says, 'The wicked shall not live out half his days.'"[65]

63   Elwood, *Ringgold Battalion*, 86.

64   McClellan MSS (L.C.) telegram dated January 13, 1862, from Lander to Colburn, from Patterson Creek, Virginia.

65   Elwood, *Ringgold Battalion*, 86.

Chapter 27

"Men, if your colonel is a damned coward, follow your general."

—Lander to his cavalry prior to a charge

Lander Chases Jackson

O n January 11 the temperature was cold, and deep snow covered the ground. At 6 P.M. Lander's infantry at Hancock followed him in an attempt to reach the Patterson Creek area before Jackson.[1] The Thirty-ninth Illinois, the Eighty-fourth Pennsylvania, and the One Hundred Tenth Pennsylvania began a forced march in wretched weather. The route covered forty miles through mountains with steep grades. At 4 P.M. the next day, they reached Cumberland. Five days later, January 17, they traveled by rail from Cumberland to New Creek, where they joined Kelley's troops, who had withdrawn from Romney.[2]

The position at Patterson's Creek lay in a sea of deep mud. Many of the men, poorly equipped for the winter and often without tents, fell sick.[3] Yet again Lander asked McClellan, "Give me Infantry. Enough to guard the road that I may advance on Jackson." According to the latest intelligence, the Confederates had passed Ungers headed for Romney, stating that their purpose was to destroy the railroad.[4] Ensconced in his headquarters in the railroad depot, Lander found the troops in a

---

1 Merchant, *Eighty-fourth Pennsylvania*, 26.

2 Clark, *Thirty-ninth Illinois*, 55.

3 Elwood, *Ringgold Cavalry*, 86.

4 McClellan MSS (L.C.) telegram dated January 16, 1862, from Lander to Marcy.

state of confusion but set to work "getting things into shape, while Jackson reached and occupied Romney."[5] He ordered Alpheus Williams to have his brigade ready to begin a five-day forced march on one hour's notice for a "job in winter bivouac."[6] This was more than McClellan could stand, especially with the low tolerance caused by the typhoid attack and McDowell's attempted coup. He wanted to know how Lander could give these orders to Williams, who had not been placed under his command, and "the nature of the service upon which you propose to employ these troops. Please answer at once."[7]

Williams felt no differently but could do no more than ignore Lander and complain in his letters home. "I have been here in Hancock watching the course of events, somewhat anxious on account of the erratic movements of my next neighbor, Gen. Lander . . . I see now, to my great surprise, by newspapers and his own reports that he has been doing great things . . . He talks in his report to Gen. McClellan of having opened the railroad from Cumberland to Hancock, while in fact I have had possession of all his road from Hancock to Cumberland for nearly four weeks, and have twice established the telegraph line over the whole route . . . I confess my astonishment, therefore, to see in the Baltimore papers today a long account of Gen. Lander clearing the line of the railroad and opening the route for Gen. Williams' brigade. . . ."

Lander had also reported his "daring and successful" reconnaissances. Williams scornfully reported to his family that he had gone to all these "daring" locations, in one instance with one other officer and an escort of only four men.[8] Self-aggrandizement in his telegraphic reports Lander had begun early in his tenure along the Potomac. After he had held command in Hancock for three days, he reported to Banks that the fire of his heavy artillery and the powerful defensive positions his men held in the brick buildings along the riverfront had kept the Confederates from crossing the river.[9]

Now, the Confederates had reached Romney with twelve thousand troops and "an immense artillery force." Lander had seven thousand infantry at New Creek and numerous cavalry, but only two troops with carbines. The rest of his division lay in the mud at the mouth of Patterson's Creek. He believed that unless he con-

5   McClellan MSS (L.C.) telegram dated January 16, 1862, from Lander to Marcy.

6   McClellan MSS (L.C.) telegram dated January 16, 1862, from Lander to Williams.

7   McClellan MSS (L.C.) letter dated January 17, 1862, from Seth Williams to Lander.

8   Quaife, *Williams Letters*, 60, letter dated February 3, 1862, from Williams to "Lew."

9   McClellan MMS (L.C.) telegram dated January 7, 1862, from Lander to Banks.

centrated, the enemy could beat him in detail and capture Cumberland. If he divided his troops to serve as railroad guards, the Confederates could, piece by piece, capture the railroad and the guards. His best prospect was to call the troops from New Creek to Patterson's Creek and attack the Confederates with his consolidated force. Although he could hold his position, the Confederate advance endangered the railroad, he feared.[10]

At this time, McClellan did not wish to force his way into the foot of the Valley. "A premature advance," like a direct advance on Centerville and Manassas, would compromise his Urbana plan by committing him to the overland route he wished to avoid, might cause the Confederates to withdraw from Manassas, and would shorten their march to Urbana. A second but more direct step toward restoring the railroad was Charles P. Stone's plan to cross the Potomac at Leesburg, capture the Rebels there, and fortify the area around it. This would position sufficient force across the Potomac to protect the flank of any crossing in the Harpers Ferry area and allow the occupation of Winchester and Strasburg.[11] Combined, Lander's, Banks', and Stone's divisions could secure the area in which the track ran south of the Potomac, Harpers Ferry to Cacapon,[12] and the Charlestown, Winchester, Strasberg spur. More troops and a safe route back would be necessary. At Harpers Ferry itself McClellan could create a safe crossing, but in the meantime he might strike a little blow for revenge in the area of Leesburg.

Stone originated the idea and the commanding general approved it.[13] In the larger picture it fit well with Lander's early suggestion that McCall march to Leesburg from his position on the right of the Army of the Potomac's Virginia line. On January 22, Brigadier General William W. Burns, one of Stone's brigade commanders, attended a court martial at Poolesville. At the end of the session he returned to his camp about three miles from Poolesville. There, he received a telegram from Stone asking him to come to division headquarters that night. In the stormy darkness he complied.[14]

"Do you know the ground between yourself and the river," Stone asked.

---

10   McClellan MSS (L.C.) letter dated January 18, 1862, from Lander to McClellan.

11   Schoff Collection (Stone MS) (Clements Library, University of Michigan) letter dated November 5, 1866, from Stone to Lossing; McClellan MSS (L.C.) letter dated January 28, 1862, from Burns to McClellan.

12   *O.R. Atlas*, 1, Plate xxvii, map no. 1.

13   Schoff Collection (Stone MS) (Univ. Mich.) letter dated November 5, 1866, from Stone to Lossing.

14   McClellan MSS (L.C.) letter dated January 7, 1862, from Burns to McClellan.

"I have made it my study," answered Burns, "and I do."

"Do you know the river and country opposite?"

"I have not so particularly observed that and think it beyond my sphere of action."

Stone then asked, "Do you know the best place to cross?"

"I think near the head of Mason's Island," the next island north of the ill-fated Harrison's Island.

"That is the very place," said Stone. "Could you command the crossing?"

"Yes," responded Burns, "the bluffs on our side can sweep the plains beyond but the grassy hill about half a mile above on the other side, which although commanded by the bluffs on our side, yet cannon *might* be placed to rake our landing, being masked by the crests of ravines from our batteries."

"What are the relative heights?"

"Eighty feet on the other side and one hundred feet on our side."

"What kind of boats do you want?"

"In the absence of a pontoon bridge," responded Burns, "flat bottom boats—plenty of them—and wire rope ferries."

"Do you know the channel near the head of the island?"

"Yes, but it would delay us to pass through it."

"What is the width of the river on the other side of the island?"

Burns gave him the approximate width.

"Could you cross over your brigade under these circumstances?"

"It would depend upon the force. Crossing guns in the face of the enemy is a most difficult operation."

Stone was not deterred. "Could you cross with a sufficient cover of artillery to keep off an opposing force and with two mountain howitzers and a squadron of cavalry march to the fort to the rear of Leesburg and carry the work containing say two thousand troops?"

"I think not."

"Why?" asked Stone. "You have 3,600 bayonets."

"In addition to the raking guns which might resist my landing, I would have some eight miles to march, would have to use a thousand of my men to keep open the communications for other purposes, and I would reach the fort with less than the military allowance for attacking works."

"You frighten me," responded Stone. "Can you rely upon your troops to charge a work?"

Burns, a graduate of West Point with service in the Regular Army, responded with the standard West Point learning. "I have seldom heard of volunteer troops attacking works successfully."

Stone's source of knowledge was the same. "I have not either. How many more troops would you want and what troops?"

"If I were to go, I would like the First Minnesota, Fifteenth Massachusetts, and Seventh Michigan added to my brigade."

"I cannot spare the First Minnesota."

The after-effects of Ball's Bluff and more sharply defined common sense tinged the conversation. Burns had already said he would want "plenty" of boats. Now, he rejected the mountain howitzers, which had been useless and lost at Ball's Bluff.

"I would not like to take mountain howitzers. I would prefer a battery consisting of four Parrott guns and two twenty-four pounder howitzers."

"You cannot take them over the roads in their present condition."

"Is it to be done so soon?"

"Yes. General Ord is to advance on the Turnpike to attack the works on the Gumspring Road and the line must be chosen while the roads are bad to give him the advantage. A force of five thousand troops will threaten them good. Six thousand troops under General Ord will attack the works on their right and rear while you simultaneously storm the works to their left and rear. They will abandon the position but we must calculate for a resistance."

"General McClellan has directed this, of course."

"Yes. We have discussed it fully. No one knows of it but General McClellan and myself." Stone then turned back to the earlier critical point.

"Could you do it with the force we discussed?"

Burns responded, "I could try, as I know that General McClellan would only order it in combination with a general plan," another point showing the flickering light of Ball's Bluff.

"I suppose it to be part of a general plan," concluded Stone.[15]

McClellan knew he must enter the foot of the Valley with force and move to Winchester and Strasburg, but he preferred to do it after he had landed at Urbana. That would probably require him to cross the Potomac at Harpers Ferry where the river was narrowest and most accessible. The Leesburg crossing would cover his exposed left flank. Although he considered an immediate crossing at Harpers Ferry premature, it would play a part in his overall plan; and he might as well investigate it at this time. The long-term plan probably explained his refusal to allow a premature, partial encounter by Lander's single division and Williams' brigade. Deep in

---

15   Schoff Collection (Stone MS) (Univ. Mich.) letter dated November 5, 1867, from Stone to Lossing; McClellan MSS (L.C.) letter dated January 28, 1862, from Burns to McClellan.

thought about his grand design against the Confederates, he would not, especially after the mess at Ball's Bluff, have authorized a minor river crossing for a non-determinative encounter under a volunteer general, especially an encounter with his skillful classmate.[16]

Jackson began to withdraw from Romney with the mass of his force on January 23 and by February 5 had evacuated Romney entirely. Lander followed, moving his headquarters to the Paw-Paw Tunnel in the mountains lining the Potomac River.[17] Having at last concentrated all his regiments in one place, Lander could create a real division. His adjutant reported to Mrs. Lander, "It has been a Herculean task to brigade, infuse life, check abuse, find among strangers the right men for the right place in this command, the general has done it and with all the regard to red tape of the most old foggied martinet."[18]

The First Brigade went to Colonel Nathan Kimball of the Fourteenth Indiana, the Second to Colonel J. T. Crittenden of the Thirteenth Indiana, and the Third to Colonel Erastus B. Tyler of the Seventh Ohio. Two of them, Kimball and Tyler, would later become brigadier generals.[19] A suitable staff Lander created from friends and men who had shown competence.[20] For cavalry he had no regiments; but he did have a collection of independent companies, two or three companies from the First Ohio, two or three companies of the First Virginia, the Morehead Cavalry, the Ringgold Cavalry, and the Russell company, the last three being independent. On January 19, he issued an order which de facto confirmed Colonel Henry Anisansel as his chief of cavalry, saying, "Colonel Anisansel 1st Virginia Cavalry is hereby complimented for his efficiency and soldierly conduct. The commanding general expects much from him in the future. . . ."[21]

16   No direct evidence supports these inferences about the place of a Harpers Ferry crossing in McClellan's strategic thinking, but they are logical conclusions from the many tiny facts of this period.

17   McClellan MSS (L.C.) telegram dated February 16, 1862, from Stanton.

18   Chase MSS (L.C.) letter dated January 24, 1862, from Barstow to Mrs. Lander.

19   Thomson, Orville, *From Phillipi to Appomattox: Narrative of the Service of the Seventh Indiana Infantry in the War for the Union* (n.p., n.d.) 74 (Thomson, *Seventh Indiana*); Warner, *Generals in Blue*, 267, 515.

20   Ecelbarger, *Lander*, 199.

21   Court martial Transcript of Colonel Henry Anisansel, First Virginia Cavalry (National Archives, Record Group 393, Number 693) transcript in general and Exhibit B. (NA-CM-Anisansel no. 693).

As soon as Jackson departed, Captain John Keys, the man Lander preferred for chief of cavalry, returned to Romney with the Ringgold Cavalry. The men enjoyed reunions with their friends in the village. They rested and fed their horses, then assembled in front of the courthouse. In a hurricane-force wind, Keys explained the mission. They were to burn at least the church, the bank, and the courthouse.

"If I carry out my orders," Keys said, "the way the wind is blowing, the entire town will be consumed. Rather than turn helpless women out of doors at this time of year, I will disobey this order."[22]

A short time later Lander learned that he could strike the rear of Jackson's wagon train and its guard in the vicinity of Bloomery Gap. He took a large force of infantry and four hundred horsemen under Colonel Anisansel toward the gap in pursuit. If he could smash Jackson's baggage train, he would repay some of the many overdue debts.[23]

Now miles south of the railroad and east of the South Branch of the Potomac, Lander did not hold a position of complete safety but was headed toward the rear of the Rebels at Romney. "It is true I have moved east but I have an excellent fighting force. Ohio & Indiana with artillery and cavalry. I shall only hold strong positions as I advance. If the enemy should outnumber me I am confident under the circumstances he cannot beat me." He had assumed the Confederates would evacuate Romney because they could not hold the position with their rear threatened. He had also assumed the evacuation would be without a fight. "Genl McClellan may rely on my not acting sharp—rather simply to show my courage . . . although I have been unduly assailed by the press [I] will not fail to do my duty to him until relieved from service—which I trust may take place as soon as practicable if I have not his entire confidence and respect. The unmilitary style of this Report must be excused by the occasion."[24] Throughout, Lander suffered increasingly from his unidentified physical ailment but remained with his troops in order to cover the railroad and keep the country clear of the enemy.[25]

But when Lander reached the Cacapon River, icy and swollen from the recent rains, the engineers reported that with the materials at hand they could not bridge it.

22   Elwood, *Ringgold Cavalry*, 88.

23   McClellan MSS (L.C.) telegram dated February 6, 1862, from Pawpaw, Virginia, from Lander to McClellan.

24   McClellan MSS (L.C.) telegram received February 6, 2:30 A.M. from Lander to Williams.

25   McClellan MSS (L.C.) letter or telegram received January 18, 1862, from Lander to Williams; MS draft report; *OR*, 5, 48, and 56, McClellan's report.

Lander "stormed, swore, and out-roared the roaring flood," the colonel of the Eighth Ohio remembered after the war. Once again the extraordinary ingenuity of the ordinary American citizen swept into the military rose to the occasion. Wagonmaster Samuel Fuller announced to Lander that he had been the "engineer" for a circus before the war. He thought he could solve the problem with the scientific principles of circus engineering, and he would not need more than a span of powerful mules and a wagon loaded with heavy ballast.

Lander responded with ecstasy.

Fuller hitched the mules to the wagon and drove them into the icy water. At the far bank he unhitched the mules, left the wagon standing in the stream, and repeated the process. When he had formed a line of wagons and laid planking across them, the infantry and cavalry crossed rapidly, leaving the artillery, ambulances, and supply wagons behind. The foot soldiers and horsemen continued the pursuit at their own paces, the infantry falling behind.[26]

All night the cavalrymen, with Lander at their head, pressed through rugged, mountainous terrain.[27] A young black and a fleeing civilian had told Lander that Confederate officers had taken quarters in houses in Bloomery Gap. About three miles short of the gap, Lander anticipated an encounter with Jackson's rear and explained his plan to the commander of his polyglot cavalry.[28] He believed he had reached a position behind the Rebels on their line of retreat.[29] Anisansel should charge through the gap, surround the houses, capture the Rebel officers, then proceed to the eastern end of the gap, which he would hold until the infantry arrived. On a mild slope he should charge mounted, and in terrain unsuited for a mounted charge, he should dismount his cavalrymen and use them as infantry.[30]

Traveling south, they neared the gap and the east-west Romney-Winchester route at first light. Anisansel threw forward a guard and advanced. Lander ordered all four hundred cavalry to charge west into the gap and west toward Romney. With Anisansel, Lander, and his staff at their head, the cavalrymen galloped along the road, probably in column, surrounding each house as they went but finding no Confederate

---

26   Sawyer, Franklin, *A Military History of the 8th Regiment Ohio Vol. Inf'y: its Battles, Marches, and Army Movements* (Cleveland, 1881) 31–32 (Sawyer, *8th Ohio*).

27   NA CM Anisansel, no. 693, 39 (Major Harry G. Armstrong, Lander's Adjutant General).

28   NA CM Anisansel, no. 693, 21 (Frothingham).

29   No source states this, but the charge west seems to confirm the fact that Lander believed he had reached a position in their rear.

30   McClellan MSS (L.C.) telegram dated February 6, 1862, from Paw Paw, Virginia, from Lander to McClellan.

officers. They passed a road on the left with a sharp angle turned east through the pass in the heights.[31] In the ordinary confusion of a mounted charge, Anisansel disappeared. The column halted. Half an hour passed. Anisansel reappeared.

Lander ordered Anisansel to send a squad of cavalry to reconnoiter westward on the Romney Road, then left Anisansel and, with his staff, headed for a nearby house, where he found John J. Cannon, an officer of Russell's company of independent cavalry, acting as a guide for the cavalry. By now, dim first light had become earliest sunrise.

"I want you to take a lantern, find out which way they went, and where they are," Lander said to Cannon.[32]

A miller told them they could find part of the Rebel column about two miles to the east on the Winchester road. Lander found Anisansel again and ordered him to reverse directions, follow the road toward Winchester, engage the Confederates, and capture their baggage train. If necessary, Lander would support him with his entire force of infantry, which had by now passed the fork into Bloomery Gap and marched a short distance along the road west to Romney.

Meanwhile, Cannon took ten men in the direction of Winchester in search of the retiring Confederates. When he reached the pickets after about a mile, he learned that the Rebels were just ahead. Back to Lander he went with his men to report. By this time the infantry had arrived, leaving the cavalry in the rear to the west.

"Tell Colonel Anisansel to turn the cavalry and go in pursuit of the enemy," Lander said.

Cannon carried the order to Anisansel, who had already reversed his column toward the fork. When Cannon delivered the order, Anisansel and Cannon went to the front of the column, where they met Lander.

Did Anisansel have any men good with the saber, Lander asked.

Yes, he did.

Anisansel should put the saber men in front for the charge.[33] Lander and his staff resumed their trip to the house.[34]

---

31   The descriptions of this encounter are a mass of confusion and the courtmartial testimony with its unclear map makes it worse. Lander apparently reached Bloomery Gap, an east-west pass in the mountains, on a road from the north and first charged west, back toward Romney, then east toward Winchester.

32   Partly direct and partly indirect discourse, all made direct discourse.

33   NA CM Anisansel, no. 693, (Cannon) 5–7.

34   NA CM Anisansel, no. 693, (Armstrong) 39–41, sketchmap by Fuller.

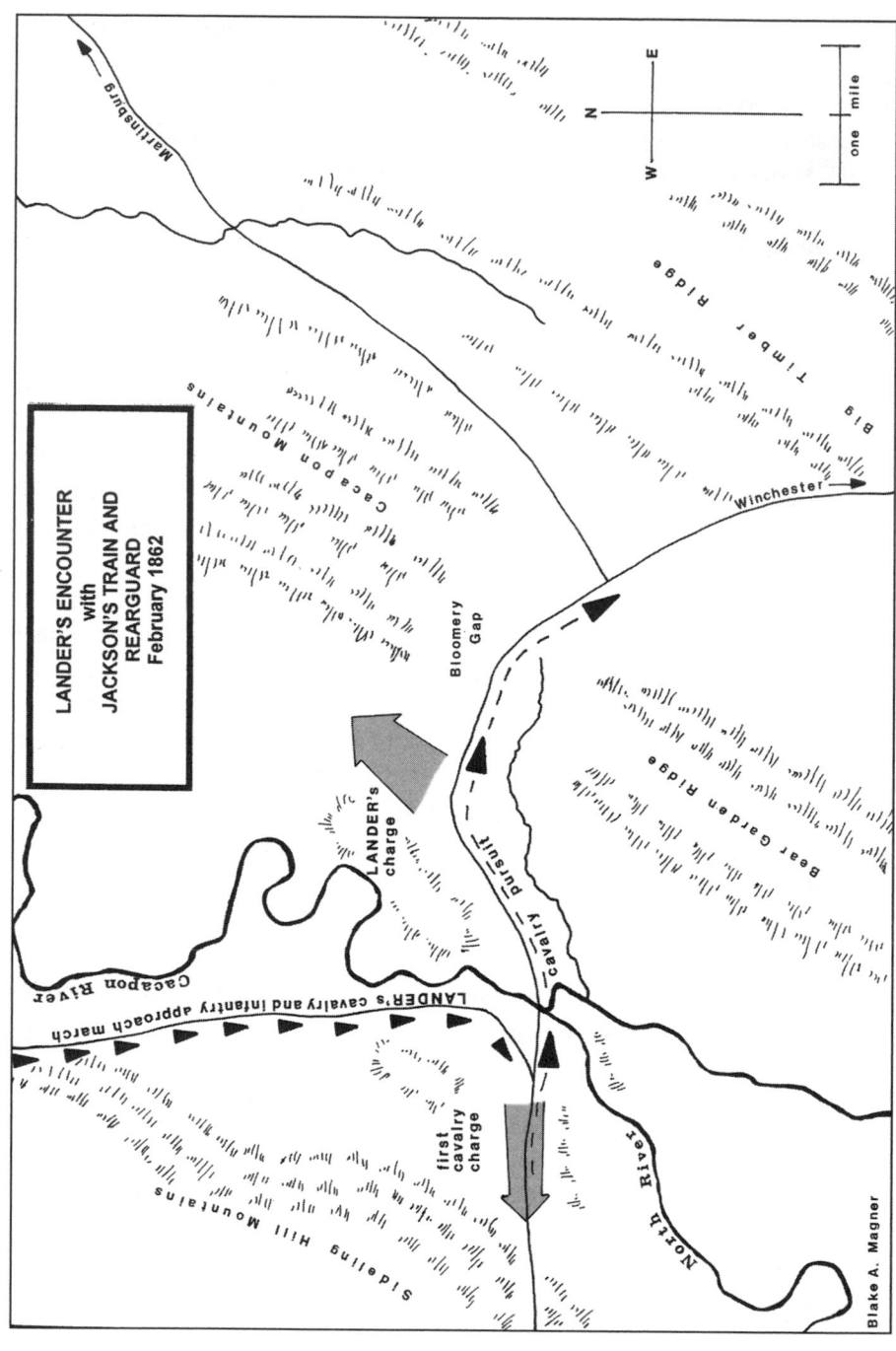

LANDER'S ENCOUNTER
with
JACKSON'S TRAIN AND
REARGUARD
February 1862

Blake A. Magner

The first sergeant of Russell's Company, then in front, told Anisansel the company had no pistol cartridges. The colonel sent it to the rear, then started into the gap.[35] His companies were variously armed with pistols, sabres, rifles, and carbines, some of them breach loaders. He called the companies with breech loaders from the rear of the column.[36]

Lieutenant Cannon, he said, should take ten or twelve men forward again, and when he heard Anisansel's bugle call, he should halt.

Cannon complied, moving about a mile and a quarter east on the road. He could see approximately three hundred Rebel infantry advancing toward him. He stopped, then looked back. No sign of Anisansel. The Confederates, perhaps a quarter of a mile to the front, divided. Approximately one company closed to within two hundred yards, then left the road for positions on the slopes. Cannon called Captain Carmen to come forward. Carmen and four or five men joined him. The remainder of the cavalry column stood still.

Cannon and his men withdrew one hundred fifty yards. Within sight of the Rebel infantry, they could see the main column of Union horse about fifty or sixty yards to the rear.[37] They began to receive infantry fire from the slopes on the sides of the road.[38]

At the rear of the column a troop of the First Ohio Cavalry and its commander, Captain Nathan D. Menkin, could hear firing in the distance. The halting way the cavalry had arrived in the gap, the knowledge that the Confederates were at hand, and the realization that fighting was about to occur made Menkin uncertain. He felt no confidence in Anisansel. The presence of General Lander he regarded as highly important and decided he should send for him. He called for Sergeant Charles W. Florence and told him to report to Lander. He should ask Lander to come forward and mention Menkin's name to avoid any mistake about the source of the message.[39]

Next in front of Menkin's company, Captain William C. Carmen, at the head of his company of loyal Virginia cavalry, could hear the firing at the head of the column. He galloped forward to find Anisansel.

Where were the Rebels, he asked.

Anisansel pointed to the left and front where bushes dotted the slope.

35   NA CM Anisansel, no. 693, (Cannon) 5–8.

36   NA CM Anisansel, no. 693, (Armstrong) 40–41.

37   NA CM Anisansel, no. 693, (Cannon) 5–8.

38   NA CM Anisansel, no. 693, (Armstrong) 40–41.

39   NA CM Anisansel, no. 693, (Menkin) 37–38.

"What are we going to do?"

If he ever knew it, Anisansel had forgotten the lesson to be learned from Captain Boyd's prompt charge to Occoquan the previous spring. He had also forgotten Lander's orders.

"General Lander is going to deploy infantry through the bushes," he said.

The head of the column continued to fire at the Confederates on the slope.[40]

Meanwhile, on the porch of the house, Lander and his staff received the message from Menkin.[41] Sergeant Florence stated that the cavalry had received enemy fire about two miles along the Winchester road and halted. This was contrary to the orders Lander had given before they reached the gap to charge on foot or mounted, depending on the terrain. Lander and his staff headed for the front of the cavalry column. They could hear a few shots from the hillsides.[42] As he rode alongside the halted column, he showed his usual excitability, not unlike a short, nasty man who would command much more cavalry in two years.

"Who in hell commands the cavalry?" he shouted.

He rode to Captain Irwin Redpath, commanding the Morehead Cavalry.

"Why in hell and damnation don't you charge?"

Redpath was not about to attempt an explanation. He pointed toward Anisansel at the head of the column.[43] Lander continued forward.

"My men! My men! What are you staying here for? Why don't you go on? Come ahead and follow me!"

As he drew alongside Lieutenant Cannon at the head of the column, he called to him, "Come on!"[44]

Galloping furiously to the head of the column, Lander shouted, "Men, if your colonel is a damned coward, follow your general!"[45]

Placing himself at the head of the column,[46] Lander, his adjutant general Major Harry C. Armstrong, Captain Carmen, a troop commander of the First Ohio Cavalry,

---

40   NA CM Anisansel, no. 693, (Carmen) 24–25. Indirect discourse converted to direct.

41   Ecelbarger, *Lander*, 239.

42   NA CM Anisansel, no. 693, (Armstrong) 40–41.

43   NA CM Anisansel, no. 693, (Redpath) 29–30.

44   NA CM Anisansel, no. 693, (Cannon) 8.

45   Cooper, Colonel John S., "The Shenandoah Valley in Eighteen Hundred and Sixty-Two," in *Broadfoot MOLLUS Illinois*, 13, 40. The exact expletive appears in the narrative as a blank, of course; but Lander's reputation for foul language and the many times narratives quote the word "damned" make this the most logical choice. Nor is the exact time of this incident clear from Cooper's narrative. It has been placed logically.

46   NA CM Anisansel, no. 693, (Carmen) 25.

and five or six cavalrymen broke into individual charges. Anisansel ordered his men to charge, then joined Lander's group. Having already established that he lacked command of his men, Anisansel started up the slope with no more than a few of them. Carmen and twenty men raced east along the road, where he was finally joined by Anisansel and a few others. Carmen himself veered away after two fleeing Confederates and captured them, then returned to the road to follow his men and the colonel.

Meanwhile, in response to Lander's call to "follow me," a few officers and five or six enlisted men galloped up the slope to the left. The remainder stood in the road at a halt.[47] As Lander and his horsemen swept up the slope, a private of Carmen's Company C captured a Confederate colonel. Playing the role of Southern aristocrat, the colonel refused to yield his sword. Lander arrived and ordered the enlisted man to disarm the colonel.

"He says he will never give his sword to a Yankee," replied the private.

Lander dismounted and grabbed the Rebel officer by the shoulder.

"Then you'll give it to me!"

Overborne in rank, height, probably strength, and certainly circumstances, the colonel unbuckled his sword and handed it to the general. Lander turned to the private.

"If you find another man like this, don't multiply words with him."[48]

When Lander returned to the road with his prisoners, Major Bannister, Lieutenant O'Brien, Lieutenant Armstrong, and a number of enlisted men joined him. His blood was racing.[49]

Meanwhile Carmen and his men, followed by Anisansel, continued east at a gallop in pursuit of the retreating Rebel wagons. Having proven he was not competent as a cavalry officer, Anisansel found his horse not a competent cavalry horse. In the road, now a ribbon of heavy mud from the recent heavy rains, his horse fell.

Half a mile later Carmen saw Anisansel at the head of a group of horsemen. Why was he returning, Carmen called. Covered with mud, Anisansel responded that his horse had fallen with him and he was badly injured.[50] Lander ordered the

---

47   NA CM Anisansel, no. 693, 41 (Armstrong), 8 (Cannon), and 25 (Carmen).

48   [Gillespie, Samuel L.] "Lovejoy," *A History of Company A, First Ohio Cavalry 1861–1865: a memorial Volume Compiled from personal Records and living Witnesses* (Washington, Ohio, 1898) 51 ([Gillespie] *Company A, First Ohio Cavalry*). The name of the author appears in the extraordinary and invaluable Dornbusch, Ohio, 4, 47, who refers to a photograph for the real name, but the photograph is missing from the author's battered copy.

49   NA CM Anisansel, no. 693, 24 (Frothingham); [Gillespie], *Company A, First Ohio Cavalry*, 51.

50   NA CM Anisansel, no. 693, 41 (Armstrong), 8 (Cannon), and 25 (Carmen).

remainder of the cavalry to advance on the Winchester road and capture the baggage train. No one moved. He repeated the order several times. Still no-one moved. He threatened to shoot them if they did not advance, then pulled out his pistol and fired it in the air. Anisansel stood passively apart from his men.

"Why don't you follow your colonel?" said Lander.[51] Lander ordered Anisansel to take one hundred twenty-five men, follow the Rebel wagons, and capture them.[52]

A mounted messenger arrived with information about Rebel fortifications on the Winchester road and a large force, supposedly Jackson's rear guard.[53]

Major Armstrong suggested to Colonel Charles Sprigg Carroll of the Eighth Ohio Infantry that he find any fortifications or Rebel force. As Carroll advanced east along the road toward Winchester, he met various outposts but with one exception could not convince any of them to come with him. Several miles later, without sighting more than a few scattered Confederate skulkers and seeing no fortifications, Carroll turned his column back. On the way he met three cavalry companies coming to join him.[54]

When Lander gave the first order to charge east, most of the men had stood still, but fifteen men, including wagonmaster Fuller, started east on the Winchester road in pursuit of the rebel baggage train. Anisansel went with them. After several miles they overtook two wagons struggling to stay ahead of them. The small party of Union cavalry captured them, shooting one of the Rebel guards. Less than half a mile beyond, approximately two hundred Confederate infantry rallied and returned. Half a mile to the rear slightly less than one hundred federal cavalrymen watched but did not respond to Anisansel's calls for assistance or a messenger carrying an order to come forward. On both sides Confederate troops inched their way down the slopes to the rear of the fifteen men and their return route. Confederate bullets struck the wagons and fell short[55] while the party tried to dismantle the fences and turn the wagons. Seeing danger from the regrouping Rebels and the disparity in numbers, Anisansel ordered his men to withdraw and leave the wagons. Meanwhile on the slopes to the rear the aggressive part of the column had captured seventeen officers, including colonels, lieutenant colonels, and captains.[56]

---

51   NA CM Anisansel, no. 693, (Frothingham) 24; [Gillespie], *Company A, First Ohio Cavalry*, 51.

52   NA CM Anisansel, no. 693, (Frothingham) 34 and (Fuller) 15.

53   NA CM Anisansel, no. 693, (Carroll) 11.

54   NA CM Anisansel, no. 693, (Carroll) 11–12.

55   NA CM Anisansel, no. 693, (Fuller) 15–18.

56   Wilson, Lawrence, with Historical Committee, *Itinerary of the Seventh Ohio Volunteer Infantry 1861–1864 with Roster, Portraits and Biographies*, 2 vols. (New York, 1907) 1, 120 (Wilson, *Seventh Ohio*); McClellan MSS (L.C.) letter dated February 14, 1862, from Lander to McClellan; *OR*, 5, 405, Dunning's report.

Still in a rage at Anisansel after the fighting, Lander reported all this to McClellan,[57] who apparently referred the letter to the War Department. If Lander were satisfied that Colonel Anisansel had acted with cowardice or had misbehaved before the enemy, replied the secretary, he could try him on the spot and carry out a sentence of death on a guilty finding. In the alternative, Lander could cashier him. "The former course is recommended as the preferable one," said the secretary, "Cowardice in an officer should receive the swift punishment of death."[58]

After Lander's successful encounter with Jackson's wagons at Bloomery Pass, the secretary of war wrote him a note saying, "The President directs me to say that he has observed with pleasure the activity and enterprise manifested by yourself and the officers and soldiers of your command. . . . Your brilliant success is a happy presage of what may be expected when the army of the Potomac shall be led to the field by their gallant General."[59]

Banks and McClellan now routinely ignored without comment Lander's barrage of ideas, but the brigadier general did not believe that he overstepped his bounds or that he offended anyone. In fact, the members of the media, "inventive" because of their need for controversial information, had reported a rift between McClellan and Lander. In a letter to Secretary of the Treasury Chase, Lander explained his relationship with McClellan, "Gen'l McClellan has no better friend than I am. I care nothing for his reprimand. He has more than made amends. What I care for are the misrepresentations of those having access to his papers. I have no time for newspaper controversy but abundant records when the time arrives. I deny criticizing the President. If I was critical it was on the 'have beens.' I said Banks *should have*, crossed, as I said three days ago. Not Banks 'should cross.'"[60]

McClellan's annoyance had not escaped him. Although the newspapers had reported a difference between Lander and McClellan, Lander felt his whole record proved that none existed. "Refer to the past," he wrote to McClellan's chief of staff, "and contradict it. I do not worship any man—am free spoken but so far as honorable man can, will do right. He knows me, and you know me."[61]

To defeat Jackson, Lander proposed yet another plan for his division and Williams' brigade. Williams should march to a point on the north bank of the Potomac

---

57   McClellan MSS (L.C.) letter or telegram received January 18, 1862, from Lander to Williams; MS draft report; *OR*, 5, 48 and 56, McClellan's report.

58   McClellan MSS (L.C.) telegram dated February 16, 1862, from Stanton.

59   Stanton MSS (L.C.) letter dated February 17, 1862, from Stanton to Lander.

60   Chase MSS (U.P.I.) letter dated February 8, 1862, from Lander to Chase.

61   McClellan MSS (L.C.) telegram dated February 20, 1862, 10:45 P.M., from Lander to Marcy.

halfway between them. Lander would build flatboats in Cumberland, then seize the Virginia shore opposite Williams and bring him across on the boats.

Meanwhile, Williams had sent Kelley a letter showing an indisposition to join Lander. Exasperated, the rambunctious Lander finally ceased asking for Williams' assistance and unleashed his well-schooled sarcasm. "My mistake in asking it at all was my misconception of the object I was ordered here for, which I supposed was to open the Baltimore and Ohio Railroad. This cannot be done from the north bank of the Potomac River."[62]

In spite of his frustrations the railroad to Hancock had come open—as had the telegraph—while Jackson and Loring had recoiled to Winchester. "As the work entrusted to me may be regarded done, and the enemy out of this Dept—I most earnestly request to be relieved. If not relieved must resign. My health is too much broken. . . . I respectfully commend Colonel [Charles Sprigg] Carroll to your notice. He is a most efficient and gallant officer."[63]

McClellan reacted as he always did to a personal problem with a man he could not, or did not wish to, replace. Again, form over substance, McClellan wrote him, "Your conduct is just like you. Don't talk about resigning. If your health makes it necessary for you to be relieved, of course you shall be. I advise, in view of possible movements, that you quietly rest at Cumberland & endeavor to recruit your health before making another move . . . I will arrange to relieve you & give you other work as soon as you are well enough."[64]

Lander had been told that sixty thousand Rebels held Winchester. "What it means I don't know, perhaps you may," he wrote to army headquarters, then asked for orders to take Winchester with authority to burn it. "I am confident I can do it with what I have,"[65] he said, even though on the best road in his vicinity he had to use double teams of the strongest wagon horses to send six guns to Cumberland and the mud was almost impassable. Then, once again, the aggrandizement of self. "No army can beat mine marching. When I came here they were slow—a few victories will make them the best troops out—they have never had a check and hurrah when I come in sight—tell the general."[66]

---

62   McClellan MSS (L.C.) telegram dated January 18, 1862, from Lander to Williams.

63   McClellan MSS (L.C.) telegram dated February 14, 1862, 8:00 P.M. from Lander to McClellan.

64   *OR*, 51, pt. 1, 531, telegram dated February 14, 1862, from McClellan to Lander.

65   McClellan MSS (L.C.) telegram dated December 19, 1862, from Lander to Marcy.

66   McClellan MSS (L.C.) telegram dated February 20, 1862, from Lander to Marcy.

On Washington's birthday, booming artillery greeted the daybreak.[67] This was the day on which the president had ordered a general advance of all the armies, including the Army of the Potomac, but the president's war order apparently had more effect on Tom Jackson than on George McClellan. Once again, Jackson began to march his entire force north from Winchester toward Bath and the Hancock "bulge." Once again, Lander's blandishments. "If he is ass enough to do this I shall move on his rear over Bloomery Furnace and beat him to death. Recent thaws have placed the roads in bad condition but I have sent cavalry reconnaissances and rest assured that you will hear a good account of this army. I shall move on the first intimation that he is north of my line."

Lander considered it his duty to risk a battle with his entire force. In preparation for a major engagement, which he expected to have within the next forty-eight hours, he recalled all his detached parties. His only weak point, he thought, remained his artillery, which, in the mud, required ten horses to the gun. "We are in the best possible condition for a fight,"[68] he wrote to McClellan.

At the end of the day, he held a dress parade at which he reviewed his entire division. He now had twenty-six guns and almost twelve thousand officers and men. As the self-appointed orator of the day he showed that he knew the importance of a personal relationship between the commanding general and his men by visiting each regiment to make a speech laced with his characteristic profanity.[69]

Although his health had improved after he left Washington,[70] all did not look or sound well. By passing near the bone but not striking it, the bullet through his calf had probably broken the leg bone without displacement. It would undoubtedly have left bits of cloth from his trousers inside the wound, but most certainly the strap from his boot would have carried germs for the infection that followed. Because no swelling or discoloration occurred and the hole apparently healed, he probably suffered an osteomyelitis, an infection of the bone rather than of the surrounding tissue. In due course, this kind of infection, untreated by antibiotics, would have become systemic but would have shown no more symptoms than the weakness and

---

67   Kepler, William G., *History of the Three Months and Three Years Service from April 16th, 1861, to June 22d, 1864 of the Fourth Regional Ohio Volunteer Infantry in the War for the Union* (Cleveland, 1886) 57 (Kepler, *Fourth Ohio Infantry*).

68   McClellan MSS (L.C.) telegram dated February 22, 9:30 P.M., from Lander to McClellan.

69   *OR*, 5, 732, extract for return of the Army of the Potomac for month of February 1862; Kepler, *Fourth Ohio*, 57; Clark, *Thirty-ninth Illinois*, 57, Merchant, *Eighty-fourth Pennsylvania*, 27.

70   Chase MSS (L.C.) letter dated February 4, 1862, from Barstow to Chase.

exhaustion about which he complained frequently in February.[71] As Lander addressed the Fourth Ohio his face showed a pallid color. His voice did not have a firm and healthy ring. And his eyes had a glassy look. Notwithstanding the breadth and depth of his lexicon of four-letter words, he spent more time than ever pouring over his bible and praying.[72]

But he was not so ill that he could no longer attend to business, especially matters that had enraged him. In spite of his earlier, laudatory general orders he had no sympathy for his inept chief of cavalry Henry Anisansel. Rumors circulated that the colonel would be court-martialed for cowardice in the face of the enemy. Everyone knew that he had not executed his orders and that he had infuriated the general.[73] Certainly he had not applied the combat characteristics of cavalry, shock action and maneuverability. Unlike Captain Boyd with his company of the First New York Cavalry at the Occoquan River, Anisansel had halted, waited for infantry, and not taken advantage of the fact that he had caught scattered, retiring infantry in no formation to resist a determined charge of cavalry armed with sabers, pistols, and breech-loading carbines. He had shown that he lacked all the characteristics of a good cavalry officer and could not confront the confusion of a cavalry attack from column in the road or the disorganization of a pursuit at the gallop. Nor did he have the confidence of his men and the immediate responsiveness that would accompany it.[74]

No matter how angry he was, Lander's mercurial temper cooled. Anisansel had no competence but had charged through Bloomery Gap, followed Lander up the slope, then joined Carmen's company in a headlong race out the road toward

---

71   Intv. medical consultant Francis M. Weld, M.D., whose great grandfather Francis Minot Weld served as a surgeon aboard the monitor *Nantucket*, then as a surgeon with the Army of the Potomac, and whose great, great uncle Stephen Minot Weld served as a staff officer to Fitz John Porter and a regimental commander in the Army of the Potomac. None of the contemporary accounts give a convincing medical diagnosis. Various accounts mention pneumonia, exhaustion, wounds at Bloomery Gap, etc. The two diagnoses in Ecelbarger, *Lander*, 211, n. 9, agree with Dr. Weld but do not include some of the explanation.

72   Kepler, *Fourth Ohio*, 57–58.

73   National Archives, Record Group 94, Records of the Adjutant General's Office, Compiled Military Service Records, First West Virginia Cavalry (Anisansel, Colonel Henry) telegram dated February 28, 1862, from Ford to Pierpont and Rosecrans.

74   Another cavalryman from another era with different mounts would present the exact opposite. He left his staff and headquarters behind, took enough men for a small headquarters unit, mounted his captured British Mammoth and a few open cars, took mobile radio trucks, and headed into the battle zone. "Thus, he could appear in the thick of any battle and take personal command without the time consuming waiting for messages . . ." His men worshiped him . . . most of the time, and his Afrika Corps became legendary. Irving, David, *The Trail of the Fox*, 103 (New York, 1977).

Winchester. He simply could not be accused of cowardice. Instead, in one charge and two specifications, Lander had him court-martialed for misbehavior before the enemy by halting before an inferior force and once he had begun the pursuit by halting again and not capturing the train.[75]

The evidence showed no hot-headed animosity like Richardson's testimony during the court of inquiry about Colonel Dixon Miles' drunkenness. Without pejorative adverbs or adjectives, it was subdued. The prosecution presented its witnesses. Anisansel presented none. But Lander's staff officers and some of Anisansel's subordinates made their animus clear. Major John B. Frothingham, an aide to the general; Major Harry C. Armstrong, his adjutant general; Lieutenant John J. Cannon, the guide for the cavalry force; and Captain Nathan D. Menkin, a troop commander of the First Ohio Cavalry did the most damage. But they did not do enough to convict the hapless colonel. The wrong charges had come before the court. If Anisansel had been charged with incompetence or poor leadership, the evidence would have convicted him easily. The testimony began on February 24 and concluded on February 28. Counsel for Anisansel, an officer on Rosecrans' staff, finally appeared at the very end and introduced the complimentary order Lander had issued when he created his staff. The court returned a simple "not guilty" verdict on both specifications with a final judgment of acquittal.[76] Nevertheless, Lander and his ineffective cavalry commander had smashed and put to flight the rear of Jackson's retreating Confederate column; and Lander had shown that he was one of the few Union officers not paralyzed by Jackson's dash.[77]

---

75   NA CM Anisansel, no. 693, Charge and Specifications.

76   NA CM Anisansel transcript in general and 44.

77   Robertson, *Jackson*, 322.

Chapter 28

"I cannot repress the desire that I feel as an American to thank you—
which I do from my heart—for the appointment of the present Secretary
of War."

—Joseph Holt to Lincoln

Stanton Becomes
Secretary of War

*T*he historian can pick his story and select the parts he wants to tell from the
tapestry of history, but the president had no such luxury. McClellan's sickness and his ill-tempered recapture of the baton formed only a series of important episodes in the multiple trials facing the head of state. While Lincoln dealt
with McClellan and the Army of the Potomac, he also had to handle the delicate task
of removing the secretary of war and choosing an appropriate replacement.

The day the major general recaptured the baton, Lincoln submitted the nomination of McClellan's friend Edwin M. Stanton to the Senate for approval as secretary of war. That night, when McClellan returned to his house to dress for dinner, a
member of his family told him Colonel Key had just been there to report that
Cameron had resigned as secretary of war and Stanton had been appointed in his
place.[1] McClellan finished dressing and went downstairs to meet his guests, the
Prince de Joinville and David Dixon Porter, an old friend, cousin of the general's
reliable confidant Fitz John and a participant in the rescue of Fort Pickens.

---

1   *M.O.S.*, 153.

After the three men had taken their seats for dinner, a member of the house staff delivered the card of Edwin M. Stanton, the new candidate for secretary of war. Appearing in the doorway of the dining room, Stanton stood for at least a minute. Finally, the general invited him into the room but left him to stand by the fireplace. Although the general did not introduce him or invite him to sit, Stanton kept his equanimity and, according to Porter, was not "the slightest disconcerted." Probably assuming that each man, an important public figure, knew or recognized the others, McClellan would have seen no need for introductions. Porter thought McClellan's conduct "extremely rude" but concluded that "Stanton felt at home and did not mind it." After approximately five minutes the young general in chief invited Stanton to join them for dinner, and the would-be secretary of war ate "with remarkably good appetite." A grudge bearer of great proportion, Stanton made a mental record of this incident. He would never forget it.[2] He would take revenge.

At some point in the evening, probably after Porter and de Joinville had left, Stanton said the president had appointed him to be secretary of war and sent his name to the Senate for confirmation. He wanted to discuss it. Acceptance of the appointment would involve great personal sacrifice, he said. He could be induced to accept it only if he would have a hand in putting down the rebellion by aiding McClellan. He said he was willing to devote all his time, intellect, and energy to helping McClellan. Together, he thought, they could soon bring the war to an end. If McClellan wished him to accept, he would, but only on McClellan's account. He had come to McClellan's house to learn his wishes.

McClellan said he hoped he would accept the position.

Stanton consented and exclaimed with great emotion, "Now we two will save the country."[3]

Next day, January 14, Lincoln visited McClellan at his house to apologize for not consulting him about Stanton's nomination. Because he knew Stanton was a friend, he said, he assumed the general would be glad to have him as secretary of war; and if he had told McClellan before the appointment, he feared "some of those fellows" would accuse him of dragooning McClellan into accepting it.[4]

---

2   David Dixon Porter MS journal (L.C.) no. 1, 174–175. The journal gives no date for this meeting except the statement that, according to "rumors," Stanton would become secretary of war, which tends to place it in this small period.

3   *M.O.S.*, 153; McClellan, George B., "The Peninsula Campaign" in *B&L*, 2, 163.

4   Porter MSS (L.C.) letter dated August 3, 1888, from Porter to Benjamin; *M.O.S.*, 161; McClellan, "The Peninsula Campaign" in *B&L*, 2, 163. The two accounts by McClellan have a minor conflict on the concern about "dragooning." *M.O.S.* describes Lincoln dragooning McClellan, and *B&L* describes McClellan dragooning Lincoln. Neither account is contemporary. The *B&L* account seems more logical and is accepted.

Lincoln now knew that the Joint Committee had a strong hostile attitude toward the major general. After he knew McClellan had recovered enough, he sent him a brief note suggesting a visit with the committee.[5] On January 14, McClellan wrote the committee, "The condition of my health is now such that I can appear before your committee when you wish."[6] It scheduled a meeting for the next day at 10:30 A.M.[7] With a touch of ironic humor the general wrote the president, "I am so much better this morning I am going before the Joint Committee. If I escape alive I will report when I am through."[8]

Oddly, the committee kept no transcript of the conference with McClellan, an entry of four lines in its Journal sufficing to record the discussion.[9] In the first hour and a half, as McClellan recalled it, he explained matters of interest to the committee, no doubt including Ball's Bluff. Although the chairman had already demanded McClellan's removal, he lied outright, saying the members had no desire to embarrass him. On the contrary, they were exceedingly anxious to sustain him and to cooperate with him in all matters pertaining to the war. They merely wanted explanations. He added, however, that he hoped McClellan understood the financial condition of the country, the feverish desire of the people for action, and the possibility of foreign complications. McClellan replied that he thoroughly appreciated the embarrassments Wade had mentioned, must decide if immediate action were advisable, had taken measures to secure an advance without delay in the West, and without any details intimated that Kentucky would very soon be a field of action.[10]

At the end of this discussion Chandler asked bluntly why McClellan did not attack the Confederates.

The major general replied that with only two bridges and no other transportation across the Potomac, he lacked sufficient means of communication with Washington.

Chandler had learned nothing from Bull Run and Ball's Bluff. He asked what the number of bridges had to do with an advance.

---

5   Basler, *Lincoln's Collected Works*, 5, 94, letter dated January 9, 1862, from Lincoln to McClellan.

6   *C.C.W.*, 1, 74, (Journal) letter dated January 14, 1862, from McClellan to Wade.

7   *C.C.W.*, 1, 74–75 (Journal) letter dated January 14, 1862, from Wade to McClellan.

8   Sears, *McClellan's Correspondence*, 154, letter dated January 15, 1862, from McClellan to Lincoln.

9   *C.C.W.*, 1, 75 (Journal), entry dated January 15, 1862. Two partial accounts of this session exist: Ives' long letter to Bennett describing his meeting with McClellan on January 15 and the Detroit Post & Tribune biography of Chandler. They are mildly inconsistent in factual content and conflict strongly in tone, but they can be reconciled.

10   James G. Bennett MSS (L.C.) letter dated January 15, 1861, from Ives to Bennett.

McClellan explained that one of the most important requirements of skillful strategy was plenty of room to retreat before making an attack.

"General McClellan, if I understand you correctly," Chandler responded, "before you strike at the Rebels, you want to be sure of plenty of room so that you can run in case they strike back!"

"Or in case you get scared," Wade added sarcastically.

Indignant, the major general delivered a lengthy explanation of the science of war, laying great stress on the need for open lines of retreat, communication, and supply. Wade could not have cared less about technical professionalism. He had a clear, simplistic idea about waging war: collect a sufficient number of men, arm them, march to the enemy, and start a fight—last man standing wins.

"General, you have all the troops you have called for, and if you haven't enough you shall have more," Wade said when McClellan had concluded. "They are well-organized and equipped, and the loyal people of this country expect that you will make a short and decisive campaign. Is it really necessary for you to have more bridges over the Potomac before you move?"

"Not that," concluded McClellan. "Not that exactly, but we must bear in mind the necessity of having everything ready in case of a defeat, and keep our lines of retreat open."[11]

Yet again, McClellan had sorely misgauged his audience. After he left the committee, Wade turned to Chandler.

"Chandler, what do you think of the science of generalship?"

"I don't know much about war," replied Chandler, "but it seems to me that this is infernal, unmitigated cowardice."

The collision precipitated by this meeting did not occur at once. Other events intervened. Stanton had arranged the promised conversation with Ives for that evening. As Ives entered McClellan's small study, Stanton introduced him.

"Now, General, we will show Dr. Ives what we think of the course of the *Herald*."

Stanton gave Ives information he had promised about "the recent changes," then discussed persons Ives had identified as candidates for the secretaryship and his own fear that difficulties might interfere with his confirmation in the Senate. He

---

11   Detroit Post & Tribune, *Chandler*, 224–225. This exchange, intended to make McClellan look like a coward, shows McClellan's thoughtful care and professionalism . . . and the supreme military ignorance of Wade and his cohorts. The necessity for an accessible line of retreat "just in case" has been proven many times. Recently, the "Black Hawk Down" incident in Mogadishu, although a small unit action, shows that a highly trained military force in a well planned operation can suffer severely when the plan goes awry and no proper arrangement for withdrawal or extraction has been made. Bowden, Mark, *Black Hawk Down, a Story of Modern War*, 338–339 (New York, 2000).

also described other contemplated cabinet changes. Chase, "who sustains McClellan," would remain and Welles, "who has been more foolish than dishonest," would not be changed unless he wished. He confirmed that the policy of the War Department would "fully accord with that of the commander in chief and the president." Joseph Holt would take Welles' place, Stanton presumed, but was not certain. Secretary of the Interior Caleb B. Smith, who wished to be on the bench and who was being pressed to be replaced by Schuyler Colfax, would go.

After Stanton left, McClellan locked the door and talked for three hours. "With much feeling,—a manner so heartfelt so evidently pure and sincere as to be absolutely touching," wrote Ives the next day to his superior, "he began by saying that on the previous day he had been summoned to meet the President and a majority of the members of his cabinet. They had demanded, peremptorily, information about the manner in which he intended to carry on the campaign. He had courteously but firmly refused to open his lips upon the subject.

"What I declined communicating to them," continued McClellan, "I am going to carry through you to Mr. Bennett and Mr. Hudson. I am going to give you *all* the knowledge I possess myself with no reserves; and if you choose to take a pen, you may make notes of what I am going to say; and I will willingly give you all the time you require to make the information complete."

McClellan added that one member of his staff, and no one else, knew his plans. He surprised Ives by saying that Ives had a claim on his confidence through family friends.

"But I particularly wish to charge you with a message to Mr. Bennett. Mr. Bennett has stood by me in the hour of the clearest anxiety of my whole life, a sadder one than I can anticipate for the future. He has done me nobly and with the whole force of his paper. He and he alone has upheld me, cheered me, and recognized me when every other newspaper heaped upon me calumny and abuse at the very time I was saving them from the horror of an invasion, which it is incomprehensible to me at this moment to explain. I shall *never, never, never* forget his kindness, and I wish him to know that I cherish him in my heart, and that I shall strive with all the energy my maker has given me to prove, as I have no doubt I shall, that his confidence has not been misplaced."

McClellan then apologized because he felt compelled to request a solemn pledge that Ives not reveal anything he was about to say except to Bennett and Hudson. Ives would be the first to have the knowledge.

Ives gave the pledge.

The major general described his national strategy involving Halleck and Buell in Kentucky and Tennessee and Burnside on the coast, all of which would set the stage for his decisive battle in Virginia.

"General McClellan's mind need not be made up now where he will fight," reported Ives, "but he will be able to do so just where he pleases and on his own ground. He will beat the rebels, and the rebellion will be ended, or at least its strength will be irrecoverably broken. The possibilities are that the Waterloo of the war will be somewhere on the Lynchburg-Winchester road to Richmond, and success is inevitable." The Union sentiment in the South would erupt, and spontaneous reactions would destroy Southern strength. He estimated Confederate strength in western Virginia at one hundred thousand to one hundred fifty thousand men. The Rebels could deploy from one hundred thousand to one hundred twenty-five thousand on the field of battle in a general action. The Federal troops, including the men in Baltimore, Romney, and other places, counting sick and incapables about the District of Columbia, was about two hundred thousand men—say one hundred ninety thousand fit for duty. If McClellan advanced with all available men on short notice, he would have one hundred thirty thousand troops. If he advanced on any other line he could not muster more than one hundred ten thousand. He believed that, when the latter had been under fire, they would be inferior to no forces in the world. His private information tallied with that published in the Richmond *Examiner*. He also understood that the ordinary Confederate soldiers would not drill and that their morale was bad.

After he mentioned the final struggle in the New Orleans corner of the Confederacy, McClellan finished with the kind of romantic flourish he had used in so many of his letters to Ellen. "They must be beaten, and they shall be beaten in Virginia, and then I will knock them to pieces at New Orleans. Otherwise, I-I-. . . ."

He clasped his hands together and smiled but did not finish. "He seems, however, to be as sure and undoubted of success, as a second Providence," added Ives.

The major general said the Rebels could have taken Washington with ease up to August 10 and gave a graphic description of the difficulties he had overcome. He was certain he had saved the capital. Then, he spoke enthusiastically about the president. He believed Lincoln's apparent weakness was the result of bon homie, which hurt nothing. Probably not knowing that the former secretary of war had satisfied McClellan fully, Ives remarked that the general must have suffered greatly under Cameron.

"Ah! Ah! Ah!" McClellan groaned with a little dissembling. "It is just that he should go in peace and that no strife about the past should be created."

Many of his staff, he said, were so enthusiastic they were imprudent. He mentioned Key as an example but did not believe Key had done anything harmful.

Ives wanted to know what support McClellan would ask of Bennett if he could see him.

"I should want Mr. Bennett to do just what he has done," McClellan said, "to preach patience, forbearance and confidence." He wanted support, especially in light of the Mason and Slidell affair, for a program to "defend our harbor fortifications." McClellan thought the program would be beneficial whether or not a foreign war occurred.

He then said that, if Ives would see him the next morning at 10, he could have documents, including the very recent letters from General Halleck and General Buell with the precise amount of their forces and other information.

"I cannot say that I advise the publication of the above," Ives wrote to Bennett, "and I would rather deprecate it; but General McClellan permitted the use of the facts, and so I tell you. He is as guileless and innocent as a child, and we must be careful not to injure him, even to promote *Herald* interests." McClellan gave Ives permission to use the telegraph for an account of his interview with the Joint Committee.[12]

The next day after breakfast Ives went again to see McClellan. "In case of the failure of any of your expeditions, or military movements," Ives asked, "what would be the remedy, and how far would it delay your operations in Virginia?"

"Scarcely any, unless the reverse should be such a one as cannot be remedied without serious loss of time." The general explained that he was preparing for a movement in Virginia, "in the same manner as though it were not connected with the grander scheme of campaign."

"Then," responded Ives, "your time for moving on the other side of the Potomac must be substantially fixed."

"Certainly," the general answered. "I think I shall advance by the first days in March whatever else may happen." Then he gravely and earnestly described sly, romantic trickery. "And now I want you to tell Mr. Bennett, that, when the time for immediate action comes, I want his whole support to help me throw dust in the most elaborate manner in the eyes of the enemy. Together with real information, you shall have pretended information for which you may be railed at as prematurely divulging secrets, but, if I live, the aid thus given me, shall become historical."

The young general laughed and rubbed his hands together as he contemplated the disinformation he would give his Southern opponents.

Ives responded that the moment of action would be unexpected to the public. It would be well for McClellan, who wished no allusion to his plans made to any one, to create some code for communicating with Bennett.

"The instant it is necessary," McClellan said, "I will get Colburn to telegraph 'Come on,' and you will know what it means."[13]

12   James G. Bennett MSS (L.C.) letter dated January 15, 1861, from Ives to Bennett.

13   James G. Bennett MSS (L.C.) letter dated January 16, 1862, from Ives to Bennett.

McClellan's gratitude for the support he had received from Bennett led him into yet another unfortunate collision with the committee: publicity the committee members would consider false and would want to disavow. According to the description McClellan gave Ives, Wade "thanked him in the name of the Committee for the frankness and courtesy of his communications." McClellan's account confirmed the naiveté he had already shown in his dealings with politicians: they appreciated his "energy, ability, and patriotism," and after the meeting, Ives wrote, "the members of the Committee have appeared radiant & jubilant. They can no longer conceal their enthusiasm, and they are unanimous in the conviction that everything is being done that the exigencies of the Country require."[14]

McClellan had made a large mistake when he described his relationship with the committee as one of cooperation and support. On January 19, the *Herald* published an account of his session with the Joint Committee[15] that could not have been more infuriating to the members.

McClellan's "firm and dignified" appearance before the committee, said the *Herald* account, caused "a most wonderful change in his favor." He showed himself to be a "man of wonderful genius and great executive ability." The committee had been "howling against General McClellan for weeks in a manner that would be unbecoming in boys . . . Confidence in the Commanding General," the *Herald* concluded, "is increasing." Worse yet, it quoted the testimony of an unnamed general who could only have been Fitz John Porter, and the account of the testimony, printed as if the *Herald* had a transcript, was inaccurate to say the least. The unnamed general supposedly testified that McClellan had "submitted his plans to a council of war."[16] The article accurately conveyed the tone the general had given to Ives; but when the committee members saw it, they must have been "incredulous,"[17] if not furious. After the

---

14   James G. Bennett MSS (L.C.) letter dated January 15, 1861, from Ives to Bennett. Ives' recitation of McClellan's narrative and characterization of his meeting with the committee has many possible explanations ranging from intentional distortion by Ives through good faith errors by one or both to intentional misstatement by McClellan. Many explanations simply have no support beyond the rational basis of a valid hypothesis. McClellan, where the largest error probably lay, most likely made the naive mistake in assessing his critics that he recorded in his memoirs, *M.O.S.*, 155 (at this time no real opposition had developed against him) and that he had given an instructive lecture solicited and well received by the committee. Not privy to the inner thoughts of the seven men, he completely misgauged their attitudes. That would change dramatically over the next two months.

15   *New York Herald*, January 19, 1862, 1, col. 1; Tap, *Over Lincoln's Shoulder*, 108–109.

16   *New York Herald*, January 19, 1862, 1, col. 1.

17   Tapp, *Over Lincoln's Shoulder*, 108.

war Henry Villard wrote harshly about Bennett that he had a "shameful record as a journalist, . . . particularly the sneaking sympathy of his paper for the Rebellion, and its abuse of the Republicans for their antislavery sentiments."[18] Knowing that McClellan was the only possible source for this account, believing the general had played them the fool in the eyes of the public, and probably inferring that McClellan had made common cause with a powerful enemy, committee members allowed their dislike for McClellan and Bennett to combine. As he had with Barlow, Astor, Key, and others, McClellan, yet again, suffered guilt by association.

This incident illustrates another of McClellan's strong characteristics, one that appeared in many circumstances and that unfortunately served him poorly. In this time of fractured and varied support for the war, McClellan had close contact with several different groups, all serving different purposes, all seeking different goals, all working in areas that could help him, all divided by their attitude toward him, and many alienated by the general in chief's favoritism. Ruled by an intense loyalty to his friends, he would play favorites. Among high-ranking officers in his army, cabinet officers, members of Congress, important civilians, newspapermen, and every other group that touched his life, McClellan preferred to deal with those he liked and respected. Others he often ignored, a practice that did not engender their loyalty and support. The unfavored men, left to their own devices, often ignored altogether, he could have made his supporters without much effort and without compromise of his principles.

This characteristic demonstrated another flaw in his personality. Like his apparent preference for wealthy, prestigious Democrats, he thought he could show favoritism with impunity. He believed it would not hurt him because he had a pure heart. But it would. The members of the disfavored groups would, like Ellet, become hostile while McClellan believed that his personal strength would always lead him to success no matter who became his detractor and that in the end they would all laud him because he would save his country—and theirs.

For two days Stanton's nomination stood without Senate confirmation. Then, on January 15, it passed.[19] A few days later, recovered but still weak from his illness, McClellan wrote his friend Sam Barlow, "Stanton's appointment was a most unexpected piece of good fortune & I hope it will produce a good effect in the North."[20]

18   Villard, *Memoirs*, 1, 161.

19   *D.A.B.*, 9, pt. 1, 518.

20   S. L. M. Barlow MSS (H.L.) letter dated January 18, 1862, from McClellan to Barlow.

The ever-critical clerk in the State Department saw this change with optimism. "Change in the Cabinet: Stanton, a new man, not from the parlor, and not from the hacks," he wrote in his diary. "It is the awakening voice of the good genius of the people. I never saw him, but I hope he is the man for the events; perhaps he may turn out to be *my* statesman."[21]

Joseph Holt, a war Democrat and Stanton's former colleague in Buchanan's midnight cabinet, wrote Lincoln, "I cannot repress the desire that I feel as an American citizen to thank you—which I do from my heart—for the appointment of the present Secretary of War. In him you will find a friend true as steel and a support which no pressure from within or from without will ever shake."[22]

And the literate George Templeton Strong wrote in his diary, "Stanton impresses me and everybody else most favorably . . . At lowest estimate worth a wagon load of Camerons. Intelligent, prompt, clear-headed, fluent without wordiness, and above all, earnest, warm-hearted, and large-hearted."[23]

Letters to Stanton addressed mainstream issues already presented to the government: treason, treachery, the West Point clique, preservation of slavery, and the need for battles without regard for casualties. Joseph Medill, editor of the *Chicago Tribune*, wrote, "You will discover scores of lukewarm, half secession officers in command who cannot bear to strike a vigorous blow lest it hurts their rebel friends or jeopardizes the precious practice of slavery. Such men for instance as . . . Gen. Stone on the Potomac . . . and indeed three fourths of all the 'West Pointers' in the army." Medill complained about "quasi loyalty" and called for "vigor, system, honesty, and *fight.*"[24]

Other events confirmed to McClellan that he and Stanton would enjoy a comfortable, cooperative working relationship, born in part from similarity of views. The day after the Senate confirmed Stanton, he and Ives met again. "I asked the War Secretary what course was to be taken with blundering abolitionist generals," Ives wrote to Bennett. "His views and those held by General McClellan respecting the matter, are nearly identical. They say that all such *must* be '*dropped*' and will be."

Stanton and McClellan agreed that the army had insufficient topographical engineers and that the deficiency could not be corrected by transferring men from the Corps of Engineers. Congress should authorize the president to appoint topograph-

21   Gurowski, *Diary*, 1, 145, entry dated January, 1862.

22   Lincoln MSS (L.C.) letter dated January 15, 1862, from Holt to Lincoln.

23   Nevins, *Strong Diary*, 3, 203, entry dated January 29, 1862.

24   Stanton MSS (L.C.) letter dated January 21, 1826, from Medill to Stanton.

ical officers from civil engineers. McClellan, the Congress, and the president could find abundant talent and learning scattered through the country and available for the federal service if the president were given the power.[25]

Short, broad-shouldered, thickly built, pig-faced, with a long brown beard sprinkled with gray and severe little eyes peering through spectacles on a large head covered by a mass of black hair, Stanton spoke in a "quick and apparently positive" manner, recalled John Pope after the war. His complexion was dark with mottling that suggested a dissolute, high style of life, but his duties would entirely absorb him and he would demonstrate "almost superhuman" work habits. His deeply religious nature had made him very familiar with the Bible and given him a firm conviction that God directed the armies of the Union.

"We owe our recent victories," he would say again and again, "to the spirit of the Lord that moved our soldiers to rush into battle and filled the hearts of our enemies with dismay."

A serious student of history, widely read, and fond of discussing historical characters, Stanton showed no ostentation about his learning. He enjoyed discussing legal questions and would listen eagerly to descriptions of cases involving his many friends, to whom he was devoted. In conversation witty and satirical, he told a story well; and with his quick intelligence he understood a thing before it was half described to him. He was impatient with those who could not explain themselves promptly and sharply, and his judgment was swift.[26]

Entering an entirely new assignment without background or experience, Stanton nevertheless had a clear picture of the task before him, a picture little different than McClellan's view of his responsibilities with the army. "To bring the war department up to the standards of the times, and work an army of 500,000 with machinery adapted to a peace establishment of 12,000 is no easy task," he wrote to Charles A. Dana. "This was Mr. Cameron's great trouble and the cause of much of the complaints against him. All I ask is reasonable time & patience. The pressure of members

25   James G. Bennett MSS (L.C.) letter dated January 16, 1862 from Ives to Bennett.

26   Piatt, Donn, *Memories of the Men who Saved the Union* (New York and Chicago, 1897) 50–57, and the entire Stanton chapter, 50–93, for a highly laudatory account of Stanton as secretary of war (Piatt, *Memories*); Cozzens, Peter, and Robert I. Girardi, eds., *The Military Memoirs of General John Pope*, 114–117 (Chappel Hill and London, 1998). The quotation, "We owe our recent victories . . . ," appears in *Doster, supra*, as it appears in the text but appeared, apparently for the first time, in *The New York Daily Tribune*, February 20, 1861, p. 4, col. 2, and was much later quoted at length in Ropes, John C., "The Peninsular Campaign," 1, 78–79, in *Campaigns in Virginia*, in Dwight, Theodore F., ed., *Papers of the Military Historical Society of Massachusetts*, 10 vols. (Boston, 1881, Broadfoot rep.).

of congress for clerk & army appointments notwithstanding the most stringent rules; and the persistence tried against all measures essential to obtain time for thought, combination, and confidence is discouraging in the extreme."[27]

The transformation of the War Department occurred at once. Stanton "banished self-seeking 'shoulder-straps' from the capital," wrote Nicolay and Hay after the war. "He expanded and verified his various military bureaus. He found some Congressmen, like some contractors, misrepresenting his peremptory refusals of the special favors they arrogantly demanded." To correct this abuse, he adopted the sunshine practice by receiving all supplicants publicly. At ten in the morning and three in the afternoon he would, with a red-headed orderly from the Fourth Pennsylvania Cavalry tending the door, stand behind a shoulder-high writing desk with a window immediately behind him.[28] He presented an appearance of irritability as if he were a schoolmaster, as if he had not slept well, and as if he would suffer no pain by refusing a request. In fact, he had a remarkable facility for saying "no" and no respect for any civil liberty or army regulation that stood in the way of suppressing the Rebellion—and destroying the planter aristocracy of the South. For one hour he would receive the seekers while the "adjutant-generals, orderlies, and clerks on duty moved gently and deferentially . . . knowing that Stanton was no respecter of persons, precedents, formulas, or tape and that he was capable of dealing heavy blows with great coolness and celerity." With this practice of receiving public applications, Stanton presided over a rapid diminution of those made by "influential people," acquaintances at the bar, corrupt persons, women in tears, and venerable old men.

Lincoln and Stanton had a comfortable, informal, personal working relationship from the outset, often visiting each other without appointment when important news came to hand. Having the personality of a bully, the strong-willed Stanton nevertheless gave acquiescence to Lincoln's stronger personality and better judgment. In the end Stanton never tested the authority or power of his chief, accepting the president's determinations even when he disagreed.[29]

Later in the war they faced a question about bounties, counting of recruits, and the draft. Stanton assigned an assistant adjutant general to explain the issue and the reason the president had the wrong approach.

---

27   Charles A. Dana MSS (Library of Congress) letter dated February 1, 1862, from Stanton to Dana.

28   Although the facts are not clear, he probably positioned his desk with the windows at his back and left his visitors with the sun in their eyes, a practice used today by skillful lawyers in conferences with their adversaries because the "view" out the window into the sun actually erodes the adversaries' resistance.

29   *N&H*, 5, 141, 142, 144, 145; Doster, *Lincoln and Episodes*, 115, 117.

"Now, Mr. President," he concluded, "those are the facts; and you must see that your order cannot be executed."

Sitting on a sofa with his long legs crossed, Lincoln waited until the secretary finished, then spoke in a positive tone.

"Mr. Secretary, I reckon you'll have to execute the order."

"Mr. President, I cannot do it. The order is an improper one, and I cannot execute it."

Showing his determination, Lincoln fixed his eye on the secretary and spoke firmly, even sharply.

"Mr. Secretary, I will have it done."[30]

For McClellan the change was significant. If Cameron had a philosophy for the post, he intended to give the major general the things he requested but exclude himself from military affairs. Stanton, altogether different, verging on hyperactivity, would take part in everything and demanded a high level of accountability. Of course, he would also expect compliance with the rules of protocol and military courtesy.

---

30   James B. Fry in *The New York Daily Tribune*, June 28, 1885, 3, cols. 1–2, quoted in *N&H*, 5, 146–147.

Chapter 29

"Statement of James Shaw relative to disloyalty of Brig. Gen. Charles P. Stone U.S.A."

—*Title of report by Pinkerton to McClellan*

Stanton Puts the
Shroud on Stone

$\mathcal{F}$or Charles P. Stone, the Joint Committee and the secretary of war had adverse evidence in quantity, and the brigadier general would add to it. On January 28, he wrote a letter to C. H. Powell of Valley Grove, Virginia. In it he mentioned that he had already forwarded another letter across the Potomac. ". . . I refrain from sending [your letter] to the hands of the General at Leesburg, because I think it would compromise Mr. Gray with the rebel authorities and cause you the certain loss of any property you may have in Loudoun Co." Stone returned the letter and suggested silence on political subjects. He said he had no objection to the letter going across the river but it would be contrary to Powell's interests.[1] This letter found its way to Lincoln.

That same day, Stanton gave McClellan a verbal order to arrest Stone and keep him in "close custody."[2] When McClellan insisted that the order be in writing, the secretary wrote it himself. He issued the order, he said, at the insistence of the Joint

---

1 Lincoln MSS (L.C.) letter dated January 28, 1861, from Stone to Powell.

2 McClellan MSS (L.C.) order dated January 28, 1861; Porter, *Stone*, 14–15 (pam.).

Committee on the basis of testimony it had taken. McClellan responded as he usually did to an order he did not like: he argued that he should not be required to execute it.

After he received the order, he and another West Point graduate discussed Stone and the committee.

"They want a victim," said the general.

"Yes," was the reply. "And when they have once tasted blood—got one victim—no one can tell who will be next."

McClellan colored visibly but remained silent.[3]

A few days later McClellan telegraphed Stone to come to Washington at once. The order reached Stone at 11 P.M. in the middle of a dark storm. Stone thought the general in chief wished to see him about the plan he had suggested for capturing Leesburg and drawing the Confederates into an ill-advised assault on a prepared position. Within fifteen minutes he was on his way, "leaving my tent and office as the order had found them," he wrote later. In the morning when he arrived in the capital and reported to McClellan, Stone was, "to my utter astonishment and disgust," not to discuss his plan for defeating the enemy but to go "before a committee of civilians, the Committee on the Conduct of the War, who, it was said, had some evidence affecting my loyalty."

McClellan relieved Stone of command of his division and went to Chairman Wade's office. He reported that Stone was in the capital, was not under arrest, and could undoubtedly answer any questions about his conduct. Firmly, he argued his subordinate's innocence, urging Wade to call Stone before the committee and confront him with witnesses or testimony. Three days later, the last day of the month, the committee recalled Stone to testify about his loyalty. "My loyalty!" he stormed four years later. He had been on the front and within hearing of Rebel picket fire continuously since June except for three short visits to Washington on business. "I was to be called before a table of civilians whose rest I had secured and who had, none of them, ever exposed a little finger for the defense of the Government." He was to "talk to them and persuade them I was loyal to the Government." After all the abuse and false charges heaped on him, he was "in no amiable temper"; and his sharp tongue so surpassed his judgment that the transcript required alteration.[4]

---

3 Beale, *Bates Diary*, 229, entry dated February 3, 1862.

4 McClellan MSS (L.C.) letter dated December 5, 1862, from McClellan to Stone; segment of draft final report; Schoff Collection (Stone MS) (Univ. Mich.) letter dated November 5, 1866, from Stone to Lossing; Irwin, "Balls Bluff and the Arrest of General Stone," in *B&L*, 2, 133.

"We do not profess to sit here as a military board," said Wade, referring disingenuously to Ball's Bluff. "We do not profess to be competent judges of these matters. But we deem that the testimony tends . . . to impeach you for not reinforcing those troops when they were over there in the face of the enemy, and, in connection with that, when you knew the battle was proceeding, that you did not go within three or four miles of it."

"From what point should they have been reenforced?" asked the general.

"We cannot help but think," said Wade, speaking for the other six, "that they ought to have been reinforced—for instance, from Edwards Ferry, or perhaps, if you had sufficient transportation, as you intimate, then right across at Ball's Bluff."

"Colonel Baker had at his disposal a force vastly superior to that of the enemy."

"I propose merely to state the heads," countered Wade, stating, in effect, that Stone's only purpose that day was to hear the guilty verdict and remain silent. "I do not desire to discuss them."

"I should like to know those heads," answered the "accused," declining to be silenced, "and I would be greatly pleased if two members of this committee or three or four or the whole of them, would just take a trip up to that ground, and look at it a half an hour, and see if you do not become thoroughly satisfied of the impracticability and false soldiership which would have been shown if we had attempted to pass troops from Edwards Ferry to the right at that time."

"We are not military men," hedged Wade.

"Yes, but you judge military men."

"Yes, sir, but not finally," said the chairman with less than half truth. "We only state what, in our opinion, tends to impeach them when the evidence tends to do so and then leave it to better judges to determine. Those two points, we thought, tended to impeach your conduct on that occasion. Another point is, you are apparently impeached. I say 'impeached.' The evidence tends to prove that you have had undue communication with the enemy by letters that have passed back and forth, by intercourse with officers from the other side, and by permitting packages to go over unexamined to known secessionists."

The Joint Committee could be excused for military ignorance, perhaps for incompetence, even for stupidity. But outright dishonest malevolence? The federal government had always stood for more than that.[5]

---

5 Stone's case has interesting parallels with the career and end of Mikhael Tukhachevsky, the core similarity being the spurious charge of disloyalty. American society, until recently a society characterized by high moral principles, never went to the lengths of the French or Russian Revolutions in its treatment of the "opposition" or the military. How far the zealous, loyal, well-intentioned, but malevolent and judgmentless Radicals would go in the pursuit of their political and

When Stone had protected Washington at the outbreak, he commanded a mere three thousand District of Columbia militia, slept a total of three hours in his own bed while Washington lay completely isolated, and dozed in his cloak at outposts or while traveling to them.[6] For the second time Stone lost control and allowed the questions to provoke him.

"That is one humiliation I had hoped I never should be subject to. I thought there was one calumny that could not be brought against me. Any other calumny that anybody can raise I should expect after what I have received, but that one I should have supposed that you personally, Mr. Chairman, would have rejected at once. You remember last winter—when this government had so few friends—who had this city, I might almost say, in his power? I raised all the volunteer troops that were here during those seven dark days of last winter. I disciplined and posted those troops. I commanded them, and those were the first troops to invade the soil of Virginia, and I led them."

The questions and answers continued, with the seven congressmen often on the defensive and the general bombarding them with intemperate statements.[7]

---

social goals remained to be seen. Stone was a West Point Democrat, Tukhachevsky a member of the minor nobility, both anathema to the revolutionary zealots. The enemies of both men fabricated evidence against them. The motivation against both was, in essence, the same: the protection of the state from disloyalty. The "charges" against Stone had as little merit as those against Tukhachevsky. Both sprang from baseless fear. A rare combination of the brilliant, creative, innovative intellectual military thinker and the first rate battlefield leader, Tukhachevsky did not owe his prominence or his high rank in the Red Army to Stalin, which left his loyalty in doubt in Stalin's mind. Tukhachevsky's close working relationship with Trotsky and his extended absence in Germany while the Germans and Russians cooperated in their clandestine work on military technology and tactics provided "evidence" of disloyalty and a patina of fact on which to base charges. Tukhachevsky's obvious brilliance made lesser men jealous and anxious to repeat rumors of a conspiracy with him at the head of it. In the Soviet Union during the latter stages of the great purge, which focused primarily on the military (1937–1941), more than thirty thousand of eighty thousand officers were arrested or executed, Tukhachevsky among them. Shimon Naveh, "Mikhail Nikolayevich Tukhachevsky," in Shukman, H., ed. *Stalin's Generals*, 257–258 (London, 1993); Glantz, David M.,and House, Jonathan, *When Titans Clashed: How the Red Army Stopped Hitler*, 11–13 (Lawrence, 1995); Ericson, John, *The Red Army* (London, 1962); MacIntosh, Malcolm, *Juggernaut: A History of the Soviet Armed Forces* (New York, 1968); Volkoganov, Dimitri, and Harold Shukman, trans. and ed., *Stalin: Triumph and Tragedy*, 318–329 (New York, 1988).

6   Schoff Collection (Stone MS) (Univ. Mich.) letter dated November 5, 1866, from Stone to Lossing.

7   *C.C.W.*, 2, 426–427 (Stone). In his account in the Schoff Collection at the University of Michigan, Stone states that his testimony was transcribed without some of his intemperate comments. Combined with the absence of a transcript of the discussion with McClellan, this suggests that the printed reports of the Joint Committee's hearings are not necessarily reliable and may have been modified to fit the committee's desires.

Confronted for the first time with accusations, Stone countered them effectively. Although he did not regain his command, he succeeded in keeping his freedom. Perhaps as long as McClellan was willing to shield him he would remain free. To all appearances he had persuaded the committee and Stanton that he had done nothing wrong. He was treated "with respect and dignity by the President and the Secretary of War." He was invited to attend a dinner hosted by McClellan for ranking staff and line officers and many members of Congress.[8] On February 7, Stanton told him that his explanation had been satisfactory, that his exculpation was complete, that no charges were being entertained against him, and that increases of his command and responsibility were being considered.[9]

But the order of arrest remained unrevoked in McClellan's hands when James Short, a civilian resident of Leesburg, crossed the Potomac into Maryland, where he was taken to McClellan's intelligence officer Allan Pinkerton. Short knew that the name of a prior informant had been leaked to the press and that the informant had suffered unpleasant local repercussions. He wished his information reported under a false name. Pinkerton filed two reports. The first, a brief letter, explained the problem with the leak and stated that Short's information would be reported under the name "James Shaw." The second, much longer, contained "Shaw's" information. A few pages from the beginning, the long report had a large center heading underscored in red and entitled, "Statement of James Shaw relative to disloyalty of Brig. Gen. Charles P. Stone U.S.A."

Stone was "very popular with the Rebel officers at Leesburg and with all secessionists in that vicinity," it said. They spoke of him as a gentleman although they bitterly denounced other officers in the Union army. Local citizens doubted Stone's loyalty to the United States government, especially for his conduct during the battle at Ball's Bluff. Flags of truce in this area were extremely frequent. Persons could cross to and from Virginia. Correspondence passed back and forth easily.[10]

Elijah White, a captain in the Eighth Virginia Cavalry Regiment, part of Turner Ashby's cavalry in Jackson's Valley army, had become legendary. At Ball's Bluff

---

8   Heintzelman MS diary (large diary) (L.C.) entry dated February 6, 1862.

9   Porter, *Stone*, 13 (pam.).

10   McClellan MSS (L.C.) letters dated February 6, 1862, from Allan to McClellan. Allan (Pinkerton) had already complained about press coverage which made performance of his duties more difficult. *Ibid.*, letters dated January 10 to 13, 1862, from Allen to McClellan. In one case two men had been brought to headquarters at 3:00 P.M. to be interviewed. A description of them and some of the information they gave appeared in the *Washington Star* that evening. McClellan MSS (L.C.) letter dated January 13, 1862, from Allen to McClellan.

"Lige" White had scouted, served as a courier, led the final Confederate charge at the cliff, and guided a group of forty infantrymen who captured more than three hundred armed Union troops at the base of the bluff.[11] Mrs. White, a Maryland resident, Stone allowed to pass back and forth across the river through his pickets at Conrad's Ferry. No other person had this freedom. In fact, Stone had committed other indiscretions involving Mrs. White. On December 5, he wrote to Colonel Edward Hinks commanding the Nineteenth Massachusetts Infantry, "Mrs. White has lost two negro servants (women), who left early yesterday morning & are said to have been seen at the camp of the 19th just before it was broken up yesterday. If they have been harbored by the men, you will please cause them to be at once turned from the camp or quarters of the Regiment, which Mrs. White will visit this morning."[12]

This correspondence apparently found its way to Governor Andrew of Massachusetts. Ten days later Hinks received a letter saying, "Your highly valued favor of 7th inst. came dearly to hand. I have seen the correspondence with Genl. Stone with much satisfaction. I was much pleased to notice the action taken by Congress in regard to the battle at Ball's Bluff. The investigation by the Committee I have no doubt redown [sic] much to your credit, and only confirms my conviction that the nations eye is on you. Your friends here are much gratified with your correspondence."[13] Shaw did not report this incident, but he did report that Captain White had sent a note across the river to his wife on the Union side by a flag of truce and that the note had been taken across by Union troops.

Shaw had been told by a Captain McCabe of the Twenty-eighth Pennsylvania that Mrs. White crossed the river by permission of General Stone. According to Captain McCabe, he had arrested a man in early September who crossed the river from the Virginia side.

"I know who you are," McCabe said. "Your name is Elijah White. You are from Virginia."

At first, a denial. Finally, the man admitted his name was White; but he denied that he was Elijah White and that he was from Virginia.

When McCabe described the man to Shaw, he fit the description of Captain White. McCabe told Shaw that he sent the man to General Stone and that Stone released him.

---

11   Patch, Joseph Dorst, Maj. Gen. (ret.), *The Battle of Ball's Bluff*, 22, 69, 76, 81 (Leesburg, 1958).

12   Hinks MSS (B.U.) letter dated December 5, 1861, from Stone to Hinks.

13   Hinks MSS (B.U.) letter dated December 14, 1861, from William D. Miller to Hinks.

According to the unanimous opinion among the Rebels, both civilian and military, Shaw reported, one Union regiment from Edwards Ferry, where Stone had his headquarters, would have produced a victory at Ball's Bluff. They felt that the Federal commander made a great blunder or played into the hands of the Confederates. Shaw also reported that Union troops had been sent across the river after dark when they were being shot by the Confederates on the bluff as fast as they arrived. The effort to send more troops continued long after any person on the Maryland side "must have known what was taking place on the Va. side . . . "

In the hotel in Leesburg, "Shanks" Evans had told other Confederate officers that Stone had recently sent over sugar, coffee, money, and other things by flag of truce for the Union prisoners in Leesburg. He reported a conversation in the hotel parlor about the flags of truce.

"I think there are a great many flags of truce coming over."

"Well, what do they want?"

"Oh, I don't know. Some correspondence for General Evans."

On another occasion, Union troops had crossed to a small island and taken blacks and two horses from a secessionist. A week later Stone returned them with a note saying that he had not come there to steal negroes or horses.

General Evans had been heard saying that Stone was a brave man and a gentleman. "Gen. Stone is too well spoken of in Leesburg to be alright," Shaw reported.[14]

McClellan decided this report contained too much incriminating information to be ignored. It seemed to him that it "to a certain extent agreed with evidence stated to have been taken by the Congressional Committee."

That night, he took Pinkerton's report to Stanton, who did not need any prodding. The secretary renewed the order to arrest Stone.

From the information in his possession, McClellan responded, he did not see how any charges could be framed. The case was too indefinite.

Stanton would not yield.[15] He wanted Stone arrested.

McClellan returned to his headquarters to draft the order. He must have been distraught at the thought of, without formal charges, arresting a trusted subordinate on the flimsiest hypothesis of disloyalty. As he drafted the order, he made error after error in one attempt after another. He ordered Stone taken to the wrong fort, put under the wrong officer, and in the sentence denying Stone all communication

14   McClellan MSS (L.C.) letter dated February 6, 1861, from Allen to McClellan (long letter).

15   McClellan MSS (L.C.) letter dated December 5, 1862, from McClellan to Stone.

omitted the critical word "no."[16] When he finally had the order in correct form, he delivered it to his provost marshal, Andrew Porter.

Between 11 P.M. and midnight the officer assigned to make the arrest took two lieutenants, a sergeant, and fifteen men from Company B, Third United States Infantry, to H Street in front of the house of Lord Lyons, the English ambassador. The officer entered to find a reception or ball taking place but no Stone. He rejoined the men on the street and marched them to a house on the west side of 17th Street between H and Pennsylvania Avenue. He disappeared inside again.[17]

Meanwhile, Stone and Colonel Isaac J. Wistar finished a four-hour conversation with Thomas P. Kimber in Kimber's rooms at Willard's Hotel. They had reviewed a new map of the rail lines in the South. Of course, the conversation covered Stone's travails as well. According to Kimber, who wrote McClellan a few days later, "He won my heart (though I had never seen him before) by his touching straightforward, and thoughtful narrative—confirmed fully by Col. Wistar. His strict military submission to whatever might come, his perfect confidence in you, that you & Gen. Scott would right him in time & not allow a partisan climber to ruin him—and his calm willingness to await the issue satisfied me he was loyal & true . . . "[18]

Near midnight Stone started for his own rooms on foot. When he arrived, he found the phlegmatic, "by-the-book" George Sykes, no doubt uniform jacket buttoned as always to the throat and wearing spotless white gloves, waiting on the street with officers and infantry in the background.

Sykes and Stone exchanged friendly greetings. They had been students together at West Point and had both served in Scott's Mexico City column. Stone congratulated Sykes on his fine command.

Speaking in his usual nasal tone, Sykes responded cordially that, although he had fine troops to command—he commanded the City Guard—his duties were very disagreeable, "and, Stone, I have now the most disagreeable duty to perform that I ever had—it is to arrest you."

"Arrest me!" exclaimed Stone in amazement. "For what?"

Sykes did not know. Indeed, he could not conceive why; but he had orders to arrest Stone and hold him in close custody.

Stone was astounded.

---

16   McClellan MSS (L.C.) drafts of order of arrest n.d. but probably February 8, 1862, to the arresting officer and the officer in command of Fort Lafayette.

17   Carter, *Four Brothers in Blue*, 45.

18   McClellan MSS (L.C.) letter dated February 11, 1862, from Kimber to McClellan.

Sykes then said Stone had better change to civilian clothes. "I may as well tell you that you are to be sent to Fort Lafayette."

"Why, Fort Lafayette is where they send secessionists."

"Yes."

"Well, this is astonishing. They are now sending there one who has been as true a soldier to the government as any in service."

"That is just what three officers of your own rank said a few minutes ago when the order for your arrest was received."

Stone entered his quarters, where he changed to civilian clothing. He said goodby to his wife with a few calming words, then returned to Sykes, his officers, and his detachment of infantry.[19]

He was puzzled. Sykes showed him no charges and no authority for the arrest except the armed guard accompanying him.[20] No one recognized him as they marched the short distance to a building occupied by some of the officers of the guard. They gave him a room on the upper floor with one of the lieutenants and a sentinel posted outside the door. In spite of the unique and disturbing circumstances in which he found himself, he slept the sound sleep of the righteous.

First thing next morning, Stone requested writing paper and prepared a letter to the adjutant general reporting his arrest, asking for the charges against him and seeking an opportunity to meet them at once. Unaware of the complex political forces raging out of control in his case, Stone felt he had become involved in "some strange misunderstanding" that the government and the army would wish to resolve. Aside from the disagreeable nature of the occurrence, he felt little uneasiness and expected to rejoin the Corps of Observation within a week.

When he learned he was to travel to Fort Lafayette under guard, he told Sykes that, if McClellan would order him to report to the fort under arrest, the order would be as effective as any guard.

Sykes was willing to accept Stone's word, he said, but someone farther up the chain of command insisted on an escort. On Sunday, February 9, Stone, a lieutenant, and two detectives departed. His escort accepted his word of honor that he would not try to escape during the trip.

19 Schoff Collection (Stone MS) (Univ. Mich.) letter dated November 5, 1862, from Stone to Lossing; *Cullum*, 2, nos. 1139 and 1237; Sykes' characteristics from Parker, Dangerfield, "The Regular Infantry in the First Bull Run Campaign," in *The United Service*, 8, 524, 529 (November 1885).

20 McClellan MSS (L.C.) letter dated December 1, 1862, from Stone to McClellan.

When they reached Philadelphia, the lieutenant had no money to pay for train tickets. Ironically, Stone loaned the lieutenant enough money to pay for the trip to jail and at sunrise on February 11 the escort delivered him to the colonel in command at Fort Lafayette and Fort Hamilton. The colonel and Stone were old friends from the Mexican War.

"In the name of God, General Stone," he exclaimed, "what does this mean?"

"I do not know, Colonel, any more than you."

The lieutenant handed the colonel the order.

"Well, well," he said as he read it, "we must carry out the general in chief's order as nearly as we can, but as to the 'comfort' of the thing at Fort Lafayette, I don't know how we can manage it."

Never having seen the order of arrest, Stone now learned for the first time that McClellan had included some direction about his comfort in it. In a boat he crossed the bay to Fort Lafayette, where the lieutenant in command received him politely in his office, receipted for him, and took his cash for safekeeping. After a good breakfast from the officer's mess at Fort Hamilton, Stone moved into his new quarters, a part of the casemate vacated by some of the soldiers of the garrison. Now, he learned that he was to be denied communication with anyone.[21]

According to No. 79 of the Articles of War, passed in the embryonic stages of the country: "No officer who shall be put in arrest shall continue in confinement more than eight days or until such time as a court-martial can be assembled."[22] This law assured Stone a speedy release, and he must have known it. But, lo and behold, a week passed and more, without a sign that he would be freed. In fact, to all intents and purposes, it appeared as if he would never be set at liberty.

On the outside, Secretary of War Stanton intercepted all attempts at communication. A purely commiserative letter failed to receive clearance.[23] A request to visit the general also failed.[24]

In the days that followed Stone's arrest Allan Pinkerton accumulated numerous reports that tended to confirm Stone's disloyalty. A refugee from the Virginia side of the Potomac reported that, as a local militiaman, he had worked on a Confederate

---

21   Schoff Collection (Stone MS) (Univ. Mich.) letter dated November 5, 1866, from Stone to Lossing; Carter, *Four Brothers in Blue*, 45.

22   War Department, *Revised Regulations for the United States Army with a full Index*, 512, Article 79 (Philadelphia, 1861, Morningside reprint).

23   Quoted in full in *Cong. Globe*, 1663–1664.

24   *D.A.B.*, 9, pt. 2, p. 72; *Cong. Globe*, 1663.

fortification within range of Stone's artillery, had hoped Stone would stop the work by firing on it, but had been disappointed when nothing happened. Stone had written a letter to a Mrs. Mason saying that her farm, which was in Virginia two miles south of Point of Rocks, would be protected; that he was pleased to be stationed in an area where no great slaughter would occur; and that he did not wish to be involved in the great battle in front of Washington, where brother would kill brother.[25] Stone had sent slaves back to millowner Smart in Virginia after they escaped during the fighting at Ball's Bluff. Smart was not loyal and his mill was, in fact, supplying the Confederate army in the area. Smart had spoken very highly of Stone.[26]

"It is an established fact," wrote one of McClellan's informants, "that the mill was not only supplying the rebbel [sic] army in that section of the country but also furnishes the rebbel [sic] army at Manassas also." Stone should have closed it, he claimed.[27] In early January, Colonel John Geary's spies reported that the Rebels relied on Stone and that they could pass information through his lines.[28]

Stone's division, the Corps of Observation, added to the inflammatory information. When the senior brigade commander, Willis A. Gorman, assumed temporary command, he made it clear that he did not consider Stone guilty of anything and that no other officer who knew Stone believed him guilty of disloyalty.[29] George Meade wrote his wife, saying, "I must believe he is a victim of political malice, and that he will be vindicated from the charge of treachery and collusion with the enemy. You know I always told you his conduct was open to criticism, and I always wondered McClellan did not open an investigation. The 'Tribune' is becoming more violent and open in its attack on McClellan and all Regular officers."[30] Charles Hamilton, a brigade commander in Banks' division and a fellow West Point graduate, felt strongly enough to assume the risk of comparing himself with Stone, saying that "Stone was no more a traitor than I was."[31]

Major Wilder Dwight in the Second Massachusetts of Banks' division had a better vantage point and a more critical eye. A family member in Boston wrote him, "We were astounded yesterday by the reported arrest of Genl. Stone. Ball's Bluff is

25   McClellan MSS (L.C.) letter dated February 15, 1862, from Allen to McClellan.

26   McClellan MSS (L.C.) letter dated February 17, 1862, from Allen to McClellan.

27   McClellan MSS (L.C.) letter dated February 12, 1862, from Lander to McClellan.

28   Dwight Family MSS (L.C.) letter dated February 19, 1862, from Wilder to his mother.

29   Davis, *History of the 104th Pennsylvania*, 39.

30   Meade, *Meade's Letters*, 1, 245–246, letter dated February 11, 1862, from Meade to his wife.

31   Dwight Family MSS (M.H.S.) letter dated February 11, 1862, from Wilder to his mother.

as much a mystery [sic] today as on the day of the battle & I have the impression Stone was in fault [but] I cannot credit the charge of disloyalty. I fear he is to be made a scapegoat to satisfy the craving for vengeance on somebody."[32] Several days later Dwight described Stone's plight to his mother: "It is odd that I should not have spoken of Genl. Stone. I have only speculations on the case and it really is not one that interests me much. I had known for months of great dissatisfaction with him in some of the officers of his command and a general want of confidence among the troops. He certainly blundered Ball's Bluff, but his own mistakes were greatly aided by the blundering of Devens and perhaps Baker. I cannot believe him a traitor, if the charges made against him are those stated in the newspaper I can reconcile them all with his loyalty, by simply supposing him weak. His line on the Potomac had certainly been leaky. He has had communication with the rebels often. He has very many friends within the rebel army. His weakness and folly may have led him into such conduct that he has laid himself open to just suspicion. It is guessing on the outside facts. There may be proofs of other things than we know. But if he is a traitor he is the stupidest traitor that every betrayed . . . There is great abolition and political hostility against Stone, and I fear this has something to do with his arrest. One thing is true. McClellan is and has been his friend. Either he has been overborne in the arrest, or he knows facts that at least demand investigation."[33]

As it was with all controversial questions in the Army of the Potomac, the views throughout the officer corps had no unanimity. A junior officer in the Tenth Massachusetts wrote home in February at the time of Stone's arrest, "I think there can be no doubt but that Gen. Stone is a great traitor and I do not think they can be too soon about hanging him and all the rest of his stamp."[34]

On the edge of the army but not a part of it, George Templeton Strong wrote the assessment of an objective but generally uninformed civilian in his diary. "Everybody was astounded by the news that General Stone had been arrested," Strong wrote. "He is now in Fort Lafayette, charged, it is said, with treasonable correspondence. Very marvelous. That there has been treason somewhere in high quarters is certain, and if Stone be guilty, I hope he may be speedily hanged. He has had certain strong Southern affinities, vehemently anti-Abolition tendencies, undoubtedly." Because many had blamed Stone for the trouble at Ball's Bluff, Strong spec-

---

32   Dwight Family MSS (M.H.S.) letter dated February 11, 1862, from Thomas Dwight to Wilder Dwight.

33   Dwight Family MSS (M.H.S.) letter dated February 19, 1862, from Wilder Dwight to his mother.

34   Blight, *Brewster Letters*, 64, letter dated February 15, 1862, from Brewster to his mother.

ulated that Stone might have turned on his country and, in spirit, joined old friends in the Confederate army.[35]

Meanwhile, McClellan ordered Stone's papers, still in his hotel room and his headquarters, collected and put in Colburn's office.[36] After a few interim days McClellan assigned Brigadier General John K. Sedgwick, a brigade commander in Heintzelman's division, to command the Corps of Observation.[37] On February 20, after receiving orders to collect all Stone's papers, Sedgwick directed Lieutenant W. R. Hyslop, Stone's aide, to deliver Stone's public and private papers to division headquarters. Gorman, who had led the division as senior brigade commander, had sealed the papers in the presence of Generals Burns and Dana, the other brigade commanders. Sedgwick made no effort to segregate the public and private papers but asked that, after they had been examined, the public papers be returned to him for the division's records and Hyslop's private letters, caught in the sweep, sent to Hyslop, an aide to Stone.[38]

Dejected at Stone's arrest, Fitz John Porter said very little about it. Through his close friendship with McClellan, Porter no doubt learned promptly about the flood of incriminating "evidence" crossing McClellan's desk. His reticence showed that he was "afraid some of the charges were true," wrote Stephen Minot Weld, an officer on his staff. "I have heard him express no opinion on the matter lately."[39]

A few days after Stone's arrest, McClellan had apparently not yet recovered from it. He could have been distraught about an unfair fate for a man whose abilities he respected. He could have worried that the committee had enjoyed its first taste of blood, that it had taken a first indirect step against him, and that he could be next. He had narrowly escaped an attempt to put his army in McDowell's hands, an effort he saw driven by his former supporter, the secretary of the treasury. He could not now have felt as confident about his position as he had in the past. After tea on February 11, he went to the White House to visit the president, who was entertaining other distinguished guests including the new senator from Illinois, Orville Hickman Browning. Not his usual charming, engaging self, McClellan said little, leaving Browning with the impression that he was "not . . . big enough for his position."[40]

---

35 Nevins, *Strong Diary*, 3, 206, entry dated February 12, 1862.

36 McClellan MSS (L.C.) letter dated February 19, 1861, from Seth Williams to Colburn, endorsement by Colburn.

37 Winslow, Richard Elliott, III, *General John Sedgwick: The Story of a Union Corps Commander*, 5 (Presidio, 1982).

38 McClellan MSS (L.C.) letter dated February 21, 1861, Sedgwick to Williams.

39 Weld, *Diary and Letters*, 60, letter dated February 18, 1862, from Weld to Hannah.

40 Pease, *Browning Diary*, 1, 529, entry dated February 11, 1862.

As always, McClellan's views remained unexpressed and unknown. Although he had disagreed with Stanton's order of arrest, he had not chosen to make Stone's fate a battleground with the new secretary of war. If McClellan's conduct could be taken as any portent of the future, it said loudly that any predicaments in which a friend found himself would be his problem to solve. He would not risk himself by powerful intercession no matter how strongly he felt about his friend's innocence.

Unlike McClellan, Stone's faithful civilian friends would not allow him to languish in prison without attempting to obtain his release. Henry M. Parker, his brother-in-law, traveled from Boston to the Army of the Potomac, where he had a lengthy conversation with Seth Williams about prompt ways to exonerate Stone. He wished an immediate order issued for a court and a hearing scheduled for the earliest possible moment. If it could take place within a week, he strongly believed Stone would be free to return to active service by the time the army moved. He wanted Stone transferred to some place other than Fort Lafayette and, accompanied by a garrison officer, allowed exercise within the limits of the fort. Stone's books and papers, now under guard in his tent at Poolesville and his rooms in Washington, should be sent to him to enable him to prepare his defense while he was in custody. Parker and anyone else appointed to be Stone's counsel needed to be able to speak confidentially to him under no more restrictions than necessary.[41] Williams reduced the conversation to a concise memorandum he gave to Colburn with a request that it be laid before McClellan at once because he expected Parker to return that afternoon.[42] Parker should be told, McClellan responded, that Stone's case was still under investigation and that his trial would be held as soon as possible.[43]

41   McClellan MSS (L.C.) memorandum dated February 19, 1862, by Seth Williams of conversation with Henry Parker.

42   McClellan MSS (L.C.) letter dated February 19, 1861, from Seth Williams to Colburn.

43   McClellan MSS (L.C.) letter dated February 19, 1861, from Seth Williams to Colburn, endorsement by Colburn.

Chapter 30

"Stanton is certainly three parts lunatic."

—George Templeton Strong in his diary

McClellan and Stanton Start Their Own War

cClellan's relations with the new secretary of war took an immediate, rapid turn for the worse. Now dealing regularly with Stanton, an important member of the cabinet, on a broad range of subjects, McClellan had a method of discourse that would not have impressed the secretary. "In . . . deliberative conversation on matters of importance," wrote one of his aides after the war, "he was decidedly cautious, reticent, and when he did speak was rather slow of utterance, unless, indeed, he was conscious of holding all the data and had carefully considered them, in which case his speech was sufficiently copious and convincing. But on new ground he was disposed to leave the exploratory talking to others . . . Unlike the president and his cabinet, all of them lawyers, professional talkers whose practice was to think and argue aloud," he preferred to think with his brain, not with his mouth, and to some of them, probably including Stanton, he "seemed hesitating."[1]

About to become an important man in an era of great moral questions, Stanton himself had few morals and no scruples.[2] Next to Lincoln, a tall man of integrity, he stood a short master of deceit and duplicity. His protestations of friendship and

---

1   Biddle, "Recollections of McClellan" in *The United Service*, 9, 461 (May, 1894).

2   Piatt, *Memories*, 78–79, 89.

support for McClellan had probably been false from the beginning and intended only to enlist support for the cabinet position. But his strident integrity on fiscal matters set him apart from Cameron. During a social visit a former law student and partner sought a government contract for a friend.

"No talk on business here, William," said Stanton. "I'll hear you at the Department tomorrow."[3]

A few days after his confirmation he wrote to Charles A. Dana, a newspaper reporter, "As soon as I can get the machinery of the office working, the rats cleaned out, & the rathole stopped, we shall *move*. The army has got to fight or melt away; and while men are striking nobly in the west, the champagne & oysters on the Potomac must be stopped. But patience for a short while only is all I ask . . . "[4]

While he described his negative feelings about abolitionist generals and protested his loyalty to McClellan in order to obtain the general's support for his nomination, Stanton met Captain Donn Piatt on the street.

Was the report about the nomination true, Piatt asked.

"Yes," Stanton responded, "I am going to be secretary of war to Old Abe."

Piatt asked how he would reconcile his appointment with his contempt for the president.

"What will you do?"

"I intend to accomplish three things. I will make Abe Lincoln president of the United States. I will force this man McClellan to fight or throw up; and last, but not least, I will pick Lorenzo Thomas up with a pair of tongs and drop him from the nearest window."

When Stanton said he would make Lincoln president of the United States, he flagged the political-military issue, meant he would "relegate the young Napoleon" to his proper position as a subordinate, and intended to restore the president to a position of primacy, probably like that espoused by Bates. At the time of his appointment Stanton already believed, as his provost marshal for the District of Columbia would write after the war, that, "a military aristocracy of the Regular Army and of immense power had arisen in the bosom of the army of volunteers. This aristocracy had as [its] head the commander in chief."[5]

3　Jerome, Edward S., "Edwin McMasters Stanton: the Great War Secretary," in *Broadfoot MOLLUS Ohio*, 7, 376.

4　Dana MSS (L.C.) letter dated January 24, 1862, from Stanton to Dana.

5　Piatt, *Memories of Men*, 57–59; Doster, *Lincoln and Episodes*, 124–125. At least some people in Washington considered Thomas' loyalty to be questionable, and Stanton, because he had no other reason to make the statement, must have been one, Gurowski, *Diary*, 1, 124, entry dated November 1862.

The secretary demanded that General Ripley, the benighted head of the Bureau of Ordnance, come to the War Department to defend a firing mechanism for an infantry weapon. When Ripley arrived, he found Stanton by the window examining the lock with a contractor.

How many had he acquired, the secretary wanted to know.

Ripley gave the number.

A Zeus-like frown.

"If you dare to adopt another musket of this kind, I'll dismiss you from the service."

"But, Mr. Secretary . . ." interrupted Ripley.

"Not another word. You can return to your bureau."

Flushed from the embarrassing abuse and "shaking as if struck with the palsy," Ripley passed through the waiting crowd, all of whom had witnessed the scene. The threat of dismissal acquired common usage.

But not all recoiled in horrified submission from the secretary's lightning bolts. A Pennsylvania judge sought an extension of leave for his son, a colonel who had not yet recovered from a wound.

Stanton turned to the colonel and in "an extremely insolent way" ordered him to be gone. The colonel limped from the meeting. The judge had seen enough of life to know a bully when he saw one. He rose from his chair.

"Sir, my son will not go to his regiment to die. He will go with me to the president, your superior officer, who will grant my reasonable request."

Stanton "stood as one in a trance" and made no response.

People willing to face Stanton's coarse arrogance and abuse might even prevail. A fat, wealthy butcher from Pennsylvania wanted a pass to deliver new blankets to his two sons and others who had lost them in a December battle. Imperative orders forbade transportation of civilians forward to the battlefield. The butcher nevertheless pushed his way through the crowd and presented his request.

Stanton refused.

He turned to the next supplicant.

The butcher refused to retire cowed.

"Well," he said. "How many sons have you got at Fredericksburg? I guess not many or you wouldn't want to freeze mine!"

Stanton issued the pass.[6]

Arbitrary, arrogant, capricious, course, and unfair, he nevertheless kept his hands free of all cliques and became a hard-working lawyer with one and only one

6   Doster, *Lincoln and Episodes*, 119, 120, 121, 123–124.

client, his country as it was embodied in its government. His client had a case, a huge case of great moment, a war to crush the South and free the slaves, as Stanton saw it; and he must win it without regard for the niceties of principle. A man with no friends to repay, he became a man with no friends and with no desire for friends. Unresponsive to high military concepts or political authority or sentiment, for all his ruthless disregard of human complaint, he never refused to alleviate real distress—at once—and took pleasure in "conferring a kindness as quickly as he is satisfied the object is deserving."[7]

In early February 1862, Stanton decided he should receive regular information about army affairs. In some cases information that affected the financial markets appeared without authorization in newspapers. He concluded that a leak existed somewhere, suspected the Telegraph Department, and assigned Assistant Secretary of War Peter H. Watson to investigate. After a week Watson reported that he could not find the leak but also reported that Thomas T. Eckert, a telegrapher, did not give careful attention to his duties and withheld important military dispatches from the president and the secretary. Stanton prepared an order for Eckert's dismissal and telegraphed Edward S. Sanford, president of the American Telegraph Company, to come from New York to take charge of the Military Telegraph.

Sanford knew Eckert, for whose abilities, faithfulness, and honesty he had high regard. He stated this to Stanton. Mindlessly stubborn, Stanton continued to believe Watson's report about Eckert; and when Eckert learned from Sanford about Stanton's dissatisfaction with his service, he immediately sent his resignation by messenger to the War Department. Stanton reacted with fury: an officer had been warned to resign before he could be dismissed. Sanford found himself in an unpleasant situation. He went to Stanton's house early Sunday morning to intercede for Eckert, then he and Eckert went to the War Department Sunday afternoon to meet with Stanton. Eckert and Sanford stood for ten minutes. Taking a page from McClellan's book, Stanton continued to write at his desk without looking at them. Finally, he turned and asked Eckert what he wanted.

"Mr. Sanford tells me that you sent for me," Eckert said, "and I am here."

In a loud voice, Stanton said he understood that Eckert had been neglecting his duties, was absent from his office much of the time, allowed newspapermen access to the office, and was unfit for his important position. He pointed to a large pile of telegrams in Eckert's handwriting and demanded to know why Eckert had not sent copies to the secretary of war when he received them.

Eckert replied that his orders from Secretary Cameron expressly required the delivery of all military telegrams to the commanding general and to no one else.

7   *Ibid.*, 115–114, 126.

Applying the tactic of a good trial lawyer whose line of cross-examination had gone astray, Stanton switched to another subject.

"Well, why have you neglected your duties by absenting yourself from your office so frequently?"

Eckert replied that he had not neglected his duties, that he had attended to them strictly and faithfully, and that any statements to the contrary were false. For more than three months he had been at his post almost constantly and had hardly taken off his clothing during that time except to change his linen. He remained in his office many times all night and seldom slept in his bed. Finally, he said, since it appeared that his services were not satisfactory, he insisted that his resignation be accepted.

Eckert felt a hand on his shoulder. He supposed it was Sanford, who was standing behind him, but when he turned, he was surprised to see the president.

With his hand still on Eckert's shoulder, Lincoln said to Stanton, "Mr. Secretary, I think you must be mistaken about this young man neglecting his duties, for I have been a daily caller at General McClellan's headquarters for the last three or four months, and I have always found Eckert at his post. I have been there often before breakfast and in the evening as well, and frequently late at night, and several times before daylight, to get the latest news from the army. Eckert was always there, and I never observed any reporters or outsiders in the office."

John Brough, a newspaper editor of Ohio, had also entered the room. He went to Eckert, shook his hand, and addressed him cordially. Then he turned to Stanton.

"I will vouch for anything Eckert says or does because I believe him to be the ablest and most loyal man for the position."

Stanton was impressed by the intercession of Lincoln, Sanford, and Brough. Deep in his character, well below his venomous instincts, his old sense of fairness and decency survived. He took from his desk a package of papers and selected one.

"I believe this is your resignation, is it not, sir?"

Eckert replied that it was.

Stanton tore it into pieces and dropped them on the floor. He opened another paper.

"This is the order dismissing you from the army, which I had already signed, but it will not be executed." He destroyed the order, too. "I owe you an apology, Captain, for not having gone to General McClellan's office and seen for myself the situation of affairs. You are no longer Captain Eckert. I shall appoint you Major as soon as the commission can be made out; and I shall make you a further acknowledgment in another manner," a horse and carriage to be purchased for Eckert's use in the performance of his official duties.

The next day Stanton detached Eckert from McClellan's staff and ordered him to move his office to the War Department and to connect all telegraph wires with the War Office building. He left enough instruments at army headquarters to handle the separate business of the commanding general.[8]

Stanton's light-hearted, happy disposition of prewar days had vanished. The extraordinary strain of his new position, wrote Don Piatt after the war, overwhelmed "the great Secretary's nervous system, and not only deepened the gloomy spells to which he was addicted, but made him so irritable and impatient that official business with subordinates often resulted in insults. All about him approached in fear and trembling. And the ugliness seemed to be contagious. The officer coming from his presence, wounded to the quick, gave to others under him the same treatment."[9]

Close association with Lincoln created no immunity against Stanton's abusive treatment. John Hay wrote to Nicolay, "Don't, in a sudden spasm of good-nature, send any more people with letters to me requesting favors from Stanton. I would rather make the tour of a small-pox hospital."[10]

McClellan found he had difficulty gaining access to the new secretary of war. While Stanton, Fitz John Porter, and McClellan were in McClellan's office, the new secretary committed "very indecorous conduct" intended, as Porter saw it, to insult McClellan in front of another officer. Whatever Stanton's real intent, brusque or malicious, both McClellan and Porter took it as an intentional personal affront; and from that day forward, Stanton and McClellan had no cordiality in their dealings. As far as McClellan and his friends were concerned, Stanton, instead of assisting McClellan, threw every obstacle in his way and did all he could to create distrust between the general and the president.[11]

When Stanton met his officers at his first reception, he affirmed his statement to Piatt.

"Now, gentlemen, we will, if you please, have some fighting. It is my business to furnish the means. It is yours to use them. I leave the fighting to you, but the fighting we must have."[12]

This attitude, which he shared with the Joint Committee, conflicted with his perception of McClellan, whose friend Sam Barlow did not help his cause. Barlow

8   Bates, David H., *Lincoln in the Telegraph Office: Recollections of the United States Military Telegraph Corps during the Civil War*, 132–137 (New York, 1907), indirect discourse converted to direct.

9   Piatt, *Memories of Men*, 62–63.

10   Dennett, *Hay Letters and Diary*, 1, 129, letter dated November 25, 1863, from Hay to Nicolay.

11   Porter MSS (L.C.) letters dated August 3, 1888, from Porter to Benjamin; and dated June 13, 1881, from Burns to Webb; *M.O.S.*, 153–154; Military Historical Society of Massachusetts MSS (John C. Ropes letters) (B.U.) letter dated March 27, 1895, from Biddle to Ropes; *M.O.S.*, 153–154.

12   Piatt, *Memories of Men*, 61.

had written to a friend describing terms on which the North could negotiate an end to the war. In his opinion the Southern leaders would accept the following:

- the president to be elected by a majority of Southern states and a majority of Northern states with proper provisions in case of non-election.
- no law to be passed affecting slavery that did not receive the vote of a majority of both the slave states and the free states.
- the war debt of each section to be borne by that section.[13]

Barlow's correspondent promptly endorsed the letter and forwarded it to Stanton.[14] Knowing that McClellan and Barlow were good friends and probably thinking they were political allies, Stanton would have assumed this program for a negotiated peace, an unthinkable end to the war, had McClellan's blessing.

"This man has no heart in the cause," Stanton said about the general in chief. "He is fighting for a boundary if he fights at all. Our great difficulty is to make him fight at all."[15]

The fighting, particularly battlefield tactics, he may have decided to leave to the military. But the management of military affairs, including the structure of McClellan's army? He would have much to say about that. Two days after he took office on January 20, Stanton met with Dennis Hart Mahan, visiting Washington on one of his periodic trips from the Military Academy. They had a long conversation about military affairs. As Mahan prepared to leave, Stanton raised two issues that held the attention of both the president and the Radical Republicans on the investigating committee: the organization of corps and the duties of a chief of staff.[16] Stanton believed these issues too important to leave to a commanding general he did not trust.[17]

13   Stanton MSS (L.C.) letter dated January 28, 1862, from Barlow to Pierrepont.

14   Stanton MSS (L.C.) endorsement dated January 28, 1862, to Stanton from Pierrepont, on letter dated January 28, 1862, from Barlow to Pierrepont.

15   Piatt, *Memories of Men*, 75–76.

16   Mahan MSS (U.S.M.A.) letter dated February 16, 1862, from Mahan to n.a.

17   The issue of corps, already one of widespread discussion and correspondence, loomed large on the military agenda of the day. Although the corps had no history in the United States, whose armies had not fielded units larger than a brigade, they had dominated the Napoleonic Wars on both sides. Everywhere he had enough men, Napoleon created them almost at once. The British army, ruled less by the unified authority of one man, muddled through brigades, to divisions, back to brigades, and at the end under Wellington to corps. Elting, John R., *Swords around a Throne: Napoleon's Grand Armée*, 58–59 (New York, 1988); Ward, S. P. G., *Wellington's Headquarters: A Study of the Administrative Problems in the Peninsula, 1809–1814*, 48–52 (Oxford, 1957).

A man who attached himself to new ideas with the fervor of a religious convert, Stanton would become intractable on those that appealed to him. Taking a page from the Joint Committee's book of charges against McClellan, Stanton began to express himself strongly in favor of the creation of corps and to identify specific candidates for corps command.[18] He toyed with the assignment of divisions to the three or four corps he might create. The sheets recording these various alignments designated no corps commanders, merely the grouping of divisions. Not an exercise in the advancement of favorites, Stanton's jottings reflected a military program with which Stanton wished to override the general in chief.[19]

Probably to persuade others that Scott was interfering with the proper development of the Army of the Potomac, McClellan claimed toward the end of Scott's tenure that he wanted to create corps for McDowell, Franklin, and Heintzelman but that Scott would not agree.[20] As always, McClellan's priorities ran deeper than the surface issue of a few corps commanders. He was not ready to appoint corps commanders; or, more likely, he did not believe the president and the new secretary ready for his choices. Stanton mentioned to McClellan that Heintzelman should have a corps when they were created. Finding himself in a dilemma, McClellan opposed Stanton's idea. On an issue so personal to the commander of the Army of the Potomac and so early in the secretary's tenure, Stanton probably felt he needed support he did not have. He thought Heintzelman should have one of the corps and urged him to press the issue with the president. At the least he convinced Heintzelman that he would have his way on the question no matter what McClellan wanted.[21]

The secretary did not limit himself to issues involving the structure of the Army of the Potomac, nor did he consider himself excluded from the areas McClellan deemed sacred to the military. In the realm of the unthinkable, tactics and strategy, Stanton urged McClellan to transfer fifty thousand men from the Army of the Potomac to the West to strengthen Buell and Halleck. He had transportation ready. McClellan would not agree "because he thinks it may interfere with his plans here although I believe he will still have enough left for any movement he can make," Stanton wrote.

---

18   Heintzelman MS diary (large diary) (L.C.) entry dated February 21, 1862.

19   Stanton MSS (L.C.) memorandum attached to draft of General War Order No. 2 and separate memorandum.

20   Chandler MSS (L.C.) letter dated March 8, 1862, from Gurowski to Chandler; Heintzelman MS diary (large diary) (L.C.) entry dated February 10, 1862.

21   Heintzelman MS diary (large diary) (L.C.) entry dated February 21, 1862.

To command the powderkeg of the West, the State of Missouri, Stanton wanted to assign Ethan Allen Hitchcock, a peculiar, even bizarre, man with a noteworthy family background. Once again, McClellan did not approve the appointment, but Halleck had requested it, and Scott had strongly recommended it. Stanton decided that, McClellan's opposition or not, he would make the appointment, and he did.[22]

Stanton believed that a strong distrust of the government had crept into the army, that the West Point graduates were predominately pro-slavery Democrats, and that with few exceptions the West Point graduates despised the rule of the abolitionists. "This feeling arose from the additional fact that West Point is more of a social feature than a military school, and as reformers are not fashionable, seldom, if ever, even respectable, the cadet had a horror of the howling Abolitionist," wrote Piatt after the war.[23]

George Templeton Strong's diary showed that Stanton's conduct would change the early laudatory comments about his appointment as secretary of war. "Stanton is certainly three parts lunatic," Strong recorded later.[24]

The secretary's foul disposition and poor memory combined to inflict suffering on his subordinates. Many people believed he took "a malevolent delight in browbeating his subordinates . . . every now and then making a spectacle of some poor officer or soldier." He called Captain Piatt to serve as judge advocate of a commission to investigate the conduct of General Don Carlos Buell in Tennessee.

When told of this, Piatt said, "This is all very well, Mr. Secretary, but I'd like to know where you find a law to sanction such a court as this."

"My noble captain," replied the secretary, his short upper lip curled slightly and his white teeth and dark eyes gleaming in an intimidating expression, "You are commissioned to obey orders, and not to study law, for it is rather late in life for you to begin that. When I need a legal advisor it is not likely I will call on Judge Piatt. If I am to be met here with the quibble of a county-court lawyer, I will find some other officer."

The sarcasm stung Piatt. In fact, he had become a judge at the age of twenty-five and had been a practicing lawyer before that. He hid the wound.

---

22   Stanton MSS (L.C.) draft letter dated February 21, 1862, from Stanton to Scott.

23   Piatt, *Memories of Men*, 75.

24   Nevin, *Strong Diary*, 3, entry dated August 10, 1862. Major General Ethan Allan Hitchcock, a fussy grandmother more interested in alchemy and spiritualism than in military service, also saw Stanton as a man without reason, short of memory, and given to outbreaks of rage at the people around him. Croffut MSS, tr. of Hitchcock MS Diary (L.C.) entry dated September 30, 1863.

"All right; but I would suggest that this is no ordinary inquiry, and a court should be made up of the ablest officers."

"That is true. You go to the list of officers not on duty and I will appoint from that."

The next day Piatt sought the secretary with a list of officers in his hand. He met Stanton on the street headed for his office. Piatt walked with him, explaining what he had done. Stanton was in a terrible mood. He did not look at Piatt or speak to him. At his office, one of his staff opened the door. Stanton entered, then slammed the door in Piatt's face. Piatt turned, saw a man he knew, and began to talk with him. A messenger appeared from the secretary's room. After looking about in a terrified manner, he asked Piatt if he were "Captain Piety."

"All but the piety."

"Well, I guess you're the man," he said. "The secretary wants you."

Piatt entered Stanton's chambers. The secretary was seated alone at the end of his table. He looked up and said, "Don, what in the hell do you want?"

"Nothing, sir. Not even civil treatment. You directed me to make out a list of officers to compose the Buell court. I have done so and only came to report the names."

"Take them to Halleck," who had come east. "That is his business," roared the secretary. "I can't run the War Department, let alone trying to run Halleck. Go to him."

"Mr. Secretary," Piatt responded quietly, "I don't mind being jumped on by you any more than if it were my elder brother, but I won't be insulted by General Halleck as you know I will be if I go as you direct."

"Insulted?" Stanton responded angrily while he hastily wrote a note. "I'll see to that. Here, take him this."

Piatt took it with him and appeared before "the great Art of War." Halleck reminded him of two lines in an old ballad:

> *His head being larger than common*
> *O'erbalanced the rest of his fat.*

Halleck read the note. Tearing it in two and dropping it in the wastebasket, he said with all the sarcasm his dull face allowed, "What is your address, Captain?"

Piatt explained his purpose. Halleck rose from his chair, bowed mockingly, and added, with such superb sarcasm that Piatt felt compelled to admire him for it, "When I need your assistance, I shall certainly send for you, *captain*."

Piatt retired as gracefully as possible and reported to Stanton.

"Damn his insolence!" stormed the secretary. "Why didn't you pull his nose?"

"Because the insult was directed to you," answered Piatt. "I was only the poor devil of a captain assigned to the duty of carrying it. I wish to God I was out of this."

Stanton was amused. He burst into laughter and said, "Oh, never mind Halleck. He can't insult anyone. Take the court he gives you, and do the best you can."

Seeing that Piatt was deeply hurt, Stanton put his arm around his shoulders "in his old caressing way" and said, "Don't mind me, we are both hasty. This is important business I give you, and I know I can trust you."[25]

Stanton's imperfect recollection caused many problems. A Jewish member of Congress named Strauss had a Jewish friend in Virginia. The friend had crossed from Confederate to Union lines and delivered himself to Benjamin Butler at Fort Monroe. When he surrendered, he had with him between fifty thousand and seventy-five thousand dollars, which Butler took in exchange for a receipt.

Later the man appeared in Washington to request his money. He and Strauss went to the War Department where they bothered Stanton greatly but without success. Finally Stanton sent for Assistant Secretary Charles A. Dana.

"Strauss is after me. He wants that money, and I want you to settle the matter," said Stanton.

"What shall I do? What are the orders?"

Stanton took the relevant papers and endorsed them on the back, "Referred to Mr. Dana, Assistant Secretary of War, to be settled as in his judgment shall deem best. E. M. Stanton."

Dana looked into the matter, determined that the man was entitled to the money, and returned it to him. The next day Stanton sent for Dana. He was angry.

"Did you give that Jew back his money?" he asked in a harsh tone.

"Yes, sir."

"Well, I should like to know by what authority you did it."

Dana responded, "If you will excuse me while I go to my room, I will show my authority to you."

Dana departed, returned with the paper, and read the endorsement aloud. Then he gave it to Stanton.

Stanton looked at it and laughed, saying, "You are right. You have got me this time."[26]

Even with Stanton's support, the Radicals lacked the power and the evidence to launch a full-scale assault on McClellan. But they could begin an implacable campaign of erosion, taking every opportunity to demand his replacement. Intentionally

---

25 Piatt, *Memories of Men*, 64–67.

26 Dana, *Recollections*, 157–161.

or not, conspiratorially or by independent choice, Stanton helped them as often as he could. Although he had no power to convey command of the Army of the Potomac, he began to offer it to others, a practice, he must have known, that would undermine McClellan's position. When Ethan Allen Hitchcock, who had attended West Point only because of the Ethan Allen heritage in his family, arrived reluctantly in Washington to accept a post as an adviser, Stanton immediately offered him command of the army.[27] And to thwart McClellan he asked others for their strategic and campaign suggestions.[28]

Like Stanton and Chase, the Joint Committee had its own candidates for major military posts. Lincoln had removed John Charles Fremont from command in the West for more reasons than his decree freeing the slaves in his area. The reports by Meigs, Blair, Pope, Hunter, Lorenzo Thomas, and others all pointed to vast waste and fraud in the administration of his department and a severe lack of military competence on his part.[29] Although without a command, Fremont did not fall to the trash-heap of discarded generals. He had many powerful supporters who expressed themselves strongly in his favor. In effect, he had demanded that abolition be a war measure. To the Radicals his attitude toward slavery proved his military capacity and qualified him for high command. Even after his travails and failings had been publicly aired in a debate conducted, in part, among major daily newspapers in New York City,[30] Fremont, the general, benefitted when the members of the Joint Committee commenced their own "investigation." As in all things, the committee began with its conclusion already in hand and proved its predispositions: Fremont was a victim of the enemies of abolition; the charges against him had no merit.[31]

---

27   Croffut MSS, tr. of Hitchcock MS Diary (L.C.), entry dated March 15, 1862.

28   Stanton MSS (L.C.), letter dated January 30, 1862, from James Shields to Stanton; and letter dated February 10, 1862, from Fremont to Stanton; Herr and Spence, *Jessie Benton Fremont Letters*, 311–312, letter dated February 7, 1862, from J. B. Fremont to Billings.

29   Tap, *Over Lincoln's Shoulder*, 83–84; Nevins, *Fremont*, 530–535.

30   Nevins, *Fremont*, 524–527; Rolle, *Fremont*, 207.

31   Tap, *Over Lincoln's Shoulder*, 86, 87, 88, 89; see generally *C.C.W.*, 3, 32, 33–43, 43–153 (Fremont). In a manner very favorable to Fremont and unlike the treatment of Stone, the Committee chose an unusual format. On the first of Fremont's appearances (January 10) he appeared with a mound of documents to support his expected testimony on predictable subjects. The Committee asked him to prepare a written statement "of such matters as you may deem important, connected with your administration of the Western Department." The Committee would then ask questions if it deemed them necessary . . . no probing, no shrewd cross-examination, no hostile, unanswerable, hyperbolic questions (*ibid.*, 32). Fremont's long statement incorporating many documents found its way into the record on January 17 (*ibid.*, 33–43). Fremont reappeared for lengthy testimony on January 30, at the end attaching another large collection of documents selected by him (*ibid.*, 43–77, testimony; 78–153, documents).

The thought that the committee should conduct an impartial, objective, inductive investigation never occurred to its members.

Meanwhile, Fremont had left the Midwest and moved with his beautiful but ferocious wife to the Astor House in New York City.[32] By his visible role on the question of emancipation, Fremont had accumulated extraordinary support: Greeley and the *Tribune*, Wade, Chandler, Lincoln's friend Orville Hickman Browning, and others. Subjected to great pressure to restore Fremont to a responsible command, Lincoln could not ignore him, especially in the early part of the war when political considerations played a commanding role in promotions and assignments.[33]

This became clear at the ball Mrs. Lincoln scheduled for February 5, which she intended to be a White House affair without equal. She invited six hundred to seven hundred guests, including Fremont and many other members of the military. Claiming that the existing state of war should preclude revelry, Senator Wade and other Radicals refused to attend.[34] Unfortunately, Willie Lincoln fell seriously ill with typhoid shortly before the event and had reached a state near death by the scheduled night.[35] When confronted with the family illness, Lincoln wanted to cancel the ball, but too many plans and commitments had been made.

Still offended by the treatment Lincoln had given them, the Fremonts declined the president's invitation. Lincoln made a personal point of sending Judge Corwin of Cincinnati with a special message expressing good will and telling Fremont that he did not wish Fremont's absence to be a subject of comment.[36] Fremont chose to treat the invitation as the equivalent of a military order. Jessie must relent and agree to attend, he insisted.

The ball took place in great splendor, women appearing in their best finery.[37] Early in the evening an announcement was made that, because of the family illness, the ball would have no dancing but would be a dinner with the usual social conversation.[38] For the number of people the rooms were too crowded, Heintzelman noted

---

32   Herr and Spence, *Jessie Benton Fremont Letters*, 298–301, letter dated December 14 and addendum dated December 14, 1861, from Fremont to Fields.

33   Meade, *Meade's Letters*, 1, 246, letter dated February 11, 1862, from Meade to his wife; Rolle, *Fremont*, 207.

34   Williams, *Lincoln and the Radicals*, 105.

35   Meirs, *Lincoln Day by Day*, 94–96, February 1862.

36   Fremont MS memoirs (U.C. Berkeley) typescript, 328; Williams, *Lincoln and the Radicals*, 105.

37   Washington *Star*, February 6, 1862, quoted in Miers, *Lincoln Day-by-Day*, 93, February 5, 1862.

38   Fremont MS rem. (U.C. Berkeley), 328; handwritten mem. by Jessie Benton Fremont, dated April 10, 1890, 9–10.

in his diary, and the supper room seemed hardly larger than his own parlor. To the annoyance of some of the guests, the cramped space delayed service, dinner not being served until midnight. In spite of the prohibition against dancing because of Willie Lincoln's condition, "the discordant old Marine Band blazed away," wrote Jessie Fremont many years later. McClellan, Heintzelman, Stone, Marcy, and other representatives of the Army of the Potomac attended. Ellen McClellan and her mother, Mrs. Marcy, appeared among the guests,[39] the sharp-eyed critics noting that the general in chief's wife wore the colors of secession, a white dress with a band of red velvet from shoulder to waist and three scarlet and white feathers in her hair.

Written almost thirty years later, Jessie's account of the ball showed her lasting bitterness. As she and John entered, she still harbored a strong resentment at the treatment given her by Lincoln when she delivered her husband's note in September. Bowing politely, she did not speak. But she knew that Willie lay upstairs dying and saw the president "haggard with anxious grief." John Fremont expressed their hopes for Willie's recovery, and they passed into the crowd.

Jessie found the guests gravitating toward her husband as the majority of the crowd congregated on the side of the East Room where he stood. "The whole talk," she wrote, "was on the necessary peremptory pursuit of the war to make the South realize that it could not maintain slavery under the protection of the North . . . many criticized the conduct of the war . . . and there was so much feeling of sorrow expressed that General Fremont's policy of Emancipation was not to be carried out,—that it was becoming embarrassing." They prepared to leave, but as Jessie began to don her wraps, Senator Charles Sumner arrived with a message from the president, who had discovered that Fremont and McClellan had never met. He wanted his generals to know each other, Sumner said, and requested that Fremont return in order to be introduced.

Sumner gave Mrs. Fremont his arm, and the three of them started across the East Room. Lincoln came to meet them, took Fremont by the arm, introduced the two generals, and introduced the two wives. Lincoln, Fremont, and McClellan stood in conversation a few minutes while the wives maintained a firm silence.[40]

Criticized for failing to drive the Confederates, for losing a battle by failure to reinforce, for allowing another force to be cut off, for the corruption of his subordinates, and for fractious ineptitude, Fremont still held the trump card: his proclama-

---

39   Heintzelman MS diary (large diary) (L.C.) entry dated February 6, 1862; Fremont MSS (U.C. Berkeley) handwritten mem. by Jessie Benton Fremont dated April 10, 1890.

40   Fremont MSS (U.C. Berkeley) Fremont MS rem. (U.C. Berkeley) typescript, 329; handwritten mem. by Jessie Benton Fremont, dated August 10, 1890, 9–10.

tion of emancipation. The conversations at the non-dancing ball showed that he would return in another high military position, whether or not Lincoln liked it.[41] Was he a threat to McClellan? Could he possibly lead the nation's largest and most important army? Even if the president opposed, would his choice be overborne by the combined force of the Radicals and the members of the Joint Committee?

Before the ball, the Joint Committee had met with the secretary of war to announce the result of its Fremont "investigation." According to Jessie, the members "told him that everything was more than explained & justified in regard to Mr. Fremont's Dept. and that they came to ask for him a command."

Stanton responded that he had awaited the committee's decision. He would arrange a position, one "of which his friends should have nothing to complain— that it would give him ample scope for his military talent & satisfy their pride as well as the Genls."[42]

On the day after the ball Fremont had an unscheduled meeting with Lincoln. The president, though distraught at Willie's illness, wanted to talk to him.[43]

Unlike Fremont, McClellan had not created enough problems to destroy his position with the president, who had no candidate to replace him and who did not want to replace him. But McClellan had a wide and powerful group of opponents, including the abolitionist Radical Republicans, particularly the members of the Joint Committee, who were the most powerful and the most intransigent. Chase stood in the background with his candidate McDowell and the Joint Committee with its favorite Fremont.

The committee's "investigation" had collected testimony from favorably disposed witnesses, carefully avoided most of the witnesses who could convict the general, and taken Fremont's testimony without the unfair treatment Stone received. On the day of the Lincolns' ball, Benjamin Wade wrote a letter that again showed the spurious nature of the claim of confidentiality. "The character of so many persons and the deep and excited feeling of the community are so involved in Fremont's case that it may be long before the committee can complete their investigations especially as the witnesses are so remote and widely scattered and it is a settled rule of the committee to keep everything secret until the final publication. But, in strict privacy, I will say this to you, that the investigation has proceeded far

---

41 Tap, *Over Lincoln's Shoulder*, 87, 93.

42 Herr and Spence, *Jessie Benton Fremont Letters*, 309–310, letter dated January 21, 1862, from J. B. Fremont to Billings.

43 Herr and Spence, *Jessie Benton Fremont Letters*, 34, letter dated February 7, 1862, from J. B. Fremont to Billings.

enough to convince beyond a doubt that no public man since Admiral Byng was sacrificed by a weak and wicked Administration to appease the wrath of an indignant people has suffered so unjustly as Genl. Fremont."[44]

The committee produced the desired exoneration. In fact, after Fremont's first session with the committee Jessie could report to a family friend, "The Committee were, a part of them, for deciding the case then & there on its reading. The Chairman, Mr. Wade, said no witnesses were needed and that it was all proved up & every charge against Mr. Fremont exploded. Some technicalities prevailed, but the thing is fixed. . . ."[45]

Fremont had joined McDowell and Hitchcock in the wings, where they waited with very different attitudes for future developments, but all with support for them to replace McClellan.

44   Dana MSS (L.C.) letter dated February 5, 1862, from Wade to Dana.

45   Herr and Spence, *Jessie Benton Fremont Letters*, 309–310, letter dated January 21, 1862, from J. B. Fremont to Billings.

Chapter 31

The New McClellan

*M*cClellan's illness led to, if it did not cause, many significant changes; and these alterations would produce many effects. At the top of the list were the differences in the working personalities of the general in chief and the commander in chief. Neither man tended to explain himself, and neither explained his new persona to the other. On military and political questions McClellan and Lincoln had begun their association at opposite ends of the pole. After their changes of personality they continued to stand poles apart. Would either of them recognize the unstated change in the other? Would recognition come in time? Would either adjust to the different circumstances? More subtle, more difficult, more impossible for virtually all men, would either recognize a change developing and give it enough time to reach productivity?

At the least the early stages of transition became perceivable in the months of February and March. From the limited encounters of the fall, the drills, and the reviews, McClellan had changed his Mexican War attitude toward a volunteer army and concluded that the Army of the Potomac had achieved readiness for an offensive campaign.

Although McClellan's strong constitution and great resilience had allowed him to nip the McDowell coup in the bud, he knew after the January meetings that he faced significantly different circumstances, that he must protect himself against

McDowell, and that he must end the rumors that Fremont, Halleck, or Wade would become general in chief in his place.

Probably governed by the usual youthful belief in his own immortality, he had never considered the need for a substitute; and the idea that he might fall before an invisible, insidious foe like typhoid would never have occurred to him.[1] For Lincoln, Chase, and others one of the most troublesome aspects of McClellan's illness had been the lack of a knowledgeable man to take his place. Much like former President James K. Polk's plan to promote Thomas Hart Benton in order to prevent Scott, a potential political competitor, from heading the Mexico City column, the rumors about successors lacked reality and substance. But they must have seemed real to McClellan and probably disturbed him. For general in chief, for command of the Army of the Potomac, and for military primacy he had a real competitor for the first time. Scott had held McClellan back by stacis and had kept his own high position by inertia, neither of which required any support, activity, or effort. Unlike Scott, McDowell had formidable active support from powerful constituents like Chase, Wade, Chandler, and the Joint Committee; and he had the potential to be an active adversary. McClellan had blocked the January "coup" because the precipitating cause, his illness, had ended and left the Radical opposition without an irresistible basis for demanding change. He had not prevailed by well-organized support.

To avoid this problem in the future, he would take the advice Chase had suggested in the letter to his daughter, Chase had presumably given him, and the Joint Committee had investigated. He would take selected subordinates into his confidence by telling them his full plans. As soon as he felt well enough, he called his best friends and most trusted subordinates, William B. Franklin, Fitz John Porter, and Baldy Smith, to meet in his house, where he spread a large map on the dining room table and in much detail explained his plans for the decisive campaign. He described the strategic relationships among operations by Sherman and Burnside on the coast, the Army of the Potomac down the Chesapeake, and the armies of Halleck and Buell in Tennessee and Kentucky. Much time he spent explaining the strokes planned for east Kentucky and east Tennessee. Consistent with his explanation to Lincoln, the president's "advisors," and Ives, he said the Army of the Potomac would move as soon as the other armies had attracted enough Confederate military attention to prevent concentration against him. He had explained this, he told them, to Halleck over the telegraph wires. But he never finished this part of the conversation, particularly the description of the coastal operations. An "attack of faintness" ended the meeting by forcing him to retire.[2]

1   Heintzelman MS diary (large diary) (L.C.) entries dated February 13 and March 8, 1862.

2   Porter MSS (L.C.) letter dated May 9, 1895, from Franklin to Porter.

As a result of the failed coup by McDowell, he resolved to abandon his pathological secrecy, explain his plans to civilians, act at once, and undertake projects he deemed prejudicial to the proper course of military affairs.

The Confederate batteries on the Potomac River, the irritation on his left, and the Baltimore and Ohio Railroad beyond Harpers Ferry, the right flank annoyance, needed relief but not for military reasons. McClellan accepted the fact that he must address these complications on his flanks even though he considered them insignificant at their worst. Between the January meetings and the end of the month, he devised solutions and set them in motion.

McClellan probably considered the Potomac batteries easy to solve. Hooker, whose division held the Maryland bank of the Potomac below Washington, had proposed various attacks on the batteries on the Virginia shore below the mouth of the Occoquan River.[3] His division alone, however, lacked the strength to hold a position across the river.

McClellan questioned R. J. Williamson, a topographical engineer who had already submitted numerous reports on the batteries,[4] about a "dash" across the Potomac with part of Hooker's division. Williamson answered a week after the last of the "illness" meetings. Confederate batteries at Evansport and Shipping Point, after months of construction, had great strength, double rows of palisades, and landward fortifications against infantry attacks. Because he had not been down the river since early December, Williamson felt less certain about other positions but knew from newspaper accounts that the Rebels had constructed emplacements at Possum Nose and Cockpit Point. He believed these could not have great strength. Even the older, larger forts could be seen from Budds Ferry to have few guns.[5]

On January 20, 1862, the day Stanton officially took office, McClellan drafted a letter to Hooker: could an assault be made on the Rebel batteries opposite his position? Even if Hooker could not hold the batteries after taking them and nothing more could be done than spike the guns and throw them in the river, "the movement would be productive of advantage," he wrote, showing a new sensitivity to public opinion. Specifically, he wanted to know the feasibility of a demonstration against the Confederate position at Acquia Creek; and he also wanted to know the number of batteries, the number of guns in each, the troops serving and supporting them, the

3 *OR*, 5, 633–634, letter dated October 30, 1861, from Hooker to Seth Williams; Heintzelman MS diary (large diary) (L.C.) entry dated May 6, 1862.

4 *OR*, 5, 373–374, 374–375, 375–376, 376, 377, 625, Williamson's reports in October and November.

5 McClellan MSS (L.C.) letter dated January 20, 1862, from R. J. Williamson to Williams.

proper place for landing, the troops Hooker would need in addition to his division, and the assistance he would need from the navy.[6] Shortly after the Senate approved Stanton and the new secretary assumed office, true to his word, he met with McClellan to press the two flank subjects.[7] McClellan received the demands peacefully and did not oppose or argue even though they might compromise his Urbana plan.[8]

Probably in response to McClellan's inquiry Hooker sent two men across the river. Just after daybreak on February 9, Colonel Charles K. Graham and a lieutenant landed at Acquia Creek. Across the mouth of the creek, they saw three batteries, one at water level and two flanking it on the heights.[9] Graham and the lieutenant reported, and the lieutenant forwarded a diagram for an attack.[10]

McClellan planned an assault but was uncertain about capturing the upper or lower batteries.[11] He feared that, if he did not simultaneously attack them all, those not taken in the first wave would quickly become too well-fortified to be captured by a direct assault, and a siege he considered out of the question.[12] Toward the end of February McClellan added an interesting new twist to an assault on the west bank of the Potomac. "We can count upon the assistance of the iron steamer *Ericson* armed with two eleven inch guns during the present week . . . It seems to me that the safest plan is to use the *Ericson* supported by the whole flotilla and a heavy force prepared to land. I can furnish here the means of landing at any point from 10,000 to 15,000 men in addition to your command . . . "[13]

The Baltimore & Ohio Railroad crossing at Harpers Ferry? In December, McClellan sent a young West Point engineer, whose real notoriety would await the postwar period, to report on the facilities for crossing the Potomac in the Harpers

6   McClellan MSS (L.C.) draft letter dated January 20, 1862, from Seth Williams to Joseph Hooker in McClellan's handwriting. The final version is in the Hooker MSS.

7   *OR*, 5, 41, McClellan's report; McClellan in *B&L*, 2, 164.

8   Military Historical Society of Massachusetts MSS (John C. Ropes papers) (B.U.) letter dated May 16, 1862, from Stanton to Dyer (the copy in Ropes' papers was taken from one of several newspapers which later reprinted the letter, but the newspaper cannot be identified).

9   Hooker MSS (H.L.) letter dated February 10, 1862, from Magan to Hooker.

10   Hooker MSS (H.L.) undated, unsigned memorandum of three pages with a map on the third page in the handwriting of Lieutenant Magan.

11   Hooker MSS (H.L.) letter dated February 15, 1862, from Marcy to Hooker; McClellan MSS (L.C.) letter dated January 20, 1862, from Williamson to Williams.

12   Hooker MSS (L.C.) telegram in cipher dated February 15, 1862, to Hooker.

13   Hooker MSS (H.L.) telegram dated February 23, 1862, from McClellan to Hooker, received February 23. Of course, the *Ericson* would be better known in a short while as the *Monitor*.

Ferry area. Lieutenant Orville E. Babcock, Class of 1861, traveled to Harpers Ferry, Williamsport, and other crossing places beyond the Ferry. The farther places provided relatively easy crossings, he reported, but the engineers could construct a bridge at the Ferry only with difficulty even though he found the river no more than two hundred yards wide. The masonry walls on both sides, the banks of the canal on the Maryland side and the embankments of the armory in Virginia, rose twenty feet above ordinary water level. Determining that India rubber pontoons would be unstable, susceptible to damage, and vulnerable to the dramatic changes in the depth of the river during rainfall, Babcock made fateful recommendations: "There is a lock leading from the Canal into the Potomac a short distance from the remains of the railroad bridge . . . I would respectfully suggest a bridge supported by canal boats . . . The boats can be locked into the river and anchored in their places immediately."[14] No one measured the width of the canal, the boats, or the locks. Local people told McClellan's engineers the locks were large enough for the canal boats. They knew everything would fit. McClellan himself had seen canal boats being "locked" into the river at other places on the canal.[15] In his report Babcock assumed a number of things: enough canal boats, lumber for bridge stringers, sufficient planking, and bridge-builders from the Baltimore and Ohio.[16]

Careful, thorough, and thoughtful, McClellan did not intend to proceed against the Confederates on Babcock's assumptions. Back went the lieutenant, this time to the men who would provide the assumed services and equipment. He began with John C. Garret, the president of the railroad company, and submitted his second report on the day after Christmas, while typhoid still held McClellan in its grasp. The railroad had sufficient employees and lumber and would make them available to the government when needed. Babcock's second report confirmed his earlier statement. "I would respectfully recommend a bridge supported on canal boats . . ." Enough ships' anchors for the canal boats could be had in Baltimore.[17]

On January 20, Banks acted on Lander's suggestions and probably on the early stages of a plan by McClellan by asking his engineers, Major D. D. Perkins and Captain James W. Abert, along with Colonel John White Geary, to assess the possibility of crossing the river at Harpers Ferry. He wanted a written report about bridging. Perkins and Abert reported that the recent rains had raised the river ten feet, which made it too high and its current too strong for a bridge of canal boats. Other means

---

14   *OR*, 5, 677, letter dated December 7, 1861, from Babcock to Marcy.

15   *M.O.S.*, 193.

16   *OR*, 5, 677, letter dated December 7, 1861, from Babcock to Marcy.

17   *OR*, 5, 692–693, report dated December 26, 1861, from Babcock to Marcy.

of crossing were no more certain or stable. Bateaux thirty-one feet long and six feet wide would provide adequate floatation for stringers.[18] In his short note forwarding the report to McClellan, Banks, too, opposed the use of canal boats for a bridge.[19]

Geary disagreed. Strong ropes or cables could be thrown across, boats attached to them with pulleys, and troops crossed to execute Lander's plan to catch Jackson in the "bulge" or Peninsula of the Potomac. He believed Leesburg could be taken by a rapid movement from Point of Rocks. Having survived the dancing, Colonel Maulsby agreed with Geary. Banks' men could march along the river road to Dam No. 5 on the canal, cross, and reach Jackson's rear. In fact, Maulsby was anxious to serve in the field under Lander.[20]

In spite of the advice from Lieutenant Comstock that barges were the superior bridging material and perhaps because of the conflicting report from Banks and his engineers, McClellan asked Barnard to report on the question. On February 1, Barnard deemed Harpers Ferry the best place to cross and canal boats vastly superior to the bateaux or pontoons suggested by Banks' engineer officers, Perkins and Abert.

Even if he could not find a satisfactory plan for an assault on the Potomac batteries, McClellan considered them an inconsequential annoyance he would cure when he unleashed his offensive.[21] He responded to Stanton's inquiry about them with an explanation of his Annapolis-Urbana-Richmond plan. This was beyond the new secretary. The major-general should develop that idea to the president, Stanton said.[22] The general in chief decided he would do it but, for him, in a new and unique way. He met with the president to unveil, for the first time, the details of his Urbana plan.[23] Lincoln had heard a general statement of this plan during the meetings earlier in the month, he had probably heard a bit about it from Chase and McDowell, and he might have seen McDowell's pre-Bull Run memorandum to Chase. He had undoubtedly read James Shields' long letter in which Shields suggested the route by way of the Peninsula between the York and James rivers.[24] Nevertheless, a change of

18   *OR*, 5, 705–706, letter dated January 20, 1862, from Perkins and Abert to Banks.

19   *OR*, 5, 705, letter dated January 21, 1862, from Banks to McClellan.

20   Chase MSS (U.P.I.) letter dated February 4, 1862, from Bannister to Chase.

21   *M.O.S.*, 197.

22   *OR*, 5, 46, McClellan's report.

23   *OR*, 5, 41, McClellan's report.

24   *OR*, 5, 700–702, letter dated January 16, 1862, from Lander to McClellan. The original, dated January 10, 1862, is in the McClellan MSS. Undoubtedly recognizing that this was support for the change of base, McClellan sent it, as one of his earliest acts after rising from his sickbed, to Secretary of State Seward; and on January 14, 1862, Seward sent it to the Secretary of War. *OR*, 5, 700, letter dated January 14, 1862, from Seward to the Secretary of War.

base by water to Urbana was a new idea the president had not had sufficient time to consider and embrace.

McClellan probably thought he could persuade Lincoln to approve the Urbana change of base with relative ease. After all, another president had agreed to a plan like it, the Vera Cruz plan for Scott's Mexico City column. The two plans had many similarities: the entire army would move by water, land in hostile territory, and make an overland march, its ultimate goal, if only to bring the opposing army to a definitive battle, being the opponent's capital. Capture of the seat of government would bring the war to an end. But Polk's plan had significant differences that probably did not occur to McClellan. First, Polk was wedded to no strategic idea for the war with Mexico, but Lincoln remained fixed on an advance against Centerville and Manassas. Second, Polk had devised the Vera Cruz plan himself and did not require persuasion; Lincoln had no pride of authorship in the Urbana route and needed to be convinced.[25] Last, the Urbana plan presented the one goblin Lincoln simply could not willingly confront: Washington unshielded by the main army.

During the January meetings Lincoln had requested information about shipping when Franklin suggested a change of base to the Peninsula, and the loyal Franklin must have reported this to McClellan. A telegram summoned John Tucker, an assistant secretary of war who understood shipping, to a meeting. McClellan wanted to know if Tucker could obtain enough transportation to move fifty thousand men, ten thousand horses, one thousand wagons, thirteen batteries of artillery, and their ordinary equipment by water at one time. Until difficulties had been described by Meigs and Van Vliet, two experienced quartermasters, the commanding general had assumed that his staff could collect this transportation easily. A few days later Tucker reported confidently that he could provide the necessary transportation.

During the illness meetings, the plan for a change of base had suffered when compared with a direct assault on Manassas because it required delay to accumulate transportation. Transportation to Manassas, the feet of the ground pounders, needed no more than a three hour call to duty. Before the end of January McClellan, Lincoln, and Tucker met to discuss this critical issue, especially the necessary time. Tucker believed that schooners and barges should carry the wagons and horses, that every schooner should have special fittings for the horses as well as forage and water, and that each transport would need water for the troops. From the time the order was given, Tucker said, more than thirty days would be required to accumulate and equip the shipping. Lincoln and McClellan pressed him for the

25   Bauer, *Mexican War*, 232; Eisenhower, *So Far From God*, 161.

shortest time. If he had favorable winds and loading went quickly, Tucker thought, the time could be shortened a great deal.[26]

Late in the month of January McClellan had begun plans to raid the Confederate batteries along the Potomac River and open the river to navigation. He had also progressed in his own plans for crossing the river at Harpers Ferry. Last, he had begun final preparations for a strategic advance to the bottom of Chesapeake Bay and a march to Richmond by accumulating shipping. These plans he had discussed with the new secretary and the "new" president, made more confident by his recent foray into the literature of the military art and the insistent speeches of Attorney General Bates. The general in chief must have been stunned when he came face to face with their first real disagreement on an issue of substance. In spite of the discussions about the Urbana or Peninsula plan, Lincoln took a step forward on his own by issuing President's General War Order No. 1 on January 27, 1862.[27] The sentimental anniversary of the birth of George Washington, February 22, he decreed, would be the day for "a general movement of the land and naval forces of the United States against the insurgent forces." The "general movement" would include the Army of the Potomac.

After the meeting in which he explained his plans to Franklin, Porter, and Smith; probably after the meeting with Tucker; and probably after he received General War Order No. 1, McClellan began work on a "white paper" to explain his plan for a change of base, clear evidence of the birth of the new McClellan and a dramatic change in his approach to his obligations as general in chief. Properly addressing his letter to the new secretary of war, he explained the two plans that had held everyone's attention at the meetings earlier in the month, the Occoquan-Brentsville direct advance on land and the Chesapeake Bay-Urbana flank sweep by water. At great length he analyzed the benefits and risks of each. McDowell's hope for vindication, a movement on the Warrenton Turnpike against the Centerville-Manassas area, he did not dignify by discussion. Frank Blair had disposed of that in his November 4 memorandum, which McClellan had sent to Lincoln; and Montgomery Blair had fiercely criticized McDowell's ideas at the

---

26   *OR*, 5, 46, McClellan's report.

27   *OR*, 5, 41, McClellan's report. Without referring to the meeting with Tucker, Basler discusses in his usual thorough detail the origin of this letter and the peculiar circumstances of its dating in Basler, *Lincoln's Collected Works*, 5, 118–125, esp. notes 1 and 2; and Sears, *McClellan's Correspondence*, 170–171, n. 1, letter dated January 31, 1862, redated February 3 by the editor. In the discussion Sears appears to be correct when the two differ, but the undated memorandum of questions from Lincoln, *Basler*, 5, 119, seems far more likely to be contemporaneous with the December 10 note.

January meetings.[28] McClellan's letter, more than twenty pages in draft, dismissed McDowell with a cursory statement at the very end. The discussion of the two plans covered roads, transportation, weather, natural defenses, the condition of the army, and the army's capabilities.

While McClellan worked on his lengthy position piece, the president embellished his own idea. Just as a new McClellan emerged from McDowell's reluctant, abortive coup in January, so emerged a new president, who now took an active, imperative role in military affairs. Still somewhat uncertain but willing to issue strategic commands, Lincoln prepared entirely on his own[29] two documents that showed he did not have full immunity against the blustering demands of the Joint Committee and the Radicals. To make President's War Order No. 1 more precise, he issued President's Special War Order No. 1, directed solely to McClellan and the Army of the Potomac.

Without regard for McClellan's Urbana plan, which he did not negate, Lincoln dealt with the issue that bothered him most, the safety of the capital. The Army of the Potomac must provide a garrison for Washington, then take its movable force to a position it would seize and hold on the railroad southwest of Manassas Junction. The date remained the same, the sentimental twenty-second of February.[30]

28   Lincoln MSS (L.C.) letter dated November 4, 1861, from Blair to McClellan. No document or other written evidence states that this letter was sent to the president; but because it found its way to his papers, the inference seems justified.

29   *N&H*, 5, 160. Nicolay and Hay state firmly that General War Order No. 1 was Lincoln's concoction and done completely on his own. They say nothing about the Special War Order and do not say the president sought or received any advice on it. The inference that he did not seems reasonable.

30   Basler, *Lincoln's Collected Works*, 5, 115, President's Special War Order No. 1, dated January 31, 1862. Crippled by a childhood injury to his back, John C. Ropes could not join his younger brother Henry in the war; but he could become, as he did, a keen, intelligent student of it. He assessed this period in the joint life of Lincoln, the commander in chief, and McClellan, the general in chief, in Ropes, John C., "Gen. McClellan's Plans," in vol. 1, 59–88, *Campaigns in Virginia, 1861–1862*, in *Papers of the Military Historical Society of Massachusetts*, 10 vols. (Boston, 1881, Broadfoot rep.). Although critical of the Peninsular plan and of McClellan's handling of his relations with the government, Ropes wrote, "There can be no doubt that the Government had behaved towards Gen. McClellan, for some months before the campaign opened, in a manner which your committee consider alike unjust to him, injurious to the morale of his army, and detrimental to the success of our arms. Few men at the head of affairs during a great war have ever given such evidence of an entire unfitness to have any general direction over military men as Mr. Lincoln and Mr. Stanton. And this inaptitude for war [Mr. Lincoln] retained to the end of his life." *Ibid.*, 76–77. Ropes characterized General War Order No. 1 as "puerile," seizure of a point on the railroad southwest of Manassas Junction as "well-nigh impossible," appointing the corps commanders without consulting McClellan as "another slight," the removal of Blenker from the Army of the Potomac as a concession to "political claims" by Fremont. *Ibid.*, 76–77.

McClellan wished to surprise the enemy with his strategic landing; but yet again, he had been correct: anything known to the president would find its way into the newspapers. Captain Alonzo Adams, one of the indefatigable organizers of the First New York Cavalry but certainly not a member of Lincoln's inner circle, found himself outside during one of the torrential downpours of the winter. The rain was heavy, the wind powerful, and the ubiquitous Virginia mud deep and gelatinous.[31]

Struggling in the driving rain as he walked from headquarters to an officer's tent, Captain Adams discovered an enlisted man stuck fast in the mud, almost motionless, and heedless of the storm. His body was a little bent, his hands joined before him, and his face shrouded by a downcast, dejected air.

"Is that you, McSourley?" Adams asked.

The enlisted man turned with a look of sorrow. He shook his head affirmatively.

"It is, an troth—an sorry am I it is me. Its no good luck brought me here, Captin."

"You had better go to your tent, out of the storm."

McSourley's face brightened as he smiled; but when he tried to pull his right foot, Adams saw the schackle, ball, and chain.

"How'd I go to my tint, an I ankered here to the mud?"

Adams knew McSourley was a brave man and not a bad man except when whiskey unleashed his temper.

"I am sorry to see so good a soldier as you undergoing such severe punishment in this storm—"

"Faith it might be worse, Captin," McSourley interrupted, with a good-natured smile. "But won't the ribils pay for this, thin! Stay awhile till I git em within length of my sabre."

No matter how much he suffered, McSourley blamed the Rebels and promised they would pay when he had them in saber range. Puzzled, Adams confessed his inability to see how the Rebels had anything to do with this punishment.

"May the Saints forgive me!" McSourley exclaimed. He raised his hands. "Would I be here only for the ribils? Bad luck to thim, and the breed o' thim; and may the divil git'm afore they git absolution." He struggled to move forward and extended his hand in a threatening manner. With much earnestness, he complained to a third man passing them, "And wasn't it the likes of you, too, that brought me here?"

Adams turned to see a black man walking to his master's tent. He thought the poor man should be an object of sympathy, he said.

---

31 Adams, *Story of a Trooper*, 262.

"An it's a mighty lot of it they gits," McSourley added quickly. "If the ribils had the naigars and the devil the pair o'thim, would'nt I be home, living in pace wid the ould woman?"

Adams could see that a discussion of Rebels and slaves would resolve nothing. He asked for the cause of McSourley's punishment. Unknowingly producing conclusive evidence about the president, plans, and the newspapers, the enlisted man stuck his hand in his vest pocket and produced a small, dirty strip cut from a newspaper. "Perhaps ye've read that before. Anyhow ye can read it agin." It was

PRESIDENT's SPECIAL WAR ORDER NO. 1.

Executive mansion
Washington, January 31st, 1862.

Ordered: That all the disposable force of the Army of the Potomac, after providing safely for the defence of Washington, be formed into an expedition for the immediate object of seizing and occupying a point upon the railroad southwestward of what is known as Manassas Junction, all details to be in the discretion of the commander in chief, and the expedition to move before or on the 22d day of February next.

ABRAHAM LINCOLN.

Adams told McSourley he could not relate the punishment to the article. The enlisted man carefully restored the paper to his pocket and smiled. He was for the president, he explained, a more sincere friend with a stronger arm than many of those who fawned and flattered him in the hope of favors. Raising his right hand he exclaimed with emphasis, "A mighty curse upon your head, Finn McGinnis!"

"So, then, it was another fight between you and McGinnis. Whiskey, I suppose, had something to do with it?"

Adams started to leave.

"Stay, Captin, stay," McSourley said anxiously, "an I'd tell ye all about it. There was a mighty dale o' talk in camp, as ye know, about Giniral Micklillin laven us an the President takin a spil at commandin the army. There was thim as said perhaps he could do that same; thin there was thim as said perhaps he could'nt do that same. Och! the whole camp was mighty agitated—ye know that. And there was Corporal Rooney and private Teddy O'Brien and Mister McSourley (misilf ye know) in the tint beyant, behavin like gintlemen, when Finn McGinnis drops in widout sayin by your lave. 'Have ye's heard de news, boys?' says he.

"'What news have ye now?' says I.

"'Gineral Micklilhin laid on the shilf and the President himsilf commands the army. Much luck may he have wid his new ockupashun,' says Finn, radin' the Prisident's order till us, and spakin derrogrutory of the President as a Gineral. 'Musha! should'nt I like to see the Gineral that oud move an army an it stuck in the mud: a good time he'd have wid his artillery, crossing strahms an his powder wit. Botherhashin to that man as would sit in his aisy chair and till the army to move an it fast in the mud,' says Finn, spakin of the President as did'nt become the likes of him."

McSourley shook his head and paused.

"And you used striking arguments in defence of the President's military capacity?" responded Adams wryly.

"Faith I did! Wus'nt it my duty to stand up for de man as commands us. 'Yer a blackguard, Finn,' says I, 'an its not sayin much for ye as a sodger that ye refuse to obey orders, anyhow.'

"'Oud ye repate that?' says he.

"'I oud,' says I, 'an more, too, bedad. An do ye mind this, Mister McGinnis. The man's no gintleman what inshults the Prisident in my tint. Doent yees git yer rashuns, and doent yees git yer pay, and doent yees git yer clothes? An seein that, is'nt it yer duty as a sodger to yeald obadience to the orders of your suparior?'

"'Is it the likes o' you that's come to tache me my duty?' says Finn.

"An did'nt myself tache him bitter manhers by knockin him down! An what does the spalpeen do but cry.

"'Murther! murther! Would ye, Mister Sourley, murther a man in your own tint?'

"'I would,' says I, 'an its that same ye desarve for yer disrespect to the President.' An its not the half murthered he was.

"Thin I was arristed and had comodashnns in the guardhouse, beyant. Thin charges, an spisafikashuns, an all that, an more too. An I was thried afore a chourt-marshal fur the half murthetrin Finn McGinnis. Musha, was'nt there a dale of lies told! The divil a woord I'd be allowed to say fur mysilf, an I innocent as the lamb. An its here I am, payin the pinality. Ye have it all, Captin. Good luck to ye; may ye niver do duty of this sort. But won't the ribils pay for this, an they within the rach of my sabre?"[32]

Had he been present, McClellan could have said, "I told you so; the Lincoln government is a conduit for information to the enemy." Writing a rare memoir

---

32   Adams, *Story of a Trooper*, 263–267.

before the end of the war, Adams commented gently but critically on the commander in chief's military skills. "Today it would be freezing cold. Tomorrow a drenching rain, filling the streams and overflowing roads . . . hail, sleet, and a fierce, cutting wind. Then snow would cover the ground, and the Army of the Potomac would lay for weeks in a mud drench . . . Subsistence wagons stuck in the mud, teamsters labored in mud knee deep, and the poor animals plunged and struggled in vain to do their work . . . Artillery could not be moved, forage teams were stuck fast in the road, and our poor animals suffered and died for want of something to eat." Commenting on the absurdity of the War Order and the Special War Order, Adams, a thoughtful and perceptive officer, wrote, "Mr. Lincoln, I am sure, must by this time, join the nation in its wish that these innocent war orders had never seen the light of day."[33] McClellan, too, must have wished that they had never seen the public light of day and become known to the Confederates.

Whatever the political expediency of an immediate offensive might have been, only the future, unfortunately for McClellan, would prove the military absurdity of Lincoln's order. It provoked McClellan's typical reaction to an order he did not like. He asked whether the special order were final or if he could submit written objections and reasons for preferring his own. Always reasonable, Lincoln agreed.[34]

McClellan continued work on the long letter he had already begun to the secretary of war, but he did not alter it to create a specific response to the special war order. When he finished, he had a fair copy made and had the final version delivered to the secretary of war. One of them sent a copy to Lincoln.[35]

Meanwhile, the president did not sit idly. Armed with military science, he devised a number of military questions and determined that, if McClellan answered them satisfactorily, he would accept the major-general's plan. Of course, the hardest part of this decision was the restoration of the condition he had suffered in March, April, and May of the preceding year: the capital without a major army between it

---

33   Adams, *Story of a Trooper*, 261–262; Blight, David W., ed., *When This Cruel War Is Over: The Civil War Letters of Charles Harvey Brewster* (Amherst, 1992) 77–78, letter dated January 15, 1862, and 85, letter dated February 19, 1862, both from Brewster to his mother (Blight, *Brewster Letters*).

34   *M.O.S.*, 228–229; *N&H*, 5, 161.

35   Sears, *McClellan's Correspondence*, 170–171, n. 1, letter dated February 3, 1862, by the editor from McClellan to Stanton. This letter has a peculiar history. Several copies of it exist. The draft is in McClellan MSS (L.C.); a final in Stanton MSS (L.C.), dated January 31, 1862; and a final in Lincoln MSS (L.C.), dated February 3, 1862. N&H give no help on the "original" original or on the date of delivery to anyone. Where the questions from Lincoln fit in the chronology remains a mystery, but their location does not seem to matter.

and the Rebels. Lincoln's five questions, all common-sense inquiries resting in part on issues raised during the conferences in January, found their way into a brief note also dated February 3, 1862.[36] McClellan probably thought the president was "taking on airs" by presuming to engage in a sophisticated military dialogue, and he probably did not take the letter very seriously. Unfortunately, the "new" McClellan did not stop to recognize the "new" Lincoln and address the new character in a new way. Unlike most subordinates trying to convince his ultimate superior, he did not take this opportunity to address the president's military concerns directly. The president had already given him permission to submit a critique-defense, and he had done it that day. He decided that he had answered the five questions in his long letter. He would write no more.[37]

McClellan's February 3 letter received no specific response. Nor did the president insist on the execution of the special war order. Both men proceeded as if they would perform the conflicting formalities of compliance and revocation, McClellan because he never obeyed an order he did not like until several repetitions and Lincoln because he never insisted on protocol. But the romance of not obeying an order from the president, an impression McClellan tried to convey for more than one incident when he wrote years later, did not give a fair picture of reality. Many conferences followed the exchange. Although no record of these discussions survives, McClellan probably explained movements that would give lip service to the order and argued for his change of base. Whatever they discussed, McClellan's unusual powers of persuasion did not fail him. His plans prevailed. He would strike the Rebel batteries along the Potomac. To do this, the government would collect as many canal boats as possible to move the Army of the Potomac. They could be quickly modified to accommodate infantry, artillery, and cavalry. He would cross the Potomac at Harpers Ferry to occupy the Shenandoah Valley as far south as Winchester and Strasberg and to guarantee the safety of the Baltimore and Ohio Railroad west. He and the president agreed that the army could change its base.[38]

With the approval of the president, Stanton advertised for transports on February 14 and ordered Tucker to charter enough to move the Army of the Potomac to its new base of operations. Tucker called for bids. That evening Meigs learned about the decision and assigned two assistant quartermasters to the project.[39]

36   *OR*, 5, 41–42, McClellan's report.

37   *M.O.S.*, 229.

38   *M.O.S.*, 237.

39   *OR*, 5, 46, McClellan's report.

But advertisements for shipping did not eliminate all other considerations, especially the president's fear about the safety of the capital. He had not recovered from the long worrisome nights when the defense of the capital rested on Charles P. Stone's thirty-five hundred District of Columbia militia. Many change-of-base plans had passed before Lincoln in January: the Urbana route, the Peninsula route, the Suffolk-Norfolk assaults. He had not approved one to the exclusion of the others.

Nor did his acceptance of the general idea preclude alternatives of execution. After Lincoln issued General War Order No. 1, McClellan and Stanton had "many, very many earnest conversations" about the impending bankruptcy of the government and fears that England and France would recognize the South. Between February 22 and March 8 Lincoln pressed McClellan for something immediate. No longer unyielding on matters of strategy that seemed so clear to him, McClellan confirmed that he would clear the blockade of the Potomac and move through Harpers Ferry to Winchester in the foot of the Valley.[40]

During this period of the "new" McClellan, the major general may have decided that a small compromise might assure firm consent to his change of base. He had always believed that seizure of the foot of the Valley around Harpers Ferry and Martinsburg would cause the Confederates to withdraw from the Manassas-Centerville position. That might alleviate the uncovered capital problem. As thorough and analytical as he was, McClellan must have known that it would also endanger the Urbana movement.[41] He certainly concluded that a pincers movement by Banks from Harpers Ferry and Lander from Paw Paw would drive the Rebels up the Valley.

Soon it would be spring. Although the Union had collected a string of remarkable victories in other theaters,[42] the Confederacy appeared to be winning the war in the East by sitting. No doubt McClellan thought the flank moves would relieve some of the dissatisfaction with his unproductive Army of the Potomac. By the middle of February McClellan had been told that the War Department could collect enough shipping for his change of base, Hooker was planning a series of landings to attack the batteries on the Virginia shore of the Potomac, Lander was operating around Paw Paw on the Baltimore and Ohio Railroad, and McClellan was readying

---

40   Military Historical Society of Massachusetts MSS (John C. Ropes papers) (B.U.) letter dated May 16, 1862, from Stanton to Dyer (the copy in Ropes' papers was taken from one of several newspapers which later reprinted the letter, but the newspaper cannot be identified).

41   *M.O.S.*, 194.

42   Gallagher, Gary W., "The Civil War Watershed, the 1862 Richmond Campaign in Perspective," in Gallagher, Gary W., ed., *The Richmond Campaign of 1862, The Peninsula and the Seven Days*, 5–7 (Chapel Hill, 2000).

Banks to cross the Potomac at Harpers Ferry. Banks and Lander would enter the foot of the Valley and advance together on Everyman's Achilles Heel, the town of Winchester.

In January, McClellan discussed crossing on canal boats with Banks and ordered him to be ready to operate against Jackson in the lower end of the Valley on short notice.[43] In all probability this developing plan accounted for McClellan's firm refusal to allow Lander to cross the river and pursue Jackson and his peremptory orders to Lander to consolidate his scattered regiments at Romney.[44]

On February 13, McClellan said to Chase, "In ten days I shall be in Richmond."

Chase, surprised at such a happy event so close, asked, "What is your plan, general?"

"Oh, I mean to cross the river; attack and carry their batteries; and push on after the enemy."

"Have you any gunboats to aid in the attack on the batteries?"

"No. They are not needed. All I want is transportation and canal boats, of which I have plenty that will answer."[45]

On February 19, a subcommittee of the enemy-within-the-gates, the Joint Committee, met with Secretary Stanton to ask why the army was idle, why large numbers of troops sat in the capital, and why the army "crowded with troops" the east bank of the Potomac when the enemy was in Virginia.

"It is a disgrace to the nation," said Wade, "that Washington is thus allowed to remain to all intents and purposes in a state of siege."

"The Committee can not feel more keenly upon this subject than do I," replied Stanton. "I do not go to bed at night without my cheek burning with shame at this disgrace, and the subject has received my earnest attention, but I have not been able to change the situation as I wish."

They sent for McClellan. Stanton explained the reason for summoning him and repeated the inquiries.

The "new" McClellan did not include the Joint Committee in the expanded group with a "need to know." He was considering the matter, he responded, but immediate action was not possible. He hoped he would soon be able to decide on a course of action.

---

43   *OR*, 5, 705–706, letter dated December 26, 1861, from Babcock to Marcy; and 712, letter dated February 1, 1862, from Barnard to Colburn.

44   *OR*, 5, 703–704, letter dated January 18, 1862, from Banks to McClellan.

45   Schuckers, *Chase*, 446, handwritten memorandum by Chase.

How long before he reached a decision?

It would depend on the circumstances. Probably as a byproduct of his earlier belief that the Rebels intended to cross the Potomac and capture Baltimore in the rear of the capital, he would not send the Washington troops to the Virginia side unless he left their rear fully protected and they had better lines of retreat. He intended to construct a temporary bridge across the Potomac as soon as possible, then make it a permanent structure at his leisure. Three bridges. That would be enough.

Wade became impatient, and when his patience disappeared, his common sense usually vanished with it. He lapsed into military silliness.

"With one hundred fifty thousand of the best troops the world has ever seen, there is no need of more bridges," he jabbed. "The Rebels are inferior in numbers and condition. Retreat would be treason. The one hundred fifty thousand men can whip the whole Confederacy if they are given a chance. If I were their commander, I would lead them across the Potomac, and they should not come back until they had won a victory and the war was ended, or they came in their coffins!"

Word by word, the secretary of war endorsed Wade's blunt, strong, plain statements. The next day, February 20, Stanton and the committee met again, this time at the Secretary's home.[46] The committee had demanded McClellan's removal around the time Stanton had taken office. In spite of Stanton's protestations about wanting to help McClellan in every way, Stanton agreed with the demand. The agreement the committee reached in Stanton's home could not have required much time: it should persuade Lincoln to replace McClellan or compel the major general to begin an immediate, active campaign.[47]

To many, McClellan seemed to embody the Great Emperor. The press dubbed him "the Little Napoleon," and men hostile to him derisively called him "McNapoleon." To his men he published announcements beginning "Soldiers," just as Napoleon had.[48] He stood for photographs in the famous Napoleonic pose, his hand stuffed into his partially unbuttoned uniform blouse. Like Napoleon, he

---

46   *C.C.W.*, 1, 84–85 (journal) entry dated February 19, 1862; Detroit Post and Tribune, *Chandler*, 226–228. The journal is entirely indirect discourse and *Chandler* is part direct, part indirect. All of both, without change in text, has been converted, where necessary, from indirect to direct.

47   Detroit Post & Tribune, *Chandler*, 218. Strangely, no transcript was apparently taken of this meeting; nor was McClellan's statement summarized in the Committee's journal, *C.C.W.*, 1, 87 (Journal).

48   Gurowski, *Diary*, 1, 212, entry dated May, 1862; compare Sears, *McClellan's Correspondence*, 58–59, Address to "Soldiers of the Army of the West," dated July 16, 1861, with Chandler, *Napoleon*, 1, 76; Roe, Frederick Seelye, *History of the First Regiment of Heavy Artillery Massachusetts Volunteers: Formerly the Fourteenth Regiment of Infantry 1861–1865*, 113 (Boston, 1917).

generally explained his organizational, tactical, and strategic plans to no one.[49] Like Napoleon, he performed prodigious amounts of work over long hours, rose early, heard staff reports, attended planning sessions, finished mountains of paperwork, met politicians and important civilians, took long rides to see and be seen by his men, and returned after dark to the paperwork.[50] But at best it was only a superficial resemblance to the incomparable Corsican.

Not a monarch, not even lesser royalty, McClellan was not a ruler-warlord but had fallen heir to a life that probably made him think he might become the American embodiment of the outmoded, Machiavellian[51] combination of battlefield commander and head of state. Confused thoughts about the presidency were not foreign to his mind or to the minds of other important persons.[52] Perhaps when he looked in the mirror he saw the next exemplar of the long line running from Alexander the Great and Caesar to Frederick the Great and Napoleon, a democratic society's counterpart to a ruler-commander. In fact, his country's constitutional theoreticians agreed with that picture. They had seen the president as the field commander of the nation's military forces.[53]

But no matter what image he carried in his mind, McClellan was not the president, nor was he Napoleon Reborn. A reserved, dignified gentleman at all times, he did not explode into the well-known and widely-feared Napoleonic rages.[54] Never would he publicly mistreat any of his officers. Served expertly, loyally, even slavishly by Marshal Louis Alexandre Berthier, Prince de Neuchatel et de Wagram, his indefatigable chief of staff, Napoleon berated the hapless Berthier, referred to him

---

49   Heintzelman MS diary (L.C.) (large diary) see generally the entries for November 1861, and December 16, 1861; *C.C.W.*, 1 , 117–118 (Heintzelman), 215 (Blenker), 146 (Wadsworth), 166 (McCall), and 131 (McDowell).

50   Chandler, *Napoleon*, Introduction, 1, xxxvi–xxxvii.

51   Gilbert, Felix, "Machiavelli: The Renaissance of the Art of War," in Paret, ed., *Makers of Modern Strategy*, 25, quoting from Machiavelli's *Discourses*, 2, 33.

52   E.g., Pisani, *supra*; Kearny MSS (L.C.) letter dated March 4, 1862, from Kearny to Parker.

53   Hunt, Gaillard, ed., *United States Constitutional Convention (1787) The Journal of the Debates in the Convention which framed the Constitution of the United States, May–September, 1787 as recorded by James Madison*, 165, 167 ff, 175 ff (New York 1908); Hamilton, Alexander, Paper no. 69, published in the *New York Packet*, March 14, 1788, in Cooke, Jacob E., ed., *The Federalist*, 464, 465, 470 (Middletown, 1961), Elliot, Jonathan, ed., *The Debates in the several State Conventions on the Adoption of the Federal Convention as recommended by the general convention at Philadelphia, in 1787*, 5 vols. (1836–1845) 2, 365; 3, 996; 4, 107ff; Story, Joseph, *Commentaries on the Constitution*, 3 vols. (Boston, 1833) 3, 340–341, 342.

54   Schom, Alan, *Napoleon Bonaparte* (New York, 1997) 379 (Schom, *Bonaparte*); Chandler, *The Campaigns of Napoleon*, 1, Introduction, xxviii, xxxvii.

demeaningly as a mere "chief clerk" and physically assaulted him in a tirade.[55] Nor did McClellan alternate hard work with the Napoleonic periods of indolence, especially the long idle periods after disappointments.[56] Unlike Napoleon, alternation between superhuman work and sloth were foreign to McClellan. He knew only the one.

A core part of McClellan's military education and a person to whom he was likened, both in compliment and with derision, Napoleon did not share much with McClellan. But another figure from the great European wars created an interesting parallel: John Churchill, Duke of Marlborough and commander of the Allied Forces on the continent during the War of the Spanish Succession. In the developing cabinet government with the queen as head of state, Marlborough had loyal and devoted supporters who preserved his position of influence with Queen Anne, including his wife, Sarah, an influential member of the queen's chamber staff, and Sidney, the First Earl of Godolphin. While serving with the army in Europe Marlborough wrote long, informative letters to his wife and created the historical record for his story. He was supremely fortunate to find as his biographer his kinsman Winston Churchill, a man with a wondrous pen that described the duke's letters: "Although no scholar and for all his comical spelling, he wrote a rugged, powerful English . . ." And in his own "rugged, powerful" English W. Churchill wrote about J. Churchill:

> . . . When in Marlborough's conduct of the war we see now violent and sudden action with armies marching night and day, and all hazards dared for a decision, now long delays and seeming irresolution, the dominating fact to be remembered is that he could not be beaten . . . Neither in his headquarters at the front nor behind him at home did he have that sense of plenary authority that gave to Frederick the Great and Napoleon their marvelous freedom of action.

But the opposition forces at home displaced Sarah and Godolphin, and Marlborough fell from favor. Would McClellan be able to manage the currents in his army and in the government behind him? McClellan's problems did not differ in kind from those that had faced Marlborough. McClellan, too, would enter a period of "long delays and seeming irresolution"[57] complicated by a weighty increase in responsibilities he

55   Chandler, *The Campaigns of Napoleon*, 1, 369; Chandler, David G., *Dictionary of the Napoleonic Wars*, 55 (New York, 1979); Schom, *Bonaparte*, 377; Rothenburg, *Art of War*, 129.

56   Schom, *Napoleon*, 377; Chandler, *Napoleon*, 1, introduction, xxxvii; 374–378.

57   Churchill, Winston S., *Marlborough: His Life and Times*, 2 vol. edition of the original 4 vols. (London, Toronto, etc., 1936, 1947 ed. rep. in 1966) 3, 18–20 (Preface), 278–295 (Churchill, *Marlborough*). Even with the voluminous correspondence and contemporary accounts, incidents cannot be dated with direct evidence, *ibid.*, 3, 278, n. 1.

might not be able to fulfill. Would McClellan find the management of his country's far-flung armies too great a task?[58]

Unlike Frederick, Napoleon, and Washington, McClellan faced powerful enemies among those who should have been his supporters and complex social and political issues that should not have been his concerns. George Washington had his venomous personal enemies in Charles Lee and Thomas Conway.[59] Scott had his James K. Polk.[60] But none matched Wade, Chandler, Barnard, Wadsworth, Kearny, Casey, the press, the Radical Republicans, the Joint Committee, and the friends who had defected. Nor had any prior military leaders faced confounding civilian questions like slavery, abolition, insurgent property, and political party affiliation.

A young man with limited political experience in general and none in politics at the highest level, McClellan had nevertheless achieved great success. Overnight he had become a major general of the Ohio militia, a major-general of volunteers, then a major general in the Regular Army. He had formulated military policy with the president, the general in chief, cabinet officers, and important politicians. He had won his country's first important victory in the war. He had been summoned to command—in fact, to create—his nation's most important army. He had deftly outmaneuvered and replaced a seasoned veteran of politics and war, capturing as spoils the command of all the armies of the United States. All this he had done from the purest and most patriotic motivations, his love for his country and his desire to serve her.[61] These were staggering accomplishments for a man in his thirties. To them must be added his uncanny ability to make the lowest enlisted man and his lowest-ranking officers revere him[62] and critical civilian observers like Henry Bellows and Frederick Olmstead admire him. All in all he merited the unanimous

---

58   Parker, Geoffrey, *The Grand Strategy of Philip II*, 14, 18–22, 27–30, 36–37.

59   Freeman, *George Washington: Victory with the Help of France*, 5, 489; Showman, *Greene Papers*, 2, 312, letter dated March 17, 1777, from Greene to Jacob Greene; 277, letter dated February 7, 1777, from Greene to Jacob Greene; 277–279, note 2; 295, letter dated February 28, 1777, from Alexander McDougal to Greene.

60   Bauer, *Mexican War*, 73–74, 235–236; Elliott, *Scott*, 432ff; Sellers, *Polk-Constitutionalist*, 2, 439–443.

61   Sears, *McClellan's Correspondence*, 70, letter dated July 27, 1861, from McClellan to his wife; 82, letter dated August 9, 1861, redated August 10 by the editor from McClellan to his wife; 85, letter dated August 16, 1861, from McClellan to his mother; 104, letter dated September 27, 1861, from McClellan to his wife; 105, letter dated October 2, 1861, from McClellan to his wife; 124, letter dated November 3, 1861, redated November 2 by the editor, from McClellan to his wife.

62   Williams, *Lincoln and the Radicals*, 192; Acken, *Inside the Army of the Potomac (Donaldson Letters)*, 58; letter dated April 11, 1862, from Donaldson to Jacob.

highest praise his country and his countrymen could give him. But he did not receive it. His failures, small when compared with his accomplishments but given too much time to grow, had begun to generate force by the end of the year. Adverse circumstances that should have been controlled by others and by his own activity provided momentum to adverse change. These small but growing problems would determine the outcome of his military career.

McClellan tended his political fences only when he felt like it, not when he should have. "I do not care to pay much attention to my enemies," he wrote one of his correspondents.[63] He declined dinner invitations from important governmental officials. He withheld himself from all visitors except those he deemed necessary to his military work. He ignored most of the people who flocked about him, but, having located his headquarters in the capital, he had put himself in the vicinity of men like Charles Ellet, who repeatedly tried to see him, whom he repeatedly brushed aside, and who then joined his detractors.

Perhaps in time the social, financial, and political issues would find their own forum and leave the army to its military duties; but in the early stages of the war all intermingled. Nor had a clear policy emerged in any one of these troublesome areas. The uncertainty caused by lack of precedent, lack of experience, political conflict, and new leadership everywhere made McClellan a lightning rod for internal governmental disputes over these hotly contested questions. He did not try to control the government's policy on slavery, abolition, runaways, or Confederate property, but he did not try to convince the disputants that he would support any policy the government fixed. He left his opponents free to argue that he had a policy of his own, that his policy was contrary to the national interest, that he wanted his policy to prevail, and that he would impose it with his army if necessary.

Most important of all, he failed to perceive the need for any kind of early military action without waiting for the perfect army, the determinative battle, or the certain victory. For reasons other than those he stated, Isaac Stevens had been right. While McClellan built his large army, he should have sought many skirmishes, raids, encounters, small battles, a continuous succession of victories and defeats, and combat activity even if it amounted to no more than motion without movement. Instead, he slowly, painstakingly built an army for the great battle that would end the war. Mistaking the small for the large, he tried to avoid even the most insignificant defeat at all cost. Avoidance of an unpremeditated general engagement passed from byword to law.

---

63 S. L. M. Barlow MSS (H.L.) letter dated March 16, 1862, from McClellan to Barlow.

But he could never have achieved his goal of the great Armageddon. Beginning slowly with Gustavus Adolphus and the Duke of Marlborough, military leaders had become increasingly willing to commit their armies to huge "decisive" battles.[64] This willingness grew as the armies changed from irreplaceable mercenaries, to national professionals, then to nations in arms. More and more easily could a nation replenish its military forces. Fed by the growing power of democracy, the *levee en masse*, and the nation in arms, the armies of democratic republics in the mid-nineteenth century could fight one battle after another, mixing defeats and victories in a continuous stream.[65] The army suffering near destruction could reappear to fight again and in a short time. As democratic political reform proceeded, armies became more renewable, battles more common, and the decisive Armageddon more impossible.

Military thinkers believed in the decisiveness of the great battle.[66] A man with an eye for history, McClellan was their student and their believer. In his letters he wrote repeatedly about the great battle he would win to end the war.[67] Oddly enough, Wade and Chandler seemed to know that the winner of this war would be the last man standing and that battles, including defeats, were more important than uninterrupted but infrequent victories.

McClellan realized none of this. Carefully avoiding any risk that he lose the Armageddon battle and waiting until he was fully prepared to win it,[68] McClellan held

---

64   Weigley, Russell F., *The Age of Battles*, xi-xiii (Bloomington and Indianapolis, 1991); Rothenberg, Gunther E., "Maurice of Nassau, Gustavus Adolphus, Raimondo Montecuccoli, and the 'Military Revolution' of the Seventeenth Century" in Paret, *Makers of Modern Strategy*, 46. In fact, Maurice of Nassau fought only one major battle in twenty years of active military life, *ibid.*, 37.

65   An example of extraordinary recovery, Prussia suffered a crushing defeat at the dual battles of Jena-Auerstadt, which cost her in casualties and prisoners seventy percent of her effective military forces. Chandler, *The Campaigns of Napoleon*, 1, xxxii, Introduction. With social reform and a secretive program of rebuilding, the advent of war between Napoleon and Austria in 1809 brought Scharnhorst, von Gneisenau, Blücher, and von Grolman to the King with a plea to "join the fight." Craig, *Politics of the Prussian Army*, 53–55.

66   Gilbert, chapter 1, and Rothenberg, chapter 2, in Paret, *Makers of Modern Strategy*, 11–63; Weigley, *Age of Battles*, generally and 536–540.

67   Sears, *McClellan's Correspondence*, 74, memorandum dated August 2, 1861, by the editor from McClellan to the president; 75, letter dated August 2, 1861, from McClellan to his wife; 115, letter dated October 31, 1861, by the editor from McClellan to Cameron; 127, letter dated November 8, 1861, from McClellan to Barlow. In the letter to Barlow he said, "I feel however that the issue of this struggle is to be decided by the next great battle . . . "

68   McClellan filed no report of the operations of the armies under his command until he had been replaced forever. The huge report he wrote with the assistance of a large "staff" provides an excellent example of his truthfulness: He described objective factual events with absolute

his forces in check except for his two abortive advances, one well planned but signaled by large reconnaissances, and the other an impromptu adventure that failed because the intelligence was faulty, the battlefield commander incompetent, and McClellan lacked terrain visualization. Unfortunately, he took no account of the impatient American: once a problem had been identified, it had to be addressed—and solved—at once. By waiting for the perfection of his army, McClellan frustrated the legitimate desires of his expectant countrymen and refused the demands of his gathering enemies. Almost any other policy would have served him better.

If the "new" McClellan were to succeed, he had to make progress with the new secretary of war as well as the president. Something more affirmative than his vague statements to the committee would be necessary. Acting his part as a "new" man, he confidently told Lincoln and Stanton that he would make a "great strategical movement" to retrieve the railroad, capture Winchester, and drive the Rebels from the foot of the Valley. This would satisfy the spirit if not the letter of the president's war order.

He would trick the Confederates by building a light pontoon bridge across the Potomac, a river liable at this season to raging changes. The Rebels would not take the threat of a crossing on it seriously. But the real plan involved barges gathered carefully in the canal south of Harpers Ferry. In accordance with the repeated recommendations of his engineers, he would cross a small force on the pontoon bridge, seize a bridgehead, lock the barges into the river, and build a bridge of canal

accuracy while personal motives were subject to the rules of casuistry. In some parts of his draft report, which is in the McClellan MSS, explanations of his conduct, therefore, the operations of his mind, appear in his own hand, appear more than once for the same event, and are in clear conflict. In the final document the explanation most favorable to McClellan survives, the less favorable, crossed out but legible, does not. His explanation for "no advance by the Army of the Potomac" after he became general in chief is disingenuous. He claims he found the Western armies in disarray and unready for the new strategic combinations he planned, *OR*, 5, 41. At best this was only partly true. In a gratuitous attack on his report and the Peninsula Campaign, his great critic John G. Barnard characterizes this as an "*afterthought*" (Barnard, *Peninsular Campaign*, 10–11, Barnard's emphasis). Barnard was, for once, probably correct; but, as always, he went too far. Barnard's continued diatribe, that coordination of the far distant western armies with the Army of the Potomac "never was . . . and never could be" *ibid.*, 10, would be conclusively refuted after the arrival of Grant. McClellan certainly believed the western armies, the strategic right flank of the armies of the United States, should distract the Confederates with a movement before his army marched, Sears, *McClellan's Correspondence*, 72–73, mem. dated August 2, by the editor, from McClellan to the president. In his letters, usually reliable from the heart, he said nothing about the unready western armies, generally, *ibid.*, 122–145; but he did complain about the usual things, *ibid.*, 127–128, letter dated November 8, 1861, from McClellan to Barlow. Other examples of disingenuous explanations of his intentions and motives, particularly the withdrawal of the Confederates from the Manassas-Centerville line, will be described in due course.

boats to Harpers Ferry, a sturdy bridge that would withstand the river and would carry infantry, artillery, supply wagons, and everything else he would need for an independent force sufficient to take Winchester.[69]

Then he would reconstruct the railroad bridge over the stone pillars in the river. The canal boat bridge, then the rebuilt railroad bridge, would immunize his supply line against the unpredictable attention of Mother Nature. Unlike Leesburg and Ball's Bluff, he would use an adequate force composed of divisions under Lander, Banks, Sedgwick, Keyes, and perhaps McCall.[70] He would cross the Potomac at Harpers Ferry with this powerful force, occupy Leesburg with a flank guard, solidify a position on Loudon Heights, march to Charlestown, bring together at Martinsburg Lander from the west and Banks from the east, then march the consolidated force on the Winchester-Strasberg position. At Harpers Ferry Banks' division would cross first; Sedgwick next with Stone's old division, the Corps of Observation; and Keyes last. Once united with Lander's division at Martinsburg they would confront Jackson's fifteen thousand with almost fifty thousand men.[71] Rumors suggested that McClellan's friend from the engineer company in the Mexican War, G. W. "Legs" Smith, and fifteen thousand Confederate troops had withdrawn from their Manassas-Centerville position and headed for the foot of the Valley, a Bull Run reinforcement in reverse. McClellan did not believe it.[72]

---

69   Kelley, William D., *Lincoln and Stanton: with special Reference to the Campaign on the Peninsula* (Philadelphia, 1885) 22 (Kelley, *Lincoln and Stanton*) (pamphlet). The chronology, once again uncertain, has been reconstructed on the most logical basis. The fundamental principle of the significant differences between a small book and a thick pamphlet fails on first glance. In his pamphlet Kelley claims on second-hand information and misguided inferences that the movement to the Peninsula was devised by Lincoln, Stanton, and Naglee and that McClellan had no part in it, indeed, no plan at all. Nevertheless, Kelley's piece contains fascinating factual material, some from first-hand observation and some from reliable second-hand sources. Used with care, it explains many things and answers many small questions.

70   Comte de Paris MS diary (small diary) entry dated February 19, 1862.

71   In none of McClellan's writings or those of his friends is this plan described in detail, but it can be pieced together from a number of sources. *M.O.S.*, 192–195; *OR*, 5, 48, 66, 712; McClellan MSS (L.C.) draft section of McClellan's Report, McClellan's handwritten account of the Harpers Ferry crossing and undated memorandum about the Potomac batteries (reprinted in Sears, *infra*, 195, and dated by Sears March 1, 1862); Comte de Paris MS diary (small diary) (A.N. de la M. de F.) entries dated February 19, 20, 25, 26, 27, and 28, 1862; Sears, *McClellan's Correspondence*, 191–192, letter dated February 27, 1862, from McClellan to his wife; Schoff Collection (William L. Clements Library, Univ. Mich.) letter dated March 3, 1862, from McClellan to Halleck; Strother, "Personal Recollections," in *Harpers New Monthly Magazine*, 34, no. 200, 172–173.

72   Sears, *McClellan's Correspondence*, 191–192, letter dated February 27, 1862, from McClellan to his wife; Kelley, *Lincoln and Stanton*, 24.

On February 25, Stanton and the Joint Committee met with the president. Taking aim at their favorite target, they made little headway. Chandler and Wade threatened to raise McClellan's sluggishness on the floor of the Senate and propose a resolution ordering Lincoln to direct an advance at once. Several other meetings followed.[73]

The constitutional niceties of separation of powers and the president as commander in chief made the Committee's threat meaningless as a matter of compulsion, and Lincoln's knowledge of these principles would have precluded any concern on this score. But the practical consequences of an ugly debate about the strategic use of the nation's largest army presented more serious concerns, especially when the general in chief was about to begin a grand operation at Harpers Ferry and follow it with an even more grand change of base.

---

73   Detroit Post and Tribune, *Chandler*, 228.

Bibliography

*I*n the past thirty years the amount of newly published primary source material on the military aspects of the American Civil War has exploded, making the task of the historian easier, more difficult, more rewarding, and more frustrating. The new does not supplant the old, but it does answer many more tiny questions. The regimentals, the slim volumes of letters from insignificant men about insignificant events, the uncritical battle studies. Before I began to sweat in their vineyard, I scorned them because they were beneath the real historian. But, in truth, they all make invaluable, if not indispensable, contributions to the researcher-writer. Along with this dramatic increase in material we enjoy a dramatic growth of scholarship and thought about our favorite subject, the dominant event of the American nineteenth century. And the vast majority of this qualitative concentration on the military aspects of the war has come from the pens of amateurs. The great theories of the era still come from the professional ranks, old and new, James Ford Rhodes, George Bancroft, James Bassett Moore, Frederick Jackson Turner, Carl Becker, John Hope Franklin, Arthur Schlesinger, James M. McPherson, and Herman Belz. But the best insights into the military questions came then and come now from the amateurs who abound in the field.

The bibliography for volume two differs from that in volume one. Earlier, descriptive paragraphs accompanied the designations for many of the sources. For those sources reappearing in volume two, the paragraph will not reappear unless a portion of it seems particularly relevant. New sources, if they warrant it, will have a descriptive paragraph.

Manuscripts

William W. Averell MSS (New York State Library and the Gilder Lehrman Collection in the Morgan Library).

John B. Bachelder MSS (New Hampshire Historical Society).

Bancroft-Bliss Family MSS (Library of Congress). The mass of Civil War material in this collection relates almost entirely to family business and personal matters, but interesting material exists in it, including a long personal narrative by Bliss about quartermaster duties during the Peninsula Campaign.

Brown, Edwin A. MSS (Civil War Institute, Carroll College, Wisconsin). Serving in the Sixth Wisconsin in the Iron Brigade with, among others, Rufus Dawes, Brown wrote long, literate letters home. A typewritten transcript of them is available. The author is indebted to Lance Herdegen, wizard of Wisconsin in the War, for his copy. Like Henry Ropes', Brown's pen falls silent at the end of a bloody day in the history of the army; and the reader feels he has lost a special friend.

Nathaniel Banks MSS (Library of Congress).

Francis Channing Barlow MSS (Massachusetts Historical Society).

S. L. M. Barlow MSS (Huntingdon Library).

James Barnes MSS (N.Y.H.S.).

William F. Barry MSS (Buffalo Historical Society). For a man who played such a large early role a distressingly small collection, primarily of official documents.

James G. Bennett MSS (New York Public Library).

James C. Biddle MSS (Pennsylvania Historical Society). Serving first as a company grade line officer, Biddle became an aide to Ricketts, then to Meade. His letters contain excellent factual material and commentary.

Simon Cameron MSS (Library of Congress).

Ezra Carmen MSS (New York Public Library).

Century Company MSS (New York Public Library). This massive collection contains the correspondence by which Johnson and Buel determined who would write articles for their legendary series. Some of the letters seeking selections contain lengthy factual accounts presumably intended to convince the two editors that the applicant had something valuable to say. The rewards of study are significant, but the burden of sifting is severe. Some of the applicants who failed the admissions correspondence test left valuable narrative material behind. Others left a disappointing but suggestive gap in our knowledge.

Zachariah Chandler MSS (L.C.).

George H. Chapman, MS Diary (Indianapolis Historical Society).

Salmon P. Chase MSS (University Productions, Inc.). Still an indispensable and invaluable collection.

Miscellaneous Civil War Collection (Huntington Library).

Miscellaneous Civil War Letters (New York Historical Society).

Edward Payson Clar MSS (Missouri Historical Society).

Schuyler Colfax MSS (Indiana Historical Society).

Comtes MS memoirs (Library of Congress). According to Comtes, he served as colonel of the Sixth United States Cavalry in the Peninsula campaign, then as colonel of the Second Ohio Cavalry, neither of which are consistent with *Cullum* or any other source.

Court-martial Transcript of Colonel Henry Anisansel, First Virginia Cavalry (National Archives, Record Group 393, Number 693).

Croffut MSS. This collection has most of Croffut's work papers for his book about Hitchcock, the most valuable being an unfortunately partial transcript of Hitchcock's diary.

Caspar Crowninshield MSS Diary (Boston Public Library).

John A. Dahlgren MSS (Library of Congress). For a naval officer, unusually informative about the army because of Dahlgren's correspondents.

Philippe D'Orleans, Comte dé Paris MSS and MS Diaries (Archieve Nationale de la Maison de France). The indispensable diaries, large and small, of the heir to the French throne. After three and one half years of frustrating correspondence, the author finally obtained permission from the royal family in Amboise and from the library staff in Paris to work in the collection. The correspondence, which must have been large at one time, is sparse, but the diaries are extraordinary.

Dwight Family MSS, particularly the letters of William and Wilder (Massachusetts Historical Society). The published letters of Wilder were edited by the family in the frustrating, restrained style of the nineteenth century. The originals will reward the extra effort.

Fourth Corps MSS (New York Historical Society). An unusually large and complete collection of official Fourth Corps records, this, like the McClellan and Hooker papers, shows how little control the Army and the government had over records in the hands of higher-ranking officers. The National Archives have no significant collection of Fourth Corps records.

William B. Franklin MSS (Library of Congress).

John Charles Fremont MSS including MS Reminiscences by John and Jessie (University of California, Berkeley). Except for the official military papers, the papers, at least in information, are equally valuable from both John and Jessie, who was born one hundred fifty years too soon and is one of the few women of the era with real ability.

William Frothingham MSS (New York Public Library). For the brief period Frothingham served as surgeon for the Fortieth New York, a literate record of daily life for officers.

John Gibbon MSS (Maryland Historical Society). A small collection of letters, many of which are quoted in the autobiography written by Gibbon after the war.

John Gibbon (MSS) (Pennsylvania Historical Society). Although Gibbon wrote one of the best memoirs of any higher-ranking officer in the Union Army, his letters will reward the work of traveling and reading.

Simon Gratz MSS Collection (Civil War Generals) (Pennsylvania Historical Society). An autograph collector who tried to obtain at least one original signature of every general officer in the Union Army, Gratz assembled at least one letter from many, if not all. Because the signature was the goal, the content is as diverse and sometimes useless as any other miscellaneous collection.

Horace Greeley MSS (New York Public Library).

Francis Vinton Greene MSS (New York Public Library).

Griess, Thomas E., MS dissertation "Dennis Hart Mahan: West Point Professor and Advocate of Professionalism, 1830–1871" (UMI dissertation services, 1969). This well-written, marvelously researched study deserves to be published; but its market is probably too small to induce a publisher to do it.

Charles Graham Halpine MSS (Huntington Library).

John P. Hatch MSS (Library of Congress).

Louis M. Haupt MSS (Library of Congress).

Samuel P. Heintzelman MSS (Library of Congress). Still indispensable.

Edward W. Hinks MSS (Boston University).

Ethan Allen Hitchcock MSS (Library of Congress).

Joseph Hooker MSS (Huntington Library).

Oliver Otis Howard MSS (Bowdoin College). A huge collection of personal and official correspondence. Howard was a vigorous and informative correspondent even after he was forced to switch hands and learn to write a second time.

Andrew Atkinson Humphreys MSS (Pennsylvania Historical Society). Engineer, staff officer, chief of staff to Meade, and corps commander, Humphreys was one of the few universally respected and admired men in the Army of the Potomac and his pronouncements on controversial issues can usually be taken as gospel limited only by human ability to observe. His collection includes both personal letters to his wife and many official documents not routinely available.

Henry Jackson Hunt MSS (Library of Congress) including "Notes for a biography of General Ricketts," by Hunt.

E. C. James MSS (Yale University). A small collection of letters by a junior officer in an engineer regiment.

Reverdy Johnson MSS (Maryland Historical Society).

August V. Kautz MS rem. (L.C.). Typewritten transcript.

Philip W. Kearny MSS (Library of Congress).

William A. Ketcham MS Reminiscences (Indiana Historical Society).

Frederick W. Lander MSS (Library of Congress).

Robert Todd Lincoln MSS (Library of Congress). The correspondence and other materials received by Abraham Lincoln, especially during his presidency. Available on microfilm.

Theodore Lyman MSS (Massachusetts Historical Society). Edited and published as *Meade's Headquarters* by Edward Meade Agassiz, Lyman's complete letters in this collection including the postwar correspondence along with one or two other sources are indispensable for the Army of the Potomac from late 1863 to 1865.

J. K. F. Mansfield MSS (United States Military Academy). A small collection of letters primarily to his daughter Mary.

Manton Marble MSS (Library of Congress). Invaluable for the long, frank letters from Fitz John Porter to Marble.

George A. McCall MSS (Pennsylvania Historical Society). Numerous official documents that did not find their way into the *Official Records* or *Broadfoot's Supplement*.

George B. McClellan MSS (Library of Congress). In spite of requests from the War Department and from Grant when the latter was general in chief, McClellan refused to deliver his papers to the government or allow access to them. Several of the "not found" documents noted in *OR* can be found here, and no good work on the Army of the Potomac or McClellan can proceed without them.

McCoun, Richard A., unpublished MS master's thesis, *George Brinton McClellan: from West Point to the Peninsula; the Education of a Soldier and the Conduct of War* (1973) 71–74 (UMI dissertation services). An interesting account for all except the Civil War period.

George G. Meade MSS (Pennsylvania Historical Society). A huge collection, much of which has been published, it is nevertheless valuable for the unpublished letters and the incoming correspondence.

T. A. Meysenburg MSS (Missouri Historical Society).

Military Historical Society of Massachusetts MSS John Codman Ropes letters (Boston University, Mugar Library). A collection that rewards every minute of study and requires little sifting, the Ropes collection, with one or two exceptions, including an extraordinary letter on First Bull Run, contains letters responding to inquiries by Ropes about incidents covered in his history of the war and are invaluable at the army, corps, and division level.

Robert H. Milroy MSS (Indiana Historical Society).

William Roby Moore MS rem (Indiana Historical Society). Moore wrote five versions of his recollections, all of which are in the collection.

Edwin D. Morgan MSS (New York State Library). Like all available governor's papers, a massive collection with particularly numerous incoming letters from persons whose letters are hard to find, e.g., the largest and most informative collection of Wadsworth letters.

MS Court of Inquiry in the case of Dixon S. Miles (National Archives).

N.a., *He Walked With Lincoln* MS biography of Edward Donald Baker (Oregon Historical Society).

National Archives, Record Group 94, Records of the Adjutant General's Office, Compiled Military Service Records, First West Virginia Cavalry (Anisansel, Colonel Henry).

National Archives, Record Group 393, vol. II, Polyonymous Successions of Commands, 1861–1870, No. 3, 3d Army Corps., no. 186, Sickles personal letters, letters received by Daniel E. Sickles, 1861–1863.

James Nesmith MSS (Oregon Historical Society). Senator from Oregon, Nesmith left a small but valuable collection of correspondence with Union officers, particularly Joseph Hooker, and other senators.

John G. Nicolay MSS (Library of Congress). In addition to Nicolay's personal letters and random memoranda, recently edited in his excellent style by Professor Burlingame, the collection contains a translation of the inscrutable Montgomery C. Meigs MS diary.

Officers MS Reports of Services (National Archives). Intending to identify ineffective officers lost in the assignment mill but holding slots that could be given to more qualified junior officers awaiting promotion, Congress passed a law requiring all general officers to submit reports of their activities during the war. For historical reasons Congress continued the requirement after the war. The result is an invaluable source for both narrative and personal information. The archives have put them on microfilm, the complete set of eight reels is available at a very reasonable price, and soon they will all be available in a multi-volume set.

Edward Otho Cresap Ord MSS (Stanford Univ.). Not large, this collection contains little more than Ord's personal letters to his wife.

Alfred Pleasanton MSS (Library of Congress).

David D. Porter MS "Private Journal of Occurrences" (L.C.).

Fitz John Porter MSS (Library of Congress). Although devoted to every detail of the court-martial and the re-trial, this collection is indispensable for the first two years of the war in the East, especially the correspondence after 1865.

William Warren Potter, M.D., MS Reminiscences (Buffalo Historical Society). *Three Years With the Army of the Potomac: A Personal Military History*. Typewritten unpublished manuscript of approximately 100 pages by an infantryman who enlisted from Buffalo.

Henry J. Raymond MSS (New York Public Library). Approximately three hundred letters which include a wide variety of correspondence over a very lengthy period of time. It also includes various letters relating to McClellan, his attempt to suppress the *New York Times*, and the attitude of certain officers toward him.

John A. Roebling MSS (Rutgers University).

Henry Ropes MSS (Boston Public Library). The best published or unpublished letters of a junior company grade officer, who served in an active Massachusetts regiment, and the surviving record of one of the many literate graduates of Harvard University who gave their lives in the cause.

Schoff Collection (Stone MS) (Clement Library, Univ. Mich.). Like the Palmer and Gratz Collections, a random, but excellent, gathering of miscellaneous collections and items.

Carl Schurz MSS (Wisconsin State Archives).

Phillip Schuyler MSS (New York Historical Society).

Winfield Scott MSS (Library of Congress).

John Sherman MSS (Library of Congress). Served as an aide to Patterson; his letters are valuable for his participation in the Valley.

Daniel E. Sickles MSS (New York Historical Society). A collection of approximately two hundred letters, a few of which have to do with the Civil War. Some, however, are extremely interesting and supply good details not found in other places. Another interesting collection of letters, primarily about the Second Battle of Gettysburg, can be found in the National Archives.

Franz Sigel MSS (New York Historical Society). Much of the valuable material is in German.

T. C. H. Smith MSS (Ohio Historical Society). Primarily a MS account from Pope's viewpoint of Second Bull Run, the best defense of Pope, an indefensible man, by anyone, then or now. Smith's narrative, however biased, deserves publication.

William F. ("Baldy") Smith MSS (Vermont Historical Society). Both MS Memoirs by Smith, one in the form of a letter to his daughter and recently published, are in this collection. But it has much more, primarily organized by and devoted to the many controversial incidents in which he participated.

Edwin McM. Stanton MSS (Library of Congress). Although they have very little personal correspondence, Stanton's papers contain valuable memoranda of important meetings and reports from his staff of diligent assistant secretaries about the Army of the Potomac.

Stevens Family MSS (University of Washington). Primarily letters of or about Isaac Ingalls and Hazard, this collection, cut short in part by Isaac's death at Chantilly, is very useful.

Charles Sumner MSS (Harvard University) (a U.P.I. microfilm of Sumner's papers is in the Butler Library of Columbia University). My schoolmate Alfred Bakhash, who veered away to Harvard when we graduated from school, kindly found an important letter for me in Sumner's massive collection in the fall of 1957.

Union Defense Committee (New York Historical Society). Active in critical ways at the beginning of the war, the committee filled many important needs when the federal government could not and touched many important people.

John Caldwell Tidball MS Reminiscences (Library of Congress and United States Military Academy). These are two parts of Tidball's manuscript reminiscences.

Charles Townsend MSS (New York State Library). A small collection of personal letters.

Wadsworth Family MSS (Library of Congress). Regrettably only a small volume of material from James survives; and in spite of the statement by Pearson in his biography, no letters exist in the Charles Sumner Papers.

James S. Wadsworth MSS (University of Rochester). Another small collection.

Gouverneur Kemble Warren MSS (New York State Library). Although, like the Porter manuscripts, Warren's collection has much of its shelf space devoted to a hearing on his removal from command of the Fifth Corps by Sheridan at Five Forks, it is still invaluable for the Army of the Potomac.

Alexander Stuart Webb MSS (Yale University, Sterling Library). Staff officer to Barry, brigade commander at the bloody angle at Gettysburg, and staff officer to Meade, Andy Webb wrote letters to his naggy wife that are cited by all but read by few, until recently, especially the postwar correspondence.

Willey MS Reminiscences (Vermont Historical Society).

William S. Tilton MSS (Boston Public Library).

Trumble MSS (L.C.) letter dated August 13, 1861, from Preston to Trumble.

John E. Wool MSS (New York State Library). A massive collection covering many years of both personal and professional affairs of the second-ranking officer in the United States Army at the outbreak. They give marvelous insight into the problems Wool inflicted on McClellan and the methods he used to do it.

Officer's Biographies, Autobiographies, Diaries, Letters, and Reminiscences

Acken, J. Gregory, ed., *Inside the Army of the Potomac: the Civil War Experience of Captain Francis Adams Donaldson* (Mechanicsburg, 1998).

Adams, F. Colburn, *The Story of a Trooper* (New York, 1865).

Agassiz, George R., ed., *Meade's Headquarters 1863–1865, Letters of Colonel Theodore Lyman from the Wilderness to Appottomax* (Boston, 1922).

Albert, Don E., *Brandy Station to Manilla Bay: A Biography of General Wesley Merritt* (Austin, 1980).

Ambrose, Stephen E., *Halleck: Lincoln's Chief of Staff* (Baton Rouge, 1962).

Anders, Curt, *Henry Halleck's War: a fresh Look at Lincoln's Controversial General in Chief* (Indiana, 1999).

(Anonymous, ed.) *War Letters of William Thompson Lusk, Captain, Assistant Adjutant General, United States Volunteers 1861–1863 M.D. LL. D.* (New York, 1911).

Applegate, John S., *Reminiscences and Letters of George Arrowsmith of New Jersey, Late Lieutenant-Colonel of the 157th Regiment, New York State Volunteers* (Red Bank, 1893).

Arnold, T. J., *Early Life and Letters of General Thomas J. Jackson "Stonewall" Jackson* (New York, 1916).

Athearn, Robert G., *Thomas Francis Meagher: An Irish Revolutionary in America* (Boulder, 1949).

Baltz, John D., *Edward D. Baker, U.S. Senator from Oregon, one of America's Heroes: Colonel E. D. Baker's Defense in the Battle of Ball's Bluff, fought October 21st 1861, in Virginia and slight Biographical Sketches of Colonel Baker, Colonel Wistar, and Colonel Stone* (Philadelphia, 1888).

Bayard, Samuel J., *The Life of George Dashiell Bayard: late Captain, U.S.A., and Brigadier-General of Volunteers, Killed in the Battle of Fredericksburg, Dec. 1862* (New York, 1874).

Benedict, George Grenville, *Army Life in Virginia: Letters from the Twelfth Vermont Regiment and Personal Experiences of Volunteer Service in the War for the Union 1862–63* (Burlington, 1895).

Blair, William Alan, ed., *A Politician Goes to War: the Civil War Letters of John White Geary* (University Park, 1995).

Blake, Henry N., *Three Years in the Army of the Potomac* (Boston, 1865). As one of the most extreme critics of virtually every general he saw and all officers as a class (with the exceptions of Hooker, Kearny, and Grant), Blake ranks with the anonymous author of *Red Tape and Pigeon Hole Generals* and Wilkeson (*Personal Recollections of the Civil War*).

Blight, David W., ed., *When this Cruel War Is Over: the Civil War Letters of Charles Harvey Brewster* (Amherst, 1992). One of the recent publications of letters, this collection has useful personal information and information relevant to the work at hand.

Bloodgood, Rev. J. D., *Personal Reminiscences Of The War* (New York and Cincinnati, 1893).

Burr, Frank A., *Life and Achievements of James Addams Beaver* (Philadelphia, 1882).

Butler, Benjamin Franklin, *Butler's Book, A Review of his Legal, Political, and Military Career* (Boston, 1892).

Butterfield, J. L., ed., *A Biographical Memorial of General Daniel Butterfield including many Addresses and Military Writings* (New York, 1904).

Byrne, Frank L., and Jean Powers Soman, *Your True Marcus: The Civil War Letters of a Jewish Colonel* (Kent, 1995). The marketing gimmick, a "Jewish" colonel, tells little about the content and without the title, the reader would have difficulty discerning the ethnic fact.

Byrne, Frank L., and Weaver, Andrew T., eds., *Haskell of Gettysburg: His Life and Civil War Papers* (Madison, 1970).

Campbell, James Havelock, *McClellan: A Vindication of the Military Career of General George B. McClellan, A Lawyers Brief* (New York, 1916).

Cannon, LeGrand B., *Personal Reminiscences of the Rebellion: 1861–1866* (New York, 1895). Cannon served as a volunteer aide on the staff of General Wool during the first two years of the war. His memoirs contain a number of interesting anecdotes about Wool's conduct in command of Fort Monroe in 1861 and the relations between Wool and McClellan during the Peninsula campaign.

Cleaves, Freeman, *Meade of Gettysburg* (Norman, 1960).

Cochrane, John, "The War for the Union" (New York, 1879) (pamphlet).

Coco, Gregory A., Ed., *Through Blood and Fire: The Civil War Letters of Major Charles J. Mills, 1862–65* (Gettysburg, 1982).

Condon, William H., *The Life of Major General James Shields: Hero of Three Wars and Senator from Three States* (Chicago, 1900). Hero worship bias is everywhere.

Corby, William, C. S. C., *Memoirs of Chaplain Life: Three Years with the Irish Brigade in the Army of the Potomac* (New York, 1992). Another of the valuable recent additions to the literature.

Cox, Jacob Dolson, *Military Reminiscences of the Civil War*, Two Volumes (New York, 1900).

Cozzens, Peter, and Robert I. Girardi, eds., *The Military Memoirs of General John Pope* (Chappel Hill and London, 1998). For this job of editing, Cozzens and Girardi deserve a medal, Pope having left so little contemporary or later correspondence.

Crary, Catherine S., Ed., *Dear Belle—Letters from a Cadet & Officer to his Sweetheart, 1858–1865* (Middletown, 1965).

Croffut, W. A., ed., *Fifty Years in Camp and Field—Diary of Major-General Ethan Allen Hitchcock* U.S.A. (New York, 1909). This book is a rambling collection of partial diary entries, letters, vignettes from newspapers, and a variety of other unidentified sources, and personal commentary. It covers the lengthy military life of Ethan Allen Hitchcock. The brief segment treating the Civil War is useful only in its demonstration of the confusion of the civilian authorities in Washington at various times, particularly 1862, and the incompetence of Hitchcock.

Curtis, Newton Martin, *From Bull Run to Chancellorsville: the Story of the Sixteenth New York Infantry together with personal Reminiscences* (New York, 1906).

Dahlgren, Madeleine Vinton, *Memoir of John A. Dahlgren, Rear-Admiral, United States Navy* (New York, 1891).

de Forest, B. S., *Random Sketches and Wandering Thoughts* (Albany, 1866).

de Forest, John William, *A Volunteer's Adventures, a Union Captain's Record of the Civil War* (New Haven, 1946).

De Montravel, Peter R., *A Hero to his Fighting Men: Nelson A. Miles 1839–1925* (Kent and London 1998).

De Peyster, John Watts, *Personal and Military History of Phillip Kearny, Major General United States Volunteers* (New York, 1869). Cumbersomely written, excessively laudatory, and often irrelevant, this biography is nevertheless the best printed collection of original source material on Kearny. Although it was written by a worshipful relative, it nevertheless also points out many of Kearny's disabilities and the restraints they imposed on his Civil War career.

de Trobriand, Regis, trans. George K. Dauchy, *Four Years With the Army of the Potomac* (Boston, 1889).

Dix, Morgan, *Memoirs of John A. Dix*, 2 vols. (New York, 1883). The war consumes only a small part of this work, another laudatory "family member" piece. It best shows the frustrations of early would-be leaders.

Donaghy, John, *Army Experience of Captain John Donaghy, 103d Penn'a Vols. 1861–1864* (Deland, 1926).

Doster, William E., *Lincoln and Episodes of the Civil War* (New York and London, 1915).

Draper, William F., *Recollections of a Varied Career* (Boston, 1908).

Dwight, ed., *Life and Letters of Wilder Dwight* (Boston, 1867). This work discloses no author on the title page or at any other specific place, but it was obviously edited and written by a close relative of Wilder Dwight, most probably his mother or his father. It gives an interesting first-hand account of the formation and operations of the Second Massachusetts Infantry and an interesting insight into certain of the higher-ranking officers in command of the Union forces in the Shenandoah Valley in 1862. It stops at the battle of Antietam, where Dwight was mortally wounded. The Dwight family papers, including letters from William and Wilder, have recently been deposited in the Massachusetts Historical Society, which allows the compulsive author to fill the annoying nineteenth century editing omissions.

Eby, Cecil D. Jr., ed. *A Virginia Yankee in the Civil War—the Diary of David Hunter Strother* (Chapel Hill, 1961). A staff officer born and raised in the Shenandoah Valley in the area of Martinsburg, Virginia, and well-known because of publications showing his familiarity with the Valley. Strother served almost entirely in the Shenandoah Valley during his military career. The diary was apparently not prepared on a day-to-day basis and entries on many days were obviously made at later times. More interesting, although requiring care and verification, are the parallel articles in *Harper's*.

Ecelberger, Gary L., *Frederick W. Lander, the Great American Natural Soldier* (Baton Rouge, 2000). Every knowable fact about Lander by an indefatigable researcher.

Eckenrode, H. J., and Conrad, Bryan, *George B. McClellan: the Man who Saved the Union* (Chapel Hill, 1941).

Eckert, Edward K., and Amato, Nicholas J., Eds., *Ten Years in the Saddle—The Memoir of William Woods Averell* (San Raphael, 1978).

Elliott, Charles Winslow, *Winfield Scott, the Soldier and the Man* (New York, 1937). The best biography of Scott by far and not likely to be replaced without the discovery of some huge cache of Scott correspondence.

Emerson, Edward W., ed., *Life and Letters of Charles Russel Lowell* (Boston and New York, 1907).

Engle, Stephen D., *Yankee Dutchman: The Life of Franz Sigel* (Fayetteville, 1993).

Favill, Josiah Marshall, *The Diary of a Young Officer—Serving with the Armies of the United States During the War of the Rebellion* (Chicago, 1909).

Ford, Worthington Chauncey, ed., *A Cycle of Adams Letters*, 2 vols. (Boston and New York, 1920).

Ford, Worthington Chauncey, ed., *War Letters 1862–1865 of John Chipman Gray and John Codman Ropes* (Boston and New York, 1927).

Forsyth, George A., *Thrilling Days in Army Life* (New York and London, 1900).

Gardner, Augustine V., ed ., *Recollections of a Civil War Quartermaster, An Autobiography of William G. Le Duc* (St. Paul, 1963).

Gibbon, John, *Personal Recollections of the Civil War* (New York and London, 1928) reprint by Morningside Bookshop. This is one of the best reminiscences written by any officer who served in any American war. It is also one of the most well-conceived, well-designed, well-written, and well-constructed personal accounts published after the war.

Gordon, George H., *Brook Farm to Cedar Mountain in the War of the Great Rebellion 1861–62* (Boston, 1883).

Gordon, George H., *A War Diary of Events in the War of the Great Rebellion, 1863–1865* (Boston, 1882). This is a continuation of Gordon's three-volume work on the Civil War, which includes *Brook Farm to Cedar Mountain*, and *The Army of Virginia*.

Gould, Edward K., *Major General Hiram G. Berry, His Career as a Contractor, Bank President, Politician and Major General of Volunteers in the Civil War Together with His War Correspondence Embracing the Period from Bull Run to Chancellorsville* (Rockland, 1899).

Gregg, Reverend J. Chandler, *Life in the Army, in the Departments of Virginia, and the Gulf, including Observations in New Orleans, with an Account of the Author's Life and Experience in the Ministry* (Philadelphia, 1866).

Gunn, Jane Augusta, *Memorial Sketches of Doctor Moses Gunn by his Wife with Extracts from his Letters and Eulogistic Tributes from His Colleagues and Friends* (Chicago, 1889).

Hagemann, E. R., ed., *Fighting Rebels and Redskins: Experiences in Army Life of Colonel George B. Sanford, 1861–1892* (Norman, 1969).

Hancock, Mrs. Almira, *Reminiscences of Winfield Scott Hancock* (New York, 1887).

Harrington, Fred Harvey, *Fighting Politician: Major General N. P. Banks* (Philadelphia, 1948).

Harris, Samuel, *Personal Reminiscences of Samuel Harris* (Chicago, 1897).

Hassler, Warren W., Jr., *General George B. McClellan, Shield of the Union* (Baton Rouge, 1957).

Haupt, Herman, *Reminiscences of General Herman Haupt* (Milwaukee, 1901).

Hebert, Walter H., *Fighting Joe Hooker* (New York, 1944).

Historical Committee, *Henry Wilson's Regiment: the Twenty-second Infantry, Second Sharpshooters, Third Light Battery, Massachusetts Volunteers* (Boston, 1887).

Hollandsworth, James G., Jr., *Pretense of Glory: the Life of General Nathaniel P. Banks* (Baton Rouge, 1998). Not the groundbreaker, but, nevertheless, the best biography of Banks.

Howard, O. O., *Autobiography of Oliver Otis Howard Major General United States Army* (2 volumes) (New York, 1907). Howard's autobiography is well-written and entertaining. It combines in a sound manner the general with the personal narrative and presents Howard's views of the controversial events in the latter half of the first day at Gettysburg.

Howe, Henry Warren, *Passages from the Life of Henry Warren Howe, Consisting of Diary and Letters Written During the Civil War, 1861–1865* (Lowell, 1899).

Howe, Mark DeWolfe, ed., *Home Letters of General Sherman* (New York, 1909).

Howe, Mark de Wolfe, ed., *Touched With Fire—Civil War Letters and Diary of Oliver Wendell Holmes, Jr. 1861–1864* (Cambridge, 1946). Holmes served first as a company-grade officer in the Twentieth Massachusetts Infantry, then as a staff officer to General Sedgwick and later General Wright when they commanded the Sixth Corps.

Humphreys, Charles A., *Field, Camp, Hospital and Prison in the Civil War 1863–1865* (Boston, 1918).

Humphreys, H. H., *Andrew Atkinson Humphreys*.

David Hunter, *Report of the Military Services of General David Hunter, U.S.A., during the War of the Rebellion made to the United States War Department* (New York, 1873).

Hyde, Thomas W., *Following the Greek Cross or, Memories of the Sixth Army Corps* (Boston and New York, 1894, 2d ed.).

Hyndman, Capt. William, *History of a Calvary Company. A Complete Record of Company "A2" 4th Penn'a Calvary* (Philadelphia, 1870).

Johnston, Joseph E., *Narrative of Military Operations During the Late War between the States* (New York, 1872).

Jones, Evan R., MS Memoirs, *Four Years in the Army of the Potomac: A Soldier's Recollections*. The author served in the Fifth Wisconsin, one of the regiments in Hancock's original brigade, and the memoirs contain a number of interesting anecdotes about Hancock.

Jordan, William B., Jr., ed., *The Civil War Journals of John Mead Gould, 1861–1866* (Baltimore, 1997). For its length and detail this is the most disappointing recent discovery and publication, especially for such an active participant in the Second Civil War.

Kennedy, Elijah R., *John B., Woodward, a Biographical Memoir* (New York, 1897).

Keyes, E. D., *Fifty Years' Observation of Men and Events Civil and Military* (New York, 1884). Although written in 1884, almost twenty years after the war, this book begins with Keyes's reminiscences from the 1830s when he served as military secretary to General Scott and ends with the withdrawal of the Union Army from Harrison's Landing in August of 1862. It is disjointed, sometimes confusing, but withal an interesting and literate account of a controversial officer's participation in the early phases of the Civil War. With the terse memoir by Smith, it is the only significant memoir of the Fourth Corps, which terminated its useful life after the Army of the Potomac withdrew from Harrison's Landing. Neither Couch nor Casey left any memoir or manuscript collection.

Keyes, E. D., *From West Point to California* (1950, Oakland). This short piece was apparently written by Keyes some years after his service in California, between the years 1849 and 1858, when he was stationed at the Presidio of San Francisco.

Kidd, James Harvey (J. H. Kidd), *Personal Recollections of a Cavalryman with Custer's Michigan Brigade in the Civil War* (Ionia, 1908). This is undoubtedly one of the very best narratives written by any participant in the Civil War and clearly one of the best cavalry accounts. Its personal vignettes of Custer, Merritt, and other officers serving in the Cavalry Corps during the war rank at the top.

Kiefer, Joseph Warren, *Slavery and Four Years of War, a political history of slavery of the United States together with a narrative of the campaigns and battles of the Civil War in which the author took part: 1861–1865*, two volumes (New York and London, 1900). Both a comprehensive history and a personal narrative, these two volumes cover a wide range of areas of the Civil War.

Lavery, Dennis S., and Jordan, Mark H., *Iron Brigade General: John Gibbon, A Rebel in Blue* (Westport and London 1993). Well researched in the primary sources, this short biography does not fill the need for a full-length biography of a devoted McClellanite who nevertheless survived the witch hunts to end the war in command of a corps.

Lewis, Lloyd, *Sherman: Fighting Prophet*, 2 vols. (Norwalk, 1991, Easton Press ed.). A long-standing biography that has stood the test of time but frustrates with sparse citations of original authorities.

Longacre, Edward G., *General John Buford* (Conshohocken, 1995). The standard, long-overdue biography by the keeper of the cavalry of the Army of the Potomac.

Longacre, Edward G., *The Man behind the Guns: a Biography of General Henry J. Hunt, Commander of Artillery, Army of the Potomac* (New York, 1977). Still the best of Longacre's many works on the Army of the Potomac.

Mahood, Wayne, *General Wadsworth: the Life and Times of Brevet Major General James S. Wadsworth* (Cambridge, 2003). Vastly more thoughtful than, and superior to, Pearson's work.

Malles, Ed., ed., *Bridge Building in Wartime: Colonel Wesley Brainerd's Memoir of the 50th New York Volunteer Engineers* (Knoxville, 1997). One of the best recent contributions to the growing Civil War literature. One could only wish for more newly discovered works like this and the Willcox letters and diaries.

Marshall, Jessie Ames, ed., *Private and Official Correspondence of Gen. Benjamin F. Butler During the Period of the Civil War*, 5 vols. (Norwood, 1917).

Martin, Samuel J., *Kill-Cavalry: Sherman's Merchant of Terror: the Life of Union General Hugh Judson Kilpatrick* (Madison, 1996).

Maull, D. W., *The Life and Military Services of the Late Brigadier General Thomas A. Smyth* (Wilmington, 1870).

McClellan, George B., *McClellan's Own Story* (Norwalk, 1995) (Easton Press ed.). The most rewarding, frustrating, taxing, informative, confusing, disorganized, copied, and baffling of all postwar memoirs. From its terse style one wonders if the earlier draft, destroyed by fire, would not have made the historian's task easier. Its real value appears only when used with the MSS.

McKinney, Francis F., *Education in Violence: the Life of George H. Thomas and the History of the Army of the Cumberland* (reprint Chicago, 1991).

Meade, George Gordon, ed., *The Life and Letters of George Gordon Meade Major-General United States Army*, 2 vols. (New York, 1913). Indispensable to the history of the army and its officers corps but like McClellan's and Gibbon's memoirs should be used with the MS.

The Memoirs of Field Marshal the Viscount Montgomery of Alamain, K. G. (New York, 1958).

Merington, Marguerite, *The Custer Story: The Life and Intimate Letters of General George A. Custer and His Wife Elisabeth* (New York, 1950).

Meyer, Henry C., *Civil War Experiences Under Bayard, Gregg, Kilpatrick, Custer, Raulston, and Newberry 1862, 1863, 1864* (New York, 1911).

Michie, Peter S., *Life and Letters of Emory Upton, Colonel of the Fourth Regiment of Artillery and Brevet Major General U.S. Army* (New York, 1885).

Miller, C. G., *Donn Piatt: his Work and his Ways* (Cincinnati, 1893). A biography of a junior but well-connected officer who spent much of his time defending the indefensible persons of the war, such as Schenk and Stanton.

Miller, Edward A., Jr., *Lincoln's Abolitionist General: The Biography of David Hunter* (Columbia, 1997).

Mitchell, Donald G., ed., *Daniel Tyler: A Memorial Volume* (New Haven, 1883).

Moore, James, M.D., *Kilpatrick and Our Cavalry* (New York, 1865).

Morse, C. F., *Letters Written During the Civil War—1861–1865* (Boston, 1898).

Myers, William Starr, *General George Brinton McClellan: A Study in Personality* (New York, 1934).

Myers, William Starr, Ed., *The Mexican War Diary of General George B. McClellan: A Campaign Journal Written in Camp and Field, in 1846–47 and Now for the First Time Published* (Princeton, 1917).

Nagle, Theodore M., *Reminiscences of the Civil War* (Erie, 1923).

Nash, Howard P., Jr., *Stormy Petrel: The Life and Times of General Benjamin F. Butler, 1818–1893* (Cranbury, 1969).

Nevins, Allan, Ed., *A Diary of Battle: The Personal Journals of Colonel Charles S. Wainwright, 1861–1865* (New York, 1962). One of the best diaries maintained by anyone during the entire Civil War.

Nevins, Allen, *John Charles Fremont: Pathmarker of the West* (New York, 1955, 2d ed.). Still the best biography of Fremont.

A staff officer [Newhall, Frederick C.], *With General Sheridan in Lee's Last Campaign* (Philadelphia, 1866).

Nichols, Edward F., *Toward Gettysburg: a Biography of General John F. Reynolds* (New York, 1958).

Nicolay, John G., and Hay, John, *Abraham Lincoln, a History*, 10 vols. (New York, 1914). Not unbiased, not fair to McClellan, not replaced by Sandburg or Randall, this indispensable work wait for the work in progress by Professor Burlingame can do it better.

Niven, John, ed., *The Salmon P. Chase Papers*, 4 vols. (incomplete), vol. 3, *Correspondence, 1858–1863*.

Nolan, Dick, *Benjamin Franklin Butler.*

Norton, Oliver Willcox, *Army Letters, 1861–1865, extracts from Private Letters to Relatives and Friends from a Soldier in the Field during the late Civil War with an Appendix containing copies of some Official Documents, Papers and Addresses of a later Date* (Chicago, 1903).

Noyes, George F., *The Bivouac and the Battlefield; or Campaign Sketches in Virginia and Maryland* (New York, 1863).

Osborne, Seward R., ed., *The Civil War Diaries of Col. Theodore B. Gates, 20th New York State Militia* (Hightstown, 1991).

Palfrey, Francis Winthrop, *Memoir of William Francis Bartlett* (Boston, 1878).

Pearson, Henry Greenleaf, *James S. Wadsworth of Geneseo, Brevet Major General of United States Volunteers* (New York, 1913).

Perry, Martha Derby, *Letters from a Surgeon of the Civil War* (Boston, 1906).

Piatt, Don, *Memories of the Men who Saved the Union* (New York and Chicago, 1887).

Pinchon, Edgcumb, *Dan Sickles, Hero of Gettysburg and Yankee King of Spain* (New York, 1945).

Pisani, Lieutenant-Colonel Camille Ferri, *Prince Napoleon in America 1861, Letters from his Aide-de-Camp* (Bloomington, 1959).

Poore, Ben: Perley, *The Life and Public Services of Ambrose E. Burnside, Soldier-Citizen-Statesman* (Providence, 1882).

Poore, Ben: Perley, *Perley's Reminiscences of Sixty Years in the National Metropolis*, 2 vols. (Boston, 1986).

Porter, Admiral David D., *Incidents and Anecdotes of the Civil War* (New York, 1885).

Porter, Fitz John, *In Memory of Gen. Charles P. Stone* (n.p., n.d.) (pamphlet).

Quaife, Milo M., ed., *From the Cannon's Mouth, the Civil War Letters of General Alphius S. Williams* (Detroit, 1959).

Revere, Joseph W., *Keel and Saddle: A Retrospect of Forty Years of Military and Naval Service* (Boston, 1872).

Rhodes, Robert Hunt, ed., *All for the Union: the Civil War Diary and Letters of Elisha Hunt Rhodes* (New York, 1985).

Robertson, James I., Jr., Ed., *The Civil War Letters of General Robert McAllister* (New Brunswick, 1965).

Robertson, James I., Jr., *Stonewall Jackson: the Man, the Soldier, the Legend* (New York, 1997).

Rockwell, A. D., *Rambling Recollections and Autobiography* (New York, 1920).

Roemer, Jacob, ed. by L. A. Furney, *Reminiscences of the War of the Rebellion 1861–1865* (New York, 1897).

Rolle, Andrew, *Fremont, Character as Destiny* (Norman, 1991).

Rusling, James F., *Men and Things I Saw in Civil War Days* (New York, 1899).

Samito, Christian G., ed., *Commanding Boston's Irish Ninth: the Civil War Letters of Colonel Patrick R. Guiney, Ninth Massachusetts Volunteer Infantry* (New York, 1998). A good recent edition to the primary source literature about the war.

Schafer, Joseph, ed. and trans., *Intimate Letters of Charles Schurz 1841–1869 (Publications the State Historical Society of Wisconsin, Collections, Vol. 1130)* (Madison, 1929).

Schmitt, Martin F., ed., *General George Crook, His Autobiography* (Norman, 1946).

Schurz, Carl, *The Reminiscences of Carl Schurz*, 3 vols. (New York, 1907–1908).

Schutz, Wallace J., and Trenarry, Walter N., *Abandoned by Lincoln, a Military Biography of General John Pope* (Urbana, 1990). More authors who deserve a medal for being willing to rewrite a biography of such a low human being.

Scott, Robert Garth, ed., *Forgotten Valor: the Memoirs, Journals, & Civil War Letters of Orlando B. Willcox* (Kent, 1999). One of the major recent publications of first-hand material about the Army of the Potomac.

Scott, Robert Garth, *Forgotten Valor: The Memoirs, Journals, & Civil War Letters of Orlando B. Willcox* (Kent and London, 1999).

Scrymser, James A., *Personal Reminiscences of James A. Scrymser in Times of Peace and War* (1915, n.p.).

Sears, Stephen W., ed., *For Country, Cause & Leader: The Civil War Journal of Charles B. Haydon* (New York, 1993). This is a superb journal of a junior company grade officer who rose to the rank of lieutenant colonel by 1864 in the Second Michigan. It gives an excellent picture of the duties and responsibilities of a junior company grade officer, the hazards of picket duty, and a variety of other responsibilities that all tend to be lost in the usual, grander civil war narrative.

Sears, Stephen W., *George B. McClellan: the Young Napoleon* (New York, 1988).

Sears, Stephen W., ed., *The Civil War Papers of George B. McClellan, Selected Correspondence 1860–1865* (New York, 1989). If this work, extremely valuable, had been published twenty-five years ago, it would have saved the author a great deal of work.

Sherman, William Tecumseh, *Personal Recollections of General William T. Sherman*, 2 vols. (Des Moines, 1902).

Small, Abner, *Road to Richmond* (California, 1939).

Snell, Mark A., *From First to Last, the Life of Major General William B. Franklin* (New York, 2002). A new and the only biography of Franklin from his personal papers, which defied the author's best efforts to find them.

Sparks, David S., ed., *Inside Lincoln's Army: the Diary of General Marsena R. Patrick, Provost Marshal General, Army of the Potomac* (New York and London, 1964).

Stevens, Hazard, *The Life of Isaac Ingalls Stevens*, two volumes (Boston and New York, 1900).

Stoeckel, Carl and Ellen, eds., *Correspondence of John Sedgwick, Major-General*, 2 vols. (n.p. 1903).

Styple, William B., ed., Nathalie Chartrain, trans., *Our Noble Blood: the Civil War Letters of Regis de Trobriand Major-General U.S.V.* (Kearny, 1997).

Swanberg, W. A., *Sickles the Incredible* (New York, 1956). The best reasonably current biography of a highly visible, always controversial officer.

Taylor, James E., *With Sheridan up the Shenandoah Valley in 1864: Leaves from a Special Artist's Sketch Book and Diary* (Cleveland, 1989). This book has a great deal more valuable historical information in it than its artsy appearance suggests.

Thomas, Mary Warner and Richard A. Sauers, *The Civil War Letters of First Lieutenant James B. Thomas, Adjutant, 107th Pennsylvania Volunteers* (Baltimore, 1995).

Thompson, Jerry, ed., *Fifty Miles and a Fight: Major Samuel Peter Heintzelman's Journal of Texas and the Cortina War* (Austin, 1998).

Tilney, Robert, *My Life in the Army: Three Years and a Half with the Fifth Army Corps, Army of the Potomac, 1862–1865, by Robert Tilney, Company D, Twelfth N.Y. Volunteers and Sergeant Company F., Fifth New York Veteran Volunteer Infantry* (Philadelphia, 1912).

Townsend, Brevet Major-General Edward D., *Anecdotes of the Civil War in the United States* (New York, 1881).

Tremain, Henry Edwin, *Last Hours of Sheridan's Cavalry* (New York, 1904).

Tremain, Henry Edwin, *Two Days of War: A Gettysburg Narrative and Other Excursions* (New York, 1905).

Trumbull, H. Clay, *War Memories of an Army Chaplain* (New York, 1898).

Tyler, Daniel, *Damiel Tyler: a Memorial Volume, Containing his Autobiography and War Record. Some Account of his Later Years and with Various Reminiscences and the Tributes of Friends* (New Haven, 1883).

Tyler, Mason Whiting, *Recollections of the Civil War with Many Original Diary Entries and Letters Written from the Seat of War and with Annotated References* (New York and London, 1912).

Walker, Charles N. and Rosemary, *Diary of the War by Robert S. Robertson, 93d Reg't. N.Y. Vols. & A.D.C. to Gen. N. A. Miles, Commanding 1st Brigade, 1st Division, 2d Army Corp, 1861–2–3–4* (Indiana, 1965).

Walker, Francis A., *General Hancock* (New York, 1895).

Wallace, Lewis, *Lew Wallace: an Autobiography*, 2 vols. (New York, 1905).

Weigley, Russell F., *Quartermaster General of the Union Army: a Biography of M. C. Meigs* (New York, 1956).

Weigley, Russell F., *Quartermaster General of the Union Army: a Biography of Montgomery C. Meigs* (New York, 1959).

Weld, Stephen Minot, *War Diary and Letters of Stephen Minot Weld, 1861–1865* (Boston, 1979, 2nd ed.). Originally prepared by Weld and published in 1912 in fifty copies for his family, this is one of the most invaluable works written by any of the participants in the war.

Whittaker, Frederick, *A Complete Life of Gen. George A. Custer, Major-General of Volunteers, Brevet Major-General, U.S. Army, and Lieutenant-Colonel, Seventh U.S. Cavalry* (New York, 1876). Custer's incomplete reminiscences of the war appear without attribution verbatim in the text.

Williams, Frederick D., ed., *The Wild Life of the Army: Civil War Letters of James A. Garfield* (Michigan, 1964).

Wilson, Calvin Dill, ed., *Sword and Gown by John R. Paxton D. D. Soldier And Preacher, A Memorial Volume* (New York, 1926).

Wilson, James H., *Life and Services of William F. Smith, Major General, United States Volunteers in the Civil War* (Wilmington, 1904).

Wilson, James Harrison, *Under the Old Flag—Recollections of Military Operations in the War for the Union, the Spanish War, the Boxer Rebellion, etc.*, two volumes (New York and London, 1912). This is one of the outstanding military reminiscences written by any general officer. However, it is marred from time to time by "if only they had . . . I would have . . . "

Wistar, Isaac Jones, *Autobiography of Isaac Jones Wistar, 1825–1907* (Philadelphia, 1937).

Wister, Sara B. *Walter S. Newhall, A Memoir* (Philadelphia, 1864). This slim volume, printed during the war after Newhall's death, contains parts of a number of interesting letters written by Newhall during the war. Newhall himself served, after a brief tour of duty in Missouri at the outset of the war, in a distinguished regiment, the Third Pennsylvania Cavalry.

Youker, J. Clayton, ed., *The Military Memoirs of Captain Henry Cribben of the 140th New York Volunteers* (n.p., 1911).

Enlisted Men's Letters, Diaries, and Reminiscences

Adams, John G. V., *Reminiscences of the 19th Massachusetts Regiment* (Boston, 1899).

Allen, Stanton G., *Down in Dixie: Life in a Calvary Regiment in the War Days from the Wilderness to Appomattox* (Boston, 1893).

(Anonymous) A Citizen-Soldier, *Red Tape and Pigeon-Hole Generals: As Seen From the Ranks During a Campaign in the Army of the Potomac* (New York, Carleton, 1864). This extraordinary book was written by a member of Tyler's brigade of Humphrey's division, Fifth Corps, after the battle of Antietam. The division was composed primarily of short-term enlisted men and was disbanded almost immediately after the battle of Chancellorsville. It should be compared with Wilkeson for its vituperative criticism of virtually every senior officer in the army.

Armstrong, Dr. Nelson, V. S., *Nuggets of Experience—Narratives of the Sixties and Other Days, with Graphic Descriptions of Thrilling Personal Adventures* (San Bernadino, 1904, Times—Mirror, P. and B. House).

Bennett, Edwin C., *Musket and Sword or the Camp, March, and Firing Line in the Army of the Potomac* (Boston, 1900).

Benton, Charles E. *As Seen from the Ranks—A Boy in the Civil War* (New York, 1902).

Billings, John D., *Hard Tack and Coffee or the Unwritten Story of Army Life* (Boston, 1887).

Block, Eugene B., *Above the Civil War—The Story of Thaddeus Lowe, Balloonist, Inventor, Railway Builder* (Barclay, 1966).

Borton, Benjamin, *On the Parallels or Chapters of Inner History: A Story of the Rappahannock* (Woods Town, 1903).

Bristol, Frank Milton, *The Life of Chaplain McCabe, Bishop of the Methodist Episcopal Church* (Cincinnati and New York, 1908).

Bryant, Charles E., and Nelson D. Lankford, eds., *Eye of the Storm: A Civil War Odyssey (Memoirs of Private Robert Knox Sneden)* (New York and London, 2000). Like *Gone for a Soldier* and *With Sheridan up the Shenandoah Valley,* this is a gimmick book sold as much for its art as its content, but the art is quite good, helps resolve geographic issues, and gives panaromic views. The content is better than the art because Sneden, although only a private, served at corps headquarters and wrote voluminously both during and after the war. There lies the difficulty. The work is not reliable as a first-hand, contemporaneous account of the war. Additions after the war Sneden sometimes lifted verbatim, without attribution, from other sources.

Calvert, Henry Murray, *Reminiscences of a Boy in Blue 1862–1865* (New York, 1920).

Coco, Gregory A., ed., *From Ball's Bluff to Gettysburg—And Beyond: The Civil War Letters of Private Roland E. Bowen, 15th Massachusetts Infantry 1861–1864* (Pennsylvania, 1994). Another excellent addition to the contemporaneous literature about the war.

Cole, Jacob H., *Under Five Commanders or a Boy's Experience with the Army of the Potomac* (Patterson, 1906).

Crotty, D. G., *Four Years' Campaigning in the Army of the Potomac* (Grand Rapids, Michigan, 1974).

Crowell, Joseph E., *The Young Volunteer: the everyday Experiences of a Soldier Boy in the Civil War* (Patterson, 1906).

Deane, Frank Putnam, 2nd, Ed., *"My Dear Wife . . ." the Civil War Letters of David Brett Ninth Massachusetts Battery, Union Cannonier* (n.p., 1964).

Don Pedro Quaerendo Reminisco, *Life in the Union Army by a Two Years Volunteer: a History in Verse of the Fifteenth Regiment N.Y.V. Engineers, Col. John McLeod Murphy . . .* (New York, 1864).

Foster, Alonzo, *Reminiscences and Records of the Sixth New York Veteran Volunteer Cavalry* (n.p., 1892).

Galwey, Thomas Francis Colonel W. S. Nye, ed., *The Valiant Hours* (Harrisburg, Pennsylvania, 1961).

Gause, Isaac, *Four Years With Five Armies, Army of the Frontier, Army of the Potomac, Army of the Missouri, Army of the Ohio, Army of the Shenandoah* (New York and Washington, 1908).

Goss, Warren Lee, *Recollections of a Private. A story of the Army of the Potomac* (New York, 1890).

Greenleaf, Margorie, Ed., *Letters to Eliza from a Union Soldier, 1862–1865* (New York, 1970).

Hamilton, William Douglas, R*ecollections of a Calvaryman of the Civil War after Fifty Years 1861–1865* (Columbus, Ohio, 1915).

Hennessy, John J., ed., *Fighting with the Eighteenth Massachusetts: the Civil War Memoir of Thomas H. Mann* (Baton Rouge, 2000). Another of the half dozen of exceptionally valuable, recently published participants' accounts.

Hill, Archibald F., *Our Boys: the Personal Experiences of a Soldier in the Army of the Potomac* (Philadelphia, 1864).

Jackson, Harry F. and O'Donnell, Thomas F., eds., *Back Home in Oneida: Hermon Clarke and His Letters* (Syracuse, New York, 1965).

Jones, Evan R., *Four Years in the Army of the Potomac: A Soldier's Recollections* (London, n.d.).

Keillor, James A., *No More Gallant a Deed: a Civil War Memoir of the First Minnesota Volunteers* (St. Paul, 2001). Like Hennessy's *Eighteenth Massachusetts* book and Malles, *Bridge Builders*, this, too, is one of the half dozen truly excellent personal accounts published in recent years. The author served in the First Minnesota and had a sharp eye for relevant detail.

Kennedy, Elijah R., *John B. Woodward: A Biographical Memoir* (New York, 1897).

Kieffer, Harry M., *The Recollections of a Drummer Boy* (Boston and New York, 1881) revised ed. 1888.

Locke, E. W., *Three Years in Camp and Hospital* (Boston, 1870).

Lockwood, James D., *Life and Adventures of a Drummer-Boy; or Seven Years a Soldier* (Albany, 1893).

Loving, Jerome M., ed., *Civil War Letters of George Washington Whitman* (Durham, 1975).

Lowenfels, Walter, ed., *Walt Whitman's Civil War* (New York, 1964).

Lyle, Rev. W. W., *Lights and Shadows of Army Life: Or, Pen Pictures from the Battlefield, the Camp, and the Hospital.* (Cincinnati, 1865, 2d ed.).

Lynch, Charles H., *The Civil War Diary, 1862–1865, of Charles H. Lynch, 18th Conn. Vol's.* (Hartford, Connecticut, 1915).

McKinney, E. P. *Life In Tent And Field: 1861–1865* (Boston, 1922).

Miller, Delavan S., *Drum Taps in Dixie—Memories of a Drummer Boy 1861–1865* (Watertown, 1905).

Noyes, George F., *The Bivouac and the Battlefield or Campaign Sketches in Virginia and Maryland* (New York, 1863).

Parker, David D., *A Chatauqua Boy in '61 and Afterward* (Boston, 1912).

Rauscher, Frank, *Music on the March, 1862–65, with the Army of the Potomac. 114th Regt. P.V., Collis' Zouaves* (Philadelphia, 1892).

Ryder, John J., *Reminiscences of Three Year Service in the Civil War* (New Bedford, 1928).

Spangler, Edward W., *My Little War Experience with Historical Sketches and Memorabilia* (York, 1904).

Stone, James Madison, *Personal Recollections of the Civil War, by One Who Took Part in it as a Private Soldier in the Twenty-first Volunteer Regiment of Infantry from Massachusetts* (Boston, 1918).

Truxall, Qida Craig, ed., *"Respects to All" Letters of Two Pennsylvania Boys in the War of the Rebellion* (Pittsburgh, 1962).

Urban, John W., *In Defense of the Union; or, Through Shot and Shell and Prison Pen* (Chicago, 1887).

Vanderslice, Catherine H., ed. *The Civil War Letters of George Washington Beidelman* (New York, 1978).

Viola, Herman J., ed., *The Memoirs of Henry Veil: a Soldier's Recollections of the Civil War and the Arizona Territory* (New York, 1993). Although only a small part of this narrative covers the war, it contains useful information on incidents and people, e.g., Reynolds and Ord.

White, Russell C., ed., *The Civil War Diary of Wyman S. White: First Sergeant of Company F. 2nd United States Sharpshooter Regiment, 1861–1865* (Baltimore, 1991). Detailed and interesting with relevant anecdotes.

Wilkeson, Frank, *Recollections of a Private Soldier in the Army of the Potomac* (New York, 1887). Wilkeson makes three points in this small book, which begins with the wilderness and ends with the early stages of the siege of Petersburg: Generalship on the Union side ranged from poor to cowardly, the volunteers from earlier years were excellent troops, the draftees and bounty troops were abysmal. Like all "exposes," everything in this book appears to be vastly overstated.

Williams, G. F., *Bullet and Shell: War as the Soldier Saw It: Camp, March, and Picket; Battlefield and Bivouac; Prison and Hospital* (New York, 1882).

Wing, Samuel B., *The Soldier's Story: A Personal Narrative of the Life, Army Experiences and Marvelous Sufferings Since the War of Samuel B. Wing* (n.p., 1898).

Wittenberg, Eric J., ed., *We Have It Damn Hard Out Here: the Civil War Letters of Sergeant Thomas W. Smith 6th Pennsylvania Cavalry* (Kent and London, 1999).

Young, Jesse Bowman, *What a Boy Saw in the Army, A Story of Sight-Seeing and Adventure in the War for the Union* (New York, 1894).

Unit Histories

Albert, Allen D., ed., *History of the Forty-fifth Regiment Pennsylvania Veteran Volunteer Infantry 1861–1865* (Williamsport, 1912).

Bacarella, Michael, *Lincoln's Foreign Legion: the 39th New York Infantry, the Garibaldi Guard* (Shippensburg, 1996). A modern regimental history about a controversial unit.

Banes, Charles H., *History of the Philadelphia Brigade Sixty-ninth, Seventy-first, Seventy-second, and One Hundred and Sixth Pennsylvania Volunteers* (Philadelphia, 1876).

Bates, Samuel P., *History of the Pennsylvania Volunteers 1861–1865* originally published as 5 vols. (Harrisburg, 1869, 1871).

Bates, Samuel P., *Martial Deeds of Pennsylvania* (Philadelphia, 1875).

Beach, William H., *The First New York (Lincoln) Cavalry from April 19, 1861, to July 7, 1865* (New York, 1892).

Beach, William H., *The First New York (Lincoln) Cavalry from April 19, 1861, to July 7, 1865* (New York, 1902).

Benedict, G. G., *Vermont in the Civil War: A History of the Part Taken by the Vermont Soldiers and Sailors in the War for the Union, 1861–1865*, 2 vols. (Burlington, Vermont, 1886).

Boyce, C. W., *A Brief History of the Twenty-Eighth New York State Volunteers, First Brigade, First Division, Twelfth Corps, Army of the Potomac* (Buffalo, 1896).

Bryant, Edwin E., *History of the Third Regiment of Wisconsin Volunteer Infantry 1861–1865* (Madison, Wisconsin, 1891). A very well-written and organized participants' regimental history.

Camper, Chas., and J. W. Kirkley, *Historical Record of the First Regiment Maryland Infantry, with an Appendix containing a Register of the Officers and Enlisted Men, Biographies of deceased Officers, etc., War of the Rebellion, 1861–1865* (Washington, 1861). Less helpful than most.

Captain, Thomas E., *Eighty-fourth Regiment Pennsylvania Volunteers* (Philadelphia, 1889).

Clark, Charles M., M.D., *The History of the Thirty-eighth Illinois Volunteer Veteran Infantry (Yates Phalanx) in the War of the Rebellion (1861–1865)* (Chicago, 1889).

Clowes, Walter F., *The Detroit Light Guard* (Detroit, 1900).

Committee, *History of the Fifty-Seventh Regiment Pennsylvania Veteran Volunteer Infantry, First Brigade, First Division, Third Corps, and Second Brigade, Third Division, Second Corps, Army of the Potomac* (Kearny, 1995 rep.).

Committee, *History of the Third Pennsylvania Cavalry, Sixtieth Regiment Pennsylvania Volunteers, in the American Civil War 1861–1865* (Philadelphia, 1905).

Cooke, S. G. and Benton, Charles E., EDS., *The Dutchess County Regiment, (One Hundred Fiftieth Regiment of New York State Volunteer Infantry, in the Civil War)* (Danbury, 1907).

Cowtan, Charles W., *Services of the Tenth New York Volunteers (National Zouaves) in the War of the Rebellion* (New York, 1882).

Crowninshield, Benjamin W., *A History of the First Regiment of Massachusetts Cavalry Volunteers* (Boston, 1891).

Cudworth, Warren H., *History of the First Regiment* (Boston, 1866).

Davis, Charles E., Jr., *Three Years in the Army: The Story of the Thirteenth Massachusetts Volunteers from July 16, 1861, to August 1, 1864* (Boston, 1894). A frank and fascinating discussion of relations with superior officers, especially McDowell and Abercrombie.

Davis, W. W. H., *History of the 104th Pennsylvania Regiment, From August 22, 1861, to September 30, 1864* (Philadelphia, 1866).

Denison, Rev. Frederick, *Sabres and Spurs: The First Regiment Rhode Island Cavalry in the Civil War, 1861–1865* (Central Falls, 1876).

Denison, Frederick, *Sabres and Spurs: the First Regiment Rhode Island Cavalry in the Civil War 1861–1865, its Origins, Marches, Scouts, Skirmishes, Raids, Battles, Sufferings, Victories, and Appropriate Official Papers; with the Roll of Honor and Roll of the Regiment* (Central Falls, 1876).

Elwood, Sgt. John W., *Elwood's Stories of the Old Ringgold Cavalry 1847–1865* (Cool Center, 1914). A large collection of interesting anecdotes.

Fairchild, C. B., *History of the 27th Regiment N.Y. Vols. being a record of its more than two years of Service in the War for the Union from May 21st, 1861, to May 31st, 1863* (Binghamton, New York, 1888).

Farrar, Samuel Clarke, *The Twenty-second Pennsylvania Cavalry and the Ringgold Battalion 1861–1865* (Pittsburgh, 1911).

Floyd, Frederick Clark, *History of the Fortieth (Mozart) Regiment New York Volunteers which was composed of four companies from New York, four companies from Massachusetts, and two from Pennsylvania* (Boston, 1909). One of the best regimental histories by and for participants.

Floyd, Frederick Clark, *History of the Fortieth (Mozart) Regiment New York Volunteers, which was Composed of four Companies from New York, four Companies from Massachusetts, and two Companies from Pennsylvania* (Boston, 1909).

Ford, Andrew E., *The Story of the Fifteenth Regiment Massachusetts Volunteer Infantry in the Civil War 1861–1864.*

Fremont, Jessie Benton, *The Story of the Guard: A Chronicle of the War* (Boston, 1863).

Gates, Theodore B., *The Ulsterguard and the War of the Rebellion* (New York, 1879).

Gillespie, Samuel L. "Lovejoy," *A History of Company A, First Ohio Cavalry 1861–1865: a Memorial Volume Compiled from Personal Records and Living Witnesses* (Washington, Ohio, 1898).

Goff, Alan D., ed., *The Second Wisconsin Infantry* (Dayton, 1994).

Gracey, Rev. S. L., *Annals of the Sixth Pennsylvania Cavalry* (Pennsylvania, 1868).

Hall, Henry, *Cayuga in the Field: A Record of the 19th N.Y. Volunteers, and Third New York Artillery Comprising an Account of Their Organization, Camp Life, Marches, Battles,*

Losses, Tails and Triumphs in the War for the Union, with Complete Rolls of their Numbers (Auburn, 1873).

Hard, Abner, *History of the 8th Cavalry Regiment Illinois Volunteers, During the Great Rebellion* (Aurora, 1868).

Haynes, Martin H., *A History of the Second New Hampshire Volunteer Infantry in the War of the Rebellion* (Lakeport, 1896).

Historical Committee, *History of the Nineteenth Regiment Massachusetts Volunteer Infantry 1861–1865* (Salem, 1906).

Holcombe, R. I., *History of the First Regiment Minnesota Volunteer Infantry* (Stillwater, Minnesota, 1916).

Hutchinson, Nelson V., *History of the Seventh Massachusetts Volunteer Infantry in the War of the Rebellion of the Southern States Against Constitutional Authority, 1861–1865, with description of battles, army movements, hospital life, and incidents of the camp, by officers and privates* (Taunton, 1890).

Hyndman, *History of a Cavalry Company: A Complete Record of Company A, 4th Penn'a Cavalry as Identified with that Regiment and with the Second Brigade, Second Division, Cavalry Corps in all the Campaigns of the Army of the Potomac during the last Civil War* (Philadelphia, 1872).

Hyndman, William, *History of a Cavalry Company: a complete Record of Company "A," 4th Penn'a Cavalry* (Philadelphia, 1870).

Imholte, John Q., *The First Volunteers: History of the First Minnesota Volunteer Regiment 1861–1865* (Minneapolis, 1963).

Isham, Asa B., *An Historical Sketch of the 7th Regiment Michigan Volunteer Cavalry From Its Organization, in 1862, to Its Muster Out, in 1865* (New York, n.d.).

James, Henry B., *Memories of the Civil War* (New Bedford, 1898).

Judd, David W., *The Story of the Thirty-third N.Y.S. Vols or Two Years Campaigning in Virginia and Maryland* (Rochester, 1864).

Kepler, William G., *History of the Three Months and Three Years Service from April 16th, 1861, to June 22d, 1864 of the Fourth Regional Ohio Volunteer Infantry in the War for the Union* (Cleveland, 1886).

King, David H., A. Judson Gibles, and Jay H. Northup, *History of the Ninety-third Regiment New York Volunteer Infantry, 1861–1865* (Milwaukee, 1895).

Kirk, Hyland C., *Heavy Guns and Light: A History of the 4th New York Heavy Artillery* (New York, 1890).

Lash, Gary G., *"Duty Well Done": The History of Edward Baker's California Regiment (71st Pennsylvania Regiment)* (Baltimore, 2001).

Lecomte, Ferdinand, *Campagnes de Virginia et de Maryland en 1862: Documents Officiels Soumis au Congres Traduits au L'Anglais avec Introduction et Annotations* (Paris, 1863).

Lowery, Roland, *The Story of Battery I First Regiment Ohio Volunteer Light Artillery 1861–1865* (Cincinnati, 1972) (pam.).

MacNamara, Daniel George, *The History of the Ninth Regiment Massachusetts Volunteer Infantry, Second Brigade, First Division, Fifth Army Corps, Army of the Potomac June 1861 to June 1864* (Boston, 1899).

Marvin, Edwin E., *The Fifth Regiment Connecticut Volunteers: a History Compiled from Diaries and Official Reports* (Hartford, Connecticut, 1889).

Mills, J. Harrison, *Chronicles of the Twenty-first Regiment New York State Volunteers, embracing a full History of the Regiment, from the enrolling of the first Volunteer in Buffalo April 15, 1861 to the final mustering out May 18, 1863* (Buffalo, 1887).

Moe, Richard, *The Last Full Measure: the Life and Death of the First Minnesota Volunteers* (New York, 1993).

Nash, Eugene Arus, *A History of the Forty-fourth Regiment New York Volunteer Infantry in Civil War, 1861–1865* (Chicago, 1911).

Newell, Captain Joseph Keith, *"Ours." Annals of the 10th Regiment, Massachusetts Volunteers, in the Rebellion* (Springfield, 1875). Presented in general in the form of a diary with extensive biographical information at the end, much of this book contains narrative material. The core of this volume was used for the later history of the regiment published shortly after the turn of the century as a result of funding by the Massachusetts Legislature.

Norton, Chauncey S., *The Redneck Ties, or History of the Fifteenth New York Volunteer Calvary* (Ithaca, 1891).

Osborn, Captain, and others, *Trials and Triumphs the Record of the Fifth-Fifth Ohio Volunteer Infantry* (Chicago, 1904).

Parker, John Lord, *History of the Twenty-second Massachusetts Infantry, the Second Company Sharpshooters, and the Third Light Battery, in the War of the Rebellion* (Boston, 1887).

Pennsylvania at Gettysburg, 4 vols. (1893–1938).

Pinkerton, Allan, *The Spy of the Rebellion* (New York, 1883).

Powell, William H., *The Fifth Army Corps (Army of the Potomac): a Record of Operations during the Civil War in the United States of America, 1861–1865* (New York and London, 1896). Exhaustive and a labor of love but not as good as the first-rate corps history by Frank Walker.

Prince de Joinville, William H. Hurlbert, ed. and trans., *Army of the Potomac: its Organization, its Commander, and its Campaign* (New York, 1862).

Publication Committee, *History of the Eighteenth Regiment of Calvary, Pennsylvania Volunteers (163d regiment of the line) 1862–1865* (New York, 1909).

Quint, Alonzo H., *Record of the Second Massachusetts* (Boston, 1867).

Reichardt, Theodore, *Diary of Battery A, First Regiment Rhode Island Light Artillery* (Providence, 1865).

John H. Rhoades, *History of Battery B, First Regiment Rhode Island Light Artillery in the War to Preserve the Union 1861–1865*, 33–24 (Rhodes, *B, First R.I. Arty*).

Robertson, John, *Michigan in the War* (Lansing, 1882).

Roe, Alfred S., *The Tenth Regiment Massachusetts Volunteer Infantry 1861–1864, a Western Massachusetts Regiment* (Springfield, 1909). This regiment served from the early stages of the war until the siege of Petersburg in 1864, when its three-year enlistment expired. The history is in part a daily diary of the activities of the regiment but includes excerpts from various personal reminiscences, letters, and diaries.

Roe, Alfred Seelye, *The Fifth Regiment Massachusetts Volunteer Infantry in its Three Tours of Duty, 1861, 1862–1863, 1864*.

Roe, Frederick Seelye, *History of the First Regiment of Heavy Artillery Massachusetts Volunteers: formerly the Fourteenth Regiment of Infantry 1861–1865* (Boston, 1917).

Sawyer, Franklin, *A Military History of the 8th Regiment Ohio Vol. Inf'y: its Battles, Marches, and Army Movements* (Cleveland, 1881).

Smith, James E., *A Famous Battery and its Campaigns, 1861–1864* (Washington, 1892). The best personal narrative by an enlisted artilleryman.

Smith, Thomas West, *The Story of a Cavalry Regiment: Scott's 900 Eleventh New York Cavalry from the St. Lawrence River to the Gulf of Mexico 1861–1865* (Chicago, 1897).

Sterling, Pound (Manson, William P.), *Camp Fires of the Twenty-third: Sketches of the Camp Life, Marches, and Battles of the Twenty-third Regiment, N.Y.V., during the Term of Two Years in the Service of the United States* (New York, 1863).

Stevens, Capt. C. A., *Berdan's Sharpshooters in the Army of the Potomac 1861–1865* (St. Paul, 1892).

Stevenson, James H., *"Boots and Saddles," a History of the First Volunteer Cavalry of the War, known as the First New York (Lincoln) Cavalry and also as the Sabre Regiment, its Organization, Campaigns and Battles* (Harrisburg, 1879).

Swinton, William, *Campaigns of the Army of the Potomac: a Critical History of the Operations in Virginia Maryland and Pennsylvania from the Commencement to the Close of the War 1861–1865* (New York, 1882, rev. ed.).

Swinton, *History of the Seventh New York State Militia*, 2 vols. (New York, 1902).

Sypher, J. R., *History of the Pennsylvania Reserve Corps: a Complete Record of the Organization and of the Different Companies, Regiments and Brigades Containing Descriptions of Expeditions, Marches, Skirmishes and Battles; together with Biographical Sketches of Officers and Personal Records of Each Man during his Term of Service* (Lancaster, 1865).

Thompson, Gilbert, *The Engineer Battalion in the Civil War: a Contribution to the History of the United States Engineers* (Washington, 1910).

Thomson, O. R. Howard, and Rauch, William H., *History of the "Bucktails" Kane Rife Regiment of the Pennsylvania Reserve Corps (13th Pennsylvania Reserves, 42nd of the Line)* (Philadelphia, 1906).

Thomson, Orville, *From Phillipi to Appomattox: Narrative of the Service of the Seventh Indiana Infantry in the War for the Union* (n.p., n.d.).

Todd, William, *The Seventy-ninth Highlanders New York Volunteers in the War of the Rebellion 1861–1865* (Albany, 1886).

Waite, Otis F. R., *New Hampshire in the Rebellion Containing Histories of the Several New Hampshire Regiments and Biographical Notices of Many of the Prominent Actors in the Civil War of 1861–1865* (Claremont, 1870).

Walcott, Charles F., *History of the Twenty-first Regiment Massachusetts Volunteers in the War for the Preservation of the Union 1861–65* (Boston, 1882).

Ward, George W., *History of the Second Pennsylvania Veteran Heavy Artillery from 1861 to 1865 (112th Regiment Pennsylvania Volunteers) from 1861 to 1865 including the Provisional Second Penn'a Heavy Artillery* (Philadelphia, 1904).

Waring, George E., Jr., *The Garibaldi Guard* (New York, 1893).

Welcher, Frank J., *The Union Army, 1861–1865: Organization and Operations*, 2 vols. (Bloomington and Indianapolis, 1989). Lack of footnotes makes this monumental and valuable work useful with trepidation.

Williams, K. P., *Lincoln Finds a General*, 5 vols. (New York, 1952).

Willson, Arabella M., *Disaster, Struggle, Triumph: the Adventures of 1000 Boys in Blue from August, 1862, to June, 1865* (Albany, 1870).

Wilson, Lawrence, with Historical Committee, *Itinerary of the Seventh Ohio Volunteer Infantry 1861–1864 with Roster, Portraits and Biographies*, 2 vols. (New York, 1907).

Woodward, E. M., *History of the Third Pennsylvania Reserve: being a complete Record of the Regiment with Incidents of the Camp, Marches, Bivouacs, Skirmishes and Battles, together with the Personal Record of Every Officer and Man During Their Terms of Service* (Trenton, 1883).

Miscellaneous

Adams, George Worthington, *Doctors in Blue: the Medical History of the Union Army in the Civil War* (Baton Rouge and London, 1952).

Adcock, F. E., *The Art of War under the Roman Republic* (New York, 1995 ed.).

Allen, Oliver E., *New York, New York: a History of the World's Most Exhilarating and Challenging City* (New York, 1990).

Ambrose, Stephen E., *Nothing Like It in the World: the Men who Built the Transcontinental Railroad 1863–1869* (New York, 2000).

Anbinder, Tyler, *Nativism and Slavery: The Northern-Know-Nothings and the Politics of the 1850's* (New York, 1992).

Andrews, J. Cutler, *The North Reports the Civil War* (Pittsburgh, 1955).

Barnard, Brig-Gen. J. G., and Barry, Brig. Gen. W. F., *Report of the Engineer and Artillery Operations of the Army of the Potomac from Its Organization to the Close of the Peninsula Campaign* (New York, 1863).

Barnard, John G., *The Peninsular Campaign and Its Antecedents as Developed by the Report of Maj.-Gen. George B. McClellan and Other Published Documents* (New York, 1864).

Bassford, Christopher, *Clausewitz in English: the Reception of Clausewitz in Britain and America* (New York, 1994).

Bates, David Homer, *Lincoln in the Telegraph Office: Recollections of the United States Military Telegraph Corps During the Civil War* (New York, 1907).

Bauer, K. Jack, *The Mexican War, 1846–1848,* (Norwalk, 1990, Easton Press ed.).

Beale, Howard K., ed., *The Diary of Edward Bates 1859–1866* (Washington, 1933).

Beasley, W. G., *The Meiji Restoration* (Stanford, 1972).

Belz, Herman, *Emancipation and Equal Rights: Politics and Constitutionalism in the Civil War Era* (New York and London, 1978).

Bickers, Richard Townsend, *Friendly Fire: Accidents in Battle from Ancient Greece to the Gulf War* (London, 1994).

Birkhimer, William E., *Historical Sketch of Artillery* (Washington, 1884).

Blaine, James G., *Twenty Years of Congress* (Norwich, 1884, 1886).

Blue, Frederick J., *Salmon P. Chase: a Life in Politics*, 180–185 (Kent and London, 1987).

Bogue, Allan G., *The Earnest Men: Republicans of the Civil War Senate* (Ithaca and London, 1981).

Bond, Brian, *Liddell Hart: a Study of his Military Thought* (New Brunswick, New Jersey, 1977).

Bowden, Mark, *Black Hawk Down, a Story of Modern War* (New York, 2000).

Bradley, Erwin Stanley, *Simon Cameron, Lincoln's Secretary of War: a Political Biography* (Philadelphia, 1966).

Bradley, Omar N., *A Soldier's Story* (New York, 1951).

Bremner, Robert H., *The Public Good: Philanthropy and Welfare in the Civil War Era* (New York, 1980).

Brimelow, Peter, *Alien Nation, Common Sense about America's Immigration Disaster* (New York, 1995).

Brinton, Crane, *The Anatomy of a Revolution* (New York, 1965, rev. exp. ed.).

Brockett, Doctor L. P., *Battle-Field and Hospital; or Lights and Shadows of the Great Rebellion including Thrilling Adventures, Daring Deeds, Heroic Exploits, and Wonderful Escapes of Spies and Scouts, Together with the Songs, Ballads, Anecdotes, and Humorous Incidents of the War* (n.d., n.p.).

Browne, Albert Gallatin, *Sketch of the Official Life of John A. Andrew* (Boston, 1868).

Burlingame, Michael, and John R. Turner Ettlinger, eds., *Inside Lincoln's White House: the Complete Civil War Diary of John Hay* (Carbondale and Edwardsville, Illinois, 1997).

Burton, Richard L., *Melting Pot Soldiers: the Union's Ethnic Regiments* (Ames, 1988).

Butler, J. R. M., ed. *History of the Second World War (United Kingdom Series)*, Kirby, Major-General S. Woodburn, *The War Against Japan: the Loss of Singapore* (London, 1957).

Casdorph, Paul D., *Prince John Magruder: His Life and Campaigns* (New York, 1996).

Casey, Brig.-Gen. Silas, *Infantry Tactics for the Instruction, Exercise, and Maneuvers of the Soldier, a Company, Line of Skirmishers, Battalion, Brigade, or Corps D'Armee*, 3 vols. (Washington, 1863).

Chandler, David, *The Campaigns of Napoleon*, 2 vols. (Norwalk, 1991, Easton Press Ed.).

Chandler, David G., *Dictionary of the Napoleonic Wars* (New York, 1979).

Churchill, Winston S., *Marlborough: His Life and Times*, 4 parts in 2 volumes (the original United Kingdom edition had 4 volumes and the original American edition had six) (London and Toronto, 1936, 1938, reprinted 1966).

Coffman, Edward M., *The Old Army: A Portrait of the American Army in Peacetime, 1784–1898* (New York, 1986).

Cohen, Eliot A., *Supreme Command: Soldiers, Statesmen, and Leadership in Wartime* (New York and London, 2002). The definition of war aims must always remain in the hands of the political representatives of the body politic. The achievement of those ends by military action should remain with the military, subject to absolute overview and supervision by the civilian government. And the line between—more correctly, the gray area in which the fuzzy line should lie—should remain as well defined as possible and should be observed by both sides. In this volume Cohen does not make a convincing or knowledgeable case for Lincoln as one of the great heads of state at war.

Cole, Hugh M., ed., *United States Army in World War II*, 94 vols., *European Theater of Operations*, 10 vols.

Comte de Paris, *History of the Civil War in America*, 3 vols. (Philadelphia, 1875).

Cooke, Jacob E., ed., *The Federalist* (Middletown, 1961).

Craig, Gordon A., *The Politics of the Prussian Army 1640–1945* (Oxford, 1955).

Craig, Gordon, and Loewenheim, Francis L., eds., *The Diplomats 1939–1979* (Princeton, 1994).

Creasy, Sir Edward, *The Fifteen Decisive Battles of the World* (Norwalk, 5th Ed. 1969, Easton ed.)

Crist, Lynda Lasswell, and Dix, Mary Seaton, co-eds., *The Papers of Jefferson Davis*, 10 vols. (incomplete) (Baton Rouge and London, 1971–).

Dana, Charles A., *Recollections of the Civil War: With the Leaders at Washington and in the Field in the Sixties* (New York, 1898).

Davis, William C., *Lincoln's Men: How President Lincoln became Father to an Army and a Nation* (New York, 1999).

Dayan, Moshe, *Moshe Dayan: Story of My Life* (New York, 1976).

Delbrück, Hans, trans. Walter J. Renfroe, Jr., *History of the Art of War*, 4 vols. (Lincoln and London, 1975 Eng. trans.).

The Detroit Post and Tribune, *Zachariah Chandler: An Outline Sketch of His Life and Public Services* (Detroit, 1890).

Deutscher, Isaac, *Biography of Leon Trotsky*, 3 vols. (New York and London, 1954–1963).

Dixon, Karen R., and Southern, Pat, *The Roman Cavalry from the First to the Third Century AD* (London and New York, 1992).

Donald, David, ed., *Inside Lincoln's Cabinet, the Civil War Diaries of Salmon P. Chase* (New York, 1954).

Donald, David, *Charles Sumner* 2 vols. (New York, 1960 and 1970), especially vol. 2, Donald, *Charles Sumner and the Rights of Man*.

Duffy, Christopher, *A Military Life of Frederick the Great*, 330–334 (Norwalk, 1992, Easton Press ed.).

Duffy, Christopher, *The Military Experience in the Age of Reason* (New York, 1988).

Duncan, Captain Louis C., *The Medical Department of the United States Army in the Civil War* (Gaithersburg, Maryland, n.d. reprint; orig 1900).

du Picq, Colonel Ardant, *Battle Studies: Ancient and Modern Battle* (Norwalk, 1997, Easton Press ed.).

Elliot, Jonathan, ed., *The Debates in the several State Conventions on the Adoption of the Federal Convention as recommended by the general convention at Philadelphia, in 1787*, 5 vols. (1836–1845).

Eltinge, John R., *Swords Around a Throne, Napoleon's Grande Armee* (New York and London, 1988).

Epstein, Robert M., *Napoleon's Last Victory and the Emergence of Modern War* (Lawrence, 1994).

Ericson, John, *The Red Army* (London, 1962).

Erickson, John, *The Soviet High Command: A Military-Political History 1918–1941* (London, 1962).

Eskew, Garnet Laidlaw, *Willard's of Washington: the Epic of a Capital Caravansery* (New York, 1954).

Farwell, Byron, *Eminent Victorian Soldiers: Seekers of Glory* (New York and London, 1985).

Featherstone, Donald, *Bridges of Battle: Famous Battlefield Actions at Bridges and River Crossings* (Loudon, 1998).

Fehrenbacher, Don E., *The Dred Scott Case: Its Significance in American Law and Politics* (New York, 1998).

Fishel, Edwin C., *The Secret War for the Union: The Untold Story of Military Intelligence in the Civil War* (Boston, 1996).

Ford, Worthington Chauncey, Ed., *A Cycle of Adams' Letters 1861–1865* (Boston, 1920).

Freeman, Douglas Southall, *Lee's Lieutenants: A Study in Command*, 3 vols. (New York, 1942).

Freeman, Douglas Southall, *R. E. Lee*, 4 vols. (New York, 1934). Replaced in tone by many, but has never lost its "Best biography by or about an American."

Freeman, Douglas Southall, *George Washington: a Biography*, 7 vols. (New York, 1949–1957).

French, William H., William F. Barry, and Henry J. Hunt, *Instructions for Field Artillery* (Philadelphia, 1861).

Fry, James B., *The History and Legal Effect of Brevets in the Armies of Great Britain and the United States from their Origin in 1692 to the Present Time* (New York, 1877).

Fuller, Major-General J. F. C., *The Generalship of Alexander the Great* (Norwalk, 1990, Easton Press ed.).

Gavin, James M., *On to Berlin: Battles of an Airborne Commander 1943–1946* (New York, 1978).

Gienapp, William E., *The Origins of the Republican Party, 1852–1856* (New York, 1987).

Glantz, David M., and House, Jonathan, *When Titans Clashed: How the Red Army Stopped Hitler* (Lawrence, 1995).

Goerlitz, Walter, trans. Brian Battershaw, *History of the German General Staff 1857–1945* (New York, 1953).

Goodman, Paul, *Of One Blood: Abolitionism and the Origins of Racial Equality* (Berkeley, Los Angeles, London, 1998).

Gordon, Harold J., Jr., *The Reichswehr and the German Republic 1919–1926* (Princeton, 1957).

Gordon, John Steele, *The Great Game: the Emergence of Wall Street as a World Power* (New York, 1999).

Green, Peter, *The Greco-Persian Wars* (Berkeley, 1996, rev. ed.).

Greene, Peter, *Alexander of Macedon: 356–323 B.C. A Historical Biography* (Berkeley, Los Angeles, London, rep. 1991).

Griffith, Paddy, *The Art of War of Revolutionary France 1789–1802* (London and Mechanicsburg, 1998).

Grimsley, Mark, *The Hard Hand of War: Union Military Policy toward Southern Civilians, 1861–1865* (Cambridge, 1995).

Hagerman, Edward, *The American Civil War and the Origins of Modern Warfare: Ideas, Organization, and Field Command* (Indianapolis, 1988).

Hagerman, Edward, *The American Civil War and the Origins of Modern Warfare: Ideas, Organization, and Field Command* (Indianapolis and Bloomington, 1988).

Hammond, Bray, *Sovereignty and an Empty Purse: Banks and Politics in the Civil War* (Princeton, 1970).

Hanson, Victor Davis, *Carnage and Culture: Landmark Battles in the Rise of Western Power* (New York and London, 2001).

Hart, B. H. Liddell, ed., *The Rommel Papers* (Norwalk, 1988, Easton Press ed.). One cannot read this book without seeing a much larger man than the "Desert Fox" of legend.

Hart, Salmon Portland, *Salmon Portland Chase* (Boston and New York, 1890).

Hearn, Chester G., *Six Years of Hell: Harpers Ferry during the Civil War* (Baton Rouge, 1996).

Herodotus.

Herr, Pamela, and Spence, Mary Lee, eds., *The Letters of Jessie Benton Fremont* (Urbana and Chicago, 1993).

Herrmann, David G., *The Arming of Europe and the Making of the First World War* (Princeton, 1996).

Hesseltine, William B., *Lincoln and the War Governors* (New York, 1948).

Hoffman, Edward M., *The Old Army: A Portrait of the American Army in Peacetime 1784–1898* (New York and Oxford, 1986).

Hofschröer, Peter, *1815, the Waterloo Campaign*, 2 vols. (London, 1998).

Hungerford, Edward, *The Story of the Baltimore & Ohio Railroad 1827–1927*, 2 vols. (New York and London, 1928).

Hunt, Gaillard, ed., *United States Constitutional Convention (1787) The Journal of the Debates in the Convention which framed the Constitution of the United States, May–September, 1787 as recorded by James Madison* (New York 1908).

Hyman, Harold M., *Stanton: the Life and Times of Lincoln's Secretary of War* (New York, 1962).

Irving, David, *The Trail of the Fox* (New York, 1977). A controversial and somewhat strange biography of Erwin Rommel.

Jones, Archer, *The Art of War in the Western World* (New York and Oxford, 1983).

Joyaux, Georges J., ed. and trans., *Prince Napoleon in America: Letters from his Aide-de-Camp by Lieutenant Colonel Camille Ferri Pisani* (Bloomington, 1959).

Julian, George W., *Political Recollections 1840 to 1872* (Chicago, 1884).

Katz, Irving, *August Belmont: A Political Biography* (New York and London, 1968).

Katz, Irving, *August Belmont: A Political Biography* (New York and London, 1968).

Keegan, John, ed., *Churchill's Generals* (New York, 1991).

Laas, Virginia Jeans, ed., *Wartime Washington: the Civil War Letters of Elizabeth Blair Lee* (Urbana and Chicago, 1991). This collection, the originals in the Firestone Library at Princeton University, consists of letters from Elizabeth Blair Lee, a member of the prestigious Blair family, reporting on "current events" to her husband, a naval officer serving at sea on the blockade.

Lacouture, Jean, Patrick O'Brian, tr. *DeGaulle: the Rebel 1890–1944*, 2 vols. (New York and London, 1990).

Langer, William L., *Political and Social Upheaval 1832–1852* (New York, 1969).

Leech, Margaret, *Reveille in Washington 1860–1865* (New York, 1941).

Lowry, Thomas P., M.D., *The Story the Soldiers Wouldn't Tell: Sex in the Civil War* (Mechanicsburg, 1994).

MacIntosh, Malcolm, *Juggernaut: A History of the Soviet Armed Forces* (New York, 1968).

Macksay, Kenneth, *Guderian: Creator of the Blitzkrieg* (New York, 1975).

Mann, Golo, Charles Kessler trans, *Wallenstein: His Life Narrated by Galo Mann* (New York, 1971).

Maverick, Augustus, *Henry J. Raymond and the N.Y. Press* (Hartford, 1870).

Maxwell, William Quentin, *Lincoln's Fifth Wheel: The Political History of the United States Sanitary Commission* (New York, London, and Thrato, 1956).

Mayer, Henry, *All on Fire: William Lloyd Garrison and the Abolition of Slavery* (New York, 1998).

McClellan, George B., *The Armies of Europe: comprising Descriptions in Detail of the military Systems of England, France, Russia, Prussia, Austria, and Sardinia adopting their Advantages to all Arms of the United States Service; and Embodying the Report of Observations in Europe during the Crimean War, as Military Commissioner from the United States Government in 1855–1856* (Philadelphia, 1861).

McClure, A. K., *Abraham Lincoln and Men of War Times: Some Personal Recollections of War and Politics during the Lincoln Administration* (Lincoln and London, 1996, 4th ed.).

McKay, Ernest A., *The Civil War and New York City* (Syracuse, 1990).

McLaughlin, Charles Capen, ed., *The Papers of Frederick Law Olmstead*, 5 vols. (incomplete) (Baltimore and London 1977–).

McLaughlin, Charles Capen, ed., *The Papers of Frederick Law Olmstead*, 4 vols. incompl. (Baltimore and London, 1986).

McPherson, James, *For Cause and Comrades: Why Men Fought in the Civil War* (New York and Oxford, 1997).

McWhiney, Grady, ed., *Grant, Lee, Lincoln and the Radicals* (Chicago, 1964).

Meneely, A. Howard, ed., "Three Manuscripts of Gideon Welles," in *American Historical Review* (1926).

Miller, William J., *The Training of an Army: Camp Curtin and the North's Civil War* (Shippensburg, Pennsylvania, 1990).

Monaghan, Jay, *Custer: the Life of General George Armstrong Custer* (Boston, 1959).

Montagu, John Drogo, *Battles of the Greek and Roman World: a Chronological Compendium of 667 Battles from the Historians of the Ancient World* (London and Mechanicsburg, 2000).

Montgomery, Field Marshal Bernard, *The Memoirs of Field Marshal the Viscount Montgomery of Alamein, K. G.* (Cleveland, 1958).

Morse, John T., ed., *Diary of Gideon Welles: Secretary of the Navy Under Lincoln and Johnson*, 3 vols. (Boston and New York, 1911).

Naisawald, L. Van Loan, *Grape and Cannister: the Story of the Field Artillery of the Army of the Potomac, 1861–1865* (New York and Oxford, 1960).

Nevins, Allan, *The Emergence of Lincoln, Prologue to Civil War 1859–1861*, 2 vols. (New York, 1950).

Nevins, Allan, and Thomas, Milton Halsey, eds., *The Diary of George Templeton Strong*, 4 vols. (New York, 1952).

New York Monuments Commission for the Battlefields of Gettysburg and Chattanooga, *Final Report on the Battlefield of Gettysburg*, 3 vols. (Albany, 1900).

Niven, John, *Salmon P. Chase: A Biography* (New York and Oxford, 1995).

Niven, John, ed., *The Salmon P. Chase Papers* 4 vols. (incomplete) (Kent and London, 1993–).

Norman, A. V. B., *The Medieval Soldier* (New York, 1971).

Oates, Stephen B., *To Purge this Land with Blood: A Biography of John Brown* (New York and London, 1970).

Palmer, Robert R. *The Age of the Democratic Revolution: a Political History of Europe and America 1760–1800* (vol. 1, *The Challenge* and vol. 2, *The Struggle*) (Princeton, 1959 and 1964).

Paret, Peter, ed., *Makers of Modern Strategy from Machievelli to the Nuclear Age* (Princeton, 1986).

Paret, Peter, *York and the Era of Prussian Reform 1807–1815* (Princeton, 1966).

Parkman, Francis, *France and England in North America* 10 vols., *Montcalm and Wolfe* (Frontenac Edition, Boston, 1902) 3 vols.

Parrish, Thomas, ed., *The Simon and Shuster Encyclopedia of World War II* (New York, 1978).

Pease, Theodore Calvin, and Randall, James G., eds., *The Diary of Orville Hickman Browning*, 2 vols. (Springfield, 1925) (1850–1864).

Pipes, Richard, *Russia Under the Bolshvik Regime* (New York, 1993).

Pollack, Kenneth M., *Arabs at War: Military Effectiveness, 1948–1991* (New York and London, 2002).

Porch, Douglas, *The French Foreign Legion: a Complete History of the Legendary Fighting Force* (New York, 1991).

Raymond, Henry J., *The Life and Public Services of Abraham Lincoln* (New York, 1865).

Reid, Whitelaw, *Ohio in the War: Her Statesman, her Generals, and Soldiers*, 2 vols. (Cincinnati, 1868).

Reese, Peter, *The Scottish Commander: Scotland's Greatest Military Leaders from Wallace to World War II* (Edinburgh, 1999).

Rice, Allen Thorndike, ed., *Reminiscences of Abraham Lincoln by Distinguished Men of his Time* (New York, 1888).

Riddle, Albert Gallatin, *Recollections of War Times: Reminiscences of Men and Events in Washington 1860–1865* (New York, 1895).

Roemer, J., *Cavalry: Its History, Management, and Uses in War* (New York, 1863).

Rothenberg, Gunther E., *The Art of Warfare in the Age of Napoleon* (Norwalk, 1995, Easton Press ed.).

Salter, William, *The Life of James W. Grimes, Governor of Iowa 1854–1858 a Senator of the United States 1859–1869* (New York, 1876).

Schom, Alan, *Napoleon Bonaparte* (New York, 1997).

Schouler, William, *History of Massachusetts in the Civil War* (Boston, 1868).

Searcher, Victor, *Lincoln's Journey to Greatness: a Factual Account of the Twelve Day Inaugural Trip* (Philadelphia, 1960).

Searcher, Victor, *Lincoln's Journey to Greatness: a factual Account of the Twelve Day Inaugural Trip* (Philadelphia, 1960).

Sellers, Charles, *James K. Polk*, 2 vols. *Continentalist 1843–1846* (Princeton, 1966).

Seward, Frederick W., *Reminiscences of a War-Time Statesman and Diplomat, 1830–1915* (New York, 1916).

Shannon, Fred Albert, *The Organization and Administration of the Union Army 1861–1865*, 2 vols. (Cleveland, 1928).

Shukman, H., ed. *Stalin's Generals* (London, 1993).

Skelton, William B., *An American Profession of Arms, The Army Officer Corps, 1784–1861* (Lawrence, 1992).

Smith, W. E., *The Francis Preston Blair Family in Politics*, 2 vols. (New York, 1933).

Spence, I. G., *The Cavalry of Classical Greece: a Social and Military History with Particular Reference to Athens* (Oxford, 1993).

Sperber, Jonathan, *Rhineland Radicals* (Princeton, 1991).

Starr, Stephen Z., *The Union Cavalry in the Civil War*, 3 vols. (Baton Rouge, 1979).

Stille, Charles J., *History of the United States Sanitary Commission Being the General Report of its Work During the War of the Rebellion* (Philadelphia, 1866).

Story, Joseph, *Commentaries on the Constitution*, 3 vols. (Boston, 1833).

Strachan, Hew, *The Politics of the British Army* (Oxford, 1997).

Stryker, Lloyd Paul, *Andrew Johnson, A Study in Courage*.

Summers, Festus P., *The Baltimore and Ohio in the Civil War* (Gettysburg, 1993).

Tap, Bruce, *Over Lincoln's Shoulder: the Committee on the Conduct of the War* (Lawrence, 1998).

Thomas, Benjamin P., and Hyman, Harold M., *Stanton: The Life and Times of Lincoln's Secretary of War* (New York, 1962).

Trefousse, Hans L., *The Radical Republicans: Lincoln's Vanguard for Racial Justice* (New York, 1969).

Triumph in the West: A History of the War Years Based on the Diaries of Field Marshall Lord Alanbrooke, Chief of the Imperial General Staff (New York, 1959).

Turner, George Edgar, *Victory Road the Rails: The Strategic Place of the Railroads in the Civil War* (New York, 1952).

Upton, Emory, *The Military Policy of the United States* (Washington, 1904).

Van Deusen, Glyndon G., *William Henry Seward* (New York, 1967).

Villard, Oswald Garrison, *Fighting Years: Memoirs of a Fighting Editor*, 2 vols. (New York, 1939).

Volkoganov, Dimitri, and Harold Shukman, trans. and ed., *Stalin: Triumph and Tragedy* (New York, 1988).

Ward, Christopher, *The War of the Revolution*, 2 vols. (New York, 1952).

Ward, S. P. G., *Wellington's Headquarters: A Study of the Administrative Problems in the Peninsula, 1809–1814* (Oxford, 1957).

Weigley, Russell F., *The Age of Battles: The Quest for Decisive Warfare from Breitenfeld to Waterloo* (Bloomington and Indianapolis, 1991).

White, Leonard D., *The Jacksonians: A Study in Administrative History, 1829–1861* (New York, 1954).

Whitman, William E. S., and True, Charles H., *Maine in the War for the Union* (Lewiston, 1865).

Widen, Peter, *Bay of Pigs: the Untold Story* (New York, 1979).

Wiley, Bell I., *The Life of Billy Yank* (Indianapolis, 1952).

Williams, T. Harry, *Lincoln and his Generals* (New York, 1952).

Wilson, Derek, *The Astors, 1763–1992: Landscape with Millionaires* (New York, 1993).

Worby, Leslie J., *Hippies: The Cavalry of Ancient Greece* (San Francisco, 1994).

The Detroit Post & Tribune, *Zachariah Chandler: An Outline Sketch of His Life in Public Services* (Detroit, 1879).

Multi-Biography

Bartlett, John Russell, *Memoirs of Rhode Island Officers who were engaged in the Service of their Country during the Great Rebellion of the South* (Providence, 1867).

Biographical Dictionary of the American Congress 1774–1927.

Brown, Russel K., *Fallen in Battle: American General Officer Combat Fatalities from 1775* (Westport, 1988).

Cullum, George W., *Biographical Register of the Officers and Graduates of the U.S. Military Academy at West Point, N.Y. from its Establishment, March 16, 1862, to the Army Reorganization of 1866–1867*, 2 vols. (New York, 1868).

Eicher, John H., and David J. Eicher, *Civil War High Commands* (Stanford, 2003).

Fiske, John, eds., *Appleton's Cyclopedia of American Biography*, 6 vols. and 6 supplements (New York, 1887–1891).

Hassler, Warren W., Jr., *Commanders of the Army of the Potomac* (Baton Rouge, 1962).

Heitman, Francis B., *Historical Register and Dictionary of the United States Army from its Organization, September 29, 1789, to March 2, 1903*, 2 vols. (Washington, 1903).

Hunt, Roger D., and Brown, Jack R., *Brevet Brigadier Generals in Blue* (Gaithersburg, Maryland, 1990).

Hunt, Roger D., *Colonels in Blue: Union Army Colonels of the Civil War, The New England States Connecticut, Maine, Massachusetts, New Hampshire, Rhode Island, Vermont* (Utglen, 2001).

Kirshner, Ralph, *The Class of 1861: Custer, Arms, and Their Classmates after West Point* (Carbondale, Illinois, 1999).

Lewry, Thomas P., M.D., *Tarnished Eagles: The Courts-Martial of Fifty Union Colonels and Lieutenant Colonels* (Mechanicsburg, 1997).

Lonn, Ella, *Foreigners in Union Army and Navy* (Baton Rouge, 1951).

Malone, Dumas, ed., *Dictionary of American Biography*, 10 vols. (New York, 1964).

Official Army Register of the Volunteer Force of the United States Army for the Years 1861, '62, '63, '64, '65 (Washington, 1865, 1987 Military Books rep.).

Powell, Lieutenant Colonel William H., ed., *Officers in the Army and Navy (Volunteer) who Served in the Civil War* (Philadelphia, 1893).

Report of the Class of 1860, Harvard College 1895–1900 (Cambridge, 1900).

Shanks, William F. G., *Personal Recollections of Distinguished Generals* (New York, 1866).

Spaller, Roger J., ed., *Dictionary of American Military Biography*, 3 vols. (Westport, Connecticut, 1984).

Spencer, John, *Civil War Generals: Categorical Listings and a Biographical Directory* (New York, 1997).

Warner, *Generals in Blue*.

Waugh, John C., *The Class of 1846: From West Point to Appomattox: Stonewall Jackson, George McClellan and Their Brothers* (New York, 1994).

Waugh, John C., *The Class of '46 from West Point to Appomattox: Stonewall Jackson, George McClellan and their Brother Officers* (New York, 1994).

Welsh, Jack D., M.D., *Medical Histories of Union Generals* (Kent, 1996).

Wilson, James G., and John Fiske, *Appleton's Cyclopedia of American Biography*, 6 vols., 6 supps. 2, 65, 261 (New York, 1887–1951).

Battles and Campaigns

Baltz, John D., *Hon. Edward D. Baker, U.S. Senator from Oregon, one of America's Heroes . . . Colonel E. D. Baker's Defense in the Battle of Ball's Bluff, fought on October 21st, 1861, in Virginia and slight Biographical Sketches of Colonel Baker and Generals Wistar and Stone* (Lancaster, 1888).

Barnard, John G., *The C.S.A. and the Battle of Bull Run: a Letter to an English Friend* (New York, 1862).

Barnard, John G., *The Peninsular Campaign and its Antecedents as Developed by the Report of Maj. Gen. Geo. B. McClellan and other published Documents* (New York, 1864).

Beatie, Russel H., Jr., *Road to Manassas: The Growth of Union Command in the Eastern Theatre from the Fall of Fort Sumter to the First Battle of Bull Run* (New York, 1961).

Chamberlain, Joshua Lawrence, *The Passing of the Armies* (Dayton, 1974).

Davis, William C., *Battle at Bull Run: A History of the First Major Campaign of the Civil War* (Garden City, 1977).

Farwell, Byron, *Ball's Bluff: a small Battle and Its Long Shadow* (McLean, 1990).

Fry, James B., *McDowell and Tyler in the Campaign of Bull Run* (New York, 1884).

Gallagher, Gary W., ed., *The Richmond Campaign of 1862, The Peninsula and the Seven Days* (Chapel Hill, 2000).

Hamlin, Augustus Choate; *The Battle of Chancellorsville: the Attack of Stonewall Jackson and his Army upon the Right Flank of the Army of the Potomac at Chancellorsville, Virginia, on Saturday Afternoon, May 2, 1863* (Bangor, 1896) (pam.).

Heller, Charles E., and William A. Stafft, eds., *America's First Battles 1776–1965*; esp. W. Glenn Robertson, "First Bull Run 19 July 1861," Chap. 4 (Lawrence, 1986).

Hennessy, John, *The First Battle of Manassas: An End to Innocence July 18–21, 1861*, 2d ed. (Lynchburg, 1989).

Holien, Kim Bernard, *Battle at Balls Bluff* (Alexandria, 1985).

Huey, Pennock, *A True History of the Charge of the 8th PA Cavalry at Chancellorsville* (Pennsylvania, 1885).

Johnston, R. M. *Bull Run: Its Strategy and Tactics* (Boston and New York, 1913).

Marks, Rev. J. J., *The Peninsular Campaign in Virginia or Incidents and Scenes on the Battlefields and in Richmond* (Philadelphia, 1864, fourth ed.). The work by Marks, written by a regimental chaplain and suspect for its sanctimonious, religious attitude toward many issues, features his regiment, the Sixty-third Pennsylvania, and its commander, Colonel Alexander Hays, who, having risen to division command, would be killed in the Wilderness in 1864.

Newell, Clayton R., *Lee vs. McClellan: The First Campaign* (Washington, 1996).

Patch, Joseph Dorst, Maj. Gen. (ret.), *The Battle of Ball's Bluff* (Leesburg, 1958).

Patterson, Robert P., *A Narrative of the Campaign in the Valley of the Shenandoah in 1861* (Philadelphia, 1865).

Pierson, Charles L., *Ball's Bluff: An Episode and Its Consequences to Some of Us* (Salem, 1913).

Pond, George E., *The Shenandoah Valley in 1864* (New York, 1883).

Wert Jeffrey D., *From Winchester to Cedar Creek: The Shenandoah Campaign of 1864* (Carlysle, 1987).

Collected Articles

Basler, Roy P., ed., *The Collected Works of Abraham Lincoln*, 9 vols. and 2 supps. (New Brunswick, 1953).

Burnett, Edmund C., ed., *Letters of Members of the Continental Congress*, 7 vols. (Washington, 1923).

Crist, Lynda C., ed., *The Papers of Jefferson Davis*, 9 vols. (incomplete) (Baton Rouge, 1992).

Papers of Jefferson Davis, 8 vols. (incomplete) (Baton Rouge and London (1971–1995).

Dwight, Theodore F., ed. *Papers of the Military Historical Society of Massachusetts*, 13 vols. (Boston, 1881) (Broadfoot Reprint).

Everett, Edward G., "Pennsylvania Raises an Army, 1861" *Western Pennsylvania Historical Magazine* (Summer, 1956).

Johnson, Robert Underwood, and Buell, Clarence Clough, eds., *Battles and Leaders of the Civil War, being for the most part contributions by Union and Confederate Officers. Based upon "Century War Series,"* 4 vols. (New York, 1956, Yoseloff-Reprint).

McClure, A. K., ed., *The Annals of the War written by Leading Participants North and South originally published in the Philadelphia Weekly Times* (Philadelphia, 1879).

McLaughlin, Charles Capen, ed.-in-ch., *The Papers of Frederick Law Olmstead*, 5 vols. (incomplete) (Baltimore and London 1972).

Military Essays and Recollections: Papers Read before the Commandery of the State of Illinois, Military Order of the Loyal Legion of the United States, 4 vols. (Chicago, 1894) (Broadfoot edition, 1992, vol. 11).

Moore, John Bassett, *The Works of James Buchanan, Comprising His Speeches, State Papers, and Private Correspondence*, 11 vols. (New York, 1960).

Pennsylvania Archives: Papers of the Governors, 9 Series (Harrisburg, 1902).

Showman, Richard K., ed., *The Papers of General Nathaniel Greene*, 3 vols. (Chapel Hill, 1980).

The War of the Rebellion: A Compilation of the Official Records of the Union and Confederate Armies, 145 vols. in 4 series (Washington, 1899).

Pamphlets and Articles

Allen, Lewis F., "Memorial of the late Gen. James S. Wadsworth delivered before the New York State Agricultural Society at the close of its annual exhibition at Rochester, September 23rd, 1864, by the Hon. Lewis F. Allen, of Buffalo (ex-President of the Society). (Buffalo, 1864).

Allen, Hon. Lewis F., *Memorial of the late Gen. James S. Wadsworth delivered before the New York State Agricultural Society at the Close of its annual Exhibit at Rochester, September 23rd, 1864* (Buffalo, 1864) (pamphlet).

William D. "Edward Dickenson Baker," *The Quarterly of the Oregon Historical Society*, vol. IX, 1–23.

Banes, Charles H., *An Address Delivered at Gettysburg, August 27, 1883, by Alexander S. Webb, at the dedication of the 72nd PA. Vols Monument. Also, a historical sketch of the 72nd regiment* (Philadelphia, 1883) (Pamphlet). Webb delivered the address; Banes wrote the sketch of the regiment.

Biddle, "Reminiscences of McClellan," in vol. xi, *The United Service* (May, 1894).

Branch, E. Douglas, "Frederick West Lander, Road Builder," *Mississippi Valley Historical Review* (September, 1929).

Chamberlain, Joshua Lawrence, *The Passing of the Armies* (Dayton, 1974).

Cullum, George W., *Biographical Sketch of Major-General Henry W. Halleck of the United States Army* (New York, 1880). This brief sketch of Halleck by his chief of staff and most ardent supporter is frustratingly short about his service as general in chief.

T. W. Davenport, "Slavery Question in Oregon II," *The Quarterly of the Oregon Historical Society*, vol. IX.

Ellet, Charles, Jr., *The Army of the Potomac and its Mismanagement* (Washington, 1861) (Pamphlet).

Glad, Paul W., "Frederick West Lander and the Pacific Railroad Movement," *Nebraska History*.

Gould, John Mead, *Joseph K. Mansfield, Brigadier General of the U.S. Army. A narrative of events connected with his mortal wounding at Antietam, Sharpsburg, Maryland, September 17, 1862* (Portland, 1895). Gould maintained a spirited correspondence on this subject with anyone who would respond to him, e.g., the Carmen MSS in N.Y.P.L.

Hicks, John D., "The Organization of the Volunteer Army in 1861 with special Reference to Minnesota, *Minnesota Historical Bulletin*, no. 5, Feb. 1918.

Hunt, Henry J., "Artillery Administration" in *Journal of the Military Institute of the United States* (1891).

Lander, Edward, "A Sketch of General Frederick W. Lander," *Historical Collections of the Essex Institute* (October, 1904, no. 4).

Lander, F. W., *Practicability of Railroads through South Pass* (House Ex. Doc. no. 70, 35 Cong., 1 Sess. IX, 18); Lander, F. W., "A Bill to Provide for the Construction of a Railroad from the Missouri River to the Pacific Ocean" (Washington, D.C., 1860).

Lander, F. W. *Remarks on the Construction of a First Class Double Track Railway to the Pacific* (Washington, D.C., 1854).

Lander, F. W., *Synopsis of a Report of the Reconnaissance of a Railroad from Puget Sound via South Pass to the Mississippi River* (Washington, D.C., 1856) (reprinted as House Ex. Docs., no. 129, 33 Cong., 1 Sess. and Senate Ex. Docs., 33 Cong. 2 sess., XIII, pt. 2).

LeComte, Ferdinand, *Campagne de Virginie et de la Maryland en 1862: Documents Officials Sounies au Congress traduits de L'Anglais avec Introduction et Annotations* (Paris, 1863). A reprint in French, with valuable footnotes by one of McClellan's European aides, of the first report of the Joint Committee about the Army of the Potomac. I am again indebted to Jennifer ("Raspberry") Pariser for the translations.

Olmstead, Frederick Law, Secretary, United States Sanitary Commission, "Report of the Secretary with Regard to the Probable Origin of the Recent Demoralization of the Volunteer Army at Washington and the duty of the Sanitary Commission with Reference to Certain Deficiencies in the Existing Army Arrangements as Suggested Thereby"(Washington, 1861) reprinted in McLaughlin, Charles Capen, ed., *The Papers of Frederick Law Olmstead*, 5 vols. (incomplete) (Baltimore and London 1977–).

Parker, Dangerfield, "The Regular Battalion in the First Battle of Bull Run," in *The United Service: A Monthly Review of Military and Naval Affairs*, xiii, no. 5 (November, 1885).

Porter, Fitz John, "In Memory of Gen. Chas. P. Stone" (n.p., n.d.).

Prince de Joinville, trans. William Henry Hurlbert, *The Army of the Potomac: its Organization, its Commander, and its Campaign* (New York, 1862).

Proceedings of the Century Association in Honor of the Memory of Brig. Gen. James S. Wadsworth and Colonel Peter A. Porter; with Eulogies Read by William J. Hoppin and Frederick S. Cozzens December 3, 1864 (New York, 1865) (Century Association, *Wadsworth Eulogy*) (Pamphlet).

Robinson, John C., and John Watts de Peyster, "Obituaries of Major General Samuel P. Heintzelman, first Commander of the Third Army Corps, and Major General Joseph Hooker," (New York, 1881).

Scheips, Paul J., *Albert J. Meyer, Founder of the Army Signal Corps: A Biographical Study*, 2 parts (unpublished Ph.D. dissertation) (U.M.I. Dissertation Services).

R. C. Schenck, "Major-General David Hunter," *Magazine of American History*, vol. 15, no. 2, February, 1887.

Shutes, Milton H., "Colonel E. D. Baker" (California, 1938) (pamphlet reprint from the *California Historical Society Quarterly* of December 1938).

Weik, Jesse W., "Side Lights on Lincoln, How Lincoln Was Convinced of Scott's Loyalty," 89 *Century Magazine* 594 (1911).

Wilkes, George, *McClellan: From Ball's Bluff to Antietam* (Philadelphia, 1863).

Williams, T. Harry, "The Attack upon West Point during the Civil War" in *Mississippi Valley Historical Review*, vol. 25, March, 1939, pp. 491–504.

Wilson, James G., "General Halleck: a Memoir" in vol. 36 *Journal of the Military Service Institution of the United States*, 553.

Wilson, William B., *A Leaf from the History of the Rebellion: Sketches of Events and Persons* (Philadelphia, 1888).

Government Documents

Adjutant General's Office, *Official Army Register of the Volunteer Force of the United States Army for the Years 1861, '62, '63, '64, '65*, 10 vols. (n.p., n.d. reprint Gaithersburg, 1987).

Congressional Globe, 36th to 41st Congress (Washington, 1860–1865).

Everly, Elaine, et al. (National Archives), *Preliminary Inventory of the Records of United States Army Continental Commands, 1821–1920, Record Group 393*, 4 vols. (Washington, 1973).

Heitman, Francis B., *Historical Register and Dictionary of the United States Army, 1789–1903*, 2 vols. (Washington, 1903).

Hewitt, Janet B., et al., *Supplement to the Official Records of the Union and Confederate Armies*, 100 vols. in 3 parts with index (Washington, 1990–1999, Broadfoot ed.).

Official Army Register of the Volunteer Forces of the United States for the Years 1861, 1862, 1863, 1864, 1865, 8 parts plus index (Washington, 1865–1867, Van Sickle reprint).

Report of the Joint Committee on the Conduct of the War, 9 vols. (Wilmington, 1998, Broadfoot ed.).

Rush, Lieutenant Commander Richard, and Robert H. Woods, eds., *Official Records of the Union and Confederate Navies in the War of the Rebellion*, 30 vols., in two series (Washington, 1894–1922, National Historical Society reprint).

Scott, Lieutenant Colonel Robert N., ed., *The War of the Rebellion: a Compilation of the Official Records of Union and Confederate Armies*, 145 vols. in 4 series (Washington, 1881, Broadfoot ed.).

Senate, *Executive Journal*, 38, Wednesday, December 11, 1861.

War Department, *Revised Regulations for the United States Army with a full Index*, 512, Article 79 (Philadelphia, 1861, Morningside reprint).

Index